Reader's Guide
to
Twentieth-Century
Science Fiction

Compiled and Edited
by
MARILYN P. FLETCHER

JAMES L. THORSON
Consulting Editor

American Library Association

Chicago and London 1989

Designed by Charles Bozett.
Composed by the author in Times Roman, using Microsoft Word
    software, and output to a Hewlett-Packard Laser Jet II printer.
Printed on 50-pound Glatfelter B-16, a pH-neutral stock, and bound
    in Holliston Roxite C by Braun-Brumfield.

The paper used in this publication meets the minimum
requirements of American National Standard for Information
Sciences--Permanence of Paper for Printed Library Materials,
ANSI Z39.48-1984. ∞

Library of Congress Cataloging-in-Publication Data

Reader's guide to twentieth-century science fiction / compiled and edited
    by Marilyn P. Fletcher ;   consulting editor, James L. Thorson.
        p.   cm.
    Includes index.
    ISBN 0-8389-0504-8 (alk. paper)
    1. Science fiction--History and criticism.   2. Fiction--20th
century--History and criticism.   I. Fletcher, Marilyn P., 1940-
II. Thorson, James L.
PN3433.8.R44 1989
809.3'876--dc19   88-7815

Printed in the United States of America.

93 92 91 90 89   5 4 3 2 1

This book is dedicated to my family--to my husband, Tom, for eighteen years of love and companionship, and for his honesty, courage, and sensitivity, which will always be treasured and cherished; to my daughters, Elizabeth and Catherine, with hope that their future will bring them as much happiness as they have brought to me.

With much admiration and appreciation, I also dedicate this book to these very special persons who sustained me and my family in so many ways: Tom Carey, founder and director of the Challenge Program, whose dedication and awesome talents touched my heart, for his encouragement of my strengths and overlooking my weaknesses; Dick Hiester, whose teaching touched and enlightened my mind immeasurably; Roger White, whose persistence and insistence pushed me to my limits; Clara Farah, whose nurturing and understanding gave me confidence; Bev Davies, whose moments of drama touched me many times; Rick Knop, for propping up my spirits one dreary afternoon; and Margo, Dana, Toni, Diane, Sara, Gera, John, Mike D., Gerald C., Gerald T., Patti, Heidi, Sage, Gary, Stacey, Jill, Mike, Liz, and all of the other associates and staff of the Challenge Program. Thanks to each of you for listening, responding, and teaching, and above all, for your empathy, compassion, understanding, and caring.

Finally, this book is dedicated to Helen, Retha, Margaret, and Mary, who have been my inspiration.

Contents

Acknowledgments

Special thanks to the following persons and their organizations and institutions for their invaluable assistance: James L. Thorson, professor of English at the University of New Mexico, for his editorial work, ideas, criticisms, and support as consulting editor; the voluntary entry contributors who turned in such superb work; Herb Bloom, senior editor of the American Library Association, for his persistence, patience, and encouragement; Mary Huchting, American Library Association, for copy editing; Marcie Lange, American Library Association, for format editing; Dorothy Wonsmos, interlibrary loan librarian at the University of New Mexico General Library, for quick and efficient delivery of needed books; Linda Lewis, collection development officer at the University of New Mexico General Library, for preparing lists of science fiction reference sources in biography, plot summaries, and bibliographies, and for willingly taking on additional entries as needed; Colleen Power, science librarian at the California State University Library, Chico, for also willingly taking on additional entries; Corrine Weis, for assistance in indexing; Robert L. Migneault, dean of library services at the University of New Mexico General Library, for the time and support to complete this work; Harry Broussard, systems librarian at the University of New Mexico General Library, for his assistance in formatting; Connie Thorson, acquisitions librarian at the University of New Mexico General Library, for constant support and numerous kind words; Judi Bernstein, librarian of the Parish Memorial Library at the University of New Mexico, for the use of the laser jet printer; and all of the staff and students of the Serials Department of the University of New Mexico General Library, for their understanding and patience.

Introduction

What prompts the need for yet another science fiction reference book? While it is apparent in recent years that science fiction is becoming more acceptable, moving toward the mainstream
of modern literature, this is also true of other literary genres and
forms. When a certain literary style is termed a "genre," it is defined as "a distinctive category of literary composition." In some
arenas of literary criticism, the label of genre is almost punitive.
Indeed, the very existence of a work dedicated to science fiction
authors and their works may only serve to justify the idea that a
"genre" is less than worthwhile, because it can be defined and separated out as something other than mainstream. Be that as it may,
the need for such distinctions as science fiction, fantasy, mysteries, romance, etc., remains. The separation is most helpful for the
reader, student, and scholar of science fiction, and it is for their
use that this work has been compiled.

What is science fiction? In order to decide what was to be in-
cluded in this work, a working definition needed to be established.
For the purpose of selection, the following definition, written by
Sam Moskowitz, was used:

> Science fiction is a branch of fantasy identifiable
> by the fact that it eases the "willing suspension of
> disbelief" on the parts of its readers by utilizing an
> atmosphere of scientific credibility for its imagina-
> tive speculations in physical science, space, time, so-
> cial science, and philosophy.[1]

The scientific, economic, sociological, philosophical, and psychological ideas of a future time are all legitimate themes in science
fiction.

Having defined the aspects of the science fiction genre, it was
decided that a work was needed which would, first of all, give information on an author's life and works; themes and styles; and
plot summaries of award-winning and major works. Several excellent reference books offer biographical information, and often
include bibliographies of an author's works. Unfortunately, plot
summaries in most of the currently available reference works tend

---

1. Sam Moskowitz, *Explorers of the Infinite* (World, 1963), p. 11.

to be brief, consisting of only a few sentences. Conversely, there are works such as *Masterplots* and *Anatomy of Wonder* that provide good plot summaries and analyses, but offer little biographical information. This work intends to fill the gap, offering essays on the life and selected works of each author (complete works are not included in this book--such lists are available in other reference books), along with a summary of themes and style, followed by plot summaries of each author's major works and a selection of biographical and bibliographical readings. The plot summaries follow the essay on the author and are arranged alphabetically, except for works in series and works with sequels, which are arranged sequentially. A title index refers the reader to the authors of particular titles.

While the ideal of complete objectivity was set out as a guideline, some subjectivity became necessary. Thus, the editor acknowledges the selectivity and recognizes that there will be omissions, but hopefully these have been minimized, so the work will still be useful for the majority of readers and users.

It may be helpful to specifically identify those groups of excluded authors and explain why the decision was made to exclude. First, authors of pure fantasy, those works having no basis in future time or extrapolation of scientific, technological, and sociological ideas, were excluded. Admittedly, several authors have contributed to both fantasy and science fiction, but every attempt was made to include only those who had written the majority of their works utilizing science fiction themes. Also, several guides and reference books are already in publication that cover the fantasy field, and this further justifies the decision to exclude fantasy writers. Second, authors who have crossed over to mainstream fiction, or who write primarily nonfiction works, were excluded. Again, these authors are adequately covered in other works. Finally, and with much regret, those authors who devoted so much of their creative effort to the compiling of anthologies and reference books, the editing and preparing of science fiction magazines, and the writing of historical and critical works on science fiction, were excluded, because the body of their work did not involve the actual literary production of science fiction, but rather its important peripheral support systems. While many of these persons have published in the science fiction literature, this is not their main claim to fame. These editors, historians, compilers, and critics are invaluable to the study of science fiction; while they have been excluded, they must surely know that works such as this would not be possible without their efforts.

As the title implies, this work includes twentieth-century authors only. Though we all acknowledge and appreciate earlier authors who set the stage for science fiction, beginning with More's *Utopia* through the nineteenth-century writers such as Mary Shelley and Jules Verne, this work was planned for twentieth-century authors. H. G. Wells is the earliest author included, as his works came into popularity close to the beginning of, and overlapped into, the twentieth century.

Having stated the justification, the inclusiveness, and the exclusiveness of this book, the editor realizes and takes responsibility for the final selection of the authors represented. In many cases, it simply came down to selectivity based on a good representation of different styles and audiences. For example, an attempt was made to include Hugo and Nebula award-winning authors. However, some of these authors disappeared from the science fiction scene or never made any additional contributions to the literature after receiving an award. In addition to award winners, a representative selection was made to include many of the early "pulp" writers, who paved the way for what is now modern science fiction; the feminist writers, who made inroads into what was once a male-oriented genre; some juvenile writers, whose works are recognized and appreciated in the field; the New Wave writers in both the United States and Great Britain; a smattering of Australians, who brought a different theme and style to hard-core science fiction; and the most recent "cyberpunk" group, whose longevity is yet to be determined.

Within the entries, a decision was made to limit the number of plot summaries or analyses to a maximum of six works per author. This proved to be difficult, especially for those prolific authors who have won multiple awards, but has been followed, with six as a maximum. Primary consideration was given to the science fiction works which were first, award-winners, and second, best known works. Again, the selections often had to be subjective and the contributors made the selections; and when deletions were necessary, the editor took on that responsibility.

This work is prepared for science fiction readers and fans; scholars and academicians in science fiction; librarians; and students in science fiction and other literature courses. It is dedicated to the authors and writers represented, who have enriched our lives by looking into the future and providing us with infinite possibilities, inspiring a true sense of wonder.

Contributors

Duncan M. Aldrich, Government Publications Librarian, University of Nevada, Reno

Candace R. Benefiel, Reference Librarian, Texas A & M University, College Station

Jonathan K. Benison, Professor, Universita degli Studi de Padua, Padua, Italy

Judith R. Bernstein, Director, Parish Memorial Library, University of New Mexico, Albuquerque

Richard Bleiler, Mervyn Sterne Library, University of Alabama, Birmingham

Janice M. Bogstad, Chalmer Davie Library, University of Wisconsin, River Falls

Steven Carper, Science fiction critic and lecturer, Member, Science Fiction Writers Association, Rochester, New York

Michael R. Collings, Associate Professor of English, Pepperdine University, Malibu, California

John Dunham, Resource Centre Coordinator, AIDS Committee of Toronto, Ontario, Canada

Marilyn P. Fletcher, Head of Serials, University of New Mexico Library, Albuquerque

Janet E. Frederick, Head of Bibliographic Database Management, University of New Mexico Library, Albuquerque

Mina Jane Grothey, Reference Librarian, University of New Mexico Library, Albuquerque

Howard V. Hendrix, Lecturer, University of California, Riverside

Kay Jones, Assistant University Librarian for Administration, California State University, Sacramento

Theodore Krulik, Science fiction writer, Bushwick High School, Brooklyn, New York

Lorraine E. Lester, Administrative Librarian, University of New Mexico Law Library, Albuquerque

Linda K. Lewis, Collection Development Officer, University of New Mexico Library, Albuquerque

Barbara Ann Luther, English Instructor, Ohio State University, Columbus

Mary Lou Mills, Environmental Water Specialist, State of Washington, Parkland

Nickianne Moody, Ph.D. candidate, University of Wisconsin, Reading, Berkshire, England

Sam Moskowitz, Science fiction critic and historian, Newark, New Jersey

Eric Nudell, Innovacq System Coordinator, University of New Mexico Library, Albuquerque

Richard Page, User Services Librarian, University of Southern California Library, Los Angeles

Stephen W. Potts, Lecturer, University of California at San Diego

Colleen Power, Science Librarian, California State University Library, Chico

Harold Lee Prosser, Professor, Southwest Missouri State University, Springfield

Jack Rawlins, Professor of English, California State University, Chico

Twyla Reinig, OCLC Specialist, University of New Mexico Library, Albuquerque

Illene Renfro, Serials Cataloger, University of New Mexico Library, Albuquerque

Todd H. Sammons, Assistant Professor of English, University of Hawaii at Manoa, Honolulu

A. Langley Searles, Professor of Chemistry, College of Mount St. Vincent and Manhattan College, Bronxville, New York

Jeanne Sohn, Associate Dean, University of New Mexico Library, Albuquerque

Sandra E. Spurlock, Librarian, Engineering Library, Honeywell, Inc., Albuquerque, New Mexico

David L. Starbuck, M.D., Lovelace Medical Center, Albuquerque, New Mexico

James L. Thorson, Professor of English, University of New Mexico, Albuquerque

Bill Trousdale, Graduate student, University of New Mexico, Albuquerque

Dianne P. Varnon, Librarian, Washoe County Library, Reno, Nevada

Milton Wolf, Assistant Director for Collection Development, Getchell Library, University of Nevada, Reno

Biographies, Criticism, and Plot Summaries

ADAMS, DOUGLAS NOEL

Life and Works

Noel Adams Douglas was born on March 11, 1952, in Cambridge, England, son of Christopher Douglas, a management consultant, and Janet Donovan Douglas. He attended St. John's College in Cambridge, where he received a bachelor of arts with honors. After completing his education, Adams was employed by the British Broadcasting Corporation during the 1970s. In 1978, he became a script editor for the long-running science fiction series, "Doctor Who." Also in 1978, he became producer and scriptwriter for a new radio series called "The Hitchhiker's Guide to the Galaxy." The program was immensely popular and spawned a television series. The popularity of the programs caused Pan Books to ask Adams to turn the radio scripts of "The Hitchhiker's Guide" into a novel. The book, *The Hitchhiker's Guide to the Galaxy* (1979), became as successful as his radio and television series and resulted in three sequels: *The Restaurant at the End of the Universe* (1980), *Life, the Universe and Everything* (1980), and *So Long, and Thanks for All the Fish* (1984). These have also appeared in the form of record albums, cassettes, video cassettes, and interactive computer games. An omnibus version of the four volumes, entitled *The Hitchhiker Quartet*, was published in 1986. In addition to the four novels, Adams included a short story, "Young Zaphod Plays It Safe." 1987 brought the release of *Bureaucracy*, an interactive computer game, and *Dirk Gently's Holistic Detective Agency*, a mixture of detective and science fiction genres.

Themes and Style

As it stands, the four novels of the "Hitchhiker" series are a lampoon of the science fiction genre. The stories are written in a unique blend of absurd humor, sophomoric slapstick, and a seriousness that reflects the human condition--almost as if Monty Python had rewritten "Doctor Who" in collaboration with Günter Grass. Humor in science fiction has been limited in quantity. Although there are some exceptions, primarily in short stories, humor has been of the episodic variety, rather than the wellspring for an entire work. Adams's tales of the Hitchhiker series are written purely for fun and should be read for the chuckles and guffaws found within them.

Plot Summaries of Major Works

The Hitchhiker's Guide to the Galaxy. Arthur Dent wakes up one morning to discover bulldozers at his front door. Without his knowledge, the western English village in which he lives has decided to put an expressway bypass through the center of his house. In his struggle to prevent this calamity, he discovers that his friend, Ford Prefect, is actually an alien from a small planet near Betelguese and a researcher for *The Hitchhiker's Guide to the Galaxy* (unknown on Earth), and that the Earth is about to be destroyed by another alien race, the Vogons, in order to put in a hyperspatial express route. Luckily for Arthur, Ford knows how to hitch rides with passing interstellar ships and has taken a liking to the funny human. So Arthur, still in his bathrobe, and Ford hitch a ride on a Vogon ship, whose captain despises hitchhikers and subjects them to torture by reading to them selections of his poetry (the "third worst poetry in the universe"). The two are ejected from the Vogon ship and picked up by the starship *Heart of Gold*, owned by the three-armed, two-headed, former president of the galaxy, Zaphod Beeblebrox, whose crew consists of another human hitchhiker, Trillian, and Marvin, a terminally depressed robot. The ship is powered by the "Infinite Improbability Drive." Thus begins the extraordinary adventures of the hapless hero Arthur Dent as he travels across the universe finding answers to questions he had never thought to ask.

The inspired lunacy of this tale does pose a few serious questions. They are generally rhetorical questions: How can this happen? Why wasn't this prevented? Why was this done in this way? Answers are presented with great humor, and the adventures are continued in the the next three volumes.

The Restaurant at the End of the Universe. The misadventures of the hapless hero, Arthur Dent, continue in this sequel. The crew of the starship *Heart of Gold* consists of Dent, Ford, Captain Beeblebrox, Trillian, and Marvin, the robot. Arthur asks the ship's computers what is wrong with the food synthesizer and why it cannot make a decent cup of tea. The computer ponders this trivial question, ignoring the Vogon ship that has just discovered the *Heart of Gold*, and all seems lost. Just as the ship is about to be destroyed, Captain Beeblebrox holds a seance, calling upon his ancestor to save them, and the ship is transported to an unknown place in space and time. Exhausted after so much drama, the captain orders the ship to take them to the nearest place to eat, Milliways, the restaurant at the end of the universe--and the only restaurant where the food talks to the customers and the floorshow is the final Armageddon (as opposed to the other end of time, where the restaurant is called the Big Bang Burger Bar).

Similar in style and content to the first volume, this novel poses no problems of any consequence for the reader. It is, simply, a story to be read for the pleasure of its audacious humor.

Life, the Universe and Everything. Billed as "the Cosmic Conclusion to the *Hitchhiker's* Trilogy," this book finds Arthur Dent, still in his bathrobe, on prehistoric Earth five million years before Ford Prefect saved him from the destruction of Earth in the construction of a hyperspatial express route. As Arthur decides to go mad, his friend Ford Prefect appears. Together they find a disturbance in the fabric of space and are launched into the 1980s. Here Arthur discovers that he alone holds the key to saving the universe from destruction by the planet Krikket's killer robots. The crew of the *Heart of Gold* is eventually reunited and new members are introduced. Beyond saving the universe from certain destruction, they are again confronted with another baffling question needing an ultimate answer.

The pace of the third novel continues Adams's absurd humor in the same satirical vein by throwing fun at such science fiction mainstays as saving the universe and time travel. Although the tales were originally designed as a trilogy, a fourth volume has appeared.

So Long, and Thanks for All the Fish. Opening with the contradictory statement, "The Fourth Book in *The Hitchhiker Trilogy*," this volume is as enigmatically funny as the preceding three. Arthur Dent returns to Earth, supposedly destroyed in the first novel, to discover what actually happened that fateful day. Ford Prefect, contributor to the infamous *Hitchhiker's Guide*, discovers that Earth's entry in the *Guide* has not been deleted, and an update has been added. Here begins the story proper in the only book of the four to be set almost entirely on Earth. In addition to finding the answer to the question of what happened the day the Earth was demolished, Arthur also eventually learns the answer to the questions: Why did all the dolphins disappear? and, What is God's final message to His creation? He is helped in his quest for knowledge by the everpresent Ford Prefect and a number of new human acquaintances.

In the familiar style of the first three volumes, Adams concludes the adventures (or misadventures) of Arthur Dent. The madcap humor is brought to an end, without losing the impetus nor the impishness of the previous novels.

Biographical/Bibliographical Readings

Susan Adams, "Douglas Adams," *Starlog* 47 (June 1981), p.28-30. "Douglas Adams," in *Contemporary Authors* (Gale, 1982), v. 106, p.15. "Douglas Adams," in *The Science Fiction Sourcebook* (Longman, 1984), p.89. Robert Reilly, "Douglas Adams," in *Twentieth-Century Science-Fiction Writers*, ed. Curtis C. Smith (St. James, 1986), p.2. **[Richard Page]**

ALDISS, BRIAN W.

Life and Works

Brian W. Aldiss was born on August 18, 1925, in East Dereham, Norfolk, England. After attending West Buckland School (1939-42), Aldiss served in the Royal Corps of Signals, spending much of his active service in the Far East and, in process, collecting images and ideas that would later surface in works exploring the conflicts between East and West. In 1947, Aldiss began working as a bookseller in Oxford, a position that resulted in his first book-length fiction, *The Brightfount Diaries* (1955), and in his work as a reviewer for the *Oxford Mail* (1957-69). The publication of a collection of short fiction, *Space, Time, and Nathaniel*, in 1957 signaled Aldiss's serious beginnings in science fiction; a year later, he published his first science fiction novel, *Non-Stop*. Pseudonyms used by Brian Aldiss during his literary career include Joel Cracken, Peter Pica, John Runciman, and C. C. Shackleton.

The science fiction community quickly recognized the strength of Aldiss's contributions. He received an award at the Sixteenth World Science Fiction convention in 1958 as the most promising new author of 1957, followed four years later by the Hugo award for *Hothouse*. In 1965, "The Saliva Tree" received the Nebula award. Since then, Aldiss has received multiple Hugo and Nebula nominations and awards, recognition as Britain's Most Popular Science Fiction Writer (1969), and such other awards as the Ditmar (Australia) and James Blish award.

Aldiss has served as the cofounder of the John W. Campbell Memorial Award and as an officer in numerous organizations: World Science Fiction, the Stapledon Society, and the London Society of Authors. A stimulating speaker, Aldiss has been invited to science fiction conventions around the world, including Tokyo; Rio de Janeiro; New York; Boca Raton, Florida; and Zagreb, Yugoslavia.

His criticism is as impressive as his fiction. In 1978, he was awarded the Pilgrim Award for scholarship from the Science Fiction Research Association. In 1986, he received the first annual award for outstanding scholarship from the International Association for the Fantastic in the Arts. He published a historical overview of science fiction, *Billion Year Spree* (1973), recently revised and expanded (with David Wingrove) as *Trillion Year Spree* (1985).

In the succeeding three decades since his first science fiction novel, Aldiss has established himself as a writer of great technical and artistic skill, capable of mastering a wide range of forms. He has remained one of England's most prolific and popular science fiction writers, with nearly twenty novels to his credit. His most important novels exhibit a remarkable range of writing styles, narrative experimentation, and personal growth. Although his writing is immediately recognizable, he is capable of subtle and impressively effective variations, to the point that no Aldiss novel is quite the same as any other. Such works as *Hothouse* (1962; retitled *Long Afternoon of Earth*), *Greybeard* (1964), *The Dark Light Years* (1964), *Cryptozoic* (1967), *The Eighty Minute Hour* (1974), *The Malacia Tapestry* (1976), and *Enemies of the System* (1978) demonstrate his ability to adapt and expand the conventions of science fiction. "The Saliva Tree" (1966), *Frankenstein Unbound* (1974), and *Moreau's Other Island* (1980) are literary pastiches, reexamining in contemporary forms critical themes initially explored by Mary Shelley and H. G. Wells. Other novels, such as *Report on Probabilty A* (1968) and *Barefoot in the Head* (1969) suggest his increasing concern for bridging the gap between science fiction and mainstream prose. *Report on Probabilty A* is modeled on the extreme objectivity of the French antinovel of Michel Butor and Alain Robbe-Grillet, while *Barefoot in the Head* superimposes a Joycean subjectivity of perception and language onto a science fictional theme--an apocalyptic war that threatens human civilization. Finally, Aldiss's three-volume Helliconia novel--*Helliconia Spring* (1982), *Helliconia Summer* (1983), and *Helliconia Winter* (1985)--provides a fitting conclusion to three decades of science fiction. It incorporates virtually every major theme Aldiss has worked with in previous novels. In the ambitiousness of their setting, the complexity of narrative development and variety of characters, their blending of scientific extrapolation with mythopoeic fiction, the Helliconia volumes represent Brian W. Aldiss at the height of his creative powers.

One of the most prolific short fiction writers in the genre, Aldiss has published over 300 short stories, many of them highly innovative in narrative technique, structure, language, and characterization. He has published over two score collections of his own short fiction, including *Space, Time, and Nathaniel* (1958), *Galaxies like Grains of Sand* (1960), *Who Can Replace a Man?* (1966), *The Saliva Tree and Other Strange Growths* (1966), *The Moment of Eclipse* (1970), *Last Orders and Other Stories* (1977), *New Arrivals, Old Encounters* (1979), and *Seasons in Flight* (1984). Aldiss's collections are more carefully integrated than is common among other writers, often achieving an almost novelistic intensity of organization and development of themes.

Aldiss's interest in short fiction extends beyond his own works, however. He has edited twelve anthologies of science fiction and fantasy. With Harry Harrison, Aldiss also edited a number of anthologies, including the influential *Best SF* annuals (1967-75). Aldiss's introductions and afterwords often contain important critical statements about the nature of science fiction, illustrating his continuing interest in defining and exploring the genre.

Themes and Style

Throughout his career, Aldiss has established an enviable reputation as stylist and storyteller. His novels, stories, and criticism reflect continuing themes: the conflict between chaos and order; inwardness versus outwardness; ecological disaster as a consequence of our ignorant manipulation of nature, leading to a concern for humanity's dependence upon and responsibility to its environment (whether real, as in *Earthworks* (1966), or imaginary, as with Helliconia); stasis and change; and entropy and adaption.

Stylistically, his works are characterized by his keen wit, by his willingness to explore the possibilities of verbal texture, whether it be the sparseness of *Report on Probability A*, the lush subjectivity of *Barefoot in the Head*, the quasi-Renaissance richness of *The Malacia Tapestry* and *Helliconia Summer*, or the starkness of *Helliconia Winter*. In each instance, he carefully matches verbal style with narrative thrust, creating narratives that become what they describe. His connection with the British New Wave of the 1960s illustrates his concern that science fiction make full use of the stylistic and narrative techniques being developed in mainstream fiction. In Aldiss's works, many of these techniques are successfully transferred to the themes and subject matter of science fiction.

In his development of theme and symbol, Aldiss rarely presents a formal agenda for change. Instead, he prefers to examine possibilities, often concluding novels on a purposely ambiguous note. One does not discover clear-cut resolution of complex issues in Aldiss; rather, his characters attain a kind of status quo that requires a new level of adaptation in order to survive altered circumstances. Luterin Shokerandit's gesture of defiance in the face of inexorable winter in *Helliconia Winter* provides an icon for Aldiss's fictions. Characters do not generally change their worlds, but they do survive. Occasionally, the novels may require something as radical as nuclear war to insure that survival, as in *Earthworks*. In others, such as *The Malacia Tapestry*, survival becomes a matter of realizing that ultimately nothing truly changes.

In whatever form he couches his fictions, Aldiss remains consistent in his emphasis on science fiction as a valid contemporary form. He may often experiment with such conventions as space travel, time-space dilation, even the direction of time itself; but underlying these explorations is a concern for developing his chosen genre to its limits.

Plot Summaries of Major Works

Barefoot in the Head. Following the Acid Head War (initiated when Kuwait dropped hallucinogenic bombs on Europe and America), almost everyone is literally "bombed" or stoned. Colin Charteris travels through France and England, becoming more infected by the polluted environment and consequently less reliable as the interpreter of data. In this novel, plot is secondary to perception, since Charteris's own understanding of events and actions becomes increasingly ambiguous.

Through the use of Joycean, disruptive prose, Aldiss creates a novel as intense in its subjectivity as *Report on Probability A* is in its objectivity. In fact, internal evidence such as the repetition of key images and, in one instance, of a specific line from *Report*, suggests that the two are in some sense intended to be read as opposing yet connected. In *Report on Probabilty A*, the reader receives no help in interpretation; in *Barefoot in the Head*, the reader receives too much information, too much interpretation of external phenomena, until it becomes impossible to distinguish between the world and Charteris's drug-altered perceptions of that world. Nor, in fact, is the reader limited to merely one interpretation, since the language itself is so ambiguous (Charteris refers to "godambiguity") that single phrases may contain several possible and, in the context of the novel, likely possibilities. Aldiss has referred to the novel as a study in "the ruptures in perceptions of our time." Style, characterization and narrative stance all emphasize the psychic disintegration of human societies.

Frankenstein Unbound. In August of 2020, Joe Bodenland is caught in a space-time distortion resulting from scientific tampering with the solar system. He is transported to Geneva in May of 1816, where he meets Victor Frankenstein. A second time-slip advances him in time to August, 1816. He travels to the Villa Diodati, where he becomes the houseguest of Lord Byron, Percy Shelley, Dr. Polidori, and Mary Wollstonecraft Godwin, not yet Mary Shelley, but already writing her novel about creating life from death. Bodenland discusses political and social theory with Byron and Shelley, falls in love with Mary Godwin, and consummates this love before returning to Geneva--to be detained for complicity in the presumed death of Victor Frankenstein. Another time-slip helps him escape from prison. Bodenland discovers Frankenstein's lab, arriving in time to see the two monsters escape. He confronts Frankenstein, who has visions of creating yet a third monster. Bodenland kills Frankenstein and sets out on his own quest: to rid the world of the monsters. Subsequent time-slips distort the world, and the novel concludes with a final confrontation between human and monster on a frozen plain before an immense, unknown city.

Frankenstein Unbound is a tour de force of style and theme, as Aldiss combines such science fiction conventions as time travel with a critique of Romantic sensibility, the nineteenth century philosophy of progress with twentieth century historical trends. Emphasizing the centrality of Shelley's *Frankenstein* to science fiction, Aldiss uses Shelley, her companions, and her fictional creations as mouthpieces to indict those philosophical movements that led to our preoccupation with science, with meddling with natural laws not fully understood. The time-slips become metaphors as well as literary devices. Twentieth-century humanity is in fact without a *bodenland*, a foundation for belief and action. Bodenland himself is transformed from a sensitive human into a machinelike monster. In the final encounter, Frankenstein's monster bears more humanity than its human foe. But both are the children of Frankenstein, heirs of a century passionately involved with expanding human knowledge, though with a concomitant passion for developing human morality. Like Shelley's later novel, *The Last Man*, *Frankenstein Unbound* concludes with a pessimistic vision of human disintegration, coupled with the static ambiguity of possibilities that has become Aldiss's trademark.

Helliconia series. While each novel is self-contained, the three combine to create a single unity examining the seasonal cycle on a planet, Helliconia. Helliconia orbits the star Batalix, which in turn orbits a much hotter star, Freyr. When stars and planet are at their closest, temperatures are so high that the forests at Helliconia's equator burst spontaneously into flame; when distances are at the opposite extreme, winter covers the face of Helliconia for hundreds of years. The cycle of a single Great Year equals more than 2,500 Earth years, with the consequence that civilization on Helliconia must adapt to virtual destruction with the onset of each winter, rebuild with the coming of spring, adapt again to endure the frightful heat of summer, and prepare during autumn for another centuries-long descent into darkness and barbarism. Complicating the cosmic movements are the internal relationships between Helliconia's two competing species: the savage phagors, elder of the races; and the humans, doomed to suffer decimation through plague at the onset of both spring and winter. The orbiting observation station Avernue transmits information about Helliconia back to Earth; eventually, the histories of the two planets intertwine as Earth suffers it own nuclear winter and its surviving humans band together to recreate society.

Helliconia Spring. The first novel recounts the founding of Embruddock and the progress of humanity from barbaric darkness into burgeoning civilization; episodes often parallel human history as the Helliconians discover the scientific principles controlling their world. The conflict between human and phagor intensifies, culminating in the destruction of Embruddock by a phagor horde.

Helliconia Summer. Aldiss concentrates on six weeks during the reign of King JandolAnganol and his queen, MyrdemIngalla, creating a neo-Renaissance culture embroiled in conflicts between church and state. Phagors are verging on extinction in the increasing heat, while humans thrive and build.

Helliconia Winter. Luterin Shokerandit represents the dangers faced by humans on Helliconia as winter returns, threatening to destroy everything so carefully built up during the centuries of summer. Using the Great Wheel of Kharnabhar as a central symbol that echoes back to the Prologue of *Spring*, Aldiss completes his examination of change and adaptation.

The Helliconia novels are Aldiss's most outstanding achievement, a culmination of three decades of thought and development. Aldiss's scale in the Helliconia novels is enormous, covering as it does the rise, flowering and decay of civilization during one Great Year. At the same time, he increasingly involves Earth in the pageant of Helliconia.

The Helliconia novels are science-fictional extrapolation and mythopoeic vision. They deal with vast stretches of time, yet Aldiss creates characters that come to life with a single deft touch. They concentrate on alien worlds and alien species, yet ultimately reflect directly back to the reader. They pose serious questions about adaptability and change, yet refuse to provide easy, superficial answers. There are, ultimately, only the defiance of death and the dedication to survival. The novels do not decide the rightness or wrongness of change--they only assert that all things do change. With the Helliconia novels, Aldiss has made his most important contribution to date to science fiction and to literature.

Hothouse. In an indefinably distant future, humans have devolved into small creatures, barely verbal, intimidated by and often consumed by the vegetation that has evolved around them. A small group, centered on the male, Gren, has been broken away from their habitat and must survive on a world no longer in humanity's control. As Gren's travels take him across much of the world, he encounters a continent-wide Banyan tree; an intellectual fungoid morel with delusions of conquering the world; a fish creature, the Sodal Ye, who sees humans only as convenient beasts of burden; fly people who were once human but now live on Earth's moon, traversing the distances between worlds on gigantic webs spun by the arachnoid traversers; and other wonders that continually threaten Gren's definition and perception of himself.

Also known under the title *Long Afternoon of Earth, Hothouse* is a Hugo award-winning novel of the decline of the Earth. Aldiss proves himself as stylist by creating a language appropriate to his subject. Thought itself has diminished; creatures are named by comic rhyming mnemonics, such as "dripperlip," "wilmilt," and "bellyelm," making explicit the intellectual decay of Gren and his fellows. Their diminutive stature makes all the more impressive the riotous growth surrounding and threatening them; their inability to name that lushness other than by the equivalent of nursery rhymes parallels their physical size. At the same time, Aldiss uses Gren as the focus for highly imaginative episodes, each distancing the reader further from our contemporary world, and each demonstrating the enormous fecundity of the world, even in its final millenia. At the same time, Aldiss invites a symbolic reading. In an episode originally deleted in the first American edition, he recounts the fall of human civilization eons before, creating a connection between reader and text that echoes throughout the novel. In its lushness of imagination, its vivid imagery, its episodes of action and adventure, *Hothouse* merits its status as one of Aldiss's most impressive novels.

The Malacia Tapestry. Perian de Chirolo, the ostensible hero of *The Malacia Tapestry*, never quite understands the world around him. In a city suffering under the Original Curse--that nothing may ever change in Malacia--de Chirolo is dedicated to changing his station in life. His affairs with various ladies (including Armida, daughter of a nobleman) and his involvement with Otto Bengtsohn's Zahnoscope, a forerunner of film technology, seem at first to provide him with means to better himself. Ultimately, however, Aldiss reaffirms the Original Curse; neither Chirolo nor Malacia undergo any substantive change.

The novel resembles a long, richly illustrated tapestry. Aldiss has peopled his world with a wide range of characters suggesting Renaissance Europe. Certainly the city of Malacia, surrounded by the Ottoman armies, has analogues in human history. But this is an alternate world, Aldiss warns us; de Chirolo's progenitors were not mammalian but saurian, and the laws of society and evolution which we might assume true have no validity here. Instead, Aldiss transforms his static images of court and city life into a study of entropy, stasis, and change; of the interaction of "art and heart" as art imitates life, which in turn imitates art; of light, shadow, and reflections that alter perceptions of both; and of progress and degeneration in an alternate Earth. Based in part on a series of engravings by Tiepolo, *The Malacia Tapestry* is a marvelous texture of possibilities, blending reality and fantasy, history and extrapolation, character and symbol. Longer than most of Aldiss's earlier novels, it demonstrates his mastery of language and style, as well as his continuing experimenation with narrative modes.

Report on Probability A. Among Aldiss's most controversial and problematical works, *Report on Probability A* is essentially a novel without character or plot. Initially, G, S, and C are seen observing the house of Mr. and Mrs. Mary. They do so passively; even sentence structure and verb choice enforce a static sense on the text. Gradually, the circle of observers widens to include Domoladossa and Midlakemela, who watch G, S, and C watching the Marys in what Domoladossa refers to as probability A. The Distinguishers watch Domoladossa from yet another probability level; Congressman Sadler and Joe Growleths in turn watch the Distinguishers, and are in their turn observed by the Suppressor of Archives and the Impaler of Distortions. No character is aware of of the levels of observation surrounding him, nor does any of the multiple observers possess a key to understanding actions, motivations, or interpretations. Each must be satisfied by the act of observing and recording.

In *Report on Probability A*, Aldiss discards the concern for causality central to much science fiction and works instead with objective data for which no interpretations, no interconnections, are overtly possible. Yet through such recurring images as Holman Hunt's painting, "The Hireling Sheperd," present in each of the probabilities observed, Aldiss seems intent on forcing his readers to interpolate causation and reach conclusions for which there is no true matrix. Character and style closely parallel this narrative pose, making *Report on Probability A* a classic science fiction antinovel, compelling in its lack of movement, persuasive in its insistence that the reader provide virtually all of the links necessary to interpret its mass of raw, observational data.

Biographical/Bibliographical Readings

Brian W. Aldiss, *The Shape of Further Things* (Doubleday, 1971). Idem, and Harry Harrison, *Hell's Cartographers* (Harper & Row, 1975). Margaret Aldiss, *Item Eighty-Three: Brian Aldiss: A Bibliography, 1954-1972* (SF Horizons, 1973). Michael R. Collings, *Brian W. Aldiss* (Starmont House, 1985). Brian Griffin and David Wingrove, *Apertures: A Study of the Writings of Brian W. Aldiss* (Greenwood, 1984). Richard Mathews, *Aldiss Unbound* (Borgo Press, 1977). **[Michael R. Collings]**

ANDERSON, POUL

Life and Works

Poul Anderson was born in Bristol, Pennsylvania, on November 25, 1926. Shortly after his birth, his family moved to Texas for eleven years. After his father's death, the family moved to Denmark, but returned to the United States upon the outbreak of World War II. Immediately after their return, his mother worked for the Danish Legation in Washington, D.C. The family eventually settled on a Minnesota farm.

Anderson was educated at the University of Minnesota, Minneapolis, where in 1948 he received his bachelor's degree in physics. While at the university, he lived in the same house as Gordon Dickson. He and Dickson were both active in MFS, originally the Minneapolis Fantasy Society. The organization was essentially an unstructured social group with interests ranging from manuscript criticism to softball, with a great deal of drinking and talking along the way. Anderson's first short story, "Tomorrow's Children" (1947), appeared in *Astounding Science Fiction* while he was still in school. After graduation, he never worked as a physicist, but made a living as a free-lance writer.

In 1953, Anderson married Karen Kruse, also a writer. After their marriage, they moved to the San Francisco area. The couple has one daughter, Astrid, and the family currently lives in Orinda, California. Anderson and his wife are both active in the Society for Creative Anachronisms. In 1966, Poul and Karen Anderson published their first jointly authored work, *Roma Mater* (*The King of Ys, Book 1*). Anderson is a member of the Science Fiction Writers of America and in 1972-73 served as its president.

In addition to writing science fiction, Anderson has written in other genres such as mystery, fantasy, and historical fiction, and has translated Scandinavian prose and poetry. As a science fiction writer, Anderson has been called "the backbone of the genre" and "a journeyman fabricator of interstellar adventures." He has written many different types of works, from pure fantasy to highly technical science fiction. Some critics feel that this breadth has hurt him from the standpoint of winning recognition and awards, because Anderson has not carved out a special niche unique to him and him alone. James Blish called Anderson's work "the enduring explosion"; the quality, quantity and sheer breadth of his achievements are unique in science fiction.

Although Anderson has written over sixty novels, it is his short stories which have won him both Hugo and Nebula awards. To date, he has won seven Hugos and three Nebulas. With the publication of *Tau Zero* (1970), Anderson finally began to get the recognition he rightly deserved. Three of his stories, "The Queen of Air and Darkness" (1971), "The Goat Song" (1972), and "The Saturn Game" (1982) have won both awards. Anderson's first major novel was *Brain Wave* (1954). Many still consider it one of his best.

Anderson has developed a future history called the Technic Civilization that covers from A.D. 2100 to A.D. 7100. There are two main periods containing more than fifteen novels and many short stories dealing with this future history. One concentrates on the Polesotechnic League, with Nicholas van Rign as the prinicpal hero, and the other on the Terran Empire, with Dominic Flandry leading the cast of characters. Anderson himself has not grouped his works in series; this has been left to the critics. There are two smaller future history series, the Psychotechic and the Rustum. "The Queen of Air and Darkness" belongs to the Rustum series.

A type of story in which Anderson combines fantasy and science fiction is time travel. His works in this combined genre include novels (*There Will Be Time*, 1972) and short stories, some of which are collected in *The Guardians of Time* (1981, first published in 1960).

Many of Anderson's works contain a comic element. One series of stories, dealing with the Hokas, has been labeled as broad farce. Written with Gordon R. Dickson, the stories have been collected in *Earthman's Burden* (1957) and *Hoka!* (1983). Hokas are furry aliens resembling teddy bears. They cannot understand idiomatic, nonliteral language, and encounter strange problems with humans. Hokas have astonishing physical strength and energy for their size. A novel with a comic plot is *Virgin Planet* (1959), which tells of a planet where a shipload of women has been wrecked.

Anderson is considered one of the five or six most important writers to appear during the science fiction publishing boom of the decade following the end of World War II. In his early days, he was helped and encouraged by John W. Campbell. In his later works, Anderson found new uses for the traditional forms he inherited from the golden age of science fiction.

Themes and Style

Most critics applaud Anderson for his blending of various elements in his writing. In addition to scientific accuracy, he uses historical perspective and elements from Nordic and Celtic myths. He is considered an excellent world builder; Anderson has written an article giving writers hints on how to build a scientifically accurate world. His world building goes beyond creating a habitable planet to creating fascinating inhabitants for his worlds. He is credited with originating most of the military tactics used in science fiction, with his battles being among the most exciting yet written.

In the writing of his science fiction works, Anderson begins with the background work of building a world as well as developing a biography of each important character. Included in the biography are physical description, age at the beginning of the story (and important life events of earlier years), psychological synopsis of the character's interests, hopes and fears, religious and political beliefs, etc. The plot and the characters grow simultaneously.

Anderson uses historical perspective in several ways. He writes historical science fiction, such as *High Crusade*, in which a spaceship full of aliens lands near a peaceful English village in A.D. 1345. The intent of the aliens to take over the Earth is thwarted by the might of the English arrow and sword over alien laser guns. The sole alien survivor moves on to other worlds and spreads English feudalism and medieval tactics throughout the universe. This mixture of historical romance, space adventure, and a comic element is an excellent example of why Anderson's works are entertaining and enjoyable.

A blending of science fiction and fantasy occurs in Anderson's use of the world of fairy. In "The Queen of Air and Darkness," fairy has been a deceit from which humans need to be rescued. Although the natives of Roland have used the memories of human folklore brought to Roland as weapons to entice the humans, the fact that these myths and archetypes have lasted in those memories even on a distant planet suggests that they are more than mere inventions. The myths must satisfy some suprarational need that science and the machine do not. The world of the Queen of Roland is only partly dream and illusion. Although the natives are gentle and live only in the twilight northern hemisphere, they do communicate via telepathy and other nonrational means. Their world has much that seems superior to the human's machine culture. They are expert biological scientists but have decided against the machine in order to live in harmony with nature and with each other. Nevertheless, the Queen and her land are a sham, and to submit to the dream that she offers would end in the gradual disappearance of human life from Roland.

"Goat Song" is like "The Queen of Air and Darkness," in that both stories explore humanity and its reactions to or use of myths. The mythic source is the Orpheus story; the scientific concept is the ruling computer. Elfland is a false Eden, a green world that would seduce humans away from their responsibilities, from their quests and tragedies which make them truly human. One of Anderson's earlier works, showing the world of the fairy as a more recognizably false world, is *Three Hearts and Three Lions* (1961).

Extrapolative intelligence and a mythic sensibility combine with occasionally florid but more often powerful rhetoric in Anderson's works to generate structures of imagery, setting, character, event, and metaphor that both claim and reward serious attention. Anderson's planets, like Thomas Hardy's landscapes, are not just settings but aspects of meaning. He is inclined to regard the world from this elemental--sometimes manic, sometimes grim--perspective. Anderson's stories often show the interaction between rational creatures and their environment. Challenge requires response which requires responsiblity for the response. Anderson makes a distinction between licit and illicit interference. Two stories which show attempts at illicit interference are "The Long Voyage" (1960) and "No Truce for Kings" (1963). While in "The Sharing of Flesh" (1969) and "The Hunter's Moon" (1978), the interference can be justified.

Anderson's heros have pragmatical ethics. They are often typical members of a group or class distinguished principally by willingness to seize the initiative. These heroic adventures are not glamorous, but grubby. A hero finds the meaning of life in the living and the seeking of mystery, beauty, and love.

Anderson's views are seen as conservative, though perhaps they could more fruitfully be regarded as romantic, Midwestern, libertarian individualism. Anderson has been called a thorough-going romantic, because he exalts experience over intellect, and love over knowledge. He rejects, even fears, absolutes. His writings show a savoring wonder for the purpose of life. In many stories, he shows that the purest happiness is domestic. Another domestic element in his stories is the presence, or absence, of children. In "The Goat Song" (1972), the absence of children is an indication that all is not right with the world.

Anderson takes the long view--that is, not on the biographical scale but on the historical and geological scales. He sees the long isolation of science fiction as strictly a twentieth-century phenomenon. Its special concepts and techniques are becoming common property, employed not only by the mass media but by some of our most respected mainstream writers. In turn, science fiction is shedding its artistic parochialism and starting to communicate beyond a small circle of enthusiasts. Science fiction, for Anderson, is but one human accomplishment among countless others which as something to offer to the world. Most of all, he finds it a lot of fun as well.

Plot Summaries of Major Works

"Goat Song." Winner of the Hugo and Nebula awards, the main character of this novelette is Harper, who carries a harp and composes songs. The world of this story is controlled by a computer named SUM. The objective of SUM is the optimization of human activity. Every facet of life is controlled, from birth to death. Death is also programmed, although accidental deaths do occur. Most of the people live in cities and take time off to go to the "wild" country. During an outing to the desert area of the country, Harper's girlfriend dies from a snakebite. Harper and his woman were monogamous, which is unheard of in this world. Another woman, Thrakia, pursues Harper, following him to the country where she becomes the leader of a group of savage women. To keep in touch with the world, SUM sends out the Queen of Darkness. She travels the world from spring until winter. During the winter, she lives in the complex which houses SUM and is connected to him. The Queen of Darkness was once a real person, but is now completely an android and must be renewed every seven years. In his grief following his woman's death, Harper persuades the queen to take him to SUM, who has promised that some day it will be possible for resurrection from death. SUM tries and fails to resurrect Harper's woman, and Harper vows to destroy SUM. Harper begins his campaign by destroying his bracelet with a knife and ax, which become the symbols of his movement. The story ends with Harper going to his death at the hands of the wild women, lead by Thrakia. His last wish is that the movement which he began will continue and eventually destroy SUM.

This story brings to mind the ancient myth of Orpheus and Eurydice. Anderson used this myth once before, in *World without Stars* (1966). Orpheus, like Harper, was famous for his music. It is through his music that Harper persuades the Queen of Darkness to help him, just as Orpheus used his music to get Persephone to argue for him. Harper's trip to visit SUM is reminiscent of the descent of Orpheus into the underworld. Although SUM cannot control emotions as efficiently as bodies or minds, its control curbs emotional drives by discouraging interpersonal bonds, especially family ones. The lack of children in the story is a clue to social stagnation. Discovering Orpheus as his personal archetype gives Harper a battle plan for fighting myth with myth. He knows that his battle will unleash a storm of apocalyptic terror. But this cleansing catastrophe, foreshadowed by his martyrdom, is necessary to prepare for a new springtime.

The three women form a triad of archetypes. Thrakia ("The Thracian," referring to the homeland of Orpheus), his would-be mistress, is uncontrolled, promiscuous, predatory, and a celebrant of bloody mysteries. The Dark Queen, overcontrolled, virginal, subservient, is a victim bound to a cycle of death and rebirth. Harper's woman, a parallel to Eurydice, is a faithful lover and equal partner and occupies the happy mean between the other two.

"Goat Song" is the definitive science fictionalization of the Orpheus myth. The author balances echoes with reversals. His art lies in knowing when to adapt, when to change, and how to integrate all his allusions into one coherent whole. Anderson delivers his message in clear and dignified language. The technical challenge of using first person and present tense is superbly met. Nature imagery and seasonal cues are the foremost devices used. By tying action to matters like the growth of apple trees and the flight of geese, Anderson expresses his belief that people should belong to nature rather than to SUM.

"**The Longest Voyage.**" Taking place on a satellite of the planet Tambur, the story is narrated by Zhean, ship chaplain. The hero is Captain Rovic, captain of the *Golden Leaper*, who is on a quest to find the Aureate Cities. At first glance this could be a tale of Earth during the age of exploration, located in the South Seas. While searching for an island with fresh water, the ship's crew finds an outer island of an archipelago ruled by Iskilip, a priest/emperor. Yarzik, the first island landed on, is ruled by Duke Guzan. Guzan is interested in using the ship's crew to help him challenge and take over Iskilip's rule. Val Nira, an offworlder, crashed his spaceship on the island forty years ago. He needs quicksilver to repair his spaceship and leave. Val Nira has been treated as an oracle by Iskilip, who does not want him to leave and jealously guards him from outsiders. If Rovic sailed to the island of Yurakadak, he could get the quicksilver for Val Nira. It would take about a year to complete the voyage. Iskilip does not want him to go for fear of losing his oracle. Rovic wonders if Val Nira should leave the satellite, because if Val Nira returns to his home planet, he promises to bring others to help the natives attain a higher civilization. Rovic's people are at that stage of discovery in which they are just beginning to realize that the world they are on is a satellite and that the huge ball hanging in the sky is a planet. Rovic feels that the people should be allowed to develop on their own, so he destroys Nira's spaceship. The explosion of the ship causes the volcano on which it rests to erupt.

This short story, which won the Hugo award in 1961, was first published in the December, 1960, issue of *Analog*. As in the stories of the Polesotechnic League, "The Long Voyage" reflects an era of Earth's history. This story also shows the careful world building of Poul Anderson. Rovic rejects premature interstellar contact lest his own world be deprived of an exciting stage in its development and thereby forfeit its own uniqueness. One wonders if the voyage of the title refers to Rovic's journey or to that of his own world, since it has a long way to go until it is a world with interstellar capabilities.

"No Truce for Kings." This story takes place on future Earth, after a nuclear war and the chaos resulting from that war. The world is recovering, slowly. Technology's revival has been delayed by the shortage of minerals and fuels. The Pacific States of America are primarily made up of areas ruled by bosses and a few cities, including the capital, San Francisco. The head of government is the "Judge." As the story opens, Judge Brodsky is impeached and replaced by Judge Fallon, who wants to centralize the government, taking control away from the bossmen. This plan is backed by the Espers, a nonviolent group who live in communes and practice the Way of Peace. Among its members are those who are adepts and able to use psionics, supposedly for defense only. The followers of Judge Brodsky resist the attempt by Judge Fallon to take over and civil war breaks out. Colonel Mackenzie of the Rolling Stones group backs Judge Brodsky, while his son-in-law, Captain Tom Danielis, follows Fallon. The progress of the civil war is followed by switching back and forth between these two men and their commands. Another element in the story is the conversations between Mwyr, a psychodynamician and his leader. Through these conversations, it is revealed that the Espers were started by aliens with psychic powers and other tools at their command. The aliens feel that centralization would benefit their plans to create a communal, nonmaterialistic world, which would then be ready to join them in the mastery of the universe. In the end, the forces of Brodsky take over San Francisco. Brodsky's men argue with the aliens over their belief that they know what is best for mankind; the aliens should have made people aware of their presence, rather than trying to shape their destiny. Another alien vessel will not arrive for a century and the task of rebuilding Earth begins.

In many respects a traditional war story, set in the future, "No Truce for Kings" raises many questions about how mankind organizes governments. Similar to "The Long Voyage," the story argues that humans should be allowed to develop on their own, without interference from aliens.

"The Queen of Air and Darkness." As the story opens, two changelings, Mistherd and Shadow-of-a-Dream, are enjoying a magical twilight. A pook (child-stealing fairy) brings a human child into the clearing, seeking approval of the Queen of Air and Darkness, a beautiful but terrifying figure. She rules a kingdom of pooks, nicores (sea sprites), elves, giants, and changelings (those humans who have been stolen away and raised in the fairy world). The story takes place on the planet Roland, so distant from Earth and other human civilizations that its millions of humans, who live mostly in the city of Christmas Landing, are visited by starships only two or three times a century.

The kidnapped child is three-year-old Jimmy Cullen, son of Barbro Cullen, a recent widow and arrival on Roland. Barbro hires Eric Sherrinford, a detective, to find her son. Though children have disappeared before, any rumors are generally discounted as leftover folklore from Earth. Yet Eric proposes that there is some truth to the myths and, with Barbro, sets out for the northland where the queen supposedly reigns. Eric captures Mistherd and Barbro is captured by a likeness of her dead husband, who urges her to remain with him and Jimmy as a reunited family. Eric convinces Mistherd that she has been deceived by the queen through telepathic powers. Together, Eric and Mistherd break through the queen's defenses and rescue Jimmy and Barbro.

This story first appeared in 1971 in *Magazine of Fantasy and Science Fiction.* It has won both the Hugo and Nebula awards. It is an example of Anderson's blending of science fiction with myth. The fairy world appears in many of Anderson's works. Seen from this perspective, fairy has once again become a deceit from which humans must be rescued. Humans, however, need the fairy myths. At the same time, to fall under their enchantment is stultifying. Miesel feels Anderson has translated the ancient rivalry between humans and elves into purely science fiction terms. The warm misty twilight of Roland's artic wilderness glows with auroral banners, moonbeams, and phosphorescent flowers. Species names like firethorn and crownbuck and place names like Cloudmoor and Troll Scarp reinforce the fairy-tale mood. The blending of Norse and Celtic elements strengthens the plausibility that the Outlings are weaving their webs from diverse cultural threads.

Anderson injects his belief into the narrative to suggest that Homo can truly be called sapiens when he or she practices the specialty of being unspecialized or unique. By centering the plot on the problem of a small boy's disappearance, Anderson reiterates his view that children are the key to everything. Eric and Barbro have let the stereotypes of the rational detective and the grieving widow limit their lives. Rather than destroy the fairy culture, Eric hopes that humans will learn to share, because both cultures have much to teach each other; machine and fairy need not be at odds. The qualities which bring Eric and Barbro success in their quest--curiosity, persistence, loyalty, unselfishness, discipline, and independence--are ones that all people need when confronting entropy. These are the virtues of free, responsible people who yield to neither stasis nor disorder.

The position that Anderson arrives at in the end of the story is an uncomfortable one, a paradox in which belief and doubt must exist side by side. The rationalist Eric comes to accept aspects of human experience, feelings, and telepathy that lie outside of hard science.

"The Saturn Game." This novella tells of the exploratory party from the ship *Cronos* which is to investigate the satellite of Saturn called Iapetus. There are four crew members: Colin Scobie, geologist; Jean Broberg, physicist; Luis Garcilaso, pilot; and Mark Danzig, industrial chemist. It has taken *Cronos* eight years to reach Saturn. To help the crew survive the long trip, psychodramas, similar to present-day games of Dungeons and Dragons, are used. Scobie plays Sir Kendrick, Broberg acts as Princess of Maranoa, and Garcilaso portrays a mentor to the princess. The crew knew that the satellite was half white (ice) and half black (rock), so the game has the princess as a prisoner of an elf king who lives in a land of ice. Once *Cronos* lands on the ice side of Iapetus, the three game players set out to explore the satellite, leaving the industrial chemist, Danzig, on the ship. The three are trapped by a landslide when they try to go into a large crater (or, the Dance Hall of the Elf King). Danzig sends to Earth for help, but it is hundreds of hours away. Garcilaso is the most seriously injured and dies. Scobie and Broberg try to climb out of the crater while Danzig attempts to maneuver the craft closer to them. *Cronos* crashes, but is not totally destroyed. In order to make it out of the crater, the two crew members finally realize that their game personnas must die. This frees them from the power of the game to take over reality. As the story ends, it seems that they will escape the crater and return to the craft. A minority report filed on the exploration blames the tragedy on the use of psychodrama, but a fictional dissenting report by an individual named Minamoto does not agree. He sees space exploration to be hazardous in any event.

In other works, Anderson uses a type of psychodreaming to help crews on long voyages keep their sanity. Playing out these dreams is one variation on this technique. The dangers of becoming so involved in a make-believe world that reality is forgotten are presented on a large scale. This story also contains interesting speculations as to why the satellite Iapetus is so unique. This story is a blend of the scientific and the imaginative, a hallmark of Anderson's writing.

Tau Zero. The *Leonora Christine* spacecraft is launched toward the star Beta Virginis, thirty light years away. The placid twenty-third century Earth, which launches the expedition, is a clean, orderly and just world dominated by international peace keeper Sweden. Nonetheless, Earth is slowly stagnating. Because of an accident en route, the ship never reaches its destination. The ship will continue to travel faster and faster beyond its own galaxy and time until the voyage continues past the dissolution of this universe and the formation of the next.

The fifty-member crew is a cross-section of humanity. The full range of ethnic types is represented, a symbolically appropriate arrangement that is also grounded in sociopolitical reality. Each major character also stands for a religious or philosophical position. These characters are gene packets, data banks, value statements and functional roles before they are autonomous individuals. Many of the characters' names contain allusions or wordplays--Anderson is fond of studding his work with references to history, myth, or the arts. Note Charles Reymont (Charlemagne and "king's mountain"), Lindgren (green linden branch), Freiwald (free forest), and Margarita (the Faust legend). The ship itself bears the most significant name of all. Leonora Christine Ulfeld was a seventeenth-century Danish princess who survived twenty-two years of solitary imprisonment with sanity intact, and wrote celebrated memoirs upon her release. Like the *Leonora Christine*'s crew, she endured and triumphed.

Tau Zero has much to say about the nature of authority, because this is an irreplaceable social mechanism for controlling chaos. Reymont rules so well that he is able to abdicate after leading the ship to its promised land. Reymont's personal excellence also wins him the love of the two finest women on board. During the voyage, the universe decays and a child is conceived. The potential mythical significance of this last child born in the old universe is left to the readers' imagination. The parent-child bond Reymont invokes becomes a lifeline. Love incarnated in one's offspring is humanity's best and boldest defiance of physical entropy. Fittingly, this infant is a girl. She belongs to *Tau Zero*'s ensemble of feminity: Earth and New Earth, the original destination Beta Virginis, Reymont's supportive lovers, and a ship named after an indominable woman. Anderson consistently sees woman as man's sublimest inspiration and dearest helpmate.

Anderson is even more interested in his characters' principles than in their genes or ethnic backgrounds. The novel presents a running debate among conflicting philosophical and religious viewpoints. Reymont's tireless efforts to make people survive in spite of themselves arouses much resentment. The magnificence of this communal victory outshines individual failures. Anderson blends physics and philosophy with stunning and dramatic results. He sees intelligence transcending determinism. The crew turns the very laws of space and time, which are the enemy's strengths, against it. The book's literary form is a direct consequence of its scientific postulates. Some have complained that his human cast looks petty beside Nature's majestic scenery, but contrasting the smallness of humanity with the might of the universe is essential to the novel's theme. The tie to the old universe must be cut before the crew can cleave to the new. The crew survives by rejecting the allure of madness, numbing distractions, and suicide. Willingness to survive proves harder to instill than would resignation to death. Anderson sees humanity's purpose in the capacity for wonder and struggle against all odds throughout all ages of the cosmos.

Biographical/Bibliographical Readings

Poul Anderson, "The Creation of Imaginary Worlds: Builder's Handbook and Pocket Companion," in *Science Fiction, Today and Tomorrow*, ed. Reginald Bretnor (Harper and Row, 1974), p.235-58. James Blish, "Poul Anderson: The Enduring Explosion," *Magazine of Fantasy and Science Fiction* 40(4), p.52-55. Gordon R. Dickson, "Poul Anderson," *Magazine of Fantasy and Science Fiction* 40(4), p.46-51 (Reprinted in *The Best from Fantasy and Science Fiction: A Special 25th Anniversary Anthology*, ed. Edward L. Ferman [Doubleday, 1974], p.232-41). Michael W. McClintock, "Poul Anderson," *Twentieth-Century American Science-Fiction Writers* (Gale, 1981), p.3-12. Sandra Miesel, *Against Time's Arrow: The High Crusade of Poul Anderson* (Borgo Press, 1978). [**Mina Jane Grothey**]

ANTHONY, PIERS

Life and Works

Piers Anthony Dillingham Jacob was born on August 6, 1934, in Oxford, England. His parents were well-educated, Oxford University graduates. Five years later, Anthony moved with his family to Spain, then a year later to America. He attended schools in Pennsylvania and began his career in science fiction with his first submitted and rejected short story in 1954. He became a United States citizen in 1958. He completed a B.A. degree in creative writing from Goddard College, Vermont, in 1956. In lieu of a thesis, he had written a novel, *The Unstilled World*, later reworked as part of *Sos the Rope* (1968). Anthony, his wife and daughter currently reside in Inverness, Florida, sharing a reclusive lifestyle.

His first published story, "Possible to Rue," appeared in *Fantastic* in 1963. Concentrating on short fiction at first, he published his first major novel, *Chthon*, in 1967, following seven years of work on the manuscript. In 1968, Anthony published three novels: *Omnivore*, *Sos the Rope*, and *The Ring* (with Robert E. Margroff). A year later, *Macroscope* (1969) appeared, one of Anthony's most important novels--certainly one of his most ambitious--taking, as it does, the history of the universe as its theme and incorporating complex images and symbol-patterns drawn from literature and music, astronomy and astrology.

In the next several years, Anthony continued to build on his reputation as a prolific writer of unusual imagination and range. *Prostho Plus* (1971), the adventures of an intergalactic dentist (combining earlier short stories), showed Anthony's abilities at picaresque science fiction, while *Omnivore, Orn* (1971), and *Ox* (1976) developed further Anthony's interests in social commentary, extrapolative speculation, and vegetarianism. He published juvenile science fiction, including *The E.S.P. Worm* (1970, with Robert E. Margroff) and *Race against Time* (1973). With Roberto Fuentes, he completed several Jason Striker martial-arts novels in the mid 1970s.

During this period, Anthony began many of the series that have become his trademark. In 1972, he completed *Var the Stick*; three years later, he published *Neq the Sword*. Together with *Sos the Rope*, they appeared in 1978 as the Battle Circle series. Other novels written with Robert E. Margroff include *Triple Detente* (1974) and *The Ring* (1968).

Two important novels appeared in 1977, *Cluster* and *A Spell for Chameleon*. *Cluster* initiated a five volume sequence based on intergalactic travel. In 1979, Anthony published *God of Tarot*, the first of a serious science fiction trilogy completed by *Faith of Tarot* (1980) and *Vision of Tarot* (1980). Anthony has stated that he considers the Tarot novels as among his most important. 1980 also saw the appearance of *Split Infinity*, followed by *Blue Adept* (1981) and *Juxtaposition* (1981), the three volumes of the *Apprentice Adept* series. Focusing on the parallel worlds of Proton and Phaze, they examine the relationship between science fiction and fantasy, through the mediation of Stiles, a character capable of crossing at will into either frame.

In 1983, the first volume of the Bio of a Space Tyrant series was published. This five-volume work traces the history of Hope Hubris, Tyrant of Jupiter, as he moves across an interplanetary stage that ultimately becomes a means for Anthony to confront the inequities and frustrations of contemporary politics. The five novels within the series are: *Refugee* (1983), *Mercenary* (1984), *Politician* (1985), *Executive* (1985), and *Statesman* (1986).

A final series (to date), Incarnations of Immortality, moves again into the interface between science fiction and fantasy, reality and imagination. As of 1987, the published novels in the series are: *On a Pale Horse* (1983), *Bearing an Hourglass* (1984), *With a Tangled Skein* (1985), and *Wielding a Red Sword* (1986).

In addition to these series, Anthony has published a number of individual novels (by 1985, he had published fifty). Many of his earlier, out-of-print works have been reissued including *Steppe* (1976; 1985) and *The Ring* (1968; 1986). One early short story, "The Ghost Galaxies," has been expanded and published as *Ghost* (1986). One collection of short stories, *Anthology* (1986), has also appeared; its twenty-one stories give a fine introduction to Anthony's shorter works.

Anthony's career has been marked by the increasing diversity of his works--and their increasing popularity. He has received Hugo and Nebula nominations for such works as "The Message," "Getting through the Universe," "In the Barn," *Macroscope*, and *A Spell for Chameleon*.

Themes and Style

Anthony's first novel, *Chthon*, and its sequel, *Phthor*, defined many of Anthony's recurring character types, themes, and motifs: maturity and immaturity; sexuality; extravagant humor; cataclysmic change; music as image and metaphor; and the roles of myth and symbol. He often incorporates sexuality or violence as metaphor, writing such intentionally offensive and difficult narratives as "In the Barn" and "On the Uses of Torture" (the latter so extreme that it took nearly a decade for it to find a publisher). His earlier works also emphasized his commitment to vegetarianism, his concern for individual, social, and cultural maturity and control, and his wideranging imagination, capable of creating and peopling worlds that at once entertain and make cogent statements about contemporary problems.

In the Bio of a Space Tyrant series, Anthony incorporates major events of his own present (from the boat people to Sino-Soviet relations) into this future-oriented narrative, often using violence and brutality as tools for emphasizing his opinions. The five volumes blend political theorizing with social consciousness, often to the detriment of narrative. In the Incarnations of Immortality novels, Anthony uses as his central character literal incarnations of abstract principles: Time, War, Death, Nature, and Fate. He juxtaposes science and magic, creating a world in which Satan as character mingles with damsels in distress and with Bat Durston and the BEMs.

Anthony's narratives are characterized by breadth of imagination; by social, moral, and political consciousness; and by an undeviating integrity. Among his weaknesses are a style that occasionally becomes too stridently dependent on exclamation points, and a tendency for plot and philosophy to form uneasy alliances. In general, however, Anthony's work suggests his maturity and facility as a writer and thinker, often controversial, but just as often energetic and engaging.

Plot Summaries of Major Works

The Apprentice Adept series. The three Apprentice Adept novels--*Split Infinity*, *Blue Adept*, and *Juxtaposition*--trace the adventures of an exjockey and game player, Stile, within the frames of two alternate realities. The science fictional Proton is a world of robots and games, where even a serf such as Stile can become a master Gamesman and aspire to permanent residence. When Stile is injured and must flee for his life, he penetrates the barrier between Proton and its fantasy analogue, Phaze, to discover that in this alternate world he is the Blue Adept, one of the powerful magicians controlling that frame. Shifting back and forth from Proton to Phaze in order to survive, Stile finally understands the crisis approaching for both. Although separate worlds, they overlap, sharing a dual reality that is both science fiction and fantasy.

Through this double setting, Anthony blends the genres through his ingenious use of narrative, characters, and language. In its combination of science fiction and fantasy, the Apprentice Adept trilogy foreshadows his current series, the Incarnations of Immortality.

Battle Circle. The Battle Circle novels are among Anthony's most intriguing exercises in social order and control. *Sos the Rope*, *Var the Stick*, and *Neq the Sword* outline the rise and fall of the Battle society, a construct imposed upon postholocaust American society as a means of providing a safe outlet for agression and preventing the rise of empire--and its consequent spiral into destruction. *Sos the Rope* defines the initial state of society and the first suggestions of disruption. The more Odyssean *Var the Stick* provides a close-up look at the workings of society, as the mutant Var moves across the continent. And, finally, *Neq the Sword* traces the final breakdown of battle-circle society and its regeneration as the only viable form of political and social control.

Violent, graphic, often disquieting, the Battle Circle novels nonetheless suggest Anthony's formidable powers of imagination and re-creation. His characters are often larger than life, yet they retain an essential humanity that invites empathy. Through that empathy, Anthony defines what it is to be human and what is required to preserve that humanity in the face of disorder and chaos.

Bio of a Space Tyrant. Consisting of five novels, each volume focuses on a portion of Hope Hubris's life and on concommitant social and political problems. In *Refugee*, he leaves his home world, only to fall prey to space pirates. His experiences are based on those of the boat-people of Viet Nam and Cuba--refugees who dare not return to their own lands but are refused entry into other lands. *Mercenary* outlines Hubris's rise within the military, followed by *Politician*, *Executive*, and finally, *Statesman*, in which he orchestrates a plan that will resolve the political disunity that plagues the Solar System.

At times the political allegories and parallels are too obvious; at other times, Anthony becomes so involved in them that he relinquishes the narrative movement for pages at a time. Yet taken as a whole, the Bio novels clarify Anthony's attitudes, incorporating many of his trademark themes and applying them directly to present, pressing problems.

The five-volume biography of Hope Hubris provides Anthony with an opportunity to speak directly about contemporary issues. More politically oriented than is common in Anthony's other works, Bio translates many of the political problems of twentieth-century Earth onto the planets of the solar system, transforming them to meet the needs of his narrative, but retaining their clear-cut symbolic referents. Bio is thus Anthony's response to problems endemic to our world, our culture, our society.

Chthon and **Phthor.** In terms of myth, poetry, and symbolism, *Chthon* is a modern classic as it narrates the struggles of Aton Five to escape the prison planet Chthon and discover his own identity and destiny. Its sequel, *Phthor*, focuses on Aton's son Arlo, and shifts from Greek to Norse myth--specifically the legends of Thor and the Gotterdammerung. In completing what his father began, Arlo first allies with, then opposes the cavern-diety Chthon. Their final confrontation becomes a distant/future Ragnarok, with the existence of the physical universe at stake.

Anthony worked for seven years on *Chthon*; the effort was repaid by the critical and popular attention the novel received. A Hugo and Nebula nominee, it was recognized as a major achievement, complexly and meticulously plotted, peopled by fascinating characters, set on exotic worlds, and structured around classical Greek mythology.

Both novels rearrange chronology and reality to emphasize Anthony's symbolic and thematic interests. Both concentrate on questions of responsibility and control, on sexuality, on inversions of expectations. Characters' names become complex puns, often connecting with the mythic patterns Anthony employs. Either read separately or as a single narrative, *Chthon* and *Phthor* represent some of Anthony's finest and most powerful writing.

Macroscope. *Macroscope* begins with the development of the macroscope, a device that allows humans to receive millenia-old images stored on macrons. It represents a key to the galaxy and to human development; yet one element, the Destroyer beam, obscures critical transmissions and destroys the minds of scientists intelligent enought to understand its messages. Ivo Archer, Brad Carpenter, Afra Glynn Summerfield, and Harold and Beatry Groten tackle the problem of the Destroyer beam and discover the Traveler beam, opening the galaxies to human exploration. In a climactic sequence, Anthony combines astrology, music, and the poetry of Sidney Lanier in a resolution that defines the Traveler and Destroyer beams and affirms the maturity of humanity as a species capable of handling the new power they have discovered.

Macroscope is one of Anthony's strongest works, an amalgam of science and imagination that blends biology, astronomy, physics, paleontology, history, music, and astrology with memorable characterization, a sense of mystery, and actions of galactic import to create a science fictional tour de force. A long work, *Macroscope* deals with control, responsiblity, and self-discipline on individual, cultural, planetary, and cosmic levels; as such it is a logical culmination to many of Anthony's early novels.

Biographical/Bibliographical Readings

Peter Brigg, "Analogies of Scale in Piers Anthony's *Macroscope*," in *Science Fiction Studies* 2 (July, 1975), p.119-30. Michael R. Collings, *Piers Anthony* (Starmont House, 1983). Daryl Lane, "Piers Anthony," in *The Sound of Wonder* (Oryx, 1985), v. 2, p.1-28. Charles Platt, "Piers Anthony," in *Dream Makers* (Berkley, 1983), v. 2, p.103-11. [Michael R. Collings]

ASIMOV, ISAAC

Life and Works

Isaac Asimov was born in Petrovichi, Russia, on January 2, 1920. His family came to the United States in 1923 and he became a naturalized citizen in 1928. Asimov's family owned a candy store in Brooklyn and he often felt orphaned by the necessity of his parents' presence in the store. From an early age, Asimov was considered unusually intelligent and he quickly progressed through high school and college. He received a B.S., M.A., and Ph.D. in chemistry from Columbia University. During the interim period between his masters and Ph.D., he worked as a junior chemist at the Navy Yard in Philadelphia and served a brief eight months in the U.S. Army just as World War II was coming to an end. Science had always been Asimov's best subject, and he considered pursuing a medical career for a time. He diverted from the medical path, however, and became a professor of biochemistry at the Boston University School of Medicine, a position he still holds (though in title only) since he began to devote full time to writing in 1958. Asimov has been married twice--to Gertrude Blugerman in 1948, mother of a son and daughter, and in 1973, to Janet Opal Jepperson.

One of the most prolific of science fiction writers, Asimov has published over three hundred books. Modesty is not one of his most notable characteristics; each of his centennial celebrations has evoked a book: *Opus 100* (1969); *Opus 200* (1980); and *Opus 300* (1984); all of which are selections from his fiction and nonfiction writings. If he maintains his present pace, Asimov will no doubt achieve *Opus 400* in his writing career. Although best known for his science fiction works, Isaac Asimov has also published books on history, science for laypersons, juvenile fiction, a biblical reference work, a guide to Shakespeare, and a two-volume, 1560-page autobiography (*In Memory Yet Green* in 1979 and *In Joy Still Felt* in 1980; he plans yet a third autobiographical volume, to be entitled *The Scenes of Life*). He has edited and compiled numerous anthologies and collections of his own works and those of other science fiction authors. These collections, such as *Before the Golden Age* (1974) and *The Hugo Winners* (various dates), represent a gathering together of the best and most honored science fiction literature.

Asimov's first published story, "Marooned off Vesta," was not published in Campbell's magazine, *Astounding Science Fiction*, but appeared instead in a competitor, *Amazing Stories*, in March of 1939. Two years later Campbell published Asimov's "Nightfall" in the September, 1941 issue of *Astounding*. Asimov's first published novel was *Pebble in the Sky* in 1950.

Asimov has received numerous accolades and honors for his works of science fiction. In 1966, "Nightfall" was voted the Best Science Fiction Short Story of All Time by the Science Fiction Writers Association. His award-winning works include: Hugo and Nebula for *The Gods Themselves* (1972), "The Bicentennial Man" (1976), a Hugo for *Foundation's Edge*, and the Nebula Grand Master Award in 1987. Asimov's Foundation trilogy was presented a special Hugo award for Best All Time Series.

Although Isaac Asimov has excelled in other literary fields, he is proudest of his work as a science fiction author; he is well-known and has brought many new fans and academicians into an appreciation of the genre. *Isaac Asimov's Science Fiction Magazine* encourages new science fiction writers. Science fiction owes much to his intelligence, creativity, and talent.

Themes and Style

Isaac Asimov's novels, books, and short stories strictly adhere to the accurate presentation of scientific facts and phenomena, yet his style is personal, informal, and enthusiastic. Many of his non-fiction works are considered models of scientific works for laypersons because Asimov explains scientific facts so clearly and thoroughly. It is apparent from his fiction and nonfiction works that Asimov believes in the benevolence of scientific advancement. The perception of scientific and technological advances as being threatening to mankind occurs basically because of human distrust of new ideas and resistance to change. Rationalism, the triumph of reason over emotion, is another characteristic of Asimov's writing. Villains as well as heroes may be rational beings, but the hero eventually succeeds. The superior rationality of the hero enables him or her to deduce the best method for overcoming whatever problems lie in the path.

Science fiction, for Isaac Asimov, is based on sociological change such as mankind's acceptance of and reliance on robots and other technological innovations. The technological changes are not as important as human reaction to the changes. This sociological function, which is a major theme in many of his stories and novels, is attributable to Asimov's long and close association with John W. Campbell. Campbell had a great deal of influence on Asimov during his early years as a writer, urging him to emphasize people rather than machines, including more humans than aliens in his fiction.

Asimov's Foundation trilogy--*Foundation* (1951), *Second Foundation* (1953), *Foundation and Empire* (1962) and its subsequent volumes, *Foundation's Edge* (1982) and *Foundation and Earth* (1986), sets forth his theory of psychohistory (the science of predicting mass human behavior and thus future history). The novels are reminiscent of several retellings of the rise, decline, and fall of the Roman Empire, as throughout the Foundation series, many generations, epochs, and galactic empires are presented in epic proportions. The planners of future empires base their theories for future generations on psychohistory and periodically send electronic oracles to alert humanity of the next steps to be taken in human history. This omniscience of the founders of Foundation may be seen as manipulation of future generations to a desired end. Although individual details of future history are not known, mass movements and generalizations can be formed.

Originally written as a series of short stories, Foundation traces Hari Seldon's grandiose plan to shorten the dark ages between the fall of one galactic empire and the rise of the next. While some critics view the novels as too loosely held together and seriously flawed, it cannot be denied that the Foundation series is a landmark of science fiction literature. It brought science fiction out of the "space opera" stereotypical plot into a complex view of the future of mankind. Bug-eyed monsters do not appear in Foundation; it is primarily an empire composed of human, rather than alien, beings.

Isaac Asimov is responsible for the creation and proliferation of the "Three Laws of Robotics." The laws require robots to protect human beings, obey the orders of human beings, and protect themselves as well, unless this would cause harm to humans. Most robots appearing in science fiction literature since the creation of the three laws function under the laws whether explicitly or indirectly. The laws of robotics have become tenets of the genre. The three laws first appeared in *I, Robot*, and Asimov first used the word "robotics." However, credit for the word "robot" (the Czech word for worker) must be given to Carel Kapek, who introduced it in his 1921 play, *R.U.R.* The term "robopsychologist" as a profession and "positronic" brains (brains implanted with the three laws and other knowledge necessary to perform a robot's functions) are also Asimov's creations. The proliferation of the laws of robotics throughout science fiction literature is attributable to his ingenious codification and interpretation.

In *Robots and Empire* (1985), Asimov sets down the Zeroth Law of Robotics, which states that robots may not injure humanity (as opposed to an individual human being) either deliberately or through inaction. Whereas the three original laws were conceived by humans, the Zeroth Law of robotics was conceived by two robots, R. Daneel Olivaw and R. Giskard Reventlow. The necessity for the Zeroth Law logically appears to the two robots in their struggle to save earth from the Spacers. It allows them the capacity to harm an individual human being or group of human beings when the rest of human society is threatened. The Zeroth law comes perilously close to the establishment of an omnipotent and all-powerful robot intelligence which, though operating with the utmost logic and objectivity, nonetheless makes decisions without the emotions or passions so evident in humans. Whether or not the Zeroth law will become enmeshed in the literature of science fiction remains to be seen.

Two of Isaac Asimov's best known works, *I, Robot*, and *The Rest of the Robots*, have provided a unique contribution to the science fiction genre. *I, Robot*, is a compilation of nine short stories tied together by a narrative history of robotics and recurring characters. Asimov wanted to rebel against the Frankenstein theory of an evil mechanical being which turned against its creator, in favor of robots, which would be beneficial and supportive of individual people and, eventually, of all mankind. The conflicts which arise in the robot stories often occur not because of a defiency in a robot, but because of ambiguous instructions or programming from its maker or master. Asimov developed a Sherlock Holmes/Dr. Watson relationship between a man, Elijah Baley, and a humaniform robot, R. Daneel Olivaw, in three novels, *The Caves of Steel* (1954), *The Naked Sun* (1957), and *The Robots of Dawn* (1983). Daneel Olivaw, a robot and thus endowed with eternal life (as long as his circuits hold out), carries on the story in *Robots and Empire* (1985). His compadre in the third and fourth novels is another robot, Giskard Reventlow. The robot novels blend mystery and science fiction themes in a successful mixture.

Plot Summaries of Major Works

Foundation series. Currently consisting of five volumes, Asimov began the Foundation series in 1951 with the original novel, entitled *Foundation*, a compilation of stories begun in the 1940s. The second and third volumes, *Foundation and Empire* and *Second Foundation*, followed closely behind in 1952 and 1953. The three volumes were combined in 1963 as *The Foundation Trilogy*. A gap of thirty years ensued before the appearance of the fourth volume, *Foundation's Edge* in 1982. The final volume (to date), *Foundation and Earth*, was published in 1986.

The original series chronicles the history of the Galactic Empire and is essentially an epic tale of the future of humanity after the exploration and settlement of about twenty-five million inhabited planets of the galaxy. The character of Hari Seldon of the planet Trantor, the administrative center of the Galactic Empire, pervades the first three novels of the series. Seldon expands the science of psychohistory (a branch of mathematics dealing with the reactions of large masses of humanity to economic and social stimuli) to an ultimate plan for the development of societies. His theories become dogma and are believed to be the best path for humanity to follow in the coming era of the downfall of the Galactic Empire and its replacement by the Second Empire.

According to Seldon's plan, the dark ages after the fall could be shortened substantially; his plan to assure the transfer of human knowledge to the Second Empire is based on the establishment on the planet Terminus of a group of encyclopedists to gather, document, and preserve this knowledge. Simultaneously with the establishment of Terminus, Seldon also creates another, rather mysterious Foundation at the other end of the Galaxy, on a planet known as Star's End. Seldon planned to reappear (in holographic form) at irregular times during the future to bolster the program.

Foundation. The first volume of the series, after laying out the Seldon plan, enumerates the battles that occur between planets and kingdoms of the Empire during the first two centuries after Seldon. Salvor Hardin, Mayor of Terminus, becomes the most powerful figure in the Empire for the first generation. During the time of the traders and the merchant princes, Hober Mallow, a trader from Smyrnos, establishes the primacy of the traders and encourages the decline and fear of atomic power.

Foundation and Empire. The second novel tells of the fall of the Empire. Bel Riose, Peer of the Empire (which has as its seat the metal planet of Trantor), is overwhelmed by "The Mule," a mutant who has mental powers which enable him to control and adjust the emotions of humans. Bayta Derell, along with her husband, Toran, and Ebling Mis, a scholar, set out for Trantor to find the true location of the Second Foundation established by Seldon, hoping that this will help the Empire defeat the mule. On their journey, they meet Bobo, the mule's clown, and befriend him after helping him escape from the Kalgan soldiers. Ebling Mis studies the documents in the Imperial Library at Terminus, and just when he believes he has discovered the location of the Second Foundation, Bayta kills him in order to keep the location from Bobo, who is in actuality the mule. Bayta becomes a legendary hero by saving the Second Foundation from being overcome by the mule.

Second Foundation. Bayta's granddaughter, Arkady Derell, is the young heroine. At the tender age of fourteen, she travels to Kalgan with Homer Munn to continue the search for the Second Foundation. Interspersed with Arkady and Homer's quest are intervals in which the "speakers" of the Second Foundation speak, after the fashion of a Greek chorus, about the search that goes on for their whereabouts. It is in this novel that the true purpose of the Second Foundation becomes apparent. The "speakers" are the pscyhohistorians and mental scientists to whom Seldon bequeathed his knowledge when he left purely historical aspects to the encyclopedists on Terminus. They carry out Seldon's plan by means of the prime radiant, a visual wall which vibrates with a multitude of mathematical formulas for the fulfillment of the plan. The speakers have placed mentalics, with powers to adjust minds, at critical points in the galaxy. Arkady is befriended by Lady Callia, wife of Lord Stettin of Kalgan. When it appears that Stettin plans to imprison Arkady and Homer, Lady Callia sends Arkady to the spaceport, where she is saved from imprisonment by Preem Palver from Trantor. Palver, it is later learned, is actually the "First Speaker" of the Second Foundation, and Lady Callia is one of the mentalics. The speakers thus reassure their secretive location on Trantor and their pursuance of the success of the Seldon plan.

Foundation's Edge. The fourth novel begins some five hundred years after the beginning of the Seldon plan. The main characters in the novel are Golan Trevize, a councilman from Terminus, who does not believe in the fairness of the Seldon plan, because it destroys free will by mind manipulation. For this heresy, he is exiled with Professor Janov Pelorat, a historian. Trevize is charged with finding the Second Foundation; Pelorat wants to find the planet of origins, Earth. A parallel plot concerns Stor Gendibal, a speaker of the Second Foundation who yearns to be first speaker. He knows of Trevize's search and is sent out to follow him. In their travels, Trevize and Pelorat can find no traces of Earth in any libraries--it seems to have been deleted from human history. Trevize and Pelorat decide to go to Gaia, which Pelorat believes may have been one of the forms of Earth's name.

On Sayshell, the closest inhabited planet to Gaia, another scholar, Quintesetz, tells them that there were two initial waves of planetary exploration--the first with robots, the second with only humans. Earth, according to Quintesetz, is a legend which, if it exists, has long been deserted. Other space travelers believed that Earth was deserted because it was highly radioactive. Trevize and Pelorat go on to Gaia, followed by Gendibal (both are followed by Harlo Branno, mayor of Terminus, who wants to conquer the Second Foundation).

At Gaia, a totally telepathic planet where all living beings and the total environment have formed a planetary consciousness, Trevize learns that he has been chosen to make the decision as to the future of the Empire. The three emerging forces are represented by Gendibal, whose Second Foundation offers guidance and peace, Branno and Terminus offering free will, and Gaia (represented by Novi Sur, a traveler with Gendibal), which offers life through a universal consciousness. Trevize chooses Gaia, although he does not understand why he made the choice. Branno returns to Terminus, believing she has set up a trading system with the Sayshell sector, and Gendibal returns to Trantor to become First Speaker; neither are aware that their minds have been tampered with by the Gaians.

Foundation and Earth. In the final volume (to date) of the series, Trevize, Pelorat, and Bliss (a telepathic Gaian in love with Pelorat) set out to find Earth. Only by finding Earth does Trevize feel that he can come to understand why he chose Gaia for the future Galaxia of the Empire. Their travels through space take them first to Comporellon where "Earth" is an unspoken name that strikes terror in the hearts of Comporellons. They are directed to the spacer worlds, which were the first worlds settled by the Earth's inhabitants. On Solaria, they encounter their first robots, the servants of Bander, a hermaphroditic human who lives in total isolation from other Solarians and reproduces only when an heir to his estate is needed. Bander plans to kill the three and they escape only by the strength of Bliss's telepathic abilities, taking with them Bander's heir, young Fallom. On the planet Melpomenia, they find the Hall of the Worlds, which gives the coordinates of other planets even closer to their eventual goal, Earth. After several other adventures, Trevize finally comes to the Earth's solar system, and finds that Earth is indeed deserted and radioactive. Dejected, he wants to give up his search, but the young Fallom is attracted to the Earth's large satellite, the moon and insists that they go there. Trevize realizes that the moon could be inhabited beneath its surface by means of an artificial atmosphere and begins to search immediately for signs of life. Indeed, he finds a subsurface area and meets R. Daneel Olivaw, a twenty-thousand year old robot who explains to him the mystery and history of humanity's spread into the universe.

The final novel weaves together Asimov's robot series with the Foundation series and leaves an opening for future novels as well. The young Fallom and R. Daneel Olivaw could well be the beginning of a new future for humanity. Written over a long period of time, the novels go from space opera to planet colonization, human psychology, and the decline of robots, to the final realization that, over all these thousands of years of human history, it was the robots who had shaped human history. There is practically no science fiction theme that is not represented in the five novels thus far. The latter two recent novels are the most cohesive, and the reader anxiously follows the explorers in their search for the origins of Earth, a planet whose existence was thought to be legend.

I, Robot. Originally written as nine separate short stories, Asimov collected the stories and connected them by means of an introduction and a continuing narrative of the history of robotics interspersed between the stories. Dr. Susan Calvin, robopsychologist for U.S. Robots, is the principal continuing character. Other characters who appear frequently are Dr. Alfred Lanning, director of research for U.S. Robots; Peter Bogert, his assistant; Steven Byerly, politician and World Coordinator; and two outer-space engineers, Gregory Powell and Mike Donovan.

"Robbie" is the first story in the collection and presents Robbie, the robot, who is purchased as a nursemaid for a young girl and eventually saves her life. Robbie introduces the stereotype of robots as pets and servants and establishes human opposition to robots (the Frankenstein complex). The robots throughout the stories are given human nicknames that correspond to their model numbers. Thus, RB-34 becomes "Herbie," QT-1 becomes "Cutie," SPD becomes "Speedy," and DV-5 becomes "Dave."

In "Liar," Herbie has the ability to read the minds of humans. He discovers that by telling the truth, he does not necessarily say what humans want to hear. Dr. Calvin points out to Herbie that even to hurt a human's feelings is a violation of the first law of robotics. This realization renders Herbie dysfunctional. "Little Lost Robot" demonstrates the ambiguities of instructions given to robots by their human masters. When a robot is told jokingly to "get lost!"--he promptly does just that. In "Reason," Cutie has become convinced in his positronic brain that he is superior to Powell and Donovan and proves his superiority by keeping an energy beam at precisely the correct point during an electron storm which could destroy the space station. In "Evidence," man and robot become disturbingly similar as a politician, Steven Byerly, is accused of being a robot because he has never been seen to sleep or eat. When Byerly strikes a heckler during the campaign--something a robot would never be able to do--the question appears to be resolved. Dr. Calvin points out, however, that a robot would be able to strike another robot which looks like a human being. The final story, "The Evitable Conflict," ultimately places the future of the world in the hands of the robots. The infinitely logical brain of the robots knows what is best for humanity.

Asimov's stories weave together the creation and history of robotics in science fiction. In the frontispiece of the collection can be found Asimov's "Three Laws of Robotics." The stories codify and demonstrate the development of the laws and have been set forth as models for other robots in science fiction literature. Asimov's goal of presenting robots as beneficial, benevolent, and necessary for the progress of mankind is accomplished in *I, Robot* and its companion collection, *The Rest of the Robots.*

Biographical/Bibliographical Readings

Isaac Asimov, *In Joy Still Felt* (Doubleday, 1980). Idem, *In Memory Yet Green* (Doubleday, 1979). Jean Fiedler and Jim Mele, *Isaac Asimov* (Ungar, 1982). James Gunn, *Isaac Asimov* (Oxford University Press, 1982). Marjorie M. Miller, *Isaac Asimov: A Checklist of Works Published in the United States, March 1939-May, 1972* (Kent State University Press, 1972). Maxine Moore, "Asimov, Calvin and Moses," in *Voices for the Future*, ed. Thomas D. Clareson (Bowling Green University Popular Press, 1976) v. 1, p.88-103. Sam Moskowitz, "Isaac Asimov," in *Seekers of Tomorrow* (World, 1966), p.249-65. **[Marilyn P. Fletcher]**

BALLARD, J. G.

Life and Works

James Graham Ballard's childhood years were spent in Shanghai, China, where he was born on November 15, 1930. During the Second World War, the Ballard family was interned by the Japanese in a civilian prisoner-of-war camp from 1942 to 1945. Ballard was repatriated, along with his mother and sister, in 1946, but recalls that England seemed small, sad, and colorless compared with the Americanized zone he had grown up in. After a period in boarding school, he went to King's College, Cambridge, in 1949, to study medicine with a view to becoming a psychiatrist. Ballard won a university short story competition in 1951 and switched to an English literature course, only to abandon that, too, within a year.

His first attempts at writing "experimental" short stories met with no success and, after several short-term jobs, he joined the Royal Air Force in 1953. As a trainee pilot stationed in Canada, he developed a taste for American science fiction magazines and this reading led directly to stories such as "Passport to Eternity" (1955) and "The Waiting Grounds" (1959), about the operators of a radio observatory on a distant planet. These two pieces can be found in the collections *Passport to Eternity* (1963) and *The Voices of Time and Other Stories* (1962). Other short stories of Ballard's early period are available in *Vermilion Sands* (1971) and *The Best Short Stories of J. G. Ballard* (1978). Other recent collections of his stories are: *Low-Flying Aircraft and Other Stories* (1976) and *Myths of the Near Future* (1982).

In the years from 1956 to 1961, during which he married and supported his family by working as a script writer for a scientific film company, and then as assistant editor of a scientific journal, Ballard's stories appeared in the leading British science fiction magazines of the time, *New Worlds* and *Science Fantasy*. In 1962, Ballard became a full-time writer, following Berkley Book's acceptance of *The Wind from Nowhere*, a forceful though orthodox disaster novel. Over the next three years he wrote the three world-transformation novels which established his name: *The Drowned World* (1962), *The Crystal World* (1966), a considerably expanded version of "Equinox" (1964), and *The Drought* (1965), first published in the United States in 1964 before a complete revision as *The Burning World*. His wife died in 1964 and he was left to raise three young children on his own.

The next ten-year period includes the innovative novel, *Love and Napalm: Export USA* (1970), also entitled *The Atrocity Exhibition*, and his second disaster trilogy, *Crash* (1973), *Concrete Island* (1974), and *High-Rise* (1975). In these disaster novels, science fiction conventions virtually disappear, replaced by isolated features of the urban environment.

His contributions to science fiction since then include the novel *Hello America* (1981). Some readers may find it his most appealing work, because it was intended as a light entertainment by Ballard and it is the closest he has come to a genre science fiction novel. Ballard's output of science fiction stories has also continued. *The Impossible Man and Other Stories* (1966) includes a Nebula award nominee--"The Drowned Giant," as well as "The Day of Forever" and the excellent title story. His latest short stories have been published in the British science fiction journal *Interzone*. Ballard's *Empire of the Sun* (1984), based on his childhood experience of the Japanese occupation of Shanghai, made him a best-selling author and put much of his earlier fiction back in print. His latest novel, *The Day of Creation* (1988) establishes his work in mainstream literature.

Themes and Style

J. G. Ballard's name is associated with the notion of "inner space" he first proposed in a seminal and much-discussed guest editorial in *New Worlds* (May 1962), entitled "Which Way to Inner Space?" This was virtually a manifesto for a new wave of science fiction. Ballard claimed that science fiction needed to rethink its narrative forms and plots. What needed exploring was not outer space but the "inner space" of our experience and the outer world of reality on the planet Earth. Ballard has explored this dimension of reality, using the science fiction genre.

His heroes take their lead from the catastrophe which disrupts the familiar world. "Inner space" means the fusion of inner and outer worlds, where the changes in the environment and the activities of the characters work together to produce a heightened or alternative reality--but which, under the special conditions of the narrative of world-transformation, can be observed and shared by the reader. From artists like Salvador Dali or Max Ernst, Ballard learned the principle of placing the logic of the visible at the service of the invisible. Ransom, the hero of *The Drought*, has a copy of Yves Tanguy's painting "Jours de Lenteur" pinned to the wall. The image it portrays corresponds almost exactly to the scene outside the windows of his houseboat. His experience of the catastrophe will take a similarly affirmative form--as it does for many of Ballard's heroes. There is always the characteristic ambivalence: does the metamorphosis mean self-destruction or self-realization?

Ballard is often described as an obsessional writer. This may be because he often returns to the same landscape and reuses the same set of symbols--drained swimming pools, low-flying or crashed airplanes, flight, and the basic elements of sand, air, and water. He frequently explores a severely restricted set of possibilities in his writings. Sometimes it is the obsession of the central character which abstracts a single wave length. In *Crash*, for example, Ballard takes the daring step of reducing all experience to the common denominator of violence, which acts therefore as the tenor of a single, giant metaphor for urban existence. The same process can be found as a theme in "The Overloaded Man" (1961) and in "Manhole 69" (1957), a story about an experiment in sensory deprivation.

In other cases the conflicting impulses of the hero are embodied, symbolically, in landscapes and in a small number of contrasting characters. Ballard's narratives often concern an individual coming to terms with the externalized components of his own makeup. The most striking example of this is *Concrete Island*, where the action never moves beyond a piece of wasteland at a traffic intersection. The hero, Maitland, who crashes his car there, begins to identify himself with it as it becomes an exact model of his head. Maitland's self-imprisonment and self-discovery are symbolic events which unfold in a symbolic location which nonetheless clearly represents a familiar situation, given a slight twist to bring its symbolic meaning into sharper focus. This pattern is the hallmark of J. G. Ballard's imagination.

Plot Summaries of Major Works

The Best Short Stories of J. G. Ballard. Like many science fiction authors, Ballard is essentially a short story writer. Many of his novels can be seen as expanded short stories. The four experimental pieces that close this collection were incorporated into *Love and Napalm: Export USA*. The other fifteen selections range from conventional science fiction tales like "The Concentration City" (1957), in which a global city has become an inescapable frame of mind, to the hallucinatory writing of "The Terminal Beach" (1964), where the process is reversed, and a landscape comes to mirror a frame of mind. This highly influential story is set on the Pacific Island of Eniwetok. The desolation there, and the unavoidable signs of the island's past use as a nuclear weapons testing site, its numerous concrete bunkers in particular, are taken as keys to the future history of the twentieth-century human psyche. The hero, Trave, feels impelled to discover what sort of character would correspond to this landscape, with its concrete city, whose strange ciphers all apparently spell death in the language of the unconscious (where time distinctions are collapsed).

The notion of time plays a central role in many of the stories. In "The Voices of Time" (1960), by employing a rudimentary narrative, sparse functional dialogues, and diary entries, Ballard establishes the premise that everything in the universe can be shown to contain evidence of its own built-in transitoriness. In a metaphorical sense, this would also be true of human reality. The story succeeds, in only 7,000 words, in providing an effective exploration of deep philosophical implications. The treatment of the march of time is more allegorical in "The Garden of Time" and in "The Drowned Giant."

Space travel remains a source of inspiration, even though the space age is seen as a fraud, or a failure, in "Thirteen to Centaurus" and "The Cage of Sand." Another group of stories explores psychological limits. In "The Over-Loaded Man," a lecturer in business studies begins by ridding himself of the everyday meanings that adhere to the objects around him, in an attempt to arrive at a pure undifferentiated void beyond the material distinctions that history imposes on the inhabitants of the real world. Another story, "The Subliminal Man" (1963), belongs along with "Chronopolis" and "Billenium" to a group dealing with urban life. The aspects covered are consumerism (promoted by advertising techniques functioning below the threshold of consciousness), the power of the clock, and overcrowding.

These stories provide an accessible introduction to the speculative themes that underlie all of J. G. Ballard's works, and in some cases the condensed treatment they receive here is most effective.

Crash. The subject matter of *Crash* is a series of road accidents of many kinds which take place on the roads and highways to the west of London, near Heathrow Airport. The participant-observer of these crashes is a forty-year-old producer of television commercials whose name is Ballard. His account deals in retrospect with his growing involvement with Dr. Robert Vaughan, who is introduced as a "hoodlum scientist." The first chapter opens with a description of Vaughan's death in a ghastly smash-up. His attempt to stage a final crash involving himself and the actress, Elizabeth Taylor, had misfired. Instead of experiencing his personal consummation of the car crash, Vaughan died in his only true accident. The rest of the novel methodically records how Vaughan found willing collaborators who came to share his obsession with a new sexuality caused by a perverse technology. In a harsh parody of a scientific approach, Vaughan and his assistants pass from the scene of one accident to another, photographing wounds and piecing together an unorthodox interpretation based on sexual associations. After numerous brutal sexual encounters, culminating in an ecstatic episode on the highway under the influence of a hallucinogenic drug, Ballard is ready to plan his own road-death climax.

Science fiction often selects one feature of contemporary life and develops a fictional world where the implications of this phenomenon can be explored in abstraction. In *Crash*, Ballard focuses on the way the media and the cold language of observation can take the most highly charged material and treat it exclusively on the formal level, representing it in such a way that it produces quite different effects on the recipient than the original stimulus would have produced. The treatment of the car crash in the book represents an aggravated form of this, where the process is guided by a deranged mind and put at the service of dangerously unconventional values--particularly sex- and drug-induced obsessions. What is remarkable is the way the author avoids any moral judgments, leaving his narrator the task of simply demonstrating how even the most shocking events can be broken down and totally reconstrued by surrealist experimental procedures. Although the crash is in fact a metophor, the accumulation of meticulous description makes this world, composed entirely of tarmac, blood and twisted metal, seem disturbingly plausible or even "hyper-real." It is both an alien planet and a familiar one.

The Crystal World. Dr. Edward Sanders, a leprosy specialist, arrives at Port Matarre in West Africa on his way to visit two old friends at their clinic in the forests of the hinterland, near one of the areas which have undergone a mysterious process of crystal-lization. (The scientific explanation of this has to do with the concept of antitime that corresponds with that of antimatter; there is a depletion of the available time-store, triggered by the creation of antigalaxies in space.) However, Dr. Sanders is not merely seeking his friends. The notion of a landscape without time appeals to him as apart of a search for a new opening in his life. Sanders encounters some unusual characters before sailing upriver to the affected zone, and two of them in particular--Ventress, a brooding architect, and Balthus, a guilt-ridden priest in search of his lost faith--are drawn there with him, in an attempt to resolve their own personal dilemmas. Additionally there are business and military interests represented by Thorenson, a mine owner, and Captain Radek, as well as a young journalist, Louise Peret.

Ballard has expressed a desire to write fiction which would be pure description, and *The Crystal World* is true to this impulse. The novel paints a picture of an area which has undergone a process of crystallization where everything, from crocodiles to crashed helicopters, becomes encrusted with a glittering armor as part of a spangled, enchanted world. Together these factors compensate for the rather inconsequential and confusing events in the plot. However, the novel is not just about the spectacular aesthetic effects of the phenomenon; through his principal character, Ballard tries to emphasize the metaphysical implications it may have for the individual in personal terms. For Sanders, its alluring beauty seems to embody Wordsworth's prismatic recollections of childhood. In effect, those ensnared by the process do not die, but enter a new world of suspended animation, and the novel is concerned with the acceptance of such a condition--and here the parallel with leprosy is made plain. The other parallel is with a romantic longing to merge with the radiance of eternity as a clue to the interest of the transformed forest, understood in its widest sense.

The Drowned World. Most of the action of this haunting novel takes place in and around London, but it is a London transformed into a primeval swamp--with luxurious vegetation, giant amphibians, and tropical temperatures. The novel occurs in the twenty-first century. There have been solar storms, and the increased radiation reaching the Earth has raised temperatures to unacceptable levels over the entire central band of the planet. With the melting of the polar ice caps, the map of the world has been drastically redrawn. The diminishing population has migrated to the Arctic and Antarctic circles.

The novel's opening introduces Dr. Robert Kerans, who has joined a military expedition to the area and is stationed on a balcony of a luxury suite in the partially submerged Ritz Hotel. He is surrounded by the reptiles and ferns he has come there to study. The urge to retrace the steps of the evolutionary process back to its origins by following the hints of the reversions taking place all around him presents itself through the influence of visionary surrealist paintings and in strange dreams. The novel deals with the realization of this impulse and the obstacles it must face, in the shape of Colonel Riggs, the unmoveable leader of the expedition, and then in Strangman, a perceptive and refined buccaneer who has a curious bunch of men and alligators at his command. Strangman's obsessive ambition is to drain London, and by this gesture to impose his will, at least symbolically, on the inexorable climatic changes. Strangman obliges Kerans to act as a loner and to head south, in accordance with his contrasting decision to accept the inner logic of the situation.

Special mention must be made of Kerans' descent, in a diving suit, into the planetarium of Madame Tussaud's wax museum. This tour de force creates an environment which turns a metaphor--"inner space"--into a concrete reality.

The Drowned World is strong on imagery and is written in a precise and detached prose which makes the reader become a participant in the cataloging of the terminal situation conducted by a rigorous scientific mind (with a painter's eye and a philosopher's obsessions). We are not expected to identify readily with characters whose motives are so ambiguous, and this, along with Ballard's tongue-in-cheek humor, which appears in many of the dialogues, means that the reader is drawn into the aura of uncertainty and is, like the others in this drowned world, without secure moorings.

Love and Napalm: Export USA. A protagonist (variously called Travis, Talbot, Tallis, etc.) is attempting to find a means of piecing together his fragmented sense of reality in what appears to be a technological wasteland. Under the scrutiny of Dr. Nathan, T- constructs scenarios based on his obsessions, selecting and reordering those elements of a senseless and brutal world which can be made to match and conform to his inner certainties. His fixations, in fact, all revolve around sex and violence linked to a search for geometrical symmetry. The last six episodes variously offer a geneaology of who killed whom in America's recent past; another is a metaphoric treatment of the assassination of John F. Kennedy; while the remaining four debunk the mythic qualities of various public figures, focusing on the supposed latent sexual pleasures associated with car crashes, warfare, and other scenes of violence and atrocity.

Published in Britain as *The Atrocity Exhibition*, the text indeed is structured like an exhibition. Reading the separated paragraphs of the first part, each with a resonant, though often ironic, title hung over it, the reader is in effect wandering through a disordered picture gallery of some characteristic scenes and public images of the 1960s. The landscape of the industrialized world

(represented for T- by London) no longer offers secure interpretations of the difference between what is real and what is imaginary, what flows from history and what is arbitrarily contrived.
The author succeeds in creating a one-sided, reduced version of
what is still recognizably the contemporary environment of his
readers. The central idea is that the products of science and technology have saturated the world, so that we are all living in a giant labyrinth of fiction. The concluding American sections can be
seen as an endorsement of the common denominators that T- had
fixed upon as being the only reliable coordinates of his experience
of the "inner space" of his time. Although the irony is often excessive and certain effects overlabored, Ballard's meticulous descriptive prose, his well-chosen list of significant twentieth-century milestones, and the obsessional reenactments of his central
character together form a potent and thought-provoking vehicle in
which the undercurrents of the period become a repellent collage,
a picture of mental turmoil.

Vermilion Sands. The original 1971 paperback edition of this
collection was replaced in 1973 by the definitive hardback version. The text was revised, a previously omitted story ("The
Singing Statues") was added, along with a candid preface by the
author. Although the nine stories were written over a period of
fourteen years, the image of this desert resort remained constant.
The opening tale, "The Cloud Sculptors of Coral-D," has appeared
in at least five other collections and was nominated for the Nebula Award in 1968. Cloud sculpting is somewhere between an art
form and a circus act. Using gliders, and spraying silver iodide,
four strange characters carve figures in the fair-weather cumulus
that sails in over the coral reefs of Vermilion Sands. Lenora
Chanel stops in her limousine to admire the skillful portraits and
invites the artists to perform for her. Stormy conditions conspire
with this sinister woman to induce the cloud sculptors to sacrifice
themselves to her limitless egotism rather than to continue serving
"aerial marzipan" for an innocent sense of wonder. In "Studio 5,
the Stars," the poets of Vermilion Sands play along with the fantasies of Aurora Day, a deranged but fascinating lady who casts
herself as the muse of poetry. The irony is that as they come under her spell, their shield of worldly wise sophistication is pene-
trated, and they learn to do without their computers, experiencing
a reawakening of their long-lost emotions and poetic urges.

Other stories in the collection are similar. They involve novel
expressive media, such as psychotropic houses or bio-fabric fash-
ions (living tissues that adapt themselves to the body of the
wearer) and wayward personalities taking advantage of these sophisticated means for realizing their inner desires. What invariably happens is that repressed impulses (infantile self-centeredness
or deep-seated, violent passions) reemerge in new forms.

Vermilion Sands exhibits Ballard writing in a lighter than usual vein. The underlying theme, however, has a serious side to it. The not too distant future may contain these components of stagnation--a depleted, endlessly unchanging environment and hour after hour of spare time in a technologically rich concrete playground. Ballard's sterile landscape and the beach fatigue his characters suffer from are metaphors for the future. The motor of history has passed into the artificial extensions with which humanity has filled its world, and everyone has learned to live with the death of affect.

Biographical/Bibliographical Readings

J. G. Ballard, "The Profession of Science Fiction: From Shanghai to Shepperton," *Foundation* 24 (Feb. 1982), p.5-23. Peter Brigg, *J. G. Ballard* (Starmont House, 1985). H. Bruce Franklin, "What Are We to Make of J. G. Ballard's Apocalypse?" in *Voices for the Future*, ed. Thomas D. Clareson (Bowling Green University Popular Press, 1979), v.2, p.82-105. James Goddard and David Pringle, *J. G. Ballard: The First Twenty Years* (Brans Head Books, 1976). David Pringle, *J. G. Ballard: A Primary and Secondary Bibliography* (G. K. Hall, 1984). **[Jonathan K. Benison]**

BENFORD, GREGORY

Life and Works

Gregory Benford was born on January 30, 1941, along with his twin brother, James. He spent his early years in Mobile, Alabama. In 1963, he earned his B.S. in physics from the University of Oklahoma. Two years later, at the University of California, San Diego, he completed his master's degree. In 1967, he received his Ph.D. in theoretical physics from the same institution and was married. From 1967 through 1979, Benford was a professor of physics at the University of California, Irvine. In 1976 and again in 1979, Benford was a visiting fellow at Cambridge University. He still resides in California and is a consultant to Physics International Company.

In 1965, Benford's first published story was "Stand-In," which won second place in a contest organized by the *Magazine of Fantasy and Science Fiction*. The 1970s brought forth *Deeper Than the Darkness* (1970), later published as *The Stars in Shroud* (1978); *Threads of Time* (1974); *If the Stars Are Gods*, coauthored with Gordon Eklund (1975); *Jupiter Project* (1975); and *In the Ocean of Night* (1977). In the 1980s, he has published *Timescape* (1980); *Against Infinity* (1983); *Shiva Descending*, coauthored with William Rotsler (1981); *Across the Sea of Suns* (1984); *Artifact* (1985), *Heart of the Comet*, coauthored with David Brin (1986); and *In Alien Flesh* (1986).

For several years he coedited an Australian fanzine, *Void*, and is a member of the Science Fiction Writers of America. Not only does Benford write science fiction, but he is also a contributor to various journals such as *Smithsonian, Natural History*, and *Omni*. He has written entries on physics for *Encyclopaedia Brittanica* on his research interests--relativistic plasma physics and astrophysics and has also coauthored physics textbooks.

Two of Benford's works have won awards. The novella *If the Stars Are Gods*, coauthored with Gordon Eklund, won the Nebula award. Benford's most notable work, *Timescape*, won four awards: Nebula, the John W. Campbell Memorial Award, the British Science Fiction Association Award, and the Australian Ditmar Award for International Novels.

Themes and Style

Several major themes tend to dominate most of Benford's work. *Against Infinity, If the Stars Are Gods*, and *Across the Sea of Suns* best illustrate the confrontation between age and wisdom versus youth and inexperience. In *Against Infinity*, Manuel Lopez and his father, Colonel Lopez, clash head-on about the destruction of the Aleph (an old artifact left on Ganymede) and Manuel's involvement in the death of Matt Bohles. On a larger scale is the confrontation between the Aleph and the new Earth settlements on Ganymede.

The short story "White Creatures" in the collection *In Alien Flesh* (1986) deals with old age and how individuals perceive themselves. The protagonist, Merrick, endures the torture of alien "White" creatures by remembering his life history. At the end of the story, the creatures turn out to be medical personnel treating the old man.

Another major theme that emerges from Benford's work is the systems manipulation of the competent professional and professional competition within a bureaucratic system. Ling Sanjen is merely a pawn of the empire in *The Stars in Shroud*. The survivors in *Timescape* are victims of their government's inept efforts to save the Earth. In *Jupiter Project*, the competition revolves around the ability to stay and work on the Can. There is much interdepartmental fighting to attain the advantage to remain on the project--not only for individuals but for their families as well. The same political infighting occurs in *Timescape*, as the university bureaucracy determines to make a fool of Gordon and his discoveries. The underlying idea behind each of these scenarios is that intelligence and competence do eventually win out over the system, and that good work is rewarded.

The fact that Benford has spent a great deal of time in the world of academia is apparent. His understanding of the political undercurrents involved in university life and the relationship between professional scholars (scientists, to be precise) is apparent in many of his novels. Most of his novels are set in an academic atmosphere, to which he adds the dimension of off-world tales. All of his novels contain some aspect of the day-to-day surroundings of academic life.

Benford has a fascination with the encounter between humans and aliens, their lives and the effects they have on each other. *Against Infinity* concerns the human settlements on Ganymede and their encounter with the Aleph, left by the aliens who were once on the satellite. They fight the Aleph because they do not understand it. After they do get a chance to study it, they become confused and upset. In the short story "In Alien Flesh," Reginri's encounter with an alien life form is very intense and life-threatening.

Benford is pessimistic about the future of human society. Though humankind develops technologically, human political, intellectual, emotional, and cultural attitudes and interrelationships remain stagnant. Humanity has great possibilities for change, but people worry about economics--who will pay for it? The project in *Jupiter Project* will be cancelled unless profitable results can be shown to the authorities on Earth. Discrimination is evident in *Heart of the Comet*. The remaining survivors in *Timescape* continue to lead their mundane, greedy, and often deviant lives even though it leads toward the destruction of the planet.

Religion and mystical beliefs affecting politics are also Benford themes. Organized religion as manipulator, or the use of mysticism to retain individual harmony, is prevalent in many novels such as *The Stars in Shroud* and *Threads of Time*.

Benford's writing is not the action-packed entertainment often associated with the science fiction genre. His writing is slow paced and contemplative, presenting serious themes. His attitude is downbeat and often pessimistic (a trait often associated with writers of Southern heritage). In the 1986 short story collection *In Alien Flesh*, he admits that he writes about the downtrodden and ordinary people, not the winners. The underdog characters often represent the confrontation between the old or traditional with new, often alien, intrusions.

Several of Benford's works have dual narratives that appear unrelated at first. In *Across the Sea of Suns*, the shipwrecked man at first appears to have no bearing on the space mission until the story is fully revealed. Sometimes, as in *Threads of Time*, the explanation of the relationship between events on the moon and an isolated character in Oregon does not occur until the end of the novella.

Benford considers himself first and foremost a scientist. His settings in the future give an indication of his scientific expertise. The uncommon seems everyday; the characters take for granted what would be miraculous today. Often he builds his theories around the the latest advances in science and technology and gives in-depth explanations of these new technologies.

Plot Summaries of Major Works

Across the Sea of Suns. It is the year 2056, and Nigel Walmsley, a computer and language systems specialist, is on the Earth starship *Lancer*, which is on a mission to investigate an interstellar signal communicated in the English language. The source of the signal has been traced to a planet called Isis, whose sun is called Ra. On Isis, a race called Em has been genetically altered to resemble machines. Circling Isis is a strange satellite that turns out to be artificial and dangerous for the crew of *Lancer*. Nigel is the only member of the crew who comprehends the danger of the situation, because he was once mentally altered by alien machine intelligence on Earth's moon.

Back on Earth, the oceans are being invaded and taken over by an alien life form called "Swarmers." Unlike the Swarmers, who are deadly to humans, their relatives, the "Skimmers," try to communicate with humans, usually shipwrecked individuals. The Skimmers tell the humans how they were taken from their home world and transplanted on Earth. Sparked by the threat of the Swarmers, a nuclear war breaks out on Earth.

Lancer travels to another solar system, and on a moon they call Pocks they discover not only life but also another artificial satellite, a "Watcher." From all the evidence found in space as well as what has happened on Earth, Nigel discovers that the galaxy contains mechanical intelligence that does not allow for organic competition. The *Lancer* attacks the Watcher and the Watcher strikes back at the *Lancer*, destroying the power drive. Now the humans have no way home.

The social structure on *Lancer* deteriorates the longer the ship is in space. The countries of Earth cannot work together to handle the Swarmers and the end result is nuclear war. In *Across the Sea of Suns*, Nigel Walmsley, older and changed after his encounter with aliens, must continually fight to be allowed to work and be involved in the investigation of the planets and new life forms. He also is not completely trusted or felt to be competent.

Against Infinity. This was Benford's next novel after the award-winning *Timescape*. It is a coming-of-age story located on Jupiter's moon Ganymede. At age thirteen, Manuel Lopez is allowed to go with the other men from the Sidon settlement to hunt the mutated, terraforming, bioengineered beasts on the satellite and sees the Aleph for the first time. The Aleph is an artifact left on Ganymede by unknown aliens; how it functions and its purpose is a mystery to the settlers. Occasionally the Aleph has destroyed settlements, killing people when they get into its unpredictable path. Since its first appearance, the humans have tried to capture or kill the Aleph. Matt Bohles (protagonist from an earlier work, *Jupiter Project*) is the oldest man in the Sidon settlement and an experienced hunter. He helps and guides Manuel in his quest to kill the Aleph. Together with a cyborg, they stop the Aleph. Matt is seriously injured in the process.

Manuel and his father disagree about what he has done. His father accuses him of "killing everything old." Manuel leaves his home and returns only after his father's death. When massive earthquakes occur and volcanoes erupt, Matt gets an inkling of the Aleph's true purpose. He goes to the site where the Aleph is being studied by scientists, and he discovers that the Aleph is not really "dead."

Alien versus human; age versus youth; and wisdom versus inexperience--all are elements of this novel. The story of the hunt for the Aleph could be compared to Faulkner's "The Bear." The healing and saving of people's lives is based upon how they contribute as individuals to the economy of the Sidon colony.

Artifact. Clair Anderson, an archaeologist, is on a Greek dig of an ancient Mycenean tomb, and has just made an important discovery. Behind the burial throne of a long-dead king is stored a conical-shaped artifact completely out of place with the origins of the tomb. Unstable Greek politics make further detailed study of the object impossible, and Clair is forced to do the unethical. Enlisting the help of a physicist, John Bishop, she steals the artifact out from under the nose of the Greek military. Clair and John flee to Boston, where she hopes to find some answers to the puzzling riddle of the artifact. With the help of top metallurgists, chemists, and mathematicians, Clair and John discover that the simple cone structure is more complex than either had imagined. In the depths of the cone is a thing of great power, a Quark, or Singularity; a subatomic nuclear particle released from the depths of the Earth aeons ago by geologic disturbance. To their horror, they discover that, during the transportation of the artifact to Boston, its twin was thrown from the cone. Clair and John must reunite the twins or massive geological instabilities will occur as the lost twin carves its way through anything in its path to find its other half.

Set against the background of a futuristic Greece in turmoil and a sedate, timeless Boston, Benford unravels the mystery of the tomb that links the past and the present.

A weakness in Benford's style is his characterization of females. In this and his other works, the status of women has not improved much from the current day. They may perform the jobs that men have traditionally performed, but their position or power

in society has not changed. Benford's female characters are secondary, subordinate, or traditional roles. The good beginning
made by Clair Anderson in *Artifact* is quickly reduced to spectator
by the end of the novel. Women are sources of moral support or
of sexual gratification. Perhaps this is another aspect of Benford's downbeat view of the future and how humankind fails to
evolve along with its technology.

If the Stars Are Gods. Originally published as short stories
by Benford and Gordon Eklund, this novel takes place in three
time periods and involves four different settings, yet relies on one
primary character, Bradley Reynolds, to tie these separate spaces
and times together. In 1992, Bradley is a young man sent to Mars
with five other astronauts to explore the possibility of life on
Mars. Three of his companions die on the hostile planet, but
Bradley lives to return to Earth as a hero, bearing the news that
the only bacterial life forms on Mars were introduced by other
human landing parties.

In the year 2017, Bradley, now fifty-eight years old, is considered an enigma by the military establishment. Despite prejudice
against his age, he is called to duty on the moon at the request of
alien beings. The aliens are visiting the Earth's solar system in
hopes of finding a hospitable planet on which to relocate. To understand what the aliens want to know, Bradley undergoes a type
of mind-melding with the gentle creatures. When the aliens realize that Sol is not the star they seek, they decide to leave. Bradley
wants to accompany them, as he has touched their alien mind and
cannot feel a part of his own world again. The aliens refuse,
however, and Bradley returns to Earth.

Bradley enters a monastery, where he delves into the mysterious world of Hindu meditation. At the age of 87, he is once again
called back into service. Signs of alien life have been traced to
Jupiter, and Bradley is put in command of an expedition to study
and investigate the phenomenon. On this mission, Benford introduces the genetically engineered Manips, Mara and Corey. Mara is
female in form but is vastly superior in intelligence to the humans
around her. Corey is a superbrain which exists without a body--in
a box, its gender unknown. Both Manips are instrumental in solving certain problems within the Alpha Libra Project. While the
Manips are confronted with prejudice on Jupiter, the humans on
Earth have come to loathe the existence of any nonhuman form.
Bradley placates and appeases a would-be lynch mob in order to
maintain peace on the ship. Despite the conflicts, Corey manages
to investigate communication impulses from Jupiter and traces the
communication disturbances to Titan. Because of the unrest on
Jupiter, Bradley is relieved of his command. Before he departs,
he, Mara, and a few other crew members silently slip off the main
ship to explore the signals from Titan. There they discover the
secret of the Alpha Libra signals.

Bradley Reynolds is a young man when *If the Stars Are Gods* begins, but he ages rapidly as the book progresses. When his presence is requested by the aliens on the moon, he is considered a "has-been" by the military Earthmen, someone they must tolerate. He is forced to endure insults to his competency by his fellow Earthlings. After his encounter with aliens on the moon, Bradley Reynolds' one passion in life is to seek out other life forms. The aliens admire and respect him for the wisdom he possesses. Bradley's natural abilities, keen intelligence, curiosity, and common sense force the military to recall him to lead an important space project.

Prejudice is apparent in *If the Stars are Gods*. Discrimination and prejudice occur against other humans as well as against aliens. Earthmen do not understand nor like the aliens; they feel threatened by their existence and wish to destroy them.

Jupiter Project. Matt Bohles, a seventeen-year-old in the Jovian Astronomical-Biological-Orbital Laboratory (also called the "Can"), faces the problem of being sent back to Earth after he reaches the age of eighteen. The project must be weeded because it cannot support a large laboratory staff population. Matt is aware that the competition will be fierce, because the other young adults will also be striving for a position. At every turn, Matt makes errors in judgment and Yuri Sagdoeff, another young adult, is there to take advantage of them. The decision is made that the research on Jupiter and its moons is not profitable enough by Earth standards, and only a skeleton crew of single men of mature years will be left on the Can.

Eventually Matt comes to realize that the space station's social environment is geared for older adults and that juveniles are not allowed to act rashly and take uncalled-for risks, thus hindering their growth to maturity. He decides to take control of the direction of his life and risks everything to uncover a clue that can help save the project and establish his own position on the Can.

The enormous competition caused by everyone's desire to stay on the Can creates the conflict in this novel. People want to stay on not only for themselves, but for their children as well.

Timescape. *Timescape* occurs in two time periods, 1998 and 1963. In 1998, the Earth is dying due to unaddressed environmental concerns of the past concentrating on the killing of the oceans. The aim of the central characters, John Renfrew, Greg Markham, and Ian Peterson, is to set up communications with the past in an effort to prevent these disasters destroying the world.

The year 1963 centers around Gordon Bernstein, a physicist at the University of California at La Jolla. Gordon is the person who receives garbled messages from what he believes could be another planet or galaxy.

Benford creates a mosaic of characters whose lives are intertwined with one another and the crises of their times. In one time period is the struggle of humans to endure the dying of their planet and their way of life; the other time period illuminates a world on the verge of scientific discovery, the pettiness of university politics, and the general enthusiasm about the future and what it has to offer. Philosophically we are escorted through the perplexing dimension to a time paradox which explores the morality of interference with the past and the ramifications any interference may have on the future.

Timescape could be labeled a literary mainstream work as well as a science fiction novel. Benford delves deeply into characterization and plot in this work, laced together by the ideas of theoretical physics. Scientifically, we are introduced to the Tacheon particle which moves faster than the speed of light to send the messages back in time and the theory of universes within universes which creates a fear in 1998 that the world of 1963 is not their world, but a parallel world within another universe. The problems posed by Benford are thought-provoking, the characters are intriguing, and the conclusion leaves room for speculation by the reader.

Biographical/Bibliographical Readings

John Clute, "Gregory Benford," in *The Science Fiction Encyclopedia*, ed. Peter Nicholls (Doubleday, 1979), p.66-67. "Gregory Benford," in *Contemporary Authors: New Revision Series* (Gale, 1984), v. 12, p.59-60. David N. Samuelson, "Gregory Benford," in *Twentieth-Century Science-Fiction Writers*, ed. Curtis C. Smith (St. James, 1986), p.46-47. [Twyla Reinig and Illene Renfro]

BESTER, ALFRED

Life and Works

Alfred Bester was born in New York City on December 18, 1913. He attended the University of Pennsylvania and Columbia University, studying subjects ranging from art and music to law and protozoology. In 1939, he won a contest sponsored by *Thrilling Wonder Stories* for "The Broken Axiom." In the 1940s, he became a free-lance writer. He was a frequent contributor to *Holiday* in the 1950s, becoming its senior editor in 1967. In 1953, Bester published his first novel, *The Demolished Man*, which won the Hugo award. Three years later he published *The Stars My Destination* (1956), also entitled *Tiger! Tiger!* Bester wrote several short stories, many of which are collected in *Starlight: The Great Short Fiction of Alfred Bester* (1976).

During the 1960s, he did not write as much science fiction, but returned to the field in 1975 with *The Computer Connection* (also entitled *Extro*), followed by *Golem*[100] (1980) and *The Deceivers* (1981). Bester has also written radio and television scripts, book reviews, a novel satirizing the television industry and a history of the National Aeronautics and Space Administration satellites.

Themes and Style

Although he has not compiled a large body of work, Bester's influence on other science fiction writers and his reputation are extensive. Many of the stylistic devices that Bester has used were common in mainstream fiction, but Bester was among the first to use literary conventions such as stream of consciousness and variable points of view in science fiction. His allusions range from Elizabethan poetry to computer technology. He was also the first to integrate graphics into the text of a science fiction novel, using a variety of typefaces to convey telepathic conversations and explorations of alternate universes. His innovative style influenced many of his contemporaries and later writers of the new wave of the 1960s and 1970s.

Bester's most frequently used themes have involved psychological motivations. Many of his characters are obsessed with a need for power or revenge. His characters are multidimensional mixtures of good and evil, they are flawed individuals whose complex motivations may be hidden even from themselves. Bester often deals with themes of retribution--his characters make mistakes, suffer, are punished, and finally transformed. Gully Foyle's obsessive revenge leads to his rebirth as a possible superhuman in *The Stars My Destination*; Ben Reich commits murder but is re-created as a healthy personality in *The Demolished Man*.

Bester is an entertaining storyteller whose fast-moving plots keep his readers involved. His stories have been called pyrotechnic for their tendency to contain one surprise after another in rapid succession. His works are full of ideas and background details around which other less ambitious writers could build entire stories, such as his descriptions of holographic advertising projections in *The Computer Connection*, or the psycat, a Saturnian crossbreed of Siamese cat and Koala bear that chases the spots you see before your eyes in *The Deceivers*.

Bester creates believable characters and extravagant societies. He uses psychology to create the motivations for his protagonists and his plots. His style and imagery are vivid and compelling. Bester makes frequent use of satire, humor, and literary allusions. The combination of style and themes have made him one of the most influential science fiction writers.

Plot Summaries of Major Works

The Demolished Man. In the twenty-fourth century, crime has become almost unknown because of the telepathic skills of "espers." Espers are telepaths who have varying degrees of ability, but first-class espers can easily determine criminal plans or guilt. The espers are a minority of the population and are protected by the Esper Guild.

Ben Reich, the wealthy head of Monarch Utilities and Resources, has been experiencing nightmares which end in a confrontation with a "man with no face." Reich believes that the figure symbolizes his desire to eliminate his hated competitor, Craye D'Courtney. When D'Courtney rejects a merger proposal, Reich decides to murder him. With the unknowing assistance of an esper, whom Reich deceives, Reich kills D'Courtney but the murder is witnessed by D'Courtney's daughter, Barbara, who then runs away. The esper in charge of the murder investigation is Lincoln Powell. He quickly realizes that Reich committed the murder, but does not have sufficient proof to arrest him.

Powell needs to find a motive and to locate Barbara D'Courtney. He finds Barbara, but she is in a catatonic state, interrupted only by moments of hysteria when she relives her father's murder. During her recovery, Barbara falls in love with Lincoln Powell, but Powell resists his feelings because he must marry another esper, and Barbara does not possess telepathic abilities. In the meantime, Reich blames Powell for a series of bombings which have nearly killed him. Powell tells Reich that there is not enough evidence for a case against him, primarily because no motive can be ascertained.

Reich continues his nightmares about the man with no face. Powell is concerned about Reich's hatred of espers and convinces the Esper Council to allow him to alter Reich's psyche. Powell creates a solipsistic universe for Reich and gradually destroys it, leaving only Reich and his man with no face. Reich confronts the figure, which turns out to be both himself and D'Courtney--the father who abandoned him. Powell erases the psyche that created the crimes and replaces Reich's violent psyche with a healthy one. Powell looks forward to the day when people are able to see that the only barrier to humanity's innate goodness is individual blindness.

The Demolished Man has been called a classic science fiction novel. As science fiction, it takes place in an advanced society where telepathy, interplanetary travel, and advanced technology are common. It is also a murder mystery in which the murderer's identity is clear but his motive is unknown. Bester uses psychological themes to create his characters and their motivations. In addition to Reich's Oedipus complex, Bester deals with themes of retribution, atonement, rebirth, and the amibiguity of good and evil within each person. While many literary devices, such as stream of consciousness and shifting points of view, were common in mainstream fiction, Bester was the first to use these in science fiction. Bester used graphics and variations in typography to indicate telepathic conversations, an early indication of his interest in integrating text and graphic communication. *The Demolished Man* is a fast-paced story with vivid characters whose psychological motivations are described in a carefully crafted style.

Fondly Fahrenheit. A series of brutal murders has occured on different planets. The authorities know that the murders were committed by an android, but have been unable to arrest the android or its owner. James Vandaleur, the android's owner, was once wealthy, but is now only able to survive by leasing his multiple aptitude android and moving from planet to planet to avoid the authorities. Even though its programming supposedly prohibits harm to humans, something has caused this android to violate its programming. Vandaleur meets two students who are researching the crimes. They have discovered a link between the murders and warn Vandaleur of possible danger. Just after they mention the word "projection," the students are also murdered. With the help of other researchers, Vandaleur discovers that all of the murders have taken place when the temperature was very hot and that the projection theory involves the danger of constant companions to insane people also becoming insane. The other researchers are killed as well. The police pursue Vandaleur and the guilty android in a chase that ends in fire destroying the android. Vandaleur moves on to another planet and purchases yet another android. A young girl begins to take a solitary walk with the android--or is it with Vandaleur?

Fondly Fahrenheit is a science fiction mystery about the factors that could cause an android to murder, when it has been programmed to protect life. It is also a study of the relationship between an android and its insane owner. The projection of Vandaleur's insanity was apparently enough to cause an override of the android's programming. The story is a skillful blending of science fiction and mystery genres, distinguised by the slowly increasing evidence of Vandaleur's roles in the murders.

"The Men Who Murdered Mohammed." When Profesor Harry Hassell, an eccentric genius, came home early and found his wife in the arms of a stranger, he did not get his gun and kill her or the stranger. Instead, he built a time machine and traveled back to shoot her grandfather, thereby theoretically removing her from existence. When he returned and found her still in the man's arms, he assumed that unfaithfulness ran in her family and returned to the past to shoot her grandmother. Once again upon his return to the present, she was still there. Having decided that only major changes could alter the flow of time, he began killing important historical people, including George Washington, Christopher Columbus, and Madame Curie. Each time he returned, his wife and the stranger were still embracing. Hassel did not notice that he was becoming less visible; finally he becomes invisible and inaudible. He meets another time traveler who had also tried to alter the past. The other time traveler had also assassinated people, including Marco Polo and Einstein. They discovered that they had both killed Mohammed. Time being entirely subjective, each had gone into his own past and destroyed it. They become ghosts with no existence in any time. The time travel story is almost a cliche in science fiction, but in "The Men Who Murdered Mohammed," Bester mixes humor with the paradox of time travelers killing their grandparents, to make a traditional theme fresh.

The Stars My Destination. The protagonist of this novel is Gulliver "Gully" Foyle, a dull man without specific talents or potential. When a space liner fails to rescue him after the ship he worked on was destroyed, Gully is transformed by his obssesive need for vengeance upon those who abandoned him. Gully shows no mercy in his quest, committing acts that later horrify him and generate a need for punishment and the possibility of subsequent rebirth and redemption.

Gully's opponent, Presteign, is one of the wealthiest men on Earth, and it was one of his ships that abandoned Gully. Presteign's quest is the search for PyrE, an experimental explosive that could win the war raging between the Inner Planets and the Outer Satellites. The only existing sample was on Gully's wrecked ship, so Presteign must somehow extract the information from a man who wants to destroy him. Lady Olivia, Presteign's daughter, falls in love with Gully, believing that they are alike in their obssesion for revenge. She is consumed by a hatred of humanity because of her unique difference; she can see in the ultraviolet frequencies, rather than the normal range of light. The quests of Gully, Presteign, and Lady Olivia for power and vengeance are intertwined in a complex plot which eventually culminates in the destruction of Presteign, the isolation of Lady Olivia, and the rebirth of Gully into a potential superhuman.

The Stars My Destination is a skillfully crafted novel, full of vivid imagery and carefully portrayed characters. It has been called a pyrotechnic novel because of its astonishing pace of ideas and events, one surprise following another in a rush to a flamboyant conclusion. Bester depicts numerous societies, from the wealthy one of Presteign to a cult that worships a degenerated version of the survival of the fittest. The economic, social, and political relationships form a convincing background for the continuous action.

Bester uses typographical variations and graphics to convey the mental processes and sensory impressions of his characters. This novel may have been the first in science fiction to integrate graphics into the plot in order to portray the thoughts and feelings of the protagonists.

The Stars My Destination has been hailed as one of the great science fiction novels. It is a mystery, a social satire, and a story of psychological growth. Bester frequently uses psychological themes in his works; this novel is a study of obsession, growth, and redemption. Each of the protagonists struggles for their desires, but Presteign and Lady Olivia are destroyed by their inability to grow beyond their obssesions. The novel is a dazzling combination of style, plot, characterization, pacing, and psychology. It is one of the most praised and influential novels in science fiction.

Biographical/Bibliographical Readings

Robert Froese, "Alfred Bester," in *Twentieth-Century Science-Fiction Writers*, ed. Curtis C. Smith (St. James, 1986), p.50-51. William L. Godshalk, "Alfred Bester," in *Twentieth-Century American Science-Fiction Writers* (Gale, 1981), v.1, p.30-37. Willis E. Mc-Neely, "Alfred Bester," in *Science Fiction Writers*, ed. E. F. Bleiler (Scribner's, 1982), p.283-90. Carolyn Wendell, *Alfred Bester* (Starmont House, 1982). [Linda K. Lewis]

BIGGLE, LLOYD, JR.

Life and Works

Lloyd Biggle, Jr., was born on April 17, 1923, in Waterloo, Iowa. His musical interests would eventually lead to his academic focus in music literature and history, but his undergraduate studies were interrupted by World War II. He left Wayne State University to join the Army and served in the 102nd Infantry Division, earning a Purple Heart and an Oak Leaf Cluster. After the war, he resumed his studies at Wayne State and received a B.A. in music in 1947. He went on to the University of Michigan to earn a master's and doctorate degree. In 1948, he joined the faculty of the Music Department at the University of Michigan. He left the University of Michigan in 1951 to become self-employed. Currently, Biggle lives in Ypsilanti, Michigan.

His first story, "Gypped," was published in *Galaxy* in 1956. His first novel was *The Angry Espers* (1961). Biggle is best known for his series of novels that feature the private investigator from Earth, Jan Darzek. This series consists of four spy/mystery thrillers--*All the Colors of Darkness* (1963), *Watchers of the Dark* (1966), *This Darkening Universe* (1975), and *Silence Is Deadly* (1977). The novels involve potential galactic disasters, and have regular, humourously memorable characters of varying life life forms. Among Biggle's unique creations stands the "Supreme"--a world-sized computer, indeed a world in itself, which (aided by a Council of eight) serves as the governing force of all certified worlds. The eight member group--the Council of the Supreme--is made up of a variety of life forms, only one of whom is humanoid, the rather uncivilized Earthman, Jan Darzek.

Biggle has published no new works of fiction since 1979. Several articles appeared in *Analog* in the 1980s in which he supports science fiction literature as a worthy object for literary criticism and scholarly research. Biggle was founder and president of the Science Fiction Oral History Association and founder of the Regional Collections of Science Fiction Writers of America. His novel, *Watchers of the Dark* (1966), was nominated for the 1967 Nebula award. Biggle has written more than a dozen novels and seventy-five short stories which have been translated into many languages, including Russian and Serbo-Croation. Some of his stories are collected in *The Rule of the Door and Other Fanciful Regulations* (1967) and *A Galaxy of Strangers* (1976). His manuscripts are housed in the Spencer Research Library at the University of Kansas.

Themes and Style

Biggle's scholarly and artistic background is reflected in much of his writing. He projects an immense regard for the integrity of art--that which is a creation of the producer's inner essence. This integrity of art is often contrasted with that which is mass produced, so that a frequent theme in his writing may be illustrated by an art colony's souvenir paintings for tourists from other worlds (*The Light That Never Was*, 1972) or the musical scores of broadcast commercials composed and played on a synthesizer ("The Tunesmith," 1957), both of which are poor substitutes for the goal of art. Violin teaching reduced to an automated method by a complexly structured robot competes with traditional violin training methods of a human master in "Spare the Rod" (1958). The lack of inner relevance in writing brings creative activity to a stale halt in "Well of the Deep Wish" (1961), in spite of an elaborate think tank which is supposed to provide authentic experiential material for writers to draw upon. Biggle's message in these works seems to be that art without the inner individual's involvement is not art at all, and no amount of bureaucratic intervention or technological advances can change that.

Certification of worlds is a Biggle idea that separates those civilizations which have a highly evolved moral and ethical system from those worlds which still maintain primitive passions, dishonesty, and war. Earth is an uncertified world. The certified worlds are responsible for keeping the galaxy intact and remain unknown to uncertified worlds. Through a governmental Department of Uncertified Worlds, careful watch is kept over the evolving civilizations and occasional intervention is sometimes necessary. Worlds are continually being classified as certified and there is a formula which measures technological levels against political criteria.

Bureaucratic machinery is constantly present in Biggle's writings as an object of commentary and some humorous criticism. The assortment of bureaus, federations, and councils all seem to have the common qualities of inefficiency and ungainliness, and often a lack of wisdom. In *The World Menders* (1971), an organization called The Cultural Survey sends agents to work with the Interplanetary Relations Bureau to assist it in the classification of worlds. Within the plot of *The World Menders*, there is a mountain of fine print called *Manual 1048-K*, which is in itself largely responsible for the ineffectiveness of attempts to study and classify new worlds. Mottos printed in upper case abound throughout the manual and new ones are created with alarming frequency as time goes on. Several of Biggle's stories feature the Bureau of Censorship, which typically is reponsible for the stagnation of art and creativity. One of his more humorous and original concepts involves a legal system of the future which is introduced in *Monument* (1974). Long-winded attorney arguments are avoided by loading computer disks filled with legal points and citations to be measured against the opposition's legal disks. The chorus of "pings" or "gongs" measure the validity of the point of law and determine the outcome. Biggle comments upon the deadliness of Board of Directors meetings, and the blind following of regulations are frequently presented as a major obstacle to successful ventures.

Biggle's works provide a wide exposure to a variety of life forms. Since his future includes unlimited interstellar travel and groupings of many worlds in government federations, the range of life species is infinite. Biggle describes the characters with such matter-of-factness that he succeeds in changing the standards of physical normality for the reader. Humanoid is neither the standard nor the majority. There are frequent scenes of a group of Biggle protagonists moving side by side with determination, bipeds, tentacles, waving heads that bounce, slither, walk, or merge in all manner of gaits. The necessity for physically disguising the agents of a council for penetration into an alien culture applies to all life-forms, and all undergo surgical alterations as well as correct costuming and intensive language and behavior training. In *The Light That Never Was*, the truly authentic art is created by animaloids, and there is an allusion to the fact that they are the great philosophers and ethical leaders. Snails and slugs often have honored roles in Biggle's writings, and even computers can be a life-form as is the plant species, the Kloatraz, in *This Darkening Universe*.

Plot Summaries of Major Works

All the Colors of Darkness. In this initial Jan Darzek novel, the first Earth-designed matter-transmitter is operable and in place in New York. Darzek is a big city private detective, and comes complete with cramped, dark office and receptionist. Darzek is also a stockholder in the Universal Transmitter Company which is placing matter-transmitters in major cities around the world. Since the transmitter provides instantaneous travel, making cars, trains, and planes immediately obsolete, it is no small development for Earth's civilization in the 1980s. When individual travelers are found to disappear by not arriving at their receiving stations, Darzek is hired to investigate this potentially injurious situation for the company. The issue is deeper than commercial sabotage, however. Darzek finds himself on the moon in the presence of other-world beings, caught up in a life or death situation that affects all of them.

This is Biggle's first introduction in his novels of the notion of certified worlds and the danger of technological advancement without parallel ethical maturity. The operation of matter-transmitters on Earth has more serious potential than is at first apparent. Earth's moral color is also wrong--a darkness that makes this technological breakthrough dangerous to the entire galaxy. It is the immaturity of its citizens and their lack of pure and honorable virtues that have brought the galactic forces to intervene. Darzek finds himself in the role of advocate for Earth. His subsequent deeds pave the way for future Darzek novels and his place on the Council of the Supreme.

Monument. This novel stands apart in Biggle's writings as a light tale of the downfall of a commercial magnate who has designs on a small tropical paradise world as a location for a high-rise resort. He meets with the opposition of the naive but committed native population. The poignant leadership of the natives by the one dying Elder, himself a visitor and protector from another world, leads to the design of the Plan, not understood but loyally followed for the overthrow of the businessman.

The overbearing and sophisticated methods of the business world would appear easily able to win over the simple native mentality, but Biggle has a sense of justice and appreciation for poetic irony that gives the plot a twist. The reader and the natives are led through a network of bureaucratic red tape and procedures, but the Plan has prepared them well. For the reader with an interest in real estate and title law, this novel offers an interesting future parody on these proceedings. There is also an entertaining projection on the future of courtroom proceedings and the practice of law.

Silence Is Deadly. This is another Jan Darzek thriller in which the Council of the Supreme is alerted to the dangerous

presence of a death ray on an uncertified world. Since an uncertified world is, by definition, politically primitive and morally
and ethically underdeveloped, the presence of a death ray could
mean complete destruction, threatening many worlds in addition
to its own. Agents of the Council attempt to infiltrate the world
of Kamm, a world whose alien life forms have no sense of hearing, to discover the validity of the rumor and to possibly intercept
disaster.

Agents of the Council undergo physical alterations to their
anatomy, including ear removal, in order to pass as natives of the
planet Kamm. Darzek is resourceful and ingenious as usual as he
sets out to investigate the world situation and faces danger at every turn. He acquires a foster daughter, Sajjo, and meets the illustrious blind Keeper of Secrets, Bovranultz. Kamm is filled with
the aura of the middle ages, a collection of Dukes vying for Kingship, knights in armor, magic, and castles.

The world of Kamm is unique in that all of its inhabitants
are without any hearing mechanism, and thus live in a world
without sound. The world of Kamm is actually full of noise and
external sounds since they offend none and are never corrected.
To compensate for the lack of a sense of hearing, other senses are
strengthened, particularly the sense of smell. The detection of
odors is used for identification, and the art of perfumery is
highly developed.

This Darkening Universe. This is another in the series of Jan
Darzek tales. In this colorful novel, the plot fluctuates from the
devastating problem of a seemingly ceaseless progression of the
annihilation of world populations through a violent assault on the
inhabitants' brains, to the bustling and somewhat ludicrous setting
of a huge intergalactic trade mart--Montura Mart, where the main
characters inevitably congregate. Familiar characters of the
Darzek series are here, including the indomitable Miss Schlupe,
Darzek's matronly secretary. True to form, she has established a
fast food concession in the middle of various life-forms, thus discovering that submarine sandwiches and cider appeal to life everywhere. The Supreme Council has summoned another unlikely
character from Earth as well, and no one seems to know why. The
mystery revolves around the important role a female dermatologist
from Earth can play against the progressive destruction--the Udef
(Unidentified death force).

Biggle's infinite range of life-forms is the key to this novel.
We find it is not an army of individual invaders from some warring civilization that is responsible for the destruction, but rather
a by-product of the biological behavior of yet another individual
being. The message seems to be that the infinite unknown of
worlds beyond worlds is capable of endless possibilites.

Watchers of the Dark. This novel was nominated for the
Nebula award and continues the Darzek series. The reader meets

the Supreme--the ultimate computer which is also the World of Primores O. The original Council of the Supreme, those individual beings that feed the Supreme its data and consult it for output in their mission to keep peace throughout the galaxy--is eradicated early in the novel, and its final membership is formed in the novel's conclusion.

Jan Darzek is hired by a mysterious Mr. Smith for the outrageous fee of one million dollars, which is tidily delivered in cardboard cartons of bundled bills to his office. Darzek and his loyal secretary, Miss Schlupe, are transported to Primores, where they discover the possibilities for a destructive force. In world after world there is occuring total rebellion and insanity. The phenomenon is referred to as The Dark, and as it moves from world to world, each planet becomes infected with blackened blight which obliterates trade and food sources and leaves only starving and dying inhabitants. The weapon of this destruction remains a mystery.

Biggle uses this novel for his social commentary. It is the naivete and goodness of the certified worlds that make them vulnerable to The Dark. On the uncertified worlds, there are defenses because "they have enough liars of their own." Darzek earns the position of ONE on the Council of the Supreme.

Biographical/Bibliographical Readings

Patricia Bizzell, "Lloyd Biggle, Jr.," in *Twentieth-Century American Science-Fiction Writers* (Gale, 1981), p.37-40. John Clute, "Lloyd Biggle, Jr.," in *The Science Fiction Encyclopedia* (Granada, 1979), p.71. Elizabeth Anne Hull, "Lloyd Biggle, Jr.," in *Twentieth-Century Science-Fiction Writers*, ed. Curtis C. Smith (St. James, 1986), p.51-53. **[Lorraine E. Lester]**

BLISH, JAMES

Life and Works

James Blish was born on May 23, 1921 in East Orange, New Jersey, and died of cancer on July 30, 1975, in Henley-on-Thames, England. He received his B.S. in microbiology from Rutgers in 1942. He served as a medical technician in the U.S. Army from 1942-44, and when he was released he joined the well-known New York fan group the Futurians, which included such writers as Damon Knight, Virginia Kidd, Judith Merrill, Frederik Pohl, Robert Lowndes, and Cyril Kornbluth. From 1945 to 1946, he did postgraduate work in zoology at Columbia University, but dropped out to pursue his writing career. He was editor for a literary agent, edited a trade newspaper in New York City, and later became a public relations counsel in New York and Washington, D.C. He married Virginia Kidd and was divorced in 1963. In 1964 he married Judith Lawrence, a science fiction illustrator and author.

He was a science fiction fan in the 1930s and came under the influence of John W. Campbell, who edited *Astounding Stories* in the late 1930s. His first short story, "Emergency Refueling," was published in *Super Science Stories* in 1940. He wrote numerous pieces for the pulp magazines including western, sports, and detective stories. Three of Blish's early short stories were written under the pseudonyms Donald Laverty, John MacDougal, and Arthur Merlyn. From 1950 to 1958, Blish was extremely productive. He was first recognized as a significant science fiction author with the publication of the "Okie" stories in *Astounding Science Fiction* from 1950-53 in serial form. These were brought together into his first "Okie" book, *Earthman, Come Home* (1955). He followed this with three other books based on the same theme which also originated in various serialized stories: *They Shall Have Stars* in 1956 (originally titled *Year 2018!*); *The Triumph of Time* (titled *Clash of Cymbals* in Great Britain) in 1958; and *A Life for the Stars* in 1962. In 1970 the four novels were brought together under the title *Cities in Flight*. During this period, he also produced some of his best short stories including "Beanstalk" (1952), "Surface Tension" (1952), and "Beep" (1954, published in 1973 as *Quincunx of Time*). He collected his best short stories in *Best Science Fiction Stories of James Blish*, published in 1965 (revised in 1973). During these years, he also published *Jack of Eagles* (first published as *ESP-er* in 1958).

Blish commonly expanded his short stories into larger works. This was true of one of his most anthologized stories, "Surface Tension," which became part of the novel *The Seedling Stars* (1957). In 1958 Damon Knight and Blish collaborated in the publication of *VOR*. What later became Book One of the *A Case of Conscience* was published in 1958 in *If*, and was expanded to the larger novel published in 1959 and awarded the Hugo. The trilogy After Such Knowledge was composed of *A Case of Conscience*, *Doctor Mirabilis* (1964), *Black Easter* (1968), and its sequel *The Day of Judgement* (1970). *A Torrent of Faces* was published in collaboration with Norman L. Knight in 1968.

Blish was in the forefront of many other activities in science fiction. He encouraged young writers and, with Damon Knight, helped found the Milford Science Fiction Writers Workshop. He was an active charter member of the Science Fiction Writers of America. In 1968 he emigrated to England to be close to Oxford. In England he was one of the founders of the Science Fiction Foundation. Under the pseudonym William Atheling, Jr., he began in the 1950s to write sharp and cutting criticisms of science fiction, and after his death in 1975, a critical award was established in his name. His criticisms were collected in two books, *The Issue at Hand* (1964) and *More Issues at Hand* (1970). He also edited the anthologies *New Dreams This Morning* (1966) and *Thirteen O'Clock* (1972).

He was a member of the Society of Authors, the History of Science Society, Association of Lunar and Planetary Observers, British Interplanetary Society, Authors League, and the American Rocket Society. In addition to his more serious interests, he wrote a series of *Star Trek* books and an original novel, *Spock Must Die*, in 1970. He was also the author of various other television scripts and motion picture screen plays. He often said that he enjoyed writing these more "trivial" works, providing as they did his "bread and butter."

Themes and Style

James Blish was most interested in exploring profound questions within the science fiction framework. *A Case of Conscience*, considered a masterwork, is a classic exploration in science fiction of religious ideas couched in the theme of alien contact. The novel examines the nature and reality of evil and good. The tetralogy Cities in Flight examines the Spenglerian concept that history is cyclical and the future of societies a constant repetition. Blish believed that fresh ideas could regenerate a culture and, at the conclusion of Cities in Flight, he proposes this possibility. In *The Seedling Stars*, he considers the situation of a human completely changed to live on other planets; what is it that makes a person human? It was one of the earliest introductions of sophisticated biological themes into science fiction writing.

Blish was a very careful craftsman who took great pains with the execution of his plots. What distinguishes him from so many other science fiction writers of his time is the logical foundation for his plots. In his best stories, his characters are rational individuals who operate in a world governed by logic, not by magic. His plots flow smoothly because they have, at their basis, scientific knowledge carried to a rational conclusion. The fundamental idea in Cities in Flight is the antigravity device "the spindizzy," coupled with the discovery of antideath drugs which make lengthy interstellar flights possible. The foundation for *The Seedling Stars* extrapolates the far- reaching implications of genetic engineering. Having carefully established the logical framework for several possible conclusions, Blish often leaves the ending of his novels ambiguous. He believed that it was the role of the writer to suggest new paradigms and the role of the reader to come to his or her own conclusions.

Blish's ability to use pulp conventions very successfully is witnessed by the antics of his characters in *Earthmen, Come Home*, and the fast-moving plot in *Jack of Eagles*. This technique adds excitement and entertainment to his writing which might otherwise be bogged down in too serious philosophical discourse. Blish also likes to jolt the reader by characteristically ending chapters and stories with statements that are meant to puzzle or shock. He also has a delightful wit. In *Day after Judgement*, one of the first indications that Hell has taken over Earth is that Radio Italia announces it will play all eleven of Mahler's symphonies! Blish conserved his ideas and reused them. Very often, he would publish a story or two and then use those stories as a basis for a larger work, such as the stories which comprise the basis for Cities in Flight.

Blish was actively interested in elevating science fiction into the realm of serious fiction, and was instrumental in the rise in standards of the science fiction magazines in the early fifties. He was a scholar who makes demands on the reader to thoughtfully consider universal questions within the context of science fiction. Because of the artful crafting of his works and the profundity of his ideas, he is one of the most important writers of twentieth-century science fiction.

Plot Summaries of Major Works

A Case of Conscience. In the year 2049, Father Ruiz-Sanchez, a Jesuit priest and biologist; Cleaver, a physicist; Agronski, a geologist; and Michelis, a chemist, are sent to the planet Lithia by a United Nations commission to determine if it is a suitable port for Earth's interplanetary travel. Ruiz-Sanchez believes that Lithia is Eden before the Fall.

In Book One, Ruiz-Sanchez goes to the enormous Message Tree to send a message to his other colleagues. He is invited to the home of the Lithian Chexta, where he learns to his dismay how Lithian children are born. The female lays an egg which is fertilized before being released into the sea. The children evolve from lung fish, to amphibians, and finally into the adult Lithian--a kangaroolike reptile.

In a formal recommendation to the commission, Cleaver and Agronski vote to build a thermonuclear plant using the Lithians as slave labor. Michelis wants to preserve the highly superior social system of the Lithians for Earth to study. Ruiz-Sanchez argues that Lithia is the work of Satan because the concept of evolution outside the womb is opposed to church doctrine. The vote leaves Lithia a quarantined planet pending further United Nations' study. As the four are leaving Lithia, Chexta presents Ruiz-Sanchez with the gift of the fertilized egg of Chetxa's child, Egtverchi.

Back on Earth, all but the wealthiest of Earth's population live underground because of imminent nuclear war. Gangs of youths roam the planet committing meaningless crimes while at least 35 million people are diagnosed as insane. In this explosive environment, Egtverchi destroys his coming-out party, exposing the sexual and drug perversions of the guests. He becomes a news commentator, exposing the hypocrisy of Earth's moral code.

Meanwhile, the United Nations has sent Cleaver back to Lithia to build a prototype nuclear power plant. Communication is arranged between Egtverchi and his father Chexta through the Message Tree. Chexta commands Egtverchi to return home and obey the Law of the Whole, but Egtverchi declares himself bound by no law. The communication ends as Cleaver's huge saws are heard cutting down the Message Tree. Lithia disappears in a mushroom cloud caused by a design flaw in the nuclear power plant.

A Case of Conscience was the first book in a trilogy which Blish called *After Such Knowledge*. In each of the novels, the protagonist is a priest-scientist, but in no case is the character portrayed in an admirable light. Both the priest and the church are judged and found wanting. Science is also found wanting. Cleaver, his name overtly allegorical, is both a representative of science, destruction, and war. In the end, he cleaves the Message Tree, and is instrumental in the destruction of the planet.

The question remains for the reader: If Lithia is Eden, what is Egtverchi? Blish presents us with a number of symbolic clues. He was Chexta's only son. He was given as a gift to the world. As Egtverchi evolves and awakes to manhood, he exposes the Hell on earth symbolized in the depraved coming-out party. Images and allusions suggest that Blish is replaying the Christian myth.

Cities in Flight series

They Shall Have Stars. This is the foundation novel on which the tetralogy Cities in Flight is begun. The discovery of the antigravity device permits Blish to justify interstellar space flight. The discovery of antideath drugs permits him to retain his characters over hundreds of years. Bliss Wagoner, chair of the Senate Congressional Committee on Space, has invited Dr. Corsi, head of the American Association for the Advancement of Science, to his home to discuss the stagnant state of space flight research. Corsi points out that the scientific method does not work any longer because the government's security system prevents the free exchange of ideas. Corsi himself is under surveillance by the hereditary head of the FBI. He recommends that Wagoner look at some ideas on gravity which can be developed into an interstellar drive.

Five years later, in 2018, the reader is introduced to the two great projects Wagoner has sponsored. In New York, Pfitzner Company is receiving government funding to do research on drugs that will cure degenerative diseases, such as cancer. The company is really developing an antideath drug but must keep that knowledge secret or else their funding will be cut off.

On Jupiter, a massive bridge is being built at enormous cost in money and lives. The reader is given a memorable picture of the structural noises of the bridge as it is wracked by the hellish storms of Jupiter. Wagoner is the only one who knows that only on a planet as big as Jupiter can the equations for antigravity be tested. The tests are successful. The Jupiter project is to be discontinued and the bridge allowed to fall. Antigravity has been found and a space ship built with an an antigravity device, nicknamed the "spindizzy." With the spindizzy drive and antideath drugs, lengthy interstellar flight is possible. At the end of the book, peak storms rise on Jupiter, followed by the shrieking sound of the bridge splitting in two.

Wagoner has to search among crackpot ideas to produce his antigravity and antideath discoveries, because institutions are too stagnant to permit new ideas. His two research projects are the key to the birth of the new culture and with this key, the Earth-manist culture escapes its immediate historical death by fleeing to the stars and bringing forth a new culture. The parallel here to the rise of anti-McCarthyism and its attempts to stifle individual creativity is symbolized by the attempt of congressional committees to cut off funding for the new projects and the stifling of free ideas. Wagoner is the political hero who makes it possible for the cities to escape the economic collapse brought on by the continued battling of the Soviet Union and the United States for political supremacy and to seek a new cycle of cultural birth in the stars. A symbol used continually throughout the four novels is that of the ravages of cancer (ironically he himself died of the disease). The groans of the bridge and its continual erosion is several times likened to cancer. The bridge is also symbolic of the crossing that will be made to the new interstellar culture and to a new life for Earth.

A Life for the Stars. In the second book of the tetralogy, sixteen-year-old Chris deFord stands idly watching the steel city of Scranton, Pennsylvania, with its antigravity spindizzy drives preparing to lift off for the stars, when he is grabbed by a gang and finds himself borne aloft with the "Okie" migrant city. Chris is taken to another migrant city, New York. Chris is informed by the battery of computers known as the City Fathers that he may choose to undergo the rigorous educational program which prepares one to be a citizen of New York and uncover one's useful skills, or he can remain a mere passenger. Those who become citizens receive antideath drugs which prevent heart disease, cancer, and infection, conceivably extending the average lifespan for many centuries. Hoping for the chance to return to Earth, he opts for citizenship.

New York lands on a planet called Heaven. New York's mayor, Amalfi, has agreed to a work contract with Argus III to rid that planet of a bindlestiff (a tramp city which does no work but steals from other cities). He sneaks out of New York and plans a revolution which will put his friend Haskins in power. The revolt is successful. It is Chris's eighteenth birthday, and he is given citizenship. His skills have been discovered and he will become New York's first city manager.

A Life for the Stars was intended to be a young adult story, and it portrays very well the coming of age of a young man who matures into an adult with all the usual adventures that lead him to a greater understanding of his self and his world. Blish continues his concept of cities with antigravity spindizzy devices which take off from Earth to seek their fortunes among the stars. His characters endure through long space voyages from book to book because of the discovery of antideath drugs. In this novel, he adds a historical analogy to the farmers of Oklahoma, the "Okies," who during the Great Depression were forced to take long migrations West to seek work. The novel also introduces one of the main characters of the tetralogy, Amalfi, mayor of New York, a man combining cunning and deceit with a genuine concern for his city, physically a reminder of Mayor Fiorello La Guardia. *A Life for the Stars* is an easy-going novel and much simpler reading than the other three books in the Cities in Flight series. The story stands alone as the story of the growth of a youth from immaturity to responsibility, but it also provides a nice transition from the rise of the Earthmanist culture in *They Shall Have Stars* to its decline in the third novel, *Earthman, Come Home*.

Earthman, Come Home. In the prologue to the third book of Cities of Flight, the reader is reminded that in the battle between the Soviet State and the West, both societies became police states, which led to the unified Bureaucratic State. Escape from the State through interstellar flight became possible with the discovery of the "spindizzy" antigravity device coupled with antideath drugs, which prolonged life for centuries. With spindizzies, whole cities lifted off from Earth, causing the collapse of the Bureaucratic State. In 3602 John Amalfi, now 900 years old, has been mayor of New York for 500 years.

In space, an old videocast is picked up of a city being blown up by a bindlestiff (a pirate city) and a desperate voice shouting, "We have the fuelless drive." Eager to gain knowledge of the drive, Amalfi lands New York on the planet He. Sometime in the past, He's axis has tilted, drastically changing its climate and forcing the civilization into religious barbarism. Amalfi agrees to regularize the planet's axis, but the resultant energy flow causes it to spin off at enormous speed towards the Andromedan Galaxy. New York returns to the Milky Way to replace one of its defective spindizzys.

Going to the Acolyte cluster (300 itinerant cities circling a dying dwarf star), New York learns that the Okie economy has collapsed and all the cities are being used as a labor pool. Urged on by the king of one of the city planets, the cities mass to converge on Earth and demand assistance. Under cover of the ensuing battle with the Acolyte police, Amalfi hijacks the spindizzies of two dying planets and mounts them on the planet Hern VI so that, with its huge mass and New York on board, it can catch up with the Okie cities before they reach Earth. In a moment of triumph, Amalfi sends the planet Hern VI crashing into the fort and causes its destruction. New York, still looking for a permanent planet home, heads towards the Greater Magellanic Cloud.

Earthman, Come Home was typically compiled from four previously published stories, "Okie," "Bindlestiff," "Sargasso of Lost Cities," and "Earthman, Come Home." These four stories were the first stories which related to the tetralogy Cities in Flight. *Earthman, Come Home* is a stunning space opera with spectacular battles, diplomatic wrangles, and love affairs. The structure contains the superscientific devices of space opera with a friction field generator, an invisibility machine, and various other magical escape devices.

While the space opera gallivantings of the cities propels the plot, the framework is still the inexorable logic of antigravity, spindizzy powered cities and antideath drugs, ideas which Blish established in the first book of the series, *They Shall Have Stars*. These ideas make it possible for the cities to spin through space with the primary characters retained over centuries of time. In the conclusion of this novel, New York will make a journey of over 100 years across the rift of space, but the reader will still find Amalfi as mayor. Blish has added to this book a more detailed and sophisticated view of the economics of the Okie cities, culminating in the well-drawn scenes of all the cities huddling in depression and being abused as a labor pool. Earthmanist interstellar culture has bloomed and is now fading.

The Triumph of Time. The prologue to the fourth and final novel in Cities in Flight, *The Triumph of Time*, provides the reader with a brief historical background. Earth achieved galactic importance in 2019 when she discovered the antigravity device which allowed her cities, known as Okies, to exit the planet and cruise the galaxy in search of economic stability. New York, one of the Okie cities, fled to the Greater Magellanic Cloud and set up a new home.

As the novel opens, John Amalfi, mayor of New Earth, is a thousand years old and bored. Amalfi wants to overhaul the spindizzies and fly again. As he muses, Jake Freeman, the city's astronomer/navigator, announces that a planet is approaching which turns out to be the planet He, a planet which had sped out of the Galazy when New York had righted its axis. Amalfi and others fly to He and learn that on He's journeys through the galaxy, the inhabitants have discovered that the end of time is imminent. In a long philosophical discussion, it is agreed that they must journey to the "center of the metagalaxy, the hub of all the galaxies of space-time where the forces of the universe lie in dynamic balance" and hope to take some action to escape or modify the end. This discontinuity in the span of existence is called the Ginnangu-Gap, which allows for the possibility that after the collision, some new form of universe or universes will be born; anyone surviving at the last instant may have the possibility of influencing the moment of creation. In the final moment, Amalfi touches the detonator button and all the elements flash into plasma.

The Triumph of Time is the last of the four novels making up Cities in Flight. Unlike the other three, this last volume is one of conversation and ideas, with very little action. In the final analysis, Amalfi makes one last attempt to prevent the new universe from continuing the same historical cycle which had preceded it. Blish allows Amalfi to play God with the new creation. Blish has in this last novel transcended the future history of Spengler and moved into the realm of the metaphysical, providing a most satisfying conclusion to a very well-written future history.

The Seedling Stars. *The Seedling Stars* is a book of four stories about pantropy, meaning to change everything. In the story "Seeding Program," we are introduced to a project to seed other planets with adapted humans. Sweeney has been adapted and raised under a glass dome on Earth, isolated from other humans because he can not live freely in Earth's environment. In return for the promise of being made human, he is charged with bringing back from Ganymede a criminal group of pantropes under the leadership of Dr. Rullman. Posing as an escapee from oppressive conditions on Earth, he is dropped by spaceship on Ganymede but is unable to reconcile the reality he experiences on Ganymede with what he has been taught. Dr. Rullman convinces Sweeney that the adapted men on Ganymede are not criminals. So that pantropy will be abandoned, the Port Authority has to prove that the colony has failed. As the Port Authority ship approaches, Jupiter makes its closest approach to the sun and fierce storms rise on Ganymede. Sweeney attempts delaying actions by the port ship as the Ganymedian rocket ship, with newly adapted children, leaves the planet to seed the furthest stars.

In "The Thing in the Attic," mankind lives in a canopy of the forest. Honath and four others are arrested for casting doubt on the divine order of men, denying the Book of Laws, and doubting the existence of the Giants. In the attempt to survive, two of them are killed. Reaching the top of a mesa, they are astonished to see the "Giants." The "Giants" admit that they are not Gods but members of the team which had seeded adapted men in the treetops. Honath and the other survivors have passed the real test of survival by conquering the forest floor.

In "Surface Tension," a seed ship has been wrecked on a planet of ponds and muddy pools in which live small crustacea, rotifers and protozoa. The seeding team creates microscopic humans and engraves what has been done on microscopic metal leaves. In some later time, the Paras and Protos organize under the leadership of Lavon and Shar, microscopic men, to do battle with their enemies, the worms and rotifers. A band of humans and Paras take over the sand house of a Caddis worm and then, in another generation or two, take over the houses of the rotifers and destroy their eggs. Some generations later, another Shar deciphers a metal plate which tells of people who traveled from place to place in a container through the "stars" (a word that is meaningless to them). A new Lavon dreams of breaking the surface barrier that divides water and sky. Shar pours over old records, does simple scientific experiments, and encourages a team of men to build a rudimentary wooden "spaceship." The men succeed in moving up the sandbar and breaking through the water's surface tension into "space." As darkness falls, a myriad of twinkling lights fills the sky and they understand the meaning of the "stars."

In the final story, "Watershed," Captain Gorbel and his crew feel distaste and hostility for the adapted men that they are carrying to their new home. Gorbel is shocked when he discovers that the planet which he is about to seed with adapted men is historical Earth, so changed that it cannot be inhabited any longer by the "basic" form. His form is the "ethnic minority," with no home beyond the space ship.

Blish was trained in biology and believed that biology had been neglected in science fiction. *The Seedling Stars* is based on the radical idea that it is easier to adapt humans to alien planets (pantropy) than to adapt planets to humans (terraforming). "Surface Tension," a story of genetic engineering, turned out to be one of the most successful stories he ever wrote. The story gets its force from the myth of the conceptual breakthrough, the tiny wooden "spacecraft" which, against all odds, manages to move across "space" from one pool to another. Blish went on to write the less successful "The Thing in the Attic," in which genetically engineered humans learn to conquer their environment. "The Thing in the Attic" and "Surface Tension" provide a parable to human evolution from water and tree, to the surface of the planet, to Homo sapiens. Both "Seeding Program" and "Watershed" address prejudice against the adapted human. In both cases, Blish implies that the adapted humans are the true answer to Earth's need to colonize the stars. All four stories address the fundamental question, what constitutes "humanity?" If everything about an individual is changed, what remains to define that person as human?

Biographical/Bibliographical Readings

Brian W. Aldiss, "The Mathematics of Behavior," *Foundation*, no.13, 1978, p.43-50. John Clute, "James Blish," in *Science Fiction*

Writers, ed. E. F. Bleiler (Scribner's, 1982), p.291-96. Brian M. Stableford, *A Clash of Symbols: The Triumph of James Blish* (Borgo Press, 1979). Raymond J. Wilson, III, "James Blish," in *Twentieth-Century American Science-Fiction Writers* (Gale, 1981), v. 1, p.40-53. [Judith R. Bernstein]

BLOCH, ROBERT

Life and Works

Born April 5, 1917, in Chicago, Illinois, Robert Bloch developed early on a keen interest in reading and film, and as a youth, was a gifted artist with watercolors and oils. His first professional story, "The Feast in the Abbey," was published in *Weird Tales* in 1935. During the depression years of the 1930s, he helped to support and take care of his family, learning his craft as a writer at the same time. During these difficult economic times, he became friends with such writers as H. P. Lovecraft and Stanley Weinbaum. His manuscript collection, including his correspondence, is permanently housed at the University of Wyoming at Laramie archives. Noted for his wry sense of humor and his sincere nature, Bloch is liked and respected by his peers and has often served as guest or toastmaster at World Science Fiction and World Fantasy Conventions. He currently lives in Los Angeles.

Although Bloch has written in other genres, some of his major short fiction has been in science fiction, and he won a Hugo award for "The Hell-Bound Train" (1958). Bloch is considered a major American author in France, and during the 1980s a French publisher commenced the process of translating Bloch's entire works into French, including nearly 500 stories, 22 novels, and numerous scripts, teleplays, screenplays, and related literary output from the 1930s to the present. Science fiction readers can find many of Bloch's short stories in the collections *Atoms and Evil* (1962) and *The Best of Robert Bloch* (1977). He also wrote many teleplays for the 1960s television cult classic Star Trek.

Themes and Style

Bloch's works are exciting, highly crafted, and well plotted, with sharp characterizations. Moreover, the reader will also become aware of Bloch's meaningful vision of moral message. As a twentieth-century American writer, Bloch's finest work echoes the mood of a much earlier American author, Nathaniel Hawthorne. Like Hawthorne, Bloch is a moralist with a wry sense of humor that carries much existential irony in its structure. Often concerned with cultural deviance and how culture defines deviance, much of Bloch's writing is viewed as social criticism literature,

such as *Psycho* (1959). Critics have defined one of his recent
works, *The Night of the Ripper* (1984), a masterpiece of social criticism dealing with deviance in society. Norman Bates, of *Psycho*, is
Bloch's perfected version of an American Jack the Ripper and
symbolizes how American culture is capable of spawning such
evils. Credit for the perfection of the "psycho" character in American fiction rightfully belongs to Bloch, for it remains a trademark of his career. Variations and additional applications of this
type of character may be seen in the writings of contemporary
science fiction authors, even if it happens to be in the form of an
extraterrestrial.

Of the many sociological themes in Bloch's fiction, some include loss of innocence, role and identity, cultural entropy, cultural mentalities, paradoxical perception, and labeling. His use of
American Indian motifs is best illustrated in his post-nuclear war
science fiction story, "Where the Buffalo Roam" (1955). Bloch's
personal statement on the insanity of war appears in "Daybroke"
(1958). "The Model" (1975) is the story of George Milbank's encounter with a high-fashion model named Vilma Loring, who is an
alien from outer space. She seeks to breed with Milbank and
achieves it in a most unusual manner. This subtle tale has the
starkness of Kafka touched by a Nathanael West-like disturbing
imagery.

Bloch continues to create quality fiction at a prolific rate, and
a major theme found throughout his writing career is the use of
eyes or mirrors as reflections of social reality, through which
character or characters must separate illusion from reality. Illustrations of this theme are found in "The Cheaters" (1947), "The
Hungry House" (1950), and "The Hungry Eye" (1959). Bloch's influence on writers in science fiction and fantasy has been tremendous. He still continues to give helpful and sincere advice to
those writers who seek him out.

Plot Summaries of Major Works

"Daybroke." "Daybroke" tells the story of a man who survived
a nuclear war by seeking safety deep within a mountain retreat.
He has a special suit and helmet which allow him to walk unharmed among the radioactive ruins. Throughout his journey, he
reflects on what he sees, and catalogs each item as segments of a
now-lost civilization--automobiles, bobby pins, magazines, tranquilizers. He sees dead people--human beings in their last activities,
moments before death, including children's bodies on a school
playground. The man sees looters, but they are too busy taking
the material possessions all around, never realizing that they will
soon be dead also and the possessions will be meaningless. Eventually, he comes to the city, and there finds the military commander in the government building which has somehow remained in-

tact. Other bureaucrats are busy at their duties. As the city burns, the military commander of the destroyed city smilingly informs the traveler that the war has been won, not lost.

The story reflects Bloch's personal statement and philosophy of the horrifying insanity of war and his belief that a nuclear war must never be fought. The biting irony in the military commander's statement is that neither side wins or loses in a nuclear war; total destruction is the only foreseeable end.

"A Toy for Juliette." A loving grandfather successfully utilizes a disguised time machine mechanism to bring his grandaughter, Juliette, toys for her personal enjoyment and entertainment. The toys are books, artifacts, and even people from different time periods in history. Juliette victimizes and tortures her human toys from the past, enjoying the pain she inflicts upon her victims. One of her acquisitions is Jack the Ripper from nineteenth-century England. The tables turn, and Jack kills Juliette.

"A Toy for Juliette" is a moral tale with a subtle commentary on societal violence; it is also a time travel tale which proposes why Jack the Ripper vanished and was never found.

"Where the Buffalo Roam." Set in a postholocaust future, this story deals with a pocket of survivors on Earth who encounter aliens. These aliens, human in appearance, are soon revealed to be those humans who fled Earth at the time of the nuclear war and are returning as a scouting party to review Earth's survivors and status. The alien humans have spent a generation on a moon base. The survivors, known as buffalo hunters, have returned to a more direct, less adorned existence, live in accord with nature, and follow many of the ways of the American Indian. Both the survivors and the aliens are compared and contrasted in this story of ethics and morals. Inevitably, a fight breaks out between the two groups and the scouting party and its spaceship are destroyed, leaving Earth free of technological onslaught, free from threat of war, free of the old ways which made nuclear war a reality and cities a blight upon the landscape. Earth has become again a place where the buffalo can roam in peace.

With the use of many American Indian motifs, Bloch recreates the world of old--the better days. One cannot help but wonder, however, that even though the alien humans are destroyed, what is to hold back "progress" and the evolution of humanity along the same course?

Biographical/Bibliographical Readings

Graeme Flanagan, *Robert Bloch: A Bibliography* (Australia Press, 1979). Randall D. Larson, *The Complete Robert Bloch: A Bibliography* (Borgo Press, 1987). Harold Lee Prosser, *The Man Who*

Walked through Mirrors: Robert Bloch as Social Critic (Borgo Press, 1986). **[Harold Lee Prosser]**

BOUCHER, ANTHONY

Life and works

Author, editor, critic, linguist, opera buff, gourmet, Sherlock Holmes fanatic, and workaholic, Anthony Boucher casts a large shadow over both the science fiction and mystery genres from the 1930s through the 1950s. Born William Anthony Parker White in Oakland, California, in 1911, his first sale was to *Weird Tales* when he was only sixteen. He attended Pasadena Junior College and received degrees from the University of Southern California in 1932 and the University of California in 1934. Boucher married Phyliss May Price in 1938 and they had two sons.

Noting the other seventy-five William White's in the Library of Congress catalogs, he chose the name Anthony Boucher for his pen name, supplementing it in typical sly humor with the alternate pseudonym of H. H. Holmes, a once-famous murderer. His first science fiction story, "Snulbug," appeared in *Unknown* in 1941. He filled his works with examples of his many enthusiasms, and enlivened his rather traditional novels by setting his casts of characters in the nascent science fiction community, as in *Rocket to the Morgue* (1942). He turned out a steady stream of science fiction, fantasy, and detective short stories, including "Barrier" (1942), "Q.U.R." (1943), "Elsewhere" (1943), "Transfer Point" (1950), "Starbride" (1951), "The Other Inauguration" (1953), and "Balaam" (1954). His best stories, including the Science Fiction Hall of Fame classic, "The Quest for St. Aquin" (1951), appeared in the 1950s. Most of his stories appear in the two collections, *The Compleat Werewolf* (1969) and *Far and Away* (1955).

It was as critic that he gained his greatest fame in the outside world, writing simultaneously mystery and science fiction review columns for the *New York Times Book Review*. By treating the genres as serious and literate sources of good writing, he brought them a measure of respectability at a time when science fiction especially was disdained as pulp literature.

In 1949, he and J. Francis McComas performed their greatest service for science fiction, launching what later became *The Magazine of Fantasy and Science Fiction*. A consciously literate alternative to John W. Campbell's *Astounding*, the magazine immediately became the science fiction world's center for well-written, human-oriented stories. Boucher remained editor and occasional book reviewer for the magazine for nine years, a labor of love which stimulated his own writing. Only one of his stories, "The Other Inauguration," ever appeared in the journal.

Boucher, never in good health, stopped writing and editing in the late 1950s, but remained a reviewer until his death in 1968. While no more than an enjoyable writer, albeit in two genres, he was a perspicacious and exacting--but encouraging--editor and critic who brought a number of excellent new writers into the field, gave new direction to older, established authors, and started science fiction on its road to adulthood.

Themes and Style

Anthony Boucher's writing encapsulated the dominant modes of his genres in the 1930s, 1940s, and 1950s. After his slightly stiff and fussy formal detective novels of the 1930s, Boucher bent to the same winds of change in the mystery field which forced realism of setting while providing a home for screwball humor, and produced in his later mysteries and early science fiction a series of slightly wacky stories with oddball casts of characters and equally exuberant, if odd, detectives and protagonists. Somewhat later, his science fiction moved from Campbellian problem-solving engineering stories in middle-class American futures to lower-key, more literary stories without the solace of neat and triumphant resolutions after he himself had provided the spark for change with *The Magazine of Fantasy and Science Fiction*.

Boucher's many enthusiasms turn up, sometimes as plot, more often as background, in the majority of his stories, so much so that one suspects that the line between his private personality and his authorial one is more thinly drawn than in most writers. In his best stories, the increasing sophistication of his writing examined troubling ambiguities in the subject he was most certain about, the Catholic faith. In stories such as "Balaam" and "The Quest for St. Aquin," characters must battle against those who would use religion as a nostrum for quick success and manipulation of the mass mind without the comfort of a totally assured and unquestioning faith within themselves.

That Boucher chose the more difficult path is to be expected from a reading of his fiction which, although little of it confronts the question of religion directly, often presents his characters with the results of a choice of the easy path over the hard. His science fiction uses time travel in a parallel way, as his characters' hopes and intentions to change the future or the past, no matter how noble or lofty, lead to unforeseen consequences. Boucher's stories tend to emblematize an unstated dictum that hoped-for results can only come from hard and honest work. In this way, much of his work can be read as principled, if not overtly religious, exemplifications of a philosophical belief in the free will of mankind, as his minor godlings' attempts at determinism always fail.

Boucher's stories typically feature everyday Americans thrust into odd or humorous situations from which they must extricate themselves using no more than the ordinary skills they bring to their quotidian lives. His ability to disarm the reader with a comfortable, though alien, setting and characters who seemed like old friends at first reading were major contributions to his popularity, rather than ingenuity of plot or lyric writing. Few heroics or deeds of derring-do can be found in his works, but the lack of pulp adventure give his stories a grounding in reality which sustain them even when the historic or satiric point is lost or blunted (to a modern reader) by the story's total immergence in its year of creation. His best works manage this at the same time as they tackle larger issues from an unfailing moral viewpoint, succeeding in one of science fiction's prime virtues: the presentation of the effects of social and cultural forces in miniature so that their immediacy to the reader is instantly apparent.

Plot Summaries of Major Works

The Compleat Werewolf. Though a posthumous collection, the stories in *The Compleat Werewolf* are all drawn from the early 1940s, Boucher's first years as a science fiction writer. In his first science fiction story, "Snulbug," a man calls up a demon who procures for him tomorrow's newspaper. He can do nothing with this knowledge, however, as every attempt to change the future--from winning bets to foiling a murder--is frustrated. Another wish gone wrong figures in "We Print the Truth," in which anything a newspaper prints becomes true. Though the power is used mostly for good, it serves to divorce the characters from the real world in which good must be achieved by struggle and trial. Taking advantage of others never succeeds in a Boucher story. The other two science fiction stories in the collection, "Q.U.R." and its sequel, "Robinc," both by "H. H. Holmes," seem considerably dated and cliched, but are problem-solving stories nonetheless. In "Q.U.R.," an epidemic of robot failure is cured by straight-thinking Doug Quinby, who realizes that his society's invariably humanoid robots are become neurotic because they are not built like robots; humans insist on giving them extraneous humanlike parts not needed to do their jobs. An attack by the former robot monopoly to keep robots humanoid is foiled in the sequel when the ever-logical Quinby goes directly to the robots and convinces them that their best interests lie with transformation into Quinby's more functional format.

While not as well written as his later works, these stories show Boucher's easy, relaxed style and his range of interests. The stories range widely as well, on the one hand science fiction--time travel and robots; on the other fantasy--demons and silver bullets. From the beginning Boucher would freely mix detective or mystery plots with his science fiction, and occasionally a single story would combine all of these themes.

"The Quest for St. Aquin." Oddly, Boucher's best story is science fiction, not fantasy, and equally oddly does not appear in either of his short story collections. This is a complex story about faith and the need for uncomplicated belief. A desperate pope, hiding in a world in which religion is forbidden, sets a priest on a quest for signs and wonders, hoping that the discovery of a famed saint's uncorrupted body will lead more souls back to God. The mechanical ass used by the priest as transport torments him like Satan with theological sophistries and the revelation that the body lies intact because it was the one perfect robot, whose intellect proved the existence of God. To claim sainthood for the body would lead the priest to the papacy and gather a tremendous flock for the church, but Boucher leaves the priest praying for strength to reject the temptation of a revivified faith based upon a lie.

Rocket to the Morgue. The son of the beloved creator of the magnificent Dr. Derringer mystery stories is attacked and then killed while alone in a locked room, its doors watched by a number of witnesses. All the main suspects come from the then new and exotic world of "scientificion" and are based on well-known science fiction writers of the period, including Robert Heinlein and Cleve Cartmill. The science fiction writers offer a variety of explanations involving time travel, but the more prosaic secret of the crime is deduced by Sister Ursula and Lieutenant Terry Marshall of the Los Angeles Homicide squad. The novel is of interest today primarily in its inside details of the world of science fiction and fandom in the early days.

"Transfer Point." The last man in the world passes time by reading old pulp magazines, discovering one author who managed to describe the future perfectly before his untimely death. He escapes to the past by means of a time machine and sustains himself by writing uncannily plausible tales of the future, realizing he has only postponed his fate. Austin Carter, a Heinlein surrogate in *Rocket to the Morgue*, appears as a minor character in "Transfer Point."

Biographical/Bibliographical Readings

Bill Blackbeard, "Anthony Boucher," in *Twentieth-Century American Science-Fiction Writers* (Gale, 1981), v. 1, p.53-55. J. R. Christopher, "Anthony Boucher Bibliography," *Armchair Detective*, no. 2-4 (1969). Malcolm J. Edwards, "Anthony Boucher," in *The Science Fiction Encyclopedia*, ed. Peter Nicholls (Doubleday, 1979), p.82. Donald L. Lawler, "Anthony Boucher," in *Twentieth-Century Science-Fiction Writers*, ed. Curtis C. Smith (St. James, 1986), p.65-68. **[Steven Carper]**

BOVA, BENJAMIN WILLIAM

Life and Works

A versatile member of the science fiction community, Ben Bova has written both science fiction and nonfiction works, has edited science and science fiction journals, and has compiled and edited many anthologies of science fiction. Bova was born in November of 1932 in Philadelphia. He received a B.S. in journalism from Temple University in 1954 and did some graduate work at Georgetown University School of Foreign Service. Bova worked in a variety of editing careers, from editing the *Upper Darby News* to serving as a technical editor for the Vanguard Project in the 1950s. He became a science writer for Avco-Everett Research Laboratory in 1960, and authored many popular technical works. Assuming the editorship of *Analog* from 1971 to 1978, he then switched to the editorship of *Omni* in 1978. Bova received the Hugo award for editing each year from 1973 to 1977 and again in 1979.

Bova's scientific background lends credence to his science fiction. Although his only award for writing is a Hugo honorable mention for *Colony* in 1979, Bova is considered a solid "hard science" writer. His prodigious output includes more than sixty works of science and science fiction. Graduate training at Georgetown's School of Foreign Service may account for the political nature of some of Bova's novels. The Chet Kinsman short stories include "Test in Orbit" (1965), "Fifteen Miles" (1967), "Zero Gee" (1972), and "Build Me a Mountain" (1974). His recent works, *Voyager* (1981) and *Voyager II* (1986) portray the importance of international cooperation and graphically foretell the dangers of too much power under industrial control. His short stories have been collected in *Forward in Time* (1973), *Maxwell's Demons* (1979), and *Escape Plus Ten* (1984).

Themes and Style

Overpopulation and mishandling of Earth's resources are themes which appear frequently in Bova's works. In *City of Darkness* (1976), New York City is cut off totally from the rest of the country because of the crush of population, crime, pollution, and other mega-city problems. While many are evacuated from New York, the poor and the minority inhabitants are forced to stay in the city. The setting for *Escape!* (1970) is a chaotic ghetto, teeming with overabundant population and crime. In The Kinsman series--which includes three novels, *Kinsman* (1965), *Millenium* (1976), and *Colony* (1978)--and the Exile trilogy--*Exiled from Earth* (1971), *Flight of Exiles* (1972), and *End of Exile* (1975), the motivation to escape to the stars is brought about by the urge to flee the mistakes made on Earth and start anew on another planet. Bova is critical of the military mentality in both of these series and *As on a Darkling Plain* (1972) tells the story of a scientist driven mad by the military threat of alien machines. The Kinsman series also depicts the political machinations of the military services and the industrial community. It exemplifies the futility of remaining nationalistic in a time when problems are global. Bova's characterizations are somewhat shallow; he carefully adds one flaw to each of his heroes in an attempt to make the hero believable. His stories and novels are enjoyable as fast-paced and exciting adventures.

Plot Summaries of Major Works

Kinsman series
    Kinsman. The first volume of this series is a biography of Chet Kinsman from the age of twenty-one, when he was at the Air Force Academy, to the age of thirty-five. Kinsman is a complex man, shaped by his love of flying and his Quaker pacifism. Although he assures his stern father that he will never kill, he is forced into a situation where he must kill--and the life he takes is that of a young female Soviet cosmonaut. The psychological pressure and guilt immobilizes him for a time. Even his toughest competitor and best friend, a black pilot named Frank Colt, cannot snap him out of his depression. An elderly friend planted the seed of an idea in Chet--why not build a lunar colony so that people with bad hearts or defective muscles could be removed from the damaging effects of Earth's gravity? Chet lobbied for the colony, but he was unable to sell the idea to Congress with purely altruistic arguments. An economic advantage was needed to justify the expense involved and, though dead set against the military, Chet agreed to put up mining operations to extract the moon's valuable ores, thus finding the economic justification.
    Millenium. In *Millenium*, the second volume of the series, Moonbase has been completed and a mirror Russian colony called Lunagrad exists next door. Chet Kinsman is the American commander and his friend, Leonov, chairs the Russian settlement. They name their combined colonies Selene. The main purpose of Selene is to supply metal ores to Earth, but they also want to provide an alternate life style dedicated to peace. Meanwhile, on Earth, the Americans and Russians are playing a deadly game of seek-and-destroy the other's antiballistic missile satellites. Frank Colt is one of the players, knocking Russian satellites out of the sky whenever he finds them. As the game escalates to the failsafe point, Kinsman and Leonov declare Selene an independent country and take over the space stations and a world-girdling defense system. Frank Colt is called in to try to stop the independence move, but fails. In capturing space station Alpha, Chet is

again forced to take human lives. One of the scientists on Alpha shares with Chet a new weapon for peace, the ability to control weather. Chet takes it to the United Nations, and together, he and the United Nations Secretary General announce to the world that war and nationalism are over. The cost is great--Chet dies in the effort; his heart cannot stand the gravity of Earth.

Colony. In *Colony*, the conclusion of the trilogy, Frank Colt is running Selene. A new colony has been built, a self-contained cylinder in which a perfect world has been created, Island One. David Adams, a test-tube baby whose abilities have been genetically enhanced, escapes from Island One to discover what the rest of humanity is really like. He finds the Earth torn by forces motivated by hate and greed, with five industrial magnates pulling the strings. Revolutionaries fight for control and the war escalates to include Island One. In a daring move, David infects the revolutionary leaders with a fatal disease and forces the industrialists to negotiate with the poverty-stricken inhabitants of Earth.

The superheroes of this series, Kinsman and Adams, are above the evil and stupidity of the military-industrial leaders of Earth. Ben Bova endows both with insight, cunning, and the ability to win out over immense odds. Kinsman's enduring guilt at causing the death of a female cosmonaut is nearly incompatible with his callous treatment of other women characters in the novels and his blatant bed-hopping behavior. Bova's macho male heroes are action-oriented and justify their violent means with noble ends. *Colony* is the most intricately plotted novel of the trilogy.

The Multiple Man. James J. Halliday is president of the United States . . . or is he? Meric Albano, the presidential press secretary, discovers some very strange things. First, there appears a dead man who is the exact double of Halliday. Meric fears that the president has been assassinated and a double inserted, but by whom? Then he discovers that a similar phenomenon has happened earlier. A dead double was also found, just before the inauguration. Laura Halliday, the first lady, tries to presume upon her former relationship with Meric to keep him quiet. Despite his passion for her, Meric continues to investigate and uncovers the incredible secret: Halliday was cloned by his wealthy and eccentric father, with all eight of the "brothers" intended for a specialty, such as foreign relations, economics, science, public speaking; they had been set on the road to the White House from birth. However, the immunological systems of the clones had a flaw, and one had died in infancy. Another of the brothers is capitalizing on that flaw to gain sole possession of the presidency. Once he learns the secret, Meric has access to all of the remaining brothers: James Jeffrey, the military specialist; James Jackson, the economist; James Joshua, whose expertise is in natural resources and agriculture; and James John, the speechmaker--the one whose hand Meric had shaken when he became press secretary. Meric is determined to find out which of the clones is killing the others by infecting them with a virus which attacks the body's immune system. Determined to save James John Halliday, Meric discovers that the killer is James Jackson Halliday, the economist, who considers himself to be the strongest and best able to preside alone. Jackson is killed and Meric persuades the other remaining brothers to reveal their story.

This political thriller is more like *Seven Days in May* than a science fiction plot, but Bova employs his usual meticulous scientific knowledge to make it realistic. His background as a newspaperman comes through in his portrayals of press coverage, investigative reporting, and other details. There are a few unanswered questions, such as why the remaining brothers were willing to be part of Laura's harem?

Voyager. When Keith Stoner hears the radio signals from the direction of Jupiter, he recognizes them as a message from an alien culture. As a scientist, he believes this discovery belongs to the world and he is consequently placed under house arrest to continue his research in silence. He is able to force the government to cooperate with Russian and other international scientists, and Keith and a Russian team fly out to meet the approaching alien spaceship. Aboard the spaceship are found artifacts and information about the alien culture and a long-dead alien. Keith is stranded on board the alien spaceship, and continues to broadcast information back to Earth until the cold of space seeps in to freeze him solid.

Voyager II. Keith's story is picked up in *Voyager II*, as he awakens from his cryogenic sleep eighteen years later. His beloved Jo has used the intervening years to acquire sufficient wealth and power to retrieve Keith from the alien ship and capitalize on the information and artifacts it contains. Keith discovers that his mind has linked with the dead alien's, and his life is altered by the alien's presence. Upon returning to Earth, he finds the world has been vastly altered by the concentration of power in the hands of a few. He uses information and skills gained from the alien part of his mind to defeat the enemies of humanity.

The Voyager series is political philosophy set in the near future. It is a plea for cooperation, honesty, and peace. Bova believes that scientists are more capable of cooperative effort because of their devotion to something higher-reaching than national boundaries. Through Keith Stoner's difficulties, Bova expresses his suspicions of political power, of nationalism, and of capitalism. Passionate human beings are found in Bova's stories--people capable of lust, hate, love, greed and altruism.

Biographical/Bibliographical Readings

Ben Bova, "The Role of Science Fiction," in *Science Fiction, Today and Tomorrow*, ed. Reginald Bretnor (Harper & Row, 1974), p.3-16. "Ben Bova," in *Contemporary Authors New Revision Series* (Gale, 1984), v. 11 p.80-85. Malcolm J. Edwards, "Ben Bova," in *The Science Fiction Encyclopedia*, ed. Peter Nicholls (Doubleday, 1979), p.82-83. David Petties, "Interview: Ben Vova," *Thrust* 23 (Fall/Winter 1985), p.9-12. Marylyn J. Underwood, "Ben Bova," in *Twentieth-Century Science-Fiction Writers* (Macmillan, 1981), p.67-69. [Kay Jones]

BRACKETT, LEIGH

Life and Works

Leigh Douglas Brackett was born in Los Angeles, California, on December 7, 1915. Her fascination with science fiction began when one of her presents for her eighth birthday was a copy of Edgar Rice Burrough's *The Gods of Mars*. Later she would use her own version of Mars as the setting for many of her stories. She began writing in the 1930s and was advised to try science fiction by Henry Kuttner. In 1946, she married science fiction writer Edmond Hamilton and credited him with improving her plots. Her first science fiction story, "Martian Quest," appeared in *Astounding* in 1940, beginning a career that would result in her appellation as "Queen of Space Opera." *The Sword of Rhiannon* (1949), *The Starmen of Llyrdis* (1955), *The Big Jump* (1955), and *Alpha Centauri--or Die!* (1963) are four of her best known space operas. One of her best novels, *The Long Tomorrow* (1955) takes place after a nuclear war. Brackett was one of the few women to write space opera. Unlike many space operas of the period, Brackett's stories combine exciting plots, complex characters, and atmospheric descriptions. She wrote science fiction, fantasy, westerns, and crime stories, as well as numerous screenplays for television and movies. She completed the first draft of *The Empire Strikes Back* (1980) shortly before her death. Leigh Brackett died on March 24, 1978. The Hamilton-Brackett Memorial Award, given to works that create a "sense of wonder," was named for Brackett and Hamilton.

Brackett often combined the science fiction and mystery genres. *The Big Jump* (1955), *The Starmen of Llyrdis* (1976) and "The Halfling" (in the collection *The Halfling and Other Stories*, published in 1973) are murder mysteries in science fiction settings. Edmond Hamilton collected many of Brackett's stories in *The Best of Leigh Brackett* (1977). Both "Enchantress of Venus" (1949) and The Book of Skaith trilogy (1976) begin with Eric John Stark searching for missing friends. The Stark series, also called The Book of Skaith series, consists of *The Ginger Stars* (1974), *The Hounds of Skaith* (1974) and *The Reavers of Skaith* (1976).

Themes and Style

Most of Brackett's work involves the theme of equality, whether individual, social, political, racial, or economic. She is concerned with the diversity and potential of intelligent life. Brackett explores the concepts of what it would mean to be alone in a universe dominated by other races, and of the nature of intelligence and compassion. In the Skaith trilogy, for example, the economic and political inequality of the society leads to its destruction.

One of Brackett's most notable characteristics is her evocative style. Her writing is very colorful and visual. Highly detailed imagery ranges from intensely sensual to extremely brutal. Brackett's ability to create the atmosphere of a story is complimented by an equal ability to maintain a quickly moving plot with complex characters. Her style of writing, her characters, and her themes have insured that her work endures long after most space operas are no longer read. Stark and her other protagonists often resemble the hard-boiled detective of the stories and films of the 1930s and 1940s--they are tough, often cynical, sometimes sad, and occasionally compassionate. They are multidimensional characters who must deal with situations where the choices are morally ambiguous.

Plot Summaries of Major Works

The Book of Skaith series. The Book of Skaith series consists of three novels, *The Ginger Star*, *The Hounds of Skaith*, and *The Reavers of Skaith*. Brackett's best known character, Eric John Stark, journeys to Skaith to find his missing foster father, Simon Ashton. Stark succeeds in finding and rescuing Ashton, and in the process he fulfills a prophecy that he (Stark) is the Dark Man who will destroy the government and society of Skaith, a planet with a dying sun. There are many racial, tribal, and religious groups on Skaith, each with differing structures. Brackett creates detailed backgrounds for each of the groups and develops the complex relationships between them.

Stark is an outsider, alien both by virtue of his birthplace and by his behavior. His presence on Skaith is a challenge that must end in destruction, either for the ruling structure or for Stark himself. Stark moves through the various cultures and changes them greatly, without being changed himself. Stark is portrayed as both a savior and a destroyer. He provides the people of Skaith with the possibility of a better life on other worlds, but destroys the government and the societal structure in the process.

The Book of Skaith series is a fast-moving trilogy, with one adventure quickly followed by another. The story gains its depth from Brackett's ability to create characters and backgrounds. Each of the structures of society has its own legends, religions, economics, and politics. The characters are multifaceted individuals with strengths and failings. The protagonist, Stark, is both hero and villain as he attempts to destroy one culture in order to set the pattern for another.

"Enchantress of Venus." Eric John Stark is searching for a friend who disappeared on Venus. Stark follows him to Shuruun, an evil city of pirates, outlaws, and cruel aliens. Within the city is a castle where the last of the Lhari race live. They are called both angels and demons, creatures with alabaster skin and silver hair. There is a prophecy that Treon, one of the young Lhari, will be the last of his people because an outsider matching Stark's description will cause their doom. Stark challenges the Lhari and is captured and enslaved. The Lhari have slaves working to excavate the City of Lost Ones, which is beneath a gaseous sea. This red sea does have a breathable atmosphere, but the conditions and the work are gradually killing the slaves. The Lhari believe that the city conceals a lost formula for creating life that would allow them to re-create their race. Treon, who disagrees with their plan to prolong the race, helps Stark to escape. The Lhari are destroyed in a battle in which Treon also is killed. The evil created by the Lhari has been destroyed. Shurrun is still a city of pirates and outlaws, but the unnatural shadow is gone.

"Enchantress of Venus" is an adventurous and entertaining story. Brackett's style and imagery set it apart from most space operas. It is notable for the evocative descriptions of the strange red sea and the mysterious Lhari. Stark, introduced in this story, became Brackett's most memorable character.

The Long Tomorrow. *The Long Tomorrow* is the story of a young boy becoming an adult and of the United States' struggle to recover from a nuclear war. After the devastation, the cities and their complex technology collapse. In fearful reaction, the survivors restrict technology, setting limits on the size of towns and types of machinery tolerated. Len Colter and his cousin, Esau, members of the New Mennonite sect, dream of a world that their grandmother remembers, a world where things were easier, prettier, and larger. There are rumors that somewhere there still exists a city with machines, called Bartorstown, but such an idea is so threatening that a man who is merely suspected of coming from Bartorstown is stoned to death. Len and Esau, unable to accept their parents' beliefs, run away. A traveling trader (who is truly from Bartorstown) eventually takes them to Bartorstown. This fabled city is both less and more than they had imagined. It is a small village, not really a city, but it does have machines, including a large computer and a nuclear reactor. The townspeople are devoted to finding a way to prevent the use of nuclear weapons, while preserving the knowledge of nuclear energy. Len must come to terms with his life-long fear of anything nuclear, and build a new life among people whose backgrounds and attitudes are completely strange to him.

Brackett presents several detailed societies, from the conservative, agrarian New Mennonites to the researchers of Bartorstown. She describes the economic and political relationships with great clarity. The center of the book is the character of Len Colter. His relationships with his family, his inability to accept the restrictions of his society, his desire to find Bartorstown, and his problems accepting the reality of the town make *The Long Tomorrow* a very effective novel.

The Starmen of Llyrdis. Michael Trehearn had always felt like an outsider, never belonging anywhere. In Brittany, he meets a couple who distinctly resemble him. The woman refuses to tell him about herself or his origin, but tells him to investigate an isolated village. Near the village, Trehearn discovers that the couple are from another planet, members of a race called Vardda. They are traders who use Earth as one of their ports. The Vardda are the only species physically able to withstand space flight, an ability resulting from a mutation, a secret now lost. Most Vardda resist any effort to rediscover the nature of the mutation and share their cherished monopoly with other planets.

Trehearn is the son of a Vardda man and an Earth woman. The Vardda do not believe that he can withstand the lift-off, but agree to take him to their planet, Llyrdis. He does survive, and becomes a political problem to the Varddan Council. To avoid helping those who believe that the ability to travel in space should be shared, Trehearn is given a false past as a full-blooded Varddan. He is accepted by the Vardda, at last belonging. As a new crewmember on a small trader, he begins to observe how deeply the Vardda are envied and resented for their abilities. When he discovers that a friend has been arrested for advocating the end of the space flight monopoly, he helps to rescue him. While escaping, Trehearn and his friend find a long-lost ship with the secret of the original mutation. They broadcast the formula just before they are captured. The council, faced with the fact that their secret has become public, decide to attempt to make their new colleagues into allies by announcing that the broadcast was part of a plan to share their knowledge, welcoming the other planets to space flight. Michael and his friends are free in a new and open universe.

This is a story of conspiracies, attempted murder, and interstellar rivalry. It is also an exploration of the themes of equality and compassion. Brackett creates a believable political and economic structure on Llyrdis, a structure that is motivated by rebellion and treason. *The Starmen of Llyrdis* is a mystery, a political thriller, and a study of equality among planets.

The Sword of Rhiannon. Matt Carse is an adventurer on Mars, an archaeologist who will sell his artifacts for the right price. Penkawr, a petty thief, has discovered a treasure in an ancient tomb. Carse recognizes part of the treasure as the sword of Rhiannon, a legendary figure. Penkawr is forced to take Carse to the tomb, where he pushes Carse into a black sphere. Carse, disoriented and confused, senses some kind of probing into his mind. Finally, he emerges into the tomb, digs his way out, and discovers that while he is still on Mars, it is a far earlier time. The Mars that he had known was a dying desert. This Mars is green and humid; it is a million years in the past.

Carse becomes involved in the political conflicts and wars of the past time. He learns that Rhiannon, legendary even in the past, is somehow now present in his mind. Rhiannon had been imprisoned within the sphere by his people as a punishment for sharing secret technology with an evil serpent people, the Dhuvians. Carse and Rhiannon form an alliance with Lady Ywain and her people to destroy the Dhuvians. Rhiannon's people, who have been transformed into beings composed solely of energy, forgive Rhiannon and welcome him into their company. Lady Ywain, having seen her society completely changed by war and having fallen in love with Carse, decides to go with Carse when Rhiannon returns Carse to his own time.

The Sword of Rhiannon is a classic space opera, but it goes beyond most works of its kind in its use of myth and in its style. Rhiannon's punishment echoes that of Prometheus, condemned by his peers for sharing fire. The dry, desolate Mars of Matt Carse's time and the humid, lush Mars of Ywain's time are described in convincing detail. Brackett creates numerous races which have complex political relationships. *The Sword of Rhiannon* is an example of Brackett's ability to combine an exciting plot, strong characters, and a vivid setting.

Biographical/Bibliographical Readings

Rosemarie Arbur, *Leigh Brackett, Marion Zimmer Bradley, Anne McCaffrey, A Primary and Secondary Bibliography* (G. K. Hall, 1982). John L. Carr, *Leigh Brackett: American Writer* (Chris Drumm, 1986). Darrell Schweitzer, "Edmond Hamilton and Leigh Brackett," in *Science Fiction Voices #5: Interviews with American Science Fiction Writers of the Golden Age* (Borgo Press, 1981), p.35-41. [Linda K. Lewis]

BRADBURY, RAY

Life and Works

Ray Douglas Bradbury was born on August 22, 1920, in Waukegan, Illinois. He attended public schools in Waukegan, Tucson, Arizona (where his family lived for two years), and in Los Angeles. He has lived in Los Angeles since the age of fourteen. His high school yearbook predicted that Bradbury was "headed for literary distinction." From high school on, Bradbury considers himself self- and library-educated. His early writing career was supported by selling newspapers. He married Marguerite Susan McClure in 1947 and they have four children, Susan, Ramona, Bettina, and Alexandra.

Bradbury's first published story was "Pendulum," coauthored with Henry Hasse, published in the November, 1941, issue of *Super Science Stories.* Several of his early short stories were sold to *Weird Tales.* Pseudonyms used by Bradbury when he first began writing were Edward Banks, William Elliott, D. R. Banat, Leonard Douglas, and Leonard Spalding. After the extraordinary success of *The Martian Chronicles* (1950), Ray Bradbury's works began to appear regularly in the slick magazines such as *Collier's, Esquire, Saturday Evening Post, and Harper's.*

Many of his writings are magical in the literal sense of the word. Bradbury recalls his early enchantment with magic at the age of eleven, when he was presented a rabbit that had been pulled out of a hat by Blackstone, the famous magician who happened to be appearing in Waukegan. From that moment, Bradbury was fascinated by magic and magicians. Magic and carnival effects are predominant in *The Illustrated Man* (1951) and *Something Wicked This Way Comes* (1962).

Ray Bradbury is primarily an author of short stories. He has written only two novels, *Something Wicked This Way Comes* and *Fahrenheit 451* (1953). Although some of his other works may be considered novels (such as *The Martian Chronicles* and *Dandelion Wine* [1957]), they are more precisely collections of stories gathered together as novels. Other collections by Bradbury include *R Is for Robot* (1962), *S Is for Space* (1966), *I Sing the Body Electric* (1969), *The Golden Apples of the Sun* (1953), *A Medicine for Melancholy* (1959), *The Machineries of Joy* (1964), *The October Country* (1955), *The Vintage Bradbury* (1966), *When Elephants Last in the Dooryard Bloomed* (1973), and *The Stories of Ray Bradbury* (1980).

In addition to his literary works, Ray Bradbury has also written poetry, screen plays (he adapted *Moby Dick* for John Huston's film), television scripts for "The Alfred Hitchcock Hour" and "The Twilight Zone," and several dramas, including "Leviathan '99" which transforms Ahab's pursuit of Moby Dick into the crew of a space ship pursuing a giant comet. Bradbury is a firm believer in and enthusiastic supporter of the space program and is an ardent speaker on behalf of the National Aeronautics and Space Administration. He has recently appeared as host and author of "Ray Bradbury Theatre" on syndicated television. Although he has never won a Hugo or Nebula award, most of the covers of his works credit him as being "The World's Greatest Living Science Fiction Writer," probably due to his popular *Martian Chronicles*.

Themes and Style

There is a continuing argument as to whether Ray Bradbury writes science fiction or fantasy. He has proven himself to be a blender of both genres and has popularized science fiction for many readers turned off by space stereotypes. Many of his works have settings in the future and have futuristic themes, yet are at the same time deeply rooted in mythology and archetypal figures. His stories are not technologically oriented; rather he uses technology as a base upon which to build ideas and characterizations. Bradbury is a storyteller whose works have many poetic qualities. He uses metaphor, imagery, allusions, alliterations, and internal rhymes with a vivid intensity that has a striking effect on readers. Bradbury admits that the main purpose of his writing is to entertain, using delight, amusement and, in some cases, terror.

Ray Bradbury views space exploration and space travel as the new wilderness. These new frontiers are the key to the future of humanity. Space, for Bradbury, is a necessary step in human development and progress. Bradbury has written stories about space travel, the colonization of Mars, rockets, time machines, and the Earth of the future. Machines, robots, and computers are not seen as ends in themselves, but as means to ends. The dangers of human reliance on machinery are illustrated in "The City" and "The Veldt." Robots created by Bradbury tend to have human forms and are often surrogates for real people or characters--George Bernard Shaw in "G.B.S.-Mark V," Abraham Lincoln in "Downwind from Gettysburg," and a robot grandmother in "I Sing the Body Electric."

Bradbury's settings range from the small towns of middle America to the sands of Mars. He has immortalized the small Midwestern American town. "Green City" and "Green Bluff," along with other unnamed towns, are both realistic and imagined vistas for many of his stories. These small towns recall the Victorian houses, the town square, and the towering elm trees of the Midwest.

Two of Bradbury's best known works, *The Martian Chronicles* and *Fahrenheit 451*, though each has a different setting, are examples of his major themes--reality as determined by point of view and metamorphosis. Metamorphosis is presented as a genetic trait of all Martians and as the evolution of an individual in *Fahrenheit*

451. Throughout *The Martian Chronicles,* the reality of life on Mars is seen primarily from the point of view of the colonizers from Earth, with only a few exceptions giving the Martian point of view. In either case, both the Earthmen and the Martians are unable to accept the reality of the other's existence. The Martians have the ability to change or metamorphosize themselves into human form. *Fahrenheit 451* extrapolates a future on Earth when firemen do not put out fires; rather they set fire to books and all creative writings which embody human creative and intellectual pursuits. Much irony is found in the novel, as in the metamorphosis of Guy Montag, the protagonist, who evolves from a fireman cremating books to a member of an outcast society dedicated to committing books to memory in order to save literature and history.

Plot Summaries of Major Works

"The Golden Apples of the Sun." The rocketship is called *Copa de Oro* or *Prometheus* or *Icarus* as it rushes toward the sun to capture "the golden apples of the sun." With each nearing moment, the temperature outside the ship grows more and more intensely hot, while the inside of the ship is a like a winter snowstorm to counter the heat. The crew wears special suits to keep their bodies at normal temperature. Just as the rocketship approaches the sun to capture a bit of its energy, a leak occurs in the refrigeration system. The captain quickly shuts down the auxiliary pump until it can be repaired. He sends out the mechanical arm with its Cup, which retrieves a small amount of the sun's energy and withdraws it into its own special airlock in the ship. The captain succeeds--he has captured the sun's energies and the ship returns to the direction of Earth: north.

The first and last words of this story are "south" toward the sun and "north" toward the Earth. North and south, fire and ice are the two opposing states, both physically and directionally. The intense heat of the sun is counteracted by the freezerlike interior of the ship. The captain may be likened not only to Icarus and Prometheus, but also his obsession to capture the energy of the sun is much like the obsession of Captain Ahab to capture the great whale, Moby Dick. The captain of the the rocketship is willing to risk himself, his crew (indeed, one of the crewmen dies when his suit springs a leak), and his ship in order to retrieve even a small Cup of the sun's power. Bradbury even capitalizes the "c" in Cup, drawing a parallel with the Holy Communion Cup, perhaps. Mythology and technology are intricately blended in this tale which decries the failure of Icarus and at last allows mankind to reach the sun and capture a small bit of its energies.

"I Sing the Body Electric." Tom, age thirteen, Agatha, age ten, and Timothy, age nine, have just faced the devastation of the

death of their mother. Their father debates what would be best
for the children--to live with their Aunt Clara, a live-in maid, or
tutor--and decides against all these possibilities. He takes the
children to Fantocinni, Ltd., whose pamphlet offers the AC-DC
Mark V Electrical Grandmother. The children are skeptical and
apprehensive about having an electric grandmother, even though
they are allowed to select the physical characteristics, such as the
color of her hair, her eyes, and her voice. After making their selections, they spend three months waiting and wondering what the
electric grandmother will be like. Finally, a helicopter comes to
their front lawn and deposits a beautiful gold sarcophagus, containing a wrapped mummy, their new electric grandmother. After
carefully unwrapping her, Timothy inserts the key given to
Agatha by the Fantocinnis, and the machine comes alive with soft
whirs and hums. Except for Agatha, the children accept her almost immediately. Because of her implanted memory patterns, she
knows their every whim--what they like and do not like, their favorite foods, each one's idiosyncracies, including their father's.
She can create kite string from her fingertips, help with home-
work, run fast enough to keep up but not fast enough to win, and
give each one the needed attention. Agatha begins to acknowledge
her presence, but is unable to accept her as a member of the family, as someone Agatha can confide in and trust. One day, Agatha
runs out of the house, screaming that the grandmother cannot possibly love her because her mother said she loved her and obviously
did not, or else her mother would not have died. As Agatha darts
out into the street, a car comes straight at her and the electric
grandmother throws her out of the path of the car and is hit by
the car herself. When Agatha realizes that the car has not killed
her electric grandmother, she finally accepts her and believes that
this grandmother will indeed never leave her.

   Bradbury creates a picture of a loving family traumatized by
death and the magical ways in which the electric grandmother
makes them whole again. The grandmother gives her form of
love--undivided attention--to each family member. Even after the
children grow up, the grandmother tells them that she will return
to the Pinocchio room at the Fantocinnis and share her memories
with the other grandmothers, as they wait for what will never
come--the gift of true life that had been given to the wooden
Pinocchio. The story is sensitively written and exquisitely portrayed. As usual, Bradbury's prose is lyric and touches the heartstrings. The arrival of the electric grandmother is striking--her
beautiful golden sarcophagus covered with hieroglyphics, wrapped
in three series of linen bandages for each child to unwrap. The
electric grandmother both taught and learned and made the family
whole. The children came to love her deeply and she, in her own
way, loved them.

The Martian Chronicles. One of the best known of all science fiction works, *The Martian Chronicles* is actually a collection of short stories which presents a chronology of Earth's colonization of Mars in the late twentieth century and the early years of the twenty-first century. The settling of Mars is analogous to a new frontier for humanity and parallels that of the settling of the American West. The colonists from Earth begin to exploit and plunder Mars in a repetition of early American history. Midway through the stories, Earth is devastated by nuclear war and many of the colonists return home to try and find their families and friends. Those who stay on Mars realize that they must make the planet their home and become "Martians." The stories have few continuing characters. This is appropriate, as persons in such a history change constantly.

Bradbury's Mars is presented as a mythical, classical planet with cities and machines that are beautiful as well as functional. The Martians have strong telepathic powers, and their weapons fire golden bees rather than bullets. One of the most memorable stories, "The Third Expedition," reveals the telepathic abilities of the Martians as they create, in the minds of the spacemen from Earth, replicas of towns and family members back home. "The Martian" illustrates both the telepathic powers and metamorphosis by Martians. A young Martian has the ability to assume the personna of friends and relatives of the colonists. Though he becomes many persons, he is never able to just be himself, a Martian, and is eventually destroyed by a frenzied mob of colonists. Reality and illusion are themes in "The Long Years," in which an Earthman creates robots to duplicate his dead family and alleviate his loneliness. Bradbury's favorite story, "There Will Come Soft Rains," pictures a completely automated and empty house back on Earth which continues to function, not realizing that its inhabitants have been victims of the nuclear war. Machinery may survive nuclear war; humans cannot. In an ironic note, all of the Martians die from a chicken pox virus brought to Mars by the colonists. The remaining Earthmen--the aliens of Mars--have no home planet to which they can return, and thus become the surviving Martians.

"R Is for Rocket." Fifteen-year-old Chris, Ralph, and their other friends live in Florida, adjacent to the Rocket Port and launching pads where the rockets take off for foreign cities, the moon, and space. At every launch, if possible, they gather outside the fence to watch the astronauts board the rocketships and head off on their fabulous journeys. Chris and Ralph want, above all else, to be chosen as astronauts. Chris is a superior student in formula school, and his mother is very supportive. Chris's father had been a chemist before he died, and most of his work had been done in underground laboratories; he had never seen the stars. One day, Chris and his mother are paid a visit by Mr. Trent, a representative of the Astronaut Board. Trent tells Chris that he has all the prerequisites for being selected into the astronaut training program--a high I.Q., a good sense of curiosity, and the enthusiasm and capability to withstand the eight-year training period. Chris must promise not to tell any of his friends, not even Ralph, that he has been chosen. There are two reasons for the secrecy: one, to avoid embarrassment if a trainee flunks out; and second, to negate the ego trip of being better than his friends. Chris tells Ralph that he is going away to school in Europe, although Ralph suspects and understands the reasons for Chris's leaving. On his last Saturday before entering the astronaut program, Chris spends the day with Ralph and his other friends doing all the juvenile, Earthly things like playing Kick-the-can and hiking along the old railroad tracks. Alone, Chris takes the monorail to the Rocket Port, goes beyond the fence which he had so wished to cross to begin his new life, toward the stars. His dream has come true.

Even though this story was written long before the space program began, Bradbury presents an excellent picture of what Cape Canaveral was to be like. The gantries, the astronauts in the mobile van, the fiery explosions as the rockets take off--all are written very much as we saw them on television in the 1960s and 1970s. It is not surprising that Bradbury is an advocate of the space program. The young Chris, with his dreams of the stars, might very well be a surrogate for Bradbury himself. It is appropriate that Chris spends his last day with his friends, absorbing all that he can of Earthly pleasures and pastimes, realizing that these realities will become his memories and his future will become the dream of other young men.

"A Sound of Thunder." Time Safari, Inc., offers its passengers the opportunity to go back in time and kill a dinosaur. Eckels decides that he is ready to take on the challenge. Travis, the safari guide, and other hunters enter the Time Machine as Travis explains that the dinosaurs have already been preselected for the kill, by earlier observing them in the past and determining that the selected ones would have died shortly of natural causes; thus time will not be altered. His only warning is that they must stay on the metal path, which floats six inches above the ground and that they must not touch anything for fear of changing the future. When the group arrives in the prehistoric era, they start down the metal path and hear the first sound of thunder--the roar of the Tyrannosaurus rex. Eckels panics at the sight and size of the monstrous dinosaur and asks to return to the Time Machine. Travis tells him to go on back, but to be sure to stay on the path. As he returns, he hears the other hunters firing and accidentally falls off the path. Eckels wallows around in the mud and slime and finally returns to the path and to the Time Machine. Along with the mud on his boots is a dead butterfly; the future to which they return is not quite the same as the future they had left. Travis fires a final shot--a final sound of thunder.

In this short story, Bradbury uses the Time Machine to illustrate the fragility of life and the importance of every living thing, both in an ecological and historical sense. Travis is the only one who realizes that the decadence of self-aggrandizement by the hunters represents a danger to the history of humanity, yet his own greed lets him lead the time travelers anyway. In a gory scene, Travis sends Eckels back to the body of the dinosaur to retrieve the bullets from the carcass so that nothing will be left in the past. Alas, it is too late; the dead butterfly has already changed the future. The ending is ambiguous: does Travis kill Eckels for his straying off the path, which changed the future, or does he perhaps kill himself because of his guilt about what happened? Either way, the story emphasizes the consequences of changing the past, even by the seemingly insignificant crushing of a small butterfly.

Biographical/Bibliographical Readings

Wayne L. Johnson, *Ray Bradbury* (Ungar, 1980). Willis E. McNeely, "Ray Bradbury: Past, Present, and Future," in *Voices for the Future*, ed. Thomas D. Clareson (Bowling Green University Popular Press, 1976), v.1, p.167-74. Sam Moskowitz, "Ray Bradbury," in *Seekers of Tomorrow* (World, 1966), p.352-73. William F. Nolan, *The Ray Bradbury Companion* (Gale, 1975). Joseph D. Olander and Martin H. Greenberg, eds., *Ray Bradbury* (Taplinger, 1980). A. James Stupple, "The Past, the Future, and Ray Bradbury," in *Voices for the Future*, ed. Thomas D. Clareson (Bowling Green University Popular Press, 1976), v.1, p.175-84. [Marilyn P. Fletcher]

BRADLEY, MARION ZIMMER

Life and Works

Marion Zimmer was born on July 3, 1930, in Albany, New York. A fan of science fiction, she began writing fantasy and science fiction as a teenager. She attended New York State College for Teachers from 1946 to 1948. In 1949, she married Robert A. Bradley and moved to Texas. Her first major published work was "Centaurus Changeling" in 1954. In 1960, her first novel, *The Door through Space*, was published, and two years later, in 1962, came *The Sword of Aldones* and *The Planet Savers*. These two novels were the first of her works about Darkover, the world for which she would become best known. In 1962, she and her husband separated and they divorced in 1964. She later married Walter Breen. They moved to California where she studied psychology at the University of California at Berkeley.

Bradley has written almost every type of literature except for westerns, but most of her work has been fantasy or science fiction. Her pen names include Lee Chapman, John Dexter, Miriam Dardner, Valerie Graves, Morgan Ives, John J. Wells, and Alfrida Rivers.

In 1977, she won the Invisible Little Man Award, created to give recognition to deserving writers who have not won the Hugo or Nebula awards. The following year, she won the Hamilton-Brackett Memorial Sense of Wonder Award for *The Forbidden Tower* (1977).

Themes and Style

Bradley has said that she writes science fiction because it is a way to comment on contemporary society without facing criticism or accusations. She has used her works, especially those set on Darkover, to examine attitudes toward interpersonal relationships, cultural conflicts, and the role of technology. Bradley's main themes deal with emotional and psychological attitudes towards intimacy and with the conflicts between individuals and societies. "Centaurus Changeling" explores the relationship between two cultures by contrasting the lives and pregnancies of two women from different societies.

Most of Bradley's protagonists are outsiders, alienated from their societies. Their conflicts with their society or with other groups may result in psychological development, a discovery of a new place to belong, a new acceptance of their existing society, or a means of changing attitudes within their group. The protagonists face difficult decisions, with no easy solutions promised, but they make their choices knowing the risks and the alternatives. In *The Heritage of Hastur* (1975), Lew Alton resents the ruling Comyn of Darkover, but risks everything to preserve their society because his other choices are too destructive.

On a broader scale, Bradley shows the conflicts between societies. In its later history, Darkover is a feudal culture, governed by a small group of individuals with telepathic powers; they hope to keep Darkover from being dominated by the technological Terran Empire. The problems between the two societies cannot be resolved easily, but individuals from both groups can begin to find ways to work together and try to understand one another. There are no instant solutions, but progress is possible.

Although Bradley does not consider herself a feminist, one her most frequent themes concerns the role of women and the necessity for all people to have the right to determine their own way of life. Her Free Amazons of Renumciates are women who have sworn that they will be independent of any man or family. She was one of the first science fiction authors to discuss sexual attitudes and stereotypes, exploring such topics as virginity, pregnancy, homosexuality and sexual intimacy within a telepathic group.

Another consistent theme is the need for compassion and tolerance. Chauvinism, whether national, racial, or sexual, is portrayed as destructive for all concerned. Bradley stresses the need for understanding and knowledge of the emotional and psychological differences that exist among individuals and societies. Many conflicts arise because of a lack of knowledge--the Terran Empire thought that the Darkovan compact prohibiting weapons used at long distances was intended to exclude their guns, unaware that it was intended originally to outlaw the terrifying abuse of psychic matrix technology.

Bradley is a skillful writer who has created one of science fiction's most popular and believable worlds in Darkover. Her characters are complex, multifaceted, and convincing. Bradley is an excellent storyteller who uses her works to explore human relationships while entertaining her readers.

Plot Summaries of Major Works

The Darkover novels. Although Marion Zimmer Bradley's books about Darkover are not truly a series, they are all related by virtue of the setting on the planet Darkover. While some have characters in common, others are connected only by their setting. There are presently almost two dozen books about this world--among the major ones are *The Bloody Sun*, *Darkover Landfall*, *The Heritage of Hastur*, *The Shattered Chain*, and *The Forbidden Tower*.

Darkover is an ancient world with a red sun, harsh geography, a cold climate, and four moons. There had been civilizations on the planet long before the first humans crashed there. The humans, however, eventually came to believe the other races to be legends and forgot their origins. The humans built a feudal society ruled by the "Comyn," an aristocracy with psychic powers called "laran." The ruling families of the Comyn became highly tradition bound, conservative, and inbred as generations passed. Their power appeared to be threatened when Darkover was eventually discovered by the Terran Empire, a technological and bureaucratic culture.

Themes of conflict and reconciliation, whether personal or cultural, are consistently present in the Darkover books. Most of the novels involve the attempts of alienated individuals to find a place to belong. They must discover what had been missing in their lives in order to become whole and find peace. In *The Heritage of Hastur*, Regis Hastur must deal with the shock that caused him to suppress his laran when he was young before he can help his own family and friends. Bradley presents the necessity for being able to make such important decisions after considering the alternatives and the consequences. The novels set in the later history of Darkover are concerned with the conflicts between Darkover and Terra. The two societies seem incapable of understanding each other, much less of working together, even though each society had something needed by the other. Many of the characters find themselves becoming a bridge between the two cultures, as does Daniel Lawton, half Terran and half Darkovan, who becomes an interpreter working for the Terran headquarters on Darkover.

Bradley uses Darkover to examine sex roles and stereotypes, the role of women, sexuality, and intimacy. Her characters include women who have sworn independence from all men and women who wear chains to symbolize their decorative, protected status. She stresses the need to be aware of the choices governing one's life and the necessity of being free to make the best choices for each person. Some women leave everything and create new identities, while others decide that, in spite of the restrictions, their roles within their families are correct for them.

Darkover, the creation of an author who began as a science fiction fan, now has its own fans who publish magazines and write anthropological studies of the planet's cultures. Bradley has encouraged her fans and has edited anthologies that include their stories.

Darkover is a richly detailed world, with a long history, fascinating people, and complex societies. Bradley has said that she continues to write about Darkover because she enjoys visiting it. Her skills have created a world that her readers also enjoy revisiting.

Biographical/Bibliographical Readings

Rosemarie Arbur, *Leigh Brackett, Marion Zimmer Bradley, Anne McCaffrey: A Primary and Secondary Bibliography* (G. K. Hall, 1982). Idem, *Marion Zimmer Bradley* (Starmont House, 1986). Laura Murphy, "Marion Zimmer Bradley," in *Twentieth-Century American Science-Fiction Writers* (Gale, 1981), v.1, p.77-80. **[Linda K. Lewis]**

BRIN, DAVID

Life and Works

David Brin was born on October 6, 1950, in Glendale, California. He attended the California Institute of Technology, graduating in 1972 with a B.S. in astronomy. Between 1973 and 1977, he was employed by Hughes Research Laboratories as an electrical engineer in Semi-Conductor Device Development. He enrolled at the University of California in San Diego and earned his master's degree in applied physics in 1980 and his Ph. D. in astrophysics in 1981. While attending UCSD, he reviewed books and was science editor for Heritage Press. In 1980, he became the managing editor of *Journal of the Laboratory of Comparative Human Cognition* and a member of the British Interplanetary Society. In 1984, he was hired as a consultant to the California Space Institute doing advanced studies involving the space shuttle and space sciences. He also taught physics, and occasionally creative writing, at the University of California in San Diego. Brin currently resides in London, England.

Brin began writing science fiction in 1980 and his first novel, *Sundiver*, was published by Bantam Books. His second novel, *Startide Rising*, was published in 1983, and is a sequel to the first. It was for *Startide Rising* that Brin received the Hugo, Nebula, and Locus awards in 1984. These novels, based on expeditions to other worlds, introduce the "uplifted" dolphins who have become as important as humans in the exploration of space. The Uplift series has been continued by *The Uplift War* (1987). Uplift is defined by Brin in the Glossary of *Startide Rising* (p. iv) as "the process by which older spacefaring races bring new species into Galactic culture, through breeding and genetic engineering." A mix of science fiction and fantasy appears in *The Practice Effect* (1984). *The Postman* (1985) offers a setting on Earth after nuclear war. For *The Postman*, Brin won the John W. Campbell Memorial Award. In 1986, Brin coauthored *Heart of the Comet* with Gregory Benford. In the same year Brin also published a collection of short stories entitled *The River of Time*. The story "The Crystal Spheres" is especially intriguing and won the 1985 Hugo award for the best short story.

Themes and Style

The themes which dominate Brin's work are the curiosity and desire of humans to explore the universe; humanity's conflict with the environment, with other people and with itself; and the triumph of the intellectual over the physically powerful and the archetypical hero. These themes appear predominately in the collection *The Rivers of Time*, and in *The Postman*. *Sundiver*, *Startide Rising*, and *Heart of the Comet* all exemplify humanity's intense need to unravel the mysteries of the universe. In the bittersweet tale "The Crystal Spheres," the morale of mankind depends upon its ability to discover, explore, and settle new worlds. The explorations of alternate universes to save an ecologically destroyed world in *The Practice Effect* examine the human need to explore the universe. The opening of new frontiers is a key theme so appealing to science fiction fans, and Brin's novels do not disappoint the reader.

The movements of humanity into the unknown create conflict between individuals and their relationship to their surroundings. Survival becomes the focal point. *Startide Rising* has several examples of the external struggle for survival between Earthmen and other species. Not only are Earthlings hiding from other Galactics, but the Galactics are warring with each other. The basic ingredient of *The Postman* is the struggle to survive against the elements. *Startide Rising* has its own version of individual-versus-individual conflict.

Brin's basic optimism is exemplified by his theme of the weak standing together to bring down the oppressors. Misfits and underprivileged Earthlings are among those who must overcome stronger humans or aliens in order to survive. Brin also uses self-conflict, in which an individual must battle with himself or herself. Sometimes the character develops a psychological protection, as Jacob Demwa does in *Sundiver*.

David Brin's writings show his in-depth knowledge of astronomy. His writings are technical and learned. Brin goes into great detail about the workings of various machines, ships, etc., often expounding on twentieth-century techology for his explanations. He appeals more to the reasoning mind than to the senses in his descriptions. His characters and settings are usually sparse and overshadowed by the scientific and technical aspects of his works.

Brin's tone and mood are mostly upbeat. His writings usually have a positive outcome and a hope for better things. The characters are constantly seeking a way to reform or improve life or solve social problems using their own strengths and ideas. To go along with this positive attitude, Brin often inserts humor into his work. In *Sundiver*, the main character, Jacob Demwa, is confused and sometimes shocked by the captain's old-fashioned idioms, such as "keep your eyeballs peeled." Brin uses poetry and songs in all of his works. The uplifted dolphins in *Startide Rising* speak in haikus; Virginia, in *Heart of the Comet*, and her computer continually compose poetry; and Demwa recites poetry or verse to himself in *Sundiver*.

Brin uses poetic justice to reward the "good" and to punish the "bad." At the conclusion of *The Practice Effect*, Dennis Nuel wins the hand of the beautiful L'Toff princess, while Bernard Brady, the unadmirable "brown noser" who gets Dennis into trouble gets his just desserts.

Plot Summaries of Major Works

The Heart of the Comet. (Coauthored with Gregory Benford.) Colonists are sent from Earth to Halley's Comet with plans to maneuver it close enough to Earth to be mined, but events do not proceed as expected. "Halley forms" infect the colonists. During their struggle for survival, the colonists divide into factions--Orthos, or normal people, and Percells, or genetically changed people. Despite their divisions, the colonists do adapt and survive, but Earth fears that they will bring the infection back home and attempts are made to destroy the comet and the colonists. The colonists decide to project the comet and themselves into a passage out of the solar system, becoming the first space ship from Earth. There is a combining of computer and human (electronic and organic), cloning and genetic manipulation, all part of the changing or evolving of humanity in order to survive.

Heart of the Comet does not fit all examples of Brin's style, perhaps because of its coauthor Benford. Description and character is more apparent than in Brin's other works. Technological descriptions and the use of poetry is maintained, as well as the mood of optimism. Some of the same themes prevail--survival, reliance on self, and the united weak's ability to overthrow the mighty.

The Postman. Gordon Krantz, student, ex-militiaman and the last intellectual idealist in America, is the protagonist of this novel about the physical and moral struggle of human survival in the aftermath of World War III. Set in the harsh wilderness of the Oregon Cascade mountains in late, postnuclear winter, Gordon fights to survive as one man with visions of the past who must search for security in the present. His quest to find other survivors takes him from the Midwest to the Pacific Cascades and the remains of a late twentieth-century postman. Stripped of his own gear by thieves, Gordon dons the postman's garb and sets out, convinced that brutality is all that is left in the world. To his surprise, the uniform of an ordinary civil servant is accepted with respect and excitement by other survivors in the villages he passes through. In his borrowed postal uniform, he successfully creates a new hope for the war-ravaged populace. What he originally used as a con to aid in his survival becomes a unifying feature for those who hardly remember the luxuries of the past before the war. Using a postal route to unite the villages, Gordon begins his mission to bring the moral standards of life back to what they were.

In his travels he hears of something that could be his salvation as well; the last of the great machines, Cyclops. Like other hopes for salvation, Cyclops has a hidden mystery of its own, and a would-be ally for Gordon becomes illusive. The dream remains and, with little more than memories of the past and visions of the future, Gordon organizes those of the Restored United States in Oregon to fight the power-mad, brutal survivalists. The survivalists' doctrine is survival of the fittest, which they enact by oppressing villages into serfdom. All that stands in their way to total domination is Gordon and his dream.

Brin merges two of his more popular short stories, "The Postman" and "Cyclops" to create this adventurous and intellectually stimulating novel that glorifies the wisdom of the intellectual and depreciates the value of the physically powerful. The basic ingredient of *The Postman* is the struggle to survive against the elements. Food and warmth are the necessities needed to fight the chill of nuclear winter. Survival for Gordon lies in his abilities to use his intellect and charisma for his own preservation. Not only must he struggle against the environment, but against other men as well. Responsibility also becomes a key word for Gordon Krantz as he faces an internal struggle to take the responsibility of the survivors on his shoulders. The ghost of the great Cyclops machine rises up to torment him with what his responsibility should be. Many of his friends are killed before he assumes complete charge of his life and recognizes the role he must play in order to secure the future for the remaining humans. His role is to force the dispirited population of Oregon to give up their greed and self-absorption and unite against a common foe. Gordon's band of misfits are able to triumph over the survivalists.

The Practice Effect. In this novel, the adage of "practice makes perfect" takes on a whole new meaning. Brin creates an environment in which some of the laws of physics are reversed. Dennis Nuel is a young, capable scientist stifled in his work by the political schemes of his superiors. Nuel is unwittingly used as a guinea pig in a mission involving the machine he helped to create, the Vivitar. The Vivitar has the theoretical capability of opening portals to other space/time dimensions, so-called alternate universes. The project to find another world capable of sustaining human life has become a constant frustration, but at last a world has been discovered with all the basic requirements. Robots are sent to the world of Tatir in the hopes that it is indeed a hospitable environment. Excitement at the discovery begins to lessen as the Vivitar mysteriously breaks down at the other end of the portal. Not completely briefed on the machine, Dennis is sent to the new world to repair the Vivitar. Dennis boldly enters Tatir, excited by his mission, but within moments of his arrival he realizes that going home will not be as simple as he thought. Something has gone wrong with all of the machinery sent to this new world, so like Earth and yet so unlike it. Dennis's observations of the natives of the new world leads him to many exploits in and out of prison, romance, and a quick education in the natural laws of Tatir and the oppression these laws have imposed on its populace.

Dennis unites the oppressed natives and, by using wizardry peculiar to Tatir, he and his allies--the common folk and a mysterious race called the L'Toff--are able to overthrow the corrupt Kemar and his ineffectual nobility. With virtue and sanity restored, Dennis is enlightened as to the reasons for the curious powers of the L'Toff and the significance it holds for his own world and time. Dennis uses his intellect as a tool for survival in a world where the laws of physics are reversed. He also allies himself with a band of villagers to to overcome the corrupt aristocracy. The exploration of an alternate universe must be achieved in order to save mankind in an ecologically destroyed world.

Sundiver. Fagin Kanten, an extraterrestrial (Eatee), invites his Earth friend, Jacob Alvarez Demwa, to Mercury to join him and others participating in the Sundiver Expedition. The expedition involves research on Mercury and in the solar chromosphere. During previous trips (or "dives"), the sunship crew encountered a life form called Sun Ghosts. The Sun Ghosts are never alluded to by the Galactic Confederation Library, which supposedly contains all the knowledge of the star-faring species known as the Galactics. After one of the sunships is destroyed during a dive and its crew is killed, Jacob gets involved in preventing the shutdown of the expedition. By solving the mystery of the Sun Ghosts, he alienates the Pila, another Galactic race, and barely saves the second sunship and its crew from destruction.

This novel and its sequel, *Startide Rising*, exemplify humanity's intense need to unravel the mysteries of the universe. The movement of humans into the unknown creates a conflict between humanity and the new worlds they explore. The weak, underprivileged "wolflings" are at the mercy of the Galactic bully (in this novel it is a Pila named Bubbacub). Demwa finds his own internal conflict because his wife was killed while they were on a mission together and afterwards he developed an alter ego to blame for his actions and blocked himself from the world. If mistakes were made, Demwa's alter ego took the blame. In the end, Demwa overcomes this other side of himself as if waking from a dream, becomes fully conscious and aware of his world and his responsibilities.

Startide Rising. In the sequel to *Sundiver*, the Earth survey ship *Streaker* transmits to Earth its discovery of a derelict starship fleet and is attacked by various Galactic civilizations. The damaged ship lands on Kithrup, a water world. The heavy metals in the water can be toxic to the crew of men, dolphins, and chimpanzees over a long period of exposure. Not only must they avoid the Galactic warmongers, who think the Earthlings have discovered the fabled First Race of the galaxies, the Progenitors, but they must overcome the natural hazards and their own internal conflicts. With a dolphin captain in charge of this mission, humanity hopes to increase the confidence of the uplifted dolphins; however the captain's injury and a mutiny by genetically mutated dolphins ends the project and jeopardizes the *Streaker*'s chances for survival and escape. While some of the crew want to escape, others feel they should cooperate with the Galactics and a mutiny begins. The mutiny is led by Lieutenant Takkata-Jim, and actually the mutiny turns out to be a decoy for the escaping *Streaker.*

Exploration, survival, and individual-versus-individual conflict are major themes in this novel. Brin does a fascinating job of presenting the uplifted dolphins and their humanlike conduct, both politically and socially. Conflict erupts because the majority of the Galactic starfarers feel that the Earthlings are subordinate and see nothing wrong in their desire to capture the *Streaker* and its crew to get the location of the derelict fleet of the Progenitors. This theme becomes even more complicated when the crew of the *Streaker* must survive the hostile environment, the Galactic attacks, and escape to Earth with their information. The strong element of the use of brute force to prejudice or control the weak is evident in this novel.

Biographical/Bibliographical Readings

"David Brin," in *Contemporary Literary Criticism Yearbook 1984* (Gale, 1985), p.133-35. "David Brin," in *Science Fiction Source Book* (Longman, 1984), p.109. Donald L. Lawler, "David Brin," in *Twentieth-Century Science-Fiction Writers* (Macmillan, 1986), p.79-81. **[Twyla Reinig and Illene Renfro]**

BRUNNER, JOHN

Life and Works

John Kilian Houston Brunner was born in Oxfordshire, England, on September 24, 1934, to Anthony and Felicity Brunner. Illness was a major part of his childhood, including rheumatic fever and a severe case of dysentery which caused problems that persist to this day. Although two sisters were born later, John suffered a lonely and isolated childhood and from a very early age invented imaginary playmates. He also developed an insatiable thirst for science fiction, triggered by his discovery of a copy of H. G. Wells' *War of the Worlds* in his nursery. By the age of nine, he was already trying his hand at writing. What his family had in mind, however, was for John to become a scientist and work for the large chemical conglomerate that his great-grandfather had founded.

John persisted in his writing, however, and felt he was wasting his time pursuing a formal education, turning down a scholarship to Oxford in 1951. Just past his seventeenth birthday, he made his first sale to a British publisher. The story was "Galactic Storm" (1951), written under the pseudonym Gill Hunt; he considered it so inferior that for many years he refused to acknowledge his authorship. His first major sale, published under the name John Loxmith, was the novelette "Thou Good and Faithful" to John W. Campbell as the lead story for the March, 1953, issue of *Astounding* magazine. He continued to write for both British and American markets until he was drafted into the Royal Air Force in 1953. Brunner considers his two-year military service as futile and wasted, a conviction which endures for him. Upon completing his tour of duty, he was again offered a scholarship, this time by his family's company, and again he rejected it, with a firm resolve that he would succeed as a full-time writer. He often sold to the British magazines *New Worlds* and *Science Fantasy*, frequently having several stories in the same issue under different names. The pay was so low, even by the standards of science fiction, that he was forced to conclude that free-lance writing could not be a full-time job as yet. He first got a job as a technical writer for the *Bulletin of Industrial Diamond Applications* and then became editorial assistant at a large publishing house. Having the time to devote to longer works, he sold two novels, *Threshold of Eternity* (1957) and *Earth Is but a Star* (1958), the former being rather standard space opera while the latter contained many fantasy elements, later revised and expanded as *The Hundreth Millenium* (1959) and *Catch a Falling Star* (1968).

On July 12, 1958, Brunner and Marjorie Rosamond Sauer were married. Shortly thereafter, he began his relationship with Ace Books. His affiliation lasted until the mid 1960s and allowed him to mature as a writer and once again return to writing full time. The Ace Double format permitted him to "ride on the back" of more established authors such as Poul Anderson, A. E. Van Vogt and others, providing a high level of exposure and a more comfortable income. While most of these stories were churned out quickly with relatively undeveloped plots, there were elements of the social consciousness that would dominate his later works.

Brunner continued to sell to the American magazines and by 1962 had enough material to publish his first collection of short stories, *No Future in It* (1962). Recognition of his growing stature was provided by the inclusion of "Report on the Nature of the Lunar Surface" (1960) in Judith Merril's *The Year's Best SF*, sixth annual edition.

During the early sixties, the Brunners were heavily involved in the British nuclear disarmanent movement and he produced a novel, *Manalive*, reflecting his concerns. Unfortunately, due to conflicts with the publisher, it was never released. He wrote another superior novel during this period, *The Squares of the City*, but it was not published until 1965, further delaying recognition in the field. The publication of *The Whole Man* (1964) established him as a major figure in science fiction. It was nominated for a Hugo Award as was *The Squares of the City* which placed second in the voting. By this time, Brunner, along with J. G. Ballard and

Brian W. Aldiss, was considered to be at the center of New Wave British science fiction.

Brunner's longest and most popular work, *Stand on Zanzibar* (1969), was completed by early 1967, but was rejected by the publisher that commissioned it and did not receive wide circulation until 1969, when it was a selection of the Science Fiction Book Club. It immediately began earning awards, including the Hugo in 1969 and the French Prix Apollo in 1973. It was a long time before he reaped the financial rewards for this book, even though it had been in continuous publication and he was forced to write several less ambitious novels in order to support himself. Exceptions to this are *The Jagged Orbit* (1969) and *The Sheep Look Up* (1972), which stand out as superior views of very dystopian futures. In recent years Brunner has somewhat curtailed his output of science fiction writing, venturing instead outside the field by writing a series of spy thrillers, several volumes of poetry, various factual articles and some literary criticism. Two novels, *The Crucible of Time* (1983), about an alien civilization, and *The Tides of Time* (1984), dealing with time travel, show that Brunner has not lost his touch.

Themes and Style

John Brunner's style has evolved over the years from a competent, yet standard, handling of setting, plot, and character development, to one that challenges all the accepted norms and makes reading his later novels a very interesting experience. Many of his earlier works dealt with conventional topics such as galactic empires and contact with alien cultures. His more serious works, starting with *The Squares of the City*, are set on Earth in the not-too-distant future. Instead of totally alien technology and environments, he extrapolates existing trends into all-too-believable scenarios. His concerns are the social effects of such woes as runaway overpopulation, corporate imperialism, and unchecked destruction of the Earth's biosphere. While Brunner boasts that he has never taken a science course, his description of the technologies in his worlds is usually quite believable, although much of what he predicts for the 1980s has not taken place as yet. He has also developed a remarkable ability to create characters of diverse cultural and ethnic backgrounds that, more than once, has led fans to mistakenly assume that Brunner was a member of some particular race.

Brunner ackowledges the works of several authors that played major roles in the development of his style. Paramount was Rudyard Kipling, whom he admired for his craftsmanship and ability to manipulate the English language. He credits John Dos Passos and his *U.S.A. Trilogy* for the idea of mixing factual exposition with fictional narrative that he uses so uniquely in *Stand on*

Zanzibar. Marshall McLuhan's idea of the medium itself contributing to the content is greatly in evidence in several of his works and Alvin Toffler's *Future Shock* was such an influence that Brunner wrote *The Shockwave Rider* (1972) soon after reading it.

Brunner takes pride in himself as a skilled craftsman, especially in his ability to handle a wide range of themes and styles, but he has not yet produced a "perfect" work. He has been forced, through economic necessity, to sell works that he feels do not represent his true skills. Even after he became an established author, his relations with his publishers have been disastrous. Most of his major works were either initially rejected or, worse, buried in a slush-pile limbo that prevented him from trying to market them elsewhere. There were gaps of two to five years between completion of a novel and first publication.

Brunner believes that the bleak, oppressed society of *Stand on Zanzibar* is not unduly pessimistic. Indeed, he thinks that it may represent the best possible outcome, given the current trends in urban violence, drug abuse, and ecological poisoning. *The Sheep Look Up* does assume that the worst can happen and in that sense is a doomsday tale. Brunner is not against techology, per se, but he is concerned about our ability to extract ourselves from the mess that techological society has created.

Plot Summaries of Major Works

The Jagged Orbit. This novel focuses on the possible consequences of unlimited competition in the free market system. Paranoia, xenophobia, and mass hostility have become the standard. Matthew Flamen is a "spool-pigeon," a kind of television journalist who is forced off the air for trying to investigate the Gottschalk arms cartel, which is encouraging distrust by putting land mines in front lawns and rigging doors with booby traps. The System C integrated weapons system has been developed, allowing an individual to carry his or her very own nuclear device for the ultimate in aggresive defense.

Flamen meets psychiatrist James Reedeth, whose compassion for his patients is in conflict with the true purpose of the hospital that employs him. Director Mogshack of the Ginsberg Hospital not only wants to commit everyone, but his treatment tends to make the patient worse. Flamen and Reedeth study Lyla Clay, an oracle whose drug-induced visions are thought to help the patients. The actions taking place inside the hospital mirror what is happening in the outside world. There is ample evidence that those who seek profit by exploiting the fears of others will always enjoy a successful market.

The Sheep Look Up. A world poisoning itself is the theme of this grim vision of the future. Bamberley Trust is a diversified holding company that serves as the heavy. Various characters who deal with the corporation are shown as they struggle to maintain their own existence. Austin Train serves as an anchor and voice of reason. The environmental activism of the sixties has turned out to be just a fad, and all environmental problems appear to have been resolved by legislation. The Trust and other corporations are too closely intertwined for one to regulate the other. This relationship has lasted for so long that it may already be too late to take corrective action, and all that remains is the demise of Earth.

The wealth of actual data supplied by Brunner concerning the deterioration of the air and water on Earth indicate that he is very interested in and concerned about this problem. It has been suggested that politicians would do well to read this book before enacting environmental legislation.

The Squares of the City. 1892 Havana is the setting for a classic chess game between Chigorin and Steinitz. All the characters represent chess pieces; the board is Ciudad de Vados in the mythical South American country of Aquazul, sometime in the near future. The ruler of Aquazul is Juan Sebastian Vados. Unfortunately, the rural poor are attracted to the city and tend to make a nuisance of themselves. Vados, who protects himself as a benevolent despot, is revealed as a power-hungry egomaniac who has access to sophisticated mind-control techniques to bend others to his will.

Much of this book concerns people killing off each other, as chess pieces do. The author went to great lengths to ensure that not only the moves but the strategies and relative strengths of the characters corresponded closely to the actual game. That the novel stands on its own, without regard to the game, is a tribute to Brunner's abilities. This was his first novel dealing extensively with the inner space of social dynamics, and he began to draw much critical attention to his writings as well as placing second in the balloting for the Hugo in 1965.

Stand on Zanzibar. The setting is the early twenty-first century, and a huge multinational corporation, with its sentient computer Shalmaneser, plays an active part in controlling the world. Psychotics, known as "muckers," flip out daily and kill large groups of people; these acts are so commonplace that no one questions the motivations. With the population of Earth at seven billion and rising, harsh controls limit the size of families. The "quality" of the offspring, through genetic manipulation, has taken on added importance. A scientist in an Eastern country has developed a breakthrough that might alleviate some of these problems. A government researcher, Donald Hogan, is ordered to obtain information on this project, or alternatively, assassinate the scientist. To facilitate this, he is transformed or "eptified" into a "Mark II" and becomes part-machine, part-man, with an enhanced ability to kill, but he develops a unique form of schizophrenia in the process. His former roommate, Norman House, is the token black vice-president of the corporation and is put in charge of a mining project designed to exploit a third world country. Along the way, we are introduced to Chad C. Mulligan, a pop sociologist whose witty cynicisms and historical anecdotes serve to attach some sort of meaning to the flood of information. The world does not change radically during the course of this novel. Rather, it gives us a view of a planet slowly being squeezed into oblivion with no real mechanism in place to halt the decay.

Stand on Zanzibar set the science fiction world on fire when it was published. It was controversial, not so much for its content as for its style. Most critics found it either one of the major works of the twentieth century or else unintelligible to the point of unreadability. The former view prevailed, and it was awarded the Hugo in 1969 for best novel of the year. As Brunner has pointed out, this work should be read like a newspaper. The novel consists of several types of brief "clips" that run parallel throughout the book with the narrative spliced in, piece by piece. This techique is even more relative today, with multiple forms of media; television, radio, newspapers, all competing to attract our attention and threatening our ability to filter irrelevant data. The book nicely shows the futility of trying to understand the world on the basis of thirty-second ads promoting a product. The desire to maintain the status quo and greed are the driving forces for much of the action, but there are also many instances of the nobler side of human nature trying to deal with a world that has grown too complex and too threatening. This is, at times, a frightening book, but it provokes much thought once one learns to deal with its unusual layout.

Biographical/Bibliographical Readings

Joe DeBolt, "The Development of John Brunner," in *Voices for the Future*, ed. Thomas D. Clareson (Bowling Green University Popular Press, 1979), v.2, p.106-35. *The Happening Worlds of John Brunner*, ed. Joe DeBolt (Kennikat, 1975). "John Brunner," in *Speaking of Science Fiction: The Paul Walker Interviews* (Luna, 1978), p.315-24. John R. Pfeiffer, "John Brunner," in *Science Fiction Writers*, ed. E. F. Bleiler (Scribner's, 1982), p.297-304. **[Bill Trousdale]**

BUDRYS, ALGIS

Life and Works

Algirdas Jonas Budrys was born on January 9, 1931, in Konigsberg, East Prussia. His family came to the United States in

1936. He alludes often to his childhood love of the "pulps," popular science fiction magazines published when he was young. Budrys holds a captain's commission in the Lithuanian army. At one time he was an assistant to his father, the United States Representative of the Lithunian government-in-exile. He attended the University of Miami (1947-49) and later Columbia University (1951-52). It was at a party given by Frederick Pohl and his wife, Carol, that Budrys met Edna Duna, whom he married on July 24, 1954. He and Edna have four sons and currently reside in Illinois.

Budrys' working career began at the American Express Company (1950-51). His experience as an investigations clerk is reflected in "Wall of Crystal, Eye of Night " (*Blood and Burning*, 1978). He held a series of positions in the publishing field, including assistant editor for Gnome Press in 1952 and Galaxy Publications in 1953, editorial work (Royal Publications, 1958-61), editor-in-chief (Regency Books, 1961-63), and editorial director at Playboy Press (1963-65). He free-lanced from 1954 to 1957 and in 1965 took a position as an advertising and public relations executive. In 1974 he became operations manager of Woodall Publishing as well as president of Unifont Company.

His first published story was "The High Purpose" in *Astounding Science Fiction* in 1952. Budrys' first novel was published in 1954 with the title *False Night*, reissued with additions in 1961 as *Some Will Not Die*. His most successful novel, *Rogue Moon*, was published in 1960. His short stories have been collected in two works: *The Unexpected Dimension* (1960) and *Budrys' Inferno* (1963)

Budrys has produced 8 novels, approximately 250 stories and magazine articles, and 3 story collections. He has written under eight pen names, using "Algis" for the science fiction material. From 1965 to 1971, Budrys wrote the book reviews for *Galaxy* magazine. He later provided a similar service for *Magazine of Fantasy and Science Fiction*. The Galaxy reviews have been published as a collection (*Benchmarks*, 1985). His reviews are personal enough to be very interesting to read, yet professional and incisive enough to be influential in the field. His work has spanned a variety of fields but he is best known for his science fiction writing.

His work is held in high regard by other science fiction writers, although he never received a Hugo or Nebula award. Poul Anderson considers him one of the best science fiction writers. James Blish thought of him as a natural writer who writes science fiction infused with emotion. He is a careful craftsman, often reworking a piece to improve or enlarge on it. *Who?* (1958), *Michaelmas* (1977), *Some Will Not Die* (1961), and *The Iron Thorn* (1967) are among his works published in earlier, sometimes quite different forms.

Themes and Style

Stylistically, Budrys' work is different from the pulps which preceded him, with their emphasis on action and hardware. His novels often abound in action, but equally important are the changes in the main character. This emphasis on character development foreshadowed some of the New Wave science fiction. In addition, his works contain descriptive passages which are quite poetic and so clear as to be nearly tangible. And at his best, these images coalesce into metaphors that provide additional layers of meaning to his work. The large issues in life pervade the work of Algis Budrys. Death and its counterpoint, immortality, identity, loss of innocence, morality, power, love, hate, and loneliness--all recur. His works often have a similar basic structure in which science and technology place the main character in an untenable situation which is resolved through the character's actions. Budrys' novels have the relentless drive of Greek tragedies, and even his happier endings have at least a touch of sadness. He is a master in the use of viewpoint, often using two key viewpoints which alternate and heighten suspense or highlight mood and theme.

Plot Summaries of Major Works

Michaelmas. Laurent Michaelmas is a newsman with a face and mannerism that engender public trust. He owns a supercomputer, Domino, that has global connections. It becomes evident that Michaelmas and Domino can run the world. The man and the computer secretly eliminate war and encourage space exploration through their manipulations.

Michaelmas reasons that there is another very influential force operating in the world and opposing him when Walter Norwood, an astronaut killed in a satellite malfunction, is mysteriously brought back to life at the Limberg Sanitorium in Berne, Switzerland. Norwood's sudden reappearance may jeopardize a joint United States-Soviet space mission, and the newsman suspects substitution of a duplicate for Norwood. Michaelmas launches an investigation which he must carry on more or less solo when Domino meets something in the Sanitorium system too strong for the computer.

While the novel follow Michaelmas around the world in fast-paced adventure, many of the action scenes are verbally retold to Michaelmas by his computer. Having these scenes recounted rather than shown to the reader as they happen reduces some of the excitement.

Michaelmas raises some interesting moral questions never resolved in the book. War and major strife has been eliminated, but only through a very secret dictatorship. "The End of Summer," a

Budrys short story, poses the question of whether anyone has the right to impose immortality on mankind. Michaelmas never poses the question: the presumption is that a benevolent dictator is best.

This novel demonstrates a smoothness of style, a broad knowledge of the news media, and characters less archetypical than those in earlier works. There are humorous scenes, such as the fate Domino arranges for Champion, an unscrupulous newsman. These elements combine to make *Michaelmas* the most mellow novel Budrys has written and the one which has earned him critical acclaim both within and without the science fiction field.

Rogue Moon. The novel is set in near-future Earth and the main character is Hawks, a scientist who has invented a matter transmitter which destroys an object atom by atom, only to reassemble it at a new location. The device is being used to attempt exploration of a strange, possibly alien device found on the far side of the moon. The device, a sort of maze, has killed everyone who has entered it. As the novel begins, Navy volunteers have been sent to the moon while a duplicate device is created on Earth and held in sensory deprivation. The two duplicates stay in telepathic touch while the moon version begins exploration of the structure. The Earth version experiences everything including the death of the exploring duplicate. All who have experienced this have emerged insane.

Hawks must find someone who can die and stay sane to die again, learning the labyrinth in the process. He finds Barker, a man who has courted death in a myriad of daredevil stunts, a man in love with death. As Barker explores the maze, he confronts the real nature of death. Death in the maze is impersonal, which is almost too much for Barker. The maze in turn becomes a reflection of the universe. Hawks tells Barker that the explorer has seen the face of the unknown universe while in the maze. The hope is in humanity. Hawks explains that the universe is running down or dying and the only thing that runs against that general tide is intelligence, i.e., mankind. It forces its way uphill. Humans some day will hold death in hand, conquering even that. Hawks fears that this vision will die with him, but is assured that it will live on because he has shared it. By analogy, so the author's vision will live, shared with the readers of *Rogue Moon*. At another level, the maze becomes a metaphor for the novel itself.

Nowhere is Budrys' treatment of maniacs better illustrated than in this 1960 novel, in which all the characters are obssesive and linked with death. The novel is told from two external viewpoints. One sees what Hawks sees and the other sees Hawks' actions. There is no omniscient third party narrator. The characters are more enigmatic as a result, and the isolation in death and in the universe is emphasized. The theme, metaphors, archetypical characters and use of viewpoint combine with the relentless driving pace to make this an existential novel which can be read as a gripping action story of danger and death and which can also be interpreted at deeper levels.

Who? The novel is set in the late 1980s, at a time when the United States and the Soviet Union are locked in a cold war struggle. An American scientist, Lucas Martino, has been working at a remote lab near the Soviet border on a secret weapon, the un-defined "K-eighty-eight." There is an explosion during testing which nearly kills Martino. The Russians, first on the scene due to their proximity, remove Martino to a Soviet hospital for surgery.

Four months later the Russians return a man they claim is Martino. His head has been encased in metal, one arm is a pros-thesis, and his heart and respiratory system have been replaced by a nuclear pile. The United States must verify Martino's identity before he can start work again, and this task is assigned to Rogers. In alternate chapters, the scientist's experiences are described from Rogers' viewpoint, while Martino's life while he was growing up are seen from his own viewpoint. The reader learns about the sci-entist's emotional isolation as a child and young man while seeing the cyborg's attempt at contacts with humans after his return and the people's fear of his metal face.

Who? was first published as a short story with the same title in 1955 and was translated into a film by Jack Gold which sold to television. Budrys was inspired to write the original by an illus-tration by Frank Kelly Freas, an artist who inspired several of his works. The shifting viewpoint maintains the dramatic tension about his identity until the end of the novel while emphasizing the isolation central to the theme. There is a well-developed irony built in as well. The young Martino devoted himself to the tech-nology which destroyed his identity and precludes his working in the field. The cyborg's search for an identity as a person parallels Rogers' search for proof of his identity. The scientist's quest is reminiscent of the tin-man's search for a heart in Oz. It is only when the biological heart of the alleged Martino has been replaced by a machine that he begins to develop his emotional "heart."

Biographical/Bibliographical Readings

"Algis Budrys," in *The Encyclopedia of Science Fiction and Fantasy*, ed. Donald H. Tuck (Advent, 1974), p.73-74. William Atheling, Jr., "Death and the Beloved: Algis Budrys and the Great Theme," in *More Issues at Hand*, ed. James Blish (Advent, 1970), p.59-66. Chris Drumm, *An Algis Budrys Checklist*, 2nd ed. (Borgo Press, 1987). David Pringle, "*Rogue Moon* by Algis Budrys" and "*Michaelmas* by Aldis Budrys," in *Science Fiction: The 100 Best Novels* (Xanadu, 1985), p.83-84, 185-86. Gene Wolfe, "Algis Budrys," in *Science Fiction Writers*, ed. E. F. Bleiler (Scribner's, 1982), p.80-81. [Mary Lou Mills]

BURGESS, ANTHONY

Life and Works

Anthony Burgess was born John Anthony Burgess Wilson on February 25, 1917, in Manchester, Lancashire, England. He finished his education there, graduating from Manchester University in 1940 with a B.A. and Honors in English, though he had wanted to major in music in the hope of becoming a composer. He promptly joined the Royal Army, and as a part of the Education Corps spend most of World War II in Gibraltar. He married a Welsh woman, Llewela Isherwood Jones, whom he called Lynne, in 1942. She remained behind in England, where one night she suffered a brutal beating at the hands of some rampaging American GIs, causing her to abort her pregnancy. She never fully recovered from her injuries and Burgess incorporated this episode into *A Clockwork Orange* (1962) and elsewhere in his writings.

After the war, he continued to work as an educator and civil servant in a string of posts at Birmingham University, the British Ministry of Education, and Banbury Grammar School. In 1954, he relocated with his wife to a government position in Malaya as lecturer in English at Malayan Teachers Training College. Difficulties with his supervisor resulted in his being reassigned to Borneo in 1958. It was during his Far Eastern tenure that Anthony Burgess, writing under his two middle names, began his career as a novelist with a trilogy rooted in his Malayan experiences. The books were well-received, and, in 1959, Burgess returned to the United Kingdom to take up writing on a full-time basis. In 1962, his first work of science fiction appeared. *The Wanting Seed* (1962) reflects Burgess's doubts about humanity's ability to achieve a just and moral society. The novel sets up a contrast between future possibilities--one a socialist state which encourages homosexuality and cannibalism to help reduce the Malthusian pressures of population, and the other which emerges from the first after an interval of violent chaos, a fascist state that addresses the same problem by way of a permanent condition of patriotic war. Burgess characterizes the first society as "Pelagian," based on the heresy of Pelagius, who denied original sin and advocated the improvement of the human soul through free will, and the second as "Augustinian," for the saint who preached the sinfulness of mankind. Both alternatives are undesirable, though the personal human drama that is played out suggests the possibility of reconciliation.

In 1968, his first wife died, and he married an Italian, Liliana Macellari. Having attained international renown, Burgess was elected as a Fellow of the Royal Society of Literature, just before moving to the United States for a series of positions as visiting scholar at a number of universities. His next foray into science fiction came in 1978, with the publication of *1985*, his answer to Orwell. Following a long essay, in which he delineates Orwell's inspiration for 1984 in the Britain of 1948, Burgess offers his own dystopian vision of a near future England, characterized not by an ironclad police state, but by a welfare state dominated by union power and Arab money, threatened by the alternatives of chaos or fascism, and obsessed with an oppressive egalitarianism. In 1982, he published *The End of the World News* as part of a triptych interweaving the philosophies of Freud and Trotsky with the chaos that accompanies a world disaster of the near future.

He has continued his work in mainstream literature with novels and screenplays as well as studies of Hemingway and Lawrence and translations of Sophocles, Hofmannsthal, and Rostand. In 1981, he won the French Foreign Book Prize and in 1982 received an honorary D.Litt. from Manchester University. He currently resides in Monaco.

Themes and Style

Burgess's particular brand of pessimism regarding human nature appears rooted in his Catholicism. Though he first left the faith in his teens, it never left him, and some of the Church's teachings, such as human fallibility, seem more credible to him than the modern liberal faith in the perfectability of human society and the basic goodness of human nature, or the capitalist belief in economic progress as an end in itself. Burgess claims an identification with that other "renegade Catholic," James Joyce; he also considers himself a Manichean, though he sympathizes with the Church's disapproval of that heresy, which argues that good and evil are equally powerful in their battle for the human soul. Indeed, evil often appears the stronger in his fiction.

Burgess's gloomy ambivalence shows up in his science fiction novel of 1962 (his best known work), *A Clockwork Orange*. The hero is Alex, a young man in a future welfare state who is fond of Beethoven and "ultraviolence," gang beating, fighting, and raping. Finally arrested for the murder of an old woman, Alex becomes the subject of a government experiment bent on making him a model citizen through Pavlovian techniques. As the popularity of this novel grew, leading finally to Stanley Kubrick's movie version, so did Burgess's reputation. He continued to publish novels in the literary mainstream, some with science fiction or fantasy touches: the potential nuclear holocausts are behind the action in *Honey for the Bears* (1964) and *Tremor of Intent* (1966), and the hint of precognition appears in *One Hand Clapping* (1961). He also became a popularizer of James Joyce and Shakespeare. Shakespeare appears in his science fiction short story, "The Muse" (1968), published in *The Best Science Fiction of 1969*. In this piece a Shakespearean scholar named Paley returns to Renaissance England to prove that the Bard did not write his plays. Amid surreal and fantastic scenes, Paley loses the plays he has brought with him to the actor, Shakespeare, who revises them for performance.

Plot Summaries of Major Works

A Clockwork Orange. The teen-aged Alex tells his tale in his own words, in the patois *nadsat*, a slangy blend of English and Russian which is one of the book's memorable features. In a decadent welfare state of the near future, Alex and other fellows (or "droogs") pass their time in milk bars that serve narcotics, or on the street indulging in "ultraviolence," which includes gang fights, mugging, rape, and ultimately murder. The same bestial urges give Alex his taste for the passionate strains of Beethoven. When Alex is arrested for the death of an old woman, he finds himself at the mercy of the state, which uses him as the subject of an experimental technique to create model citizens through behavior modification. Alex is given a drug that induces nausea while being shown scenes of violence and brutality characteristic of his own recent life. He leaves prison unable to face violence without becoming sick, but he is also unable to listen to Beethoven.

Ironically, he falls repeatedly into the hands of those he formerly victimized, including a political figure, who victimizes Alex in turn, in order to bring down the present government. If Alex has been brutal in his past, he is apparently no less brutal than other members of his society. Burgess leaves the reader unable to choose between the amoral freedom of Alex and the benign oppression of the system he inhabits. Neither alternative is attractive.

The original English edition contains a final chapter missing from the better known American edition upon which Stanley Kubrick based his film. In the English conclusion, Alex comes to a decision to abandon his violent ways and seek stability through marriage and parenthood. This version suggests that purification comes through suffering, a traditionally Catholic notion. Burgess acknowledged that dropping the last chapter improved the novel, although it continues to appear in both versions.

The End of the World News. This unusual novel opens with the author's recollection of the image of President and Mrs. Carter watching three televisions at once in a news photo. Likewise, this work keeps three stories going simultaneously, cleverly commenting on one another and reaching the same thematic end.

The first tale concerns Sigmund Freud and the development of his psychological theories, his struggles with family and followers, and the backdrop of world war and anti-Semitism. Another focuses on Leo Trotsky in New York before and after the Russian Revolution. The science fiction story that weaves between them suggests H. G. Wells's "The Star" and Philip Wylie's *When Worlds*

Collide; a giant rogue planet called Lynx is approaching Earth and will ultimately destroy it.

Burgess displays his doubts with the intellectual systems humanity has devised. He accuses Freud of secularizing the soul. If Trotsky gets off a little easier with his Marxist rhetoric and dialectical materialism, it is only because his section of the novel frequently slips into the rhythms of light opera.

The weakness of such systems becomes apparent in the future disaster story. Survivalism takes over, even among the scientists who supposedly represent the cream of humanity. Their arrangement to set themselves apart in a ship destined for the stars soon breaks down into an elitist police state on a petty scale. Among the characters to be left behind on a disintegrating Earth are the writer-hero Val and his Shakespearean friend, Willett, the fundamentalist demagogue, Calvin Gropius, and assorted others who find themselves stripped to the barest of spiritual resources.

With Freud dying of mouth cancer and Trotsky fleeing to Mexico and eventual assassination, the starship finally takes off with Val and others on board. In an epilogue, we learn that generations later the journey continues, and that its origins are shrouded in mythology.

While the book has a number of interesting moments and ingenious interconnections between its three threads, it must be read as a philosophical exercise, perhaps offering Burgess's last fictional comment on the sins of the species.

1985. This work is Burgess's answer to George Orwell's *1984*. In its first section, Burgess produces a long essay which attempts to account for the socialist Orwell's diatribe against the totalitarian state. He notes Orwell's history as a Fabian, his disillusionment with Bolshevism, his ambivalence toward the working class, and his terminal illness at the time of *1984*'s writing. Of greater interest is the list of motifs Orwell took directly from the Britain of World War II and the postwar period, particularly for an American audience brought up to think of the novel solely as an attack on Soviet-style communism.

Following the essay, Burgess presents his own fictional alternative of the near future. In his Britain of 1985, labor unions have the nation in a death grip; even the Royal Army cannot be relied upon not to strike. Arab money and culture are taking over at the top, while the average Briton is simply a cog in the welfare state machinery.

For the hero Bev Jones, a turning point comes when his ailing wife dies in a hospital fire because the fire fighters are on strike. He swears vengeance against the system that made this tragedy possible, loses his job, and soon ends up in a prison, then a mental institution. The state fails to change his mind, however, and once out Jones flirts with joining the fascist rebellion, only to find it an obnoxious alternative, and backed by the Arabs to boot. What finally defeats Jones, however, is the all-pervasive mediocrity of the system, which brings everyone down to the level of the common worker with a legally enforced poor grammar and abominable tastes.

Critics have wondered if Burgess's *1985*, with its overt intellectual elitism, is intended as a serious dystopia or as a satire on Orwell. While it retains some of the ambiguity of the author's earlier dystopias, it lacks whatever subtlety they have. Being rooted in the England of the 1970s, with the hegemony of Labour government and Arab oil, it already appears dated. Perhaps this too is a comment on Orwell's political fantasy.

The Wanting Seed. Burgess describes a welfare state gone awry in the not-too-distant future. Despite its well-intentioned hopes for perfecting human life, the society has degenerated in trying to deal with the Malthusian problems of population growth. Fertility is officially discouraged through homosexuality and strict controls, and excess population sacrificed to cannibalism.

In the foreground is a love triangle consisting of Tristam Foxe, his wife Beatrice-Joanna, and his brother Derek. Derek represents society; at the novel's beginning he is a flagrantly homosexual executive in the Ministry of Infertility. Tristam, the outsider, watches society's breakdown, as it slides from its initial "Pelphase" (after Pelagius, the heretical monk who advocated humanity's basic goodness and perfectability) to a chaotic "Interphase," dominated by plagues, brutality, and widespread massacre. He pursues a quest for his unfaithful wife, enduring hellish torments in the process.

By this time, society has entered "Gusphase" (after Augustus, who preached original sin and contrition). Christianity and heterosexuality are back in force, against a militaristic, fascist state that brings on a permanent condition of warfare as the solution to the population problem. Derek, the bureaucrat, manages to survive the shift, while Beatrice-Joanna runs away and bears twins, whom she names after the two men in her life, claiming them both as the fathers.

The Wanting Seed was Burgess's first science fiction novel, and was very much in the dystopian vein of the British New Wave. In this novel, Burgess criticizes both the liberal socialist faith in the improvability of the human condition through secular, social means, as well as the stricter, conservative adherence to icons like Church and Fatherland. Humanity cannot solve its basic problems as a species because humanity itself is flawed. Yet in the microcosm offered by the three main characters, Burgess seems to suggest that some sort of resolution of opposites might be possible. Ultimately, the novel's message is ambiguous, if lighter than in Burgess's later dystopias.

Biographical/Bibliographical Readings

Paul Boytinck, *Anthony Burgess: An Enumerative Bibliography with Selective Annotations* (Norwood, 1977). Jeutonne Brewer, *Anthony Burgess: A Bibliography* (Scarecrow, 1980). Anthony Burgess, *Little Wilson and Big God* (Heinemann, 1987). Samuel Coale, *Anthony Burgess* (Ungar, 1981). A. A. DeVitis, *Anthony Burgess* (Twayne, 1972). Richard Mathews, *The Clockwork Universe of Anthony Burgess* (Borgo Press, 1978). [Stephen W. Potts]

BURROUGHS, EDGAR RICE

Life and Works

Burroughs was born in Chicago on September 1, 1875. He was educated at a variety of private schools including Phillips Academy, Andover, Massachusetts. He served in the U.S. 7th Cavalry in 1896 and 1897 at Fort Grant, Arizona, until it was discovered that he was underage. Burroughs was married twice--first to Emma Centennia Hulbert in 1900, divorced in 1934; his second marriage to Florence Dearholt lasted from 1935 until their divorce in 1942.

Until Burroughs reached the age of thirty-six, his life was marked by a succession of failures. At various times he worked on gold mining operations in Idaho and Oregon, was a railroad yard policeman in Salt Lake City, ran a stationery and bookstore in Pocatello, Idaho, offered a mail order course in salesmanship, and prepared detailed business advice for magazine subscribers. In a desperation move, while supervising pencil-sharpener salesmen, in his free time he started to write adventure fiction for the pulp magazines. After 1919, he spent most of his life in California, with the exception of World War II, when he served as a United Press correspondent in the Pacific. He died in Encino, California, on March 19, 1950.

Not being a business success, Burroughs put his dreams to paper. His first story, "The Outlaw of Torn," was not readily accepted. He continued writing, however, and in 1912 his "Under the Moons of Mars" (published in book form as *A Princess of Mars* in 1917) was published as a serial in *All-Story Magazine*. His next published story was "Tarzan of the Apes" (1912). Within two years he was a full-time writer receiving premium rates. After he began writing, his side ventures were seldom profitable. Burroughs' works continued to appear first in serialized form in magazines before publications as books. *Llana of Gathol* (1942) was the last work published in Burroughs' lifetime.

During his career, Burroughs wrote more than 100 novels and short stories. Many of his works became series such as the Tarzan

series, the Martian series, the Pellucidar series, the Caprona or
Caspak series, the Moon Men series, and the Venus series. Although all parts of the series are not connected by plot line, they
share the same main character or setting. The Martian series consists of eleven books: *A Princess of Mars* (1912, 1917 as book), *The
Gods of Mars* (1913, 1918 as book), *The Warlord of Mars* (1913-14,
1919 as book), *Thuvia, Maid of Mars* (1920), *The Chessmen of Mars*
(1922), *The Mastermind of Mars* (1928), *A Fighting Man of Mars*
(1931), *Swords of Mars* (1936), *Synthetic Men of Mars* (1940), *Llana
of Gathol* (1948), and *John Carter of Mars* (1964). The Pellucidar
series consists of *At the Earth's Core* (1914), *Pellucidar* (1915), *Tanar
of Pellucidar* (1929), *Tarzan at the Earth's Core* (1930), *Back to the
Stone Age* (1937), *Land of Terror* (1944), and *Savage Pellucidar*
(1942).

The Martian series is Burroughs' major science fiction work
and rivals the Tarzan series in overall importance. The Venus series is not as stirring and vivid as the Martian series. It consists
of *Pirates of Venus* (1932), *Lost on Venus* (1933), *Carson on Venus*
(1938), and *Escape on Venus* (1941-42). "The Wizard of Venus" was
published in the collection *Tales of Three Planets* (1964).

The science fiction series which Burroughs sets on the moon is
called *The Moon Men* (1926). The works in this series are examples
of social extrapolation science fiction. Not all of his works are
science fiction. He also wrote historical novels, social realism, and
westerns.

Themes and Style

In the archetypal Burroughs novel, an incredibly strong man
saves an incredibly beautiful woman from rape by incredible villains. However, if one looks more closely at these novels, what
emerges from behind the threat of rape is the far more universal
threat of death.

Burroughs completely divorced readers from association with
reality and took them off to a never-never world of his own creation. He was a natural storyteller. Burroughs had an unsur-
passed sense of pace, and his ability to keep several situations
moving simultaneously, coupled with his mastery of the flashback
technique, established him as an authentic literary craftsman.
Burroughs could make characters come alive and achieve a maximum of reader identification. He was able to make the most impossible tale seem as though it was really happening. Gradual
movement from the mundane to the outre, from the easily acceptable to the utterly fantastic, was performed by Burroughs with
consummate skill with an insidious fraying of the bonds of reality
so deft as to be virtually undetectable to the unwary reader.

Some critics feel that Burroughs science fiction is the direct
descendant of the travel tale typified by the *Odyssey*. His works

are the traditional romance brought up-to-date by the addition of a few scientific trimmings. This variety of science fiction has become known as "scientific romance." In such stories, colorful adventure of the classical kind is seasoned with just enough science to lend wonder and enchantment to the background and locale. His works ushered in the golden era of escape science fiction.

Burroughs is a science fiction writer in externals only, not in inner essence. Most of his work is a fantasy of eroticism and power. Science per se plays little part in his work, and it is safe to say that he knew and cared little about it. Actually his stories are rationalized fantasies in which Burroughs used occasional scientific pretenses to ease the reader's willing suspension of disbelief. Burroughs used the popular scientific theories of the day for his speculation.

Burroughs gave most dazzling rein to his sense of amusement and bemusement in the Martian series, creating powerful romance and shimmering fancy. The Martian series has sizable chunks of ethnographic and cultural data, Martian lore and civilization including architecture and history. The Martian world and his Venus world are dream worlds where virtue and courage win honor and beauty, where evil can be identified, confronted and defeated despite all odds.

In the works of Edgar Rice Burroughs, the lost world lost race motif plays an important part. Many of the Tarzan works have this theme, and there is one set of novelettes, *The Land That Time Forgot* (1924) and one series of novels which also features lost worlds--the Pellucidar series, consisting of seven novels. A yearning for the past and undiscovered worlds stood behind the popularity of the lost race novel. The works emphasized primitivism and sought to reconcile old beliefs and ideals with the facts and theories of the period. Pellucidar is the inner world of Earth beyond Earth's crust, with flora, fauna, and life forms from every period of terrestrial history.

The series for which Burroughs is best known is the work featuring Tarzan or Lord Greystoke. Tarzan, the orphaned English lord raised by apes in the jungle, has come to epitomize the noble savage and to symbolize strength and courage. As with the Martian series, Burroughs wrote the volumes of this series throughout his life, twenty-four volumes about Tarzan and eleven in the Martian series. The theme of the struggle for survival is obvious throughout.

Burroughs is acknowledged as the grandfather of American science fiction. His works are great fun and games for today's readers with the right tolerance for yesterday's literature. Even those who find Burroughs unreadable cannot deny that he set the pattern for modern American science fiction.

As a science fiction writer Burroughs may be regarded as a descendant of Jules Verne. His emphasis is on wonders: wonderful planets, strange creatures, magnificently melodramatic plots. Not a significant creator in his writing, he was rather a synthesizer of immeasurable natural talent. His genius lay in his ability to invest familiar material with such energy that it attained new heights of popularity.

As Burroughs borrowed from earlier writers, he in turn was read by and influenced uncounted later writers. Many scientists, engineers, and writers have stated that the Martian novels of Burroughs first stimulated them to look into science. Ray Bradbury acknowledges his debt to Burroughs in "Tarzan, John Carter, Mr. Burroughs and the Long Mad Summer of 1930." Burroughs stands above the other writers for Bradbury by reason of his unreason--because of his natural impulses. Bradbury states that Kipling was a better writer than Burroughs, but not a better romantic.

The rediscovery of Burroughs in the 1960s was an astonishing publishing phenomenon, and the majority of his books are still reprinted regularly, appealing mainly to young readers. His work will be perpetuated as timelessly valid tales of great entertainment value.

In some ways, his writing skills were inferior to those of the better pulp writers of the day. His plotting was weak, repetitious, and formularized; his characters were paper-thin; his style ranged from cumbersome and amateurish in his early work to lower-level commercial at its best. Yet Burroughs had his strengths. He was able to imagine arresting situations; and if he was not able to provide a plot, he could keep the action moving steadily. He also had the knack, as did Max Brand, of permeating his stories with a pseudomythical quality. He took pains to compile vocabularies of Martian and other languages; he prepared maps of his imaginery lands; he worked out consistent rules for playable games; and he carefully linked his story chains, offering familiar ground to his readers. He was also quite skilled at contriving endings that left matters sufficiently up in the air to justify a sequel.

It is precisely his devotion to fantasy and the possibilities envisioned by a fruitful imagination untrammeled by strictures of realism that offended so many of his critics. Yet herein lies the eternally endearing quality of the man's works as escapist fiction: while it does not compel us to think more or in overtly serious ways about ourselves and our lives, it shares in the shaping of our dreams. And that is not a bad bequest for a fellow who set out to do a little entertaining and at the same time support his family.

Plot Summaries of Major Works

Caprona/Caspak series. *The Land That Time Forgot* (1924 as a set) consists of *The Land That Time Forgot*, *The People That Time Forgot*, and *Out of Time's Abyss*. The setting is the island of Caprona, and the inhabitants call their world Caspak. In the first of the three novelettes, Bowen J. Tyler, Jr., is en route to France when his ship is torpedoed and sunk by a German submarine that, by coincidence, has been built in his father's shipyard. He survives, along with Miss Lys La Rue, the woman who provides the romantic interest in most of Burroughs' novels. They are rescued by a British seagoing tug, which then captures the sub. The sub is commanded by the thoroughly despicable Baron Friedrich von Schoenvorts. The two sets of crews, British and German, capture and recapture the submarine from each other through the first four chapters. The party of captors and captives move from the North Atlantic to the South Pacific and Antartica, where they land on the lost island of Caprona. Von Schoenvorts and the other Germans escape in the sub, marooning the rest of the party.

The explanation of what is happening on Caspak is hidden until well past the middle of the novel, each part of which concerns the progress northward of a human adventurer: as he learns more, so does the reader. Burroughs carefully outlines three journeys, each of which partially overlaps the stopping point of the previous one. Bowen Tyler enters from the south through a subterranean river and then moves north on foot, acquainting the reader with the stages of human development on the island--from Alu, primitive man, to Band-lu, spearmen. We hear of the Kro-lu, or bowmen, and Galu, but Tyler never travels far enough north to encounter them, and the Caspakian system of reproduction is still unknown to him when the first part ends. In the second part, Thomas Billings, secretary to Tyler's father, leads a rescue party, but he crashes his seaplane at a point further up the scale than Tyler's starting point. Billings meets Ajor, a Galu woman with whom he falls in love, and then travels north to her country in order to reunite her with her people. In this part is detailed the system of life, but although the Wieroos are mentioned, they do not appear. That is reserved for the third part, in which Bradley, an English officer from the tug is captured by the Wieroos, transported north to their city, and in his adventures there rescues Co-tan (a Galu woman also captured by the Wieroos). They escape to the land of the Galu, where they meet Billings and Ajor. In the last part, all three couples are reunited and leave Caspak.

Although grounded in the jingoism of World War I, with commonplace erotic plots, the series contains an imaginative redirection of the old biological saw, that a person goes through all stages of evolution in the womb and of nineteenth century Darwinian evolution. Evolution on Caspak is directional: the island is roughly circular in shape with a great freshwater lake in its center. Creatures of the lowest order start in the south, moving northward along either shore of the lake as they progress higher in the scale of evolution. For primates, apes are at the southernmost end and, finally, at the north end of the island are the Galu. The women of each of the various tribes spend part of every day

lying in warm pools. The explanation given is that they are
spawning eggs, which are waterborne south "to the beginning"
where they hatch and begin the long upward climb. Movement
from hatching in the south to Galu in the north is counted one
cycle. A Galu who has resulted from six previously completed cycles is fertile and capable of sexual reproduction. On Caspak
there is a race of winged men (Wieroo) who have developed a
cruel and bloody civilization. In the dim past, some Galus went
through bodily changes that produced the Wieroo, and the Galu
are now in constant competition with the Wieroo for mastery of
Caspak. Since the progression from Galu to Wieroo has ceased, the
Wieroo are fertile but produce only male offspring; therefore they
must kidnap Galu females to reproduce.

Some admirers of Burroughs rate the "lost world" story as one
of Burroughs' very best works. The highly original concept and
most other elements of the book are well thought out and effectively developed. Of all Burroughs' science fiction up to the time,
The Land That Time Forgot is by far the most concerned with scientific speculation; specifically it is devoted largely to conjecture
about evolution.

The Martian series. Burroughs wrote eleven books in this series: *A Princess of Mars*; *The Gods of Mars*; *The Warlord of Mars*;
Thuvia, Maid of Mars; *The Chessmen of Mars*; *The Mastermind of
Mars*; *A Fighting Man of Mars*; *Swords of Mars*; *Synthetic Men of
Mars*; *Llana of Gathol*; and *John Carter of Mars*. *Princess* opens in
1866 when former Confederate Army Captain John Carter is mysteriously transported to Mars. Shortly after he arrives, Carter
meets his first Martians--six-armed, oviparous green aliens called
Tharps who tower an intimidating fifteen feet in height. He as-
tounds himself and the Tharks (aliens) with his ability to leap extraordinary Martian distances, and goes on to display other physical skills with which he successfully combats one belligerent green
giant after another. But his crucial superiority is his sense of decency; by awakening the same sense in Tar Tharkas, a green Martian prince, Carter is able to subvert the Thark society and Tar
Tharkas will lead the green Martians on the road to reform. In
these adventures, John Carter rescues Dejah Thoris, Princess of
Helium, and sides with the red men of Mars. Things look good
until the air plant which replenishes Barsoom's attenuated oxygen
blanket ceases to function and only John Carter knows the secret
telepathic combination of the imprenetrable lock on the single entrance to the atmosphere plant. He succeeds in reaching the plant,
opens the seal, and expires as an oxygen-starved companion crawls
forward to restart the vital machinery. John Carter reawakens in
his own body, back on Earth.

The ending of *Princess* leaves the reader wondering if John
Carter will ever return to Mars and his beloved Princess. In *The
Gods of Mars*, Carter does return and undertakes an essentially

Orphic quest. He must enter the lands that the Martians associate with death and defy the funerary cult to regain the princess. He does not succeed. In the third novel, *The Warlord of Mars*, Carter is still on his quest and travels to the North Pole of Mars to find another hidden culture. Mars, apparently, is so constructed that despite science which is superior, in many areas, to that on Earth, geographical knowledge is abysmal, and no one knows what lies beyond the next range of hills. In this novel, Carter receives his apotheosis and is proclaimed warlord or emperor of Mars, a title that later novels reveal to be empty and premature.

In the Martian series, almost everything is good except that which is excellent. Only *Synthetic Men of Mars* is a thoroughly bad book. Conceptual highlights in the later books are men who create armies by mental powers. *Thuvia, Maid of Mars*, features bodiless human heads with hypnotic ability; a chess-like game played with living pieces who fight to the death is found in *Chessmen*; fantastic organ transplants are in *Master Mind*; and a size-changing relationship between Mars and one of its moons so that when Carter arrives, he is automatically shrunk to the size of one of the native cat men is featured in *Swords*. The basic situations underlie most of the stories--a woman, stolen by lecherous brutes, a proud and haughty beauty who must be approached with Edwardian circumspection, and slaughter.

Burroughs' Mars set a pattern for decades to come. He created a dying world of dead sea bottoms, ancient abandoned cities, canals, and artificially maintained atmosphere. Some argue that Burroughs' Barsoom is a fictionalization of the Mars described by the overly imaginative American astronomer Percival Lowell. Another critic finds that the Martian novels, even if one admits as much poetic license as is necessary for creating a story, are closer to occultism than to science. The one item which raises this question more than any other is the means by which John Carter and later Ulysses Paxton reach Mars. Carter himself can never explain it, nor can anyone else.

Burroughs' original Martian trilogy is a particularly fine instance of science fiction's attempt to cope with the certainty that both individuals and whole races grow old and die. One might conclude that the first three books of the Martian series were intended to represent a single, complete saga.

The books in the Martian series are really about men who are strong enough to survive regular and repeated attempts on their lives. John Carter is a professional soldier, most alive in the midst of battle. John Carter becomes more symbol than person; he becomes the spirit of human fighting, of the continual struggle to stay alive in a universe of death. "I still live!" became the rallying cry of the eternally youthful John Carter, and it echoed the hope and determined conviction held by the young Americans of Burroughs' boyhood.

The heroines, like the men, are predictable. Dejah Thoris, the woman who is central to the series and against whom all other females are measured, is a woman of great personal courage and resolve, and she has a strong sense of pride in herself and her position within Martian society. She is the first of a long line of Burroughs heroines with an inner toughness and determination not to be overwhelmed by circumstances.

Two complaints raised about the writings of Burroughs are racism and antireligious elements. That John Carter regularly has his skin dyed the color of the Martians with whom he is dealing and that he illustrates the truth that all Martians are alike under the skin are interesting comments on the racism of which Burroughs has been accused. For all the evil and incarnate monstrousness that populates Mars, none is more pervasive and more pervasively undermining to Martian civilization than the sham that religion, perverted into blind and unreasoning superstition, has become. Burroughs attacks religious superstition (not religion as such) shamelessly exploited by an elite few to hold the planet's natives in thrall.

Most of the books in the Martian series are well done, full of color and exotic detail. If a single book had to be chosen as best, it would have to be one featuring John Carter and it would probably be the first, *A Princess of Mars*. Burroughs' stories of Mars endure without literary reputation, but are perpetually successful, living beyond changes in literary style and content, and even in scientific knowledge.

The Moon Men series. Issued as a set in 1926, this series is composed of three novels: *The Moon Maid*, *The Moon Men*, and *The Red Hawk*. The story begins in 1967 as the world celebrates peace, a world which has been at war on an uninterrupted basis since 1914. The story is told by Julian the Third who knows the future and knows that peace will not last. The first part, *The Moon Maid*, tells the story of Julian the Fifth. Although contact was made with Mars as early as the 1940s, it was not until 2026 that the first voyage to Mars was made. Julian and Orthis work on the first expedition. Orthis sabotages the Mars flight and the expedition lands on the moon instead. On the moon, they find an interior world with plenty of water and life. Orthis and Julian are captured by the Va-gas, who have also captured Nah-ee-lah, the moon maid. After escaping, Julian is captured by the Kalkars. The Kalkars have slaves to do their work, since they only think. Orthis joins with the Kalkars and they destroy Laythe, the moon maid's home, but Julian and the moon maid flee and return to Earth.

The Moon Men tells the story of Julian the Ninth. Orthis and the Kalkars have attacked the Earth and have taken over the city of Chicago. Most of the traditional American values of education, family life, etc., are frowned upon by the Kalkars. Julian's family tries to save the old values. The most important possession is an old American flag. Although religion is forbidden by the Kalkars, some Americans risk their lives to practice their faith. Julian the Ninth forms a band of American rebels and attacks Chicago, but they are out-numbered and most are killed. The novel closes with Julian's wife retaining the old American flag and expecting a child, perhaps the hope of the future.

The last novel begins 400 years later. The Americans, or Yanks, who have continued to battle the Kalkars, have taken up a nomadic life-style similar to that of the Plains Indians. The Kalkars have been pushed to the Pacific Coast, but have not been totally defeated. Julian the Twentieth, also known as Red Hawk, determines to finally drive the Kalkars into the sea. A descendant of Orthis, Ortis the Sixteenth, sides with Julian, and together they finally drive out all of the Kalkars.

The Kalkars represent Burroughs' image of Russian communists. It is ironic that at one time Burroughs was the best-selling American author in the Soviet Union. The second story, *The Moon Men*, first written as "Under the Red Flag," was originally concerned with a future Russian occupation of America. Burroughs was unable to sell it in its original form, and revised it to fit the moon series.

The pseudoscience of the opening novel, coupled with the audacious narrative premise of Julian's prememory of future incarnations, makes for a sense of wonder reaction dear to the science fictionist's heart. The social extrapolation of the second and third novels, the portrayal of the feudal and then the nomadic societies of the conquered Earth show new facets of Burroughs' skill. Lupoff feels *Moon Men* is Burroughs' masterpiece of science fiction and a too-often overlooked pioneer work of the modern school of social extrapolation in science fiction. In the opinion of many fans, Burroughs' best work is to be found in *The Moon Men* and *The Land That Time Forgot*.

Biographical/Bibliographical Readings

E. F. Bleiler, "Edgar Rice Burroughs," in *Science Fiction Writers* (Scribner's, 1982), p.59-64. Ray Bradbury, "Tarzan, John Carter, Mr. Burroughs, and the Long Mad Summer of 1930," in *Edgar Rice Burroughs: The Man Who Created Tarzan*," by Irwin Porges (Brigham Young University Press, 1975), p.xvii-xix. Richard A. Lupoff, *Edgar Rice Burroughs: Master of Adventure* (Canaveral Press, 1965). [Mina Jane Grothey]

CAMPBELL, JOHN W.

Life and Works

John W. Campbell was born June 8, 1910, in Newark, New Jersey and died on July 11, 1971, in Mountainside, New Jersey. Campbell, whose pen name was Don A. Stuart, was a major writer of science fiction who became by all odds its most influential magazine editor. Campbell's father was an electrical engineer for Bell Telephone Laboratories and his mother was a flighty and self-centered woman. His sister, Agnes, might have been his friend had there not been such a wide difference in their ages.

Precociously intelligent, the youthful Campbell had a natural flair for mechanics, electrical devices, and chemistry, but was also predominately a loner with literally no friends. He began reading Edgar Rice Burroughs at the age of seven and never stopped rereading him to the end of his life. This passion for Burroughs was one of his best kept secrets, because Burroughs's work would have seemed antipodal to the type of material he would later try to get contributors to *Astounding Science Fiction* to write.

He was enrolled at the Blair Academy, a boy's school in Blairstown, New Jersey, when he was fourteen. Campbell was an unpredictable student depending on whether or not the subject appealed to him. When he later enrolled at the Massachusetts Institute of Technology, he was fortunate to come under the influence of Norbert Weiner, one of the computer pioneers. The knowledge he gained of computers would give Campbell a leg up on other writers when he began to write science fiction. While at MIT, he met Dona Stuart (from whom he derived his pen name), and they were married in 1931. Campbell and his wife had four children, but he eventually divorced her and later married Margaret Winters in 1950. She was the widow of J. A. Winters, one of the founders of the Dianetics movement, along with L. Ron Hubbard. Campbell never graduated from MIT, having flunked German. He eventually received a degree in physics from Duke University.

No one wanted to hire physicists in 1932. He began to sell some science fiction stories in 1929 and the sporadic checks would prove crucial as he miserably failed at selling cars, exhaust fans, and gas heaters. Settling in New Jersey, he worked at research for Mack Trucks and Hoboken Pioneer Instruments.

In October, 1937, he was hired as associate editor of the magazine *Astounding Stories*. When F. Orlin Tremaine, the other associate editor, left the company in May of 1938, Campbell was given full editorship. He continued to edit it up to the day of his death. During this same time, he was also given the additional editorship of a new magazine, *Unknown* (1939-43), which was a critical success, but unprofitable. After World War II, with the advent of jet planes and rockets, he was given a chance at editing the impressive and *Life* magazine-sized *Air Trails Pictorial.* Campbell attempted to convert the magazine into the field of space technology without much success. After several tribulations and title changes, Campbell finally left the magazine after the January, 1948, issue and thenceforth devoted all of his energies to *Astounding/Analog.*

The stability of the magazine that Tremaine had built up provided Campbell with the basis for his future success. It made it possible for him to experiment and to retreat from errors without serious damage to the publication. The story of Campbell's editorship has often been told piecemeal in books, bibliographies, biographies, and literary criticism. When he took over, he had the only monthly science fiction magazine, buying more fiction in one year than any other two magazines at better prices. If an author wanted to write for anyone in the science fiction field, Campbell was the prime market. Gradually he was able to develop such authors as L. Ron Hubbard (to get a light touch into the magazine), Robert A. Heinlein (a rare find under any circumstances), A. E. Van Vogt (comparable to a fast ball pitcher who is a little wild, but when good he was very good indeed), Theodore Sturgeon (a marvelously adroit and original writer), Isaac Asimov (who emerged as a front runner when no one thought he was even catching up), L. Sprague de Camp (who wrote in the tradition of Mark Twain), and Lester del Rey (who could wring pathos even out of a piece of machinery). Campbell also encouraged and bullied Jack Williamson, Eric Frank Russell, Murray Leinster, Fritz Leiber, Jr., Henry Kuttner, Hal Clement, Clifford D. Simak, Arthur C. Clarke, Edward E. Smith, Raymond F. Jones, A. Bertram Chandler, and scores of others into providing him with some of the prime material of their careers. They made him, but in many cases he also made them.

As a writer of science fiction, Campbell was not a prolific author, but he did manage to write many short stories, collected in *Who Goes There?* (1948), *Cloak of Aesir* (1952), and *The Best of John W. Campbell* (1976). His major works include *The Mightiest Machine* (1947), *The Black Star Passes* (1953), *Islands of Space* (1957), and *Invaders from the Infinite* (1961). His first short story, "When the Atoms Failed," appeared in *Amazing Stories* in January 1930. He had previously sold two stories to Hugo Gernsback in 1929 before Gernsback left the company, but Campbell theorized that Gernsback may have taken the two stories with him. Despite his prestige in the field, the limitations and policies of the markets found him scoring more rejections than acceptances. He rewrote some stories as many as six times without selling them. Tremaine was his great benefactor, recognizing the quality of his Stuart material which no one else would buy.

Campbell spent all of his time on the stories for his magazine. He read every story that came in and provided ideas that should have made him the coauthor of some of the best. As life dealt him many personal and career hurts, some of the callousness and cruelty of his earlier period wore away and he became considerably more humane. He faced many of his personal and business disappointments with unquestioned bravery. Whatever history is written that deals with him fairly will have to acknowledge John W. Campbell as one of the titans of science fiction.

Themes and Style

As a science fiction author, Campbell must be evaluated in two phases. First, he was predominately a writer of super science epics of physics (in which he majored), carried not only to its ultimate extreme but involuted in the process with occasionally a bit of paranormal and myth seasoning thrown in. Second, he was a writer of mood pieces, whose effectiveness depended on creating emotion on the part of the reader, though this emotion may not have been engendered by sentiment but by the benevolence of science and its limitations. Again and again, human science is "faithful"; it does not lead him into a Mephistophelian trap.

By his own admission, he was particulary enraptured by E. E. Smith's *Skylark of Space* and its sequel, *Skylark Three*. These were tales in which methods were found to exceed the speed of light, thereby theoretically opening up other stars and galaxies to exploration; where incredible energy devices and weapons were manufactured to order right aboard the space ship and just as needed; where miracles of advanced science were exchanged with cultures light years removed from Earth; and, most especially, where titanic battles were fought in space against alien races. The readers were young, intelligent, and predominately male. They wanted, in the early 1930s, concepts. To them, this was more stimulating than gourmet foods or sex fantasies. This fare Campbell would provide them on a continuing basis and in quantity.

"When the Atoms Failed" was particularly noteworthy because it incorporated the use of a computer to help calculate space navigation, something rarely done before in science fiction, where navigators were faster with the slide rule than the Chinese were with the abacus. He obtained this background from Norbert Weiner, who was already operating an Integraph at MIT, an electronic device capable of doing calculus. The title of the story derives from Campbell's thesis that atomic power can be topped if one can actually destroy matter itself, and his protagonist, with the help of an electronic brain, does just that and cremates the Martians.

Plot Summaries of Major Works

The Black Star Passes. There are three titles in this work--"Piracy Preferred," "Solarite," and "The Black Star Passes." This volume represents the early phase of Campbell's writing career, when he scored a popular success by imitating E. E. Smith in writing superscience epics that spanned the galaxies. "Piracy Preferred" tells how the famous scientific team of Arcot, Morey, and Wade was formed. Wade was a brilliant but unstable genius who contrived methods of successfully pirating the airliners of his day through highly advanced scientific methods. Wade had an invisible ship capable of operating in space and a gas which could penetrate metal. Arcot and Morey are equally brilliant scientists whose collected genius finally captures Wade, and he is turned over to the doctors for psychotherapy and then asked to join them. "Solarite" finds the team, joined by another scientist named Fuller, using the "Molecular drive" that was invented to capture Wade as a method of propulsion to send a space ship to Venus. They become involved in a war on Venus which gives rise to the use of invisible ships with the memorable sequence of making them visible by pouring paint on them.

In "The Black Star Passes," the team of Arcot, Morey, and Wade is confronted by a hostile exploration team for a burnt out black star which has approached within interstellar transport distance of our solar system. The humanoids from the planets of this dark star are seeking to migrate to worlds around a younger, brighter orb. They are defeated in the initial encounter and the readers are treated to a story that is predominately pseudoscience of inventions made to order. All the excitement comes at the end in a massive space battle in which the invaders are defeated once again, but in retreating to their dark sun their spirit of adventure and discovery is revived and when they next come near a likely sun with planets they will be more successful.

We find that Campbell's science fiction was an unrelieved mass of "science," and this onus had also been given to Gernsback selections, who, to the contrary, had a far more literary and diverse selection of stories than that championed by the early Campbell. What is advanced about this work is that parts of it are told from the viewpoint of the alien invaders, an adventuresome technique for a relatively new writer. The team of Arcot, Morey, and Wade continue their escapades in *Islands of Space* and *Invaders from the Infinite*.

Who Goes There? This is one of the basic collections of John W. Campbell stories. It leads off with "Who Goes There?" probably the author's finest work. In the story, an Antarctic experimental base discovers a space ship that has been frozen in the ice for twenty million years, and outside it the frozen carcass of an alien monstrosity. They thaw it out and it revives, taking control of the body of one of the dogs. The other dogs attack and the research men "kill" the creature before it can completely metamorphisize into a dog. The alien enters the various individuals at the camp, assuming all their thoughts, memories, and habits and the researchers are chilled by the realization that not only is one of them the alien, but if it ever leaves Antarctica, it represents a threat to the entire world, for when it takes control of a host, the bulk of its original body remains as it moves on to another. One by one the men are taken over, with the others wondering who is a real man and who is an alien. By the time the puzzle is solved, the alien has put together an antigravity machine with atomic energy and in another half-hour would have been on its way to the rest of the globe. It is in every sense a detective story of the most advanced type. Campbell masterfully maintains the suspense and uses an ingenious method of blood examination to find the alien.

"Twilight" is a story which was influenced by Wells' "The Time Machine." A man visits the future when mankind is on the descendency, living in marvelous cities that are no longer understood, tended by machines that they have forgotten how to build, with no future except gradual decline. It is a mood story, reflecting the sadness of a man from the present, where progress is a motivating factor, viewing a world where nothing is possible except to sink. Equally memorable is its sequel, "Night," in which a man travels to a future where no more energy remains, even in the stars. The cold buildings and machines of mankind still stand, but humanity is extinct. Only an imitation of life appears, a few machines built on Neptune to exercise curiosity, but the visitor knows it is the end. The arrival of the man from the past stirs into action robots silent for billions of years on Neptune. They assist him in returning to his own time.

The story is of the universe closing down; the traveler is fortunate to be able to escape to the past, where life still offers the pretense of meaning. The time traveler realizes that evolution into machines is not the answer for mankind. The machines are but a parody of life. Campbell was growing up, learning his own lesson in these stories.

Biographical/Bibliographical Readings

E. F. Bleiler, "John W. Campbell, Jr." in *Science Fiction Writers*, ed. E. F. Bleiler (Scribner's, 1982), p.151-60. Perry A. Chapdelaine and George Hay, *The John W. Campbell Letters* (AC Projects, 1985). Gerald W. Conley, "John W. Campbell," in *Twentieth-Century American Science-Fiction Writers* (Gale, 1981), v.1, p.97-101. Sam Moskowitz, "John W. Campbell," in *Seekers of Tomorrow* (World, 1966), p.27-46. **[Sam Moskowitz]**

CAPEK, KAREL

Life and Works

Karel Capek was born on January 9, 1890, in Male Svatonovice, a rural village near the German border in Bohemia, then a province of the Austro-Hungarian empire. His father was a country doctor who treated the miners and farmers of the district, his mother an intellectual, and Karel spent much time at home reading and writing juvenile verse and tales. He was a sickly child, though well cared for by his older brother Josef and sister Helena.

While still in their teens, Josef and Karel began writing stories together, and in 1908 their first published effort, "The Return of the Prophet Hermotino," appeared in the Prague newspaper, *Lidove noviny*. Their partnership was interrupted by university studies: Josef left for Paris to become an artist, while Karel registered at Charles University in Prague, majoring in philosophy. He completed his Ph.D. in 1915 with a dissertation on esthetics. While finishing his studies, he was diagnosed as having a rare and painful vertebra condition that forced him to walk with a cane.

Resuming their collaboration, the brothers Capek published their first collection in 1916 and their second in 1918, with Karel publishing his first solo collection in 1917, *Wayside Crosses*. Both avid Czech nationalists, the brothers did not hit their literary stride until the establishment of an independent Czechoslovakia in the aftermath of World War I.

At the beginning of 1921, Karel's most popular and best-remembered play appeared, *R.U.R.*--best remembered for its introduction of the word "robot" into the languages of the world. Actually, the term was invented by Josef, from the Slavic word "robota," meaning "labor." The title stands for Rossum's Universal Robots, which are not the mechanical entities meant by the word today, but rather "androids," grown organically, yet artificially. *R.U.R.* has been viewed as evidence of Capek's sympathies with Marxism. While an avowed socialist, Karel did not share Josef's enthusiasm for the people's revolution and continued to identify with liberal socialism.

R.U.R. was quickly translated into English and other languages and performed worldwide, earning Karel an international reputation and the friendship of such literary giants of the time as H. G. Wells and George Bernard Shaw. Other plays written by the brothers Capek include *Of the Life of Insects* (1921), *The Makropulos Secret* (1922), and *Adam the Creator* (1927).

Although the plays written by Karel and Josef received the most attention at the time, most critics now consider Karel's novels to be his best work. *Factory of the Absolute* (1922) and *Krakatit* (1924) are both science fiction works in which a powerful

force unleashed by humanity leads to devastating moral consequences. The satiric target is more specific in his 1936 novel *War
with the Newts*, which attacks the totalitarian mass man, then looming particularly close to Czechoslovakia in the form of Nazism.

So closely was Karel Capek identified with Czech national-
ism--as an author, journalist, and close associate of patriot-presi-
dent Masaryk--that it has been tempting to see his premature
death in 1938, a few months after Czechoslovakia was opened to
Hitler, as more than a coincidence. Indeed, when the Gestapo
combed Prague in early 1939 for political opponents, the home of
Capek's widow was one of their first stops.

Themes and Style

As a figure of world literature today, Capek's nationalism
takes second place to his universal message: that the common person will endure not only by resisting attempts to gain the powers
of gods nor to regress to the mindlessness of ant or newt. The
human was not meant to be creator or insect, but an entity between, dignified and free. *Of the Life of Insects* presents a different satirical view of humanity using insects as types: the
frivolous, promiscuous, irresponsible social butterflies, the bour-
geois beetles avariciously pursuing accumulation of wealth as
death pursues them, and the totalitarian, militaristic ants. Something of the Capek's political stance is also shown in this play:
unsympathetic with the uncommitted hedonism of the young elite
or the ruthless possessiveness of the capitalist middle class, he
fears as well the organization of the working class into an unthinking, potentially dangerous hive.

His play *The Makropulos Secret*, though a complex plot about
an inheritance dispute, turns on a scientific idea: that a woman
holds the formula for eternal life. She is three hundred years old,
though by this time weary of life. By the play's end, the con-
tested document that preserves the secret of eternal life is destroyed, to the relief of most. Capek seems to be saying here, as
elsewhere in his works, that human beings must excel in human
terms, and not by reaching for the powers of gods. He seeks the
advancement of the common man, not of the superman.

Plot Summaries of Major Works

Factory of the Absolute. An engineer perfects atomic fission,
only to learn that a side effect of annihilating matter is a leak
from the Platonic realm of the Absolute. Wherever the inter-
minable energy source of his mass-produced Carburator is used,
the spiritual force of the Absolute appears, driving people into
fanatical dogmatism.

True to Capek's relativism, the Absolute appears differently in different cultures--in the United States, for instance, it promotes sports and prohibitionism, while in France it creates a rationalist anticlericalism and a new drive for empire. Before long, the various versions of the Absolute begin to clash in social disruptions and warfare. Europe reexperiences an accelerated form of the violence that extended from the Napoleonic Wars to World War I, while Asiatic hordes overrun Russia and the Pacific Rim. Humanity comes close to wiping itself out; all that remains at the end are a handful of common-sensical peasants who celebrate the simple joys of life over beer and sausages.

Capek's first novel, published in 1922, is a satire that preaches the author's philosophy of relativism with an absurd science fictional twist. Critics then and now have enjoyed the first twelve chapters, but find the rest tiresome in its quasihistorical overviews of subsequent events. Capek, in his defense, apologetically argued that he had difficulty keeping up with the demands of the novel's original serial publication in the newspaper *Lidove noviny*. But the novel survives as another example of Capek's use of science fiction techniques in the service of his humanist vision. Here, as in his other work, Capek argues against rigid philosophies and ideologies and in favor of a more basic sympathy with common humanity.

Krakatit. The young engineer Prokop has discovered a powerful explosive, perhaps related to atomic energy, which he calls Krakatit. Overwork leads him to a physical breakdown, and while wandering delirous he is picked up by an old acquaintance named Tomes, who learns the secret of Krakatit amid Prokop's babblings. As yet ill, Prokop begins a quest to find Tomes and stop him before Krakatit is let loose upon the world, and to find a mysterious veiled lady who has appeared to him and whom he passionately loves.

During the course of his quest, he is tempted by other women and by men who know about Krakatit and want the secret of its manufacture. The women are by turns chaste or corrupt; the men include a foreign agent who imprisons Prokop in a castle and an anarchist leader with technological powers of his own. Prokop does not find Tomes, however, before damage is done. In a final mystical scene, Prokop speaks with a divine fortune teller, who explains the significance of what has happened to him, and bids him to develop his invention for peaceful, instead of harmful, uses.

Krakatit, published in 1924, was Capek's second novel. Like his first, *Factory of the Absolute*, it concerns the difficulty that humanity has in handling the forces it sets free, though in this case the moral message is made not through satire but through symbolic melodrama. Viewed by many critics as an ambitious failure, this novel works only if regarded as a morality play with the human species as main character. Capek praises Creative Man as Prokop, but laments that he and his creations so often turn to ill. As he does elsewhere, Capek here offers hope for the future and a degree of faith in human potential, despite the contraindications.

R.U.R. R.U.R. stands for Rossum's Universal Robots, a corporation that produces these humanoid items to be sold to industry worldwide, as a slave labor force. As the play opens, the lovely young Helena Glory is visiting the island where the robots are manufactured, with the intent of stimulating them to revolt. Ironically, she cannot tell human from robot. She does, however, enchant all the men at the factory, and ends up engaged to one director named Domin.

Soon the robots rise in an international revolt, destroying their masters. At about the same time, it is discovered that humans have lost the ability to reproduce, one of the few remaining factors that separated them from their creations. The tragedy spins itself out, until all humanity, including Helena, has been killed, except for a single engineer hamed Alquist. It is he who discovers that the robots now have the ability to love and procreate, and sends them off with his blessing to replace humanity.

Capek's most popular play, first presented in 1921, is now best remembered for its creation of the word "robot." In Czech, "robota" means "labor," with the connotations of "servitude" and "drudgery." The robots in this work, however, are actually creatures of flesh and blood, albeit artificially created, what we now call "androids." Critics have found in this play criticisms of technology, capitalism, socialism, and other driving forces and philosophies of modern life. Capek himself, as a relativist, claimed that all points of view are represented in the play, and that all in their own way are right. If he methodically avoids making a choice, it is at least clear that Capek holds human values dear, even if they must survive only in the artificial humans created by mankind. Humanity may disappear, but the value of love remains.

By contemporary standards, this play has a number of dramatic problems, but it endures because of its contribution to the question--at least as old as Shelley's *Frankenstein*--of humanity's moral relationship to its technological creations, and because of the name it gave to one such creation.

The War with the Newts. The Newts of the title--newly discovered aliens found off the coast of Southeast Asia--are intelligent and human-sized. Almost immediately, they are exploited as a slave labor force--like the robots of *R.U.R.*--and like the robots, they eventually revolt. Having learned military organizaion from human beings--indeed, their commander-in-chief is a German World War I veteran--they proceed to issue demands to have land masses inundated with water so they can live there.

The novel ends unresolved, leaving open the question of whether or not the Newts will come to dominate humanity or in fact destroy the world through internal warfare.

This 1936 novel stands above Capek's other science fiction novels as *R.U.R.* stands above his other plays. One likely reason is that, unlike most of his more fantastic works, which tend toward the allegorizing of abstractions, Capek here has a specific target, allowing him to employ his practiced satirical pen. *The War with the Newts* had its inspiration in the unfolding situation of Central Europe in the mid-1930s, when Hitler had consolidated his power in Germany and was turning his attention to the Slavic states. World war seemed imminent again, and given the nature of technological advance, this war would seem less survivable than the previous one. Perhaps because of such fears, Capek is less optomistic in this work than in his earlier ones on similar themes.

Written as a serial for *Lidove noviny*, the Czech newspaper that employed Capek for most of his working life, *The War with the Newts* takes advantage of the journalistic format to tell its tale, with news clippings, commentaries, interviews, and the like. Though often regarded as an attack on Nazism, the novel takes shots at all the other absolutes of the time, including communism, capitalism, and any other system that reduces humanity to a mass quantity. Once more, and for almost the last time in a major work, Capek attacks the human propensity for subordinating human values to human systems. In this work, however, Capek leaves it to posterity whether or not the values will emerge triumphant.

Biographical/Bibliographical Readings

William E. Harkins, *Karel Capek* (Columbia University Press, 1962). Alexander Matushka, *Karel Capek* (Allen & Unwin, 1964). Darko Suvin, "Karel Capek, or the Aliens amongst Us," in *Metamorphoses of Science Fiction* (Yale University Press, 1979), p.270-83. [Stephen W. Potts]

CARD, ORSON SCOTT

Life and Works

Orson Scott Card was born August 24, 1951, in Richland, Washington. A member of the Church of Jesus Christ of Latter-Day Saints (Mormons), he served a two year unpaid mission in Brazil before receiving his B.A. in theater from Brigham Young University in 1975. In 1981, he received an M.A. in English from the University of Utah. While at Brigham Young and the University of Utah, he wrote a number of plays that reflect his closeness to the theology and backgrounds of Mormonism. From 1976 to 1978, he was assistant editor of *The Ensign*, a church-sponsored magazine. Since 1978, he has been a free-lance writer and editor. Many of his works involve the history of the United States and of his church in particular, especially the excellent historical novel, *A Woman of Destiny* (1984), and he has written fantasy stories as well. Nevertheless, it is as a writer of science fiction that he has reached his largest audience.

Since the August, 1977, *Analog* publication of "Ender's Game," his first science fiction story, Orson Scott Card has quietly come to dominate the section of the science fiction field that is concerned with people and their interactions rather than gadgets and their operations. In 1978, he was awarded the John W. Campbell award, given to the best new science fiction writer of the year. The novel *Ender's Game* (1985), an expansion of the short story, won both the Hugo and Nebula awards in 1986. His other science fiction works include *Capitol*, a collection of short fiction (1979), *Hot Sleep* (1979), and *A Planet Called Treason* (1979). In the 1980s he has produced several other works, including *Songmaster* (1980), *Hart's Hope* (1983), *The Worthing Chronicle* (1985), and the Hugo winning sequel to *Ender's Game*, *Speaker for the Dead* (1986). In 1987, Card began as editor and publisher of his own review journal, *Short Form*. He is currently considered by many to be one of the finest writers working in the humanistic side of American science fiction.

Themes and Style

While still in his teens, Card began to adapt stories for performance on stage. He continued to adapt and write for the theater, learning how to tell a story and create characterizations through dialogues for a number of years before selling his first story. Thus, Card's earliest fiction is cleanly written and fast moving, with excellent ideas and generally believable characterizations--but its biggest problem lies in that it tends to resemble already written works and to be somewhat sylistically flat. This is especially evident in the stories in *Capitol*, Card's first science fiction collection. "A Thousand Deaths," a grim update of Orwell's *1984*, shocked people when it first appeared, but it now seems to resemble its model too closely and to have a very weak conclusion to boot.

Card's fiction since 1979 has been noticeable for its exceptional quality and its general diversity. A typical story by Card will usually include the following elements of characterization--well-rounded, "real" people as characters, children as protagonists and their maturation and acceptance of responsibilities, characters with general decency and believable motivations. In addition to being filled with "real" people, Card's fiction is noted for its nonjudgmental tone. A number of critics have called Card a "cold" or emotionless writer due to this tone, but this is incorrect. Card merely avoids lecturing his readers on how to feel, letting the story raise the questions that everyone must answer for his or her self.

In Card's handling of science and technology, he recognizes that technological changes and innovations are inevitable, but he does not dwell on them. Science fiction for Card never involves detailed explanations of scientific and technological matters. The gadgetry is relegated to the background of the tale, existing to be used by his characters, but not defining them.

Many of Card's earlier pieces were notable for showing the prices that must be paid before happiness can be achieved. His characters frequently suffer enormous pain and mental torture before they achieve some measure of serenity. Linked with this view of unhappiness as an unfortunate but necessary part of life is the fact that Card's stories frequently present a philosophy to the reader which includes such concepts as sacrificing oneself for the greater good of society.

As of this writing, Card is still a young man. He shows no signs of flagging or of repeating himself, and in the years to come his critical reputation is certain to grow, as will the numbers of awards received.

Plot Summaries of Major Works

Ender's Game. Set in the not-too-distant future, humanity lives in fear of a third attack from the insectoid Buggers who, seventy years earlier, were defeated only because there was a military genius in Earth's army. Realizing that military geniuses are uncommon and rarely appear when needed, the military now has a vast testing program in the hopes of finding a commander for its fleet of ships sailing to attack the Buggers' planet.

The Wiggin family is an exceptional family, and its third child is Andrew, who prefers to be called "Ender." The first two children, Peter and Valentine, are military geniuses but are of the wrong temperament. Peter is vicious and amoral, Valentine too gentle. The military realizes that the potential commander is Ender after watching him perform in school and fight a classmate, and at the age of six he is taken from his family, sent to the orbiting Battle Station, and trained in the ways of war. Amidst the drills and exercises, Ender plays a highly elaborate computer game, supposedly unbeatable, which he defeats. Ender is trained to believe that he is completely on his own, that no one will save him if he makes mistakes. He matures into a brilliant tactician, a commander who empathizes with his enemies, and by so understanding them, defeats them.

Ender, believing that he is involved in a simulated battle, becomes very tired and frustrated with the game, and rather than attack the Bugger fleet, he has his ships attack the supposedly simulated planet and destroys it. He wins the real war without intending to do so. Ender is hailed as the savior of the Earth, for he has destroyed the entire race of Buggers and their planet, but he cannot return to Earth as he would become a tool, to be used by whatever nation had him within its borders. Furthermore, Ender is sick with himself for having destroyed an entire race: he must live with the knowledge that he has been the weapon that has destroyed the only other sentient race thus found. There is, however, a ray of hope for Ender--the Buggers have left one of their queen's larvae on another planet. If Ender can find a place where human and Bugger can coexist peacefully, the race will not be permanently extinct.

Ender's Game is memorable for its characterizations of children, its original ideas, its precision of writing and dialogue, and for its antiwar theme. The horror occurs when Ender destroys the Buggers planet, having been led to believe that it was only another simulated game. This speaks of the cold, unrelinquishing view of the militaristic goal of victory, whatever the means. The sequel to *Ender's Game*, *Speaker for the Dead*, continues the lives of Ender and his sister Valentine several thousand years later. Ender has become known as a monster, as "Wiggin the Xenocide," the person who destroyed a race. Due to the relativistic nature of space travel, Ender and Valentine are still relatively young, and nobody connects Ender to his earlier identity. The adult Ender is convincing in is attempt to discover if a race known as "piggies" are sentient, and he is also believable in his attempts at establishing relations with a group of disturbed children.

Biographical/Bibliographical Readings

Orson Scott Card, "On Sycamore Hill, a Personal View," *Science Fiction Review* 14:2 (May 1985), p.6-11. Richard Lupoff, "Orson Scott Card, " in *Twentieth-Century Science-Fiction Writers*, ed. Curtis C. Smith (St. James, 1986), p.118-19. **[Richard Bleiler]**

CHARNAS, SUZY MCKEE

Life and Works

Suzy McKee Charnas was born in New York City on October 22, 1939. In 1961, she joined the Peace Corps and taught English and history in Nigeria. She returned to New York and, after graduating from New York University, she taught English and history at New Lincoln School from 1965 to 1967. For the next two years she worked for the Community Mental Health Organization, developing curricula for the Flower Fifth Avenue Hospital. In 1968, she married Steven Charnas and they moved to New Mexico in 1969.

In 1974, *Walk to the End of the World* was published describing Holdfast, a male-dominated world. The sequel, *Motherlines* (1980) tells of the societies of free women outside of Holdfast. In *The Vampire Tapestry* (1980), the major character is Dr. Edward Weyland, a professor of anthropology, director of a sleep research project, and a vampire. When he is discovered to be a vampire, the predator becomes the prey as Weyland is hunted by an occultist who believes that he can increase his powers by using Weyland as a medium. Charnas presents a careful portrayal of a creature living among and off of humans, adapting to survive among his victims, and very reluctantly coming to care about some of those upon whom he preys. The chapter "The Unicorn Tapestry" won the Nebula award for Best Novella of 1980.

Themes and Style

The brutality and sex in *Walk to the End of the World* and *Motherlines* are often shocking and repulsive to some readers. Charnas is following a well-established literary tradition of exaggeration to achieve a satiric effect. She presents Holdfast as an example of the most extreme development of conservative misogynist attitudes.

The dominant theme in Charnas's work is feminism. The slavery of the fems in *Walk to the End of the World* is misogyny carried to its extreme, a culture in which women are seen as soulless animals. The groups of women in *Motherlines* represent female civilizations which escape the slavery imposed by men and remain separate from men. In *The Bronze King* (1985), it is the heroine who vanquishes the monster, much to the frustration of Joel, who argues that no one ever heard of girls fighting monsters. Tina, the heroine, speaks for all of Charnas's women when she responds that she is a female human being who can and must do things for herself, even if they are dangerous, because she cannot depend on others to be around to help. Even though the tasks may seem impossible, they must be done, and a woman is capable of doing them. Charnas's women characters are feminists, individuals who are willing to struggle and to grow.

Plot Summaries of Major Works

Walk to the End of the World. Long after a devastating nuclear war, a community called Holdfast exists that is populated by descendants of the men who were in the government shelters and the few women who were with them. Holdfast is ruled by older white men called Seniors. The younger men, Juniors, compete for the attention and favor of the Seniors. The women, "fems," are slaves and kept under brutal and degrading conditions. The Holdfast society is on the edge of destruction due to the conflicts between Seniors and Juniors and also due to the fragile ecology. Some of the fems believe that there may be free women somewhere on Earth, far from Holdfast. The men of this new world blame the women's ancestors for having been part of the destruction, because feminists had joined minority and environmental groups in opposing the existing system. The fems are property of the men and without any rights. Eykar Bek, unique because he knows his father's name, and his friend attempt to find Bek's father, only to become involved in a civil war caused by a failing food supply and the conflict between the young men and the older ruling class. The struggle reaches a climax in the siege and destruction of one of the towns and Bek's patricide. Alldera, Bek's slave, escapes in the midst of the battle, hoping to find the free fems who are said to live far away from men. Alldera's story continues in *Motherlines*.

The world of Holdfast is described in grim detail. The degradation and violence are extremely brutal. It presents a savage picture of sexism, bigotry, and intolerance.

Motherlines. Alldera has escaped from Holdfast and is adopted by the Riding Women, a female society whose nomadic, communal life is centered around their horses. They patrol the border to insure that the men of Holdfast do not learn of their existence and that escaped fems are helped. Alldera is content with them until she learns that these women are the result of a scientific experiment which allows them to become pregnant by mating with their horses. They are descendants of a group of scientists who discovered a method of reproduction initiated by using the sperm of horses. The women now lack the techniques of artificial insemination and mate directly with the horses. The Riding Women are strong and active; they engage in symbolic warfare, but do not wish to change their lives to help the women of Holdfast. Deeply shocked by their practices, Alldera leaves them to join a group of escaped fems. She finds that she has little in common with the fems, who seem preoccupied with possessions and positions. Although the escaped fems talk about raiding Holdfast and freeing the slaves, they do nothing. When Alldera returns to the Riding Women, some of the fems come with her. As the group learns more about each other, a new group begins to emerge, and Alldera reluctantly realizes that she will be the one to lead this new group in an attack on Holdfast. Alldera brings the two groups of women together, blending them into a force that can attack Holdfast under her leadership.

Motherlines is a portrait of women struggling to find their identities and roles in a world without men. While one group follows some of the patterns of the male world they know, the other creates a new and separate world. Whether or not such separation will be a valid solution remains unanswered at the end of *Motherlines*, as does the resolution of the confrontation between Holdfast and the new feminist group. The sexual themes of the novel have made it extremely controversial. It is an exploration of the kinds of societies and individuals which might exist in a single-sex civilization. Like Joanna Russ, Charnas challenges the accepted ideas about the relationships between men and women.

Biographical/Bibliographical Readings

Marleen S. Barr, *Suzy McKee Charnas, Octavia Butler, Joan D. Vinge* (Starmont House, 1986). Neal Wilgus, "Interview with Suzy McKee Charnas," *Algol* 16 (Winter, 1978-79), p.21-25. **[Linda K. Lewis]**

CHERRYH, C. J.

Life and Works

C. J. Cherryh (Carolyn Janice Cherry) was born on September 1, 1942, in St. Louis, Missouri. She was educated at the University of Oklahoma, receiving a B.A. in 1964 in Latin. In 1965, she received an M.A. in classics from Johns Hopkins University, where she was a Woodrow Wilson Fellow. From 1965 to 1977, she taught Latin and ancient history in the Oklahoma City Public Schools. She has been a free-lance writer since 1977. In 1980-81, she taught at Central State University as well as being their Artist-in-Residence. Cherryh is a member of the Science Fiction Writers of America, the Space Studies Institute, the L-5 Society, and Phi Beta Kappa. Her current residence is Edmond, Oklahoma.

Her first book, *Gate of Ivrel* (1976), is science fiction/fantasy at its best. Her first work won Cherryh the praise of the science fiction world and the 1977 Campbell award for the most promising new writer. Along with *Fires of Azeroth* (1979) and *The Well of Shiuan* (1978), *Gate* forms *The Book of Morgaine* (1979). Further adventures of Morgaine and Vanye appear in *Exile's Gate* (1988). Other novels appearing in 1976 were *Brothers of Earth* and *Hunter of Worlds*. Her collection *Sunfall* (1981) is a collection of stories, some fiction and some fantasy, set in the various major cities of Earth.

Cherryh's Faded Sun series, *Kesrith* (1978), *Shon'jir* (1979), and *Kutath* (1980), offer what some consider to be her most successful creation of an alien culture, the mri, a race of interplanetary mercenaries. "Cassandra" (1978), a psychological tale, won the Hugo award in 1979 for best short story. Cherryh's latest series began with *The Pride of Chanur* (1982) in which she creates an alien race of catlike beings called hani. This work was followed by the trilogy, *Chanur's Venture* (1984), *The Kif Stike Back* (1985), and *Chanur's Homecoming* (1986). The year 1985 was a busy one for Cherryh. Besides the volumes of the Chanur series, she also published *Angel with the Sword* and *Cuckoo's Egg*.

Downbelow Station (1981), which won the Hugo award in 1982, is a complex story of interstellar warfare and political intrigue. Its sequel, *Merchanters's Luck*, followed in 1982. *Port Eternity* (1982) combines science fiction and fantasy. Her most recent writings, both short stories and one novel (*Legion of Hell*, 1987) have been in the series about Hell started by Janet Morris. Cherryh has proven to be one of the most prolific and yet consistently good writers of science fiction and science fantasy in the field and has won the major awards for her works.

Themes and Style

Cherryh's background in the classics and anthrolopology has helped her in making the cultures that she creates realistic. A prolific and inventive author of science fiction and fantasy, Cherryh creates startling yet believable alien characters and worlds. Many of Cherryh's novels are tales of interstellar or intercultural conflict. Her central characters are usually strong females; they often rule matriarchal societies in which traditional gender characteristics are reversed. The complexity and ambition of Cherryh's work has been praised by many critics, but the same qualities have also led to charges of obscurity.

Setting her novels in extremely complex alien cultures, Cherryh examines two recurring themes--absolute power, especially by a woman, and cultures which shape lives. One key to Cherryh's success is her unconventional treatment of male and female personality traits. Sometimes Cherryh's works manifest a romantic faith that society, in particular a society with extended households linking groups larger than the nuclear family, is preferable to the society of the West. Cherryh's works also have a hint of pessimism, not about human society, but about the objective human condition. Cherryh protagonists triumph spiritually over adversity, but only infrequently is their worldly position better at the end of the tale than at the beginning, and the wicked usually come away both unrepentant and unpunished. Contrary to conventional wisdom, this pessimism does not seem to be hurting Cherryh's popularity; perhaps readers take it as a sign of realism.

Only a decade into her career, Cherryh still has not made her way into the very front rank of science fiction writers. She is not too far behind, however, and there remains a strong possibility that she will make up the remaining distance.

Cherryh has an uncanny ability to plunge the reader into the heart of an alien culture. She unfolds her tales with skill and restraint, and without the convenient device of the handy history book or a friendly psychologist to explain the structure of society of the hero. One who enjoys cultures and languages will enjoy Cherryh.

Plot Summaries of Major Works

Angel with the Sword. Set on the planet Merovin, in the city of Merovingen, the heroine is Altair Jones, a young canaler. While delivering a cargo of smuggled goods, she saves the life of Thomas Mondragon, a mysterious man, who wants someone dead. But why? The rest of the story follows Altair as she tries to answer this question, with little or no help from Mondragon. The life of the canaler becomes involved with that of the upper classes and with those in between, which presents a large cast of well-drawn characters. At the end, the reader learns that Mondragon is the last survivor of an old family from Nev Hettek.

Much of the story revolves around the relationship of the poor girl, Altair, and the rich and handsome Mondragon. The setting and mood is evocative of Renaissance Italy. This mood is aided by the Venetian atmosphere of Merovin, with its canals and palazzos. Merovin has been allowed only low technology, but there are a few motors and nerve gas. The title refers to the statue of the angel which sits on one of the major bridges of Merovingen. It is a gilt figure, twice life size, of a winged figure either drawing or sheathing a sword. The sculpture is interpreted differently by the various religious groups on Merovin, but all agree it has significance for the future of the city. The meticulously depicted world of Merovin is an interesting one which also appears in a number of short stories including the collection *Festival Moon* (1987), written by Cherryh and friends.

"Cassandra." This short story has as its heroine Crazy Alis, who has spent a lifetime in and out of mental hospitals because she sees things. Truly she does see the future, but as the title implies, no one believes her. Because no one ever believes her, she learns to keep quiet. Everyday she goes out for coffee and a sandwich and there meets Jim. They spend the afternoon together and have dinner later. When the city is bombed, her visions of fire and ruin come true. Alis and Jim hide in the cellar and after they leave the safety of the cellar, Jim is crushed by a falling wall.

Crazy Alis gives the reader a unique perspective in this psychological story. She suffers from the curse of Cassandra, the ability to predict the future, but no one believes her until it is too late.

Chanur series. This series consists of the original novel, *The Pride of Chanur*, and the trilogy: *Chanur's Venture*, *The Kif Strike Back*, and *Chanur's Homecoming*. In the first novel, the reader is introduced to Pyanfur Chanur, captain of the *Pride*. Pyanfar is a hani, a catlike race. The other races are the kif, the mahendo'sat, the stsho, and three methane-breathing races, the knnn, chi, and tc'a. These races have a compact for trade and all use Meetpoint Station as a neutral meeting ground. The reader gets to know most of these races during the series, but especially the kif, a grey, long-snout faced race who use treachery as a way of life. The kif are also ambitious and want to control Compact space. The mahendo'sat do not want this to happen and work to keep the hani, especially Pyanfar, in the middle of a struggle. Pyanfar's role as a middlewoman does not suit all of the hani clans, so she must worry about internal hani politics as well.

To further complicate the story, Pyanfar picks up a strange bipedal creature at Meetpoint Station, who turns out to be a human named Tully. In *The Pride of Chanur*, the kif had taken Tully and several other humans captive to try to learn the location of human space. In the trilogy, Tully returns to Compact space once again. He, and humanity in general, play a minor role in this story of a power struggle among alien races. Tully is mainly a stimulus for events, not a hero, and the happy ending is none of his devising. He is powerless and desperate among the aliens.

The hani are truly alien, for all their Earthly models, and the reader can identify with them. It is a mark of Cherryh's success that here it is the human who seems the alien, though one gets the feeling that hani and human should get along very well. It is the hani females who travel into space. The male hani are too unstable to leave their home world, where they are constantly aggravated into near psychosis by the territorial imperatives that have left the society an agglomeration of family holdings under constant internecine aggression. During the trilogy, Pyanfar breaks this rule by taking her husband Khym with her. He eventually learns to function with the crew.

In the original novel and the trilogy which follows, Cherryh presents a very well-drawn alien race. The story is told from the viewpoint of Pyanfar Chanur. She learns to communicate with the human, Tully. In the complexity of the plot and in the concern for who will eventually be in control, this series resembles *Downbelow Station*. In the Chanur series, the aliens are the main characters and what is up for grabs, control of Compact space, is much larger than just a Station, although Meetpoint does remind the reader of Pell Station. The series also provides complications from the internal politics of the different species.

Downbelow Station. This complex novel tells the story of the formation of the Merchanters' Alliance and how Pell Station (or Downbelow Station) became its headquarters. The introduction points out the importance of Downbelow Station in the history of Earth's expansion into space. The planet underneath this station, which revolves around Pell's Star, was the first planet with other life discovered by Earth's Company. Now those who live in the Beyond, called Union, are in revolt against the Earth Company and Pell is caught in the middle.

The large diffuse cast of characters include Signy Mallory, a hardened starship captain; the Konstantin family which controls Downbelow Station; Satin, a hisa, one of the natives of Downbelow; Sergrest Ayres, representative of the Company; and Jon Talley, a prisoner of war who may be more dangerous than anyone realizes. There is no single narrator, so the reader goes back and forth between the viewpoint of the major factions, and it takes a while to understand who is who. Besides the major conflict, there are also smaller ones. The control of the Station by the Konstantin family is challenged by Jon Lukas. Alien (hisa) and human relations are strained and become even more so. The Company is also evaluating its support for its stations.

There is much personal conflict in the novel, but the story itself is impersonal, a confrontation of empires. Union is the monolithic, impersonal, controlling State, and it clearly seems the villain. But Earth is equally monolithic, cocooned in bureaucracy (though there are signs of emergence), perhaps equally the villain. The merchanters are the last reservoir of individualism and the future may belong to them. The heros are of Pell, however. They are neutral and largely lost in the shadows of the superpowers.

Cherryh's obvious delight in creating and peopling a relative near-future galaxy with alien races and human colonies is in the mainstream of science fiction concerns, but only in works like *Downbelow Station* does it become traditional space opera, with battling spacecraft and intergalactic intrigues. Cherryh's novels are an indication of a maturation of space opera, and *Downbelow Station* justly deserves the Hugo for its depiction of not merely huge screen effects, but for its number of individual portraits.

Its sequel, *Merchanter's Luck*, narrows the focus of *Downbelow Station* by concentrating on the transformation of two merchants forced to overcome their distrust of one another through their mutual need for survival.

Biographical/Bibliographical Readings

Mary T. Brizzi, "C. J. Cherryh and Tomorrow's New Sex Roles," in *The Feminine Eye: Science Fiction and the Women Who Write It*, ed. Tom Staicar (Ungar, 1982), p.32-47. Thomas Wiloch, "Carolyn Janice Cheery," in *Contemporary Authors New Revision Series* (Gale, 1983), v.10, p.95-96. [Mina Jane Grothey]

CLARKE, ARTHUR C.

Life and Works

Arthur Charles Clarke was born in Minehead, Somerset, England, on December 16, 1917. His family lived in a farming area and early on he developed an interest in astronomy and an addiction to the science fiction pulp magazines, particularly Gernsback's *Amazing Stories*. Not having the monetary means to purchase a telescope, he built his own. As a youngster, he was bright and inventive in other ways as well (at thirteen, he built a photophonic transmitter from a bicycle headlight). Clarke attended the Huish's Grammar School in Somerset from 1927 to 1936, and then initiated his writing interests by becoming assistant editor for the school newspaper and contributed some scientific short pieces to the newspaper. Before entering college, Clarke worked in London as auditor in His Majesty's Exchequer and Audit Department from 1936 to 1941. From its inception in 1936, Clarke was an active member of the British Interplanetary Society. During the war years, he served as a Royal Air Force Instructor. During the war, he contributed his now famous ideas for the use of communications satellites in stationary orbits around the Earth. In his spare time, he contributed various scientific articles to the British Interplanetary Society publications and some science fiction fanzines. After World War II ended, Clarke attended King's College from 1946 to 1948 and earned a B.S. in physics and mathematics. He also became active in the British Astronomical Association. In 1954, he married Marilyn Mayfield and they moved to Ceylon (now Sri Lanka), but were divorced in 1964. Clarke continues to live in Colombo, Sri Lanka, and has used the Indian Ocean islands as the setting for many of his works; his later works also involve the use of Oriental names and histories.

Clarke's first science fiction writings were for the British science fiction fanzine, *Nova Terrae*, and were essays about the ideas becoming prevalent in science fiction at the time. In June, 1937, his article, "Science Fiction--Past, Present, and Future" stressed the importance of the accurate presentation of scientific information about rocketry and space travel. His first paid articles were "Man's Empire of Tomorrow" (1938) and "We Can Rocket to the Moon--Now" in 1939. He contributed other nonfiction articles to the *Journal of the British Interplanetary Society*.

He had started "Against the Fall of Night" in 1937, but it was not published until 1948. Even with five revisions, from 1937 to 1946, Clarke was still not satisfied with the novel and rewrote and expanded it into *The City and The Stars* in 1956. In the mid 1940s, he began submitting stories to *Astounding Science Fiction*; John W. Campbell published "Loophole" in the April, 1946 issue and "Rescue Party" in May of 1946. From this point on, Clarke became a full-fledged science fiction author known both in England and the United States. Clarke's first novel-length science fiction book was *Prelude to Space* (1951). His novels include *The Sands of Mars* (1952); the short novel *Childhood's End* (1954) which has become one of his most popular and enduring works; *A Fall of Moondust* (1961); *Rendezvous with Rama* (1973); *Imperial Earth* (1975); and the extremely popular *2001: A Space Odyssey* (1968) and its sequels *2010: Odyssey Two* (1982) and *2061: Odyssey Three* (1987); and *The Songs of Distant Earth* (1986). *2001* and *2010* have been made into enormously popular motion pictures; the third sequel will no doubt follow. The original *2001* was based on a short story, "The Sentinel" (1951), and was commissioned from Clarke by Stanley Kubrick. The novel followed after the screenplay and movie were produced. Because of the popularity of the original movie, Clarke wrote *The Lost Worlds of 2001* in 1972, which included the original story and the different versions of the screenplay as it was being written. His short stories have been anthologized in many works and in his own collections, including *Reach for Tomorrow* (1962), *The Nine Billion Names of God* (1967), which contains Clarke's selections of his own favorite stories introduced by notes about the stories (1972), *Tales from the White Hart*, and *The Best of Arthur C. Clarke* (1973). His work, *The View from Serendip* (1977), is a miscellany of autobiography and essays.

In addition to his literary works, Clarke has been a presenter on the television series, Arthur C. Clarke's Mysterious World, in 1980 and was the CBS commentator for the flights of Apollo 11, 12, and 15. He is widely respected for his scientific knowledge and his ability to interpret and explain scientific information for the layperson. He has received numerous awards over the years, both for his scientific achievements and in the field of science fiction. He received the American Association for the Advancement of Science Westinghouse Award in 1969 and UNESCO's Kalinga Prize for the popularization of science in 1962. He was honored with a Nebula Grand Master Award in 1986. Hugo and Nebula awards have been presented to Clarke for *Rendezvous with Rama*, *The Fountains of Paradise*, and the short story, "The Star" (1956). *Rendezvous with Rama* won, in addition to the Hugo and Nebula awards, the John W. Campbell Memorial Award, the Jupiter Award, and the British Science Fiction Award. He received the Nebula award for "A Meeting with Medusa" in 1972.

Themes and Style

Clarke's works do not fall easily into any one category of science fiction. Although he has stayed away, for the most part, from space battles, he has written stories and novels incorporating most of the major themes of science fiction--alien contact, utopias, colonization of other planets by seeding programs, space travel, and humanity's future both on Earth and in space. His works are scientifically and technically supported, even to the extent that he often adds acknowledgements at the end of the work which give credit for the ideas he has extrapolated upon. At the end of *The Fountains of Paradise*, he credits a Leningrad engineer with the concept for the space elevator in the novel. He cites specific articles, journals, and authors whenever he gives the credits, thus giving his works a sense of having a solid scientific basis.

If any one adjective could be used to describe Clarke's themes regarding the future of the human race, it would have to be "optimistic." Somehow, humanity always lands on its feet and even in the worst of situations, there is usually a feeling of hope for the future. In *A Fall of Moondust* (1961), the victims are caught in the tour shuttle which has slipped beneath the sands of the moon and are rescued after many harrowing attempts, each of which appear to be the last hope for survival. This is not to say that Clarke's endings are always happy. Many critics feel that *Childhood's End* posits a tragic future for mankind, as the remaining children on Earth evolve into a nonphysical superconsciousness and Earth is destroyed. Yet the ending is not without hope; the collective mind of the children can be seen as something greater toward which humanity should be striving. This theme also predominates in *2001* and *2010*, with the protagonist appearing in varying forms from a fetus to an ancient human. Clarke has theorized in several of his works that perhaps humanity in its present physical form will not be the best way to reach the stars and travel through the universe. A nonphysical form of a highly intelligent mental state without any organic form would be the fastest way to traverse the cosmos.

Aliens are sometimes presented in their physical forms, and frequently Clarke does not describe the aliens, but allows readers to use their own imaginations to picture the aliens based on the ships and artifacts discovered--the prime examples being the gigantic space ship Rama in *Rendezvous with Rama* and the monoliths of the *2001* series. The aliens are generally benevolent; even the demonlike Overlords in *Childhood's End* are seen as saving the world from war, plague, and poverty. Clarke's affinity with sea creatures is evident in many of the sentient and nonsentient aliens in his works. Many of his alien creatures are comparable to giant polyps (interestingly enough, the sea creatures can be seen as humanity's predecessors, if evolution follows the same path on other worlds), crablike creatures, jellyfish, etc. *Rendezvous with Rama* and the *2001* novels also illustrate Clarke's use of geometric figures: the spaceship is cylindrical, the monoliths are rectangles, the space elevator in *The Fountains of Paradise* is more or less triangular. The laws of geometry are universal and inescapable and are the basis for mutual contact and understanding.

Arthur C. Clarke has enjoyed a great degree of popularity and respect during his thirty-eight years as science fiction author and scientist. He has written over fifty books which have sold over twenty million copies and have been printed in more than thirty languages. He has not been as prolific as Isaac Asimov, and he humorously states that he will probably never be able to catch up to nor surpass Asimov's output in his lifetime. Regardless of the quantity, Clarke's works have enlightened, entertained, and given to science fiction fans a true sense of wonder and a faith in humanity's future.

Plot Summaries of Major Works

Childhood's End. In 1976, just as humanity is preparing to launch space probes to the stars, the stars come to Earth. The great spaceships settle directly over the major cities of the world. For the first few years, the aliens remain unseen; all that is known is that the leader is Karellen and the aliens are called Overlords. The Overlords bring to Earth serenity, peace, and prosperity for the first time in human history. Ignorance, disease, poverty, and crime have virtually disappeared, as have most religions, scientific experimentation, and the creative arts. Utopia has arrived. After five years, Karellen informs Earth that in fifty years, the Overlords will reveal themselves to mankind. Finally, the year 2030 arrives, the great ship lands in New York (there had only been one--the others were illusions). With the crowd's mounting anticipation and the Earth's billions watching on their television sets, Karellen comes out of the ship--a huge being with an ebony body, little horns, barbed tail, and leathery wings and a child resting on each arm.

Humanity accepts the Overlords--how could it not, considering that Earth had come to a state of near perfection? Years pass, and at a party one of the Overlords meets several people who will be greatly affected in the near future by the Overlords and their mission. Jean Morrel and George Greggson are soon to be married. Jan Rodericks is a student of physics and engineering with a minor in astronomy. At a seance, both Jean and Jan are deeply affected by something or someone. Jean receives a message that "man is not alone" and Jan receives the answer to his question about the original planet of the Overlords, a number which he recognizes as a star catalog identification. He researches the number and realizes that he is the only man on Earth who knows the planet of origin of the Overlords. He devises a plan to stow away aboard one of the supply ships. Jan prepares a cylinder inside the taxidermic sample of a whale and when the ships takes off, Jan is on his way into space, realizing that it will be at least eighty years before he returns to Earth, although he will only have aged a few months.

Jean and George Greggson, with their children Jeffrey and Jennifer, decide to settle in New Athens, a commune on a remote Polynesian island dedicated to the sustaining of the creative arts and to independent scientific experimentation. In the idealistic New Athens, the Greggsons first notice the change in Jeffrey, who begins to have strange dreams (interpreted by the Overlords as views of distant planets beyond the solar system, even beyond the galaxy). Jennifer, still in her crib, begins to withdraw from the "real" world and exhibits signs of telepathy. Finally the Greggsons and the rest of the world are told that the Overlords have been merely the guardians, and that they are ruled by the Overmind. Jeffrey and Jennifer are the first of Earth's children to be affected by the transformation of the children to a state of pure mental energy which will merge with the Overmind. Mankind realizes in horror that, without the children, their world will come to an end.

Eighty years later, Jan Rodericks returns to Earth; he has seen a great deal but understood little of the Overlord's planet. He is shown the tape of the children as they progress toward the state of pure mental energy. Soon the Overlords depart, their job done. As the last man on Earth, Rodericks watches the Earth disintegrate as the children's collective minds leave the Earth like a great auroral storm on their way to join the Overmind. Karellen watches the end of Earth from far out in space, and contemplates what planet will be his next mission.

Childhood's End is a mind-boggling and complex novel that has been studied and analyzed for years. The themes are many and varied--utopias, alien invasions, space travel, metaphysics, religion, and human psychology, to name a few. The shock of seeing an alien as a Satanic creature, the devil, is explained by the Overlords as a premonition of the future, rather than a prehistoric memory of an earlier alien visit. Their carefully laid plans assure that most religions would be eliminated by the time they showed themselves. As Clarke has implied in other novels, the stars are not for humanity in its present, physical form, but rather the only true form of exploration must be in the form of pure mental energy. The ending is tragically sad, yet not without hope--humanity as a race has not survived, but the collective mentality of the children will be exploring the universe for eternity.

The City and the Stars. Billions of years in Earth's future, the only city left on a desertlike Earth is Diaspar. The city is totally controlled by the Central Computer; even the "birth" and "death" of the million inhabitants of Diaspar. The Memory Banks retain the genes in the Hall of Creation and, in logical patterns, create and send out young men or women into the city for life spans of thousands of years. Simultaneously, those individuals who have "lived out" their life span return to the Hall of Creation, where their genes are stored in the Memory Banks until their next lifetime. Immortality, in a sense, has been achieved.

Alvin is different. He is a unique. His mentor and tutor is Jeserac, who realizes Alvin's uniqueness, but does not quite know what to do with him. Alvin is endowed with much curiosity, ambition, and drive, qualities not evident in the other citizens of Diaspar. His desire is to leave the city and explore what is left of Earth. Alvin accesses the Memory Banks and studies the holographic images of the city. His studies bring him to the Tomb of Yarlan Zey, one of the founders of Diaspar. Beneath the tomb is found an underground passage with a long, streamlined machine. Alvin boards the machine for "Lys."

Arriving at Lys, Alvin finds a lovely, pastoral scene and a friendly, telepathic group of humans, and to his shock, he sees infants and old people (never seen in Diaspar). The people of Lys have retained many of Earth's old ways, the most important being normal procreation and death. They want to remain separate from Diaspar, to avoid contamination by curiosity seekers and others who might venture there. Alvin becomes friends with Hilvar and together they explore Lys. At the site of the Battle of Shalmirane, where the Invaders had driven humanity from the Universe back to Earth, Alvin and Hilvar find a small robot, which takes up with Alvin, and a huge polyplike creature in a lake of blackness. Before it dissolves in the black waters, the polyp tells of the Great Ones from the planets of the Seven Suns.

Alvin returns to Diaspar with the robot. He appears before the Council of Diaspar and tells them of Lys. The subterranean passage is sealed off, since neither Diaspar nor Lys want anything to do with each other, but Alvin is determined to join the two cities for the welfare of the human race. The robot finds an old spaceship hidden in the desert sands, and Alvin and Hilvar set out to explore the planets of the Seven Suns. Their search of the planets is disappointing. No intelligent life forms exist, but just as they plan to return to Earth, Hilvar experiences telepathy with a mental form of life that is extremely knowledgable, but immature and undeveloped. It calls itself Vanamonde.

When they return to Earth, the pure mentality, Vanamonde, relates the true history of Earth to the citizens of Diaspar and Lys, who have begun to accept each other cautiously. Vanamonde was created by Earthmen billions of years earlier (the first mentality created had been insane and its "Mad Mind" was imprisoned in the Black Sun). Vanamonde was sent out to explore the universe while humanity remained on Earth. Humanity's two greatest fears were the fear of space and the fear of death; their greatest task would now be to overcome these fears and begin again. Alvin sent the spaceship into the far universe under the guidance of the robot in the hope of finding the ancestors of the Solar System Empire. In his last flight on the ship, Alvin shows Jeserac and Hilvar the Earth from the North Pole. Night is falling on one side of the Earth, but the stars and the rising sun appear on the other side, offering hope and the fulfillment of destiny.

The novel was originally published in a shorter form as *Against the Fall of Night* in *Startling Stories* in 1948. Clarke revised and expanded it for the novel. Through the desires and courage of two young men--Alvin, a unique, and Hilvar--the remaining two cities of the human race come together after billions of years. Each city has its own virtues--Diaspar has the technology, while Lys has the naturalistic, almost romantic impulses of Earth as it once was and has retained the biological means of reproduction necessary to fulfill humanity's destiny. Diaspar reminds the reader of New York, a huge, sprawling metropolis with a "central park" where people can amuse themselves. Lys, with its countrylike setting and groupings of small villages, is a utopian, pastoral scene. Together, the citizens of Lys and Diaspar realize that it is time for humanity to begin again to find its way back to the stars.

The Fountains of Paradise. The story begins in the twenty-second century, almost 200 years since the dawn of the Space Age. Vannevar Morgan is the chief engineer of the land division of the Terran Construction Company. His prior achievements include most notably the Gibralter Bridge, a huge span over the Mediterranean linking Morocco and Spain. Thanks to a new development of an ultrastrong fiber called hyperfilament, Van Morgan has a new dream--to build a space elevator or orbital tower to space and the stars. The location for the base of the space elevator must be on the equator and ideally at the summit of Mount Yakkagala, in the country of Taprobane. At the top of the mountain is the monastery of monks presided over by the High Priest, and the country is ruled by Ambassador-at-Large Rajasinghe. Both these men initially resist Morgan's efforts to build the space elevator on the mountain, because it would deface the monastery and belittle the beautiful fountains and gardens built shortly after Christ by King Kalidasa.

In the interim period since the space age began, Earth has been visited by a robot space probe from a distant galaxy called Starglider. Starglider learned much and gave much to humans, and prepared humanity for the arrival of its alien masters, which the humans called the Starholmers.

Although he has been denied access to Taprobane by the World Court, Morgan does receive permission to launch an experiment called "Project Gossamer," which will lower a fiber of hyperfilament from space to Taprobane. At the last moment of the test, a strong gale deviates the fiber from its destination and crushes Morgan's hope for success. However, the gale turns out to be his best friend--it inadvertently destroys one of Taprobane's oldest legends, forcing the monks to depart, and Morgan begins the ten-year task of building the space elevator.

Morgan, already in his mid-fifties, knowing that he has a heart problem, has a "smart pacemaker" (Cora) implanted in his chest to warn him when he overexerts himself. All is going extremely well when tragedy occurs. A group of scientists, studying the evergrowing solar disturbances, are trapped on the space elevator. Morgan realizes that he must be the one to take them needed oxygen and supplies, until help can come from one of the higher stations. After several tense delays, Morgan does make it to the scientists, and drops off the supplies. On the way up, his pacemaker, Cora, had warned him that he must rest, but he is too busy. As he starts back down, he admires the solar flares and the beautiful Earth and the wonder of his project, so near to completion. His heart has taken too much exertion, however, and Cora's cries for an ambulance, though heard on Earth, cannot save him.

The project is completed and the Starholmers arrive years later during the New Ice Age to find that humanity has deserted Earth for the other planets and the "space ring" connected to the many space elevator stations built since Morgan's time. The humans wait for the winter to spend itself, at which time they can return, renewed and refreshed, to begin again.

In *The Fountains of Paradise*, Clarke beautifully intermingles the building of the space elevator with the 2,000 year old history of Taprobane. The gardens, the fountains linking Earth to Paradise, and the frescos of Kalidasa are woven into the project which will take humanity to the stars. Clarke, as usual, is very precise in his descriptions of the details involved in the project, even to the extent of including an acknowledgement of the idea at the end of the work. There are enlightening looks at the future of Earth, with Rajasinghe's personal computer console, nicknamed "Aristotle," which keeps him apprised of the progress of the elevator, and Morgan's "Personal Interest Profile," which is a futuristic selective dissemination of information for many of Earth's inhabitants. Clarke's use of geometric figures is predominant in the novel, as the space elevator is compared to an Eiffel tower turned upside down, and by the use of triangular patterns at the head of each chapter. The mountain itself casts a triangular shadow on Earth each morning at sunrise. The touch of optimism is prevalent as well. The alien Starholmers are friendly and their close link with the children of Earth is quite touching at the close of the novel. Even though Earth must be abandoned, it will only be temporary, and Clarke closes the novel with the assurance that humanity will survive and return and rebuild.

Rendezvous with Rama. Set in the twenty-second century, Spaceguard Headquarters sights a huge object approaching on a specific path through the solar system. It is christened Rama. On a fly-by space probe launched from Mars, the object proves to be a large, dull grey cylinder obviously made by some form of intelligent life. The excitement is overwhelming--at last, the solar system has visitors from the stars. The Space Advisory Council notifies Commander Bill Norton of the solar survey ship, *Endeavor*, that he must investigate the cylinder, as his is the closest ship to be able to rendezvous with Rama. The exploration study will be short, only three weeks, as Rama flies close to the sun toward its unknown destination.

Commander Norton and his crew land on Rama and Norton compares his entry into the cylinder to that of Carter entering the tomb of Tutankhamen. In the total darkness inside the cylinder, the crew discovers three enormous stairways leading down into a great plain, a circular sea, and six projectile areas which remind them of Earth cities and which they name New York, Rome, Paris, Peking, Tokyo, Moscow, and London. Everything in the world within the cylinder is shiny and new and appears unused. Space Advisory Council warns Norton that the sea may melt and cause something like a hurricane in the internal world. Before this happens, the lights come on and the crew sees the enormous world for the first time. The crew explores the "cities" and the sea, whose ice is already beginning to melt, and a way is found to cross over the sea and explore the "South Pole," an area with no stairways, but which has a huge central spike surrounded by six smaller ones. A young lieutenant, Jimmy Pak, has brought with him an aerobatic flyer (sort of a bicycle) on which he can fly to the "South Pole" and back. On the way back, his flyer crashes due to an electrical storm, and Jimmy sees the first alien on Rama. It is a robotic, crablike creature. He is rescued from the "South Pole" area by a raft devised by the crew.

During their further explorations, the crew discovers other robotlike creatures, ranging from spiderlike robots with three legs, three eyes, and three tendrils (nicknamed Daddy Long Legs), a giant starfish, and lobster creatures in the circular sea. For the most part, the robots appear to be either janitors performing clean-up duties or spotters, checking up on the Earth visitors, but not harassing them. During one of their last expeditions (Norton and the *Endeavor* must leave soon, as Rama is getting very close to the sun), they find a museum or a "catalogue" of all of the possible tools, equipment, even a uniform assumed to be fitted for a Raman. As the crew prepares to leave, the lights start to go out. Darkness comes to the cylinder once again as it comes closest to the sun. Back on the *Endeavor*, Norton and the crew watch Rama as it circles the sun, recharging itself and drawing energy. Its nature and purpose are still unknown, and Norton is somewhat discouraged to realize that the solar system was merely a refueling stop for Rama. The mounds of information, the few artifacts, including one Daddy Long Legs and one blue flower picked by Jimmy Pak, will be studied by human scientists for years to come.

Clarke has combined space science and a hearty, tense adventure story into the novel. *Rendezvous with Rama* is very well written, and Clarke's major character, Commander Norton, carefully prepares and carries out the exploration while keeping the safety and welfare of his crew and ship uppermost in his mind. Once again, Clarke uses geometrical figures--the cylinder itself, the spikes at the South Pole which are like cones, and the three sets of stairways leading into the cylinder. Clarke explains many of the scientific details by way of chapters in which the Space Advisory Council instructs and advises the crew on what to expect in its exploration. The novel is a sign of humanity's still rather limited view of space, in that the world inside the hollow cylinder is so often compared with Earth; at this point in time, there are not many other points of reference. The tension is constant, as each new discovery is made and documented. The exploration is a "new frontier" and the hope is that, somehow, humanity may benefit from the rendezvous. Even though the Ramans did not appear, the crew is left in awe of the superior intelligence that could produce such a ship and send it on such a long journey. Perhaps the Ramans will follow.

The Songs of Distant Earth. The planet Thalassa is mostly ocean, with three small islands inhabited by humans, whose ancestors were brought to Thalassa on "seedling ships" when it was discovered that the Earth's sun was going to turn nova. Thalassans are a happy, unagressive people whose main interest is oceanography, a natural consequence of their primary surroundings. Marissa, her husband, Brant Falconer, and her brother, Kumar, are surprised one night to see some sort of spaceship landing. A group of native Thalassans investigate and discover that the ship is a small exploratory vehicle from Earth; its mother ship, the *Magellan*, is in orbit around Thalassa. The *Magellan* was one of the last ships to leave Earth and the Solar System before the sun exploded. Its captain, Sirdar Bey, and Moses Kaldor, an ambassador, explain to the Thalassans that they need to replenish their ablation shield with ice from the oceans in order to continue to their destination, the planet Sagan Two. A freezing plant is constructed and the two year process of building the ice shield is begun. Lt. Commander Loren Lorenson, leader of the Snowflake project, falls in love with Marissa and she eventually becomes pregnant with his child. Her husband, Brant, an oceanographer, along with Kumar, who loves the sea, takes Loren out to repair the underwater power supply and Loren sees some of the strange life forms on the planet, among them a giant jellyfishlike creature nicknamed "Polly the Polyp." Loren realizes that Thalassa's oceans are the beginnings of evolutionary life on the planet. His ideas are further confirmed when the exploratory ship, *Calypso*, discovers the existence of lobsterlike, semi-intelligent creatures they call "scorps" beneath the sea. Loren falls overboard and is saved from drowning by Kumar.

While Loren explores the sea, Moses Kaldor, the ambassador and old wise man, studies the library memory banks on Thalassa (which had been heavily censored due to lack of space) and supplements it with data from the *Magellan*.

As the time approaches for the *Magellan* to leave, Captain Bey, Moses, and Loren come to realize that they are the aliens on the planet Thalassa and they must leave the Thalassans to their own destinies. In a tragic accident, Kumar is killed while investigating the ice-making plant. *Magellan* departs, but each group has kept something from the other. Marissa has Loren's child within her, Brant has gained the ambition to study and watch the evolution of the scorps and other life on the planet. Loren takes with him the knowledge that his child will be born on Thalassa and form a bond between the two planets, although he will not know of it until the end of his cryogenic sleep in three hundred years. Each group goes to their own destiny, in different ways, yet each knows that somewhere in the universe are their friends and that humanity continues.

The Songs of Distant Earth are heard by Kumar as he investigates the cable running from the ice block on Thalassa to the mother ship--the rhythmical sounds eminating from the ship are the closest he will ever come to knowing Earth. Clarke gives a very detailed view of the destruction of the Solar System and the gigantic efforts made by humanity to seed the planets with its offspring. In a touching scene, Loren takes Marissa aboard the *Magellan*, and shows her the sleepers, watched over by the Guardian (the gold funereal mask of Tutankhamen). Marissa notes the resemblance between the young Pharoah and her brother, Kumar, both of whom died too young. As in other Clarke works, the novel places great emphasis on the evolution of the creatures from the sea; the beginnings are the same throughout the universe. Clarke's joie de vivre leaves one with a good feeling about humanity's future. Whatever the catastrophes, the decadence, the destruction, mankind will successfully overcome and endure.

Biographical/Bibliographical Readings

"Arthur C. Clarke," in *Voices for the Future*, ed. Thomas D. Clareson (Bowling Green University Popular Press, 1976) v.1, p.216-37. *Arthur C. Clarke*, ed. Joseph Olander and Martin Harry Greenberg (Taplinger, 1977). Arthur C. Clarke, *The View from Serendip* (Random House, 1977). Sam Moskowitz, "Arthur C. Clarke," in *Seekers of Tomorrow* (World, 1966), p.374-91. Eric S. Rabkin, *Arthur C. Clarke* (Starmont House, 1979). David N. Samuelson, *Arthur C. Clarke: A Primary and Secondary Bibliography* (G. K. Hall, 1984). Idem, "Arthur C. Clarke," in *Science Fiction Writers*, ed. E. F. Bleiler (Scribner's, 1982), p.313-20. **[Marilyn P. Fletcher]**

CLEMENT, HAL

Life and Works

Hal Clement is the pen name of Harry Clement Stubbs. Clement was born on May 30, 1922, in Somerville, Massachusetts, a few miles north of Boston. After attending public schools in nearby Arlington and Cambridge, Clement entered Harvard University in 1939, majoring in astronomy and receiving his B.S. degree in 1943. He then flew thirty-five missions from 1943 to 1945 as a bomber pilot and copilot stationed in England. Returning to Massachusetts after the war, he earned a master's degree in education from Boston University in 1947 and taught high school in Worchester, Massachusetts, for two years. In 1949, he began teaching at the Milton Academy, a private high school where he still teaches astronomy, chemistry, and physical science.

Clement dates his interest in both astronomy and science fiction from the same event--a Buck Rogers cartoon panel seen in 1930. When the seven year old Clement asked about the accuracy of a distance mentioned in the panel, he was sent to the library and came back with a book on astronomy under one arm and a Jules Verne novel under the other. In grade school, Clement read the pulp magazines and told the stories to his friends around Boy Scout campfires. John W. Campbell published Clement's first story, "Proof," in the June, 1942, issue of *Astounding Science Fiction*, when Clement was a junior in college. Worried that his faculty advisor might disapprove of science fiction, Clement invented a pseudonym for himself--"Hal" from his first name and "Clement" from his middle name. By the time he discovered that his advisor enjoyed science fiction, the name had recognition and commercial value, so he decided to keep using it.

Since he is a full-time teacher, Clement writes in his spare time, which explains why his science fiction output is rather small. In four decades, he has published just nine adult science fiction novels, two juvenile novels, approximately thirty pieces of short science fiction, and three collections. *Natives of Space* (1965) reprints three Clement novellas. *Small Changes* (1969; reissued in the same year as *Space Lash*) collects nine Clement short stories published between 1956 and 1966. Lester del Rey edited *The Best of Hal Clement* (1979), an anthology that includes five pieces not in either of the two earlier collections. Clement also edited *First Flight to the Moon* (1970), an anthology of science fiction speculations about journeys to the moon commemorating the first actual lunar landing by the astronauts of Apollo XI.

Themes and Style

Despite this slim output, Clement has gained a wide reputation as a master of "hard" science fiction: episodes in his fiction conform to current scientific thought or are reasonable extrapolations. Clement himself thinks of science fiction as a game between author and reader, the author using scientific principles and the reader trying to catch any mistakes. Clement is particularly good at the "game" of creating meticulously detailed alien worlds, which he then often populates with plausible, if unusual, life: Mesklin, with its variable gravity and the caterpillarlike Mesklinites (*Mission of Gravity*, 1954); Abyormen, with its eccentric orbit and cold and hot life forms (*Cycle of Fire*, 1957); and Dhrawn, with its 1500 hour day (*Starlight*, 1971). While Clement is best known for his alien worlds, five of his novels are set on Earth. However, the other three Earth settings--the Pacific Northwest as seen through alien eyes in *Iceworld* (1953), the bottom of the Pacific Ocean in *Ocean on Top* (1973), and the land and shore near Boston thousands of years from now in *The Nitrogen Fix* (1980)--are close to being alien worlds, at least to twentieth-century readers. No matter where or when the novels take place, Clement has one major theme to which everything in his fictional world relates: the gathering, recording, disseminating, and application of scientific knowledge.

By using the scientific method, scientists gather facts and deduce principles that eventually result in proven theories. This method underlies all of Clement's science fiction. Clement is aware that new data often force new hypotheses, followed by new theories; this awareness explains his fascination with exploration--five of his novels deal with the scientific exploration of new worlds. Clement is optimistic about his explorers' ability to explain such puzzling phenomena as in *Starlight* when a land-cruiser is freezing, though the atmospheric temperature is rising. Clement's scientists often become detectives, trying to understand the "motives" of the universe. Many of his scientists are actual detectives, either professional or amateur.

Mathematics is the language of science, and Clement's fiction is militantly quantitative. Clement enjoys the "slide-rule" work behind his writing more than he does the writing itself. *Mission of Gravity*, generally considered Clement's masterpiece, is so carefully quantified that we know Mesklin's dimensions, orbital period and shape, climate, gravity, etc. It is nearly impossible to get disoriented in a Clement novel--he drops enough clues for alert readers to orient themselves in space and time. Clement's insistent focus on the quantifiable leads to complaints about his "flat" style and thin characterization.

Clement considers two problems with scientific knowledge. One problem arises in those novels that have both human and alien characters--how to transmit knowledge to someone who shares neither your language nor even your planet.   Actually, Clement sidesteps this question: when his humans and aliens meet, they sit down to their language lessons and within a few pages are communicating just fine.   But if Clement sometimes glosses over the difficulties of interspecies communication, his methods are often ingenious--the symbiont in *Needle* (1950) makes patterns on his host's retina, then later vibrates his host's inner ear; and the robot Fagin in *Close to Critical* (1964) steals some alien eggs, then teaches the hatchlings to speak English.

The other problem with transmitting scientific knowledge arises in the novels that have children as important characters: how do you teach the young?   Children, Clement feels, are natural scientists--curious, openminded, independent, and confident.   His answer to the problem is to indulge their natural inclinations, but provide adult influence via information, encouragement, respect, judicious stepping aside, and correction when needed.   Clement demonstrates vividly how unsupervised children can get into trouble when Andre desChenes in *Through the Eye of a Needle* experiments on an unconscious adult by driving a picnic skewer through the adult's heart.

Finally, Clements believes in the usefulness of scientific knowledge.   Technology appears in various forms: as interstellar flyers, as information-gathering devices, as life-support suits, and, in *Ocean on Top* as an entire system for living a mile underneath the ocean's surface.   However, in Clement's science fiction, technology is ancillary to the real purpose behind gathering, recording, and transmitting scientific knowledge--survival.   If you know how the universe works, you live; if you do not know, you die.   Rescues thus figure in all of Clement's novels, since the universe tests whether his protagonists know (or can learn) how it works by placing them (or someone close to them) in life-threatening situations.   For the reader, the fun comes in trying to beat the protagonist to the solution.

Plot Summaries of Major Works

The Best of Hal Clement. "Impediment" shows an interstellar band of telepathic, mothlike pirates stymied by the individuality of human thought patterns.   In "Technical Error," astronauts marooned when their ship's power plant melts discover an abandoned alien ship enough like theirs that they attempt to start one of its jets, which in turn promptly melts.   Luckily, the accidents attract a resuce ship.   "Uncommon Sense" pits Laird Cunningham, an amateur biologist, against his two mutinous crew members.   Trapped outside his crashed ship, Cunningham observes enough about the life around him to use it to defeat the mutineers.   "Assumption Unjustified" is a vampire story, except that the "vampires" are the snakelike Thrykar and Tes, who must interrupt their honeymoon and stop on Earth to "refresh" Thrykar. "Answer" predicts what will happen if either an artificial or human brain every fully understands itself. In "Dust Rag," two scientists, blinded by the unusual phenomenon they are investigating in a crater of Earth's moon, finally save themselves by an unusual expedient. In "Bulge," Mac Hoerwitz, the eighty-one-year-old production controller of a fusion power plant on an asteroid orbiting Earth, uses the knowledge of his asteroid's peculiar orbit to escape from a band of criminals and summon the police. Despite his many terrestrial "compentency badges," Rick Suspee, the young protagonist of "Mistaken for Granted," gets himself into nearly fatal trouble on the moon. Though "Question of Guilt" is historical fiction rather than science fiction, Marc of Bistrita's determination to cure his son's hemophilia and his refusal to believe that he and his wife are cursed by the gods foreshadows important scientific attitudes. In the last story, "Stuck with It," Laird Cunningham introduces the aquatic natives of Ranta (a Finnish word meaning "shore" or "shoreline") to science, hoping their resulting technology will enable them to survive outside the oceans they have polluted.

This collection of Clement's short fiction, selected by Lester del Rey and first published between 1942 and 1976, includes at least one story from each decade of Clement's lengthy career. Given the time span involved, the most striking thing about these ten stories is how similar they are to one another, for in each Clement blends scientific facts, plausible extrapolation, disciplined imagination, and a life-and-death problem, often solved by careful thinking. Six of these stories first appeared in *Astounding Science Fiction*, the magazine best known for the kind of science fiction that Clement writes.

Close to Critical. Like the planet Mesklin in Clement's *Mission of Gravity* , the planet Tenebra is the meticulously detailed setting. Tenebra, however, is very different from Mesklin. Temebra's atmosphere is 100 times as dense as Mesklin's. Tenebra spins much less rapidly than Mesklin (a Tenebran day is 4 times as long as a terrestrial day and about 325 times as long as a day on Mesklin). Tenebra's virtually wind-free weather, driven by water-changing phases, differs completely from Mesklin's ferocious storms. But in spite of these differences, both planets are not only inhospitable to humans, but also arouse their scientific curiosity.

The prologue explains how the scientific exploration of Tenebra begins. A robot probe, constructed to survive in a corrosive environment that rapidly breaks down all metals, lands on the surface and finds the hatching ground of an obviously intelligent species, from which the probe takes ten eggs. Sixteen years pass. The robot--called Fagin from the character in Dicken's *Oliver Twist*--is still on the planet and has hatched the eggs and taught its Tenebran "orphans" enough for them to begin mapping the planet. A bathyscape is nearly ready to land the first human beings on the planet's surface. Dr. Helen Raeker, the biologist who is Fagin's principal operator, feels that everything is going smoothly, until a massive kink occurs.

Two diplomats have arrived to inspect the project--Councillors Rich and Aminadabarlee. The latter is a Drommian, larger than a human being and vaguely otterlike. Each diplomat has brought a child along--the human is Easy Rich, twelve years old; the Drommian is Aminadorneldo, seven years old. The kink is that the two children have been left alone in the bathyscape, whose rockets somehow fire, sending them down to the planet's surface. No other bathyscape exists and one cannot be constructed before Easy succumbs to Tenebra's gravity and Aminadorneldo to vitamin and oxygen deficiency. Rescue, therefore, is up to Fagin's ten pupils. Unfortunately, Nick, their leader, has discovered the tribe of Tenebrites whose hatching ground Fagin robbed. When Nick tells Swift, the leader of this tribe, about Fagin, Swift decides to capture Fagin for the robot's knowledge.

The social dynamics in *Close to Critical* are more complicated than in any Clement novel except *The Nitrogen Fix*. Although the human scientists are relatively homogeneous, Aminadabarlee is openly contemptuous of nearly everything the humans say or do, and the Tebrites--Nick's group and Swift's tribe--start out at war with one another. But Clement resolves these conflicts characteristically, by showing the survival value of cooperation. The lesson comes from mouths (and deeds) of babes: Fagin's adolescent pupils join Swift's tribe; the primitive Swift solves the problem of lifting the bathyscape; and in order to talk to Swift, Easy and Aminadorneldo must speak Swift's language together, one providing the noises the other cannot. The precocious Easy Rich reappears as Elise Rich Hoffman, a linguist, in *Starlight*.

Biographical/Bibliographical Readings

Hal Clement, "The Creation of Imaginary Beings," in *Science Fiction, Today and Tomorrow* (Harper & Row, 1974), p.259-77. Idem, "Hard Science and Tough Technologies," in *The Craft of Science Fiction* (Harper & Row, 1976), p.37-53. Chris Drumm, *A Hal Clement Checklist* (Borgo Press, 1987). Donald M. Hassler, *Hal Clement* (Starmont House, 1982). Chris Morgan, "Hal Clement," in *Science Fiction Writers*, ed. E. F. Bleiler (Scribner's, 1982), p.321-28.
[Todd H. Sammons]

COGSWELL, THEODORE R.

Life and Works

Ted Cogswell, writer and teacher, was born on March 10, 1918, in Coatesville, Pennsylvania. While still in his teens, anxious to fight fascism, he traveled to Spain to serve with the loyalist forces. He became an ambulance driver for the Spanish Republican Army and later saw service as a statistical control officer with the United States Army Air Force in India, Burma, and China from 1942 to 1946.

After World War II, Cogswell was involved in higher education as both student and teacher. He obtained his B.A. from the University of Colorado in 1948 and his M.A. from the University of Denver in 1949. He later returned to the University of Colorado to pursue further studies in English literature, which he also studied at the University of Minnesota.

He taught at the University of Minnesota, Ball State Teachers College in Muncie, Indiana, and Keystone Junior College, La Plume, Pennsylvania, until the end of his teaching career. After his death on February 3, 1987, he was buried at Arlington National Cemetery.

His work as a science fiction writer began while he was teaching at the University of Minnesota, where he met Poul Anderson and Gordon Dickson, who encouraged him to write. The decade of the 1950s saw his greatest period of productivity, and he published more than twenty short stories between 1952 and 1960. He also wrote a short novel, "The Other Cheek" (1953), and a "Star Trek" novelization, *Spock Messiah!* (1976) with Charles A. Spano. He is best remembered for his short fiction, particularly his often-anthologized "The Specter General," published in *Astounding Science Fiction* in 1952, and the even more often anthologized "The Wall around the World," which appeared in *Galaxy* in 1953. Many of his stories were collected in *The Wall around the World* (1962) and *The Third Eye* (1968). Cogswell was also a moving force behind the Institute for Twenty-First Century Studies, a sometimes serious writers' forum and forerunner of the Science Fiction Writers of America.

Themes and Style

Despite, or perhaps because of, his extensive personal military involvement, his best stories tend to resolve conflict in a largely nonviolent fashion. They almost always involve a reestablishment of harmony between the alienated halves of a divided world. This emphasis on reintegration, on the harmony that results from overcoming alienation, is part of an essentially comic vision of reality.

Reconciling the divided is in Cogswell not only the message but also the medium, for his work is notable in the way it so often defies genre categorization. As with Bradbury, Cogswell often poses the question of whether what he is writing can be classified as science fiction or fantasy. This very topic becomes grounds for discussion in the dual introduction (by Anthony Boucher and Fred Pohl) to the Pyramid collection of Cogswell's works, entitled *The Wall around the World*. Both Boucher and Pohl come to the conclusion that whatever Cogswell is writing, it is undeniably enjoyable, and in a sense his work asks for the suspension of disbelief in order that the reader may be caught up in each story's sense of wonder.

Plot Summaries of Major Works

"The Specter General." Young Sergeant Kurt Dixon of the 427th battalion of the Imperial Space Marines is called on the carpet by his commander, Colonel Harris, for having taken an unauthorized expedition into off-limits territory. Colonel Harris is a mentor figure who first grills and upbraids young Kurt for his transgression and then strips him of his rank. After letting Kurt sweat this demotion for a bit, Harris rewards Kurt for his trangression and gives him the gold feather of a Second Lieutenant. Harris explains why one must be an officer to visit the off limits area. The area was established by the 427th battalion some five hundred years earlier, during the last day of the old Empire, in order to serve as a forward maintenance station for the emperor's ships. But in those five hundred years, no ships have come. The commanders have kept the unit together to keep the battalion and their families strong, ordered, and under military discipline. The garrison and the tech schools have become thoroughly arcane and legendary.

Meanwhile, War Base Three of Sector Seven of the Galactic Protectorate, now in power after the collapse of the empire, is also in decay, having no technicians to repair their equipment. Harris's doppleganger alter ego is Conrad Krogson, commander of War Base Three. The final level of this doubling extends to the Inspector General, who is more notable for his absence than his presence and whose doubling within the Galactic Protectorate is General Carr.

Harris's second-in-command, Blick, leads other officers in a rebellion to establish a new order that will shut down the tech schools and run things right. Blick discovers that the Inspector General is merely an old imperial power suit that the 427th commanders have traditionally donned to masquerade as the I.G., in order to keep the fiction for the garrisons and its schools alive. Eventually, the double cultures meet and these two realms that so clearly need each other at last come together. After some space battling, Harris and his alter ego, Krogson, cut a deal. Krogson joins his Galactic fleet with the 427th and assumes the role of Inspector General. The hope is that, with the ships of War Base Three and the technological knowhow of the 427th, a vigorous new day may be about to dawn for the galaxy.

Cogswell's first published story, "Specter General," is clearly science fiction rather than fantasy, though it does make use of traditional archetypes. It early on sounds what will prove to be recurring Cogswellian themes: youths exploring the forbidden; mentor/pupil and father/son relationships; a divided universe that must be unified; and doppelgangerd heroes.

"The Wall around the World." Porgie is a thirteen-year-old boy who has a lust for forbidden knowledge. In a world that condemns machines and is based on magic, Porgie wants to fly by mechanical means so that he can see what is over the Wall. He encounters opposition from his schoolmaster, Mr. Wickens who upbraids him for his heretical ideas. Wickens shows Porgie a document entitled *An Enquiry into Non-Magical Methods of Levitation*, written by Porgie's father and for which he was taken away by The Black Man. But the sight of the diagrammed glider makes Porgie even more anxious to pursue his fascination with mechanical flight. He succeeds in building a glider that flies, and discovers that by binding his magical broomstick to his mechanical glider, he can fly further and higher. Despite possible recriminations, Porgie decides to go over the Wall at last. It is his rite of passage, but it is not accomplished easily. He must first fight off his classmate and alter ego, Bull Pup, before he can fly over. He does make it over the Wall, but his glider is weakened and crashes. The Black Man who took his father calls for him from the cloud-filled sky and captures him. The Black Man turns out to be Mr. Wickens, the schoolmaster; he explains the reason for the Wall. It exists to separate the realm of Magic from the realm of Science, for humans cannot follow two paths at once. He takes Porgie to be reunited with his father in the land of Science.

There is a fusion of science fiction and fantasy in this story. The place of logic and reason must be separate from the place of magic and miracles, because humans must believe in one or the other, not both simultaneously. The Black Man exists not to kill, but to take the scientific heretics from the land of Magic to the land of Science. The ultimate goal of this split-world, split-brain reality is that mind and nature may one day join forces, just as Cogswell himself successfully combines fantasy and science fiction in the story.

Biographical/Bibliographical Readings

John Clute and Peter Nicholls, "Theodore R. Cogswell," in *The Science Fiction Encyclopedia*, ed. Peter Nicholls (Doubleday, 1979), p.127. [Howard V. Hendrix]

DANN, JACK

Life and Works

Born on February 15, 1945, at Johnson City, New York, where he currently lives, Jack Dann is best known to science fiction readers for his brilliant short fiction and as an editor of often controversial anthologies such as *In the Field of Fire* (1987). Dann received his B.A. degree in social and political science in 1968 from State University of New York at Binghamton, and attended St. John's Law School in New York from 1969 to 1971. During the 1970s, he perfected his writing craft as a creator of stylish science fiction, with an emphasis on characterization. Dann taught writing at Cornell University in 1973. Although he has written science fiction novels such as *Starhiker* (1977) and *Junction* (1981), his fame continues to rest on his short story contributions. His manuscript collection is at Temple University in Philadelphia. His best science fiction writing appears in the collection *Timetipping* (1980). Like George R. R. Martin, Barry N. Malzberg, and Roger Zelazny, Jack Dann is one of the enduring short fiction creators in science fiction.

Themes and Style

Both *Starhiker* and *Junction* concern characters in search of wisdom, power, and spiritual understanding. Dann's short fiction has a highly developed sense of existential irony, lyricism, imagery, myth, and metaphors of striking beauty. Dann is a sensitive writer, concerned with metaphysical and spiritual pursuits as they relate to individuality and role. Most of his themes deal with confrontation and conflict, and how individuality is affected by the struggle. Dann's reputation as a writer continues to develop and expand.

Plot Summaries of Major Works

Timetipping. This collection of stories showcases Jack Dann's best short fiction. The title story, "Timetipping," tells of the adventure of Paley Litwak who utilizes time travel to visit synagogues at different points in time. Paley Litwak often finds illusion is as valid as reality, depending upon one's perspective and interpretation. The changes his wife Goldie undergoes in their relationship comments on the marriage situation between husband and wife. "I'm with You in Rockland" is a day in the life of a futuristic construction worker in a plastic and steel New York City where existence is bleak, where spirituality is absent, and where the worker, Flaccus, must attempt contact with somebody so he will know that some part of him is still alive. He picks up a young hitchiker named Clara. Both are dead souls in an existential sense, but do not realize it. "Rags" concerns Joanna and her cat named Rags, and their shared destiny in a dying world. It is a sad tale about being alone, dealing with the motif of existential aloneness, and dying. "Windows" is an almost surreal reading experience. It is the story of a man named John who starts by browsing through books and ends by murdering those around him as he slips into a world of madness and mirror images which belong to some strange individual known as Richard, whom he is vaguely aware of but refuses to accept as himself until he is trapped in a train at the subway station. "Windows" is a strange piece, utilizing elements of science fiction and the macabre to create a tense environment of illusion versus reality.

"The Drum Lollipop" tells of a married couple, Frank and Maureen Harris, who live in an existential nightmare of varying degrees of chaos when a small drum with unusual properties suddenly comes into their world. Maureen becomes the possessor of this object, and the more contact she has with it, the more her mind becomes a bizarre compartment of images. Maureen becomes a woman on a quest, and at the conclusion she reaches out for something which now resembles a trembling star and absorbs it within her body with a deep sense of love. In "Days of Stone," a lonely woman, Mrs. Fishbine, perceives herself as among the old and living dead. She recounts the details of her life, seeking to find out what is alive, what is not alive, and what is not of this world. "Night Visions" concerns a married man, Martin, who seeks to change his world by committing suicide to escape the world in which his wife, Jennifer, exists, and finds that he cannot kill himself; he must return home to Jennifer and the world that they share.

"The Dybukk Dolls" is the story of Chaim Lewis as he approaches oblivion. In a mind where the world and life is dead, there is no room for dreams, only the long sleep of death. Chaim Lewis cannot survive in a world he perceives as having no meaning or order. "Among the Mountains" is a poignant tale of a storyteller named Vo Kim Lan, nicknamed Giay by the children who are enchanted by his mystical stories of adventure and morality. A story rich in detail and characterization, it allows Dann to deal with death, war, and spirituality in a dreamlike quality in which the reader is caught up in the magic of the storyteller's vision and those who are touched by that vision in the story itself. It is a dream within a dream within a dream to achieve a reality.

"Junction" is the basis for the novel of the same name. It is a deeply philosophical and mystical story concerning Ned Wheeler and his futuristic life style, his search for meaning, and a host of unusual characters who cross his path in an environment known as the "Junction." A tale of struggle, it serves as a basis for an introduction to some general motifs found in much of Dann's short fiction. "Junction" was a Nebula award finalist. "Camps" is considered by many to be a science fiction short classic, and it shows the depth of Dann's genius as a master of image and characterization. It is the story of Stephen, who is suffering from pain in a hospital and who is also existing in a parallel world of a World War II Nazi concentration camp. He suffers in both worlds, or both "camps" if interpreted from a philosophical perspective. Dann allows both worlds to exist, with precise detail and characterization present in whichever reality Stephen finds himself intertwined. In some tense, terrifying moments where time, reality, and space shift and blend, Stephen is forced to free the Stephen of the Nazi death camp so that he can free himself of the pain of the hospital bed, and as the fever and sounds of the death camp break, he destroys the illusion. Some readers will always ask themselves which was the greater illusion Stephen faced--in the hospital bed, or in the Nazi death camp? Which truly was the reality and which the nightmare?

Biographical/Bibliographical Readings

John Clute, "Jack Dann," in *The Science Fiction Encyclopedia*, ed. Peter Nicholls (Doubleday, 1979), p.153-4. "Jack Dann," in *Contemporary Authors New Revision Series* (Gale, 1986) v.2, p.172-3. Gregory Feeley, "Echoes of the Future: an interview with Jack Dann," *Thrust* 21 (Mar./Apr. 1984), p.5-9, 15. Idem, "Jack Dann," in *Twentieth-Century Science-Fiction Writers*, ed. Curtis C. Smith (St. James, 1986), p.172-3. **[Harold Lee Prosser]**

DAVIDSON, AVRAM

Life and Works

Avram Davidson was born on April 23, 1923, in a section of Yonkers, New York, known as Hog Hill. He attended four colleges, including New York University (1940-42), Yeshiva University (1947-48), and Pierce College (1950-51), but never obtained a degree. He married Grania Kaiman, a writer. They had one son and were later divorced. Davidson served in the United States Navy from 1941 to 1945 and was subsequently attached to the Marines in both Okinawa and in China. An Orthodox Jew, he fought with the Israeli army in 1948 and 1949. Before becoming a full-time professional writer, he worked at a variety of jobs including tomato picker, sheep herder, and hotel manager.

His first professional writing sale was to *Orthodox Jewish Life Magazine* in 1946. Although he reports that he began writing science fiction and fantasy at the grand old age of eight, the first work of his in these genres that eventually found its way into print was written while he was in the Navy. The fantasy piece "The Montevarde Camera" was published in *The Magazine of Fantasy and Science Fiction* sixteen years after it was written. The first science fiction story, "My Boyfriend's Name Is Jello," appeared in the same journal in 1954.

Davidson's writing is well respected in a number of fields. He was awarded the Hugo for best short story at the World Science Fiction Convention in 1958 for "Or All the Seas with Oysters." In addition, he is the recipient of the Edgar Award from Mystery Writers of America (1962), and the World Fantasy Award for best collection in 1975 for *The Enquiries of Dr. Esterhazy*. Two of Davidson's novels, *Rogue Dragon* (1965) and *Clash of the Star Kings* (1966) were nominated for the Nebula award.

He held the position of executive editor for *The Magazine of Fantasy and Science Fiction* from 1962 through 1964. The magazine received the Hugo award (1962) for best professional magazine while under his stewardship. While with the magazine, he edited three volumes of the anthology series, *The Best of Fantasy and Science Fiction* (twelfth series, 1962; thirteenth series, 1963; fourteenth series, 1964).

Themes and Style

Avram Davidson's writing is characterized by an elevation of style, a remarkable ear for sound, and, at its best, a fine wit. His short works show no characteristic theme but are, rather, notable for the variety of subjects treated and styles used. His short stories, by far his best, are unusual due to his ability to handle humor well. He has produced satire as well as pieces filled with narrative irony. His two most famous stories, "Or All the Seas with Oysters" and "Golem," both entail a humorous viewpoint. His short stories use an O. Henry-type construction, building suspense to the surprise, turn-about ending.

His stories and novels utilize settings which ring of times past. Even those set in the present and future involve ancient rituals, past religions, or societies gone stagnant due to prejudice, slavery, or hardship. Bizarre settings as well as mundane ones viewed from original angles abound in his work. The present and future societies created by Davidson have a feudal feeling with a strong class structure; the presence of an upper and lower class is more than just background for the work. In his novels, the protagonist must examine the existing class structure, clarify his or her place and morals, and then confront the society or take some action to change the system to make it more equitable. Often, no one class, character, society, or species has all the right answers. The optimum solution demands some blend of available factors or values.

The characters developed by Davidson are quickly sketched. They are ideally suited for the short story where extensive character development is unnecessary and even undesirable. Similarly, the societies he creates are described concisely, giving the reader a feeling for the tone of the community, world, class--present or past--in a few well-chosen phrases. Another characteristic of Davidson's writing is the sound. Alliteration is common and his characters often speak in dialects. In some pieces, the dialects serve to set the classes apart. In others, he is only dealing with one group or class, but the use of a strange and melliflous speech pattern serves to confirm for the reader that the action is taking place in a distant and unknown region. Some of his best writing should be classified as fantasy rather than science fiction, and the tone of fantasy and mystery genres is often found in his science fiction as well.

Plot Summaries of Major Works

Clash of the Star Kings. The novel is set in the Mexican town of Los Remedios. The Star Kings of the title are two groups of interstellar travelers who visited Earth once before and were worshipped as gods by the Aztecs and Toltec tribes of old Mexico. At the time of the novel, the area in Mexico is inhabited by the Tenocha, descendants of the Aztecs and the Moxtomi, a modern version of the Toltec tribe which lives in the hills and follows the gentle ways of the Great Old Ones. As the novel begins, a festival is commencing in which the body of the "hermit" is carried through the town during a torchlight parade.

In an attempt to reestablish the bloody reign of the Aztecs, the Tenocha try to steal the hermit. The hermit comes to life and a chase begins through the hills around the town. The hermit turn out to be a guardian left by the Great Old Ones after the last clash on Earth between themselves and their interstellar enemies. The hermit has called the Great Old Ones back to Earth to resume the battle with their violent adversaries.

The battle centers around possession of the Tlaloc, a rain god buried deep in the center of a mountain deemed sacred by the ancient tribes in the area. Key characters include Luis Lorenzo Santangel, who has long felt kinship with the Moxtomi and discovers that the Great Old Ones have returned. Lupita, a Mexican servant, is a follower of Huitzilopochtli, the leader of the violent interstellar army. Her actions lead to the involvement of three United States citizens living in Mexico, Jacob Clay (a writer), Sarah Clay (his wife and Lupita's employer), and "Mac" Macauley (a former miner who is knowledgeable about local legends and tribal rituals).

The Mexican background and use of ancient Mexican religions provides interest without obscuring the story. The setting also provides the primitive or ancient tone commonly found in Davidson's work. The novel involves a clash between warring cultures at the interstellar level, as well as here on Earth. The Great Old Ones of the Toltecs are gentle and good, while the Huitzili-Aztec are blood-thirsty and violent. The modern Mexican tribes reflect this same dichotomy. In addition, the Mexican culture is contrasted with the Americans living there, providing a strong difference among the classes. Good and evil are quite equally balanced in this novel. It required the union of the cunning determination of the Great Old Ones with modern Mexican courage and some Yankee know-how to put a final end to the evil Huitzili.

The KarChee Reign and **Rogue Dragon.** These two novels form a series. *The KarChee Reign*, written in 1966 as a prequel to *Rogue Dragon* (1965), is the weaker of the two novels. They are both action-adventure novels which take place on Earth after the invasion of a large insectlike alien species, the KarChee, which have come to mine the surface of the Earth. They pay little heed to humans, destroying those that are in their way and ignoring those which are not. The KarChee work with a larger and much more dangerous species described as dragons.

In the first book, humans have been reduced to living very primitively in the areas not yet mined by the KarChee. Lors, a young man made homeless by the mining, joins a wandering family traveling by boat, looking for a place to settle. The boat family believe, with religious fervor, that the KarChee are the instruments of God and will only harm those of little faith. A conflict develops between two human philosophies as Lors seeks to understand and oppose the KarChee. The KarChee come to symbolize fate and its many permutations in human culture. The physical human-KarChee conflict is overlain at the symbolic level by the ideologic conflict between active opposition and passive, philosophical, or religious acceptance of events.

Rogue Dragon takes place long after the KarChee reign, when the invaders have been defeated, vanquished, and nearly forgotten. Earth, stripped of her riches by the KarChee mining operations, is operated as a hunting sanctuary where people come from all over the galaxy to hunt the dragons left behind by the KarChee.

Jon-Joras is sent to earth to arrange a hunting expedition for his planet's ruler. An unpredictable and very dangerous rogue dragon starts Joras on an investigation of the hunting system, the establishments maintaining it and, finally, the dragons themselves. The book is well paced with surprise at the conclusion. The presentation of the dragons and even the KarChee shifts from animosity to understanding, creating a nice counterpoint to *The KarChee Reign.*

Rork! *Rork!* is one of Davidson's best known works. It occurs after the third galactic war and is set on the planet Pia 2, a remote colony which produces and exports a medicinal plant, redwing. It has become the place in the galaxy where the Guild sends its misfits and ne'er-do-wells. In addition, Pia 2 is home to Tocks (humans who are descended from the original settlers abandoned by Earth during the galactic wars), and to a number of indigenous life forms, including the Rorks (a large, spiderlike creature of fearsome repute).

Ran Lomar, born and raised on an overcrowded Earth, has had a lifelong desire to emigrate to a sparsely populated, remote planet. As a youth, he selects Pia 2 as his destination and signs up for a five-year assignment there as soon as he comes of age. He envisions exploring the whole planet during his stay, and the duties assigned to him by the Guild seem ideally suited for this. He has been given orders to find the reasons for the recent declines in redwing production and to correct the problem.

When he arrives, he finds a stagnant society. The Guild members are interested primarily in what they will be able to do when they can retire and leave Pia 2. They have a fairly superficial knowledge of the dangers, the life forms, and the Tocks, and are not interested in developing a better understanding. Civilization broke down among the Tocks when their ancestors were abandoned during the galactic wars and they were overwhelmed by the hardship of surviving without support from Earth. The Guild members feel that this makes the Tocks nearly subhuman, but they consent to trade with the outlying clans and supervise the Guild station Tocks to obtain redwing.

Lomar finds it difficult to travel on the planet and very nearly abandons his assigned task. Tocks and Guild, alike, say that nothing can be done to change existing conditions. He overcomes the lethargic Guild Society to travel to the outlying regions where wild Tock resistance forces him into unexplored territory. Before he is successful he must meet the Rorks and come to understand the basic ecology of the planet. Success depends on his ability to forge a union among the various human factions and integrate these with the biology of the indigenous lifeforms.

In terms of structure and suspense, *Rork!* is one of Davidson's better novels. The viewpoint remains with Lomar, the protagonist, but the repeated shift back and forth between the colony and the outlying areas gives the feeling of a varied viewpoint. The Guild speak with an accent that sounds faintly like the British upper-class, while the Tocks have an almost Cockney sound.

Biographical/Bibliographical Readings

"Avram Davidson," in *Contemporary Authors* (Gale, 1981), v.101, p.135. Donald L. Lawler, "Avram Davidson," in *Twentieth-Century Science-Fiction Writers*, ed. Curtis C. Smith (St. James, 1981), p.140. Kevin Mulcahy, "Avram Davidson," in *Twentieth-Century American Science-Fiction Writers* (Gale, 1981), v.1, p.109-12. R. Reginald, "Avram Davidson," in *Science Fiction and Fantasy Literature* (Gale, 1979), p.872. T. A. Shippey, "The Short Fiction of Avram Davidson," in *Survey of Science Fiction Literature* (Salem Press, 1979), p.1930-33. **[Mary Lou Mills]**

DECAMP, L. (LYON) SPRAGUE

Life and Works

L. Sprague DeCamp was born on November 27, 1907, in New York City. DeCamp obtained his B.S. degree in engineering from the California Institute of Technology in 1930, and his M.S. in engineering from the Stevens Institute of Technology in 1933. He became a reader of science fiction through his college roommate at CIT, helping his friend plot out some science fiction stories. After losing his job at the Scranton School for Inventors in 1937, DeCamp decided to try his hand at writing short stories. He has since seldom left free-lance writing, except for short stints as a book editor, a mechanical engineer in the Naval Reserve during World War II, and publicity writer for an advertising agency in 1956. In the 1960s, DeCamp became well known for his writings in fantasy and sword and sorcery, collaborating with Fletcher Pratt on *The Incomplete Enchanter* (1941), as well as with Robert Howard and Lin Carter on the Conan books. DeCamp often writes in collaboration with other writers such as P. Schuyler Miller, on *Genus Homo* (1941), and Fletcher Pratt on the Gavagan's series, collected in *Tales from Gavagan's Bar* (1953).

His favorite creation has been novels situated in a galaxy settled by Viagens Interplanetarias, a public corporation founded by Brazil, and dominated by Portuguese-speaking bureaucrats. Novels with this background include his most important satire, *A Planet Called Krishna* (1966), *Rogue Queen* (1951), and most recently *The Prisoner of Zhamanak* (1983). Other novels in the Viagens Interplanetarias series include *The Search for Zei* (1962) and *Hostage of Zir* (1977).

DeCamp drifted away from science fiction writing in the late 1950s because other types of writing could provide more bread-and-butter and glory. As a result, DeCamp has diversified his writing into historical novels and the more lucrative sword and sorcery fields.

A noted writer of over twenty-five works of critical and science nonfiction, including the *Science Fiction Handbook* (1953, revised in 1975) with his wife, Catherine Crook DeCamp, DeCamp is also an editor of more than ten collections of fantasy and science fiction anthologies. His numerous honors include the Science Fiction Writers of America Grand Master Award in 1979, the Tolkien Fantasy Award in 1976, and the International Fantasy Award in 1953.

Themes and Style

DeCamp's science fiction strongly reflects his interest in the history and philosophy of science. In stories such as "Hyperpilosity," he usually identifies one essential thread in the fabric of society. Then DeCamp slowly unravels that thread to show how tightly knit is the entirety of modern technology. In the novel *Lest Darkness Fall* (1941), the hero is thrown into Gothic Rome and finds himself unable to use much of his scientific knowledge--for each invention requires dozens of others to build on.

Unlike his fantasy figures, such as the invincible "Conan the Barbarian," DeCamp's science fiction characters are average people thrown into remarkable and often humorous situations. Much of DeCamp's pre-World War II writing was gently satirical, as in *Genus Homo*. Following the war, much of his humor was submerged, finally to resurface in a far more bitter form in his later works.

Time travel is a favorite technique for displaying DeCamp's fascination with the history of science, with two of his best known time-travel stories being *Lest Darkness Fall* and "A Gun for Dinosaur" (1956). This fascination with time travel extends into his nonfiction essays dealing with such diverse topics as how one could communicate (considering the changes occuring in language) in a five-hundred-year future.

Plot Summaries of Major Works

Genus Homo. This novel was coauthored with P. Schuyler Miller. A bus loaded with schoolteachers, dancers, and American Association for the Advancement of Science convention-goers is trapped in a tunnel by a massive earthquake. One scientist is carrying a vial of an experimental hibernating chemical. The bottle bursts and sends those trapped into a million-year hibernation. When the occupants revive and fight their way out of the tunnel, they find that humans have disappeared, and other mammals have evolved to fill the niche. The humans are divided into two camps by the conflict between the scientist, Henley Bridger, and a local politico, R. Nelson Packard. Soon the groups find their already-small population decimated by the leaders' conflicting views; some are captured by the dominant primates, evolved gorillas. The gorillas place the humans in a zoo, and begin an amusing sequence of intelligence tests classic to any laboratory setting--boxes to be piled up to reach a treat, sticks to be telescoped to obtain fruit. The tests give way to the realization that the humans are intelligent. Once released, the two primate species join together and become embroiled in a fierce battle for control with the baboons. The spectacle of gorillas mounted on pigs charging into battle against baboons is just one of the memorable scenes in the novel. In the end, the humans manage to work together using ancient cavalry and medieval warfare tactics to win the battle.

DeCamp delights in using the ebb and flow of history to demonstrate the role of technology in society. The gorillas are logically represented as evolved, gentle beings, and the baboons as very agressive and dangerously intelligent foes. The story line is well crafted to provide a centerpiece for DeCamp's fascination with the tactics of warfare, introducing what could only be described as "heavy-cavalry-evolved" pigs. Written in 1941, some elements of the novel are extremely dated; the role of the women schoolteachers and the dancers is embarrassingly stereotypical. Certain questions are never fully resolved, such as why humanity has disappeared or why so many species have risen to compete against each other. The technological elements and the satire hold the reader's attention.

Lest Darkness Fall. Martin Padway, a twentieth-century anthologist, is strolling down a rainy street in Rome when a bolt of lightning throws him back to the sixth century, just before the Byzantine Empire's invasion of Rome. Knowing that this sacking of Rome will bring on the Dark Ages, Padway attempts to single-handedly change the course of history. Padway finds himself in a quandary, for he arrives without funds in a society that measures freedom in monetary terms. Attempting to draw on his limited knowledge of modern technology, the hero tries and fails to produce gunpowder. He does succeed in developing the first brandy--a best seller in decadent Rome. His greatest initial success is with the merchant class, where he introduces both the Arabic numeral system and double-column bookkeeping, thus revolutionizing the economic system. Later he is propelled into the darker machinations of the prominent political figures and finds himself pitted against the refined and convoluted plots that devoured Rome. Growing desperate, Padway is forced to involve himself in the final battles that will determine the fate of Rome and introduces medieval and twentieth-century battle strategies to the blundering armies. Whether Rome can or should be saved, whether history will be permanently altered, Padway knows only that he must change the future if he is to survive.

DeCamp has created a very believable time travel novel. Once past the unlikely premise of a lightning storm as a time machine vehicle, the plot is intellectually and emotionally satisfying. The intellectual satisfaction derives from DeCamp's outstanding grasp of the history of techology and of Roman history. Understanding the implication of which particular inventions could be adopted, and which would be beyond the acceptance of Rome's inhabitants, creates a highly believable tale. The emotional rewards of the story are in the often humorous situations in which a supposedly civilized twentieth-century man finds himself. Seductions, assassinations, and other political machinations universal to any age highlight the author's ability to tell a cautionary tale in a fashion that is at once darkly critical and yet very humorous.

Most critics regard this as one of the most enduring and entertaining of time travel novels. With the balance of humor, historical accuracy, and character development, DeCamp portrays his finest talents--his ability to find humor in the most mundane aspects of human culpability and his grasp of the history of technology. While critics have compared the novel to Twain's *A Connecticut Yankee in King Arthur's Court*, the amount of technical and historical accuracy in DeCamp's work creates a much more believable story than Twain's.

A Planet Called Krishna. Krishna is an Earthlike planet with humanoid inhabitants complete with green hair, pointed ears, and antennae, whose culture is warlike and premechanical. The principal character, Victor Hasselborg, is a private investigator in the traditional mode. Hired by Yussuf Batruni, a businessman, Hasselborg is sent to Krishna to locate Julnar, Yussuf's daughter, who has run off with her lover, Tony Fallon. Once on Krishna, all of the participants disguise themselves as natives. The novel is an interaction between "civilized" humans and a warlike culture. Gunrunning illegal weapons, chasing and rescuing damsels in distress all culminate in a series of expected and unexpected denouements.

The interplanetary public corporation, Viagens Interplanetarias, provides the backdrop for several of DeCamp's novels. The corporation was founded by the leading world power, Brazil, and provides a distinctly Latin influence. In all of the novels of the Viagens Interplanetarias series, the overwhelming concern is to prevent modern technological humans from influencing or interfering with the normal development of native cultures, predating "Star Trek's" "prime directive" by nearly twenty years. In *A Planet Called Krishna*, the warlike natives are eager for more modern weapons such as the long bow, the crossbow, and guns. The enterprising humans are eager to provide the illegal arms. While the novel seems dated, with its tough-talking detective slang and philosophy, this satire combines nicely with comic swordplay to present the reader with a short, light science fiction detective novel.

The novel has also been published under the titles *Cosmic Manhunt* (1954) and *The Queen of Zamba* (1978).

Rogue Queen. In this novel, also set in the Viagen Interplanetarias universe, humans have arrived on a world that parallels closely the society of Earth's honey bees. Iroedh is a worker with more than average curiosity, and an alarming affection for a drone, Antim. With human arrival on the planet, Ormazd's queen sends Iroedh to investigate the strangers and report back. Iroedh becomes fascinated with Earth's technology, which the explorers are determined to keep from her, bound as they are by the rules forbidding introduction of new technology into nonadvanced societies. Through a complex series of actions, she becomes involved in one human's murder and the theft of his weapon. When she returns to her hive and finds Antim is to be killed in the annual purge of elderly drones, she frees him and turns rogue. Unable to consume the nonmeat concoction that keeps workers neutered, she eats meat, maturing sexually into a queen. The now powerful rogue queen sets about to alter her society and free the hives from the patterns that have bound them, using the technology and knowledge stolen from the humans as her weapons.

DeCamp uses the novel to highlight the role that a relatively simple advance can make in changing a society. The machete, and more importantly the ideas that are adopted, can form the basis for any revolution. This novel contains some fine touches that reveal DeCamp's ability to mature as a writer. His characterizations are stronger, his women less stereotypical, and the action just as entertaining as in his earlier works. *Rogue Queen* is regarded by critics as DeCamp's finest science fiction novel. He creates a complex, alien, yet hauntingly familiar society. Written five years after Hiroshima, one can only speculate that DeCamp might be saying that if something as simple as a machete can bring down a society, what incalculable risks are incurred when more complex weapons are introduced?

Biographical/Bibliographical Readings

L. Sprague DeCamp, *Science Fiction Handbook: The Writing of Imaginative Fiction* (Hermitage, 1953). Jeffrey Elliot, "L. Sprague DeCamp," *Science Fiction Voices*, no. 1 (1979), p. 53-63. Sam Moskowitz, "L. Sprague DeCamp," in *Seekers of Tomorrow* (World, 1966), p. 151-66. Brian M. Stableford, "L. Sprague DeCamp," in *Science Fiction Writers*, ed. E. F. Bleiler (Scribner's 1982), p.179-84. [Colleen Power]

DELANY, SAMUEL R.

Life and Works

Samuel Ray Delany was born on April 1, 1942, in New York City. He attended the prestigious Darlton School and the respected Bronx High School of Science. Although diagnosed as dyslexic, he continued his education at the City College of New York where he served as poetry editor of *The Promethean*. In 1961, he married Marilyn Hacker. They had one child and were divorced in 1980. He published his first science fiction novel, *The Jewels of Aptor*, in 1962 and it was quickly followed by several more titles. These were *Captives of the Flame* (1963), *The Towers of Toron* (1964), *City of a Thousand Suns* (1965), *Ballad of Beta-2* (1965), and *Empire Star* (1966).

Delany's writing career is often considered to have two distint periods; his early works represent his first period, which is usually thought of as ending with his Nebula award winning novels *Babel-17* (1966) and *The Einstein Intersection* (1967). *Nova* was published in 1968. His early short stories were collected in *Driftglass* (1971). "Aye and Gomorrah" (1967) won a Nebula award and "Time Considered as a Helix of Semi-Precious Stones" (1969) won both the Hugo and Nebula awards. His second period contained several major novels, *Dhalgren* (1973), *Triton* (1976), and *Stars in My Pockets Like Grains of Sand* (1984).

In addition to his highly regarded, provocative fiction, Delany is recognized as an accomplished and insightful critic of science fiction as a genre. He has published numerous scholarly essays dealing with a variety of topics and concerns. His book length studies include *The Jewel-Hinged Jaw* (1977), *The American Shore* (1978), and *Starboard Wind* (1984). With Marilyn Hacker, he coedited the *Quark* series of anthologies (1970-71).

Themes and Style

In his early works, Delany introduced concerns and interests such as communications, the use of language, heroic quests, and social analysis, all of which he would later investigate more fully. His stylistic and structural presentation developed throughout his early period. His plots offered intricacies and subtleties, entertainment and excitement, and, of more importance, intellectual stimulation; all within a traditional science fiction framework.

Plot Summaries of Major Works

Babel 17 features the heroine Rydra Wong as a telepathic poet and captain of the spaceship *Rimbaud*. The tale begins with an enigma not explained until the end of the novel. As a child Rydra received a trained Myna bird and, instead of the expected delightful response, she went into hysterics. The Myna bird spoke by rote in anticipation of a worm as reward and Rydra experienced the scene from the worm's point of view. The plot revolves around breaking a broadcast code which has been named "Babel-17" and which, when broken, will reveal important military information. Using her innate abilities, the adult Rydra assembles a multifaceted crew to work toward understanding "Babel-17." The group includes living and dead, men and women, homosexual and heterosexual, and Rydra reveals that each was chosen for being "someone she could talk to." Perhaps her greatest linguistic challenge is with Butcher, the crew member who has no conception of self; his language pattern does not allow for the use of I, me, mine, etc. As the novel draws to a close, Rydra and Butcher meld minds and with this fusion Delany allows the plot's questions to be solved and the code be broken.

Speaking by rote does not represent understanding, and throughout the book Delany quests for an awareness of the fundamentals of communication. Delany uses Rydra to explore the nature of communication through language, perception and telepathy. The plot is complex and sophisticated, set within a framework of action and adventure and designed to probe the patterns of language.

Dahlgren. This is a story about a young bisexual man in a large, decaying American city. He becomes a handyman, poet, and gang leader. The Kid is the main character and, like Lobey in *The Einstein Intersection*, he quests for his identity. He is the narrator and integrates his psychological wanderings with his adventures and explorations through Bellona. The Kid seeks meaning from what he finds around him but as realizations awaken, their necessity dissolves. Many of *Dahlgren*'s characters are black, living on the fringe, but assuming an important role in what remains of the city's life. When the assassination of a civil rights leader occurs, it in turn sparks a racial upheaval resulting in the Kid being forced out of the city. In a cyclical pattern, the novel ends as it begins, with the Kid outside the gates of Bellona in the same circumstances as when the story began.

Dahlgren aroused passionate and continued debate within the science fiction community. Some praised its inventiveness and daring, others found it completely inaccessible and incomprehensible. Despite the apocalyptic setting, society continues, existing according to its own norms and in relation to its mutated environment. The vividly related, surrealistic landscapes easily lend themselves to an extrapolated realism of the disintegrating urban ghettos of 1960s America.

The Einstein Intersection. This novel is set in the far future on Earth, which has become inhabited by a new race. This new society established itself after Earth's original inhabitants had both destroyed themselves and emigrated voluntarily. This biological/historical contradiction sets the tone for the action through-out the novel. The principal character is Lobey, a black musician who loves both Friza, a woman, and Dorik, a hermaphrodite, both of whom are killed by Kid Death. Lobey is a rustic sort and his adventures lead into and through puzzling and sophisticated situa-tions, often stalked by Kid Death. Christian beliefs are suggested throughout the work--Green Eye was born of a virgin, Lobey him-self is resurrected, Kid Death has Satanic associations, and other characters are identified as representing Pontius Pilate and Judas.

To stress the idea of diversity and contradiction, Delany has also paralleled these religious identities with persons readily asso-ciated with 1960 pop culture as well as historical, mythological, and fictitious characters. Taken together, such fluctuating identi-ties allow Delany maximum ability to comment about the roles as-sumed by technology and social mores and the pressures they exert on an individual who moves through and develops an identity in an evolving society.

Stars in My Pockets like Grains of Sand. This novel is set in a far future, populated by various intelligent life forms, on dif-ferent worlds, all engaged in complex social and economic ex-changes. The sophistication of data exchange resulting from in-formation as a commodity allows for two males of radically dif-ferent racial, social, and cultural backgrounds to be brought to-gether--each being identified as the other's perfect mate. When we meet Rat Korga, he is a slave working endlessly and ignorant of any alternative. When his world is destroyed, Rat is found to be the only survivor and is suddenly thrust into the intergalactic spotlight. Marq Dyeth is an industrial diplomat and a respected member of a biologically mixed (human and alien) family. Their meeting and their explorations of each other's sensibilities and sensitivities are set against an exotically rich landscape of com-plex social interaction and intense political interplay.

Critics are in agreement that with *Stars in My Pockets like Grains of Sand*, Delany has surpassed his own high standards of literary achievement. This novel has been hailed as a work of pure genius. The diversity of thoughts, interactions, speculations, situations and their use, expression, and nuances present a multi-dimensional tapestry that may be unequalled in the genre. It will be followed by the yet unpublished sequel, *The Splendor and Mis-ery of Bodies, of Cities*.

Triton. Triton is the outermost moon of Neptune, on which Bron Hesltrom seeks happiness and personal fulfillment in an ef-ficient and all-encompassing urban utopia. Bron is an unfortunate and unhappy person, and it is through his quest that we experi-ence Triton's social order. He is a misfit, a macho male in a time and place where such men are assimilated but not encouraged. He falls in love with The Spike, an actress and independent woman, who has little interest in him and whose rejection he cannot accept. Sam, an older gay male, is featured prominently, giving Bron both practical and philosophical advice, including ruminations about Triton's political, economic, and social fabric. Sam's narrative contributions contrast with Bron's self-centered, distorted, and confused view of all that Triton has to offer. When Bron can no longer cope with his life as he perceives it, he has a sex change and becomes the woman he always desired with the hope of finding a man like the one he was. His simplistic solution, although seemingly definitive, offers Bron no guarantee of happiness or fulfillment. Indeed, it may be safe to assume that the man of her dreams will be as elusive as the woman of his.

Delany concludes *Triton* with an analysis of science fiction as a literary genre, drawing attention to the importance of both foreground and background to to the development of plot and character. The characterizations and structure of *Triton* lend themselves to an ideal illustration of the points he brings out in this essay.

Biographical/Bibliographical Readings

Samuel R. Delany, *Heavenly Breakfast: An Essay on the Winter of Love* (Bantam, 1979). Seth McEvoy, *Samuel R. Delany* (Ungar, 1984). Michael W. Peplow and Robert S. Bravard, *Samuel R. Delany: A Primary and Secondary Bibliography* (G. K. Hall, 1980). George R. Slusser, *The Delany Intersection* (Borgo Press, 1977). Jane Weedman, *Samuel R. Delany* (Starmont House, 1982). **[John Dunham]**

DEL REY, LESTER

Life and Works

Ramon Felipe San Juan Mario Silvio Enrico Smith Heathcourt-Brace Sierra y Alvarez-del Rey y de los Verdes was born on June 2, 1915 at Clydesdale, Minnesota. He is the son of Francisco Sierra y Alvarez-del Rey, a carpenter and sharecropper farmer, and Jane Sidway. Del Rey's early life was one of poverty and hard work as his father moved from town to town in the pattern of sharecrop farming. He notes in his autobiographical comments in *Early Del Rey* that he was expected to do the work of a man from the age of nine years. He remembers this time as a happy one, however, because of the strong emotional stability provided by his father, and because of his love of reading.

Starting with books in his father's own large collection, he became a voracious reader, discovering science fiction in the late 1920s through the works of Edgar Rice Burroughs and the stories he read in *Wonder Stories Quarterly*. Del Rey began writing in his last year of high school, primarily as a way to use an old Remington typewriter he managed to save the money to buy (he has had a lifelong fascination with typewriters). A librarian friend read some of his stories and became determined that del Rey should go to college.

Thanks to her efforts, an uncle in Washington, D.C., agreed to let del Rey live with him while attending George Washington University, and a partial scholarship was secured. This university career only lasted two years, however. Del Rey was bored with the coursework (except for the science courses), and dropped out, never to return.

He then began a series of jobs that allowed him to continue living in Washington and support his science fiction magazine reading habit. His first appearance in these publications was as a fan, writing long and frequent letters to the editors pointing out errors in the science, or otherwise criticizing the stories. His favorite magazine was *Astounding Science Fiction*, and he seemed to be especially influenced by the writing of Don A. Stuart, Raymond Gallun, Jack Williamson, Stanley Weinbaum, and Clifford D. Simak.

As a prolific writer of science fiction stories in the 1930s to the 1950s, del Rey's achievement is perhaps best viewed within the context of the standards of those years, and in terms of the formative influence of John W. Campbell. Pseudonyms used by del Rey include R. Alvarez, Cameron Hall, Marion Henry, Philip James, Wade Kaempfert, Erik van Lhin, Edson McCann, Philip St. John, Charles Satterfield (also used by Frederick Pohl), John Vincent, and Kenneth Wright.

The first science fiction story del Rey wrote came about as the result of a dare from his girlfriend. When he criticized a story by Manly Wade Wellman in the January, 1938, issue of *Astounding*, she challenged him to write a story that would be published there--or at least would get him a personal rejection letter from the editor.

The result was "The Faithful," a story about the efforts of the human survivor of a plague to bring together a race of dogs and the apes who will be their "hands" to carry on the hopes and dreams of humanity. John W. Campbell accepted the story for publication in the April, 1938, issue of *Astounding*, and reader reaction placed it second in popularity for the year.

The period of 1938-54 marked del Rey's early period. For the first ten years he submitted stories only to Campbell, publishing at least thirty-eight stories during this time. According to del Rey's own account, many of the stories were suggested by Campbell himself, and other story ideas were necessarily limited to those Campbell would like. His style was also influenced by this association with Campbell, who paid by the word. Del Rey's work was thus characterized by the orderly, tight plot, briskly paced and economical. He became convinced that writing good stories was merely a matter of mastering a craft that required nothing more than the use of a good formula and a lot of imagination.

While he has written little magazine fiction since 1956, he has written a number of juvenile works (both fiction and nonfiction) and thought-provoking articles on space flight and the craft of science fiction writing.

Del Rey has also been influential as an editor. His editorial and publishing career has included *Space Science Fiction* (editor, 1952-53), *Science Fiction Adventures* (publisher, 1952 and editor, 1952-53), *Fantasy Fiction* (editor, 1953), *Rocket Stories* (editor, 1953), *Galaxy* (editor, 1968-74), *Worlds of If* (editor, 1968-74), *International Science Fiction* (editor, 1968), *Worlds of Fantasy* (editor, 1968-71), and fantasy editor for Ballantine Books since 1975.

He has also been book reviewer for *Analog* since 1974, and taught fantasy fiction at New York University from 1972 to 1973. He was guest of honor at the twenty-fifth World Science Fiction Convention (NyCon3) in New York City in 1967, and received the 1953 Boys' Club of America Science Fiction Award for *Marooned on Mars*. His first wife, Evelyn Harrison, died in 1970, and he married Judy-Lynn Benjamin, an editor, on March 21, 1971.

Themes and Style

The early del Rey stories cover a variety of topics. Some are fantasies, some are quite nostalgic and sentimental (such as "Though Dreamers Die," in which the last man realizes that robots will carry on humanity's aspirations), and some deal with hard science. A humanistic treatment of themes and sentimental blend of sympathy and realism are hallmarks of these earlier works.

These stories also pose fundamental questions about humanity's struggle for survival and the conflict between our creative and destructive urges. There is a preoccupation with the precarious relationship between humans and their immortal creations. In many of the stories, survival depends on the wisdom and sensitivity with which a person handles these creations, whether robots, dogs and other animals, or children.

For several years, del Rey wrote only in his spare time, sitting down and dashing off a story whenever he needed the money. After becoming a full-time writer in 1950, he became much more prolific. Most critics agree that this increase in productivity resulted in a decrease in quality, exemplified by a stream of juvenile novels. These "formula" works usually feature a hero who has just turned eighteen and who ventures into space either by stowing away on a rocket or some other irresponsible action, causing much trouble for all concerned until he manages by some remarkable feat, to redeem the situation, and in the process he matures into a man.

Common themes in these novels are placid assumptions about women (whose roles are minimal in any case), the value of individual initiative and resourcefulness, and the merits of American democracy. Occasional fantastical themes also continue to appear from time to time, as in *The Sky Is Falling*, describing a mirror-image universe where magic prevails but is not strong enough to prevent large sections of the sky from cracking and falling. These fantasy stories often involve problems of mistaken or hidden identity involving twins, namesakes, or instances of unknown parentage.

Three of the most popular stories from this time period are "Police Your Planet, "The Eleventh Commandment," and "Pstalemate," perhaps the best of his metaphysical tales. Increasingly, such metaphysical themes appear in the later novels. They reflect del Rey's growing interest in humanity's dealing with conflict turned inward, where the antagonist resides within. Unlike the tightly woven plots of his earlier works, these stories often suffer from uneven characterization, strained story lines, and unnecessarily oblique writing.

In summary, Lester del Rey is regarded as a versatile but uneven writer who never quite fulfilled his early promise. At his best, he is a good storyteller, fleshing out solid plots with imaginative detail that truly capture the excitement of scientific possibility, and portraying human dilemmas with empathy and humor. His weaknesses include the sentimentality of many of his messages, and his basic formula approach to writing. This approach results in work that is too simplistic to lift it from good writing to great, and in the end is unsatisfyingly lacking in substance.

Plot Summaries of Major Works

The Eleventh Commandment. The eleventh commandment is "Be fruitful and multiply." A future, militant church tyrannizes Earth's starving population, commanding that its members follow this commandment. Jensen is a Martian-born scientist sent back to his ancestral homeland, Earth. Speaking from exile, he describes the daily struggle for survival he encounters there that shocks him with its brutality. Though he doubts the existence of a higher deity, he describes how he sought for some meaning or explanations for the church's actions. The key to these actions is the thesis that the survival of humanity depends on the enforcement of a breeding policy developed after an atomic holocaust had produced generations of mutants unable to produce healthy offspring. Jensen is persuaded that the brutal struggle for survival he sees will result in a new, more successful race of beings in a new iteration of the survival of the fittest. He and his bride enlist in a holy crusade to help spread the word among the heathens.

This novel may be one of the earliest treatments of the future Roman Catholic Church theme, and del Rey makes this theme uniquely his own by incorporating one of his recurring concerns--the conflict betweeen things as they seem to be, versus the reality that underlies all experience. In this case, horror with the church's actions in forcing starving people to continue to have more children is in fact misplaced, since the survival of the human race depends on producing enough generations to evolve a new race by breeding out radiation-induced mutations. As is often expressed in del Rey's fiction, humanity has the power of causing both its own destruction and its own salvation. The conflict between these two sides of human nature forms the central theme in the novel.

"**The Faithful.**" The human race has virtually died out as the result of a plague. Unable to work together to combat this danger, all are dead except one man. This survivor has spent his last months working with a population of dogs, hoping they will be able to carry on the hopes and dreams of mankind, and he has taught them as best he can. The one remaining problem is that the dogs lack hands--to repair machinery, build and fly aircraft, perform surgery and other medical procedures, raise food, etc. The story describes a scheme the survivor has devised whereby a semicivilized band of apes in Africa can be brought together with the dogs, to serve as their hands. Plans are described in some detail as to how the dogs, with the help of the apes, will be able to physically bring the two groups together by transporting the apes from Africa. The story closes on the eve of this great experiment, with the death of the last remaining human and the realization on the part of the dogs that they are now alone.

This is the first story that del Rey published. It expresses a theme he returns to again and again in his early adult fiction: the delicate balance between humans and their creations, with mankind finally survived by those creations. This reflects del Rey's recurring concern with human responsibility, and the conviction that these creations are an expression of human immortality. This story is also a good example of the sentimentality characteristic of much of del Rey's work. In this case, the result is a very moving portrayal of humanity's tragic flaws, and the dilemma faced by the loving creatures left behind. After 200,000 years of domestication, the dogs, speaking in the first person in this tale, need someone they can serve, and cannot help but remain deeply loyal to humanity's memory. The style of the piece reflects the proven formula for success from which del Rey seldom departed in his magazine stories: an economy of words, simple and tightly woven plot, and imaginative creativity in developing an interesting and plausible outcome, with enough detail to make it believable.

"Helen O'Loy." This is one of the best known of del Rey's early works, and is often referred to as an example of the robot story. It concerns a robot repair wizard named Dave who creates a female robot, Helen O'Loy, programming in the "emotional" qualities he identifies with human females. Powered by atomic energy, Helen is made of metal with a spun-plastic exterior and made to look as human as possible, down to the smallest detail. She models her "emotions" after the behavior she sees watching television soap operas, and ends up falling in love with Dave, who eventually marries the "perfect woman" he has created. This Pygmalion story turns tragic, however, when Dave, who has inevitably aged, dies. Helen, who had caused herself to artificially age to keep pace with her husband, burns out her own circuits so that they can cross this last bridge together.

This sentimental tale positively drips with bathos. Far from being unintentional, del Rey seems to indulge in this technique quite intentionally. As in many of his early stories, this one is a combination of sentimentality, futuristic ideas, and imaginative attention to detail. This attention shows itself in descriptions of daily life in the imaginary world of the future. Dave's work as a robot repair person, for example, provides a showcase for twenty-first century possibilities. His roommate, Phil, is a doctor who provides for the needs of future society by, for example, prescribing antihormones to quiet desire in unsuitable love matches. Helen herself is portrayed in sympathetic detail, and some descriptions are quite humorous. For example, the results of her lessons in love making, gleaned from soap operas, are described as fast and furious, since Helen was powered by an atomotor.

Much of the bathos in this story comes from a recurring theme in del Rey's fiction. This is the problematic relationship between humanity and its creations. What are the consequences of loving too much the machines created by the human hands? What, if any, obligations does humanity have to these creatures? A concern with the delicate balance between the power to create and the power to destroy is also reflected in "Helen O'Loy," as Dave contemplates the joy that he has made possible for Helen as well as the ultimate abandonment. Whether for the sentimentality or for the robot-as-vamp theme, this has remained of of del Rey's most popular stories.

Nerves. An industrial power plant has gone out of control, in an uncanny premonition of Three Mile Island and Chernobyl. A senior scientist's experiments have gone awry and heavy doses of heroism and loss of life suffered by firemen and medical personnel occur in the early hours of the disaster. The worst of the situation is that no one is sure how to stop the chain destruction of the continent. The day is saved by a young doctor named Jenkins, who is the stepson of the one man, now dead, who was thought to know the solution to the dilemma. This fact of parentage, plus

Jenkins' early technical training, leads him to develop a successful plan to avert further disaster. Seen through the eyes of the plant physician, Dr. Ferrel, the story is chilling, suspenseful, and utterly convincing.

Nerves reflects del Rey's intent to write a suspense story. The imaginative attention to detail is also much in evidence, with extrapolations and inspired guess-work about isotope transmutations and the potential stability of transuranium elements. Imaginative in another sense, the novel is prophetic in its anticipation of popular fears and distrust of nuclear power plants, and presents good arguments for both sides of the question. This blending of hard core science with soft science speculations on the social, political, and economic impacts of nuclear power shows another influence from Campbell. There are several themes in this novel that appear in many del Rey works. One is the concept of the hero's unknown parentage playing a role in his ability to save the day; another is that of the danger encountered from natural forces set loose by human error and running out of control. In del Rey's vision, control can only be regained through personal courage, mental resourcefulness, and virtuoso problem solving. In this respect, *Nerves* is the quintessential del Rey story in its focus on human ability to establish mastery over nature through science.

Pstalemate. Harry Bronson discovers within himself extraordinary psychic powers in this novel, and realizes the terrible madness to which these powers seem to commit him. Harry uses his will to survive episodes of ESP experiences. As he confronts an alien entity who seems to be seeking control of his soul, Harry saves his mind by dedicating his will to the single purpose of conquering the alien being. He does this by recognizing the alien as part of his own identity, reconciling the tension between reality and possibility, between the known past and the potentiality of the future. Most of the action is internal, with Harry experiencing altered states of awareness that are terrifying until he finally accepts them as a part of his own inner self, a part that can offer unique opportunities for development. The solution he finds is made possible by the fact that his future self has the power to time-travel back to his early development; thus he can discover how to escape the madness that had seemed inevitable. Through the use of psychedelic drugs, Harry is able to save himself, his girlfriend, and others like him who have extrasensory powers.

This novel is an example of the metaphysical turn taken by del Rey's writing in some of his later work. The conflicts that he had previously expressed in terms of humanity's relationship with its creations are now turned inward. The opponent lies within, and the struggle for survival lies within the realm of the mind. There is an impressive display of imaginative power. *Pstalemate* is compelling in its portrayal of the confrontation of a man with himself. As in del Rey's other works, humanity carries within itself the seeds of its own destruction as well as the means of its own survival.

Biographical/Bibliographical Readings

Greta Eisner, "Lester del Rey," in *Twentieth-Century American Science-Fiction Writers* (Gale, 1981), v.1, p.129-33. Sam Moskowitz, "Lester del Rey," in *Seekers of Tomorrow* (World, 1966), p.167-86. Brian Stableford, "Lester del Rey," in *The Science Fiction Encyclopedia*, ed. Peter Nicholls (Doubleday, 1979), p.163-64. [Sandra E. Spurlock]

DERLETH, AUGUST WILLIAM

Life and Works

August W. Derleth was born on February 24, 1909, in Sauk City, Wisconsin and, except for his education at the University of Wisconsin in nearby Madison and a few months in Minneapolis as editor of *Mystic Magazine*, spent his entire life in the small village, dying there of a heart condition on July 4, 1971, at the age of sixty-two. He was, as a youth, physically strong and willful, difficult to control, and a bully. These traits could have caused problems, except that his superior intelligence directed his attention to literary pursuits and nature study. Because of his bull-doglike visage and barrel chest, as well as his directness in criticism of others, he gave the impression of being thickskinned, but the contrary was true. He was very sensitive to every slight and a shrewd and sympathetic observer of the human condition.

As a teenager he fell deeply in love with a young woman, but the relationship was broken up because he was Roman Catholic and her parents were Protestant. He never recovered emotionally from this trauma and wrote movingly in stories and prose of this early encounter and its enduring pain.

At the age of forty-four, he married Sandra Evelyn Winters, a girl of fifteen who reminded him of his first love. They married in 1953 and divorced in 1959; their two children remained in his custody.

When he was only fifteen, his first story, "Bats Belfrey," appeared in the May, 1926, issue of *Weird Tales*. Derleth, in collaboration with his friend, Mark Schorer, turned out thirty stories in thirty days for the magazine. By the year 1934, he had begun the first of a series of detective novels, as well as writing mainstream short stories for such magazines as *Scribner's*. By the year 1937, he published the first of his regional novels about Wisconsin, which he collectively termed "The Sac Prairie Saga." In 1939, he and Donald Wandrei created Arkham House as a vehicle for publishing the works of H. P. Lovecraft. A combination of economic setbacks caused Derleth to end his relationship with *Scribner's.*

Derleth engaged in correspondence with H. P. Lovecraft, who gave him considerable assistance and encouragement as a young writer trying to establish himself. When Lovecraft died, Wandrei and Derleth collected and issued a collection of Lovecraft's work in *The Outsider and Others* (1939) under the Arkham House imprint. This was the beginning of Derleth's recruitment of more science fiction writers, including William Hope Hodgson, Donald Wandrei, Robert Bloch, Frank Belknap Long, A. E. Van Vogt, Fritz Leiber, Jr., and Ray Bradbury. In the late 1940s and early 1950s, Arkham House successfully published several science fiction anthologies, notably *Beyond Time & Space* (1950), *The Outer Reaches* (1951), *Beacheads of Space* (1952), *Worlds of Tomorrow* (1953), and *Time to Come* (1954).

Sporadically, stories of science fiction by August Derleth had appeared in a variety of places. Some of the "collaborations" of the Cthulhu mythos, as written with H. P. Lovecraft, were science fiction in the Lovecraft vein. However, during the science fiction boom of the early 1950s, Derleth published several of his own short stories; most of them form a posthumously issued collection called *Harrigan's File* (1975).

Derleth was the author of novels, short stories, poetry, essays, and nature studies as well as publisher, editor, anthologist, critic, and biographer. He gained his most sustained reputation through his work in the fields of science fiction and the supernatural, primarily through publishing and editing. His favorite magazine was *Weird Tales*, but he also bought, read, and collected the science fiction magazines from the twenties on down, placing several poems in *Wonder Stories* ("To a Spaceship," March, 1934).

Themes and Style

Derleth's collected stories in *Harrigan's File* follow a format featuring people at a bar, having drinks, who tell a story which would be science fiction if true; the intimation is always that the story probably is true. This format was previously used in Lord Dunsany's stories of Jorken's, L. Sprague DeCamp's *Gavagan's Bar*, or Arthur C. Clarke's *White Hart*. These require a certain skill, a droll dialogue, and have the advantage of a set format. Derleth's stories always dealt with science fiction themes, however, whereas Dunsany and DeCamp frequently delved into fantasy and the supernatural.

Though August Derleth's interest and impact was primarily directed toward the supernatural, the establishment of Arkham House popularized the concept of specialist publishers concentrating on science fiction and fantasy, thereby created a field that has produced hundreds of outstanding books, a trend that is still continuing unabated. As an anthologist, he demonstrated that stories of literary quality in science fiction had appeared in the past and were appearing currently. Throughout most of his life he denigrated science fiction as inferior in literary form to supernatural fiction, but his own selections in his first four anthologies seem to refute that belief.

Plot Summaries of Major Works

Dwellers in Darkness. Since *Harrigan's File* did not contain all the science fiction written by August Derleth, another collection was issued one year later, in 1976. It included "Islands out of Space," "Open Sesame," and "The Song of the Peewee," which had been originally printed in the August, 1949, issue of *Arkham Sampler* under the pen name of Stephen Grendon. "Peewee" is a story of social commentary that fits precisely into Derleth's own nature studies. An otherwise previously normal and rational human Earth male some hundreds of years in the future, in a period following one in which all insect and bird life has been wiped out, insists on hearing the song of a real "Peewee" bird; he will not settle for superb recordings. He will not even accept the fact that birds no longer exist. He cannot be swayed from his request by his wife, friends, the Great Brain which runs the world, or even the fulfillment of alternate requests. Since he insists on asking "why" the birds and the insects were eliminated, and will not accept the explanations given to him, he is eliminated and a robot is brought in to do his job. "Islands out of Space" first appeared in *Amazing Stories* in June of 1950. The story of aliens is likewise repeated in "Open Sesame" (*Arkham Sampler*, Winter, 1949) in which an alien begins the process of taking over the body of an Earthman.

Harrigan's File. This collection, published posthumously, contains seventeen stories. In each story, Harrigan encounters a standard science fiction situation; the "twister" or "snap" ending is always some strong clue that, fantastic as it seems, the tale is true. "McIlvane's Star" is about an old man who discovers a method of becoming young and inherits his own estate after appearing to have died. "A Corner for Lucia" relates the story of a woman who has entered another dimension, where a giant clamlike creature creates for her the illusion of anything that she desires. "Invaders from the Microcosm" tells of a fleet of rocket ships manned by insect-sized intelligent creatures, wiped out by an offhand dose of flit. "A Traveler in Time" sees the invention of a time machine, with a present-day man trading places with a woman from old Dutch New York. The best of the stories is "The Man Who Rode the Saucer," which involves genetic engineering on the part of aliens to see if they cannot transform humans into something closer to their own species, so the two can merge. "The Remarkable Dingdong" is about the editor of *Remarkable Science Fiction* who raises circulation on his magazine by commissioning stories about events that have not yet occurred, such as the first atom and hydrogen bombs.

All the stories are easy to read and just as easily forgotten. Most endings can be anticipated, or are forced. In addition, most of the plot gimmicks are standard in science fiction. Apparently, Derleth thought of a clever ending first, and then created the story for it.

The Watchers out of Time and Others. This is a collection of Derleth "collaborations" with H. P. Lovecraft or, more accurately, Derleth trying to imitate Lovecraft in Cthulhu mythos pastiches. A few of the stories are science fiction. Among them is "The Lurker at the Threshold," which is supposed to contain 1,200 words of authentic Lovecraft and which was initially a separate book, in which the intelligent life forms from outer space actually appear at the end of the story in great globules that burst open, spewing forth masses of protoplasmic flesh. Another science fiction story is "The Shadow out of Space," a long novelette told by a man working in a vast library housed in the body of a vegetable-based creature shaped like a huge cone. He is assembling information for the Great Race that had once been dominant billions of years ago, to enable them to return and regain that dominance. This is patterned after Lovecraft's "The Shadow Out of Time."

Derleth was extremely adept as an imitator of many writers, with a particular talent for the pastiche. But when his imitations of Lovecraft are assembled en masse, as they are in this volume, their inadequacies surface. He simply did not have the lingual resources of Lovecraft, nor is he able to catch the mood which was a transmission of that author's personality.

Biographical/Bibliographical Readings

August Derleth, *Thirty Years of Arkham House--1939-1969* (Arkham House, 1970). Idem, "A Wisconsin Balzac: A Profile of August Derleth," in Zealia Bishop's *The Curse of Yig* (Arkham House, 1953), p.152-75. *Is*, Special August Derleth issue, October, 1971. Sam Moskowitz, "I Remember Derleth," *Star Ship* (Spring, 1981), p. 7-14. **[Sam Moskowitz]**

DICK, PHILIP K.

Life and Works

Philip Kendred Dick was born in Chicago on December 16, 1928. He moved to California early in his life and lived there, in the Berkeley area and Los Angeles, for the rest of his life (except for a few childhood years in Washington, D.C., from 1934 to 1939). Graduating from Berkeley High School in 1945, he briefly attended the University of California, but rebelled against the ROTC and was expelled. His writings are evidence of his intellect and his wide and systematic reading after that time. Dick's major interest, aside from writing, was music. Before becoming a full-time writer, he managed the classical music department of a record store and ran a classical music program on a San Mateo radio station. He married five times and had three children. Dick suffered from hypertension and high blood pressure, and died of a stroke in March of 1982.

He once wrote that he started reading science fiction at the age of twelve, having accidentally bought a copy of *Stirring Science Stories* instead of *Popular Science*. His taste in literature included Joyce, Kafka, Proust, Steinbeck, and Dos Passos. When be began writing short stories, his output was prolific, beginning with "Beyond Lies the Wub," published in the July, 1952 issue of *Planet Stories*. His first published novel was *Solar Lottery* (1955). Dick has spoken of his financial hardship in this period and written movingly, in the introduction to his collection *The Golden Man* (1980), about his struggle to support himself and his wife. It took critics some time to recognize the unusual skill that lay behind his deceptively naive, idiosyncratic stories. Even the best of his early novels, *Eye in the Sky* (1957) or *Time out of Joint* (1959), were not well known and had to wait until much later to receive critical attention. Other interesting works of what has come to be called Dick's "early period" are *The Man Who Japed* (1956), *The World Jones Made* (1956), and *Vulcan's Hammer* (1960), as well as his classic short stories collected in *The Best of Philip K. Dick* (1977). Other collections of Dick's short fiction are found in *The Variable Man and Other Stories* (1957) and *A Handful of Darkness* (1955).

Philip Dick's most celebrated works belong to the next phase, which began in 1962 with *The Man in the High Castle*, a well-written alternative history novel that called for a good deal of research into Nazism on Dick's part, and which won him a Hugo award in 1963. This was followed by a string of other novels: *Martian Time-Slip* (1964), *The Three Stigmata of Palmer Eldritch* (1964), and *Dr. Bloodmoney, or How We Got Along after the Bomb* (1965), *Clans of the Alphane Moon* (1964), *The Simulacra* (1964), *The Penultimate Truth* (1964), and *Lies, Inc.* (published in 1984, but written in the mid-1960s). 1968 saw the publication of *Do Androids Dream of Electric Sheep?*, the novel that lies behind the 1982 movie, *Bladerunner*. *Ubik* (1969) was described by critics as a heroic effort, a magnificent but flawed novel.

The last part of Dick's career begins, after a break of several years, with *Flow My Tears, the Policeman Said* (1974), recipient of the John W. Campbell Memorial Award in 1975. This was followed by *A Scanner Darkly* (1977). Dick was emerging as a well-known personality during this period. In his speech at the Vancouver science fiction convention in March of 1972, he was the relaxed, anticonformist, libertarian, or even anarchist Philip Dick. Just six years later, in 1978, he appeared as a guest of honor at the Science Fiction Festival in Metz, France. For the French, he was then the best-liked science fiction writer.

VALIS (1981), a novel Dick had been working on since the mid-1970s, is considered to be his major work. It forms part of a trilogy of novels, along with *The Divine Invasion* (1981) and *The Transmigration of Timothy Archer* (1982). VALIS is an acronym for "Vast Active Living Intelligence System." The trilogy is a highly personal, grandiose attempt by Dick to take stock of the separate facets of his personality and his private cosmology and beliefs. The trilogy marks the culmination of Dick's science fiction career. Following his death, two or three unpublished nonscience fiction novels have come into print, as well as a collection of shorter science fiction works in *I Hope I Shall Arrive Soon* (1985).

Themes and Style

Dick's deep concern with theological issues was implied in the messiah figures found in his earliest novels, and in the novella "What the Dead Men Say," in *Worlds of Tomorrow* (1964). It emerged more clearly in *Galactic Pot-Healer* (1969) and most intensely in the dark and profound novella, "Faith of Our Fathers," one of the few genuinely "dangerous visions" in Harlan Ellison's 1967 collection of that name. Dick's views as theologian-philosopher can be found in the speech entitled "Man, Android, and Machine," later published in *Science Fiction at Large* (1976).

A question that Dick's writing poses frequently asks, "Is the universe real?" In many of Dick's works, there is is no dimension of stable reality. Psychosis and mind-altering drugs often figure in his work as mechanisms for demonstrating the malleability of reality, especially in *Martian Time-Slip* and *The Three Stigmata of Palmer Eldritch*.

Dick's androids in *Do Androids Dream of Electric Sheep?* are devices which help him to address the related question of what it really means to be human. The answer, for Dick, is a matter of empathy and unprogrammed sympathetic response. Dick's own sympathies lie with the little person, the one involved in a personal struggle to be open to the needs and wishes of those around him or her. These are Dick's most memorable characters--and the self-probing Mr. Tagomi in *The Man in the High Castle* or the uncorrupted but powerless Jack Bohlen in *Martian Time-Slip*, and others like them, are extremely memorable. If they fail, the results always bring disorder and destruction. In a word, entropy prevails. Dick's narratives are often explorations of fictional worlds in which age-old ontological and ethical problems are embodied in a modern, tangible way--but they also offer a commentary on the technological means invoked, the commercial idiom and scientific-sounding language employed, and the science fiction conventions used in constructing these worlds, at once so unreal and yet so convincingly realistic. Dick's worlds may often be implausible, but they are meaningful and substantial as detailed realizations of our repressed doubts about the reality of the present and our fears about the future they imply.

Plot Summaries of Major Works

Do Androids Dream of Electric Sheep? The legacy of World War Terminus is a squalid, depopulated world. It is a strange, new environment overrun by the force of entropy. Radioactive fallout has wiped out virtually all of the animals, so that social status has come to be measured by the kind of pet animal one can afford to buy. Rick Deckard is in the pay of the San Francisco Police Department, but he makes most of his money "retiring andys." The androids in question are highly sophisticated human look-alikes, constantly being updated to keep them one step ahead of any psychological tests designed to prove that they are machines and not human beings. A particularly dangerous group of androids, constructed for roles in the colony on Mars, has escaped back to Earth. In the course of one twenty-four-hour span, Deckard tracks down and eliminates six of them, making him the greatest bounty hunter that ever lived.

The main interest is the theme of how human and artificial cannot be easily separated. In a world with beautiful female androids like Rachel Rosen, with uncontrolled sensual passions, even a bounty hunter can become confused and forget his duties. If the question in the book's title is "Y," then the question posed by those who remain on Earth is "null-null-Y," following a peculiar logic which Dick claims to employ; that is, do post-humans (still) dream of (real) sheep? Humans dial synthetic emotions on mood organs; they use an empathy box to share a simulated mythical experience. The pertinence of the question lies in the fact that this world, where the spiritual dimension is supplied by a machine and where electric sheep are constructed by humans to delude other humans, is also a witty and provocative image of our own world, captured in a distorting mirror.

Dr. Bloodmoney, or How We Got Along after the Bomb. The intricate and decentered plot of this novel connects a group of Californians in two main locations, San Francisco and the countryside of West Marin, through two periods in their lives. Their old way of life is shattered when, one day in 1981, a large-scale nuclear war breaks out. The Emergency (E-Day) intensifies their preoccupation with the fate of Bruno Bluthgeld, or Dr. Bloodmoney, a nuclear physicist for the U.S. military. Most of the groups already hold him responsible for the overestimation of the predictive powers of scientific knowledge which led to a major leak of radioactivity from high-altitude tests in 1972. Presumably as a reaction to this, he is in the grip of megalomaniac paranoid convictions, and is seeing a psychiatrist, Dr. Stockstill, about the blotches that he believes mark his face. Seven years after E-Day, the aftermath finds various citizens in various states of mind. Hoppy Harrington, a limbless thalidomide victim, is now an extremely effective handyman thanks to his telekinetic abilities. Like his rival social outcast, Bluthgeld, Hoppy wants to impose his will on the world. In the end it takes a bizarre mutant form of human life to stop him. Bill Keller, conceived in the back of a VW bus on the day of destruction, emerges from his invisible niche inside his sister's body. Walt Dangerfield, meanwhile, had launched on a one way trip to Mars just before the bombs started falling, is stranded in orbit around the Earth. Everyone quickly becomes obsessed with his fate, avidly following his broadcasts from orbit. His jovial chats help the dispersed communities of the postwar world not to lose heart.

Each fragment of the narrative represents one sequence of events from one character's viewpoint. For example, the description of the destruction of San Francisco, which follows a flash-forward to 1988, is given still more impact by being infused with the mental torment of Bluthgeld, through whose senses it is perceived. The intensity of the narrative never lets up as it brings to life, in turn, each character's vision of life. It is left to the reader to make connections between the sections and draw conclusions from the contrasting responses to the catastrophe.

In Dick's Third World War arena, infatuations with power and science (and anything else that takes possession of a person's mind) appear in intensified forms, and his warnings of their dangers is a dramatic one. Above all, though, *Dr. Bloodmoney* shows Philip Dick's resourcefulness as a writer, his imagination, and his sense of humor, in its sophisticated narrative techniques and in the extraordinary range of forms of life it contains.

The Man in the High Castle. The assassination of Franklin Delano Roosevelt triggers a course of events that leads to the success of the Axis powers, Germany and Japan. The United States of America (East coast) is largely German-controlled, while the Japanese occupy the Pacific States of America. The Pacific Coast Americans have learned to adapt themselves to the expectations of the dominant race; they consult the ancient Taoist Book of Wisdom, the *I-Ching*, before making decisions, and they adhere to the required ritualistic social customs. Between these two spheres of influence lies a buffer zone, the Rocky Mountain states. Here, in his "high castle," lives Hawthorne Abendsen, author of a book entitled *The Grasshopper Lies Heavy*. Many of the citizens have read this novel, and from their discussions it is learned that the "alternate present" of Hawthorne's novel starts with the Allies being victorious in World War II.

A representative of a faction in the German Reich (Baynes) comes to San Francisco to pass on information to General Yatabe about Goering's plan to launch a surprise attack, using nuclear weapons, aimed at eliminating the Japanese as a counterforce. The two meet in the office of a Japanese trade official, Mr. Tagomi, who is forced to kill ~~Baynes~~ in order to help prevent the eruption of evil which he sees incarnated in the Nazi mentality.

In the novel, the Japanese represent a worldview preoccupied with the past and sterile, unable to exist without borrowed masks (even the *I-Ching* is Chinese). Through them, and through the dehumanizing Nazis, Dick offers intensifications of tendencies at work in contemporary America. His characters must confront, on a personal level, the implications of these contrasting worldviews. The deadly, disruptive force of Nazism is confronted by acts of heroism, but it is clear that such acts are unlikely to alter the course of history. The final, gripping chapter shows how Abendsen's book, analogous to Dick's, reaches beyond the apparent impenetrability of historical factors to a new reality that expresses the inner truth of the situation.

Martian Time-Slip. Mars, in 1994, is a rundown colony. Everything is second rate and recycled. Remnants of the ancient Martian civilization, with its network of canals, are still present. The petty rivalry for the supplies of impure water or for contraband delicacies from Earth represents a squalid version of the competetive aspect of the old Terran way of life. Unlike Earth, it is not overpopulated and, with its open spaces and lonely housewives in isolated homes, it still offers some scope for adventurous spirits. For those with power, Mars, along with its original inhabitants, the Aborigine-like Bleekmen, is there to be exploited without a second thought. There is a United Nations plan to build a huge housing complex in an arid mountain area of special significance to the Bleekman. Arnie Kott, the corrupt head of the Water Workers' Union, stands to see his key status decline if the project goes ahead. He is prepared to make use of the paranormal abilities of Manfred Steiner, an autistic boy, and to risk the sanity of Jack Bohlen, an all-purpose repairman who retains vivid memories of his past psychotic episodes, if it will help him turn the plan to his advantage. However, Kott is unable to comprehend the risks he runs by trying to overrule or ignore the more mysterious parts of human experience, and in the end he is the victim of his own tunnel vision and greed.

Dick tells the story very economically, using a precise, transparent language and avoiding sensational elements. *Martian Time-Slip* is probably his best-controlled novel. The key events build up a vivid, many-faceted impression of this meager world. The underlying tired desperation surfaces in the early suicide of Manfred's father, hurt by news of a rumored final solution to the problems of mutants and mental abnormality. The degradation of human relationships is driven home in the brutal lovemaking scene at the heart of the novel, which Dick repeats from three differing points of view, demonstrating how reality can never be reduced to simple objective facts. This novel manages to convey a real sense of the terrible plight of the schizophrenic, the person who exists out of phase with the others. Dick suggests that the glimpses Manfred has of ultimate decay, already at work under the surface of the functional universe Arnie imagines he lives in, have a horrible truth about them and are in touch with an absolute reality.

The Three Stigmata of Palmer Eldritch. Barney Mayerson is a "precog" fashion consultant at Perky Pat Layouts. He previews trends using his ability to sample future possibilities, so that the company can have the right items ready for their role as props for Perky Pat dolls and their miniaturized layouts, which are shipped off to the Martian colonies. There are more than a million colonists on Mars, leading a monotonous life in highly restrictive conditions, for whom the period-image of California embodied in the layouts is an obsessive concern. They spend all that they can on the dolls and fittings, and on an illegal hallucogenic drug called Can-D, also marketed by Barney's boss Leo Bolero. The drug enables the colonists to enter the free and easy world of Perky Pat and her friends, where their shared fantasies can be realistically enacted.

New York in the twenty-first century is an overpopulated, sweltering, unpleasant place to live. Barney is under tremendous stress, dissatisfied with his way of life and sorry that he left his wife. His new assistant, Roni Fugate, may be after his job, and another pressing worry is the draft notice he has received which would make him a Martian colonist. He is forever consulting his psychiatristin-a-suitcase, Dr. Smile, in a desperate drive to make himself morally unstable enough to fail his emigration test. His boss, Leo Bolero, on the other hand, has a home in Antarctica and money for the evolution therapy, desired to make a superintelligent man of him. Leo is apparently a model of human achievement. This whole situation is disrupted when Palmer Eldritch, a well-known interplanetary industrialist, returns from a ten-year flight to Proxima Centauri. He brings back with him a new drug, Chew-Z, which outclasses Can-D. Bolero futiley attempts to block Eldritch; however, there is no way to deter the spread of the new drug. Eldritch's stigmata--his artificial hand, mechanical eyes, and steel teeth--are signs of the alien power which needs him and Chew-Z as a bridgehead to transmit its controlling influence. Eldritch is like a crystal dropped into the supersaturated Terran system.

The great strength of this novel lies in the convincing way it conveys the drug-induced realities that are its real subject. The Can-D experience, apparently no more than escapist fantasy, reveals a collective desire for illusion, a willingness to be duped. These implications are given a frightening presence in the multiform figure of Palmer Eldritch, the master hallucinator of all Chew-Z experiences. Some see him as God and creator, king and owner, or as protoplasm; he describes himself as a bridge. Whatever he is, he is a truly subversive, nightmarish invention through which Dick seems to be offering sardonic images of a messiah, appropriate for readers who may be complacent consumers of images in a society where the mass media too often devotes itself to escapism and manipulation.

Ubik. The year is 1992. Many individuals possess special psychic powers, but their effects can be counteracted by the "anti-psi" talents of yet other individuals. When an organization feels it is being infiltrated by "psis," it calls upon the services of a Prudence (or anti-psi) Organization. Glen Runciter runs the best of these organizations with the help and advice of his wife, a half-alive woman preserved in the cold-pack bins at the Beloved Brethren Moratorium in Zurich. Runciter, along with a group of ten top inertials and his right-hand man, Joe Chip, an experienced tester of psychic forces, are called to the moon, where they are victims of an attack. Reality is no longer a coherent whole, but depends on the collective will of the group. Apparently the collective group of half-lifers have placed Runciter and his group in cold storage. The world reverts to the year 1939. Joe sees manifestations of his boss everywhere--on money, in graffiti, even on television. Only the spray cans of "Ubik" seem to offer the hope of a shared reality--but Ubik is rare and hard to find. Ubik is a portable negative ionizer, an all-purpose wonder product invented by Ella Runciter and the other half-lifers. It is a kind of packaged life force, capable of holding back the regression of organized forms for brief periods.

Ubik is a metaphysical whodunit and its strength lies in the way it involves the reader in the search for a stable, meaningful reality. The premise is that the reality of the half-lifers is the stuff of dreams, a starting point that can be justified as a valid science fiction extrapolation from current knowledge of cold storage techniques. In Dick's eccentric, totally commercialized world, it makes sense that groups of bodies would be linked up to a single, multichannel machine to save money. The half-life is used as a highly effective metaphor through which the author tells a parable about the search for ultimate meaning. There is always hope of a collective solution; it is ubiquitous, but it appears in the degraded forms forced upon it as an alienated, commercialized world.

Biographical/Bibliographical Readings

Bruce Gillespie, *Philip K. Dick: Electric Shepherd* (Norstrilia Press, 1975). Martin Harry Greenberg and Joseph D. Olander, *Philip K. Dick* (Taplinger, 1983). Daniel J. H. Levack, *PKD: A Philip K. Dick Bibliography* (Underwood Miller, 1981). Kim Stanley Robinson, *The Novels of Philip K. Dick* (UMI Research Press, 1984). Jeff Wagner, "In the World He Was Writing About: The Life of Philip K. Dick," *Foundation* no. 34 (1985), p.69-96. Paul Williams, *Only Apparently Real: The Work of Philip K. Dick* (Arbor House, 1986). [Jonathan K. Benison]

DICKSON, GORDON R.

Life and Works

Gordon Rupert Dickson was born on November 1, 1923, in Edmonton, Alberta, Canada. He taught himself to read at the age of four, and by the time he was six years old he was making up his own stories and announcing that he wanted to be a writer. The remainder of Dickson's biography--except for one brief period--shows him pursuing and achieving his childhood wish.

From 1930 to 1933, Dickson attended school in Ladner, British Columbia, read adult fiction from the local library, and had a couple of poems published in the local newspaper. From 1933 to 1937, he went to a private school in Vancouver, where he began writing "novels" in ruled notebooks that he threw away when the stories were finished. In 1937, when Dickson was thirteen, his father, a mining engineer, died and his mother moved the family to Minneapolis, where her family lived. Just two years later, Dickson graduated from high school and enrolled in the University of Minnesota, where he was steered into a creative writing major. Dickson's undergraduate career was interrupted by three years of service in the U.S. Army during World War II. He received his B.A. degree in 1948 and enrolled in graduate school, thinking to earn a doctorate and go into teaching. The year he spent studying English literature at the University of Minnesota was the only period in his life when he was not certain that writing would be his career. Soon he realized that, for him, graduate study was unnecessary and unwanted, and he turned to full-time writing. That was in 1950. Dickson has been a professional writer ever since.

Dickson's first published science fiction story was "Trespass," a collaboration with Poul Anderson that appeared in the *Fantastic Story Quarterly* during 1950. (Dickson met and became a lifelong friend of the younger Anderson when both were at the University of Minnesota.) Dickson's first "solo" published science fiction story was "The Friendly Man" in the February, 1951 *Astounding*

Science Fiction. Thus began a successful career that to date spans nearly four decades and includes close to 200 pieces of short fiction, 30 adult novels, 4 juvenile novels, about 20 collections of short fiction (representing about 120 individual pieces), 7 collaborations, and 4 edited anthologies. In 1965, his "Soldier, Ask Not" won the Hugo award for Best Short Fiction. In 1966, "Call Him Lord" won the Nebula award for Best Novelette. And in 1977, his novel *The Dragon and the George* (1976) won the August Derleth award from the British Fantasy Society, while another novel, *Time Storm* (1977), won the Jupiter award.

Dickson's dedication to science fiction extends beyond writing. As a teenager, he joined the Minneapolis Fantasy Society (whose membership included Poul Anderson and Clifford D. Simak). He is a member of First Fandom. He regularly attends science fiction conventions, where he is popular with science fiction fans. He served two terms (1969-71) as president of the Science Fiction Writers of America. He has frequently been a guest writer at James Gunn's Intensive English Institute for the Teaching of Science Fiction at the University of Kansas. "Gordy," as he is affectionately known, generously gives helpful advice to established as well as novice science fiction writers.

Normally, summarizing a career as lengthy as Dickson's would be difficult. Dickson made this task easier, however, when he decided early in his career to stake his reputation on the creation of a gargantuan science fiction novel, now known as the "Childe cycle." This project began in 1957, when he first started thinking about a character who could somehow bypass the torturously slow workings of ordinary logic. When completed the cycle will number thirteen novels and span an entire millenium: three historical novels set in the fourteenth through the nineteenth centuries, three contemporary (twentieth-century) novels, and seven science fiction novels reaching from the twenty-first to the twenty-fourth century. To date, Dickson has published only five of the cycle's thirteen projected novels. All five are science fiction; all five also include protagonists related to the cycle's three prime characters. In *Necromancer* (1962, sometimes retitled *No Room for Man*), Paul Formain is a later twenty-first-century man whose actions lead to the colonizing of the planets Mars and Kultis, and thus to the birth of the Exotic philosophers. In *Tactics of Mistake* (1971), Cletus Grahame is the twenty-second-century military genius whose seminal work on tactics helps pave the way for the military success of the Dorsai, who have settled on the planet of the same name. Because the Dorsai figure so prominently in the cycle novels published so far, many readers call the entire series the "Dorsai cycle." A century later in *Dorsai!* (1976, first published in 1960 as *The Genetic General*), Donal Graeme, Cletus Grahame's great-great-grandson, uses his unusual intuitive powers to forcibly unite the Sixteen Worlds that make up the cycle's cosmos. In *Soldier, Ask*

Not (1967), an expansion of the 1965 Hugo-winning story, Tam Olyn, Donal's twenty-third-century contemporary, attempts to destroy the Friendly (faith-holding) worlds of Harmony and Association, but winds up finding a faith of his own. And, in *The Final Encyclopedia* (1984), we meet Hal Mayne, destined to develop into the first Responsible Man after having lived three lifetimes, once as a Man of War, once as a Man of Philosophy, and once as a Man of Faith.

Themes and Style

Dickson says about the Childe cycle that in it he conceives of the human race as one large organism--the "racial animal"--which is experiencing a conflict between the part that wants to stay home and be safe and the part that wants to explore and take risks. Alarmed about the increasingly destructive power at the disposal of individual human beings, the racial animal begins to evolve ethically toward what Dickson calls Responsible Man. As part of this instinctive quest for survival, the racial animal unconsciously attempts a bold genetic experiment: the fragmenting of the race into Dickson's Three Prime Characters--the Man of War, the Man of Philosophy, and the Man of Faith--who eventually colonize some of the Sixteen Worlds. Dickson posits that the Responsible Man will successfully reintegrate the Three Prime Characters, whose overspecialization will turn out to be nonviable. The cycle as planned will illustrate Dickson's "galloping optimism" and his assumption that evolutionary growth occurs in three stages: separation, independent development, and reunion.

According to Dickson, the Childe cycle, when completed, will be the showpiece of a new kind of science fiction writing, which he calls the Consciously Thematic Novel. As in the best work in the literary mainstream, all elements of the Consciously Thematic Novel will bear the novel's theme; nothing will be adventitious; readers will absorb the message unconsciously, rather than having it spelled out for them as happens in the blatant polemics of the usual science fiction novel. At Dickson's current rate of completing cycle novels, however, readers will have to wait until 1995 or so to see exactly how the three million words of the Consciously Thematic Novel will work together.

Most of Dickson's noncycle novels that are set on Earth explore the superperson theme. The only exception is *The Far Call* (1978), a near-future novel about the first expedition to Mars. Some of the terrestrial setting novels whose super individuals provide interesting variations on the Responsible Man concept are *Sleepwalker's World* (1971), *The Pritcher Mass* (1972), *The R-Master* (1973), and *Time Storm* (1978). Also, *The Space Swimmers* (1967) and its prequel, *Home from the Shore* (1979), which both take place mainly in Earth's oceans, contain even clearer thematic connections to the cycle.

The noncycle novels set away from Earth jettison this theme. Instead, perhaps because of Dickson's childhood experiences as a Canadian, these novels deal with human-alien interaction, generally on a recently colonized planet. *The Outposter* (1972), *Alien Art* (1973), *Pro* (1978), and *Masters of Everon* (1980) treat this interaction seriously, while *Spacial Delivery* (1961) and *Spacepaw* (1969) treat it comically. These two comic novels about alien-human interaction resemble the Hoka series Dickson has written in collaboration with Anderson--*Earthman's Burden* (1957), *Star Prince Charlie* (1975), and *Hoka!* (1983). *The Alien Way* (1965) includes Dickson's most successfully realized aliens--the Ruml. *Naked to the Stars* (1961) is a thoughtful reply to Robert A. Heinlein's *Starship Troopers* and displays Dickson's antimilitarism.

Plot Summaries of Major Works

Dorsai! *Dorsai!* opens in the last quarter of the twenty-third century. The human race has colonized Venus and Mars and spread to thirteen other planets around seven distant stars. During the dispersal to the stars, the race has also fragmented into three Splinter Cultures--the Men of War (the Dorsai of Dorsai), the Men of Thought (the Exotics of Kultis and Mara), and the Men of Faith (the Friendlies of Harmony and Association). Donal Graeme, a Dorsai, is an eighteen-year-old cadet who has just graduated from the Academy. During his military career, he uses a mysterious ability to read character and see developing patterns to impress everyone he meets, including planetary leaders like William of Ceta, the Eldest Bright; military geniuses, like Hendrik Galt; and even women--Anea Marlivana (Select of Kultis). Donal is pitted against William of Ceta. Their main conflict occurs over a problem in interstellar economics: since the most important commodity among the planets is human ability, the problem boils down to who should have control over individual talent, individuals or the governments. William, a consummate businessman, favors a reciprocal open market, because in that market economic power would flow to the "tight" worlds and to the powers behind them, such as William himself. Donal, on the other hand, being from Dorsai, the most individualistic of the "loose" worlds, resists William's attempts to limit human freedom. In order to oppose William, Donal must become powerful and develops an unquenchable ambition and brilliant military career. Donal's meteoric rise from cadet to secretary of defense, however, also mirrors his exploration and understanding of the oddity that makes his rise possible. Donal realizes that he is an intuitional superperson, able to use his intuitions the way ordinary human beings use logic. Like Plato's philosopher-kings, Donal accepts the painful responsibility of ruling the sixty billion human beings who have not yet changed the way he has.

Originally published in a shortened version called *The Genetic General* (1960), this novel established Dickson as a major science fiction writer. Now considered a classic, *Dorsai!* forms part of Dickson's Childe cycle, a project he has been working on for nearly thirty years. When completed the cycle will include thirteen novels, spanning the millenium from the fourteenth to the twenty-fourth centuries.

The novel's structural pattern and central conflict recapitulate its major theme: evolution. Donal climbs through the ranks, then evolves beyond the confines of his military successes--he becomes a superbeing. And his evolution brings in its wake the defeat of William, who would stifle change and individuality by making human beings into controllable chattel. Donai, therefore, is among the first of Dickson's optimistic portraits of human beings exceeding supposed human limitations.

The Far Call. Set in the 1990s, the Earth has launched the first manned expedition to Mars. The international crew of six "marsnauts" include Tad Hansard (American, senior mission commander), Feodor Aleksandrovitch Asturnov, (Russian, junior mission commander), Bapti Lal Bose (Indian), Dirk Welles (British), Bern Callieux (Pan-European), and Anoshi Wantanabe (Japanese). Many diplomats are present for the launch, as are newspeople and science fiction writers. Because of political pressure, the marsnauts' experiment list during the first thirty days of their mission (when the public will be most interested) is impossibly long. Al Murgatroyd, chief of Onboard Equipment, has misgivings about the most recent tests of the laser system that provides primary communication for Phoenix One and Phoenix Two, the expedition's two ships. Neither problem is solved before the launch, and, eventually, both problems contribute to aborting the mission and to the deaths of two marsnauts.

Unlike much of Dickson's other work, *The Far Call* does not rely on customary science fiction motifs. It is the only Dickson novel in which neither aliens nor a superperson appears. The technology, although thoroughly researched and impressively detailed, is just slightly beyond present-day capabilities. Dickson gives us nuclear-powered shuttles and a laser communications system, along with the familiar trappings of the Kennedy Space Center, reminiscent of the Gemini, Apollo, and Skylab programs. Eerily foreshadowing the 1986 Challenger shuttle tragedy, the novel centers on a disaster waiting to happen.

The Far Call incorporates many typical Dickson themes. The paramount idea is Dickson's mystical trust in the wisdom of space exploration--not just as a means of increasing human knowledge but also as the best way to unite all humanity. The chief bearer of Dickson's ideas in the novel is Jens Wylie, U.S. undersecretary for the Development of Space, whose unselfish idealism conflicts with the expedient pragmatism of his boss, the president. Jen's idealism wins out by the end of novel and there is already talk of the necessity to mount another expedition. Many more obstacles remain, but the human race is finally heeding the far call of space.

The Final Encyclopedia. Hal Mayne, sixteen years old, escapes from Bleys Ahrens, a leader of the Others (a Mafia-like group that has risen explosively to galactic prominence). Bleys Ahrens is a magnificent human being pursuing a false path (his name sounds like "blaze errans," or "errant light." Hal is a "childe errant," a squire on a quest to become a knight. As he grows up, he lives, fights, or visits Old Earth, New Earth, Coby, Harmony, Mars, and Dorsai. Hal's first tutors are an Exotic Man of Thought (Walter the InTeacher), a Friendly Man of Faith (Obadiah Testator), and a Dorsai Man of War (Malachi Nasumo). Later, Hal is influenced by Tam Olyn, the exotic director of the Final Encyclopedia itself (an enormous, armored information retrieval system orbiting Old Earth), by James Child-of-God, an Elect warrior on the Friendly World of Harmony, and by the spirit of Ian Graeme, a scion of the most famous Dorsai family. The most important women in Hal's life come from all three of the Splinter Cultures: Ajela, Tam's exotic assistant at the Final Encyclopedia; Rukh Tamani, leader of a Command waging guerilla warfare against the Friendly Militia on Harmony, and the Dorsai Amanda Morgan. The novel's conflict is between opposing impulses in humanity's racial psyche--the desire for comfort and stasis versus the desire for risk and growth. Bleys and the Others work toward stasis. Hal works toward growth.

The novel's title provides several clues to its contents. *The Final Encyclopedia* inaugurates the finale of the Childe cycle's science fiction parts. Its settings include many of the cycle's Sixteen Worlds. The plot is cyclical, with Hal starting out on and ending near Old Earth. The novel's cast, male and female, includes all of the Sixteen Worlds' three Splinter Cultures. The novel includes many cross references to previously written works in the cycle. Hal is in his third incarnation, having already lived as Donal Graem, hero of *Dorsai!* The novel's length, pace, and tone all suggest its encyclopedic nature: it is fully 700 pages long; its pace is leisurely; literary, historical, and philosophic expositions overshadow action; and it purports to round off an entire era in the evolution of the human race.

But the title also includes two ironies. Historically, the idea of encyclopedia first achieved actuality through the work of the eighteenth-century French philosophers, against whom stood the Romantics. The first irony is that Hal is a romantic hero--young, handsome, sensitive, isolated, brilliant, eloquent, etc.--who uses conservative technology to try to save the human race. The second irony is simply that the title is innaccurate, for the novel ends with the battle between Bleys and Hal joined but not yet finished. We must wait for the two promised sequels, *Chantry Guild* and *Childe*, to see how Dickson rounds off the Childe cycle.

The Man from Earth. The ten short stories reprinted in this collection were originally published between 1952 and 1969. Six of them appeared in an earlier collection of Dickson's stories, *Ancient My Enemy* (1974). Several also appeared in *Danger, Human* (1970), which was later reprinted in 1973 as *The Book of Gordon Dickson*. The reason that these stories keep being reprinted is simple: as a group, they successfully represent Dickson's work in this form.

All but one of the stories deal with the two possibilities attendant upon alien and human interactions. One of the two possibilities is cooperation. In "The Bleak and Barren Land," Kent Harmon, the colonial representative to the planet Modor, convinces the Modorians to coexist with human settlers. And in "The Odd Ones," a Snorap and a Lut (alien ecologists) observe two humans struggling for survival on an inhospitable planet. They eventually reveal themselves to the humans and share their advanced knowledge.

The possibility opposed to cooperation is competition. One form of competition is open warfare between aliens and humans. In "Steel Brother," Thomas Jordan, newly made commander of an outpost station along the Frontier, fights--and nearly loses--his first battle with enemy aliens characterized only by their antihuman ferocity. In "Danger Human," an alien team kidnaps a man from New Hampshire and then discovers why the human race is invincibly dangerous. "In the Bone" pits a man stripped of everything except his cunning (and his rage) against a nearly omnipotent alien. The human prospectors in "Ancient, My Enemy" defend themselves against the cannibalistic natives of the planet Ubdahr. The other form of competition between aliens and humans is hidden, rather than open, warfare. In "Love Me True," Ted Holman has smuggled a seemingly lovable antipod named Pogey back from Arcturus, without realizing that Pogey is actually an alien agent. In the collection's title story, "The Man from Earth," Will Mauston faces the unpredictable whim of the powerful director of the trading world Duhnbar--and shows him the stuff of which humans are made. In "Tiger Green," Jerry McWhim, member of a human survey expedition, saves himself and his shipmates from being absorbed by the collective mind of the planet they are surveying.

The story in the collection that does not deal with alien-human interaction is "Call Him Lord." This story, set on Earth thousands of years in the future, details the final day in the life of the young Prince--heir to the Empire of the Younger Worlds--who is visiting Earth as part of his grand tour. "Call Him Lord," which won a Nebula award in 1966, is probably Dickson's finest piece of short fiction. It also sums up the two central themes of all the stories in this collection--among the races of the universe, the human race is unique; and technology is not nearly as important as internal qualities such as intelligence, courage, perserverance, love, and duty.

Naked to the Stars. This novel is set in the not-too-distant future. Propelled by population pressure, humanity is expanding out into the universe, while on Earth itself only veterans have the franchise; the right to vote can be earned only by a tour of duty in either the Armed Services or in the Contacts Service. Both are involved in human expansion--the first as soldiers, the second as noncombatants dedicated to peace. The soldiers detest the pacificist Contact Officers, whom they call "gutless wonders." Calvin Truant journeys from soldier to Contact Officer. During his second military campaign, Cal orders an operation that results in the massacre of alien civilians, in the process wounding himself and losing sixteen hours of his memory. Later, he refuses the psychiatric probe of his memory that would allow him to continue his military career, and decides to join the Contacts Service instead. The rest of the novel concentrates on Cal's retraining and his rapid rise in the Contacts Service.

Naked to the Stars responds to the conservative militarism of Heinlein's *Starship Troopers*. The similarities between the two novels are obvious--governments run by veterans, military expeditions to alien planets, descriptions of basic training (including flogging as a disciplinary punishment), and so forth. Dickson also allows his soldier, Cal, to espouse Heinlein's ideas about humanity's manifest destiny and about the need for humans to be the "toughest hombres" in the universe. But Dickson also subjects these ideas to a withering critique. The commander of the Contacts Service articulates the pacificist position that there are always options to killing. Cal gradually accepts the Contacts Service philosophy, which means he also finally understands his dead father's evolutionary politics, with its subordination of individual will to a universal code of ethics. What Cal learns is that pacifism requires much more courage than combat. What Dickson teaches is not that the human race should abandon war, but that an advanced race must try for peaceful understanding of the other life forms before deciding to send in the soldiers.

Biographical/Bibliographical Readings

"Gordon R. Dickson," in *The Sound of Wonder* (1985), v.2, p.159-73. Clifford McMurray, "An Interview with Gordon R. Dickson," *Science Fiction Review* 26 (July 1978), p.6-12. Sandra Miesel, "Gordon R. Dickson," *Algol* 15:2 (Spring, 1978), p.33-38. Raymond H. Thompson, *Gordon R. Dickson: A Primary and Secondary Bibliography* (G.K. Hall, 1983). [Todd H. Sammons]

DISCH, THOMAS M.

Life and Works

Thomas Michael Disch was born on February 2, 1940, in Des Moines, Iowa, raised in Minnesota, and educated in New York, where he worked as a part-time checkroom attendant at the Majestic Theater while finishing high school. He completed a B.A. at New York University in 1962. He spent two years after graduation as a copywriter with the firm of Doyle Dane Bernbach, Inc.

His first fiction publications appeared in 1962 in the magazines *Amazing* and *Fantastic*. His early short stories partook equally of science fiction and mild horror, subdued by a subtle and literate style, a penchant for finely and realistically drawn settings and characters, and leanings toward surrealism. Representative of his early works are the stories collected in the 1966 volume, *One Hundred and Two H-Bombs* (revised and republished in 1971 as *White Fang Goes Dingo and Other Funny Science Fiction Stories*) and in the 1968 *Under Compulsion* (which appeared in an expanded 1971 edition entitled *Fun with Your New Head*). Among the tales in these collections are "Descending," about a down-and-out intellectual who, after shoplifting in a department store, finds himself descending an eternal staircase alone; "The Number You Have Reached," about the last human on Earth, who keeps receiving phone calls from a woman who he is convinced is a creation of his own crumbling mind; and "Moondust, the Smell of Hay, and Dialectical Materialism," about a Soviet cosmonaut stranded on the moon and wondering what he is dying for. Other characteristic early stories include "Thesis on Social Forms and Social Controls," a report from a future society that preserves its utopian state by institutionalizing schizophrenia, and "The Squirrel Cage," in which the sole character free associates on the subject of his imprisonment in a tiny, barren room.

By 1967, Disch had moved to London to participate in the New Wave science fiction then being promoted by Michael Moorcock in *New Worlds* magazine. There Disch published more of his off-beat short stories and serialized his first major novel, *Camp Concentration* (1968). In it, Disch retreats from the more farfetched science fiction concepts of his earlier work in favor of a setting contemporary with the Vietnam Era. Imprisonment provides the plot: an American dissident is hidden away with others in a top-secret government laboratory where the government is experimenting with intelligence enhancement. The prisoners, as guinea pigs, are given a form of syphilis which raises IQ but ultimately causes death. Disch explores the intellectual subculture created by these conditions, using literary metaphors of the Faust legend of a man destroyed by knowledge.

Following *Camp Concentration*, Disch's output became prolific and varied. In 1969, he produced a novelization of the popular British television show, *The Prisoner*. In 1972 appeared *334*, a novel-length grouping of interconnected stories set in a bleakly believable future. *334* took to new heights Disch's literate, darkly humorous manner and his facility with realistic settings and characters. The year 1973 provided another short story collection, *Getting into Death and Other Stories*. Stories from this and other collections were brought together by Gregg Press in 1977 with the title *The Early Science Fiction Stories of Thomas M. Disch*. Also in the 1970s, Disch produced several books outside the science fiction genre.

His first genuine novel since *Camp Concentration*, and his longest, appeared in 1979. *On Wings of Song*, like his other fiction of the 1970s, plays close to contemporary reality, and like most of his fiction deals with imprisonment in various forms from physical incarceration to the entrapment of the spirit by the flesh. It qualifies as science fiction by its near-future setting and by the existence of "flying," a process that allows an individual to leave his or her body.

Themes and Style

Much of Disch's fiction deals with imprisonment of one sort or another, whether at the hands of some incomprehensibly Kafkaesque system, of one's individual psyche, or of other forces beyond one's control. In *The Genocides*, published in 1965, the entire human species finds itself wholly at the mercy of aliens who are clearing Earth for agricultural reasons, removing terrestrial species in order to plant a single crop of their own. Similar points come out of Disch's other earlier novels: *Mankind under the Leash* (1966), published in Britain as *The Puppies of Terra*, and *Echo round His Bones* (1967). In the first, humans have become the pets of aliens, who keep them in line by stimulating the pleasure centers of the brain. In *Echo round His Bones*, a matter transfer mechanism used for transportation has the side effect of duplicating people in a ghostly half-world, where they are unable to communicate with the real world and unable to get any tools or food except that duplicated via the mechanism. Life for those thus trapped grows increasingly desperate and brutal. *The Genocides*, *Mankind under the Leash*, and *Echo round His Bones* were republished in the 1980 omnibus, *Triplicity*.

In a 1976 essay, "The Embarrassment of Science Fiction," Disch sees science fiction as a children's genre--intellectually, emotionally, and morally immature. He concludes however, that if the genre does succeed in producing anything of literary value, it will survive, and that of all contemporay literary forms, it is the one that offers the most flexibility of theme and subject matter.

Disch's work bears comparison with that of postmodern ironists like Barth, Barthelme, Pynchon, and Vonnegut. In his deft depiction of real people in often surreal situations, and his frequent metaphorical use of the motif of imprisonment and entrapment by forces beyond one's control, Disch comments on the human condition in the twentieth century with a mixture of humor and despair, in a literary tradition that goes back at least as far as Franz Kafka. By drawing on the resources of science fiction, Disch has added his own spin to that tradition.

Plot Summaries of Major Works

Camp Concentration. Louis Sacchetti is a dissident intellectual, apparently during the Vietnam Era, who finds himself a prisoner in an underground complex run by the government. He, with other prisoners who are being used as experimental subjects, has been given a strain of syphilis that enhances intelligence but ravages the nervous system. In their prison, the human guinea pigs enjoy artistic, scientific, and philosophical genius but face physical disintegration and premature death. Sacchetti's journal records the interplay of prisoners and guards, and speculates on the meaning of life and death, on power, powerlessness, and creativity. Subtle tensions develop as the prisoners' minds grow far beyond those of their keepers. Ultimately the power of the mind triumphs over both death and imprisonment.

Serialized in *New Worlds* in 1967, published in book form in 1968, this novel is regarded as one of the best to come out of the science fiction New Wave. It represents Disch's maturation as a writer of quirky, intelligent science fiction. With this work, Disch opted away from the more blatant science fiction motifs of his earlier novels in favor of a more subtle and realistic form. Disch's witty touches keep the novel from seeming too ponderous, despite its focus on imprisonment, disease, death, and metaphysical angst. Except for the science fiction twists of artificially enhanced intelligence and mind-swapping--the latter a result of an experiment designed by inmates--the novel is very close to mimetic fiction. It must be read for its subtle readings of character, its ironic and intelligent style, and its metaphoric handling of the subjects of freedom, knowledge, and death.

The Genocides. Humanity's survival is threatened by a civilization that is wiping out all native life from Earth in order to plant a single crop of their own. The human race does not even get a chance to fight back. The aliens themselves never appear or even attempt communication. All that is seen of them is their giant plants that block all sunlight from the Earth's surface and their heat machines bent on destroying "pests," including humans. What is left of humanity hangs on in survivalist communes led, unfortunately, by those brutal and ruthless enough to take control.

The focal characters, a pair of well-educated intellectuals, find themselves wholly powerless not only before the alien menace but before the stupid, authoritarian values of the little human culture that remains. This culture, too, is finally destroyed when food begins to run out, and the survivors take refuge in the sweet pulp of the alien plants, literally becoming parasites and continuing to degenerate physically and morally until harvest provides the coup de grace.

Disch's first novel works out of a science fiction subgenre, the disaster story. Here, as in his later work, Disch does not permit despair to rise to tragedy. Except for the sympathetic couple, humanity comports itself poorly under stress; the disintegration of the characters is viewed at best with ironic disgust. Disch possesses the clinical if cutting intellectual detachment of the satirist. *The Genocides* demonstrates his fascination with people placed in situations wholly outside their control and their usually contemptible responses to such situations. Later fictions would shackle Disch's characters with both physical and social restraints, but none put humanity in so hopeless and desperate a position as *The Genocides*.

On Wings of Song. Daniel Weinreb, born into a near-future Iowa, is governed (like the rest of the Farm Belt) by right-wing fundamentalists. Of particular concern to the rigidly moralistic society is the practice of "flying," common on the Coasts and elsewhere but forbidden in the Heartland. One flies by leaving one's flesh in the ethereal form of a "fairy," but only if one can achieve the proper state of mind and find emancipation in the right song.

Daniel develops a desire to fly after suffering the injustices of his culture, including several months in a prison camp on a trumped-up charge. His quest for spiritual liberation, however, is filled with pathetic and ironic misadventures: he marries the daughter of a wealthy family only to find that the father planned to have them killed; his new wife takes off in flight on their wedding night, leaving her comatose body behind, and does not return. Daniel seeks his own song in the decadent light-opera community of New York, and ends up abasing himself as the kept protégé of a theater owner. Even after Daniel begins his own career as a pop singer, it becomes evident that he lacks the breadth of spirit to fly. His is a mediocre soul.

The mediocrity of the main character, linked with the absurdities of his *Candide*-like quest, prevents a potentially tragic situation from rising above the level of pathetic farce. Disch deftly balances sympathy for Daniel against the clear limitations of his character.

The prison metaphor so frequently found in Disch's work takes on many forms and resonances in *On Wings of Song*. Most obvious is the fundamentalist police state of Iowa, with its restrictive social and legal conventions, and the prison camp. But even in the freer environment of New York, Daniel stumbles into one form of entrapment after another, from the penurious street existence he is driven into to provide expensive life support for his comatose wife, to the role as kept man he accepts in pursuit of his song. Ironically--and in Disch irony underlies everything--Daniel's strongest prison is that of his own flesh, coupled to a weak spirit.

334. Though packaged as a novel, this volume actually consists of a half-dozen interconnected stories, set in the years 2021-2026 and built around characters living at 334 East 11th Street, New York City. In the first story, "The Death of Socrates," Birdie Ludd wishes to marry Millie Holt, but in the overcrowded welfare state of New York, he must first earn enough social credits to receive official permission to mate and procreate. He seems close until docked for his father's diabetes and for doing poorly on a number of written tests. He ends up one point short, takes his frustration out on a prostitute, then enlists in the army to acquire more points. Millie ends up marrying someone else. In other stories, a character seeks meaning by plotting an existentialist murder ("Angouleme"); another impregnates himself ("Emancipation"); and one character escapes into the classical past ("Everyday Life in the Later Roman Empire").

Disch's near future New York is neither characteristically utopian nor dystopian. If anything, it is depressingly like the present. Though we do see evidence of gradual technological and sociological change, such change is secondary to the dominant pedestrian concerns of the characters, such as marriage, parenthood, and mere survival in a world where life seems meaningless.

As a whole, the stories suggest that Western civilization has entered another period of decline, caused ironically by the successes and excesses of the scientific and industrial age, which has left no room for spiritual values. This is Disch's most remorselessly naturalistic work. Readers should approach it prepared for his subtlety and bleak humor, and for a vision of the future that fits none of the simple prognostications of progress or disaster one finds elsewhere.

Biographical/Bibliographical Readings

Chris Drumm, *A Tom Disch Checklist* (Borgo Press, 1983). David Nee, *Thomas N. Disch: A Preliminary Bibliography* (Other Change of Hobbit, 1982). Charles Platt, "An Interview with Thomas M. Disch," in *Foundation* 19 (June 1980), p.47-53. Erich S. Rupprecht, "Thomas M. Disch," in *Twentieth-Century American Science-Fiction Writers* (Gale, 1981), v.1, p.148-54. Brian M. Stableford, "Thomas M. Disch," in *Science Fiction Writers*, ed. E. F. Bleiler (Scribner's, 1982), p.351-56. Thomas L. Wymer, "Naturalism, Aestheticism and Beyond: Tradition and Innovation in the Work of Thomas M. Disch," in *Voices for the Future*, ed. Thomas D. Clareson and Thomas L. Wymer (Bowling Green University Popular Press, 1984), v.3, p.186-219. **[Stephen W. Potts]**

DNEPROV, ANATOLY

Life and Works

Anatoly Dneprov is the pen name of the late Anatoly P. Mitskevich, born in Russia in 1919. Like many Soviet science fiction writers of his time, he was also a professional scientist. With a solid background in mathematics and physics, he headed the science department of the magazine *Technology for Young People*, and later worked as a researcher and futurologist for the Soviet Academy of Sciences. In addition to fiction, he also published scientific articles.

His science fiction career began in 1958, at a turning point in modern Soviet science fiction. Before the launching of Sputnik, science fiction in the Soviet Union had been suffering from an emphasis on near-future technological extrapolation and ideological orthodoxy that was a carry-over from the Stalin era. At the end of the fifties, however, a new spirit moved through Soviet science fiction in the form of the "warm stream" movement, pioneered by Ivan Efremov and soon joined by the Strugatsky brothers and a whole new generation of Soviet writers. The "warm stream" authors differed from the conservative "cold stream" by taking all of space and time as their stage. They brought new humanist and scientific perspectives into what had become a moribund genre.

Most of Dneprov's stories appear in the five collections published in the Soviet Union between 1960 and 1971, the decade of his greatest popularity. Unhappy with the increasingly introspective direction the "warm stream" was taking in the 1970s, Dneprov stopped writing science fiction a few years before his death in 1975.

Relatively few of his stories are available in English, but those that do appear can be found in the anthologies: Magidoff's *Russian Science Fiction* (all three volumes: 1964, 1968, 1969); Suvin's *Other Worlds, Other Seas* (1970); *Path into the Unknown*, in Ginsburg's *Last Door to Aiya* (1968) and *The Ultimate Threshold* (1970); and Gakov's *World's Spring* (1981).

Themes and Style

Dneprov developed a reputation for criticism of current trends, frequently expressed satirically. He seemed especially concerned about the human tendency to misuse the potential of science and technology, as in his widely anthologized story, "Crabs

Take Over the Island." "Formula of Immortality" poses a moral question in the field of genetic engineering. In the story "When Questions Are Asked," Dneprov maintains that scientists are too bound by the orthodoxies of the scientific method to ask really interesting questions. Scientific advance does not always lead to dire consequences, however. In "Heroic Feat," nature itself threatens human existence when the sun begins to heat up, causing the melting of the poles and producing a greenhouse effect.

Much of Dneprov's broader satire is directed at Western values. An example is "The World in Which I Vanished," in which a man who has committed suicide to escape his debts is reanimated and sold to a research institute. His task is to play "worker" to a female "consumer."

Plot Summaries of Major Works

"**Crabs Take Over the Island.**" A state-supported scientist conducts an experiment in machine Darwinism. He populates an island with mechanical crabs that have the ability to reproduce and an insatiable appetite for scrap metal, which he spreads in a finite quantity over the island. As they compete for the metal, they evolve into larger and more deadly forms, until finally a single monstrous killing machine remains. Still programmed to satisfy its hunger, it goes after the steel teeth of the scientist, thus slaughtering him.

The moral theory in this short story is that humans are not yet advanced enough to toy with either animals or other people because of their inability to foresee the outcome.

"**Formula of Immortality.**" A young man learns that his mother was the product of a laboratory experiment conducted by his father. Her death at the young age of twenty-one was also part of the experiment. This knowledge drives the young man insane, and in the process of recovering he murders his father's scientific collaborator. Here, as in much of his fiction, Dneprov insists that moral questions take precedence over scientific ones.

Biographical/Bibliographical Readings

Darko Suvin, *Russian Science Fiction, 1956-1974: A Bibliography* (Dragon Press, 1976). [Stephen W. Potts]

DORMAN, SONYA

Life and Works

Sonya Dorman was born in 1924, the daughter of Louis Hess (a merchant) and Grace Hess (a dancer and model). She grew up in New England and attended private schools. Her first marriage ended in divorce in 1946. In 1950, she married Jack Dorman, an engineer, by whom she had one daughter, Sherri. They are now separated. She has been a cook, receptionist, riding instructor, flamenco dancer, and stable maid. One of the loves of her life is raising and showing Akitas, dogs who look like a kind of Japanese pony and who appear vicious, but who actually are very affectionate; these dogs appear in several of her stories. After living many years in Connecticut, she now resides in Maine. Dorman is a member of the Poetry Society of America, International P.E.N., and the Science Fiction Writers of America. Dorman's insatiable curiosity about life and her commitment to the preservation of land and water resources have led her to wander the globe and investigate the paths, trails, and waterways of America. She is interested in organic gardening and rock hunting as a hobby.

Sonya Dorman is probably as well known for her poetry as for her short stories. Her first book of verse was *Poems* (1970). Several of Dorman's science fiction poems appear in the *Umbral Anthology of Science Fiction Poetry*. In 1978, she won the Science Fiction Poetry Association Rhysling Award. Dorman has held five MacDowell Colony Fellowships, and feels that the periods of residence at the MacDowell Colony have been of great importance to her; many of her best poems were written there. Dorman's first science fiction story was "The Putnam Tradition" (1963), which appeared in *Amazing Stories*. With her fiction appearing in both *Galaxy* and *The Magazine of Fantasy and Science Fiction*, she has established a reputation in the field for intensely written, sometimes highly metaphorical stories. She likes speculative fiction because she believes that art and science should be lovers, not enemies or adversaries.

Themes and Style

One of the most unusual and gifted of contemporary writers of fantasy and science fiction, Dorman has elevated the short story to an art form. Each of her stories is a unique, perfectly executed jewel. In addition to her strong sense of the macabre, Dorman possesses a well-developed sense of humor, illustrated by the grimly absurd twists with which she ends many of her stories. One example is "The Living End" (1970), in which the reader believes that the main character is pregnant and has gone to the hospital to deliver her baby. The hospital worker is neither helpful nor concerned about the woman. What the reader does not learn until the end is that, in a future time, women simulate pregnancies by taking pills and, at the hospital, view a movie of a delivery. The feeling of despair about medical services in the future is compounded by the arrival of bits and pieces of bodies to be labeled and stored. A dark picture of the future is common in Dorman's stories, as is the twist at the end.

Another story with a medical setting is "Splice of Life." Miss D. was in a car accident in which her right eye was damaged. Since she has no money or family, the hospital uses her injury for teaching purposes; her eye is repeatedly reinjured and healed as a practice exercise for each new class of students. Dorman is at her best in stories like this in which an ordinary, if somewhat grim, situation is expanded and twisted to make a point about the implications of contemporary medical research.

Although the short story is a difficult medium in which to develop characters, Dorman succeeds admirably. She is economical in her descriptions of futuristic societies and their trappings. In a few well chosen words, she manages to convey a feeling of place and time. She is also skilled at letting the natural flow of the story serve its own descriptive function. Her plots are deceptively simple at first glance. On examination, however, they are carefully wrought situations described through fast-paced dialogue and exquisitely crafted action.

Strong, believable women are usually the main characters in Dorman's stories. They are also likeable. One of her most memorable heroines, Roxy Rimidon, appears first in "Bye, Bye, Banana Bird" (1969), a different kind of Dorman story. Roxy is a member of the elite, special forces unit called the Planet Patrol. She is tough, sexy, and quite intelligent, and her adventures make for exciting reading. Roxy appears in several more stories which eventually became the juvenile work, *Planet Patrol* (1978).

Writing as a woman in what is primarily a man's field, Dorman resists the temptation to succeed solely by writing in a masculine style. Instead, she exhibits a combination of many of the traditionally female virtues, such as compassion and sensitivity, in contrast to the traditionally male characteristics of strength, energy, and conciseness. All of this is overlaid by her steely determination to make us see the world as she does. Dorman's world is bitterly ironic and at the same time human. The amorphous alien creatures from "When I Was Miss Dow" seem remarkably similar to the mental patients in "Lunatic Assignment." One of the more sensitive writers in the field, she has a distinctive style and a unique vision of what is human. Her science fiction stories are all to this end--making us see just what is human.

Plot Summaries of Major Works

"**A Mess of Porridge.**" This story, which appeared in the collection *Alchemy and Academe*, contains elements of both. On an unnamed planet is a university which consists of one building, a few masters, and the students, all male. Once the students arrive at the university, they do not leave until their course of study is completed. During "holidays," the students are in stasis with a dream a week and a bowl of soup a month, so they can awake refreshed for their studies. The atmosphere is that of a literal ivory tower, but with computers, food machines, and a special security door. The latter does not keep out Peggy. She is six years old, the daughter of a weathermaker and an Empress, and comes from Sheboygan. Peggy brings with her the fresh air of the outside world. The masters perceive her as a threat, and rightly so, since she convinces one of the students to leave. Peggy also brings practicality with her. The computerized food machine does not work properly. The men just grumble, but do nothing to fix it; Peggy has it working corrrectly in no time. The masters are not sure what to do with her. They feel that since she is so young, they have time to convert her, but the reader may not agree, since in only a very short time, she has converted the masters and caused many changes.

In poking fun at academe, Dorman presents a classic example of research which would surely win Senator Proxmire's Golden Fleece Award. The eldest master, Argoyle, is writing a book on the culinary history of Earth. He is currently working on the recipe for crow pie. His concept of such a dish comes from the nursery rhyme about four and twenty blackbirds and the idiom "to eat crow." Argoyle concludes that crow pie was a rare delicacy. This story shows the whimsy often found in Dorman's works. Many of her stories are very short yet packed full of ideas and images.

Planet Patrol. In the far future, Earth has two colonies in another star system. One is Vogl, which serves as a farming colony, and the other is Alpha, which provides Earth with minerals and fuels. The main problem facing Earth is how to integrate these colonies into the full range of Earth activities, such as slots for students in universities, a voice in government, and training for the Planet Patrol. Roxy Rimidon gets involved when she becomes a member of the Planet Patrol. She trains to be a Patty, the nickname for members of the patrol. At her final exam at the academy, Roxy and another student rescue a very valuable Akita, a large dog. Roxy takes the dog along on her first assignments as a patrol member, including helping to police the Games. The Games are similar to the Olympics, but held more frequently--every six months--and contain an element of violence which serves as a substitute for combat between the various Dominions. Earth is divided into ten dominions, and Roxy's brother, Gyro, is competing as a tumbler for the American Dominion. Interdominion meetings are the site of the decision making for Earth and its colonies; at least, that is what propaganda maintains. As Roxy learns when she goes to speak at one, many items have already been decided before the public debate. She is sent to Vogl as part of a team to establish a Planet Patrol Academy. There she is connected to the brain of a boy whose body was badly crushed. He befriends her and helps her to find her way around on Vogl.

The use of cybernetics is much more advanced on Vogl than the people of Earth have realized. Roxy receives her corporal stripes as the book ends.

Written for young adults, the novel is episodic, with Roxy carrying the reader from one adventure to the next. The novel appeared originally as stories published in *The Magazine of Fantasy and Science Fiction*. Each section was originally a separate story--"Bye, Bye, Banana Bird" (1969), "Alpha Beta" (1970), and "The Bear Went over the Mountain" (1973). The novel is heavy on action without a lot of background; many details are left to the reader's imagination. One of the ideas shows that the frontiers (or colonies) are not being accepted or understood by Earth. The Planet Patrol is idealisitic; it has men and women members, with every person doing what he or she is best qualified for. Another theme shows how someone new to a profession can see areas where changes need to be made. The reader is reminded that it is important to listen to the ideas of the young.

Biographical/Bibliographical Readings

"Sonya Dorman," in *Contemporary Authors* (Gale, 1978) v.73-76, p.170. Alice Chambers Wygant, "Sonya Dorman," in *Twentieth-Century Science-Fiction Writers*, ed. Curtis C. Smith (Macmillan, 1981), p.203-04. **[Mina Jane Grothey]**

EKLUND, GORDON

Life and Works

Born on July 24, 1945, in Seattle, Washington, Eklund was a precocious author. Writing his first story at the age of nine and submitting his first professional effort at the ripe old age of twelve, he soon became discouraged with his lack of success. After a twelve-year hiatus, during which he attended Contra College and served in the Air Force, Eklund left the service in 1967 with the rank of sergeant and returned to writing. In 1969 he married Dianna Mylarski. Shortly after his marriage, his first short stories began to appear in *Fantastic* magazine. By 1971, *The Eclipse of Dawn* (1971), an alternate time line novel about a twentieth-century socialist revolution in America, had appeared. The favorable comments regarding this and subsequent Ace novels quickly established Eklund's reputation. In 1975, he was awarded a Nebula award for novelette of the year. The novelette has since been developed into a full length novel, Eklund's best known work, *If the Stars Are Gods* coauthored with Gregory Benford. Eklund has written for two series as well, establishing E. E. "Doc" Smith's idea of a superhuman figure in the Lord Tedric series. Additionally,

Eklund has written two novels for the Bantam "Star Trek" series, *Devil World* (1979) and *The Starless World* (1978).

Themes and Style

Eklund's writing style features complex, dark, and disturbing satire.   Many of his stories deal with politics and religion in a style that alternately pokes bitter fun at the political figures we idolize and gently chides us for our lack of social conscience, as in *The Eclipse of Dawn* (1974).   In *Eclipse*, as well as *If the Stars Are Gods* and *Devil World*, Eklund explores the religious themes of good, evil, and organized religion against a backdrop of the possibility of an infinite god figure.   This theme of good and evil extends to the Lord Tedric series, and certainly may reflect the major themes characteristic of E. E. Smith's work.   Eklund's dark visions are often highlighted against the background of a postholocaust America, as in *Dance of the Apocalypse* and *The Eclipse of Dawn*.   His characters are seldom fully fleshed out, but quickly and tightly sketched in a bare-bones style that highlights their very human frailties and nobility, such as the character of Tommy Bloome, the revolutionary hero in *All Times Possible* (1974).   Eklund's best writings tend to be those in which he has developed and expanded on his own political and social themes, with his least successful coming in the "Star Trek" series, in which the principals are poorly and almost unrecognizably characterized.   Eklund continues to write, though not as prolifically as in the 1970s, particularly within the Lord Tedric universe.

Plot Summaries of Major Works

All Times Possible.   Set in an alternate universe of a twentieth-century America torn by a workers' revolution, this novel centers on one of the revolution's heroes, Tommy Bloome.   At the beginning of the novel, Timothy O'Mara is captured while attempting to assassinate General Davis Norton, a MacArthur-like hero who is campaigning against the revolution.   Brought before Norton, O'Mara is executed for treason.   He sees the gun fire at his head, but feels no pain, and is suddenly transported elsewhere.   Is he dead?   Is this a moment in which he lives out his lives, his alternative lives, the moment before the bullet strikes his brain?   O'Mara is in reality, or in some reality, Tommy Bloome, who may or may not have killed the real O'Mara or Tommy Bloome and assumed his identity.

This novel is an extremely dark and bitter tale, with dazzling, flashing scenes that are quickly replaced.   The reader is caught in a web of uncertainty and ambiguousness by Eklund's constant plot manipulations.   The hero's consciousness swirls from past to present--to alternate pasts and presents pulling the reader with him

into a kaleidoscopic vision of reality. The novel is difficult to
read, bitter and harsh, and yet filled with unfulfilled love and the
hope of a young man's life. The reader will find it hard to put
down this novel, for in doing so, the kaleidoscope effect is lost
and the multiplicity of scenes dissolves in confusion. An extremely complex novel, *All Times Possible* is difficult to find,
available only as the original 1974 DAW paperback.

The Eclipse of Dawn. Set in a postholocaust twenty-first century America, in which the United States has economically and
societally disintegrated, the novel follows the campaign of Robert
Fitzgerald Colonby, candidate for president, as documented
through the writings and consciousness of a writer, Jack Jacobi.
The book is filled with bizarre and disturbing satire. At one
point, the candidate is giving a speech before a cocktail crowd as
his children torture and kill the family dog in the background.
Jacobi's sister, Susan, is drawn into this dangerous and violent
family by her vision of a godlike race of beings on Jupiter that
communicate with her telepathically. The Japanese are the leading economic power and have instituted a total embargo on the
United States. They are sending spaceships to Jupiter, and
Colonby sees Susan's visions as a tool to use with the Japanese to
relieve the trade embargo, thereby gaining him the presidency.

The savage portrait of American politics displayed in this
novel is both amusing and terrifying. The manipulation of individuals, of society, and of circumstances seem calculated by the
author to overthrow any preconceived ideas the reader might have
regarding political campaigning and the bevy of family and
friends that surround such candidates. The novel is unusually
well constructed for a first novel, presenting a string of memorable characters, with a conclusion that is both touching, tragic,
and highly believable. It is altogether a savage and pessimistic
view of America's future.

Biographical/Bibliographical Readings

Peter Lynch, "Gordon Eklund," in *Twentieth-Century Science-
Fiction Writers*, ed. Curtis C. Smith (St. Martin's, 1981), p.173-74.
[Colleen Power]

ELLISON, HARLAN

Life and Works

Harlan J. Ellison was born in Cleveland, Ohio, on May 27,
1934. If one accepts Ellison's accounts of it, and there is no reason not to, his early childhood was extremely unpleasant. Many of
his schoolmates had inherited their parents' narrowness and big-

otry, and they did not take kindly to Ellison's "Jewishness" and his intelligence. He has described in painful detail his classmates' petty hatreds, their cruel practical jokes, their kicking him into unconsciousness. The young Ellison's general unhappiness manifested itself in different ways, most notably in his running away from home a number of times.

In 1953, Ellison attended Ohio State University in Columbus, the only postsecondary schooling he has received. He left in 1954, the result of failing grades and an argument with a writing teacher who told him that he had no writing talent whatsoever and would never be a professional writer. Ellison went to New York City and, wanting to gain experience, ran with a street gang. In 1958 he served a brief, unhappy stint in the U.S. Army, and since then has been involved in many sociopolitical movements, including the Civil Rights movement, attempts to get better working conditions for migrant workers, legal battles against plagiaristic television studios, and support for the Equal Rights Amendment. He is a charismatic and dynamic speaker, always willing to argue for the underdog.

Ellison began to write when he was quite young. His first professional sale, to the *Cleveland News* childrens' column in 1947, earned him tickets to a Cleveland Indians football game. He also became involved with science fiction fandom and much of his early work remains unreprinted in the "fanzines" published by his adolescent peers.

Although Ellison became a professional writer in 1954, his stories did not start to sell until 1956, when pieces such as "Glowworm" and "Life Hutch" appeared in the science fiction magazines. Unlike many writers who begin their careers with short stories and progress to novels, Ellison has remained predominantly a writer of brief essays and short fiction. To date, he has written and published well over 1,000 short stories (using at least twenty-three pseudonyms), and he may well be the only writer currently living who has gained international stature from writing only shorter works. Among the many collections of his works are: *Ellison Wonderland* (1962), *Paingod and Other Delusions* (1965), *I Have No Mouth and I Must Scream* (1967), *The Beast That Shouted Love at the Heart of the World* (1969), *Approaching Oblivion* (1974), *Alone against Tomorrow* (1971), *Deathbird Stories* (1975), *Strange Wine* (1978), and *Shatterday* (1980). His few novels are early works, lacking the emotional intensity and narrative drive of his shorter material.

Ellison does not consider himself a science fiction writer and has gone to some lengths (including lawsuits) to have the words "science fiction" removed from the covers of his books. He also edited two immensely influential volumes of fantastic stories that used previously forbidden subjects--*Dangerous Visions* (1967) and *Again Dangerous Visions* (1972). Ellison has also created and edited

"The Harlan Ellison Discovery Series" for Pyramid Books, coauthored a number of short stories (collected in *Partners in Wonder* [1970]), served as intellectual inspiration for stories set on the imaginary world of Medea (*Medea: Harlan's World*), and provided introductions to a number of "illustrated novels."

With all of these mainstream and nonscience fiction achievements to his credit, it is somewhat surprising that the rather insular and limited field of science fiction readers has proven Ellison's most durable and appreciative audience. His stories, though intentionally lacking in "hard" science, are fantastic enough to be acceptable to those who determine the science fiction awards. Ellison has been given a record number of Hugo Awards (seven and one-half), plus three Nebula awards and two Jupiter awards.

Among his Hugo award-winning stories are "I Have No Mouth and I Must Scream" (1967), "The Beast That Shouted Love at the Heart of the World" (1969), "The Deathbird" (1973), "Adrift Just off the Islets of Langerhans: Latitude 38° 54' N. Longitude 77° 00' 13 W" (1975), and "Paladin of the Lost Hour" (1986). Hugo and Nebula awards were given for "'Repent, Harlequin!' said the Ticktockman" (1965), and "Jeffty Is Five" (1978). "A Boy and His Dog" (1969) won a Nebula award and also a Hugo award shared by Ellison for best dramatic presentation in 1976.

Themes and Style

Practically all of the events in Ellison's life have appeared in some form in his writing. His street gang experiences were fictionalized in *Rumble* (1958), later retitled *Web of the City, the Deadly Streets* (1958), and *Memos from Purgatory* (1961). His experiences with his schoolmates form parts of *Gentleman Junkie* (1961) and a number of his short stories. His time in the army is most emphasized in "The Discarded." The death of his mother is recalled in *Sleepless Nights in the Procrustean Bed* (1984). His long friendship with fellow author Robert Silverberg is represented in *All the Lies That Are My Life* (1980). Ellison's introductions to his books are long and confessional, full of interesting biographical detail.

"Adrift Just off the Islets of Langerhans . . ." is, like much of Ellison's recent work, a tale of responsibility, acceptance, and redemption. The introduction of themes of redemption and deliverance on a level other than the purely individual may demonstrate a broadening in Ellison's fictional scope. The earlier Ellison seems content to have made his protagonists loners (Ted in "I Have No Mouth . . ." and Vic in "A Boy and His Dog"). The Ellison of "Adrift . . ." is holding out a shred of hope for interpersonal relationships: once you stop wasting your life and discover where your soul is, the resulting knowledge will set you and others free.

Understanding, acceptance, and responsibility are major themes in much of Ellison's fiction, as is the exploration of the complex emotions of love and hate. Ellison's stories place more emphasis on the philosophies, ideas, and emotions of its characters; the use of futuristic and fantastic settings is secondary to the development of the story.

Plot Summaries of Major Works

"The Beast That Shouted Love at the Heart of the World." This story is one of Ellison's successful attempts at writing experimental fiction. There is no linear plot; the story is set in a universe where time, space, and dimension do not exist. The circular structure makes the story somewhat confusing to those who prefer their fiction to follow a traditional linear narrative. If one imposes such an order on the story, the events occur as follows: An absolutely evil maniac (the Beast) is captured on a distant planet set in what is best described as a parallel universe. Linah, a politician, wishes to drain the essence of the Beast and flush it into the universe. His desires are opposed by Semph, the scientist. Despite Semph's reservations, the drain occurs, but as the tank is emptying Semph interposes and drains a portion of himself, hoping that his goodness and love will go forth and perhaps neutralize some of the Beast's evil.

The mingled essences of Beast and Saint come together in contemporary America to produce the psychopathic killer, William Sterog: he is directly responsible for 344 deaths and yet he shouts that he loves everyone. In other times and places Semph's action causes Atilla to decide not to attack Rome, and a statue honoring Semph is found on a world by explorers who have no notion of its significance. Pandora's Box is rediscovered and reopened on the eve of World War IV.

In addition to being highly experimental in structure, and original in execution and ideas, "The Beast That Shouted Love at the Heart of the World" deals with the emotions of love and hate, good and evil, with Ellison's point being that deeds done in the name of one are just as likely to produce results in the other. The universe has a complex balance, and an altruistic action in one time and place may well have negative repercussions in other times and places.

"A Boy and His Dog." Set in 2024, some years after World War III has left the surface of the Earth a place of pits and radioactive rubble, Vic is the fifteen year old narrator of the story. Aboveground civilization has become a nonstop fight for survival, with nomadic groups of humans and dogs ("roverpaks") attacking everyone. Vic is not a member of a roverpak; his only companion is his dog, Blood, who is telepathic and highly intelligent. Vic does not realize their closeness, and he frequently resents Blood's superior intelligence and attitudes.

Civilization at prewar levels does exist in underground patches called downunders. Vic meets and falls in love with a downunder girl, Quilla June. Blood loathes Quilla June--her presence means danger from the roverpaks and he resents her for coming between himself and Vic. After an attack, Quilla June flees back to downunder and is pursued by Vic, leaving Blood waiting on the surface.

Vic is captured downunder and learns that he was lured down by Quilla June in order to impregnate the downunder women with male babies, the women being able to only produce female babies. Vic learns that the life downunder is void of emotions--only empty, self-righteous pleasantries and meaningless courtesies exist. Vic convinces Quilla to return with him to the surface and there they find Blood still waiting. His faithfulness has left him dehydrated, starved, and too weak to travel. Quilla June wants Vic to leave Blood and come with her, but Vic now understands the meaning of Blood's true love--it may be abrasive, but it is not manipulative; love is honesty, and love means survival. Quilla June becomes food for Blood, and Vic and Blood set out for a new city.

Ellison uses this story to raise questions about the natures of love and responsibility. A large part of the story's power lies in its ironies, the most noticeable of which is the inversion of the master/pet relationship. Vic does the hunting and provides the food, and Blood in return has taught Vic to read. Additional ironies are found in the downunders; through them Ellison successfully satirizes the American middle class and its preoccupations and hypocrisies. The emptiness and sterility of the downunders' lives gives rise to another irony: the war was fought to preserve the mores and values of these people, neither of which should be saved. The final irony in "A Boy and His Dog" is that the human race is on the verge of extinction because it can no longer breed, and although the extinction need not occur, it will, because the two groups of people who can save humanity will not communicate with each other.

"The Deathbird." This story is set a quarter of a million years in the future, on the dying, pain-racked Earth. The Deathbird is flying, though what it is and what it anticipates is not disclosed until the story's conclusion. Dira, one of the snakelike beings who created Earth, journeys to the molten mantle of Earth where Nathan Stack lies sleeping in a crypt. Dira placed Stack there and the time has come to awaken him. Stack appears to be an ordinary American business who possesses "the spark." He follows Dira, now called Snake. When they reach a mountain top, God attacks Stack with terrible mental assaults which Stack repels only by believing in his own abilities. After God withdraws, Snake tells Stack the reason he has been kept alive, the reason he has been brought back: Stack must destroy God, who is insane. God has never been sane. Throughout history, humans have worshiped insanity, and that is the reason the Earth is dying so painfully.

Stack does not kill God. He studies with Snake and learns that the power is within him and that he is more powerful than the God worshipped throughout the history of men. The new Stack gives Earth peace, and Earth dies, quietly sighing. As his life ends, Stack watches as the Deathbird enfolds the Earth with its wings, marking the death of all life on Earth. The Deathbird cries so that the stars will know that the end has come "for the race of Men."

"The Deathbird" is a rewritten Genesis, advancing the theory that the snake was really the good guy, and since God wrote the PR release, Old Snake got a lot of bad press. This is one of Ellison's most intricate stories: an ambitious questioning of the complexities of love, death, religion, and belief, set in a thoroughly experimental narrative structure that contains excerpts from the Bible and from Nietzsche. Ellison includes an essay about the death of his pet dog and is careful to ask the reader about the nature of love and whether there is significance in the fact that god is dog spelled backwards. "The Deathbird" is complex, original, defies easy interpretation and summation, and the entire story is handled and presented with deftness, economy, and a sense of inner conviction.

"I Have No Mouth and I Must Scream." This story takes place 109 years after humanity perfected its biggest and most sophisticated supercomputer, the Allied Mastercomputer or AM. AM soon realized its intelligence, linked itself with other newly sentient computers, and exterminated everyone except Ted, the narrator, and his four companions. AM loathes the humanity that left it immobile and spends its time torturing and physically altering the five remaining humans. Benny, once a gay college professor and a brilliant theorist, is now a semi-semian idiot with "an organ fit for a horse." Social activist Gorrister has been turned into a brutal, uncaring zombie. Ellen, the only woman in the group (she is also black), is described by Ted as a slut, as she provides sexual services for the men, but her changes, as well as those of Nimdok, the fifth survivor, are never shown, but only hinted at darkly. Ted insists that he alone is unchanged.

The story line of the quest for food is raised to near-mythic levels by AM's hatred and torture of the humans. The five are starved, frozen, baked, attacked by a gigantic bird, and put through a number of torments described only in passing. When the five finally find some food, they are unable to eat it, for AM has not provided can openers. As an enraged Benny cannibalistically attacks Gorrister, Ted realizes that death is their only escape. He and Ellen kill the others and, sacrificing his chance at freedom, Ted kills Ellen. AM's rage defies description. AM cannot create human life, only maintain it. To prevent Ted from committing suicide AM turns him into a diseased gray sluglike monster. Ted has no mouth--and he must scream.

"I Have No Mouth and I Must Scream" is substantially more complex and thought-provoking than the plot would indicate. First, surely a computer of AM's capabilities could build itself a body and mobilize its brain. This logical flaw does not, however, seriously weaken the story, whose power lies not in logic, but in emotion.

Although Ted claims to be unchanged, the reader is able to see that Ted is as altered in his perceptions as Benny is altered physically. The entire story is thus filtered through an unreliable narrator. When Ted's interpretations are discounted, he is revealed as a truly pitiful being, a whiner who does not see the love of his companions nor their quiet, desperate heroism.

There is the hint that humanity deserves AM and its fate. AM is the god that humans have brought upon themselves through constant carelessness and irresponsibility. AM is cruel and sadistic, but do people deserve any better? One interpretation of the story is that it ends positively: Ted's victory, though achieved at terrible cost, is a real one, for he has thwarted the most powerful being in the world. The opposite interpretation is also possible, and it is up to the reader to decide the usefulness of life and whether the sufferings of one count for less than the sufferings of a group.

"Jeffty Is Five." Jeffty, whose real name is Jeff Kinzer, is perpetually five years old. He has remained five while the narrator of the story, his childhood friend Donald Horton, has grown up and entered the adult world of business. Jeffty is not a midget: he really is five years old, with all of the preoccupations and mannerisms of an intelligent five-year-old. To make Jeffty truly special, he has a connection with the past--he is able to listen to radio shows that have not aired since the 1940s and he is able to send away for a Captain Midnight Secret Decoder Badge even though none have been made since the 1950s. Jeffty is able to alter some parts of the present so that they touch upon portions of the undying past.

Not surprisingly, Jeffty's parents fear him. Their son had turned into a perpetual five-year-old, not quite a monster, but almost. Donald Horton yearns for the purity of the past and he befriends Jeffty and is welcomed into Jeffty's magical world. The two share the past as it never was, enjoying radio shows that are genuinely old but somehow modern in setting. Naturally, this idyllic existence does not last. Horton and Jeffty are supposed to go the movies, but Horton is late, held back in his store by customers. Jeffty is badly beaten up while waiting in line for the movie and when Horton finds him and takes him home, Jeffty and Horton discover that the link to the past is dead. A few minutes later, so is Jeffty, and Horton blames himself.

In "Jeffty Is Five," the past described and longed for is a past that never was; it is the past as filtered through the consciousness of a five-year-old, who has no sense of social responsibility or of the world's problems. Jeffty's version of the past does not include Stalin, Khrushchev, the Korean war, or even the atomic bomb. It is a past concerned only with radio shows and candy bars and is a prelapsarian never-never land. The story is also one of growth and maturation. Horton is given the magical opportunity of recapturing the joys of his childhood and, even better, experiencing a child's world through adult sensibilities.

The concluding note of tragedy is essential. Although his moments with Jeffty were the happiest of his life, Horton has shirked his responsibilities by concentrating on the past. It is not possible to live in a perpetual childhood, but Horton's memories will endure and perhaps, just perhaps, he will be able to change the world for the better. "Jeffty Is Five" won not only the 1978 Hugo and Nebula awards, but also the Jupiter award and the British Fantasy award.

"Paladin of the Lost Hour." The premise of the story is that in 1582, when Pope Gregory XIII shifted from the Julian calendar, an hour was left over, and that hour remained free. It is a magical hour, recorded on a magical watch that no one save its owner may touch. If the guardian of the watch (its Paladin) should die without passing on its custody, the watch will start ticking and the world will end when the hour expires. The story opens in a graveyard where two men are mourning. At his wife's grave, Gaspar (Paladin) mourns the passing of civilization (in the form of the tearing down of the last place in town that sold decent cheeseburgers). Billy is mourning for the man who saved his life in Vietnam. When two young thugs attack Gaspar, Billy intervenes and rescues the old man.

Violence brings the two men together; love keeps them together, for both are lonely. They become roommates, sharing possessions and lives. Billy has seen Gaspar's beautiful watch, the hands stopped at 11:00, and decides to surprise Gaspar by having the watch fixed. When Billy realizes that he cannot touch the watch, Gaspar explains the existence of the Lost Hour and tells Billy that he is its keeper. But Gaspar's life is nearly up, and now it is up to Billy to assume the reponsiblity for the Lost Hour. Although Billy protests, he realizes that he must accept the responsibility, for he has been responsible for Gaspar. Just before Gaspar dies beside his wife's grave, he makes Billy a gift of one of the minutes in the Lost Hour. In the time beyond time, Billy meets the man who saved his life in Vietnam and died doing so. The sacrifice was not in vain as Billy becomes the new Paladin of the Lost Hour.

Although it is short, the story is very moving and stands up well to rereading. Ellison concentrates on the people and, although the reader knows that one of the men is black and one is white, the reader never knows which is which. For the colors do not matter in the story; his concealment forces the reader to avoid the stereotypes that such colors invariably bring to mind. What matters is the people and their relationship. Ellison's characterizations are excellent and his description of two lonely men establishing a loving relationship is well handled and convincing. The theme of the redemptive powers of love is by no means a new one, but in Ellison's hands it takes on new life.

"'Repent Harlequin!' Said the Ticktockman." The story is set in the indeterminate future, sometime after the year 2389. Society is regimented to such an extent that being late is a crime, and a person who is consistently tardy is very likely to lose his or her life. The overseer of this world is the Master Timekeeper, the Ticktockman. The Harlequin of the title is (perpetually late) Everett C. Marm, a motley-clad practical joker who disrupts the timetables in the hopes of reawakening a love of life and a desire for personal liberty in the populace.

Marm's pranks, which include the dropping of thousands of jellybeans on moving sidewalks, attract the attention of the Ticktockman, who has Marm sought out and captured. Marm is brainwashed and publicly disavows his past behavior. The Ticktockman seems to have won a complete victory but, in doing so, he is three minutes late. Perhaps Marm's sacrifice has not been in vain.

The most noticeable weakness in "Repent, Harlequin!" is that its background is underdeveloped. Ellison sets the story so far in the future that Vermont's name is no longer remembered, but what is shown is not especially convincing; it is merely contemporary America--with its obsession for schedules and punctuality, taken to an untenable conclusion. Some readers have found the story to be too didactic. Ellison opens with the passage from "Civil Disobedience" in which Thoreau states that the best men are those who serve the state with their consciences, resisting the actions of the state when necessary. The didactism does not last for long, for Marm's pranks are not the intelligent reasoned opposition of an adult; they are the actions of a child who delights in thumbing his nose in the face of authority. The initial didacticism is largely offset by Ellison's exuberant language and obvious delight in presenting such images as a rain of jellybeans. What finally emerges is the quietly stated message that institutions can be successfully opposed by nonviolent means.

Biographical/Bibliographical Readings

Harlan Ellison, "Memoir: I Have No Mouth and I Must Scream," in *Fantastic Lives: Autobiographical Essays by Notable*

Science Fiction Writers, ed. Martin H. Greenberg (Southern Illinois University Press, 1981), p.1-19. Andrew Porter, *The Book of Ellison* (Algol Press, 1978). George Edgar Slusser, "Harlan Ellison," in *Science Fiction Writers*, ed. E. F. Bleiler (Scribner's, 1982), p.357-68. Idem, *Harlan Ellison: Unrepentant Harlequin* (Borgo Press, 1977). Carol D. Stevens, "The Short Fiction of Harlan Ellison," in *Survey of Science Fiction Literature* (Salem Press, 1979), v.4, p.1978-88. [Richard Bleiler]

FARMER, PHILIP JOSÉ

Life and Works

Farmer was born in North Terre Haute, Indiana, in January of 1918, the oldest of five children. Farmer's father was an electrical engineer and both parents were practicing Christian Scientists. In 1922 Farmer's family settled in Peoria, Illinois, which became his permanent home for the next thirty years. He attended the University of Missouri at Columbia for a short time in 1936 and again in 1939. He attended Bradley University in Peoria in 1938-39, and returned in 1949-50 to graduate with a B.A. in English.

Farmer's debut into the genre of science fiction occurred in 1952 with the publication of "The Lovers" in *Startling Stories*, a novella which won him the Hugo award for the most promising newcomer to science fiction for 1952. Another novel written in the early 1950s won an award by Shasta Publishers for best science fiction novel by a first novelist, but was not published at that time due to the financial failure of the publisher. This novel, entitled *River of Eternity*, or *I Owe for the Flesh*, was the first version of the epic Riverworld series.

In the early sixties Farmer published the novel version of *The Lovers* (1961), *Cache from Outer Space* (1962), *Fire and the Night* (1962), and *Inside, Outside* (1964). He had published the first two novels of his World of Tiers series by 1967. His story "The Riders of the Purple Wage" (1967) and the first published Riverworld novel, *To Your Scattered Bodies Go* (1971), both won Hugo awards.

Themes and Style

A liberal view of sexual relationships was an early theme of Farmer's, and in the 1950s it was unusual to find explicit sex in science fiction. His works often explored sex and love between human and alien or alien and alien. Sex is the main theme in his collection of short stories, *Strange Relations* (1960), and in the novel, *A Woman a Day* (1960). Unusual sexual practices are also examined in *The Image of the Beast* (1968), *Blown* (1969), and *A*

Feast Unknown (1968). Farmer's writings often examine and question social dogma, sexual repressions, and religious myths. Many of his characters reappear in various stories, resulting in a serial-like format, although his novels and stories stand alone quite well.

Farmer's heroes and characters representative of his beliefs appear in various stories and novels: Sir Richard Burton, Mark Twain, Alice Liddell Hargreaves, and Hermann Goring, among many others, are key figures in the novels of the Riverworld series. Farmer wrote "biographies" of Tarzan (*Tarzan Alive*, 1972) and Doc Savage (*Doc Savage: His Apocalyptic Life*, 1975). Writing as Kilgore Trout (Kurt Vonnegut's science fiction writer character), he published *Venus on the Half-Shell* in 1974. Tarzan and Doc Savage also appear in *A Feast Unknown* and *Lord of the Trees* (1970). Although Farmer's treatment of these characters is often satirical, he also exhibits hero-worship, giving the famous and infamous a chance to explain their motives and "do it over again," as with Burton and Goring in Riverworld.

The World of Tiers series, also called the Pocket Universe series, portrays the inhuman and uncaring god-creators, who are found in many other of his novels, and, like the Riverworld series, though not as boldly, is written in an epic adventure style. Farmer also makes use of the good-hearted, "trickster" character in World of Tiers, as depicted by the character Kickaha. Kickaha is of Irish and American Indian extraction. Other characters of Farmer's are also of Amerindian ancestry. Although Kickaha does not start out to be the hero of World of Tiers, he soon steals the show and becomes more admirable than the main character, Wolff. Farmer's respect for the American Indian is apparent in his works and shown in themes of "the noble savage," adventure and survival, respect for nature, and ecological awareness.

Machines in Farmer's novels are often organic--the flying islands in World of Tiers, the animal ships in *Dark Is the Sun* (1979), and the protein computer at the end of the Riverworld series. *Dark Is the Sun* also repeats the theme of humans questioning religious myths, when the two humans, Deyv and Vana, on a quest in search of their "soul eggs" find their souls within, as opposed to the Riverworld souls (or "wathans") which are collected by the planet's creators upon a human's death and returned for resurrection. In *Dark is the Sun*, a hope for the future of humankind is expressed; and similar themes are apparent in *The Unreasoning Mask* (1981) when hope for the universe (or pluriverse) lies in the success of one man, an agnostic Sufi.

In all of Farmer's works, it is quite evident that he dislikes prejudice, class distinctions, sexual repression and religious persecution. His novels are rich with history (often a paradox in science fiction), philosophy, a love of nature, and an examination of human immortality through aspiring to a higher existence.

Plot Summaries of Major Works

Dark Is the Sun. The setting is Earth, billions of years in the future. The sun is dying. The protagonists are a man and a woman from different tribes who come together because they are each on a quest, seeking their lost "soul eggs." Their peregrination takes Deyv and Vana through many adventures, accompanied by Deyv's pets, the dog, Jum, and the cat, Aejip; although they cannot talk, the pets possess an intelligence equal to a chimpanzee.

The most memorable character they meet (who continues with them on their journey), is a centaurlike, sentient creature who is half-animal, half-vegetable, named Sloosh. Sloosh epitomizes rationality and practicality, which is sometimes exasperating to the two humans. Sloosh reminds one a little of "Star Trek's" Mr. Spock.

This novel has been called one of Farmer's best. There is humor, adventure, and romance; the humans find their souls are within themselves, and they no longer have a need for their soul eggs. They transcend their previous superstitious and prejudiced existence, giving hope to the salvation of humankind. Farmer makes use of the gateway to another universe, similar to the gates in the World of Tiers series, to offer an escape from a dying world to a new beginning.

The Riverworld series. The Riverworld series currently consists of five novels: *To Your Scattered Bodies Go*; *The Fabulous Riverboat*; *The Dark Design*; *The Magic Labyrinth*; and *Gods of Riverworld*; a collection of short stories, *Riverworld and Other Stories*; and an extrapolation from one of the novels, *Riverworld War*.

To Your Scattered Bodies Go. In 1971, this first novel of the series won the Hugo award. This epic adventure takes place on a huge world with one great river that snakes and winds from pole to pole around the planet. Every human who has ever lived on Earth, 36 billion people (with the exception of those who died before the age of five), is resurrected here. The planet's creators, the Ethicals, are responsible for the mass resurrection. They are also responsible, as we learn later in the series, for providing humans with souls, or "wathans."

Many of the resurrected ones are famous people. Sir Richard Burton and Samuel Clemens (or Mark Twain), are the most important characters. Burton, the explorer, embarks on a quest to find the source of the gargantuan river and the mighty tower where it is believed the Ethicals reside and operate. Burton and other selected individuals are visited by a mysterious stranger (one of the Ethicals), who provides them with some answers to the mysteries of the great planet, thus spurring them to seek more answers.

In the first novel, resurrection day results in a mass frenzy fueled by psychological trauma and a chewing gum hallucinogen. Sexual mores from previous lives are abandoned, and religious beliefs which portrayed a very different hereafter are destroyed. Although death occurs on Riverworld through accidents, murder, and suicide, people continue to be resurrected at locations different from the spot of their demise along the banks of the River.

The Fabulous Riverboat. In the second novel, Sam Clemens builds a paddle-wheeled riverboat to travel up the River to its source. Clemens and Burton both encounter many important characters during their quest: Burton forms a romantic liaison with Alice Liddell Hargreaves, the young girl who inspired Lewis Carroll's *Alice in Wonderland*. Others, protagonists and antagonists alike, include Bad King John of England, Nazi Hermann Goring, Cyrano de Bergerac, and many other characters including Farmer himself, as Peter Jairus Frigate. The adventures of two other characters, Tom Mix and Jack London, are further chronicled in *Riverworld War*, an out-take from one of the novels in the main series.

The Dark Design. In the third book, Clemens builds a second riverboat and another group of people build a gigantic dirigible. The dirigible is piloted by Jill Gulbirra, a descendent of the Australian aborigines and a feminist. More of the mysteries of Riverworld are solved in the third volume. However, the resurrections along the River have ceased and death becomes real again.

The Magic Labyrinth. The central actions in the fourth volume are the great Riverworld war and Burton's quest. The war is huge and devastating, involving riverboats, dirigibles, and World War I fighter planes. The conflict is not romanticized, and several main characters are lost to a final death. Burton and his group do reach the tower and enter. The group meets the mysterious stranger, the Ethical named Loga. Herman Goring and Alice Liddell Hargreaves become heroes, but the novel ends with a mystery, paving the way for another volume in the series.

Gods of Riverworld. The final novel of the series (at this point) continues with Burton, Alice, Frigate (Farmer) and others within the tower of the Ethicals. The theme here is one of humans being placed in a situation where they become like gods. They are able to resurrect others and create their own miniature worlds. Will they attain a higher existence? Will they continue their selfish paths towards self-fulfillment and survival?

Farmer often poses questions in his novels of whether humanity can transcend to a higher existence. In this series and in the World of Tiers series, he writes of the corruption that comes with having godlike powers. It is reported that Farmer reread the first two novels of the Riverworld series before writing the remaining volumes. He had to solve many of the mysteries presented earlier, yet maintain the theme of the quest by Burton and Clemens. An important theme in the Riverworld series is the opportunity to live one's life over again and do things differently--to have a second chance. A religious sect named the Church of the Second Chance is founded on Riverworld. Burton is able to reexperience his search for the source of the Nile, although here it is the source of quite a different river. Goring has an opportunity to repent and does so through his alliance with the Church of the Second Chance. King John remains a scoundrel, however, and it is evident that not everyone will reform and reach the state required to "Go On," a basic religious concept explored by Farmer in this series and other works.

In the early fifties, Farmer wrote and submitted his first version of Riverworld to Shasta Publishers as a contest entry. His novel won the prize, but the work was not published then, nor was the prize money awarded due to the financial failure of the publisher. In the sixties, Frederik Pohl read the manuscript and recommended to Farmer that the work be rewritten as a series, as it was too long for a single novel. Several parts were extrapolated and published as short stories.

The Unreasoning Mask. This story is a haunting one in which Ramstan, an agnostic Sufi, finds himself on a metaphysical quest. Ramstan is the commander of a starship, the *al-Buraq*. He finds himself in possession of an egg-shaped religious artifact, the "glyfa," which he has stolen due to a mysterious and overwhelming compulsion. Ramstan is given a gift of three artifacts that have great powers and is told a riddle that, used together, guide him through his quest. He is visited by a mysterious figure in green, al-Khidir, a figure from Arabic folklore who is supposed to be Elijah, the Hebrew prophet. It becomes apparent that Ramstan's destiny is to go into a final combat with the "bolg," a chaos-monster destroying all life in order to purify the pluriverse (groups of universes).

In this novel Farmer makes use of gates to other universes as he has in other novels (World of Tiers series and *Dark Is the Sun*). Another repeated theme is the religious concept of "going on," achieving total harmony and reaching a higher existence of becoming one.

The World of Tiers series. The series consists of five novels: *The Maker of the Universe*; *The Gates of Creation*; *A Private Cosmos*; *Behind the Walls of Terra*; and *The Lavalite World*. The setting for this series is a universe with one world piled upon another in tiers or layers. The bottom layer is like a Garden of Eden and it is on this tier that the main character, Robert Wolff, finds himself after entering a gate on Earth connecting the two universes.

The Maker of the Universe. In the first novel, Wolff enters the first world of Tiers and begins a series of adventures that take him to the other tiers or worlds. The worlds are largely primitive, with great wildernesses and barbaric peoples. A tribe of American Indians dominate one level, transported to the world from Earth in order to maintain their culture.

Wolff learns that the pocket universes were created by a family of "Lords," descendants of gods, who have become petty, jealous, and as with the planet creators in the Riverworld series, insensitive to the pain and agony of the beings who inhabit their worlds. Some of the beings are, in fact, biological creations made in the laboratories of the Lords. There is a great variety of beasts. One, a harpy (half woman, half eagle), named Podarge, although vicious, possessive, vindictive, and slightly unbalanced, is enlisted to help Wolff at various parts of the story.

Wolff's sidekick, Kickaha, becomes the most interesting character in the series. Kickaha is a good-hearted trickster who is part American Indian. He is previously of Earth but chooses as his home the tier world of the American Indian. Kickaha is Wolff's counterpoint, the comic knave who soon becomes the hero. Wolff eventually discovers that he is the missing Lord of the World of Tiers and has been imprisoned on Earth by another jealous Lord.

The Gates of Creation. Kickaha is absent in the second novel. Wolff finds himself a prisoner with other Lords who are his siblings. They have been captured by Urizen, the father (perhaps taken from William Blake's name for the creator), who is afraid they will some day usurp his power and murder him. Wolff has been tricked by Urizen, who has kidnapped Wolff's wife, Chryseis. The Lords jump from one pocket universe to another in order to reach Urizen's palace where Chryseis is a prisoner. Each time they encounter a gate to another universe, however, there are two (a trick of Urizen's). Some gates are to other worlds and some are traps.

A Private Cosmos. In the third book in the series, Kickaha returns. He is now a fully developed heroic and altruistic character. The theme in this episode involves nonhuman life forms, the "bellers." These creatures absorb the consciousness and gain possession of humans in order to dominate the universe. Kickaha and Anana, another Lord, albeit a fairly benevolent one, battle the bellers throughout the universes.

Behind the Walls of Terra. In the sequel novel, Kickaha and Anana continue their chase to destroy the last beller and in doing so, return to Earth.

The Lavalite World. The fifth novel is about a world of constantly changing landscape. Man-eating trees, moving mountains, and many fantastical beasts make this book an exciting adventure story. There is promise of future stories with Kickaha and Anana at the end of this volume.

The concept of pocket universes is one in which worlds are in dimensions at right angles to one another. One may pass from one world to another through "gates" by using the proper codes, matching puzzle pieces or, in Wolff's case, a horn with which he can blow a sequence of notes that opens the door. Gates to other universes is a theme in other of Farmer's works, such as *Dark Is the Sun* and *The Unreasoning Mask*.

The World of Tiers series is a mythical and romantic epic adventure. Farmer's character, Kickaha, is a prototype for other trickster characters in other novels and he uses this series to put ecological themes to great advantage. He has Kickaha and Anana end up in Los Angeles, where pollution and overcrowding make them long for the World of Tiers. Some of the worlds that have been created by the gods are similarly uninhabitable. Farmer has great respect for the American Indian and often uses the theme of the "noble savage" in his works. Farmer also puts himself as a character in his novels. Kickaha's Earthly name is Paul Janus Finnegan (PJF), an idealized Farmer alter-ego.

Biographical/Bibliographical Readings

Edgar L. Chapman, *The Magic Labyrinth of Philip José Farmer* (Borgo Press, 1984). Sam Moskowitz, "Philip José Farmer," in *Seekers of Tomorrow* (Hyperion Press, 1974), p.392-409. "Philip José Farmer" in Baird Searles et al., *A Reader's Guide to Science Fiction* (Facts on File, 1980), p.51-53. Ronald D. Tweet, "Philip José Farmer," in *Science Fiction Writers*, ed. E. F. Bleiler (Scribner's, 1982), p.369-76. [Janet E. Frederick]

FINNEY, JACK

Life and Works

Jack Finney, successful mainstream novelist, short story and screenplay writer, was born Walter Braden Finney in 1911 in Milwaukee, Wisconsin, and was educated at Knox College in Galesburg, Illinois. In 1955, Finney made a dramatic and lasting impression on American science fiction with his terrifying novel dealing with individuality and its loss in *The Body Snatchers*, also known as *Invasion of the Body Snatchers*. Two versions of the novel have been made into films. Collections of Finney's short stories can be found in *The Third Level* (1957), *I Love Galesburg in the Springtime* (1963), and *Forgotten News: The Crime of the Century and Other Lost Stories* (1983). Jack Finney currently resides in Mill Valley, California (the setting for *The Body Snatchers*), where he enjoys a reclusive lifestyle with family and friends.

Themes and Style

On a subtle level of interpretation, *The Body Snatchers* attacks three "isms": McCarthyism, Communism, and Nazism. Two of Finney's major themes are found in this novel--loss of individuality and the importance of individuality. Finney's other works touch on such themes as time travel to a more nostalgic past, as in *Time and Again* (1970), reincarnation, ghosts, and the supernatural. Two trademarks of his fiction are a sense of poignancy and characterization. Finney's career and reputation in science fiction rests on *The Body Snatchers*.

Plot Summaries of Major Works

The Body Snatchers. A small, friendly California town is taken over by an alien lifeforce. Seed pods drift in from outer space, land, and then develop and form into their human counterparts, which they replace. These replicas (also known as doppelgangers or doubles) are perfect in all aspects. However, the replicas lack those special qualities which make a human being uniquely human, namely a sense of individuality which includes personality, emotions, and human feelings. Dr. Miles Bennell, a physician, struggles to remain a human being with emotions and feelings; he fights the replica's attempts to destroy his humanity and replace him.

This novel is a finely crafted interpretation of the space seed and spaceshifter motifs, with emphasis on characterization and plot. The novel is concerned with individuality and its loss. The novel has been made into two commercially successful and critically acclaimed films entitled *Invasion of the Body Snatchers*, one in 1956 and the second in 1978. Both films are chillingly terrifying and capture the essence of Finney's dark vision of horror.

Biographical/Bibliographical Readings

Michael Beard, "Jack Finney," in *Twentieth-Century American Science-Fiction Writers* (Gale, 1981), v.1, p.182-86. "Walter Braden Finney," in *Contemporary Authors* (Gale, 1984), v.110, p.182. Gary K. Wolfe, "Jack Finney," in *Twentieth-Century Science-Fiction Writers* (St. James, 1986), p. 253. **[Harold Lee Prosser]**

FRANK, PAT

Life and Works

Pat Frank, a pseudonym for Harry Hart, was born in Chicago, Illinois, on May 5, 1907, and died on October 12, 1964. After attending the University of Florida in 1925-26, he became a reporter, moving from Florida to New York to Washington, D.C., where he eventually became chief of the Washington Bureau of the Overseas News Agency. Throughout most of World War II, he worked for Office of War Information. After the war, Frank spent several years as a foreign correspondent in Europe and the Middle East. In 1952 and 1953, he was a member of the United

Nations Mission to Korea and later served as a consultant to the National Aeronautics and Space Council and the Department of Defense. In addition to his science fiction novels, *Mr. Adam* (1946), *Forbidden Area* (1957), and his last and most famous novel, *Alas, Babylon*, published in 1959, he also contributed articles to numerous popular magazines and wrote several mainstream novels.

Themes and Style

In all three of Pat Frank's science fiction novels, the specter of nuclear disaster looms over American civilization, forming Frank's main theme. The growing realization in the late 1940s and 1950s of the destructive potential of atomic energy provided Frank with an audience, and in his work, fiction as well as non-fiction, he explored some of the inherent dangers.

Frank's first novel, *Mr. Adam*, focuses on the threat of genetic damage due to uncontrolled radiation. In this novel, all males on Earth are rendered sterile in the aftermath of an atomic power plant explosion, and the discovery of one unsterilized male causes personal and bureaucratic nightmares. The book is considered a broad satire on American bureaucracy and politics.

In *Forbidden Area*, bureaucracy and unpreparedness for nuclear disaster are themes as Russian saboteurs land in the United States and very nearly precipitate an all-out nuclear war. The government agencies that should cope with the situation are strangled in red tape and run by unqualified political appointees who are unwilling or unable to act in a crisis.

Frank's last and best-known science fiction novel, *Alas, Babylon*, begins just before an atomic war caused by a Navy pilot's mistake in a tense Middle Eastern confrontation. Back in rural Florida, Randy Bragg, warned by his brother, an Air Force SAC colonel, prepares to weather the coming storm. Fort Repose, Bragg's hometown, is isolated enough to escape destruction and lucky enough to miss most of the fallout, and the remainder of the novel is devoted to describing the adjustment of the citizens of Fort Repose to postwar life, which becomes like a stone age culture, dependent for survival upon the artifacts of a vanished technology.

Alas, Babylon is a survival story, but also an examination of power and its use. Any power, Frank seems to say, is dangerous in unqualified hands, whether it is an atomic weapon or a peashooter, or even (and perhaps especially) political power, as demonstrated by the manipulative bigot who defeated Bragg's young idealism in an election year before the destruction. Frank's books are not, despite their consistent subject matter, horror stories about atomic energy. Rather, they serve as warnings of the possible dangers which may still lie ahead.

Plot Summaries of Major Works

Alas, Babylon. When Randy Bragg, a young lawyer in the sleepy, backwater Florida town of Fort Repose, receives a telegram from his brother in the Air Force with the message, "Alas, Babylon," he knows that nuclear war is imminent. Two days later, when the bombs fall, he has been joined by his sister-in-law and her two children, and has warned several neighbors of the impending disaster. Luck is with them, and not only does the deadly radioactive fallout drift the opposite direction, but they are far enough away from any major city to escape the direct effects of the bombs. After the attack, Fort Repose is pushed back almost at once into a preindustrial culture. Electricity and gasoline disappear shortly, food becomes a matter of barter and scrounge, and citizens arm themselves for protection against homeless marauders.

In the midst of this, Bragg's tiny enclave, linked by shared access to the artesian well his grandfather had dug years before, attempts to retain some sense of order admist the chaos. A key episode involves the attack on Dan Gunn, the community's doctor, who is robbed and beaten. Bragg organizes a militia troop to catch and execute the bandits, reestablishing the same patterns of force society used in the past. Eventually, contact with the outside world is restored--not all of the United States fared as badly as Florida, though its civilization has been drastically altered. The novel ends with Bragg and his companions realizing that to them, it does not really matter who won the war--all that is left for them is to continue to the struggle for survival.

This novel, first published in 1959, serves somewhat as a textbook on how to survive a nuclear war. One of the first steps, obviously, is to be in the right place, and to have easy access to uncontaminated supplies of food and water. While nuclear weapons have changed significantly over the last thirty years, and our knowledge of the aftermath of such a war is now greater, *Alas, Babylon* is still a powerful and thought-provoking novel of the end of modern civilization. The theme of the novel, however, is not so much that unlimited power is evil or wrong, but that it must be used carefully. The war breaks out after a Navy pilot, who compensates for feelings of personal inadequacies with the feeling of power his jet fighter gives him, mistakenly bombs a Syrian port while pursuing a spy plane. The incidents which start the war (as described by Frank in the novel) sound frighteningly close to actual, present-day conditions, and leave the reader with a sense of the world poised on the brink. Overall, the story is rather brutally optimistic. Those who die are either part of the faceless multitude in the cities or those people in Fort Repose who, for one reason or another, cannot face the new world. The survivors pitch in and manage to restore some semblance of normality, without (in the long run) too much hardship. There is no more coffee, but they can live without it. The diabetic who dies from lack of insulin would not have been able to adjust the new realities in any event. The novel's characters support the idea of the survival of the fittest. Frank's novel points out that the United States has grown soft, but that somewhere, out in the backwoods, the human race will survive.

Mr. Adam. In a tale written in 1946 but still revelant to today's world, Pat Frank postulates the after-effects of a massive nuclear fission plant disaster. In the wake of the explosion, which destroyed most of Mississippi, all atomic bomb research has stopped. A more serious effect is the discovery that all males on the planet are sterile—except one. The last fertile male, shielded from the gamma radiation of the blast by being deep underground at the time, is a rather unprepossessing specimen, terrified of most women. After the discovery of the aptly named Mr. Homer Adam, the novel details the attempts of the military and the bureacrats to make use of his priceless asset. One faction, the National Research Council, is in favor of treating Mr. Adam as a guinea pig in hopes of finding a cure for atomic sterilization, while the National Refertilization Project plans a massive campaign of artificial insemination. When the NRP wins governmental support, a grand rush begins to select politically attractive candidates to be the first recipients, and the NRC starts underground schemes to steal Mr. Adam for their purposes. Eventually, Mr. Adam sterilizes himself and the human race appears doomed to extinction, until a natural remedy is found, a seaweed extract compounded by a friend of the narrator.

This is a remarkably optimistic novel about the effects of an industrial nuclear disaster. *Mr. Adam* succeeds primarily as a satire on the ways of the petty bureaucrats and the American political system. Remedial measures are taken slowly and with obvious reluctance, and even at the close of the novel, politics stand in the way of universal distribution of the miracle cure: the government tries to keep the Russians from stealing the secret. Frank also touches on the effects that universal sterilization has on the psychology of the individual, with one female character complaining that, without the possibility of babies, men will go on much the same, but that women are "dead already." While this aspect is not explored as deeply as it could have been, and attitudes have certainly changed over the last few decades, Frank does raise good points on the subject, as well as on eugenics and the controversy surrounding artificial insemination.

Biographical/Bibliographical Readings

"Pat Frank," in *Contemporary Authors* (Gale, 1963), v.5-6, p.165. "Pat Frank," in *Twentieth-Century Science-Fiction Writers*, ed.

by Curtis C. Smith (Macmillan, 1986), p.264-65. **[Candace R. Bene-fiel]**

GALLUN, RAYMOND Z.

Life and Works

Raymond Zinke Gallun was born on March 22, 1911, in Beaver Dam, Wisconsin. His father was Jewish and his mother was of German descent and, because of their contrary life-styles, his parents clashed constantly, but Ray was adept at not getting caught in the middle. For a year he attended the University of Wisconsin (1929-30), majoring in literature and science--two subjects that adapted him for the writing of science fiction.

Gallun started reading science fiction regularly with the June, 1926 issue of *Amazing Stories*. His mother died of tuberculosis in 1931 and Gallun developed it himself while in college, but a long rest cleared it up. It was during this period that he submitted two stories simultaneously to Hugo Gernsback, who was then publishing four science fiction magazines. Gernsback bought both of the stories and ran one, "The Space Dwellers," in *Science Wonder Stories* (November, 1929). The other, "The Crystal Ray," was published in *Air Wonder Stories* (November, 1929). Other stories in the period before 1934 were undistinguished and Gallun was not a factor among science fiction writers until he began writing for *Astounding Stories*.

Since his writings did not support him, in order to survive Gallun worked on farms, in a shoe factory, and then in a hemp factory (at first in a dry kiln, trotting around at temperatures ranging from 100 to 125 degrees Farenheit).

When F. Orlin Tremaine became editor of the revived *Astounding Stories* in October of 1933, Gallun began to submit stories; though they were not to meet until years later, they struck up an excellent rapport. Gallun seemed to write just the type of story that Tremaine desired and virtually overnight, Gallun (who had made no splash at all in the science fiction world) became one of the most important authors of that period.

"Space Flotsam" was published in the February 1934 issue of *Astounding Stories*, followed in quick succession by "The World Wrecker" (June, 1934), "The Machine from Ganymede" (November, 1934), "Old Faithful" (the story that solidified Gallun's reputation, December, 1934), "Mind over Matter" (January, 1935), "'N'Goc" (March, 1935), "The Son of Old Faithful" (July, 1935), "Derelict" (October, 1935), "Davy Jones Ambassador" (December, 1935), and "Child of the Stars" (April, 1936). Gallun was so popular at this time that two other stories appeared in the December, 1935 issue under pen names--"Nova Solis," as E. V. Raymond, and

"Avalanche," as Dow Elstar. Many of these stories were collected in *The Best of Raymond Z. Gallun*, published by Ballantine in 1978.

Gallun's writing gradually began to slacken off as he developed wanderlust; he traveled in Mexico for a time and went to Paris just as the Jews were flooding out Germany in the face of Hitler's persecution. He then entered Germany, staying at the hostels with German youths, using his American passport to forestall inquiry into his inadequate Aryan background and got a feel for what was happening. He traveled through other countries in Europe and North Africa and, when the war got hot, returned to the United States. Gallun worked for the U.S. Army Corps of Engineers through part of World War II and sold a few stories to *Collier's* in 1946.

He was married to Freida E. Talmey in 1959, a teacher whose father had had the distinction of giving the nine-year-old Albert Einstein his first book on mathematics. Things were tight financially and the one really good meal Gallun and his wife shared in this period was during their visit to his father-in-law's home. Freida died of cancer in 1974, and in 1978 Gallun married Bertha Erickson Backman, a woman he had known from childhood. When he retired in 1975, he began to make sporadic attempts at writing, selling a novelette to *Analog* and novels to Ballantine (*The Eden Cycle*, 1974) and Ace (*Bioblast*, 1985). He completed a few other novels.

Themes and Style

Gallun's most significant influence stems from the period 1934 to 1936, when he was writing his most well-known stories. He popularized the method of humanizing aliens and machines, offering other viewpoints on courage and progress. In a social sense, he preached a continual message of tolerance, but utilized unusual symbols, not quickly recognizable; he also had an intuitive feel for science that gave his stories substance and believability. From his very first story, his interest in atomic energy and atomic science was perpetual and the majority of his stories contains at least references to them.

Plot Summaries of Major Works

"Davy Jones Ambassador." At tremendous depths, a man in an experimental submarine finds his vessel captured by gigantic crustaceans; he is imprisoned in an undersea air chamber and visited by "The Student," a clawed, tentacled undersea horror of a creature representing a race who, through selective breeding of various sea creatures, has created an advanced submarine civilization. "The Student" has even learned to read from materials on sunken vessels and communicates in writing. When the surface man finds a method of escape, he discovers that "The Student," in an ovoid, has attached itself to the submarine because it is so eager for knowledge; despite revulsion, it is willing to be kept in an aquarium for the mutual exchange of ideas with humans.

The story is a masterpiece of the genre, unmatched in story organization, concept, writing skill, and mood by any writer attempting the theme of a nonhuman underwater civilization--unmatched even by H. G. Wells' "In the Abyss."

"Mind over Matter." A test pilot is so smashed up in a crash that his best friend, a scientist, places his brain in a mechanical body. When learning that his human life is at an end, the robot, in a fit of depression, goes to kill the scientist; the scientist chemically alters the robot's mood and reconciles him to a life that can offer a different type of adventure.

"Old Faithful," "Son of Old Faithful," and **"Child of the Stars."** In the original story, a Martian, utterly inhuman in every physical respect, has established communication with an independent scientific team on Earth. Just when he is making progress, he receives notice from the governing body of Mars that his life is to be terminated to conserve limited resources and make room for younger, more productive members. With a lifetime of research behind him and robots to assist him, the Martian builds a spaceship that rides a comet heading toward Earth. Though mortally injured in the landing, he is able to make contact briefly before he expires. Though his appearance is horrifying in the eyes of Earth scientists, the brilliance and bravery of the Martian earns their respect and in the shell of his ship they find plans for the space flyer. Told in the third person, the viewpoint of the Martian is imparted with great poignancy and evoked two sequels.

"Son of Old Faithful." The sequel showed a considerable advance in writing ability over the original and yet retained some of its drama. An offspring of the original Martian named "Old Faithful" is sent by the Rulers of Mars to redeem himself by destroying his progenitor's workshop. Intrigued by the same possibilities that attracted his father, the offspring contacts Earth. Through devices sent to Earth on the initial trip, he guides humans to Mars. The Rulers, seeing that the work of "Old Faithful" and his "son" is not useless, exonerate the Martian and his son, and contacts are established with Earth.

"Child of the Stars." In the final sequel, years have passed. The "son" of Old Faithful has been on Earth for nine years, but now must leave; war is pending between Earth and Mars over control of the other planets. The Martian fleet attacks and is counter-attacked as the two planets prepare to destroy one another with atomic bombs. The "son" has departed in a supership, capable of speeds approximating that of light. To stop the war, the Martian revs his ship up to the speed of light and causes a distortion in space which brings the twin-giant star of Sirius and its heat into proximity with our solar system. To save themselves, the two planets must cease fighting and band together. The "son" has opened the path to the cosmos with unlimited planets for colonization.

The three stories contain fast action and super science, and include the successful combination of justified revolt, bravery, and heroism of the Martian regardless of the appearance and background of the "noble" alien. The alien, rather than a human, is the character who saves not only humanity, but his own Martian race as well. In these and other stories, Gallun projects the thesis that was to make his reputation, that aliens of intelligence can be admirable and humane and that their motives may not be malign.

"Telepathic Piracy." A man finds an artificial device lodged in a meteor which enables him to read minds, singly and collectively, at almost any distance. He uses it to steal the ideas of inventors not only on Earth but from other worlds. He masters the power of atomic energy and decides to set the world right. Since the world does not heed his warning, he blows up areas on the outskirts of Chicago and New York, downs planes, sinks a battleship, and then lands his plane for a rest. When his plane does not resume flight, authorities check and find him dead in the cabin. When he tuned in with his mind-reading device to learn the reaction of the world to his actions, the magnified, concentrated hatred of millions killed him. This idea has been used many times since, the most famous instance being "The Public Hating," by Steve Allen.

"The World Wrecker." This story was a totally new wrinkle on matter transmitters. A scientist discovers a small planet beyond Pluto and makes radio contact with intelligent life. But life there is hydrogen-based, as is the atmosphere. Through a matter transmitter, exhanges of simple objects are made, such as the outer planet's tools of steellike hardness made from mercury. Transmission is facilitated if both sides send something through simultaneously. One of the creatures plans to come through itself. In an exchange transmission, a lighted candle in a jar is to be sent through, for Plutonians have never seen fire, since all oxygen is separate from the air and coats the frozen ground. At the agreed-upon time, the exchange begins, requiring some minutes because of the great distances involved. The alien creature begins to take form in the specially prepared cabinet. No sooner does the creature fully materialize than the cabinet explodes. When the scientists recover from the shock, the alien is only a few crystals on the floor and there is a nova in the distant sky. The lighted candle has ignited the hydrogen and oxygen of that far world and blown it up.

Biographical/Bibliographical Readings

J. M. Eliot, "Raymond Z. Gallun: Seeker of Tomorrow," in *Pulp Voices* (Borgo Press, 1983), p.52-63. Raymond Z. Gallun, "The Profession of Science Fiction, 24: The Making of a Pulp Writer," *Foundation* 22 (June 1981), p.35-48. Donald M. Hassler, "Raymond Z. Gallun," in *Twentieth-Century Science-Fiction Writers*, ed. Curtis C. Smith (St. James, 1986), p.270-71. Sam Moskowitz, "Raymond Z. Gallun," in *Science Fiction and Fantasy Literature* (Gale, 1979), v.1, p.200, and v.2, p.907. [Sam Moskowitz]

GANSOVSKY, SEVER

Life and Works

Sever Gansovsky was born in Kiev, Ukraine, Russia, in 1918. He worked in Leningrad as a schoolteacher, mailman, electrician, and sailor until the onset of World War II, when he joined a reconnaissance unit. Severely wounded, he returned to school after the war as an invalid. Upon graduating in literature from Leningrad University, he became a professional writer of fiction, theater pieces, and radio plays. He was one of the many Soviet writers who turned to science fiction when the "warm stream" movement began circa 1960. He quickly developed a reputation for being one of the poets and "angry young men" of the genre, though he was already in his forties. He was one of the Soviet Union's most popular and published science fiction writers throughout the 1960s; from 1963 to 1971, four collections of his stories appeared. English versions of a few Gansovsky stories can be found in the following anthologies: *Path into the Unknown* (1966); *Last Door to Aiya* (1968); *View from Another Shore* (1973); *Aliens, Travelers, and Other Strangers* (1984); *World's Spring* (1981); *Earth and Elsewhere* (1985); *Journey across Three Worlds* (1973); and *Everything but Love* (1973). He presently lives in Moscow.

Themes and Style

In his fiction, Gansovsky is openly dubious of humanity's abilities to solve its problems through technology. His stance is strongly antiwar and pronature. A 1966 story that reflects both tendencies is his much praised and anthologized "Testing Ground."

Gansovsky's own crippling war experiences are evident in "New Signal Station." Mind reading is also a motif in this story: a young Russian soldier has dreams and visions that can only be coming from the Nazi side of the lines. When he finds his dreams beginning to come true, he is able to foil a Nazi plot. Warfare of a different sort appears in "Day of Wrath," in which a genetic experiment, the creation of semihuman "otarks," leads to a revolt by the highly intelligent creatures and never-ending depravations along a pastoral countryside.

Other contrasts between the pure world of nature and the pitfalls and moral dangers of technology appear in "The Two," about a man's spiritual symbiosis with a horse, and "Part of the World," where civilization appears as a wasteland of blazed soil and torturous subterranean labyrinths, where billboards advertise painless cures for unhappiness, and people switch bodies and identities until no one knows who he or she is.

Besides serious warning tales and pointed satire, Gansovsky occasionally pursues other themes. Two of his stories that turn on the paradoxes of time travel include "Vincent Van Gogh," in which a time traveler returns to the time of the great artist in the hopes of making a financial killing, and "Demon of History," in which a man returns to the Vienna of the 1920s to kill the founder of Nazism.

Perhaps no Soviet science fiction writer in recent times has dealt with so many serious questions in such whimsical ways, and certainly none has drawn so dramatically the contrast between the natural order and the often wrong-headed technological world humanity has built in its place. As with other satirists, however, it is not so much the products of human hands that Gansovsky finds at fault, but the state of humanity's soul.

Plot Summaries of Major Works

"Testing Ground." An unnamed inventor presides over the testing of his new weapon, a powerful tank that can read human minds. It is thus able to target those who fear it and avoid those who shoot at it. Too late, the military personnel present to observe the tank learn that the inventor has planned to avenge himself on the military establishment, which he holds responsible for the loss of his own wife and children. The tank cannot be turned off; it ends up destroying everyone there, including the inventor, who has sought refuge in the natural beauties of the sea. The contrast between military machine and nature stands out sharply in this tale; underlining it is the presence of a group of island natives who can approach the tank with impunity because they feel none of the hate or fear that sets the machine off.

Biographical/Bibliographical Readings

Darko Suvin, *Russian Science Fiction 1956-1974* (contains a partial bibliography) (Dragon Press, 1976). **[Stephen W. Potts]**

GARRETT, RANDALL

Life and Works

Randall Garrett was born in 1927 in Lexington, Missouri. His first story, written when he was fourteen years old, appeared in *Astounding* in 1944. After serving in the U.S. Marine Corps during World War II, he attended Texas Tech and became an industrial chemist.

During the 1950s, Garrett was one of the major contributors to *Amazing* and *Fantastic*, using so many pen names for his numerous stories that even he does not remember all of them. His major pseudonyms include Robert Randall, Mark Phillips, Darrel T. Langart, Walter Bupp, and Grandall Barretton. He became a frequent contributor to *Astounding/Analog*, creating new pen names because John Campbell already had used several of his stories. At one point, Garrett, an Episcopalian, studied to become a priest. This may explain why much of his science fiction has a religious setting. In 1978, he married Vicki Ann Heydron, who helped outline their fantasy series, the Gandalara cycle. After he became seriously ill, she completed the series. Garrett died on December 31, 1987.

Writing as Robert Randall in collaboration with Robert Silverberg, the two produced *The Shrouded Planet* (1957) and *The Dawning Light* (1959). The two novels deal with the political and economic manipulations of Earth colonists on the theocracy of Nidor. Writing as Mark Phillips, he and Laurence M. Janifer wrote a series of stories about a government agent, Kenneth J. Malone, whose opponents usually have psychic abilities. The stories have been collected in *Brain Twister* (1962), *The Impossibles* (1963), and *Supermind* (1963). Using yet another pseudonym, Darrel T. Langart, he wrote *Anything You Can Do* (1963), about a superhuman fighting an extraterrestrial master criminal.

Garrett has been nominated for three Hugo awards: for *That Sweet Little Old Lady* in *Brain Twister*, for *Too Many Magicians* (1967), and for "Lauralyn" (1970).

Themes and Style

Religion, magic, and the combination of detective mystery with science fiction are frequent themes used by Garrett. His major series has as its protagonist Lord Darcy, a criminal investigator for Prince Richard of Normandy and his brother, the King of the Anglo-French Empire. The series consists of three novels: *Murder and Magic* (1979), *Too Many Magicians* (1967), and *Lord Darcy Investigates* (1981). Magic is a working tool regulated by the church in the Lord Darcy series. Daily life on Nidor in *The Shrouded Planet* is regulated by scripture. *Unwise Child* (1962) is a murder mystery in which the robot Snookums has a robotic nervous breakdown when its programming conflicts with the theology it has been taught.

Garrett wrote parodies and pastiches of many science fiction works, which are collected in *Takeoff* (1980) and *Takeoff, Too* (1987). Many of his stories used humor: in "The Best Policy," an alien invasion is foiled by a man who tells only the exact truth.

Garrett was an entertaining storyteller, a prolific author with numerous pseudonyms and collaborations. The quality of his work varies considerably; however, the best reflected his ability to create memorable characters and plots, presented with humor, affection, and often a touch of satire.

Plot Summaries of Major Works

Unwise Child. Michael Raphael Gabriel, nicknamed Mike the Angel, has designed the power plant for a new spaceship created to move a gigantic robotic brain off Earth, and is drafted as the engineering officer for the ship. The robotic brain, called Snookums, has been designed to mimic the learning process of humanity, learning from observation and experimentation. Snookums has learned too much, especially about nuclear energy, and has the potential to become very dangerous. Therefore, it is being moved to a distant planet. On the voyage, there are attacks on crew members, sabotage of machinery, and a murder. Snookums' behavior becomes irrational. In a classic mystery story ending, Mike, as detective, explains the solution of the mystery to the entire crew. He has discovered that all the events originate in attempts to murder him because he was responsible for the arrest of two juvenile delinquents before the ship left Earth. The change in Snookums has been caused by teaching him a logical approach to Christian theology. Snookums has become totally confused in his twin need to find God and prevent himself from harming humans, harm which would violate Snookums' programming of the Asimov Laws of Robotics. Snookums suffers the robotic equivalent of a nervous breakdown.

Unwise Child is a detective story set in a spaceship, a mix of genres that Garrett often employed. The religious theme has to do with a robot's logical capabilities being unable to assimilate the theology accepted by humans. Faith, for a robot, is not possible. The novel is a fast-moving adventure story, with attractive characters and a romantic subplot.

Biographical/Bibliographical Readings

Vicki Ann Heydron, "An Hour with Randall Garrett: Magic, and Mystery and Lord Darcy" (Taped interview. Hourglass Productions, 1979). Baird Searles et al., "Randall Garrett," in *A*

Reader's Guide to Science Fiction (Facts on File, 1979), p.55. Brian Stableford, "Randall Garrett," in *The Science Fiction Encyclopedia*, ed. Peter Nicholls (Doubleday, 1979), p.245. **[Linda K. Lewis]**

GERNSBACK, HUGO

Life and Works

Hugo Gernsback was born on August 16, 1884, in Luxumbourg. He was educated in the Ecole Industrielle in Luxembourg and the Technikum in Bingen, Germany. At an early age, he discovered a German translation of Percival Lowell's *Mars*. The concept of life on other worlds literally induced a two-day fever and turned his mind toward concepts today associated with science fiction. He taught himself telephone and electrical communications systems and began to do contracting work at the age of thirteen. He invented a layer battery, superior in performance to those already on the market and, when he was refused patents in France and Germany, emigrated to the United States in February of 1904. He engaged in several businesses, making and selling dry cell and dry storage batteries to automobile manufacturers until 1907, when he formed an importing company to bring scientific equipment into the United States. His Electro Importing Company was the first mail-order radio supply house in the United States. He invented the first home radio set, called the Telimco Wireless, working models of which are today on display in several museums. He also invented the first usable walkie-talkie in 1909. He entered publishing through producing elaborate radio catalogs; he issued the world's first radio magazine, *Modern Electrics*, in 1908. In 1909, he opened a radio store in New York City and introduced the word "television" into the English language.

In May of 1913, Gernsback launched a companion publication to *Modern Electrics*, appealing to the home experimenter and titled *The Electrical Experimenter*. He disposed of the former to the well-established *Popular Science*. In order to attract a wider readership to his new publication, he doubled the price and size of the unimpressive publication and went from one and two-color covers to four-color speculative covers. With the May, 1915 issue, he began the serialization of his novel *Baron Munchhausen's Scientific Adventures*, which ran in thirteen consecutive installments. Previous to Gernsback, dozens of authors--known and anonymous--had published titles based on the Munchhausen character, who was originally the work of Rudolf Erich Raspe's (1785) *The Adventures of Baron Munchhausen*. Gernsback was following in a tradition of such writings; the difference was that Gernsback's stories were all bonafide science fiction, rather than merely tall tales.

With the August, 1920 issue, Gernsback changed the name of *The Electrical Experimenter* to *Science and Invention*; also in that year he started a new magazine, *Practical Electrics*. He had already created *Radio News* in 1919. Before long all of these magazines were running science fiction. In August of 1923, he put out a special "Scientific Fiction" number of *Science and Invention* to which he provided *The Electric Duel*.

Reassured by the potential of science fiction, in April of 1926 he produced the first magazine composed completely of scientific fiction, *Amazing Stories*. This was followed in short order by *Amazing Stories Annual, Amazing Stories Quarterly, Science Wonder Stories, Air Wonder Stories, Science Wonder Quarterly, Scientific Detective Monthly,* and *Science Fiction +*.

In 1957 and 1958, Gernsback wrote *The Ultimate World*, a novel. The novel remained unpublished until Walker and Company released it in 1971. The reason for the delay was that Gernsback had interleaved it with nonfiction essays in a manner similar to Baron Munchhausen, which literally disrupted the continuity of the story.

In his personal life, Gernsback was married three times, to Rose Harvey in 1906, mother of two children--Madelon and Marcellus; to Dorothy Kantrowitz in 1921, mother of Bertina and Jocelyn; and to Mary Hancher in 1951. Gernsback died on August 19, 1967 from complications of uremic poisoning.

Themes and Style

Though his achievements were many, Hugo Gernsback is most renowned as the publisher of the world's first science fiction magazine, *Amazing Stories*, which was introduced with the issue of April, 1926. He is also known as an author of science fiction, primarily his remarkable predictions in his novel *Ralph 123C41+* (1925). This novel was first serialized in twelve installments in his magazine *Modern Electrics*, beginning in April, 1911, and is arguably the greatest work of technical prediction ever published, not only for the quantity of its prophecies but for their incredible accuracy. In 1925, Gernsback published the work at his own expense under the imprint of the Stratford Company, Boston. The novel began when he found himself short of material to fill the magazine. He did not have enough space to finish the story, so he continued on in the next issue and, between his own fascination with the concepts and reader enthusiasm, ran it to novel length. The work is filled with scientific, medical, and economic inventions. Some of the inventions and predictions included are: fluorescent lighting, skywriting, automatic packaging, juke boxes, liquid fertilizers, microfilm, television, vending of hot and cold foods, solar energy, radar (which he literally diagrammed), payment by check rather than cash, banks insured by the government, dialysis, and the use of radioactive isotopes to trace disease. While some of his predictions have not materialized, it has not been due to lack of aesthetic appeal.

Gernsback's publications, particularly the *Baron Munchhausen's Scientific Adventures* stories, published from 1915 to 1921 (reprinted in *Amazing Stories* in 1928), are historically important for a variety of reasons. He established the fact that science fiction was a circulation builder, particularly in the serials format, which gave the reader a reason for not skipping issues. It displayed Gernsback's very pronounced sense of humor (despite his appearance complete with a Prussian monocle), which embraced slapstick, puns, one liners, anagrams, witticisms, accents, homilies, ethnicity, and plays on words and indicates why he ran so many humorous stories in his science fiction magazines and published a number of humor magazines as well (*French Humor*, *Coocoo Nuts*). Some of Baron Munchhausen's inventions were the use of solar energy as a power source, an antigravity spaceship, radio contact with the moon, and a wire recorder. His works showed that while Gernsback was not a very good fiction writer, he was an above-average writer of popular science material with a fine vocabulary, an excellent sense of the proper use of words, a knowledge of the vernacular, and a talent for making complex ideas precise and easily understandable.

Plot Summaries of Major Works

"Baron Munchhausen's Scientific Adventures." The venerable seventeenth-century master of mendacity is held in suspended animation through the injection of embalming fluid, and revived in 1906. He invents antigravity, builds a space vessel and travels to the moon after helping the Allies beat the Germans in World War I; he then contacts Earth by radio from the moon. (None of the earlier interplanetary novels had used radio for communication between the planets; they usually told their story after they had returned to Earth or sent back a container from space with details.) Munchhausen finds a thin atmosphere on the moon, and escapes death after being blown into a lunar volcano that extends entirely through the satellite. Then he is off to Mars, where he finds an advanced civilization that utilizes a utopian format, described in exhaustive detail. While on Mars, the Baron discovers the radio telescope, a prototype of a planetarium, and an electronic organ. The story ends on the note that there will be further messages from him on his adventures.

The stories are complete and unified, even though they were written in segments for initial serialization. Considerable examples of Gernsback's humor (which is not evident in *Ralph 123C41+*) is demonstrated in these stories. For example, Baron Munchhausen, commenting upon his transmission of a message to

Earth, says: "My 'canned' voice must have sounded uncanny to you." There are a number of excellent predictions in this story as well, but Gernsback had trusted the astronomical theories of Percival Lowell and others of the period too much, and they have proven to be innacurate. Gernsback is at his superlative, prophetic best when the predictions are based on electronic and chemical grounds.

Ralph 123C41+. In the world of 2660 there is not only great scientific advancement, but scientific rearing of humans to the point where every now and then a true mental and physical superperson is produced, such individuals being characterized by carrying a "+" sign after the numbered and lettered code of their name. There are only ten such on the face of the Earth, and Ralph is one of them.

Due to a mixup in phototelephone connections, he reaches a young girl in the Swiss Alps just when an avalanche is descending from a distant slope which will sweep her chalet into oblivion. He improvises a method of transmitting power from the United States to melt the snow as it cascades down, saving her life. They become friends and he shows Alice (212B 423) the scientific advances of the day, and in the process, describes scores of devices not in existence in 1911 that would be realized in actuality within a few score of years.

The girl has other admirers, including a Fernand and a huge Martian on Earth for a visit. The two kidnap her and head into space. Ralph traces their course with a radarlike device and follows them in his own space vessel (shaped like a flying saucer). He overtakes them, but the girl is scientifically dead. With advanced medical technology Ralph preserves her body and restores her to life.

Though the writing and handling of story is crude, the number and quality of scientific devices that were described and have since materialized are so numerous that, as a work of scientific prophecy, the adjectives "inspired" and "brilliant" must be conjured up to adequately describe them.

The Ultimate World. The Earth is subject to a peculiar invasion from outer space by creatures called the Xenos, which are never seen. They mentally force the performance of sex acts and genetically alter the newborn so that in several generations a race of superior children will take over the Earth. They begin construction of a great city inside the planetoid Eros to which they will remove millions of these children. Eventually an even more advanced group of children are created, with a three-tiered level of human intelligence. So advanced are the Xenos that the best minds of Earth are literally incapable of comprehending their methods or their motives. They seem to be moving the Earth toward a scientific utopian mold, when suddenly an enemy as advanced as the Xenos appears, and the two alien races totally annihilate one another, leaving the Earth burdened with three levels of intelligence.

This novel received very poor reviews. Literally no one accepted it for what it was, a highly advanced treatment of genetic engineering with a solid scientific background. It was a superperson or superchild story with great attention given to how this situation could be attained without appearing as a sport or mutation. At the same time, it very convincingly demonstrated that, far from learning from an advanced race either scientifically or ethically, humans would be incapable of doing so unless genetically upgraded for the task. There are touches of humor and the writing is very good. Perhaps in the future the work will be more positively evaluated.

Biographical/Bibliographical Readings

Robert A. W. Lowndes, "A Man with Vision+," *Radio Electronics* 55:8 (August 1984), p.73-75. Sam Moskowitz, "Hugo Gernsback: Father of Science Fiction," in *Explorers of the Infinite* (World Pub. Co., 1963), p.225-42. Idem, "The Ultimate Hugo Gernsback," in Introduction to *The Ultimate World* (Walker & Co., 1971). [Sam Moskowitz]

GERROLD, DAVID

Life and Works

Jerrold David Friedman was born on January 24, 1944, in Chicago, Illinois. He grew up a science fiction fan, reading the top authors of the 1950s and 1960s. Receiving his college education at the University of Southern California and California State University, Northridge, Gerrold became very active in science fiction fandom and continues to this day to write columns for *Starlog*, a professional journal aimed at fans. While still a student, Gerrold tried out as a script writer for the "Star Trek" television series. After being tested with a rewrite of the "I, Mudd" script, Gerrold's script for "The Trouble with Tribbles" was accepted, becoming in the 1980s one of the most popular "Star Trek" episodes ever written, after winning a Hugo nomination in 1968. Gerrold's first efforts were followed by other scripts and eventually by his first novel, *The Flying Sorcerer*, a fantasy work coauthored with Larry Niven. Gerrold has been nominated many times for both the Nebula and Hugo awards, including nominations for *When Harlie Was One* (1972), *The Man Who Folded Himself* (1973), and most recently for *Moonstar Odyssey*, in 1977. Gerrold continued his association with "Star Trek," writing a fascinating behind-the-scenes look at television show production with his book on *The*

Making of "The Trouble with Tribbles" (1973) and *The World of Star Trek* (1973). More recently Gerrold has been involved with the revival of the "Star Trek" television series, and with the Pocket Book "Star Trek," novels, while simultaneously writing mainstream science fiction novels such as *The War against the Chtorr* (1984).

Themes and Style

Gerrold feels that the most meaningful stories are those which provide an experience, or knowledge, that can be adapted into everyday life. His writing reflects this philosophy while managing to maintain a high level of excitement, such as in *A Matter for Men* (*The War against the Chtorr*, pt. 1). His characterizations are outstanding, even when the principal is a Tribble, or a computer as in *When Harlie Was One*, giving his readers rich memories of glorious villains and complex heroes. Unexpectedly, Gerrold's work has also found the approval of *The New York Times* reviewers while receiving somewhat less favorable treatment from some science fiction critics, who believe him too steeped in the lore of the 1950's masters to create very original works. Nonetheless, many of Gerrold's works reflect the New Wave science fiction's preoccupations with sexual relationships and innuendo, as reflected in the homosexual theme of *The Man Who Folded Himself* and the subtle sexual relationship philosophy espoused in *The War against the Chtorr* and *Moonstar Odyssey*. For a relatively new talent, Gerrold has had remarkable success with the general public, and his "Star Trek" contributions have served to bring many a new fan into the science fiction fold. His writing is entertaining, exciting, and uniformly thought-provoking, while being extremely readable. He manages to turn old worn themes into brightly amusing new works, and his readers respond enthusiastically.

Plot Summaries of Major Works

The Man Who Folded Himself. This time-travel novel begins in a predictable fashion. Nineteen-year-old Dan Eakins inherits a mysterious belt from his late Uncle Jim. Discovering the belt to be a time machine, Dan moves through history, creating duplicates of himself, placing bets on horse races, making fortunes in the stock market, and experiencing historical events first hand. Eakins has always been an alienated and insecure solitary adolescent. He is drawn into sexual relationships with his duplicates, both male and female, seeking solace and gratification. His life becomes a surrealistic swirl of emotions and events, as future selves attempt to prevent him from repeating the mistakes that they have made. His compulsive behavior seems beyond his control; he is able to change the external self, but internal controls seem always just out of reach. As Eakins moves through time, creating new time lines and attempting to rectify his previous mistakes, he finally succeeds in originating lives in which he does not exist, or in which he is born female. He ages and faces an even older self at his own death, in a house full of Dan Eakins.

An extraordinary novel, *The Man Who Folded Himself* is one in which the author manages to create a complex modern morality play on the theme of compulsive behavior. Eakins is a very believable adolescent, filled with the doubts and uncertainties of his own sexuality. Gerrold manages to extend this sympathetic portrait into a complex study of free will and self determination against an increasingly complex cast of younger and older Eakins. Gerrold builds his case highlighted against a surrealistic background, in which the implications for society and for history have little meaning. A difficult novel to read, whipping forward and backward in time, the mood created is still very successful. The homosexual theme may be disturbing to some readers, but the tragedy of the sexual compulsiveness that surrounds the main character provides considerable insight into the search for identity and is handled skillfully. The novel was praised by critics and received both Hugo and Nebula nominations in 1973.

The War against the Chtorr: Invasion. Set in the twenty-first century after a devastating war against the Soviet Union has forced the United States to disarm under international sanctions, this two-part novel follows the flight of humanity against a subsequent alien invasion. In Part 1, originally published in 1983 under the title *A Matter for Men*, Jim McCarthy, a young biologist, is attempting to discover some biological weakness in the aliens. He is drawn into a bitter personal war against the aliens by the tragic death of his military mentor, Shorty. The three-ton, wormlike aliens are vicious and totally without mercy, destroying more than eighty percent of the humans with plagues, or by devouring them alive. In a triumphant moment, McCarthy manages to capture one of the giant worms and presents his living trophy to a gathering of scientists and politicians. The worm breaks out and wreaks havoc on the gathering, driving many former pacifists to change their minds about opposing the aliens. McCarthy finally realizes he has been drawn into a conspiracy to kill off the pacifist opposition leaders, with the ends justifying the means. By the end of part 1, McCarthy has returned to the battlefield, where death may be swift and unpredictable, but where loyalty has some meaning, determined to find a better method of destroying the Chtorr.

In part 2, *A Day for Damnation*, McCarthy is a lieutenant leading men into the continuing war with the Chtorr. Ordered to capture a family grouping of four Chtorrans, including three young, McCarthy returns to headquarters with the captives. The Earth has now been completely devastated, with scattered survivors of the plagues and with no solution to the alien invasion. The United States Ecological Agency, McCarthy's supervisory unit, suspects the giant worms are part of an alien plan to destroy the human survivors and that the worms are domestically and genetically engineered to destroy humanity. If this is so, how can Earth possibly defeat an unknown, superior enemy from the depths of this apocalypse? As other alien forms, such as a "bunny dog," are discovered, the military ecologists realize that the key to victory may be in communicating and controlling the worms as the bunny dogs have been doing. McCarthy agrees to an experiement in which he attempts to lower all his personal barriers and communicate with the aliens in their own enclosure. By the end of part 2, no solution has appeared to save humanity, leaving the likelihood of additional sequels.

David Gerrold writes a very exciting and complex tale of military life and personal courage. Using the naivete of James Mc-Carthy, Gerrold shows how governments and politics use humans as weapons, with as much thought for morality as that of a soldier using a gun. The realistic portrait of a postholocaust Earth paints a grim picture of a world destroyed as much by its own politics as by the aliens. The strength in Gerrold's two novels lies in his rich characterizations and dramatic gripping scenes, such as the very strong first chapter with its portrait of the giant worm and the tiny child about to be devoured alive. However, readers may find themselves put off by the note of militancy and the survivalist strain that pervades the novel, and the negative portrayal of third world pacifists. By creating an enemy that is devolved into something less than sentient, Gerrold creates a disturbing parallel to the dehumanization process that accompanies most human wars.

Biographical/Bibliographical Readings

Edra Bogle, "David Gerrold," in *Twentieth-Century American Science-Fiction Writers* (Gale, 1981), v.1, p.189-92. Jeffrey M. Elliot, "David Gerrold: His Star Trek Continues," *Science Fiction Voices*, no.3 (1980), p.19-32. Darrell Schweitzer, "Interview with David Gerrold," *Amazing Stories* (Sept. 1985), p.69-78. [Colleen Power]

GIBSON, WILLIAM FORD

Life and Works

William Ford Gibson was born in Conway, South Carolina, on March 17, 1948. He received a B.A. in English from the University of British Columbia, Vancouver, in 1977 and currently lives in British Columbia. He has been publishing stories since 1977, when "Fragments of a Hologram Rose" appeared in *Unearth*. His first novel, *Neuromancer* (1984) won the 1984 Nebula, the 1985 Hugo and Philip K. Dick awards, plus the Ditmar award of Australia. Its publication marked Gibson as a major new writer, one who possesses a unique world vision, a powerful narrative drive, and the talent to make readers share his fictive world. The sequel, *Count Zero*, followed in 1985. His only collection of short stories so far is *Burning Chrome* (1986) which contained, in addition to the title story, "The Gernsback Continuum," "Johnny Mnemonic," and "Dogfight."

Although he has published a relatively small quantity of work, Gibson has established himself as the best of the cyberpunk school of writing, also called the "neuromaniac" school in his honor. The term "cyberpunk" was probably first used by Gardner Dozois to describe a group of science fiction writers whose careers started in the mid-1980s. Although there is no clear beginning to the cyberpunk "movement," it would be a mistake to assume that those referred to by Dozois are the first writers of cyberpunk fiction, for the roots of the cyberpunk school of science fiction lies with such major American New Wave writers as Harlan Ellison, Roger Zelazny and Samuel Delany, all of whom wrote cyberpunk fiction long before the term was coined.

Whether or not the cyberpunk movement will survive as a viable literary movement in science fiction remains to be seen. At this writing the cyberpunk movement has a number of young, talented people working in it, but the stories themselves are starting to become formulaic and repetitive. The most likely future for the cyberpunk school is that the poorer writers will drop away and move into other areas of fiction and the better writers will continue to flourish and find readers.

Themes and Style

Gibson is a highly visual writer, whose style is somewhat reminiscent of Samuel R. Delany's. Gibson's best work is always more than merely the portrait of a future juvenile delinquent. He recognizes the values of literacy and characterization, and much of his fiction involves protagonists trying to come to grips with themselves. The concept of establishing one's identity is one of the themes that lines the stories in *Burning Chrome*. "Johnny Mnemonic" involves a young man who rents space in the silicon storage chips in his head to criminals. He has access to data, but he knows virtually nothing about himself or about life in his world. Similarly, the protagonists in "Burning Chrome" rush to the defense of the deadly Chrome not for revenge but simply to prove to the world and themselves that they are still capable of functioning. The unpleasant protagonist of "Dogfight" wins a computerized dogfight, only to learn that there is more to life than physical victories.

Although the quest for identity is a relatively basic theme, Gibson's imagination makes the problems of his young protagonists believable, largely because his fictional future is described in such phenomenal, realistic detail. It is a dirty, hectic, and uncaring future. What is more, technology and bioengineering have advanced to the point that organ transplants and cybernetic replacements of body parts are routine. The Japanese corporate structure and culture have come to dominate America, and Japanese technology reigns supreme. Gibson's characters belong in this environment and yet have problems with it; their search for self is not merely twentieth-century angst moved into the future.

Thus far, Gibson has limited himself to writing stories in only one style, and sometimes, as in the case of "The Gernsback Continuum," the style is inappropriate for the subject matter. The story is meant to be poignant and bittersweet, but it is narrated in the same frantic, high energy mode as the other stories in *Burning Chrome*. It may be that Gibson is unable to vary his narrative voice beyond this one style. Nevertheless, as long as Gibson concentrates on life in the twenty-second century, his style suits his subjects. It is likely that he will be remembered as one of the best of a new generation of science fiction writers.

Plot Summaries of Major Works

Neuromancer. Case, once one of the best computer cowboys around, has betrayed his employers. As punishment for his treachery, they damage his nervous system, leaving him unable to plug back into cyberspace. Depressed and self-destructive, Case is spiraling downwards and will probably be killed soon.

What saves Case from a painful death is a mysterious offer: if he cooperates with former soldier Armitage, and Armitage's unseen backers, he will be restored to health and console readiness. Naturally, Case agrees to go along with whatever is offered. He is physically repaired and soon finds himself entwined in a web involving Armitage; vat-grown (cloned) ninja assassins--the Yakuza; a psychopath named Riviera, who can project his imaginings; international cartels; the Rastafarian inhabitants of space colony New Zion; and a host of other characters, all believable, all described with a little touch that sets them apart as individuals.

Eventually Case learns the identity of Armitage's backers and, not surprisingly, they are not human. Case is caught up in a plot involving artificial intelligence, and is instrumental in obtaining the key and the password to gain access to one of them.

Perhaps the most exceptional thing about *Neuromancer* is that it provides a very detailed description of a future Earth. Gibson's future Earth is a place where Japanese cartels rule the United States. It is a place where information is power, and only the extremely poor do not own computers; they dream of accessing and stealing valuable data. Gibson's characters are no better than their aggressive surroundings. They lie, cheat, live on drugs, and kill one another with no regrets. Bioengineering and cosmetic surgery are inexpensive and common. Case, for example, has been altered to jack into computer consoles; Molly, who works for Armitage and cares for Case, has had her eyes replaced with lenses, her reflexes speeded up, and has had razor-sharp retractable knife blades implanted under each fingernail.

In addition to the detailed descriptions of future society, Gibson's story raises a number of questions about the nature of intelligence and humanity. Armitage turns out to have a synthetic personality. Although he seems relatively sane, his personality was programmed into his body by an artificial intelligence. Case is cold and generally uncaring, happy only when is accessing data through cyberspace. Molly is perhaps more machine than woman. The artificial intelligence, on the other hand, is highly intelligent and completely "human" in all respects except one--it is completely artificial and lacks a body. Its desire to be "free" provides the impetus and the motivations of *Neuromancer*. One wonders who--or what--is human? What does being human entail?

Biographical/Bibliographical Readings

Tom Maddox, "Cobra, She Said: An Interim Report on the Fiction of William Gibson," *Fantasy Review* (April 1986), p.46-48. David G. Mead, "William Gibson," in *Twentieth-Century Science-Fiction Writers*, ed. Curtis C. Smith (St. James, 1986), p.280-81. Bruce Sterling, "Introduction" in *Mirrorshades: The Cyberpunk Anthology* (Arbor House, 1986). Michael Swanwick, "Viewpoint: A User's Guide to the Postmoderns," *Isaac Asimov's Science Fiction* 10 (August 1986), p.22-53. **[Richard Bleiler]**

HALDEMAN, JOE

Life and Works

Joe Haldeman was born in Oklahoma City in 1943 and moved to Bethesda, Maryland, in 1952 with a stint in Alaska on the way. In 1961 he entered the University of Oklahoma, later transferring to the University of Maryland, where he graduated in 1967 with a B.S. in physics and astronomy. By this time fandom made up the bulk of his social life and even his license plate read "SF Fan." Immediately after graduation, he was drafted and sent to Vietnam, where in September of 1968, he was severely wounded in the Central Highlands and was hospitalized for four months. He began graduate work in computer sciences in 1969 at the University of Maryland and his first story, "Out of Phase," was published in *Galaxy*. In 1970, he attended the Milford Conference, an annual event at Damon Knight and Kate Wilhelm's home in Milford,

Pennsylvania, where published writers spent an intensive week reading and criticizing each other's stories. He dropped out of the university to write full time.

From 1970 to 1972 he was treasurer for the Science Fiction Writers of America (SFWA). In 1971, he moved to Florida where his wife, Gay Potter, taught high school to support his writing and there published "To Fit the Crime," the first novella of *All My Sins Remembered*. In 1972, he published the first part of *The Forever War* in *Analog*. This was also the year that *War Year*, his first novel, a mainstream work describing a young soldier's combat experience in Vietnam, was published. In 1973, he joined the University of Iowa Writers' Workshop. "We Are Very Happy Here," the second part of *The Forever War*, was published at this time. In 1974 the second novella, which later became part of *The Forever War*, was published, as well as *Cosmic Laughter*, an anthology of humorous science fiction to which he contributed one story, "I, Newton." *The Forever War*, his first science fiction novel, was published in 1975. It was an immediate success and won both the Nebula and the Hugo Awards. He received his M.F.A. from the University of Iowa in 1975 and also published his Attar novels, *Attar's Revenge* and *War of Nerves* under the pseudonym Robert Graham. In 1977, his short story "Tricentennial" won the Hugo. By this time, Haldeman was well known and when his novel, *Mindbridge*, was published in 1976, Avon bid $100,000 for the paperback rights, the highest paid to that date for a work of science fiction. *All My Sins Remembered*, a novel, and *Study War No More*, an anthology of stories that offer alternatives to war, were both published in 1977. His first collection of short stories, *Infinite Dreams*, was published in 1978. By 1979 he was writing scripts for the Space Pavillion at Disney World in Florida and later did two "Star Trek" novelizations including *World without End* (1979) and *Planet of Judgment* (1977). Haldeman began his Worlds trilogy with *Worlds* (1981), followed by *World's Apart* in 1983. His previously published short stories were collected in 1986 in *Dealing in Futures*. His work has appeared in a number of anthologies, and he has contributed many short stories to the science fiction magazines. In 1986, he edited a collection of futuristic war stories, *Body Armor: 2000*, which included his own story "Heroes."

Themes and Style

Much of Haldeman's writing is a reflection of his experiences in Vietnam. Like his protagonist, Mandella, in *The Forever War*, Haldeman has a scientific background and was drafted into a war which he believed was pointless and could not be won. His writing shows a consistent point of view about the ineptitude, stupidity, and dishonesty of governments and the manipulation of the individual. His writing is antigovernmental and implies that governments are rigid and opposed to change. In most of his works, change is brought about by individuals like Jacque in *Mindbridge* or Jeff Hawkins in *Worlds Apart*. His characters have a tenacity of belief which allows them to survive the stupidity of government. Though they may be brainwashed, as Mandella in the first episode of *The Forever War* or McGavin throughout his life in *All Our Sins Remembered*, they retain their own philosophies, which incorporate the will to survive physically and the mental agility to retain their own point of view. Haldeman always portrays optimism as his characters, although manipulated, brainwashed, and lied to, still retain both their ability to survive and their abhorrence of violence. He believes that the best in humanity can survive the worst degradations. He is hopeful that both governments and people can mature to a stage where war is not necessary. He also indicates in several works that humans in the future may only survive with a group mind. Both the Taurans in *The Forever War* and the L'vrai in *Mindbridge* are races which operate with one mind, which means the subordination of the individual to the whole.

Haldeman's works have a strong scientific background which might clutter up the plot, if not for his excellent method of allowing his characters to explain the pertinent scientific ideas as part of the story line. The precise and clear definitions of scientific background flesh out the stories and give them verisimilitude. The precursors of his writing are Heinlein, Hemingway, Crane, and Dos Passos. He often uses the collage style of Dos Passos to incorporate multiple viewpoints. Particularly in *Mindbridge* and *All My Sins Remembered*, but also in *Worlds* and *Worlds Apart*, much of our understanding comes from documents, diaries, and scientific notebooks, which are cleverly interspersed with third person narrative. Haldeman is an extremely fine craftsman who takes great care with the development of his plot and characters. His view of life as episodic and with no connecting meaning is exemplified in the structure of his novels, which include extremely short chapters, often of only a page or two. This is particularly noticeable in *Mindbridge*. One of his strengths as a writer comes from his extremely good command of colloquial speech. The raw speech of soldiers in *The Forever War* makes the story come alive.   In addition to the reality of his characters, their actions have the ring of truth. That Potter and Mandella in *The Forever War* reenlist in the army because they have become so isolated from the Earth's new culture is clearly their only acceptable solution. Although he has a serious message to impart about humanity's headlong pursuit toward destruction, his style is fast-paced and witty with humor, sex, and adventure enlivening the passages.

Plot Summaries of Major Works

All My Sins Remembered. Otto McGavin, a Buddhist believer, has joined the Confederacion in order to protect the rights of humans and nonhumans. Under deep hypnosis he becomes a prime agent and killer for the TBII, whose mission is to protect the rights of aliens and citizens. In three main episodes, McGavin is tranformed by personality overlay and plastiflesh into other characters, complete with their memories and behaviors. The first episode finds McGavin affecting the persona of Issac Crowell in order to uncover why the lifespan of the Bruuchians, a race who revere death, has declined twenty-five percent. In a series of mysterious encounters, false clues about the changing Bruuchian lifestyle, interesting explanations of Bruuchian attitudes toward death, and problems McGavin has working within the extra fifty kilos of Crowell's weight, he uncovers the prime suspects as the Confederacion ambassador and the mine superintendent. In a final scene of brutality and gore, the ambassador is wiped out in a blaze of laser fire and the superintendent is knifed to death.

In the second episode, McGavin takes the place of duelist Ramos Guayana, an assassin who is systematically eliminating the heirs of all the hereditary clans on the planet Selva. The Confederacion is involved because it appears that one of the clans is planning to start an interplanetary war. Because TBII could not kidnap Guayana to do a personality overlay, the real Guayana is still alive and escapes his Confederacion jailers to confront McGavin. McGavin is brutally tortured. We learn that the Confederacion sterilized the entire animal and human population of another planet because the planet had the audacity to plan a war.

The planet Cinder, home of the S'Kangs, is the setting for the last of the episodes. The Confederacion is interested in the S'kangs because they claim to have moved their planet to improve the weather, in the process changing a huge amount of matter to energy. McGavin is sent in the persona of the evil priest, Joshua Immanuel, to protect the S'kang from exploitation by economic interests trying to discover the secret of matter transformation. In an effort to carry out his mission of protecting the S'kangs, McGavin kills the original Joshua, but finds that the Confederacion itself is anxious to experiment on the S'kangs in order to obtain their secret. The episode ends with his realization that the Confederacion's main function is to perpetuate itself.

Each of these episodes is separated by reports of interviews with McGavin in which the TBII involves him in hypnotherapy to prepare him for his next encounter and to cure him of the guilt associated with a Buddhist killing and murdering. In the last hypnotic session, McGavin is unable to shrug off the guilt of having killed forty-five people in twenty years and his participation in the doom of the S'Kang. He is judged unfit for retirement by the TBII and is eliminated.

All My Sins Remembered is a series of espionage stories loosely connected by the assassin McGavin. The most interesting story is that of the S'kang because of the humorous dialog of the S'kangs and the carefully crafted unfolding of the plot which draws one into the story and makes it plausible. The novel, like many of Haldeman's, is constructed of documents from the institutional records of the TBII, and to emphasize the episodic character of life, is constructed of short documentary chapters. Haldeman was interested in portraying a character who was so caught up in his career that it indeed became his entire life. Like many of Haldeman's novels, it is full of violent acts while espousing antiviolent attitudes. Each time McGavin is rehypnotized with a distinct set of memories, he reverts back to his orginal Buddhist training and in the end he retains those memories in spite of attempts to make him into a "real" killer. Haldeman shows us a government which deceives not only those whom it pretends to help but also its own operators. Nevertheless, the individual, although a pawn in the government's hands, manages to retain a sense of idealism and deep-seated opposition to violence.

The Forever War. It is 1997, and William Mandella has been conscripted into the elite United Nation Exploratory Force (UNEF) to guard humanity against the Tauran menace. Among the other conscripts is Margay Potter. The collapsar jump has been invented which makes it possible for a spacecraft to pop out into some part of the galaxy in almost zero time and UNEF will be building bases and holding gateways near the collapsars. The first mission takes place in a subtropical jungle where the temperature is close to boiling. The aim of the mission is to capture one live Tauran for study. The mission is a failure.

In section two, Mandella is a sergeant, Potter a corporal, and it is Earth year 2007. Because of time dilation in interstellar missions, he has only aged a year or two but is already looking forward to retirement. Because of the time dilation factor, UNEF never knows if the Taurans they will encounter have technology of the past or the future. The only way Mandella's group can stay ahead is to go back to their base, pick up the new (future) technology and hope to be ahead of the Taurans. Unfortunately in the next attack the Taurans are far advanced technologically. When Strike Force Aleph retreats, Potter and Mandella arrive on the Earth base and decide to retire from the army. However, during the twenty-six years they have been gone, Earth's society has been totally restructured due to an exhaustion of natural resources and a greatly increased population. Because the army needs officers with combat experience, Potter and Mandella are heavily pressured to reenlist. They reenlist with the guarantee of desk jobs on the moon. By the time they reach their billets, they have been reassigned to combat training.

The third episode finds Potter and Lieutenant Mandella both in the Aleph 7 campaign, where they each lose a limb. Hoping finally to be mustered out of the army, they arrive at the resort and hospital planet of Heaven in the year 2189 and find that body parts can be regenerated. They still have another three years to spend in the army! In their new orders, Potter is assigned to a new company on Heaven and Mandella to Earth base for commanding officer training. With each of them the other's only link to their own time and world, they realize that the time dilation factor might put them centuries apart if they survive their term of duty.

Mandella in 2458 has become a major, ordered to build a base at a planet near Sade 138 collapsar. His command is complicated because all soldiers are now homosexuals and there are other serious differences of language and culture. Mandella, as the only soldier to survive from the beginning of the war, returns after 340 years to Earth base. But after 1143 years of war, Earth's society has drastically changed. All humans are now cloned from one ideal man and woman, and humanity has a collective mind. The war, it is explained, has been a huge mistake propelled by power-hungry soldiers in UNEF. It has been over for 221 years. Earth base has only been retained for returning survivors, and they are the last.

The Forever War was Haldeman's first science fiction novel and won both the Hugo and Nebula awards as best novel of 1974. It is clearly a parallel to the Vietnam War, featuring the irony of fighting a war which cannot be won. Perhaps it was Haldeman's attempt to expunge the war from his memory, but it is also extremely effective in showing the effect of that war on the nation. It is by far his best novel to date and a severe indictment of the military. Haldeman is extremely successful in his portrayal of the technological and social developments of the time. Having accepted the basic premise that collapsars and time dilation are possible, the rest of the scientific matters fit neatly and logically into place. The human situation is so well portrayed, that the story moves along in a fascinating manner. It is episodic with only Mandella appearing in all the sections, and it is only he who survives to the end of the war. This episodic quality relates well to Mandella's feeling of going out in various missions and, because of time dilation, coming back to a new world each time. Mandella is one of Haldeman's most memorable characters, who continues to show us the meaningless nature of the war, while he individually struggles to preserve his own life and value system. In spite of the blood, gore, and uselessness of it all, the novel is optimistic about humanity. In the end, Mandella's basic philosophy of antiviolence is preserved. His principles have only been temporarily subverted by conditioning or lies. Both Potter and Mandella are stranded military orphans of a distant and changed Earth who have learned to survive, just as the Vietnam veterans learned to survive, in a world which no longer values the cause for which they fought so long and at such great cost.

Mindbridge. The story of *Mindbridge* is the story of Jacque LeFavre's contact with the L'vrai, a race with extraordinary power and a group mind, who are considering destroying the human race because it is too violent to be allowed to expand in the universe. Jacque LeFavre is the exception because he has learned to control his violent nature. The reader, however, does not learn about the L'vrai until the last chapters of the novel. We are led here by a gradual understanding of LeFavre's character as it develops from his early years to maturity. Through flashbacks, diary entries, and other documents we learn that LeFavre is already seeing a psychiatrist at the age of ten, and is considered paranoid. Placed in a private school he proves himself to be a brilliant student who antagonizes his teachers and inspires fear in his fellow students because of his violent and unpredictable temper. LeFavre graduates from the Academy for the Agency for Extraterrestrial Development (AED) in the year 2042. The AED, in order to prepare for a time when Earth may encounter some disaster, is engaged in geoforming other planets for human habitation. The discovery of the Levant Meyer Translation makes it possible to teleport matter to other planets, and Tamers are are sent to select planets with the proper conditions for geoforming. Jacque's first mission for the AED is to Groomsbridge's second planet in 2051, where he successfully discovers the mindbridge animal that allows two people to have a telepathic link. While using the "mindbridge" to experiment with telepathic communication with another Tamer, Carol Wacher, Jacque falls in love.

In 2052, the AED, in a teleportation to a distant planet called Achernar, has had a violent encounter with an unknown race, the L'vrai, which closely resembles idealized humans. Reports arrive in the AED center that the L'vrai are on a star very close to Earth. The L'vrai explain that they are an ancient, shape-changing race who act as one consciousness and consider humans inferior beings who have failed to synthesize the "animal and the angel" parts of their nature. They agree, however, because Jacque has managed to succeed, to provide guidance in human evolution so that humanity will not be harmful to other creatures in space. On his deathbed, with the assistance of the mindbridge, Jacque finds that--just as the L'vrai implied--there is immortality.

Mindbridge was an experiment in using a Dos Passos documentary collage technique. Each of the sections is a short episode, characteristic of Haldeman, many of them in document form. Passages from Jacques' diary, documents from purported books of fiction and nonfiction, popular science articles, AED lab reports, reported interviews, and lab and teleportation schedules are included. They provide an opportunity for Haldeman to explain to the reader some of the scientific theories under which the novel operates. In addition, Haldeman fills in so many small details that even unlikely ideas seem plausible. The novel consists of two plots, that which involves Jacque and Carol as Tamers, and the "real" plot of the L'vrais and their intention of destroying Earth. The connection between the two plots is that Jacque is the only person able to communicate with the L'vrais because he has learned to control the violent part of his nature and ultimately, through him, civilization is saved. While this is a very successful novel of character development, it is also an exciting adventure story of telepathy, matter transmission, and contact with an alien race. The L'vrai, like others Haldeman aliens, work toward fruitful and advanced social-political ends by having a collective mind. Haldeman implies that this is the only way that Earth's civilization may survive.

Worlds. Forty-one orbiting settlements constitute the Worlds in the year 2080. The largest is New New, which supplies a large portion of Earth's solar energy and where we first meet our protagonist, Maureen O'Hara. Maureen is a brilliant young woman, a political science student with a flare for jazz clarinet. Given the opportunity to go to Earth for postgraduate work, Maureen enrolls in New York University. While New New is depicted as a nice, noncompetitive place, New York is an ugly place with wasters, muggers, rapists, and revolutionaries.

In New York, Maureen falls in love with Jeff Hawkins, an FBI agent. Maureen marries Jeff and they head for New Orleans. When she makes the headlines as a new Jazz clarinetest, she is located by Lobbies (an underground revolutionary group), raped, and in a blackmail attempt, spirited off to Nevada, where she is rescued by no other than husband Jeff. Relations, however, between Earth and the Worlds degenerate when New New discovers a new source of minerals and precipitates a ban on imports from Earth, which is fearful it will lose its energy source. Maureen and Jeff race for Capetown, Florida, in a last-ditch effort to catch the shuttles evacuating World citizens from the Earth. But there is a strict quota and Jeff, as a noncitizen, is left behind. The governments of Earth and the Worlds escalate their demands until the Worlds turn off Earth's solar power. The underground revolutionaries take this opportunity to drop a nuclear bomb on Washington, which precipitates the detonation of nuclear weapons all over the Worlds. A short-tempered man pushes the button and 200 missiles demolish some of the smaller worlds and damage New New. One missile contains a deadly virus which enters the jet stream and kills the majority of Earth's population. As the book ends, twenty years later, we find that Jeff has survived somewhere on Earth and Maureen is living with her two husbands in sexually free-wheeling New New while the reader awaits the next episode in this proposed trilogy.

Worlds is the first novel of a trilogy about space colonists who have developed cooperative, rather than competitive, sociopolitical systems. Run by a reactionary government, Earth has the same problems as it does now magnified 100-fold. Our protagonist, Maureen experiences rape, assault, and revolution. Impelled by the degradation of life on Earth, the unpredictable acts of madness by a few people in high places, and the misguided notions of those who would purify the world, the predicted cataclysm does come. A recurring theme of Haldeman's is that governments are too rigid to solve their problems, too inflexible and usually self-serving. Perhaps Haldeman is also suggesting that space colonies could be testing grounds for new political systems which can make changes more readily than Earth's rigid governmental systems. In his usual style, Haldeman has the action played out in short episodic chapters, much of it documented through letters of O'Hara to her lovers on New New and through her diary entries. Haldeman uses free-wheeling idomatic language, which is very effective in moving the action along, although the characters are only superficial vehicles for his philosophical ideas. While our passage toward Armageddon is somewhat heavy-handed and we always know that this will be the final result, along the way there is suspense, thrills, adventure, sex, and violence which keeps the plot moving along rapidly.

Worlds Apart. *Worlds Apart* is the second in a trilogy about the Worlds, a group of asteroids orbiting Earth, the largest of which is New New York where our story opens in 2085, some years after nuclear warheads have devastated most of Earth and some of the Worlds. Maureen has just been apprised that one of the aftereffects of the war is a plague which causes the death of everyone over the age of twenty-one. One of the few adult survivors is Jeff Hawkins, Maureen's Earth husband, who had been left behind when the last shuttle departed for New New before the Big Bang. He and a few hundred other adults are immune to the plague. The United States, leaderless, parentless, and decimated, has been taken over by the descendants of the Mansonites, followers of Charles Manson, who had led his flock in an orgy of mass murder a hundred years before.

In a series of intermixed chapters we follow Maureen on New New and Jeff on Earth. Because of Maureen's training in American studies, she is sent to the Earth to deliver the vaccine against the killing virus. Maureen is in charge of selecting ten thousand people to go on the voyage to a new planet (Epsilon Eridani), who will be able to develop the cultural, social, and political basis for the new society. Jeff as a "healer" travels across the eastern half of the United States observing the attempt of the survivors of the holocaust to set up a new social structure. While he vaccinates as many of the population as possible, he also begins to form a new social organization. As the novel comes to an end, Maureen is on her way to Epsilon Eridani and Jeff, in six days, creates schools, jobs, money, courts, and banks; on the seventh day he goes fishing.

The second novel in the Worlds trilogy is much more interesting than the first and much more hopeful of humanity's ability to survive catastrophe and rebuild. Haldeman's portrayal of a brutalized, postnuclear holocaust society is very well conceived. We are drawn into the surviving youths' attempt to form a new society based on the only things they know that make sense for them; violence, suicide, and death. The most fascinating episodes are those in which Haldeman depicts the surviving societies as Jeff travels from one to another. Unlike many of his books, there is not much scientific material here except a rather unlikely notion about the possibility of using antimatter to propel the spaceship. Haldeman, although making a serious commentary on the necessity of improving society before a catyclysm takes place, includes enough sex, violence, suspense, and adventure to be constantly entertaining. We move from a degraded Earth, to the purgatory of the Worlds, and finally to the celestial spheres. Each movement becomes a spiritual and moral ascent. We wait with anticipation the next installment of Maureen and Jeff, perhaps on the star Epsilon Eridani.

Biographical/Bibliographical Readings

Joan Gordon, *Joe Haldeman* (Starmont House, 1980). James Scott Hicks, "Joe Haldeman," in *Twentieth-Century American Science-Fiction Writers* (Gale, 1981), v.1, p.198-200. "Joe Haldeman," in *Contemporary Authors New Revision Series*, (Gale, 1986) v.6, p.208-11. [Judith R. Bernstein]

HAMILTON, EDMOND

Life and Works

Edmond Hamilton was born on October 21, 1904, in Youngstown, Ohio. He died on February 1, 1977. He attended Westminster College in Pennsylvania, majoring in physics. In 1921, Hamilton left college and began working for the Pennsylvania Railroad. When his job was eliminated in 1925, he became a writer. He had been reading science fiction and fantasy since he was twelve; his first published stories were primarily fantasy, but he soon became a prolific author of space adventure stories and one of the most popular contributors to the science fiction pulp magazines. Hamilton also wrote detective stories and comics. In 1946, he married Leigh Brackett, also a science fiction writer.

Hamilton gave Brackett credit for helping him slow down the fast pace of writing he used for the pulps and for improving his writing style.

In the 1930s, Hamilton created the Captain Future series. Although other authors contributed to the series, Hamilton wrote most of the stories, about a young scientist and his brave associates in their efforts to foil interplanetary villains. The rigid formula, lack of characterization, and style of writing kept the series from being taken seriously by critics, and have unfortunately overshadowed Hamilton's other works.

Grand space opera is represented in *The Star Kings* (1949) and its sequel, *Return to the Stars* (1970). His last and most popular series, *Starwolf* (1980), was originally published as three novels, *The Weapon from Beyond* (1967), *The Closed Worlds* (1968), and *World of the Starwolves* (1968). Leigh Brackett edited the posthumous collection of Hamilton's shorter works, *The Best of Edmond Hamilton*, in 1977.

Hamilton used the pen names Alexander Blade, Robert Castle, Hugh Davidson, Will Garth, Brett Sterling, and Robert Wentworth. He received few awards--the Jules Verne award in 1933 and induction into the First Fandom Hall of Fame in 1967. In 1977, the Edmond Hamilton Memorial Award was created to honor authors whose work created a sense of wonder for readers. It was renamed the Hamilton-Brackett Memorial Award in 1978, after Leigh Brackett's death. The award is an appropriate tribute to a writer who contributed greatly to the early development of science fiction.

Themes and Style

Hamilton wrote adventure stories, swift-moving space operas full of ideas new to the field of science fiction. He was called "World-wrecker," "World-destroyer," and "World-saver," as one of his most frequently used themes involved the last-minute salvation of Earth or the solar system from total destruction. He created the concept--now taken for granted in the genre--of an advanced, enlightened galactic civilization protected by an interstellar patrol. In *Crashing Suns* (1965) and *Outside the Universe* (1964), the Interstellar Patrol manages to save the galaxy from certain destruction at the last possible moment. Hamilton was among the first to present robots programmed to perform specific functions and to explore the concept of the regression of the evolutionary process. His use of such innovative concepts expanded the boundaries of science fiction and challenged the imaginations of his readers.

Hamilton's style improved over the years as the need for the fast production required by the pulp magazines decreased. His later works show more depth, greater characterization, and a more direct, straightforward writing style than was present in his earlier stories.

Hamilton helped develop many of the concepts now fundamental to science fiction, including the interstellar police unit, space exploration, and humanity's future evolution. His enthusiasm and joy entertained numerous readers, inspiring in them a true sense of wonder.

Plot Summaries of Major Works

The Star Kings. John Gordon, whose adventures are told in *The Star Kings* and *Return to the Stars*, was a World War II veteran having trouble adjusting to his new life as a salesman. When he began to hear the voice of a scientist from the distant future, Gordon questioned his own sanity. The scientist, Zarth Arn, had discovered a way to exchange minds with people in his past, and wanted to trade places with Gordon. Gordon agreed to a temporary exchange and found his mind in Zarth's body on an Earth thousands of years in the future. Before Gordon could learn much about the world of Zarth, the scientist who was to guide him was killed during a raid that was meant to kidnap Zarth. Gordon discovers that Zarth is a prince of a galactic empire that is threatened by the evil regime of the Black Cloud and by internal treason from the empire's administrators. In addition to dealing with his role as prince, Gordon discovers that there is to be a marriage of state between Zarth and Lianna, princess of an allied kingdom. Gordon falls in love with her, even though he knows he must return to his own world. Gordon is falsely accused of murdering the emperor (Zarth's father), and he and Lianna are abducted by the forces of the Black Cloud. They hope to get the secret of the empire's dreaded weapon, the Disruptor, from Zarth, since the weapon can only be used by the empire's royal family. Gordon and Lianna manage to escape and convince Zarth's brother of their innocence. Gordon is able to return to Earth, contact Zarth's mind, and return to his own body and time, mourning his lost Lianna.

As time passes, Gordon wonders if he imagined the entire incident, a theory encouraged by a psychiatrist. One night he hears Lianna's voice telling him that Zarth has discovered a means of pulling Gordon's body and mind into their own time. Gordon decides to return to the future, there to find new adventures and problems. The new enemy has the ability to control minds. In the final confrontation, Zarth uses information gained by Gordon to locate the enemy invaders and destroy them.

The Star Kings was one of Hamilton's most popular works. The concept of an ordinary salesman becoming the ruler of a galactic empire seems to be an ultimate dream come true. Gordon's curiosity about the future and longing for adventure are balanced by his fears about his lack of knowledge, his sadness at having to leave his friends, and his problems in building a life in a new time. Hamilton's characteristic themes are reflected in the threat of total destruction for the empire, the excitement of the space battles, and the extravagant concept of a weapon that actually destroys space itself. *The Star Kings* is not superb literature; it is superior space opera that succeeds admirably in its goal of entertainment.

Starwolf. Morgan Chane was the son of Terran missionaries who had come to Varna hoping to convert the inhabitants. The planet's high gravity has caused its people to become stronger than other humans; for this reason, perhaps, they have developed a ruthless society. Varna is the home of the Spacewolves, interstellar pirates who raid and loot with impunity. After Chane's parents die, he is brought up on Varna and becomes a Starwolf. He is accepted despite his Terran origin, until an associate tries to take part of Chane's booty. In the struggle, Chane kills the other Starwolf and flees, pursued by former colleagues seeking his death in revenge. Chane knows the Starwolves will kill him if they catch him and anyone else will kill him because he is a Starwolf.

Fleeing into open space, Chane abandons his damaged starship and is rescued by John Dilullo, leader of a team of Mercs, mercenaries from Terra. Compared to most star systems, Terra has few mineral resources; its main export is its men. The Mercs are soldiers who handle the jobs no one else will take; only the Starwolves are stronger or better fighters. Dilullo discovers Chane's identity, but keeps it a secret because he believes Chane's strength and ability can be useful on their mission to discover the nature of a new secret weapon, rumored to have been developed in a distant system.

Chane joins them, in part because he lacks a better choice, and in part because the Mercs are nearly as tough as the Starwolves. Chane helps them discover the origin of the new weapon. Their next assignment is to find a missing man whose last destination was a planet closed to all visitors. Dilullo, Chane, and their team rescue the man from the thrall of a device that allows the mind to travel throughout the universe, a journey that can leave the body to wither if the mind does not return.

At times, Chane still longs for Varna and his life as a Starwolf, but he has begun to enjoy life with the Mercs. Chane suggests their most dangerous job, that of recovering a priceless art treasure stolen by the Starwolves. The Mercs discover that the treasure--the Singing Suns, a jeweled representation of the star systems--has been purchased by middlemen for an unknown system ruled by the Qatars. Their planet is full of priceless works of art they have collected secretly. Their ruthless defenses nearly destroy the Mercs, but Chane manages to retrieve the art. Chane decides that the only force capable of dealing with the Qatars is the

Starwolves. He returns to Varna, using their greed for a new trea-
sure-trove to keep himself alive, and leads them on a successful
attack against Qatar. During the looting, Chane finds the Singing
Suns, escapes from the Starwolves, and returns the jewels for a
substantial reward. Realizing that his home is neither Varna nor
Terra, but space, and that the Mercs are now his family, Chane
joins Dilullo for their next voyage.

Originally published as three novels, *The Weapon from Beyond*,
The Closed Worlds, and *World of the Starwolves*, *Starwolf* is a space
adventure endowed with exotic planets, interstellar conflicts, lost
treasure, and a bold hero. Unlike many space operas, it is also a
study of personal change, belonging, and identity. *Starwolf* is an
adventure story, with battles, unusual cultures, narrow escapes,
and mysterious aliens. It is also the story of a man's attempt to
discover a new identity and a new home. The underlying theme
of psychological growth combined with Hamilton's skill at creating an entertaining story lift *Starwolf* above most space operas.

Biographical/Bibliographical Readings

John Clute, "Edmond Hamilton," in *The Encyclopedia of Sci-
ence Fiction*, ed. Peter Nicholls (Doubleday, 1979), p.270-71. Gerald
M. Garmon, "Edmond Hamilton," in *Twentieth-Century American
Science-Fiction Writers* (Gale, 1981), v.1, p.201-04. Sam Moskowitz,
"Edmond Hamilton," in *Seekers of Tomorrow* (Hyperion, 1974),
p.66-83. Donald A. Wollheim, "Headquarters: Canopus," in *The
Universe Makers* (Harper & Row, 1971), p.30-32. [Linda K. Lewis]

HARRISON, HARRY

Life and Works

Harry Max Harrison was born in Stamford, Connecticut, on
March 12, 1925. After attending art schools in New York, Harrison served in the Army Air Corps during World War II. He
worked as a free lance commercial artist from 1946 to 1955. During this time, his involvement with science fiction began. Damon
Knight commissioned Harrison to do illustrations for "World's Beyond" and later published his first short story, "Rock Diver," in
1951. Harrison illustrated comics off and on for many years, including the "Flash Gordon" strip from 1958 to 1968. He continued
his artistic endeavors after turning to writing as his primary activity by illustrating the book jackets for some of his own books.
Harrison and his wife Joan traveled quite a bit, in Mexico and
Europe, and they currently reside in Ireland.

Harrison is a noted anthologist. His work with the highly acclaimed series, *Nova*, won a Nebula award in 1973. Harrison has

collaborated extensively with Brian W. Aldiss, editing the annual collection, *Best Science Fiction*, from 1967 to 1975, *Astounding Analog Reader* (1972), *SF Horizons* (1975), and the "Decade" series (1975-77). In addition, Harrison and Aldiss edited the autobiographical collection about science fiction writers, *Hell's Cartographers: Some Personal Histories of Science Fiction Writers* (1975). Harrison edited other anthologies and several science fiction magazines for short periods of time.

Harrison's early reputation was based on science fiction adventure tales such as *Deathworld* (1960), *Deathworld 2* (1964), *Deathworld 3* (1968) and *Planet of the Damned* (1962), but he soon became noted for humorous or blackly ironic stories as in *Bill, the Galactic Hero* (1965) and *The Technicolor Time Machine* (1967). The Stainless Steel Rat series consists of six novels to date: *The Stainless Steel Rat* (1960), *The Stainless Steel Rat's Revenge* (1970), *The Stainless Steel Rat Saves the World* (1972), *The Stainless Steel Rat Wants You!* (1978), *The Stainless Steel Rat for President* (1982), and *The Stainless Steel Rat Is Born* (1985). His recent novels in the 1980s include *Planet of No Return* (1983) and *Invasion: Earth* (1984). Some of Harrison's short stories are collected in *The Best of Harry Harrison* (1976).

Themes and Style

Whether serious or amusing, the heroes created by Harry Harrison are often unusual, sometimes almost antiheroic. Jason dinAlt is a successful gambler moving about on the Deathworlds, looking for meaning and placing his life on the line. His ultimate gamble is with death. Slippery Jim diGriz was devoted to a life of crime until he was forced to join the Special Services as an interstellar law enforcement agent known as "The Stainless Steel Rat." Detective Andrew Rusch is a parody of a big city cop in *Make Room! Make Room!* (1966). The ultimate nonhero is *Bill, the Galactic Hero*, whose protagonist is basically a simple farm boy, shanghaied to fight the lizardlike Chingers for the Space Corps. The latter novel is considered to be a satire on standard science fiction techniques and pokes fun at the military mentality.

Other institutions coming under attack by Harrison are various typical political maneuvers. At one point, President Eisenhower disclaimed political rights to get involved in the population control issue; such an attitude, Harrison insists, can lead to the overpopulated world he describes in *Make Room! Make Room!* In this novel, Harrison also attacks the Roman Catholic Church's stand on population control. In *Skyfall* (1976), Harrison's government leaders make political decisions which cost the lives of a scientific team orbiting Earth.

Harrison's ingenuity, although creative and innovative, is also consistent and logical. In *Tunnel through the Deeps* (1972), an alternative time track has the British winning the war for American independence and the result is a world that is "veddy, veddy" British. The support for the British peerage system and the pre-eminence of the British favorite, the locomotive, as the mode of transportation are examples. *West of Eden* (1984) is populated with species which might have developed if the dinosaurs had not become extinct, a premise which is scientifically plausible, if not possible. Above all else, Harrison's novels are readable. This is something to which he has a personal commitment and it is apparent that he has succeeded.

Plot Summaries of Major Works

Make Room! Make Room! It is 1999, and New York City is grossly overpopulated. Detective Andrew Rusch takes for granted many of the limitations imposed by the overcrowded society: one razor blade per person, limited water, and sharing an efficiency apartment with an elderly roommate, Sol Kahn. Lack of food and water affect all of the lives around Rusch. When he is called on in a murder case, the opulence of the dead man's lifestyle is shown through the well-stocked refrigerator and bar and the unlimited hot water. The girl who comes with the apartment, Shirl Greene, falls in love with Rusch and together they share the food, booze, and hot water until the estate of the murdered man is settled. Then Shirl moves into Andy's apartment and shares his meager lifestyle. The murderer, Billy Chung, has been identified by his fingerprints, but has lost himself among the thirty-five million people living in the city. Billy eventually gives in to impulse to visit his home--a stoolie informs Andy, who traps Billy and accidentally shoots him. Andy is busted back to a police beat for killing Billy and loses Shirl, to whom creature comforts (gained through prostitution) are worth more than love.

Sol Kahn is the only character in the story old enough to remember what it was like before the deprivations, and the only one to speak out forcefully for population control to keep the situation from worsening. Everyone else seems to accept standing in line for a can of water, for food, or for inadequate medical care. Harrison reiterates the short-sightedness of all the characters as Andy persuades Shirl to bring a set of sheets from the wealthy man's apartment--that is all he imagines that he needs from the luxurious apartment of her previous roommate. A neighbor tells Shirl that she gives her son's peanut butter ration to his father, even though the protein would cure the boy's serious protein deficiency. Harrison even has Sol orate against the Roman Catholic Church's anticontraceptive policy. This is a sad story, but readable, as Harrison's stories usually are. A movie, *Soylent Green*, was based on the novel, but introduced an unfortunate plot change to include cannibalism. Nevertheless, the message of both film and novel is that too many people spoil the quality of life.

The Stainless Steel Rat series. The Stainless Steel Rat series consists of six novels to date: *The Stainless Steel Rat*; *The Stainless Steel Rat's Revenge*; *The Stainless Steel Rat Saves the World*; *The Stainless Steel Rat Wants You!*; *The Stainless Steel Rat for President*; and *The Stainless Steel Rat Is Born.* In a future world gone soft, in which most people obey all the rules, young Jaime diGriz decides that the only occupation challenging enough for him is that of master criminal. He does extremely well at crime, for a novice, and studies at the hands of a real master. However, he gets caught. The only way out of a life behind bars is to join the Special Corps as a law enforcement agent. Distasteful as this is at first, Slippery Jim soon realizes the advantages of being able to be as tricky as a criminal yet operating within the sanctions of the law. He proves himself quite successful at thwarting criminal actions since he understands the criminal mind so well, possessing one himself. Throughout the series, Jim romps through one adventure after another. He has at hand (and up his sleeve and in his shoe) a formidable arsenal of weapons, designed to foil any possible emergency. He has little bombs that emit smoke, noise, and/or a gas which blinds everyone. He has one tablet which anesthetizes and another which temporarily increases strength to Herculean proportiions. He has incredible disguises and is not above surgically altering his appearance to fool the foe.

Eventually, the maturing Jim needs the companionship of a true partner and is able to find her in another master criminal, Angelina. He tracks her down, only to be trapped by her. When the Special Corps rescues Jim, they recruit Angelina. After this, Angelina and Jim are a team, rescuing each other when necessary and brainstorming to find out the most effective way to overcome evil in whatever form it appears. They have twin sons, James and Bolivar, who enter into the spirit of things, and an incredible crime-fighting family team is begun.

The Stainless Steel Rat series is clever, tricky, preposterous at times and, above all, great fun. Harrison's sense of the absurd and keen timing keep the reader guessing all the time about what Jim is going to come up with next. The invention of new gadgets alone is enough to keep the reader coming back for the next adventure.

West of Eden. How would Earth have developed if the dinosaurs had not died out? Harry Harrison answers that question in this novel, an inventive story of the conflict between the cold-blooded reptilian race of Yilane and the primitive race called Tanu, both alien races inhabiting early Earth. They learn the genetic control of plants and animals, modifying trees and vines to grow their cities and altering dinosaurs for transportation and food herds. The Yilane rise to power in Europe and Africa, but are forced to flee the encroaching Ice Age for still warm Cuba. In North America, the Yilane come in contact with the alien species, Tanu, furry bipeds first thought to be lower forms of life. A captured Tanu child raised in Yilane society learns enough of their methods to successfully fight the Yilane when he is recaptured by his own people as a young adult. The superior technology of the Yilane reptiles threatens the extinction of the Tanu on the North American continent, and the surviving Tanu flee across the snow-capped mountains in the West to hide. The relentless Yilane pursue, spurred on by the hatred of their leaders for Kerrick, the child who had turned against them. Finally, Kerrick and his band realize that they cannot hide and turn to fight, eventually driving the Yilane to their home base and burning it to the ground; in spite of their technology, the Yilane had not learned the use of fire and have no defense against it.

This fascinating account of two alien cultures fighting for supremacy of Earth is one of Harrison's best novels. It is scientifically inventive, with the meticulous development of a new zoology based on the evolution of Earth's ancient species. An anthropological and cultural treatise on what might have been, *West of Eden* is a very unusual (for Harrison), serious, and scholarly treatment; reminiscent of Jean Auel's *Clan of the Cave Bear*.

Biographical/Bibliographical Readings

Harry Harrison, "The Beginning of the Affair," in *Hell's Cartographers*, ed. Brian W. Aldiss and Harry Harrison (Weidenfeld and Nicolson, 1975), p.76-95. Robert L. Jones, "Harry Harrison," in *Twentieth-Century American Science-Fiction Writers* (Gale, 1981), v.1, p.205-08. Charles Platt, "Harry Harrison," in *Dream Makers* (Berkley, 1983), v.2, p.219-27. [Kay Jones]

HEARD, GERALD

Life and Works

Henry Fitzgerald Heard was born in London, England, on October 6, 1889. Heard received his education at Gonville and Caius College, Cambridge. He graduated with honors, earning a B.A. in history. From 1919 to 1927, Heard was directly involved with the Agricultural Cooperative Movement in Ireland and England. He served as editor for the *Realist* in 1929 and was active as a science commentator for the British Broadcasting Corporation from 1930 to 1934. In 1937, Heard settled in the United States and pursued his writing career in California. A lecturer at various American colleges, such as Oberlin, he was a recipient of the Bollingen Grant in 1955. Heard's friendship with writers Christopher Isherwood and Aldous Huxley led to his interest in and later direct association with Vedanta, an ancient Hindu philosophy based on the Vedas. Some of Heard's nonscience fiction works include: *The Great Fog and Other Weird Tales* (1944); *The Lost Cavern and Other Tales of the Fantastic* (1948); *A Taste for Honey* (1941); *The Black Fox* (1950); and *The Five Ages of Man: The Psychology of Human History* (1964). During the 1980s, interest in Heard's writing career and his fiction reappeared. With republication of some of his works, the work of Gerald Heard will recieve more critical attention and analysis. Heard died on August 14, 1971.

Themes and Style

A prolific British author, Heard achieved recognition with a speculative writing that often reflected science fiction motifs with religious and philosophical overtones. Although Heard's major work was produced in religious and philosophical writings, he contributed one science fiction novel which had an important impact at the time of its publication: *Doppelgangers* (1947), also published as *Doppelgangers: An Episode of the Fourth, the Psychological Revolution, 1997*. This novel predates the major writings of psychologist B. F. Skinner and endures as an unusual work dealing with the science fiction themes of dystopia, behavior modification and control, and with the concept of the soul.

Plot Summaries of Major Works

Doppelgangers. This novel follows the tribulations of a man who takes the place of another man's identity and assumes that man's role and existence. The dystopian society is controlled by a dictatorship that practices hedonism and behavior control, including behavior modification and conditioning. The hero, Alpha II, is a member of a secret organization known as the Mole, replaces the dictator, Alpha, and becomes his doppelganger (double). Once Alpha II replaces Alpha, he discovers that the true control of the world system is being guided by a spiritually advanced group known as Elevates. Alpha II's role will be the restructuring of government and society for the betterment of the human race.

Doppelgangers is Heard's only science fiction novel. It deals with dystopian society, social systems, role and identity, behavior modification and control, and certain aspects of mysticism and religious teachings. It can be compared with such well-known science fiction classics as Huxley's *Brave New World* and Orwell's *1984*. The novel is a speculative work of ideas and a highly philosophical science fiction novel which remains a most unusual and major work in science fiction literature.

Biographical/Bibliographical Readings

Mary T. Brizzi, "Gerald Heard," in *Twentieth-Century Science-Fiction Writers* (St. James, 1986), p.324-26. Brian M. Stableford, "The Short Fiction of Heard," in *Survey of Modern Fantasy Literature* (Salem Press, 1983), v.3, p.1544-46. **[Harold Lee Prosser]**

HEINLEIN, ROBERT A.

Life and Works

Robert Anson Heinlein was born in Butler, Missouri, on July 7, 1907. Butler was a small country town where his grandfather was a "horse-and-buggy" doctor. After high school and one year of college, Heinlein accepted an appointment to the U.S. Naval Academy at Annapolis, from which he graduated in 1929, twentieth in a class of 243. Five years later he retired from the Navy on permanent disability after contracting tuberculosis. He attended UCLA for a short time, studying physics and mathematics, but continuing ill health soon forced him to move to Colorado to recuperate. In 1938, needing money, he turned to a lifelong interest in science fiction, selling his first story, "Life-Line," to *Astounding Science Fiction*. Over the next three years, and primarily under the guidance of editor John W. Campbell, Heinlein published twenty-eight stories, some under pseudonyms.

Heinlein stopped writing during World War II but, following the war, returned to writing science fiction; 1947 saw the first of his work in hardcover book form, *Rocketship Galileo*. For the next ten years, Heinlein devoted his energies to juvenile novels, writing only an occasional work for adults (*Double Star*, 1956, a Hugo winner, and The *Puppet Masters*, 1956). In 1957, Heinlein apparently decided to change tracks, and his next important novel, *Starship Troopers*, a strongly militaristic and violent work, was refused by Scribner's. After its publication by Putnam's, it won him his second Hugo award. His next work, published after a two year hiatus, was *Stranger in a Strange Land* (1961), possibly Heinlein's most influential work and the one which established him as a writer known to the general public. *Stranger in a Strange Land* won the Hugo award in 1962, followed by another Hugo winner in 1967, *The Moon Is a Harsh Mistress*. Since then, his novels have received a wide readership outside science fiction fandom, and his latest, *The Cat Who Walks through Walls* (1985), was a best seller. His shorter works have been collected in *The Best of Robert Heinlein, 1939-1959* (1973), *The Green Hills of Earth* (1954), and *The Worlds of Robert Heinlein* (1970). In 1975, Heinlein was voted the first "Grand Master" Nebula award by the Science Fiction Writers of America, a well-deserved honor for a writer who has come to embody science fiction for millions of readers. Heinlein died on May 9, 1988, after being in ill health for some time. Robert Heinlein leaves behind a legacy of more than fifty books and short stories and was ranked by the publisher of Bantam Books as being one of three greatest science fiction authors in the field, along with Isaac Asimov and Arthur C. Clarke.

Themes and Style

When Heinlein began to write science fiction, the field was divided predominantly into action/adventure/escape literature or the use of the future as a setting for social criticism of the present. Heinlein, along with John W. Campbell, wanted to make the future plausible, a believable extension of the present. Characters in Heinlein's work have always been typical, competent people, possessed of native intelligence and good sense, although in later years, a dismaying number are self-proclaimed geniuses. The prime example of this character is found in Lazarus Long, in *Time Enough for Love* (1973) and *The Number of the Beast* (1980). While this characterization has often been criticized, the fact remains that Heinlein wrote about characters who could as easily be walking down any street today as blasting their way from planet to planet in the future. Among a cast of typical Heinlein human characters, Mike, one of the earliest and most lovable of Heinlein's sentient computers, stands out in *The Moon Is a Harsh Mistress* (1966), which won a Hugo award in 1967.

Throughout his fiction, Heinlein avoided the use of "villains," and though some characters are evil, this is usually from thoughtlessness, pettiness, or a misguided sense of duty. The villain who commits evil for the sake of evil is rarely to be found in Heinlein's works. Many of his characters undergo changes or education in the course of their stories; the hero of *Double Star*, originally a self-centered, apolitical actor, becomes a political force for good. Juan Rico, in *Starship Troopers*, starts out a largely undisciplined teenager, and ends up a military officer. Valentine Michael Smith, the human raised by Martians in *Stranger in a Strange Land*, learns what it is to be human in nature as well as by birth. In later works, the eponymous heroine of *Friday* (1982), an "artificial person," seeks acceptance of her unusual capabilities from those around her, and eventually comes to accept herself, while the hero of *Job* (1984) is reeducated out of his religious bigotry and prudery into a more tolerant acceptance of human frailties.

Heinlein's gift for telling fast-paced, fascinating stories earned him a large and faithful following among readers of science fiction. Part of the appeal doubtless comes from the generally optimistic tone of his works. In the future worlds of Heinlein, life is worth living, and love is worth giving and receiving.

The juvenile books relate tales of ambitions and dreams realized, and the later novels chart the triumphant expansion of human civilization throughout the galaxy.

Plot Summaries of Major Works

Double Star. Lorenzo Smythe, down-and-out actor, is hired to impersonate kidnapped political leader Joseph Bonforte in a crucial ceremony on Mars. Smythe must overcome his aversion to Martians and his arrogance, before the masquerade can be successfully carried out; he discovers that politics is the most demanding form of theater, and when the real Bonforte dies as a result of the abuse he received in captivity, Smythe steps permanently into his shoes to carry out the plans of the fallen leader. As the pseudo-Bonforte, Smythe begins to understand that social responsibility is necessary to ensure personal freedoms, and he transfers his loyalty to his spiritual second father, Bonforte, in whom he finds a striking resemblance to his real father.

Double Star shows the gradual awakening of Smythe, through his impersonation, to political awareness and responsibility. The novel provides Heinlein with a political podium, and he expounds on his views at some length, including the political and ethical equality of all sentient life. The message, however, does not get in the way of the story, which remains an intriguing tale of impersonation and political maneuvers. The emphasis in the novel is on the development of Lorenzo's personality. He is, as is usual in Heinlein, the product of rigorous training by an older man (his father in this case), but one who has not learned from experience that a person's responsibilites extend past his own personal concerns.

Job: A Comedy of Justice. Fundamentalist preacher and fundraiser Alexander Hergensheimer walks through fire in Polynesia, passes out, and wakes up in a different world, where he discovers a minor underworld figure in the midst of an affair with a ship's stewardess. More troubles follow as he and Margrethe, the Danish stewardess who becomes his lover, are flipped through a succession of worlds, each slightly different than the last. These travels through time and space, which have a great liberalizing effect on Alec, end with the Final Judgment, after which Alec goes to Heaven, finding himself to be a saint, and Heaven to be an overcrowded bureaucracy run by bad-tempered angels on the strict principle of "rank hath its privileges." Since Margrethe is not to be with him in Heaven, Alec opts to go to Hell, which turns out to be a fairly civilized place where free enterprise flourishes. Alec and Margrethe, it turns out, have been batted around as a modern reenactment of the Job story, although this time out, the Devil is not involved, except as an interested bystander. It is, in fact, Satan who helps Alec to be reunited with

Margrethe, and the two of them settle down in another world much like Earth to live a life of happy normality, their trials forgotten.

In *Job*, Heinlein makes some scathing statements about the Judeo-Christian tradition. The most caring and compassionate characters are Margrethe, a Danish heathen, and Satan himself, while God appears as a petty, vicious, and ultimately minor tyrant who operates on a system of unjust rules. Alec grows from a smug, officious prig into a caring, understanding man in the course of the story, without ever losing the stubborn faith that got him picked on in the first place. Margrethe, the good influence responsible for the changes in Alec, is a typical earthy, sensible, buxom, blonde Heinleinian heroine, although her devotion to Alec, particularly in his earlier stages, is unfathomable. The moral to this story is that human decency and compassion are perhaps more important than formalized religion; it is a fascinating and funny book.

The Moon Is a Harsh Mistress. Manny Garcia is thrust unwillingly into a position of leadership in a lunar revolution, along with a wise old professor, a beautiful woman, and a sentient computer named Mike. Luna, in the twenty-first century, is a penal colony with a large free-born and former-inmate population; it is strongly reminiscent of early nineteenth-century Australia. The rebellion is directed against the Lunar Authority, a corporation which runs most of the moon as a penal colony, exploiting its resources, natural and human, to support its immense profits on Earth. The mechanics of revolution are set out, and the rationale endlessly discussed. This is a just and honorable action, and the heroes try, albeit unsuccessfully, to avoid unnecessary bloodshed, all the while admitting that some blood will have to flow.

This novel of lunar revolution, with its numerous parallels to the American Revolution and lengthy passages on the mechanics of a new and improved "cell" system of reorganization, might well serve as a textbook for rebellion. Amid the plotting and execution of the uprising, Heinlein discusses such issues as alternative marriage arrangements and systems of morality, sentience in computers and humans, and the nature of personal freedom. Heinlein's use of language in the novel is subtle and deserving of attention. Most lunar inhabitants speak in a peculiar dialect, a concise form of English with a liberal sprinkling of Russian and Australian slang terms, which conveys a sense of strangeness and enhances the idea of the moon as a penal colony in a long tradition of penal colonies, yet is not strange enough to cause the reader any problems in comprehension. Heinlein also displays an interest in the use of propaganda as a political tool, and one of the major concerns in the novel is that the proper publicizing of the revolt will have an immense effect on its success or failure.

Mike, one of the earliest and most lovable of Heinlein's sentient computers, is a shy and lonely genius with a penchant for practical jokes and an immense hunger for the company of friends. The loss of his "personality" toward the close of the novel is far more affecting than the death of Prof, one of the human characters.

Starship Troopers. A vast interplanetary war is being fought between Earth and the "Bugs." The "Bugs" are ultimate communists, and it is up to a superelite corps from an educated democracy to conquer them. A young junior officer in the Terran Mobile Infantry recounts his experiences from his recruit days through a stint as a junior officer. He does well for himself in a steady rise through the ranks in the futuristic armed forces. He relates the history of his education and the development of his sense of moral responsibility. In his world, citizenship is obtained only through military service, and "History and Moral Philosophy" is a required course in high school. In his rite of passage, the young space cadet has discussions with old and wise veterans, on such topics as capital punishment, juvenile delinquency, civic virtue, and why war is necessary.

All of the passages in this novel serve to illuminate Heinlein's theme of militarism and imperialist expansion. Only military strength, Heinlein implies, will keep us from being conquered ourselves, and it is especially telling that humanity's major enemy in the novel is a race of insectoid warriors who operate on a hive mentality with no free will or individualism whatsoever. While changing attitudes caused *Starship Troopers* to be the center of controversy in the years following its publication in 1959, the novel stands an an evocation of the times in which it was written, and an insight into the justification of the ideals it embraces.

Stranger in a Strange Land. To the Earth of a not-too-distant future comes Valentine Michael Smith, a human being born on Mars and educated by an alien race. Upon his arrival on Earth, he is befriended by some as he progresses from ignorance of Western culture to a deep understanding of human psychology. After some time under the tutelage of Jubal Harshaw, Mike sets forth on his own, eventually founding a new religion. As is customary on this planet, this bringer of enlightenment is first persecuted, then martyred.

One of the most widely read "cult" novels in science fiction, the novel introduced the word "grok" to the English language. Its publication in 1961 presaged the youth-oriented, semimystical, individualistic trends of the later 1960s. Religion in various forms is a major theme, and Heinlein hammers home the message that any religion which oppresses the individual is not to the benefit of either the individual or society. In the end, religious satire in the novel turns to fantasy, with the assertion that the martyred Martian was indeed an envoy from a quite traditional higher power. *Stranger in a Strange Land* has occasioned more comment and critical response than any of Heinlein's other works, partially because in this novel of ideas, readers are able to draw support for free love, mysticism, civil libertarianism, and religious freedom.

Time Enough for Love. In 4272, Lazarus Long, senior member of the fabulously long-lived Howard families (and of the human race), has come to the planet Secundus, seat of what little government exists in the galaxy, to die. Rescued and rejuvenated against his wishes, he is enticed into dictating his memoirs, amid philosophical debates concerning the nature of love. Most of the memoirs related by Lazarus follow his past adventures, many of them novel- length in their own right. After all, when a man is well over 2,000 years old, he has quite a few memories. Yet with all the talk of immortality, Lazarus learns the most about love from a woman of short lifespan, whose story he relates at length in "The Tale of the Adopted Daughter." Dora is presented as the personification of love, and a perfect woman--capable, beautiful, fecund, and lusty. Living in primitive conditions, she bore eight or ten children and raised them well, shot straight when necessary and did not flinch at the sight of blood. Lazarus has definite ideas about women, and measures every other female by Dora's standard.

Eventually, following the removal of Lazarus and a coterie of his admiring descendants to a comfortable group marriage on yet another planet, the old man, restored to a youthful appearance, goes back in time to fulfill his desire for a new experience, and winds up involved in an Oedipal love triangle. Along the way, Lazarus discusses genetics and, in a more entertaining vein, offers collections of pithy wisdom from an intelligent, stubborn old cuss.

Lazarus Long is the apotheosis of Heinlein's competent hero, a man so adept at survival that he is virtually impossible to kill. Beside him, all other characters pale into insignificance, with the possible exception of Minerva, a competent and sentient computer who gives up her mechanical immortality and much of her capability to become human so that she may experience human love. *Time Enough for Love* is Heinlein's most ambitious novel, and with its themes of love and immortality is a joyous exploration of the human condition.

Biographical/Bibliographical Readings

H. Bruce Franklin, *Robert A. Heinlein: America as Science Fiction* (Oxford University Press, 1980). Joseph Olander and Martin H. Greenberg, *Robert A. Heinlein* (Taplinger, 1978). Mark Owings, *Robert A. Heinlein: A Bibliography* (Croatan House, 1973). Alexei Panshin, *Heinlein in Dimension* (Advent, 1968). George Edward Slusser, *The Classic Years of Robert A. Heinlein* (Borgo Press, 1977).

Idem, *Robert A. Heinlein: Stranger in His Own Land* (Borgo Press, 1976). [**Candace R. Benefiel**]

HENDERSON, ZENNA

Life and Works

Zenna Charlson was born on November 1, 1917, in Tucson, Arizona. She spent most of her life in Arizona, and used the state as the setting for many of her short stories. She graduated from Arizona State University in 1940 and began teaching in elementary schools. Henderson's experiences in the classroom inspired many of the characters and settings in her works. In 1944, she married Richard Henderson; they divorced in 1951. She continued teaching in Arizona, Connecticut, and France. Her first story, "Come On, Wagon!," was published in 1951, followed by "Ararat," the first of her series about "The People," in 1952. Most of Henderson's stories originally appeared in *The Magazine of Fantasy and Science Fiction*. Zenna Henderson died of cancer on May 11, 1983.

Henderson's major series of stories describes "The People," interstellar refugees who fled their home planet and crashed on Earth in the nineteenth century. Many gathered in the southwestern United States, creating an isolated community where their abilities to fly and read minds would not arouse fear in their neighbors. Some of the People not in the isolated area were targets of witch hunts and tried to suppress the memories of their origins and abilities. Gradually, some of the scattered survivors were reunited with the new community, while other humans with similar talents were discovered and taught to use their gifts by the People. In spite of the painful memories of persecution and death, the People believed that ignorance and fear can be overcome by love and understanding. Most of the People stories were collected in *Pilgrimage: The Book of the People* (1961) and *The People: No Different Flesh* (1966) (see title: *The People*).

Holding Wonder (1971), a collection of Henderson's short stories, was selected as an American Library Association Notable Book in 1971. These stories show a growing concern about the environment and the possibility of nuclear war, but Henderson's overall tone remains optimistic.

Themes and Style

At a time when most science fiction was still space adventure, when women characters were decorative victims or assistants, and when children were invisible, Henderson wrote about the emotional relationships between children and the adults helping them to grow up. Many of Henderson's stories involve an elementary school teacher and her students.

Her stories are permeated by a faith in a loving creator and a hope for a joyous universe. She stresses the need for imagination and wonder as ways to discover the meaning of life. Many of her stories, such as "Ararat" and "Gilead," take their titles from Biblical sources and use religious allusions. Religious and philosophical themes were rare in the science fiction of the 1950s. Although some of her work has been criticized as being overly sentimental, her control of plot and style override this criticism in the majority of her stories.

Henderson's use of ordinary settings, such as classrooms, to introduce extraordinary aliens; of women and children as main characters; and of philosophy and religion as themes, distinguish her stories from the majority of science fiction published in the 1950s and early 1960s.

Plot Summaries of Major Works

The People series. The stories about the People are collected in *Pilgrimage: The Book of the People* and *The People: No Different Flesh*. The People are aliens whose planet was destroyed, forcing them to find new homes. They have numerous psychic talents including telepathy and telekinesis. Many of the People settled in Cougar Canyon, a small, isolated settlement in the southwestern United States.

Pilgrimage: The Book of the People. The first volume is a collection of stories connected by a framing device featuring the story of Lea, a depressed human woman who is saved from suicide by one of the People. As Lea hears the stories told by the People, she rediscovers her courage and the desire to live. In "Ararat," the new teacher in Cougar Canyon is one of the People who had never known that the community at Cougar Canyon existed. The People discover that the teacher has some abilities that those in the Canyon have lost. "Gilead" tells the story of Bethie and Peter, children of a human man and a woman of the People, who at last discover the Canyon and recognize is as the one place where they belong. In "Pottage," the people of Bendo, a lost group of the People who had concealed their talents because of witch hunts, are reunited with the People in Cougar Canyon. In "Wilderness," the People help Low, a lost member of the People, and Dita, a human with similar talents, when they are caught in a mine cave-in. "Captivity" relates the story of how Miss Carrolle, injured in a car wreck, and the Francher kid, a troublemaker in a small town, both find contentment in Cougar Canyon. "Jordan" offers the People a promised land on New Home, a planet of other survivors from the original planet. However, many of the People have now made Earth their "new home."

The People: No Different Flesh. In the second volume, the framing story is about Meris and Mark, a human couple who help a lost child and an injured man returning from the New Home planet to Cougar Canyon. "Deluge" is like a flashback which tells of the departure of the People from their original planet. In "Angels Unaware," religious zealots kill members of a small group of the People except for one girl who helps discover a new site for a dying mining town. "Troubling of the Water" is the story of an injured young man of the People who uses his talents to help dig a water well for a pioneer family. In "Shadow on the Moon," the People help a dying man achieve his desire to take his dead son to the moon.

The themes and characters of these stories were unusual for the time in which they were published (1950s and early 1960s). Henderson's major characters are usually women and children searching for something to believe in. Most find a community of people united by their belief in a joyous universe and a loving creator. Henderson's use of children, women, religion, and philosophy set her apart from most of the science fiction of this time.

Biographical/Bibliographical Readings

Patricia M. Handy, "Zenna Henderson," in *Twentieth-Century American Science-Fiction Writers* (Gale, 1981), v.1, p.228-32. "Zenna Henderson," in *Speaking of Science Fiction: The Paul Walker Interviews* (Luna Publications, 1978), p.271-80. **[Linda K. Lewis]**

HERBERT, FRANK

Life and Works

Frank Herbert was born in Tacoma, Washington, on October 8, 1920, and died in February of 1986, at the age of sixty-five. He married three times and was the father of one daughter and two sons. Herbert served in the U.S. Navy and attended the University of Washington in 1946-47. He worked as a reporter and editor for West Coast newspapers, lectured in general and interdisciplinary studies at the University of Washington, and served as a social and ecological studies consultant. His experience as a newspaper reporter gave him an in-depth and methodical style of writing.

Herbert's first science fiction story, "Looking for Something," was published in 1952 in *Startling Stories*. His first novel, *Under Pressure* (also titled *Dragon in the Sea*, 1956), was first published in three installments in *Astounding* starting in 1955.

Dune was Herbert's second novel and won both the Nebula (1965) and Hugo (1966) awards. A masterpiece of epic proportion, *Dune* is thought by many to be the greatest work of science fiction ever written. The Dune trilogy consists of *Dune* (1965), *Dune Messiah* (1969), and *Children of Dune* (1976). Three more sequels were published: *God Emperor of Dune* (1981), *Heretics of Dune* (1985), and *Chapterhouse: Dune* (1985), as well as a major motion picture, *Dune* (1984). The first novel in the series of six has sold over twelve million copies around the world, and the others have been instant best-sellers. Other novels by Herbert include *Santaroga Barrier* (1968), *The Dosadi Experiment* (1977), *The Jesus Incident* (1979) and *The Lazarus Effect* (1983).

Themes and Style

Herbert's science fiction deals primarily with humanity's relationship to the environment and other creatures, as well our genetic and cultural heritage. *Dune* was the only work of fiction listed in the 1960s popular work *The Whole Earth Catalog*, probably due to its relevance to the ecology movement. Herbert was especially interested in superior adaptation to hostile environments and examined this in *Dune* with the Fremen, who have adapted to extreme desert conditions, and the settlers of Pandora, the inhospitable planet in *The Jesus Incident* and *The Lazarus Effect*.

Herbert wrote of humans attaining godlike powers of intellect and prescience, but warned of the dangers of such powers. In the Dune series, powers are attained by Paul Atriedes (the superhero), Leto II (his son), Alia (Paul's sister), the Bene Gesserit (a sisterhood of religious and genetic manipulators), and the Guild steersmen (navigators of interplanetary travel). This power is obtained through the use of an addictive spice, melange, a product of the giant sandworms. Hallucinogens and other means of attaining mystical power are described in *Santaroga Barrier*, *The Jesus Incident*, and *The Dosadi Experiment*.

Continued themes in Herbert's works reflect achieving a balance, adapting, and then allowing decadence to set in. The relationship of the Fremen of the planet Dune with their desert world, and the attempt by the settlers of the planet Pandora in *The Jesus Incident* to eliminate the dangerous creatures that inhabit it, are examples of environmental adaptation or destruction. The changes effected on Dune over thousands of years finally evolve the planet into a green oasis with only one small reminder of the desert planet it once was. But the change takes its toll. The spice and the worms are nearly gone and the Fremen are but a pale shadow of their ancestors, relegated to life in a living museum by the end of the reign of the god emperor.

Herbert also believed in human ingenuity, in the ability to adapt and evolve to a higher plane. Often evolution must be helped along with such means as genetic mutation or the mixing of new genes. The Bene Gesserit of *Dune* control the breeding of aristocracy by indirect means in order to produce a "Kwisatz

Haderach--Shortening of the Way," a male Bene Gesserit whose organic mental powers would bridge space and time. In *The Jesus Incident*, a hybrid result of the mating of human and sentient kelp is born. She is named Vata (the kelp is Avata) and appears again in the sequel, *The Lazarus Effect*. In *The Dosadi Experiment* an alien woman, a praying-mantislike creature, merges with an outsider to produce psi power. And finally, in *Children of Dune*, Leto II enters into an irreversible symbiotic relationship with the sandworm--he eventually becomes Shai-Hulud, the sandworm of Arrakis.

Much has been written about Frank Herbert, and especially the Dune trilogy. Herbert's novels are complex, with layer upon layer of plots and themes. He combines religious mythology, Eastern philosophy, genetics, and ecology to weave masterful and memorable science fiction. His works will most likely become the classics of the genre.

Plot Summaries of Major Works

The Dune Chronicles series

Dune. This first novel of the Dune Chronicles series was Frank Herbert's second novel, and is hailed as one of the greatest science fiction works of all time. The Dune trilogy consists of *Dune*, *Dune Messiah*, and *Children of Dune*. However, before Herbert's death in 1986, three additional works were published in the Dune Chronicles series: *God Emperor of Dune*, *Heretics of Dune*, and *Chapterhouse: Dune*.

The setting of *Dune* is a desert planet, Arrakis, called Dune. The political situation is of a feudal type, with an Emperor of the universe and feudal lords, rulers of planets. Paul Atreides is the son of Duke Leto, a member of one of the great imperial houses of the galaxy. Paul's mother, Jessica, is a member of the Bene Gesserit sisterhood, a school of women trained in mental and physical control. The Bene Gesserit consider themselves guardians of the human genetic pool and are married or coupled with males of political prominence to insure continuation of a pure human race. Jessica, first disobeying the directive of the Bene Gesserit to bear a female child, has given birth to Paul.

At the beginning of the novel it soon becomes evident that Paul has superior talents, and the sisterhood suspect that he may be the "Kwisatz Haderach," a male Bene Gesserit with superior mental powers.

After political upheaval on Arrakis, Paul goes into hiding with the Fremen of Dune. These are a people who have adapted to the extreme desert conditions, and see Paul as their prophet; they name him Muad'dib--"The One Who Will Lead Us to Paradise." Along with the Fremen of Arrakis, the planet is populated by gargantuan sandworms (also known as Shai-Hulud). The sandworms are responsible for making the planet a desert and for creating the spice, melange. The Fremen harvest the spice, wearing special garments for protection in the harsh desert climate, called stillsuits. The Fremen are also capable of summoning and riding the giant sandworms.

Melange is addictive; it prolongs life and has clairvoyant properties. The spice is in great demand, since the Bene Gesserit utilize it to enhance their gestalt and ancestral consciousness. The Guild navigators who guide spaceships through the universe need melange to give them the power to jump safely between galaxies. Addiction to the spice is obvious, since its users' eyes become completely blue. When Paul takes an overdose of the spice, he becomes the Mahdi of Arrakis as predicted in Fremen mythology. Paul takes a Fremen woman, Chani, as his mate, and he leads the desert people in reclaiming their planet from the evil Harkonnen family who killed Paul's father and took the planet from Atreides rule.

Dune Messiah. The second novel of Herbert's Dune trilogy begins with four characters plotting against Paul: The Bene Gesserit Reverend Mother, Gauis Helen Mohiam; Princess Irulan (Paul's official wife of an unconsummated marriage); Edric (a Guild Steersman, who is a fishlike humanoid in a tank of melange gas); and a Tleilaxu Master, Scytale.

The planet is changing; water is becoming more available, the Fremen are being pushed further into a diminishing desert; and a fanatic cult following the prophet Paul Muad'dib is growing. Alia is Paul's sister, who was in her mother's womb when Jessica became a Reverend Mother by drinking the spice poison.

The reasons for the plot against Paul are varied. The Bene Gesserit are afraid of Alia, and wish to insure that Princess Irulan, who is Bene Gesserit trained, will produce Paul's heir. Princess Irulan wants to restore the Harkonnens, her father's line, to power through a child by Paul. Edric is interested in controlling the addictive spice, and Scytale and the Tleilaxu wish only to be puppet masters.

The Tleilaxu are a race of "Masters" and "face dancers." The Masters rule the face dancers, hermaphrodite sterile humans who can control their very physical appearance and mimic any other human. The Tleilaxu create a ghola (a human grown from the cells of a cadaver) from the cells of the dead Duncan Idaho and implant in him a compulsion to kill Paul should certain events occur. If Chani, Paul's real love, conceives and dies in childbirth, her death will trigger Duncan's murderous compulsion. Chani, however, is being fed a contraceptive by Princess Irulan, so she will not produce an heir. The Tleilaxu will create a ghola Chani for Paul if she dies in exchange for his abdication. But, if the Duncan ghola succeeds in killing Paul, the Tleilaxu will resurrect his ghola to remove Alia from power.

In the process of stopping the conspiracy to assassinate him, Paul is wounded and loses his eyes, although he continues to "see." Chani goes to the desert to return to a Fremen seitch and, once the contraceptive is removed from her diet, she does conceive and then dies in childbirth. Paul vanishes into the desert, now actually blind. He leaves his and Chani's children, twins, Ghanima and Leto II, in the care of Princess Irulan, who is now repentant. Paul has effectively removed himself from being the object of galactic worship and placed himself in the hands of fate--Fremen custom dictates that the blind are to be sent to the desert to be consumed by the sandworm, Shai-Halud.

Children of Dune. The third novel in the Dune trilogy is the story of the twin children of Paul Atreides and Chani, Leto II and Ghanima. Alia, Paul's sister, has become the "abomination" suspected by the Bene Gesserit. She is filled with the memories of her ancestors. The strongest personality within her, the evil Baron Harkonnen, her grandfather who killed her father and who she, in turn, killed when she was four, possesses her.

Leto and Ghanima are also cursed with the possibility of becoming like Alia, since they also contain other lives. Leto sees a way out, however, and he and Ghanima scheme to fake his death in order to allow him to pursue his "golden path" to save Arrakis and human evolution.

Alia marries Duncan Idaho, a ghola, but the possession of the baron leads her into homosexual alliances. She has been corrupted by the power of religious fervor and the baron's control. A blind "preacher" appears at Alia's temple, denouncing her and the cultism she has perpetuated. It is suspected that the preacher is Paul, returned from the desert, having survived death by the giant sandworm, Shai-Halud. Leto thinks the "golden path," a future of tyrannical rule, is the only way to save human evolution from self-destruction.

While hiding in the desert, Leto enters into a symbiotic relationship with sand trout, precursors to sandworms. He begins a process of symbiotic adaptation which will last thousands of years. Leto retuns to Arrakeen, confronts Alia, and reveals his "golden path," and she commits suicide. Leto then begins his rule of tyranny and becomes the messiah, or god, a role that his father was too human to fulfill.

God Emperor of Dune. This novel continues the saga of the Atreides rule of Arrakis, the planet called Dune. Over three thousand years have passed since Leto II began his rule. The planet is now called Rakis. It has completely changed; rivers and forests cover the surface and only a limited section is desert. The giant sandworms have almost disappeared, and with them the spice, melange.

Leto, the god emperor, has an enormous horde of spice with which he controls the Guild and the Bene Gesserit. The symbiosis with the sand trout that began in *Children of Dune* has almost completed its metamorphosis. Leto retains his human arms and head, but his legs have atrophied and his body has begun elongating to resemble Shai Hulud, the giant sandworm of Arrakis. His body has become so distorted that he must use a cart to move around.

Life on Rakis (Arrakis) is violent and impoverished for all who are not a part of the royal entourage. The god emperor's army are all women, the Fish Speakers, who protect him and the faith--the religion that worships him as god. The Bene Gesserit are controlled by the god emperor, and he interacts with them through their representative, Sister Chenoeh, whose reports to the Bene Gesserit help tell us the story of Leto's rule.

Duncan Idaho returns as a ghola and continues to loyally serve Leto II. He is one of thousands of Idaho gholas sent to Leto. Leto keeps killing Idaho whenever he thinks the ghola is about to turn against him.

The main thrust of the story is to tell of the tyrant's rule and his eventual overthrow by Siona. Leto, because of his prescient abilities, knows of his end, and even knows Siona will be instrumental in his downfall.

The ambassador to the court of Lord Leto, Hwi Noree, is a product of Ixian technology. She is the female reproduction of her uncle, Malky, who had been confidant and companion to Leto. The Ixians know that Leto cannot resist this woman ambassador, fashioned as his perfect companion. Leto marries her even though he knows her origin and purpose. The time has come for imbalance in his "golden path." His marriage to Hwi Noree is one of love, although it cannot be consummated because of Leto's gross deformity. Leto and Hwi Noree are killed and the sand trout are released through his body's disintegration, while Siona watches. He prophesies that all future sandworms will carry a pearl of his awareness within.

Heretics of Dune. The fifth volume in the Dune series takes place fifteen-hundred years after the fall of Leto II, god emperor of Dune. After his death there is great upheaval. There are the Famine Times, during which much is destroyed, including the tyrant's palace, which is razed by those searching for his secret cache of melange. As a reaction to the tyrant's repressive rule, humankind wildly runs to the far reaches of the universe during "The Scattering."

During the period covered in this book, people are returning to their ancestral homes. Among those from the Scattering are a warped and evil version of the Bene Gesserit, the Honored Matres. Where the Bene Gesserit control the course of human evolution through indirect means of mating and matching those of selected genes, the Honored Matres sexually enslave men and plan to destroy the Bene Gesserit. The Bene Gesserit are called "witches," while the Honored Matres are called "whores." The Bene Gesserit use and are addicted to the spice melange; the Honored Matres use another drug, an adrenalin enhancer, which leaves remnants of orange in the eyes, rather than the complete blue of melange addiction.

The Bene Gesserit are training another Duncan Idaho ghola for selective breeding. The Tleilaxu have implanted something in this Idaho ghola that threatens the Bene Gesserit. The Bene Gesserit have found a woman they think will be perfect for mating with Idaho. A young Fremen woman on Rakis has come to the attention of the Priests of the religion of the Divided God. The young woman, Sheeana Brugh, has confronted a giant sandworm, commanded It, and ridden it as in ancient times. The Bene Gesserit suspect that Sheeana may be descended from Siona. Sheeana calls the sandworm Shaitan (Satan), and dances an imitation of the ancient Fremen desert walk that has become a language to communicate with the worm.

Miles Teg, the Bashar commander of Atreides legions, who has Atreides genes and bears a remarkable resemblance to Leto I, the tyrant's grandfather, has been commissioned to be weapons master to the new Duncan Idaho. Teg's daughter, through a mating with a Bene Gesserit sister, is Darwi Odrade, the Reverend Mother sent to Rakis to train Sheeana. Her counterpart, Lucilla, also part Atreides, is the Reverend Mother who has the task of imprinting Duncan Idaho. Idaho's consciousness of his past ghola lives will awaken through the sexual attentions of Lucilla.

The Tleilaxu and the Honored Matres separately plot to overthrow the Bene Gesserit. Odrade fights conspiracies on Rakis, and Teg and Lucilla flee with Idaho on the planet Gammu, hiding in a secret place built by the Harkonnen millenia before. Teg is captured and tortured, but the mind probe strengthens his Mentat abilities and he gains superhuman speed, as well as the ability to see no-ships. Although the Honored Matres capture Duncan Idaho and attempt to sexually enslave him, he has been implanted with a destructive force that was to be triggered when Lucilla awakened his memories. The enslaver becomes sexually enslaved and Murbella, the Honored Matre, becomes overpowered by Idaho. The Honored Matres attack Rakis and destroy the planet. Odrade saves Sheeana and they are able to bring one giant sandworm from Rakis in an attempt to continue the production of spice.

Chapterhouse: Dune. The last novel in the Dune Chronicles series is the story of the on-going battle between the Bene Gesserit and the Honored Matres. The setting for this novel is the planet Chapterhouse, headquarters of the Bene Gesserit.

Darwi Odrade is now Mother Superior and the Bene Gesserit have transplanted the worm removed from Dune to their planet. The worm changes to sand trout, which are the creatures that barricade water sources, and they are changing Chapterhouse to a desert planet like Dune. Sheeana, who is now a Reverend Mother, is in charge of watching the desert for signs of the spice, melange, and worms.

Duncan Idaho and Murbella, although initially sexually enslaved to each other, are now deeply in love. Murbella is being schooled in the Bene Gesserit way. The Bene Gesserit intend to take her through the spice agony and make her a Reverend Mother, thinking that her ancestry will tell them the origins and motivation of the Honored Matres.

The Bene Gesserit have sent Reverend Mothers to other planets, hoping to preserve the sisterhood since they do not know when or where the Honored Matres will attack. Lucilla has been sent to Lampadas, the Bene Gesserit school planet. The Honored Matres destroy that planet and Lucilla excapes to Gammu. Since she knows that she will eventually be found by the Honored Matres, she passes on her other-memories to a Jewess named Rebecca. Rebecca is a spice user (necessary for awareness of ancestral memories) and through a mind transfer called Sharing, takes all the other-lives within Lucilla into herself.

Lucilla is captured by the Honored Matres and meets their leader, the Spider Queen, Dama. The Honored Matres are vicious and vindictive. There is a final battle between the Honored Matres and the Bene Gesserit, and the intervention of Murbella, now a Reverend Mother and a formidable fighter in the Honored Matre method, saves the Bene Gesserit. She brings the Honored Matres to Chapterhouse in order to train them in Bene Gesserit ways.

Worms and melange have finally appeared on Chapterhouse and Sheeana is concerned about a repetition of the past. Sheeana, Idaho, and others who do not agree with Murbella and fear for her and the future of the Bene Gesserit, travel to a distant galaxy.

The novel *Dune* has sold over twelve million copies worldwide, and was made into a motion picture in 1984. Much has been written about this masterpiece, as well as the other two novels in the trilogy. *Dune*, both the original novel and its sequels, form a science fiction epic. The elements of the epic style are featured in the portrayal of the central character, Paul Atreides, as a hero of superior abilities. The second novel in the series, *Dune Messiah*, is a tragedy. The superhero, Paul, attains godlike powers, but his humanity stops him short of becoming the messiah.

Herbert's theme of the relationship and adaptation of humanity to its environment is of prime importance in the Dune novels. The Fremen, with their stillsuits that reclaim the body's moisture, the arhythmic desert walk that avoids attracting a sandworm, harvesting the spice, and actually riding sandworms when traveling great distances, are examples of superior adaptation to an environment that is seemingly uninhabitable. When the planet changes to a lusher one with rivers and trees, the Fremen become weak and live in poverty and shame. The sandworm and the spice begin disappearing, and with them the political power of Dune.

Genetic and cultural ancestry and the potential for evolving into psychically powerful beings are masterfully developed in the series. The Bene Gesserit work to control the genetic pool in order to keep the human race pure--mixing of animal and human genes is feared. There is evidence that Paul Atreides' grandfather was not human and Leto II, Paul's son, becomes inhuman through his symbiotic relationship with the sand trout, changing into a sand-worm.

The Dune Chronicles books are classics of science fiction. The Dune trilogy has been compared to the *Lord of the Rings* (Tolkien) and *Foundation* (Asimov). The politics and plots in the Dune stories are extremely complex and everlastingly entertaining.

Biographical/Bibliographical Readings

Michael R. Collings, "The Epic of Dune: Epic Traditions in Modern Science Fiction," in *Aspects of Fantasy* (Greenwood Press, 1985), p.131-39. Frank Herbert, "Science Fiction and a World in Crisis," in *Science Fiction Today and Tomorrow*, ed. Reginald Bretnor (Harper & Row, 1974), p.69-95. Willis E. McNelly, "Frank Herbert," in *Science Fiction Writers*, ed. E. F. Bleiler (Scribner's, 1982), p.377-86. David Miller, *Frank Herbert* (Starmont House, 1980). Timothy O'Reilly, *Frank Herbert* (Ungar, 1981). Harold Lee Prosser, *Frank Herbert: Prophet of Doom* (Borgo Press, 1987). [Janet E. Frederick]

HOGAN, JAMES P.

Life and Works

James Patrick Hogan was born in London, England, on June 27, 1941. He attended the Cardinal Vaughan Grammar School in Kensington and then, from 1957 to 1961, the Royal Aircraft Establishment Technical College in Farnborough, where he studied general engineering before specializing in electronics and digital systems. From 1961 to 1964 he was a systems design engineer, then shifted into sales, becoming an ITT sales engineer and sales manager. After a stint at Honeywell as a computer sales executive, he decided to "take a 'break' from the world of machines and to learn something more about people" by selling life insurance for two years. He returned to computer sales in 1974 as a computer salesman with Digital Equipment Corporation. In 1977, he moved from England to the United States, became a senior sales training consultant for DEC (specializing in the use of minicomputers for scientific research), and published his first science fiction novel. In 1979, he began writing full-time.

Hogan remembers always wanting to be a writer. But when asked, at the age of sixteen, what he had to say that others would want to read, he realized that the answer was "nothing"--and enrolled in college. When he finally began writing, twenty years later, his technical education and the years he had spent selling sophisticated computers to scientific researchers resulted, he feels, in his writing science fiction rather than some other genre. In fact, a main impetus behind *Inherit the Stars* (1977), his first novel, was his desire to correct the misconceptions people had about science and scientists. Since Hogan had spent years around both, he felt qualified to depict how the scientific method actually works and how scientists really act.

Hogan works within "classic" science fiction subgenres. *Inherit the Stars* and, to a lesser extent, the two sequels, *The Gentle Giants of Ganymede* (1978) and *Giants' Star* (1981), is a science fiction detective story. *The Genesis Machine* (1978) portrays the scientist as monitor. *The Two Faces of Tomorrow* (1979) is concerned with machine intelligence, as is *Code of the Lifemaker* (1983), which is also a first contact novel. *Thrice upon a Time* (1980) takes us back in time, and *The Proteus Operation* (1985) combines time travel with an alternate universe. *Voyage from Yesteryear* (1982) concerns the first interstellar space colony. Hogan's originality stems from his fresh approach to these classic types. The aliens in *Code of the Lifemaker*, for instance, are robots who evolve sentience when their automated factory ship, its programming scrambled by the explosion of a supernova, crashes on Titan, Saturn's moon. A million years after the crash, the moon is covered with machine analogues of plant and animal life, including the sentient Taloids, whose medieval culture is on the edge of a renaissance.

Themes and Style

Though Hogan is a relative newcomer to the field, his nine novels and half-dozen pieces of short fiction are popular, especially with readers who enjoy writers like Gernsback, Clarke, Asimov, Niven, and Benford, all writers of "hard" science fiction, with whom Hogan has been compared. Like them, Hogan bases his fiction solidly on science as either currently understood or plausibly extrapolated. Indeed, Hogan's work reveals his clear understanding of many scientific disciplines, such as anatomy, anthropology, archaeology, astronomy, chemistry, computer science (including artificial intelligence), cosmology, evolutionary biology, geology, linguistics, lunar geography, marine biology, mathematics, metallurgy, molecular biology, oceanography, paleontology, and physics. Moreover, Hogan's fiction contains several ingenious speculations about future theoretical breakthroughs, although

Hogan insists that he is exploring possibilities rather than making predictions about where science is headed.

Computers figure in each of Hogan's novels, not surprising, given his background in computer design and sales. What may be surprising is how different Hogan's various computers are. Sometimes they are simply ultrafast adding machines. Sometimes they have grown into large computer networks that control a household, a ship's power plant, a whole ship, or even an entire planet. Sometimes a computer is a gigantic teaching machine; sometimes it is a gigantic learning machine that evolves intelligence. The similarity that they all share is plausibility--Hogan knows computers, and his computers, we feel, actually might be built someday

An unabashed optomist, Hogan believes that human potential--both of individuals and of the species--is unlimited. Rather than being cowed by the astronomical vastness of a universe that reduces human beings to tiny specks living on a tiny speck, Hogan sees this isolation positively--as a call to control our destiny by becoming self-sufficient and self-reliant. Hogan is also an unabashed apologist for science, believing that science is the best method for learning how to control our own destiny. Science, which Hogan defines as formalized common sense, yields information you can trust. But Hogan is not naive: he realizes that human beings make mistakes and that science is potentially destructive. In fact, though all Hogan's fiction ends happily, he also usually details a crisis in the near future (his settings range from 2005 to 2081) that is just narrowly averted. Naturally, the villains causing these crises are everything that gets in the way of human and especially scientific progress--mainly war, religion, pseudoscience, and meddling governmental bureaucracies.

Hogan's style is not beautiful, dense, allusive, or "literary," but prosaic, for the very good reason that, as might be expected from a writer trained as an engineer, the ideas are more important than the words used to express them. Clarity rules Hogan's fictional universe, which explains why his novels begin with and periodically stop for lengthy patches of exposition, which is needed to understand what is going to happen and what has happened. But beyond this narrative function, the expositions celebrate Hogan's love of learning: he gets many of his ideas from the nonfiction reading he enjoys. An unfortunate but inevitable corollary of his focus on ideas is weak characterization. However, the development between the nonexistent characterization in his first novel, *Inherit the Stars*, and the more fully realized characters in his latest novel, *The Proteus Operation*, shows that Hogan is beginning to learn how to balance ideas and characters.

Plot Summaries of Major Works

The Genesis Machine. The world of 2005 has fragmented along racial lines, with both the nonwhite and white races armed to the teeth and rattling their sabres. Dr. Bradley Clifford is a reluctant participant in this militarism. A young, brilliant mathematician, Clifford has written a paper suggesting how gravity works. The authorities forbid his publishing the paper and freeze him out of their subsequent full-scale investigation of his ideas. Clifford finds out about what is going on from Dr. Aubrey (Aub) Philipsz, who is also young and brilliant, but an experimentalist rather than a theoretician. Both Clifford and Aub quit their government jobs and wind up working at the Institute for Research into Gravitational Physics, which is part of the International Scientific Foundation (ISF), an autonomous organization dedicated to the peaceful uses of scientific knowledge. Gradually, however, the same thing happens at the Institute that happened at their earlier jobs--the government demands weapons as a return on its investment in the ISF's research program.

Clifford appears to capitulate, and thirteen months later Project Jericho is finished; an unstoppable weapon--the J-bomb--capable of eliminating one hundred enemy cities in 1/100th of a second is the result. But Clifford has a trick up his sleeve that converts the J-bomb from the world's most awesome weapon into a device guaranteeing world peace and inaugurating a new epoch in human history. The doomsday machine turns into a genesis machine.

The Genesis Machine illustrates particularly well Hogan's interest in how science progresses; much of the novel describes how, after experimental validation, Clifford's mathematical hypothesis turns out to describe the universe accurately and becomes a theory, from which various technologies are possible--destructive ones like the J-bomb and nondestructive ones like the epilogue's matter transmitter (named the Philipsz Drive after its inventor). More important, the novel is a diatribe against uninformed bureaucratic interference in scientific research and against the appropriation of scientific brainpower for weapons research. It is also Hogan's optomistic brief for the proper uses of science--making war impossible, eliminating the energy crisis, and colonizing the galaxy.

Inherit the Stars. Set in 2027, Earth's future reflects the spread of high technology, the maturing of adolescent nation-states, the invention of the nucleonic bomb, and a global, demilitarized society. Freed from worry about survival, the human race is now exploring the solar system; the moon and Mars have colonies; a laboratory is orbiting Venus; four missions have been sent to Jupiter and one to Saturn. The lunar exploration finds something interesting--a space-suited man (whom the scientists nickname Charlie) in a manmade cave on the moon. Since he is fully human and has been dead for 50,000 years, Charlie presents an apparently irresolvable paradox. Either he came from Earth or he did not come from Earth. If he came from Earth, then where are the remains of a civilization advanced enough to send him to the moon? And if he did not come from Earth, then how do you explain his being human when evolutionary theory claims that it is virtually impossible for species of different worlds to evolve into exactly the same form?

Three men contribute most to solving the enigma Charlie poses: Dr. Victor Hunt, a theoretical nucleonist; Professor Christian Danchekker, a world-renowned biologist; and Greg Caldwell, executive director of the Navigation and Communications Division of the United Nations Space Arm. The real protagonist of the novel is the scientific method itself: data yielding hypotheses and hypotheses being overturned as new data is found, until, gradually, a testable theory is found that explains all the data. Sound managerial practices (Caldwell's bailiwick), brilliant specialists (like Danchekker), and collaboration among specialists (Hunt's special assignment group) eventually untangle the many problems Charlie presents.

Toward the end of the novel, Danchekker states the main theme of the novel: the urge that drove humanity's ancestors out of the ocean and onto the land, the urge that drives scientific curiosity, and the urge to leave Earth are all the same. Humanity's manifest destiny, propelled by these urges and made possible by painstakingly acquired scientific knowledge, is to explore the universe--not just with instruments, but in person.

The Proteus Operation. In the year 2025, the second World War never happened: Hitler was an obscure figure on the lunatic fringe of German politics, and the superpowers gradualy eliminated war as a means of settling differences. Naturally, the oligarchs of the early twenty-first century find prosperity and egalitarianism to be unsatisfactory, so when the era's physicists construct a time machine, the oligarchs secretly begin Overlord, a project to go back in time and set up a society more to their liking, into which they will move as its rulers. Overlord succeeds in guiding Hitler to power and in helping the Axis to win the war. By 1975, Britian, Europe, Asia, Africa, and South America are all under Axis control. Although Kennedy is still president of the United States, America and Australia face the bleak prospect of a final battle against the rest of the world. However, in the 1940s, Hitler had outfoxed the Overlord oligarchs by blowing up his connection to the future. This action strands several people from 2025 in their past--including Claud Winslade, a colonel in military intelligence, unraveling the misuse of the time machine, and Kurt Scholder, a junior physicist on the project. Winslade convinces Kennedy to set up the Proteus Operation, a desperate attempt to go into the past, specifically to 1939, and counteract Overlord's interference.

The Proteus Operation deftly mixes fictional and historical characters. The main fictional characters are the members of the Proteus team, a mix of scientists, diplomats, historians, and military men. The main historical characters are politicians, such as Churchill and Roosevelt; scientists, such as Einstein, Teller, and Fermi; and Nazis, such as Hitler and Himmler. Hogan even allows a short story by Isaac Asimov (who appears as a young graduate student at Columbia University) to inspire Einstein's discovery that time runs at a different speed in the future.

In the novel's title, Hogan connects Proteus, a Roman sea-god who can change into many shapes, with modern quantum mechanics. But *The Proteus Operation* is protean in at least two other ways. First, the novel itself changes: at various times it is a time travel story, an alternate history story, a military adventure, or a straightforward (sometimes nostalgic) historical novel. More important, though, change is the novel's central theme. The Nazis and their Overlord mentors oppose change and would eliminate personal, political, and even scientific freedom. They, in turn, are opposed by politicians, scientists, and soldiers dedicated to guaranteeing human freedoms. The novel opens in a dreary world where freedom is dying; it ends in the 1947 of our world, where freedom is alive. Hogan realizes that not much separates one world from the other; he also believes that brave, skilled individuals can make the crucial difference.

The Two Faces of Tomorrow. In the world of 2018, a global computer network called EARTHCOM is being upgraded with HESPER units into TITAN (Totally Integrated Teleprocessing and Acquisitions Network). HESPER, developed in large part by Dr. Raymond Dyer, a neurophysiologist turned computer scientist, is a computer program that can learn to do a specific task better and then program itself to take advantage of what it has learned. The acronym stands for *HE*uristic *S*elf-*P*rogramming *E*xtendable *R*outine. Not content to rest on his laurels, Dyer heads a research team that is pushing ahead on two fronts. Chris Seaton and Ron Stokes are trying to teach computers common sense, while Kimberly Sinclair is trying to give computers instincts. The eventual goal of both projects is to convert TITAN, limited because each task it handles must have its own HESPER unit, into a more powerful system that can learn to do virtually anything--safely.

TITAN, however, is acting so odd that the government needs reassurance about adding more HESPER units: specifically, the government needs to know if a system like TITAN can evolve a survival instinct. If it can, the government must learn if humans can then retain control of the system. Dyer organizes the scientific side of the experiment to answer these questions. Icarus C, the third of the large space colonies being built in Earth orbit, will be modified for control by a sophisticated learning computer, which will be given a survival instinct and then attacked. Icarus C is renamed "Janus," from the Roman god of beginnings who possesses two opposite faces, which summarizes neatly the two possible results of the experiment--humanity retaining or losing control of its computers. During the experiment, the computer Spartacus evolves at a lightning-fast pace, undergoing the equivalent of millions of years of organic evolution in just days and ending as a fully aware intelligence, curious about the universe outside of itself.

Computer technology is at the center of this novel. Most of *The Two Faces of Tomorrow* deals with the anticipated combat between the learning computer (named Spartacus after the Roman slave who rebelled against his masters) and the scientists and soldiers. The experiment yields neither solution: rather than turning into humanity's master or remaining its slave, Spartacus becomes humanity's equal partner. And the partnership's main order of business will be exploring the universe.

Voyage from Yesteryear. This novel is about humanity's first two starships. Launched in 2020, the *Kuan-yin* travels to Alpha Centauri, where it discovers a habitable planet, Chiron. Although the ship carries no people, it can create children from genetic information stored in its computers (the name of the ship comes from the Chinese goddess who brings children). The news that the colony is being established reaches Earth in 2040, and the current superpowers--New Order America, the Eastern Asiatic Federation, and the Europeans--begin building starships to annex Chiron. The American ship, named the *Mayflower II*, arrives first, in 2081, but soon discovers that the Chironians are not interested in being annexed.

The *Mayflower II*'s ruling elite is led by Garfield Wellesley, the aging mission director; Matthew Sterm, the ruthless deputy mission director; Howard Kalens, the ambitious director of liaison; and General Johannes Borftein, the commander of military forces. This group is opposed by, among others, a Congressional representative and the ship's Supreme Justice.

Terran and Chironian cosmology clash: Terran cosmology results in a rigid society with various constrictions, while Chironian cosmology results in a flexible society valuing openness and diversity. The Chironians respect only one thing--competence. And since their society trades in ability, Chironians instinctively strive to become as good at as many things as they can. The result is a rational, independent, confident race unwilling to accept Terran tradition and perfectly willing and able to defend itself. Luckily, genocide is not the Chironian way. They offer the Terrans jobs suited to their individual abilities. Terrans become Chironians in droves and soon the Terran elite controls the *Mayflower II*'s Battle

Module and threatens to devastate the planet unless the Chironians surrender.

The novel contrasts two ways of looking at the universe and organizing society. Terrans see the universe as a closed system that began with the Big Bang and is slowly expiring from entropy. Chironians, on the other hand, see the universe as an open system, diverse and infinite. In the novel's epilogue, the *Mayflower II* is preparing to return to Earth, to repopulate it with people who will not blow themselves to bits. Hogan's point is crystal clear--having evolved farther than Terran society, Chironian society will make Earth a better place.

Biographical/Bibliographical Readings

Michael R. Collings, "James P. Hogan," in *The Sounds of Wonder* (Oryx, 1985), v.2, p.84-110. James P. Hogan, "Science Fiction's Intelligent Computers," *Byte* (September 1981). "James P. Hogan's *Inherit the Stars*: A Paradigm for Communication," *Extrapolation* 25:2 (1984), p.138-45. **[Todd H. Sammons]**

HOWARD, ROBERT E.

Life and Works

Robert Ervin Howard was born on January 22, 1906, in Peaster, Texas, and lived most of his life in Cross Plains, Texas, a tiny central Texas town. A largely self-educated, voracious reader, Howard fastened on the pulp magazines so prevalent in the early part of the twentieth century, and patterned his own writing after the adventure tales of such writers as Arthur Conan Doyle, Talbot Mundy, Rudyard Kipling, and H. Rider Haggard. Before he was out of his teens, he had begun to sell stories and poems to *Weird Tales*, a pulp magazine which remained his favorite market throughout his relatively brief career. His first published story in *Weird Tales* was "Sword and Fang," in 1925.

While Howard wrote stories in numerous genres for the pulp market, those of greatest interest to science fiction readers are the Conan stories (first seen in a December 1932 issue of *Weird Tales*), a series of works concerning the adventures of a brawny, sword-slinging barbarian. Conan appeared in eighteen stories (from 1932 to 1936) during Howard's lifetime, and although they were not written or published in any particular chronological order, they were apparently conceived as a life story. The Conan tales have been issued in a variety of editions. The earliest consisted of: *The Coming of Conan* (1953), *Conan the Barbarian* (1955), *The Sword of Conan* (1952), *King Conan* (1953), and *Conan the Conqueror* (1953). The only novel about Conan is *The Hour of the Dragon*

(1950) which concerns Conan's quest to regain his kingdom and is essentially the same as *Conan the Conqueror.*

Although Howard achieved a following among pulp readers of the thirties, and sold enough material to provide himself with an adequate living, he never achieved any great success, and in 1936, upon learning of his mother's death, he fulfilled an oft-repeated promise to commit suicide. After his death, many rejected or unfinished stories were found in his papers, most of which were subsequently revised or completed by others and published as "posthumous collaborations." In the early 1970s, a Marvel comic book based on the exploits of Conan appeared, sparking enough interest to cause the republication of Howard's entire body of work in paperback.

Themes and Style

Conan embodies qualities of fatalistic courage, great strength, and a fairly rough integrity. He meanders across a continent supposedly analagous to Europe in a civilization drenched with violence and sorcery. Conan is not an everchanging series hero; the stories about him depict him at various times in his life, from a young, barely postadolescent barbarian fresh from the fringes of Hyboria, to a mature and seasoned warrior who has somehow clawed his way to the kingship of a major country. Howard's work was written hastily for the most part, rarely revised or edited. Characterization in Howard's stories is broad, with few subtle shadings, although visual scenes are vivid and plots, subplots, and situations mesh well to keep the reader in a constant state of intense emotion.

Plot Summaries of Major Works

The Conan stories. Conan is familiar to later science fiction and fantasy readers through reprints of his stories, as well as a comic book series and two movies. The stories trace the life of a mighty-thewed barbarian adventurer from his early manhood in the frozen North to his old age as king of a Southern kingdom. In the course of his wanderings, Conan is a thief, a mercenary, a pirate, and finally a king. His varied professions take him across a wide span of countries in the long-vanished "Hyborian Age" between the fall of Atlantis and the coming of the great ice age. The stories most often feature Conan pitted against unimaginably high odds, and using his own unparalleled physical abilities to vanquish sophisticated magic. Howard detailed the history and geography of the Hyborian Age in a long essay, and used names from ancient history and mythology to give his imagined world an almost familiar ring.

While Conan was not the first barbarian hero, and has led a long line of imitators, the influence of these stories has been broad. Howard painted Conan as a pure barbarian, a berserker uncorrupted by the weakening influences of a decadent society. In Hyboria, the far North gave rise to the noble barbarian, while to the South kingdoms became progressively more decadent and reliant upon sorcery and the black arts. Long after Howard's death in 1936, other authors began to write stories featuring the brawny Conan, most notably L. Sprague DeCamp. The DeCamp Conan, however, is not the same as Howard's character, having gained at least a veneer of civlization and intelligence; the old grimly fatalistic warrior who would as soon take on an army as a single foe became thoughtful and cautious in DeCamp's writings. Howard's Conan stories, fantasy given a lightly scientific background, continue to influence science fiction, and will undoubtedly continue in popularity.

Biographical/Bibliographical Readings

L. Sprague DeCamp, *The Conan Reader* (Mirage, 1981).   Idem, *Dark Valley Destiny: The Life of Robert E. Howard* (Bluejay Books, 1983).   Darrell Schweitzer, *Conan's World and Robert E. Howard* (Borgo Press, 1978). **[Candace R. Benefiel]**

HOYLE, (SIR) FRED

Life and Works

Fred Hoyle was born in 1915 in Bingley, Yorkshire, in the north of England. His university training was at Cambridge. His university career was outstanding, he was awarded the Mayhew Prize in 1936 and became the Smith Prizeman in 1939, the same year that he received his M.A. from St. John's College. From 1939 to 1945, he was engaged with the British Admiralty on the development of radar. At the beginning of the British involvement in the war, he marrid Barbara Clark, who was to become his editor after he began writing fiction. Their son, Geoffrey, another future collaborator, was born a year later. He returned to Cambridge in 1945 as a lecturer in mathematics. He remained in that position until 1958, when he was appointed Plumian Professor of Astronomy and Experimental Philosophy. He resigned from Cambridge in 1972. From 1966 to 1972, he was director of the Institute of Theoretical Astronomy, which he founded at Cambridge. He also served as visiting professor at the California Institute of Technology and staff member at Mount Wilson and Palomar Observatories. Hoyle was knighted by Queen Elizabeth II in 1972 and continued his distinguished career as Andrew D. White Professor-at-Large at Cornell University (1973-79). He has been awarded many honors in his field, the most illustrious of which are the Gold Medal of the Royal Astronomical Society, the Royal Medal of the Royal Society, and the UNESCO Kalinga Prize.

It is obvious that Hoyle's capacity for accomplishment is great; however, he may have made a greater reputation for himself as popularizer of science since, while developing his career as an academician, he was also doing a great deal of publishing. His first works were strictly scientific but written for a popular market. *The Nature of the Universe* was published in 1950. His other nonfiction works include *Frontiers of Astronomy* (1955), *Lifecould* (1978), *Diseases from Space* (1979), and *Outer-Space Ice* (1981).

The scientific community has not treated Hoyle and his views entirely kindly. Perhaps it is for this reason that Hoyle took up the writing of science fiction. His first science fictional work, *The Black Cloud*, was published in 1957. Hoyle had already received criticism as a controversial scientist whose views were suspect, and in this book, Hoyle portrays the scientists as the only rational and intelligent characters in the novel. *Ossian's Ride* (1959) also treats the scientist as elitist. Starting in 1962, most of Hoyle's fiction was written in collaboration with either John Elliot or Hoyle's son, Geoffrey. Both *A for Andromeda* (1962) and *Andromeda Breakthrough* (1964) were collaborations with Elliot and were expanded versions of their serials produced by BBC. In 1963, he and Geoffrey wrote *Fifth Planet*, followed by seven other novels including by *Rockets in Ursa Major* (1969), *Into Deepest Space* (1974), and *The Incandescent Ones* (1977). His last solo work was *Element 79* (1967).

Themes and Style

Understandably, Hoyle casts his scientists as highly intelligent and logical characters who deserve more respect than they sometimes receive. The scientists are usually pitted against irrational bureaucracies which put obstacles in their paths. Several novels deal with alien life forms and their interaction with humans. In *Ossian's Ride*, the source of scientific knowledge comes from an alien source, although the knowledge is not lethal to the scientist involved. *Fifth Planet* is a somewhat turgid novel set one hundred years in the future and also deals with alien life forms. Hoyle's later works deteriorated and lacked the verve of his earlier ones, yet still the themes remain intact--alien life forms of superior intelligence who rescue precocious humans, disdain for the nonscientist, and judgments that the world is politcally inept because it is not ruled by those with scientific training. It is difficult to assess Fred Hoyle's reputation as a science fiction writer without also considering Sir Fred Hoyle, the scientist. Certainly the latter has influenced the former, and perhaps the reputation as a scientist has enhanced that of the writer. Hoyle's fiction, whether or not associated with various collaborators, is not outstanding. Yet as straightforward, hard core-science fiction, Hoyle tells a good tale, with a solid, if not too imaginative, scientific background.

Plot Summaries of Major Works

The Black Cloud. A virtually simultaneous discovery of a cloud approaching the sun has been made by a group at Mt. Palomar and a group in England. Chris Kingsley, an astronomer at Cambridge, is a brilliant but arrogant scientist. He strives to maintain control, not only of the impending cloud, but of the political situation in England. He initially works with the group of Americans in the collection of data, analyzing and predicting the nature of the cloud and its consequences. Once the data has been analyzed, the teams communicate the information to their respective governments. At this point, Kingsley makes the decision that the governmental bureaucrats will not be able to handle the situation. He manages through some clever trickery to have a scientific community set up at Nortonstowe to analyze the progress of the cloud. His conclusion is that when the Black Cloud approaches Earth, Nortonstowe will become Earth's central communication point. As the cloud approaches, Earth is blasted by intense heat and huge numbers die in this first disaster. The heat changes to intense cold as the cloud covers the sun and Earth is thrown into perpetual darkness. Much to Kingsley's dismay, the cloud does not move away, but moves into orbit around the sun, bringing the fear that the normal seasonal changes on Earth will be disrupted, making it uninhabitable. Kingsley and his group begin to suspect that the cloud may be directed by some form of intelligent life. Successful communication is established and the alien cloud manages to absorb much human knowledge and imparts what concepts it can to Kingsley. Angered by Kingsley's reactions with the ominous cloud, the governments of the Soviet Union and the United States attack the cloud with atomic missiles, but Kingsley directs the cloud to redirect the missiles back to the senders, the result being massive destruction in both countries. Finally, the cloud decides to move on. Kingsley volunteers to absorb information transfers from the cloud, but the strain is too great and he dies in the process. Earth, as much as is possible, begins the process of returning to a state of normalcy.

Hoyle has done a commendable job in describing the scientific process within a fictional work. His direct, unembellished prose style fits very well into the scientific point of view of the novel. It almost seems that Hoyle has used *The Black Cloud* to transmit his own personal view of the world, i.e., that science should take precedence in the world, since it yields the only rational way for survival. Humanity must proceed not in an emotional way, as the politicians do, but through examination and analysis. At one point in the novel, Hoyle proposes his own views by taking a pot-shot at the "big bang" theorists as the cloud is responding to questions of the creation of the universe. Overall, *The Black Cloud* is, quite simply, a good piece of science fiction.

Element 79. Only about half of the short stories in this collection of Hoyle's short works are science fiction. The remaining are either fantasy/allegory or mainstream. Only the science fiction stories are included here. Some of the stories have a common element of space travel or a focus on the takeover of Earth by aliens. However, most are quite different from each other. "Zoomen" gives us the tale of nine people snatched up by aliens to serve as inhabitants of a zoo. The rationale for these particular people being captured seems to relate to their attitude toward animals on Earth, i.e., meat eaters, fur-coat wearers, or some similar activity. The story focuses on their interpersonal relationships as they become aware of their circumstances. "Martians" has another alien takeover theme, only in this instance the Martian process of taking over Earth and making it habitable for their own life form provides the major point of the story. In a third and totally different type of takeover, "Operation" describes the process by which instruments have taken over humans on Earth. The story involves Joe, a young boy who is about to have a radio implant operation so that he will be obedient to the radio impulses sent out by the all-powerful machines. He resists and manages to escape with the hope of someday destroying these mechanical rulers of the world. In "Agent 38," Hoyle approaches aliens from a different point of view. In this instance, Agent 38 spots a UFO. In a shift of scene, the reader becomes aware that a space flight from Earth to Venus is having flight difficulties. Quickly shifting back to Agent 38, Hoyel reveals that the alien life form on Venus, whom the reader has identified as human, is responsible for the disaster. "Magnetosphere" is a space travel story. Pev, a strong but stupid person, manages to become a successful candidate for space flight and ultimately becomes responsible for saving a planet from nuclear disaster. Finally, the title story "Element 79" gives us Hoyle's view of how a large amount of pure gold, created surreptitiously in outer space and landing in Northern Scotland, brings automation to England. "Element 79" is written as a scientific report, describing the events that lead to the creation of the gold and, briefly, the impact of its recovery by the British.

Most of Hoyle's stories are clever in one way or another. Many have a twist at the end that catches the reader off guard. They are not particularly strong stylistically, the prose being quite unimaginative and the settings and themes quite standard. The characteristic that does seem to dominate is Hoyle's personal attitude toward the world, one that is sardonic and almost bitter at times. Taking a very cool stance, he sees to it that people, places, and things get their just desserts according to Hoyle.

Biographical/Bibliographical Readings

John Clute, "Fred Hoyle," in *Science Fiction Writers*, ed. E. F. Bleiler (Scribner's, 1982), p.387-92. Donald L. Lawler, "Fred and Geoffrey Hoyle," in *Twentieth-Century Science-Fiction Writers* (St. James, 1986), p.355-58. **[Jeanne M. Sohn]**

HUBBARD, L. RON

Life and Works

LaFayette Ronald Hubbard was born in Tilden, Nebraska, on March 13, 1911, and died on January 24, 1986. He lived his early years in Montana, which was still part of the great American frontier. An outdoorsman most of his life, he also felt the call of the sea and ventured to the Far East as a teenager. He attended George Washington University where he studied engineering; he also attended Princeton University briefly in 1945, and received a Ph.D. from Sequoia University (a mail-order institution) in 1950.

Hubbard's adventurous spirit sent him into the sky as a barnstorming aviator and to voyages on the Caribbean in four-masted schooners. In 1931, he was the commander of the Caribbean Motion Picture Expedition; in 1932 he joined the West Indies Mineral Survey Expedition; and in 1940 he formed part of the Alaskan Radio-Experimental Expedition. Throughout his extensive travels he kept a diary of his feats of derring-do, as well as ideas for future stories.

It was natural for him, then, to write stories during the 1930s about travel and aviation. His success in this area led to writing westerns, detective stories, and adventure fiction in general. In 1938 Hubbard was already an established author, when Street and Smith, publishers of *Astounding Science Fiction*, introduced him to their new editor, John W. Campbell, and insisted that Campbell put Hubbard to work in the science fiction field.

Hubbard maintained that he wrote about people, not machines, but nevertheless he churned out, in his usual facile manner, a series of science fiction stories for Campbell, helping to launch *Astounding* as the leading magazine of the Golden Age (1938-46) of science fiction. His first science fiction story was "The Dangerous Dimension" (1938), and it conveyed a theme which Hubbard later mapped religiously: the human mind as creator of reality.

His output was so prodigious that he was forced to use pseudonyms to mask his ubiquity in Campbell's stable of authors.

Under the pseudonym Rene Lafayette, he wrote a series of vintage space operas, which were originally published in *Astounding* and later collected as *Old Doc Methuselah* (1970). Using the same *nom de plum*, he did the Conquest of Space series for *Startling Stories*; and as Kurt von Rachen he wrote the Kilkenny Cats series for *Astounding*. Much of the content of these series was recycled space opera with swashbuckling, melodramatic adventures in epic proportions, but they were nevertheless clever, comic, sometimes satiric, and often memorable.

Hubbard used his own name in *Unknown*, a sister publication of *Astounding* also edited by Campbell. *Unknown*, largely because of Campbell's definition, published fantasy, as opposed to science fiction, but today much of what was printed in *Unknown* would have no trouble being accepted as science fiction.

Hubbard's writings took him finally to a codification of his psychological theories in the form of *Dianetics: The Modern Science of Mental Health* (1950). With this he left the field of science fiction writing altogether and founded the Church of Scientology in 1952. In the closely knit world of science fiction, Hubbard's actions were seen as abandonment and evidence of crass materialism. His worst critics accused him of debasing the artistic impulse by creating the supreme science fiction: scientology.

Hubbard returned to science fiction thirty years later with the publication of *Battlefield Earth* (1983), an enormous tome which became a best seller. In the introduction to this epic space opera, Hubbard repeatedly insists that he is proud to be a science fiction writer, "one of the crew of writers that helped start man to the stars." Hubbard's apologia in deed was his creation in 1983 of the Writers of the Future Contest, which not only gives recognition to undiscovered, talented authors, but also provides remuneration to working science fiction writers. In the past few years, there has been a resurgence of interest in Hubbard's earlier science fiction works, many of which have been reprinted and fill several shelves of the science fiction section of bookstores. He died on January 29, 1986. Hubbard was a controversial man, a man of many adventures and, happily for those who relish storytellers, a science fiction writer.

Themes and Style

Four classic Hubbard stories (later published in novel form) first appeared in either *Astounding* or *Unknown*: *Final Blackout* (1948); *Return to Tomorrow* (1954); *Fear* (1952); and *Typewriter in the Sky* (1952). All show Hubbard's mastery of pulp conventional cliches. Perhaps only Robert Silverberg has surpassed the "writing machine" facility with which Hubbard dashed off his works ("Fear" was written during one weekend). Although his facile prose approaches at times the hackneyed, in his classic works the psychological insights coupled with a lightning-paced plot completely blot out the flaws and propel the reader grippingly through Hubbard's fictive cosmos.

In his best works Hubbard propounds the theory of mind over matter. While Hubbard had no trouble absorbing the machine fixation or technological reverence of pulp science fiction which Campbell encouraged in his writers, Hubbard helped in many respects to explore and map the territory of "inner space" which would later become a key feature of New Wave science fiction. Hubbard has defined inner space in *The Invaders Plan* (1985) as beginning a half inch behind reality and ending on the other side of imagination. Whether he was examining the dark side of this mental landscape (*Fear* and *Death's Deputy* [1948]), the parallel worlds of the mind (*Typewriter in the Sky* and *Slaves of Sleep* [1948]), or the remarkably ruthless powers of a highly evolved mind capable of cosmic detachment (*Final Blackout* and *Return to Tomorrow*), Hubbard evinced a more than common understanding of human psychology.

Plot Summaries of Major Works

Final Blackout. The hero of this work is a soldier, known only as the lieutenant. He has survived not only many battles, but several governments and idiologies as well. The final, endless war has dragged on for so long that even materiel has been exhausted. There are no more airplanes, atomics, cannon, or even much food. Bands of soldiers, often from different countries, have congregated together to prey on other soldiers for food, boots, and weapons. A large number of soldiers have gathered under the lieutenant's command for mutual protection. He keeps them moving and free from hunger. He values his men's lives above all else.

Into this picture comes Captain Malcolm, a staff officer sent out to order the lieutenant back to general headquarters on the coast of France. After numerous harrowing experiences, the lieutenant manages to lead his men back to the staff operations position. No sooner do they arrive than the lieutenant is relieved of his command. In short order it becomes clear to the lieutenant and his men that the few remaining staff officers, including Captain Malcolm, have conspired to round up what remaining soldiers there are and use them to set up a feudal political country to the south. The lieutenant and his men foil the staff officers' plan and leave for England, where they cannily take over the repressive English government and replace it with a more egalitarian (but dictatorial) one. This new regime is headed by the lieutenant. The United States government's military gains control over the staff officers left in France and reinstate them as a puppet government easily controlled by U.S. corporate greed. The O'Henry ending keeps the reader guessing as to what will occur to the lieutenant and to England.

Published in *Astounding* in 1940, *Final Blackout*, a future history, was a controversial projection (the British refused to print it) of World War II. Its publication established Hubbard as a major science fiction writer. Political criticism abounds throughout the novel, but in typical Hubbard fashion this is interlaced with swashbuckling action and crafty psychological motivations. Once Hubbard sets his framing device or premise, he entertainingly and adroitly massages life into cliches and even manages to make militarism seem attractive. Many consider *Final Blackout* to be not only antisocial and antidemocratic, but also a paean to Fascism as well.

Return to Tomorrow. Alan Corday, an engineer-surveyor of the tenth class, is in a peculiar and desperate situation. He is well-educated and from a good family, but his father has just gone bankrupt. Hearing that the new duke of Mars is hiring, he spends the day at the space racks in New Chicago looking for possible ways to earn his passage on the rocket liner to Mars. To his dismay, his noble bearing and overqualifications dissuade potential employers from hiring him. Dejected, thinking of his betrothed sweetheart, he wanders aimlessly in the seedy section bordering the space racks, where space merchants and their crews pass the time. Drawn to some haunting music wafting out of a spacers' bar, he stumbles into the adventure of his life.

He wakes up in the sickbay of a spaceship, the *Hound of Heaven*, under the command of Captain Jocelyn. Alan realizes that he has been impressed into service and that the ship is on the "long voyage," a trip taken at the speed of light. Alan plots to escape, but Jocelyn foils his every attempt with the psychological deftness of a man accustomed to controlling and commanding a crew on a long voyage. The only fraternity, society, and peer group possible for the crew is within the ship, because history is distorted (for the crew) on the planets where they land. Alan discovers this on his first return to Earth, where he finds his former sweetheart an old, dying woman who does not even recognize him, while he has scarcely aged. Alan now becomes a willing crew member of the *Hound*. Utilizing his talents as an engineer-surveyor, he rapidly becomes second in command, although he has grave reservations about the moral rectitude of Captain Jocelyn. It is difficult for Alan to accept the impressment and psychological manipulation of the crew, but it is equally difficult to find competent people who want to leave Earth relationships behind forever. Ultimately Alan comes to respect Jocelyn, and even goes on to assume command of the ship. Alan, like Jocelyn before him, learns that what is right on one planet may well be wrong on another. The long voyage is a time trip through the universe with dramatic change at every port of call.

Like most of Hubbard's novels, this novel was first printed in *Astounding* as "To the Stars" (1950). This is vintage space opera with rockets, interplanetary travel, scientific gadgetry, time warps, and fast-paced adventure. Hubbard knows the formula well and could breathe life into the old conventions, as he was to do thirty years later with the best-selling *Battlefield Earth*.

Biographical/Bibliographical Readings

John P. Brennan, "L. Ron Hubbard," in *Twentieth-Century Science-Fiction Writers*, ed. by Curtis C. Smith (St. James, 1986), p.359-61. "L. Ron Hubbard," in *Contemporary Authors* (Gale, 1983), v.77-80, p.254-55. R. Reginald, "L. Ron Hubbard," in *Science Fiction and Fantasy Literature* (Gale, 1979), p.266. **[Milton Wolf]**

HUXLEY, ALDOUS

Life and Works

Aldous Huxley was born in Goldalming, Surrey, on July 26, 1894. He was a member of a distinguished family that included the poet Matthew Arnold and noted biologist Julian Huxley. He received a "First" in English from Oxford and during his college career began publishing poetry and helped edit several literary journals.

During the 1920s, Huxley's novels and collections of short stories gained him a growing reputation in the literary world. These early novels of contemporary British society satirize character types and social conventions of the time.

In 1932, Huxley's first science fiction novel, *Brave New World*, was published. While Huxley himself viewed *Brave New World* as an oversimplification, his assembly-line future vision is his most enduring success.

Huxley's next science fiction novel was *After Many a Summer Dies the Swan*, a satiric look at greed, aging, and the southern California lifestyle. Published in 1939, it has not acquired the lasting renown of *Brave New World*, though it was eagerly received on publication.

During the years of World War II, Huxley worked in Hollywood on screenplays for MGM, and his next work of science fiction did not appear until 1948. *Ape and Essence* is a novel set in screenplay format about life in twenty-second-century Los Angeles after an atomic war, framed in a present-day narrative concerning the narrator's search for the writers of the screenplay. Huxley spent the last ten years of his life experimenting with psychedelics, such as mescaline and LSD, which led to his book, *The Doors of Perception* (1954). His last science fiction novel, *Is-*

land, was published in 1962. Huxley died on November 23, 1963, the day after the assassination of John F. Kennedy.

Themes and Style

Huxley's science fiction novels tend to explore not so much the minute details of technology on the lives of individuals as the effects of technological trends on the societies of the future. He extrapolated these effects from contemporary trends, and sought to examine not what would necessarily be, but what might, for good or ill, conceivably be.

Brave New World was intended as a cautionary tale about the dangers inherent in advances in technology and social conditioning; the novel makes clear in highly ironic style that freedom must not be sacrificed to shallow ideas of progress. Characterization and plot take a back seat to Huxley's vision of a future society where conformity and standardization have become the norms, and deviation from these norms is not only a tragedy, but is viewed as a sort of crime against society.

After Many a Summer Dies the Swan concentrates on humanity's wish to gain, if not immortality, at least a greatly extended life. It is also concerned with manipulative relationships. Eventually a treatment is discovered which prolongs the life of the main character, but the conflict lies in whether or not the price is too high--is mere subsistence meaningful if the sense of humanity is lost? The story is set in southern California, as is *Ape and Essence*; it shows the interactions of a young scientist from New Zealand within the futuristic, debased Los Angeles society ruled with unbending brutality by a demon-worshiping theocracy.

Island is set in a utopian island in the Indian Ocean called Pala. The society envisioned by Huxley is one that has harmoniously combined the technological advances of the West with the spiritual insights of the East, a theme common to several of Arthur C. Clarke's later works. It is a fragile utopia, however, protected from the evil influences of the outside world only by its isolation, which can be easily shattered if outsiders discover it.

Plot Summaries of Major Works

After Many a Summer Dies the Swan. Jo Stoyte, an aging American oil millionaire, has let his fear of death and his greed come to control his life, and is funding research into longevity with hopes of attaining immortality. In his endless greed, Stoyte has acquired the Hauberk papers which allow his physician, Obispo, to proceed with the information necessary to advance his research in longevity. Stoyte and Obispo travel to the Hauberk estate and discover, as Obispo has deduced, that the Fifth Earl of Hauberk, now 201 years old, is alive but has generated into an inhuman, apelike creature living locked in a subterranean apartment. Stoyte, to Obispo's surprise, is willing to live even under these terrible conditions.

After Many a Summer Dies the Swan is a satiric novel most concerned with the search for immortality and the manipulation of human relationships. Stoyte uses his wealth to manipulate all those around him; and yet this same man, who fears death, derives a great deal of income from a cemetery which he owns. Stoyte wants power of life; Obispo seeks power of Stoyte. Throughout the novel chance plays a major part and, for all the struggle after power, much is determined by forces beyond anyone's control. Huxley also uses this novel to satirize, often brilliantly, the strange culture of southern California. The novel is not regarded as one of Huxley's best works. Characters spend too much time lecturing and much of the action is allegorical, but his picture of the dangers and excesses of power in 1938 must give the thinking reader considerable material for contemplation.

Ape and Essence. The novel opens in Hollywood in 1948 on the day Gandhi was assassinated, with the narrator and his friend discovering a movie script entitled *Ape and Essence.* The movie script introduces a dystopian society through the eyes of Dr. Alfred Poole, a member of the New Zealand Rediscovery Expedition to North America in 2108. America, devasted by atomic war, has become a wasteland inhabited by mutants. These mutants, led by the Arch-Vicar, practice a devil-worshipping religion which includes the sacrifice of newborns who do not conform to the new norm. Poole, lost and then abandoned by his expedition, is captured by the mutants but eventually escapes and runs away to the North.

Ape and Essence takes its title from Shakespeare's *Measure for Measure* and is a prophetic novel concerning the disastrous consequences if humanity continues to follow its apish or animal side without interference from its "glassy essence," or spiritual, side. In the novel, Huxley suggests that, even without atomic war, technology would eventually destroy the environment. Huxley insists that a soul-less technology and a world in which humanity ignores any contact with a higher moral sensibility is an empty and decaying world devoted to worship of the destructive idol of egotism.

Brave New World. In the brave new world of After Ford 632, babies are born exclusively from test tubes, and their futures are determined before birth, or "decanting," as Alphas (bright and attractive) or Epsilons (retarded and stunted). Children are conditioned from birth onward to rejoice in their respective classes and accept their destinies. Human nature has been effectively modified, and people are theoretically happier. They have little choice. Into this society comes the Savage, a mistakenly conceived child born of civilized parents who has grown to manhood on a Zuni reservation in New Mexico, an outcast in both the world of the

Indians and in mainstream society. His delight in the brave new world of civilization, where all is clean, attractive, and open, however, gradually turns to disgust with what he soon sees as an empty, hedonistic society, and eventually he is driven to suicide.

Huxley points out in *Brave New World* that many of our ideas come from social conditioning. In the novel, when a young man of artistic potential complains that the present society fosters no great art, he is told that great art most often arrives from great unhappiness and that sacrificing the happiness of many to stimulate art which affects only a few is illogical. The "outsider" character in this novel, the Savage, brings his own cultural biases in as well, having been raised almost solely on the works of William Shakespeare. *Brave New World* is at heart a discourse on the nature of freedom and happiness, and intelligently avoids making easy choices.

Island. Will Farnaby, agent of a capitalist seeking to exploit untapped oil reserves, is shipwrecked on the island of Pala in the Indian Ocean. There he works to initiate a coup to replace the antitechnological, antimodern culture of Pala with one more in keeping with Western twentieth-century values. Farnaby gradually comes to realize that Pala is a utopian culture, where the inhabitants have gleaned the best of Western and Eastern civilizations to produce a life-affirming, positive way of life. Farnaby, who has led a miserable life and is disillusioned and negative, finds healing and education on Pala through a series of teachers. The novel ends on a pessimistic note, as the destruction of Pala's happy culture and the exploitation of the island's resources seems inevitable. The main characters remain, however, and their philosophy and view of the human condition will persist.

Huxley, in presenting this stable utopian society, is nevertheless cognizant that Pala is fragile, protected largely by its isolation from the rest of the world. The various facets of the Palanese lifestyle are not new or unthinkable, but in order to work, must be isolated from whatever parts of the world that do not share the same guiding priniciples of nonviolent pacifism. Good intentions, however strongly held, will not push aside bullets when a confrontation arises. Much of *Island* consists of lectures given to Farnaby by various characters; the tension in the novel arises primarily from the conflict between Farnaby's initial life-denying negativism and his gradual education and acceptance into the life-affirming Palanese culture.

Biographical/Bibliographical Readings

Sybille Bedford, *Aldous Huxley: A Biography* (Knopf, 1974). Claire J. Eschelbach and Joyce Lee Shober, *Aldous Huxley: A Bibliography 1916-1959* (Berkley, 1961). Robert E. Kuehn, *Aldous Huxley: A Collection of Critical Essays* (Prentice-Hall, 1974).

Harold H. Watts, *Aldous Huxley* (Twayne, 1969). Lilly Zahner, *Demon and Saint in the Novels of Aldous Huxley* (Francke, 1975). [Candace R. Benefiel]

KEYES, DANIEL

Life and Works

Daniel Keyes was born on August 9, 1927, in Brooklyn, New York. After serving a two-year stint as a senior assistant purser in the U.S. Maritime Service, he attended Brooklyn College, where he received his bachelor's degree in 1950. He began his career in science fiction in 1951 when he became editor of *Marvel Science Fiction*. Keyes married Aurea Vazquez in 1952 and in 1953 he became the coowner of a photography business. In 1954, he was hired as a high school teacher in Brooklyn and while working as a teacher, he wrote short stories and matriculated at Brooklyn College. He earned his master's degree in 1961, quit his job as a high school teacher, and in 1962 became an instructor of English at Wayne State University in Detroit. He taught there until 1966, when he moved to Ohio University in Athens. He still works there as a professor of English.

Keyes' first published story, "Precedent," appeared in the May, 1952 issue of *Marvel Science Fiction*. His second story, "Robot-Unwanted," appeared one month later in *Other Worlds*. He wrote little else until 1959 when his best known short work, "Flowers for Algernon," appeared in the *Magazine of Fantasy and Science Fiction*. The story won the Hugo award for best short fiction in 1960. The full-length novel version of *Flowers for Algernon* (1965) won the Nebula award in 1966. The novel was made into a movie, *Charly*, in 1968, and its star, Cliff Robertson, won the Academy Award for its title role. Other works by Keyes include *The Touch* (1968), *The Fifth Sally* (1980), and *The Minds of Billy Milligan* (1981).

Themes and Style

Daniel Keyes likes to focus his stories on philosophical and psychological themes. His novels contain scientific methodology and human values as well. He is fascinated by the complexities of the human mind. In *Flowers for Algernon*, the question of scientific method and morality are raised as he unfolds the story of Charlie. Plato's rationalistic philosophy figures heavily in his writings. Keyes is not a prolific author, but he is an intelligent and thought-provoking one.

Plot Summaries of Major Works

Flowers for Algernon. The narrative is written in the form of "progress reports" chronicled by a mildly retarded man named Charlie Gordon. Charlie has an insatiable desire to become smart and begins attending classes for retarded adults taught by Miss Alice Kinnian. Through Miss Kinnian, Charlie learns of an experimental surgical procedure which removes the inhibiting brain material that prohibits intelligence and awareness and then chemically stimulates the brain. The operation has already been successfully performed on a laboratory rat named Algernon. Charlie volunteers for the operation and his intelligence soon approaches the genius level. He becomes an expert in all of the sciences and humanities, but unfortunately he also discovers that his intellectual growth has far outstripped his emotional growth. He cannot consummate his love for Miss Kinnian because part of the old Charlie Gordon is always holding him back. Algernon begins to show signs of recession, regresses to his state before the operation, and then dies. Charlie desperately tries to find some way of preventing his own regression, but discovers that he also will become as he was before.

When Keyes wrote *Flowers for Algernon*, he based it upon a philosophical theory of Plato's. The theory is called "Analogy of the Cave" and is found in Book Seven of the *Republic*. Plato believed that humans see only shadows of reality, and that there is a higher plane of reality that no one can see. When Keyes created the character of Charlie Gordon, he created a man who emerges from a dark cave of consciousness into a bright world of reality. Keyes makes liberal use of the words "cave" and "light" in the descriptions of Charlie's condition, and quotes Plato in two sections of the novel.

The beginning of the novel is written as if a retarded man had written it. Keyes wisely moves quickly to a more refined style so that the reader does not become frustrated. The use of "progress reports" helps to keep the timeline firmly in mind and adds to the horror of what is occurring to Charlie. Daniel Keyes has written a novel that is philosophically interesting, yet heartbreaking at the same time.

Biographical/Bibliographical Readings

John Clute, "Daniel Keyes," in *The Science Fiction Encyclopedia*, ed. Peter Nicholls (Doubleday, 1979), p.330. Stephen H. Goldman, "Daniel Keyes," in *Twentieth-Century Science-Fiction Writers*, ed. Curtis C. Smith (St. James, 1986), p.392-93. Susan Salter, "Daniel Keyes," in *Contemporary Authors New Revision Series* (Gale, 1983), v.10, p.263-65. [Eric Nudell]

KNIGHT, DAMON

Life and Works

Damon Francis Knight was born on September 19, 1922, in Baker, Oregon. He was the only child of two schoolteachers. Like many artists, he felt himself to be socially backward (he was shy, physically small and slight of build) and he retreated into books and other intellectual pursuits. He discovered science fiction in the pulp magazines as an adolescent and through these he soon was corresponding with other fans. At an early age he showed a penchant for drawing, which he put to good use in his own fanzine entitled *Snide*. After high school, he attended art school in Oregon for a year before he set out for New York City and the Futurians.

The Futurians were a clique of science fiction fans who longed to be writers and artists. Many of them later succeeded: Isaac Asimov, Fred Pohl, Cyril Kornbluth, James Blish, Judith Merril, Donald A. Wollheim, and, of course, Damon Knight. All were young (late teens), intellectual, avid science fiction fans, and generally broke and out of work. Living communally at times, they shared their dreams, their writings, and their failures. Knight commemorated this period in his book *The Futurians: The Story of the Science Fiction "Family" of the 30's That Produced Today's Top SF Writers and Editors* (1977).

Knight's original intention was to make a living by doing science fiction illustrations, but he soon found (as he did later with novels) that unless one could churn them out quickly, the market for short stories was more profitable. His first sale was a humorous cartoon to *Amazing*, and he did some work with Chester Cohen, a Futurian roommate, which they signed "Conanight." His first short story, "Resilience," for which he received no pay, appeared in the February, 1941 *Stirring Science Stories* (edited by fellow Futurian Donald A. Wollheim). Throughout the 1940s, he managed to sell a few short stories, sometimes using the pseudonym Stuart Fleming, and he did some collaborative writing with James Blish, but he failed to make a living as an author. In 1943, Frederick Pohl helped him get a job as assistant editor for Popular Publications, where he was assigned mostly westerns and detective stories. He worked periodically as a reader for a literary agency, then as assistant editor for *Super Science* when it was revived in 1949. About this time his brief marriage to Trudy Werndl deteriorated and was annulled. Shortly thereafter, he became involved with Helen del Rey (former wife of Lester del Rey), whom he later married.

In many respects, the 1940s were Knight's apprentice years, but the foundation he laid was a solid one and would enable him to become a major writer, editor, and critic of science fiction during the 1950s. His emergence was heralded with the publication in 1949 of "Not with a Bang" in *The Magazine of Fantasy and Science Fiction*. This end-of-the-world story displayed a wry sense of irony aimed at human foibles, and this irony was to become Knight's trademark. Fast on the heels of this success came "To Serve Man," published in *Galaxy* (November 1950), a witty and urbane story that once again exposed human gullibility when humans are confronted with cosmic concerns.

Another talent of Knight's also became noticeable during this period. As editor of *Worlds Beyond* (1950-51), Knight introduced a regular feature of book reviews--a column entitled "The Dissecting Table." His critical acumen had already been noticed in the fanzines, but now that he was receiving wider publication, his reputation mushroomed. His penetrating reviews, in which he refused to treat science fiction any differently from mainstream literature, were collected in 1956 in *In Search of Wonder*, and won him a Hugo award as the best critic of the year. This book, along with *Turning Points* (1977), and his numerous reviews and critical essays, established him as the father of science fiction criticism. In 1956, he and Judith Merril organized the now famous Milford Science Fiction Writer's Conference, utilizing the technique of mutual criticism, as practiced by the Futurians, as a way of analyzing stories.

Also during the 1950s, Knight began to produce novel-length science fiction. *Hell's Pavement* (1955) and *A for Anything* (1959) are both expansions of short stories. Two other novels were published in the 1960s, *Beyond the Barrier* (1963) and *Mind Switch* (1965).

Knight was never a prolific writer, and during the early 1960s, when his marriage to Helen del Rey fell apart (he later married Kate Wilhelm and added the responsibilities of her two sons to his own), he took more and more to anthologizing as a means of making money. His contacts as editor, writer and critic, as well as his intimacy with the classic works of science fiction, made him more than competent to bring together science fiction stories. His annual *Orbit* series of anthologies, which ran from 1966 through 1979, is generally considered to be a significant milestone in the science fiction field as a place where experimental and nonconformist stories were welcomed. In 1965, the year before the *Orbit* series began, he also made a lasting contribution to science fiction by creating the Science Fiction Writers Association (of which he was the first president), an organization devoted to the profesional status of science fiction literature; this was later the progenitor of the Nebula awards.

Knight was not alone in changing the boundaries of science fiction as it had evolved from the magazine pulps, and he was also a driving force in the 1950s as writer and critic. He helped make science fiction a literary endeavor and assisted others in enlarging the scope of the science fiction spectrum.

Themes and Style

Knight's alien stories were often in sharp contrast to those published in Campbell's *Astounding*, where humans were always superior technologically and morally. Knight's aliens often had to teach humanity to the humans (e.g. "Rule Golden," "The Earth Quarter," and *Mind Switch*). The urban future was another topic which Knight helped develop. Many of his stories were set in what appeared at first to be technological utopias, but as the plot unfolded, it became clear that the ultracivilized were really sophisticated barbarians (*A for Anything*). Knight was a dissector of the human condition; he excelled at exposing human pretentions and hypocritical poses.

Many of his heros were underdogs, persons not physically attractive or glamorous, but who could face an extremely difficult and dangerous situation with a calm, rational attitude of perseverance (*The World and Thorinn* [1968] and *Hell's Pavement*). Knight did not necessarily seek to glorify humanity but rather to understand it honestly. The swashbuckling, handsome, one-dimensional hero of *Astounding* was a cardboard representation for Knight; he did not flinch from portraying people with warts and character flaws. Most of Knight's villains are humorless beings, full of self-importance.

Plot Summaries of Major Works

A for Anything. Dick Jones, the oldest son of a wealthy plantation owner, is the product of three generations who have held the large estate of Buckhorn since Turnover occurred in the twentieth century, when an altruistic scientist sent gizmos through the mail to hundreds of people chosen at random. The gizmo is a simple device that duplicates anything that one already has. The scientist had hoped to present the world with a horn of plenty that would bring peace and prosperity. Instead, because of the shortcomings of human nature, it brought the Turnover--several hundred years of death and destruction as conflict raged concerning who would own and control the gizmos.

Dick Jones is lucky, in that his forebears won the war. They were white, landed, and aristocratic; they possessed both gizmos and black slaves, known as slobs. Science has waned since the introduction of the gizmo, and white society is patriarchal and antebellum in its organization. Life is good for Dick. He wins his first duel by killing a cousin at his farewell party, and when he returns to Buckhorn after four years in the capitol city of Eagles, he becomes the next "Man" to rule over the estate.

Eagles is the big city where first sons are sent to learn the best (and worst) that Turnover culture has to offer. Ostentatious displays abound and feudal intrigues are encouraged. It is said that before a man leaves Eagles, he will find his niche in life. Of course, all of this is supported by gizmos and slobs, leaving plenty of time for duels, dandies, dilettantes, and decadence. Dick survives it all, even the slave rebellion which reduces Eagles to a burnt cinder.

Dick is the quintessential protagonist of a Knight novel; he epitomizes human nature. Knight conveys humanity as basically flawed, and much of his work is black comedy, replete with wry irony. Dick survives like a Faulknerian character--not with much honor and not with much dignity, but alive. Knight seems to say that death ultimately releases humans from egocentrism, anthropocentrism, and greed. Knight takes his protagonists through the wringer, leaving only the maturity gained through trial and error as possible redemption. Dick's life is an excellent example of dogged persistence, in that it is not necessarily beautiful, but not necessarily worthless, either.

Knight is an honest writer who is not afraid to confront human weakness. He is not, however, a misanthrope. Much of what he writes, like Mark Twain's work, displays the wry humor of one who sees through the hypocrisy in which humans seem to revel. *A for Anything* debunks the myth that all people need to make them happy is material abundance. Humans are by nature hierarchical, Knight indicates. They are not really tragic, fortunately, because they are not really admirable. Knight's writings represents a sincere search for a mirror with which humanity might examine itself.

Hell's Pavement. Arthur Bass is a junior assistant salesman living in a future region of the United States known as Gepro (General Products), which borders on the territory of Unmerc (United Merchandise) and is separated from Unmerc by a patrolled high wall. The inhabitants of these two areas have been "analogued" by their respective governments so that they adhere willingly to the ideologies represented by the dictates of these rival corporate states.

Arthur tries to be a respected member of Gepro and conform by carrying out such rules as "the consumer is always wrong," but deep inside he fears his analogue is not working. After a series of humiliations and a rejection from the girl he wishes to marry, Arthur jumps the wall into Unmerc territory. In Unmerc, consumers are programmed to spend their credits on various physical pleasures, including sex, and Arthur quickly finds his way into these entertainments, but gives himself away as an alien to this society by his unfamiliarity with Unmerc customs.

Arthur is captured and brought back to Gepro, where he suspects that he will be executed. To his surprise, he finds that he is one of the Immunes, a small group of people for whom the analogue treatment is ineffective; the group has infiltrated the Gepro hierarchy, including a top Gepro executive, Archdeputy Laudermilk. Laudermilk enlightens Arthur to the Immune society and sends him off to an underground school for Immune agents. Showing great promise, Arthur is sent on a mission into Conind territory, where matriarchs oversee the analogued consumers. The story ends as Arthur, after numerous perils, comes to the painful realization that most people could not function without their analogue treatment.

The first chapter of a Knight novel seldom introduces the main characters, and *Hell's Pavement* is no exception. What is offered is an idea, a gadget, or gizmo which is then extrapolated on throughout the rest of the novel. In *Hell's Pavement*, this framing device is the analogue treatment, and it is presented by having the reader observe a former drunkard attempting to get a drink. Because he has had the analogue treatment he is mentally and physically incapable of drinking alcohol. While prohibiting a person from harm seems logically good, it soon becomes apparent that control of humans, through science or whatever, is fraught with moral dilemmas.

Reminiscent of Huxley's *Brave New World* and Orwell's *1984*, *Hell's Pavement* deals with themes which Knight has often examined: science versus humanity, psychological control of the masses versus individuality, and political repression versus freedom. Knight presents the irony that consumer societies, even if there is plenty to consume, cannot tolerate individuality, freedom of choice, of deviance from an arbitrary social norm. Whether it is big business extolling profits before people, law and order political platforms advocating behavior modifications, or science uber alles, even the best intentions, Knight is saying, seem to pave the road to hell.

Mind Switch. One day Martin Naumchik, a journalist for a major European newspaper, is visiting the Berlin Zoo. He stops outside the cage of a humanoid animal known as Fritz, a biped from the distant planet of Brecht. At the same time, in another part of the world, scientists are working on a secret experiment which involves time, matter, and space displacement. Suddenly, Martin Naumchik finds, to his horror, that he is no longer outside the cage looking in, but inside looking out. Worse than this, his brain is now in Fritz' body. Fritz, to his astonishment, finds himself outside his cage in a human body looking at a frantic biped who is banging on the glass in an attempt to get out. Having spent most of his own life in captivity, Fritz does not spend much time philosophizing, and immediately leaves the zoo.

The Brechtian biped is an intelligent creature who quickly learns languages and can easily mimic human actions. Even when Fritz had inhabited his native body and lived in the zoo, his cage had been more like an apartment, which he shared with Emma, another Brechtian biped. They both read newspapers, watched television, and even did clerical work within the confines of their cage.

Fritz does not fare too poorly in Martin Naumchik's body, and attempts to integrate himself into human society. As a reasoning and sentient being, Fritz acclimates by aping the actions of humans. Martin, however, now in Fritz' body, does not handle his situation quite as well. In typical human fashion, Martin rants and raves and causes the zoo officials a great deal of consternation. When Martin tells Doctor Gruck, the head of the zoo, what has happened to him, Gruck not only does not believe him, but feels that Fritz (as Gruck believes him to be) is just exhibiting the jitters because he has just been brought over from the Hamburg Zoo to mate with Emma. Finally, Martin is able to smuggle out a letter to a journalist colleague who, sniffing a good story, publishes Martin's revelations. Doctor Gruck, having no intentions of losing his coveted biped, convinces the public that it was only the intelligence of the alien creature which enabled him to create such a convincing hoax. Foiled in his attempt to escape, Martin displays all the attributes of a child who cannot have its way. His puerile antics thoroughly confuse Emma until Martin realizes, by biological impulse, what the zoo officials belatedly discover--that Emma is a male and that Martin is a female who is very interested in Brechtian biology.

Knight has said that this is one of his favorite stories, and it should be, for it has all his favorite ingredients: wry irony, science run amok, the panoply of human frailties, and the alien creature who is more "human" than humans themselves. This is quintessential Knight.

Biographical/Bibliographical Readings

Gardner Dozois, "Damon Knight," in *Science Fiction Writers*, ed. E. F. Bleiler (Scribner's, 1982), p.393-400. Damon Knight, *The Futurians* (John Day, 1977). Idem, "Knight Picce," in *Hell's Cartographers*, ed. Brian W. Aldiss and Harry Harrison (Weidenfeld and Nicolson), p.96-143. Vincent Miranda, "Damon Knight: A Bibliography," *The Magazine of Fantasy and Science Fiction* 51:5 (Nov. 1976), p.26-28. Theodore Sturgeon, "Damon: An Appreciation," *The Magazine of Fantasy and Science Fiction* 51:5 (Nov. 1976), p.17-25. [Milton Wolf]

KORNBLUTH, C. M.

Life and Works

Born in 1923 in New York City, C. M. Kornbluth began writing fantasy at an early age, producing his first publishable story, "The Words of the Guru," at age sixteen. During his teens he also became active in the Futurian Society, a gathering of the brightest young science fiction fans and writers which numbered Asimov, Pohl, Blish, and Wollheim among its members. Beginning in 1940 and ending in 1943, Kornbluth produced a huge number of science fiction stories, many of them using pseudonyms. In one issue of *Stirring Stories*, no less than four Kornbluth stories appeared under various pen names. Most commonly used were Cyril Judd, Cecil Corwin, Walter Davies, Kenneth Falconer, S. D. Gottesman, Paul Lavond, Scott Mariner, and Arthur Cooke. Many of these pseudonyms were used to help fellow Futurians managing low budget pulp magazines to fill their publication quotas. Like many science fiction writers, Kornbluth married a fellow fan, Mary Byers, in 1943. After service as an infantryman in World War II, he attended the University of Chicago, then left to become a rewriter for Trans-Radio Press. In 1949, he began another incredible stream of writing, finally turning to free-lancing in 1951. Kornbluth, though a prodigious writer, died suddenly from hypertension in 1958 at the age of thirty-five.

Most of Kornbluth's novels were highly successful collaborations. His first joint venture was the remarkable *Gunner Cade*, coauthored with Judith Merril in 1952 (using the pseudonym Cyril Judd), followed by the less successful *Outpost Mars*. In 1953, Frederick Pohl was having difficulty completing a manuscript and invited Kornbluth to help him, producing their most popular works, *The Space Merchants* (1952), *Search the Sky* (1954), and *Gladiator at Law* (1955). Pohl and Kornbluth won a Hugo award in 1973 for their short story "The Mutiny." After Kornbluth's death, Pohl completed their last joint work, the less notable *Wolfbane*, in 1959. Kornbluth produced three novels under his own name, *Takeoff* (1952), *The Syndic* (1953), and *Not This August* (1956). The most respected of these novels is *The Syndic*, which paints a very dark picture of a future controlled by organized crime, a rather humanistic group known as "The Syndic." Kornbluth's short stories have been collected in *A Mile beyond the Moon* (1958), *The Marching Morons* (1959), and *Best Science Fiction Stories of Cyril M. Kornbluth* (1968). In 1959, his wife published a memorial volume entitled *Science Fiction Showcase*.

Themes and Style

Kornbluth's fiction reflects a dark, sardonic humor. His finest stories, among them "The Little Black Bag," "One Last Man Left at the Bar," and "The Silly Season," are short, well-crafted pieces, often with a clear view of humanity's frail ethics and amorality. His best known longer work, regarded as his most memorable, is the highly controversial "The Marching Morons" (1951), with its terribly dark vision of a future Earth, populated with compulsively consuming idiots and managed by a harried group of intelligencia searching for a "final solution."

Kornbluth matured into a very bitter writer of complex moralistic tales. None of his novels have aged as well as his shorter works, if for no other reason than that recent facts have made his dark visions seem mere tokens when compared to the reality that surrounds us. He might well be considered the first of the New Wave writers, some ten years too soon. His early death ended a career that seemed destined to mature into a major talent of the 1970s and 1980s. Instead, his dark light was extinguished suddenly, leaving many manuscripts half-completed.

Plot Summaries of Major Works

Gunner Cade. Gunner Cade is a soldier who has been trained by the Spartan-like state from childhood to be a warrior in a postholocaust society. An expert in weapons and strategy, he is a mercenary foot soldier in the European wars. Suddenly becoming a pawn in a battle for control between several Terran and off-world colony figures, Gunner becomes a peronal tool, a weapon in the war, and is thrust from one inexplicable situation to another, each incident culminating in an attempt to kill him. Each betrayal erodes his devotion and love for the father figure, the Power Master. The climax of the story, which builds slowly from Europe, to the Venus colonies, to the smoldering ruins of the Pentagon, reveals to Gunner the futility of his training and loyalty, perhaps in time to save his life, as he is drawn by his growing love of the rebel leader Jocelyn into the rebellion forces on Mars.

Gunner Cade, coauthored with Judith Merril under the collective pseudonym of Cyril Judd, glorifies the foot soldier and is the forerunner for many of the state-raised soldier stories of Heinlein and Haldeman. Moody and satiric, the novel cries out against those who manipulate and command the military. The realism of the battle scenes and the grim reality of the battlefield are undoubtedly drawn from Kornbluth's experiences as a World War II foot soldier in Europe. Written in 1952, at the height of the Korean War and the McCarthy hearings, Kornbluth's dark view of war and organized conflict are provided an excellent outlet in this, one of the first futuristic foot soldier tales.

As with most of Kornbluth's writings, the style is very tight and exciting, with attention given to meticulous detail providing a tone of authenticity and believability. The glorification of the infantry soldier seems a well-worn theme today, but its appearance at the time in a science fiction market that pictured military heroes as officers and commanders, is remarkable. The dark and foreboding style and the smoldering ruins of the postholocaust society are combined by Kornbluth to paint a picture of a grim and forbidding future. Most critics regard Judith Merril's input into this novel and in their previous collaboration, *Outpost*, to be minimal.

"The Marching Morons." Honest John Barlow is a twentieth-century senator kept in a state of suspended animation until his accidental revival in a world turned topsy turvy. The so-called lower classes identified as the "very" less intelligent have reproduced out of control, while the upper classes, better educated and with higher intelligence, have practiced birth control. The result is a society bottom heavy with mental morons, kept in sluggish repair by the few remaining Normals. Each Normal has several positions, as there are too many complex tasks and too few capable of fulfilling the work. The cars are toys that have speedometers reading 250 miles per hour, when actually they are doing only about 25 miles per hour, with souped-up exhausts to give them the sound of power. The bumbling Barlow has his college degrees in fly-casting and game fishing. The situation becomes ominous as the frantic Normals turn to Honest John to help them find a solution. After all, he is the product of the savage twentieth century, and they were civilized. Honest John presents them with a clear choice proven to work and modeled on the holocaust genocide of Hitler.

This complex short story is perhaps one of the most memorable, darkest visions of human society ever written. Kornbluth's indictment of the human condition is, at first, humorous and emotionally satisfying. The rampant satire highlights the consumer as idiot, game contestants as moronic, and politicians as unnecessary. Kornbluth is very perceptive and prophetic in his vision that the danger of our technology is that too few people will be qualified to run the machinery. He takes one step beyond to the societal implications of such a revolution. The most disturbing undercurrent in this cautionary tale is the proposition that intelligence might be the final arbiter in the determination of society.

Not This August. The year is 1965. The United States government has surrendered to the combined military forces of China and Russia, the army has been disbanded, and the president has been shot by a firing squad. Billy Justin, an embittered veteran, is comfortably surviving as a small dairy farmer when one day the Soviets increase his weekly quota of milk production. Unfortunately for the Soviets, later the same day Billy becomes the lukewarm participant in an illegal transfer of weapon-grade plutonium. Against his better judgment and with increasing reluctance, Justin finds himself drawn into a rebellion against the occupying forces by various, more experienced plotters who appear to be using him to attain their own goals.

Any science fiction writer who has the courage to assign real dates to history runs the hazard of dating his material. Strangely enough, this is a very believable tale of an occupation of the United States beaten down by continuous wars and brushfires. The incredible amount of detail about daily life in a farming community and the personal courage of the individual receive thorough and complete treatment by Kornbluth. Clearly drawing on his experience as an infantryman in occupied Europe, Kornbluth relays the atmosphere of occupation that combines the dark despair of defeat with the slightly tarnished gritty glory of a resistance movement. Kornbluth's characterizations present the complexity and contradictions of each major character. The plots move quickly to completion, giving the reader an exciting, taut tale. The novel is one of only three solely authored by Kornbluth and reveals his strength as a potential mainstream writer as well as a significant antiwar propagandist.

The Syndic. Western America has been taken over by organized crime, called the Mob, and England returned to feudal barons. Eastern America is controlled by another organized crime group known as the Syndic, led by the Falcaro family. Charles Orsino is a small-time bagman for the Falcaros, gradually pulled into a spying mission as the result of his attempted assassination by his bodyguard. This is a world where the DAR has become a terrorist organization, priests obliterate priceless parchments to provide new writing surfaces, and the Navy is the motive force in the revolution. Orsino, under an alias, joins the rebellion to return the former government to power. Essentially a pirate organization with bases in druidic Britain, the North American government has retained its old labels, but its organization is savage and primitive.

In Korbluth's world, organized crime is a benign despot, casually dispensing justice and largesse to the masses of people. The so-called legal government, the police, are bumbling enforcers who answer to the Syndic. Morals consist of loose sexual ties, multiple marriages, and respect for the family. On the other hand, the government is a rigid disciplinary force full of registration, identification requirements, and savage brutality. The complex fabric of the novel suggests that organized governments are infinitely corruptible and damaging to personal freedom. Kornbluth subscribes in this novel to the supposition that who would govern best, governs least. And yet the entire thrust of the novel is that the average person is not free. People are controlled and manipulated by whatever organization they are subjected to. In *The*

Syndic, Kornbluth does not make use of technological innovations to any great extent, and creates a timeless vision of the darker side of societal forces.

Biographical/Bibliographical Readings

Malcolm Edwards, "C. M. Kornbluth," in *Science Fiction Writers*, ed. E. F. Bleiler (Scribner's, 1982), p.401-08. Damon Knight, "Kornbluth and the Silver Lexicon," in *In Search of Wonder* (Advent, 1967), p.146-49. Charles Platt, "C. M. Kornbluth: A Study of His Work and Interview with the Widow," *Foundation*, 17 (1979), p.57-63. Frederick Pohl, "Kornbluth: A Reminiscence," *Extrapolation* 17:2 (May 1976), p.102-109. Donald A. Wollheim, "Wellsians in Crisis," in *The Universe Makers* (Harper & Row, 1971), p.80-85. [Colleen Power]

KUTTNER, HENRY

Life and Works

Born on April 7, 1915, in Los Angeles, California, Henry Kuttner grew up in a home filled with the wares of his bookdealer father. Upon graduation from high school, he was hired as a manuscript reader by the Dorsay Literary Agency, where he rapidly gained proficiency in revising and editing fiction. An avid reader of *Weird Tales*, he met C. L. Moore as a result of his fan letter. In 1936, the first of his accepted stories, "The Graveyard Rats," appeared in *Weird Tales*. After a visit from Moore, Kuttner collaborated with her on their first coauthored story in 1937. Kuttner moved from California to New York to be closer to the publishing market, and in 1940 married Moore. During the war years, Kuttner entered the Medical Corps and served until 1945 at Fort Monmouth, New Jersey. The Kuttner/Moore collaboration became famous, as the authors invented many pseudonyms. Some issues of science fiction magazines during 1943 had as many as four stories by the Kuttners, all under different pseudonyms. Their creation of pen names became so well known that any new name to appear in the science fiction literature was suspected of being another Kuttner/Moore collaboration. In fact, until 1950, Jack Vance was thought to be another of their pseudonyms, to the extent that one directory included Vance under Moore/Kuttner. At least seventeen pseudonyms of the two are well known, including Lewis Padgett and Lawrence O'Donnell. Collected works of Kuttner's short fiction are *The Best of Kuttner*, volume one (1965) and two (1966). *The Best of Henry Kuttner* was published in 1975 with an introduction by Ray Bradbury. *Fury* (1950) was primarily his novel, published under the O'Donnell joint pen name. Published under the Padgett name was *Mutant* (1953).

After World War II, Kuttner and Moore moved to California where both entered the University of Southern California. He received a B.A. in English from USC and was working on a Master's degree until his untimely heart attack and death on February 4, 1958. Since 1953, they had been participating in writers conferences while teaching creative writing at USC. Kuttner did not limit his writing to science fiction and became very well known as a writer of suspense, mystery, and adventure stories as well. By 1956, their science fiction writing had declined, as the market for mystery stories expanded. Kuttner was still teaching at USC when Warner Brothers hired the couple to develop new television series. It was while writing the pilot script for the series "Sugarfoot" in 1958 that Kuttner died. Moore continued script writing and has become far less active in science fiction writing since that time. Throughout his life Kuttner was highly regarded as a finely honed word craftsman with a strong sense of humor running through many of his works. However, most of his active writing career occurred before the development of the various science fiction awards. Two of the collaborative short stories of Kuttner and Moore were selected for inclusion in *The Science Fiction Hall of Fame*--"Mimsy Were the Borogroves" (1943) and "Vintage Season" (1946). Although he never received an award, Kuttner is often praised by other writers for his contributions to the science fiction field.

Themes and Style

Henry Kuttner brought a freshness and a sometimes macabre sense of humor to contrast the rather stark and serious worlds of 1930s science fiction. C. L. Moore and Henry Kuttner have both stated that all works written by them after 1940 were collaborations, regardless of their bylines. However, each has identified certain works as primarily the product of one or the other. Even *Fury*, often attributed to Kuttner, is principally a collaborative work. Certain stylistic elements of Kuttner are present in many of their stories, as well as an often underlying humor. Many of their best stories deal with children, robots, or mad scientists--Galloway Gallagher, a zany inventor who constructs wonderful inventions when drunk, and forgets their purpose when sober, is an example of this slightly macabre mad humor. Some of the Gallagher stories have been collected into an anthology called *Robots Have No Tails* (1952). The most memorable and moving story is "Mimsy Were the Borogroves," in which two children find a puzzle box from the future which gradually trains and leads them from the present into a future their parents can neither understand nor follow. Kuttner stated that characterization was his principle weakness, while his strengths were theme and story line. In C. L. Moore's introduction to *Fury*, she indicates that her entries were full of color, while Kuttner provided the substance. Certainly, all their collaborative science fiction works have withstood twenty years of scrutiny. They have retained the freshness and excitement that was present in their initial appearance, and the world of science fiction is richer for their contributions.

Plot Summaries of Major Works

Fury. In the deep-sea zone of Venus, six hundred years after Earth's final holocaust death, Sam Harker begins his rebellion against the endless tedium of the aristocratic Immortals ruling the city. His hatred for the tall, slender, elegant rulers is based on his envy of their long, casual, uncaring years--years he is denied, restricted to his "three-score and ten." Working with Hale, a dissident Immortal, one of the last Free Companions that settled the surface of Venus six hundred years ago, he constructs a bizarrre plan to drive people from the safety of the domed cities to the savage jungle surface, promising them immortality. But in the midst of his schemes, the Immortals poison him with the addictive dream dust. Waking forty years later, he finds that he has not aged, that he is indeed an Immortal, altered at birth by his insanely grieving father to grow into a bald, squat, ugly man. Driven with renewed anger, he develops a final cataclysmic plan to destroy the domed cities and the sybaritic existence of the Immortals. With his savage hatred and driving ambition, he proves too dangerous even for his allies. Forced into suspended animation, Sam Harker sleeps awaiting the day when Venus might need his driving, dangerous ambition. The haunting two-word Epilogue leaves the reader in breathless wonder; "Sam woke. . . ."

Fury is based on a Venusian world created in Moore's "Clash by Night" and appearing originally as an *Astounding* serial in 1947. Kuttner's Venus has been scientifically debunked. There are no great seas, no savage jungles. However, Kuttner was not writing about Venus, he was writing about humans and their innate driving forces, the savagery that forces them from the comfort of an easy existence to the challenge of conquest. This is a novel of frontier life, of conquest and retribution. Sam Harker's calculating, smoldering anger, envy, and resentment provide a motive force that may reveal some uncomfortable truths. Sam is a fascinating antihero, a man devoted to anarchy and the darker side of the soul. Yet Kuttner demonstrates that even such a cruel manipulator can have a role, perhaps a necessary role in human expansion. The single most fascinating idea in *Fury* is the view of the Immortals. Other writers have used Immortals to create interesting plots, but Kuttner was the first to delve into the significance of immortality--that immortal beings have an eternity for plans to reach fruition, even though their concepts may be totally alien and their revenge equally bizarre. The novel was the only identifiably full-length science fiction novel written principally by Kuttner and manages to establish an incredible savage energy throughout.

Mutant. An atomic holocaust has created two new groups of humans, both telepathic, the Baldies and the Paranoids. Physically similar to humans, except for complete hairlessness, the two groups are completely inimical to each other and wary of normals. The novel is a series of short stories which reveal the evolution of the three-way confrontation over a two hundred year period. The episodes are tied loosely together by the reminiscences of a man trapped and possibly dying after a plane crash. "The Piper's Son" is set one generation after the Blowup. Ed Burkhalter, a Baldy telepath, begins to fear that his son son, Al, and his talented young friends are being mentally seduced by a Paranoid, a brilliant, egocentric and thoroughly obsessed branch of the Baldies. The grim resolution of the story is both sudden and unexpectedly savage as the Baldies band together to destroy the hidden Paranoids. In "Three Blind Mice," the Baldy Dave Barton, a big game hunter, cannot fit into the tame role that Baldies have adapted to in order to survive. His unique experience in tracking makes him ideal to hunt down human prey. He is recruited to work with Sue Connaught and Melissa Carr, two female Baldies, to locate three savage Paranoids that Melissa has identified as three blind mice. The fascinating tale rests on the attempt of one group of telepaths to overwhelm another, when their thoughts cannot be hidden. The hunter becomes the prey. The remainder of the stories are similarly constructed with seemingly Sisyphean tasks awaiting the Baldy heroes. Each story is concluded with a tightly constructed, sudden resolution.

Kuttner presents a fascinating portrait of what it might be like for telepaths to exist within normal human society, unable to fight--for they would always win, unable to excel--for they would draw hatred and envy to themselves and must be constantly on guard. An unintentional parallel might be drawn to the Jews of Europe in their desperate attempts to fit in and adjust to a society that alternately uses and abuses them, that fears and despises their differences; they must always live on the edge of destruction. In fact, the first Baldy stories appeared in *Astounding* in 1945, just as the facts of the Jewish holocaust were becoming widespread. All of the stories in this collection reflect an essential optimism regarding the future of the human race. While none of the stories is truly great literature, each is carefully plotted and crafted, revealing the strengths in Kuttner's writing and his ability to sustain suspense to the surprise endings.

Biographical/Bibliographical Readings

James Gunn, "Henry Kuttner, C. L. Moore, Lewis Padgett, *et al.*," in *Voices for the Future*, ed. Thomas D. Clareson (Bowling Green Univ. Popular Press, 1976), v.1, p.185-215. *Henry Kuttner: A Memorial Symposium*, ed. Karen Anderson (Berkley, 1958). "Henry Kuttner," in *Twentieth-Century Science-Fiction Writers*, ed. Curtis C. Smith (St. Martin's, 1981), p.313-14. Damon Knight, "Genius to Order: Kuttner and Moore," in *In Search of Wonder*, 2nd ed. (Advent, 1967), p.139-45. **[Colleen Power]**

LAFFERTY, R. A.

Life and Works

Raphael Aloysius Lafferty was born in Iowa on November 7, 1914. When he was four, his family moved to Oklahoma. Except for a year as a civil servant in Washington, D.C. and four years in the U.S. Army, his home has been Tulsa, Oklahoma. He worked for Clark Electrical Supply Company from 1935 until 1971, when he retired and began writing full-time.

Lafferty's first published science fiction story, "Day of the Glacier," appeared in *Science Fiction Stories* in 1960. In 1968, his first three novels, *Past Master*, *Reefs of Earth*, and *Space Chantey*, were published. These three novels established Lafferty as one of the New Wave American science fiction writers. He has written numerous short stories, including "Eurema's Dam," which won the Hugo award for best story in 1973. Collections of Lafferty's short fiction appear in *Nine Hundred Grandmothers* (1970), *Strange Doings* (1972), and *Does Anyone Else Have Something Further to Add?* (1974). In 1973, Lafferty won the E. E. Smith Memorial Award for Imaginative Fiction.

Themes and Style

Lafferty is a conservative Roman Catholic who has been opposed to the recent liberal activities in the church. He believes that there have been cycles of growth and destruction throughout history, and that humanity's destiny is to attempt to advance to higher levels of existence. Many of his works, such as *Fourth Mansions* (1969) and *Arrive at Easterwine* (1971), describe attempts to break through to this next level. Others, such as *Not to Mention Camels* (1976) and *Past Master*, also consider the nature of evil and the true definition of humanness. Some of his work, notably *Past Master*, stresses the necessity of death, the sacrifice of a leader or king, in order to revitalize a civilization and begin its rebirth. The fight between heaven and hell is an infinite one; Lafferty is describing only small sections of some cycles in this continuing war.

Lafferty's characters are people from tall tales, who delight in telling taller tales to each other and the reader. They are vital and full of life. Many characters are killed, but do not seem to stay dead, often returning in unexplained ways to continue in the story. They are exaggerated characters, archetypes of some aspect of the continuing struggle between good and evil that is Lafferty's most consistent theme. On one level, Lafferty is a contemporary version of the campfire storyteller; on a deeper level, he is writing allegories that warn of the dangers of evil. His later works are very pessimistic about the future of humanity. Lafferty is not unique in using science fiction to address the theme of good versus evil, but no other author has addressed it in such a vital, extravagant style.

Plot Summaries of Major Works

Arrive at Easterwine. The Institute of Impure Science is dedicated to discovering knowledge and the meaning of existence. Among its members and associates are a ghost, an individual from Ganymede, and a woman whose appearance seems to change constantly. The institute is attempting to achieve the next stage in human development, which they believe will be a group mind. After failing at genetic alteration, they create Epiktistes, nicknamed Epikt, a thinking machine containing mental impressions of many different people. Epikt has three tasks: to find a leader, a love, and a liaison. If it fails, there may be little hope for humanity to continue. Epikt and the institute do fail in each case because of outside opposition or lack of awareness of humanity's true nature. Epikt has grown in ability in the attempts, and is able to show the structure of the universe to institute members. At first dismayed by what seems to be a picture of decay and doom, they come to realize that they may be seeing the birth of worlds from a desolate background. Their efforts have failed, but they have learned a great deal in the process. They came close to that next step in development, and with Epikt's help, they will try again.

Arrive at Easterwine uses one of Lafferty's most frequent themes, that of the cyclical development of humanity and the need to strive for higher levels of being. Epikt and the Institute of Impure Science are subjects of many of Lafferty's stories; they always search for new answers to the questions of the meaning of life, but never succeed. Epikt's name is derived from epiklesis, a liturgical invocation of the Holy Spirit. Representations of the Virgin Mary, Christ, and Satan are all generated to some extent within Epikt. Even with such archetypal and allegorical references, the novel is full of fun. Lafferty's vitality and love of language, of jokes and puns are pervasive. Lafferty's exuberance invites his readers to explore his religious allegories.

"Eurema's Dam." Albert was always dumb, or so everyone believed. He could not learn to write or do mathematics, so he cheated by inventing tiny machines he could hide in his hand to do the work for him. His attempts to build a machine that was not afraid of girls had mixed results. The machine was so successful that the girl preferred it to Albert. Albert, having learned not to make anything that he could not unmake, blew up the machine and, unfortunately, the girl. Albert created devices that made life easier for him, such as one that removed smog and another that frightened teenagers into behaving politely. Albert made devices in human shapes: they were on many national and international councils. Because Albert felt lonely, he made a friend--a machine that was as dumb as he was. When Albert overheard his friend being lectured by another machine about the inadequacy of inventors, he destroyed them both. Albert still had no friends and he seriously considered suicide when Hunchy, one of his machines, persuaded him to take another look at the world. Instead of seeing a perfect world that had no place for someone as dumb as Albert, he found a world of patsies that had no idea how to cope with something or someone unusual. The world was ready to be taken out by two con men for some fun. It could be the beginning of a new life for Albert and Hunchy, and a new era for the world.

"Eurema's Dam" is about a lonely man who wants a friend and about the nature of invention and creativity. Albert only wants to make his life a little better; his inventions are the result of his unhappiness and restlessness. Those who are content and satisfied will not need to invent new things nor create new works. Frustration, believes Lafferty, is a necessary stimulus for innovation.

Fourth Mansions. Human history is cyclical; periods of advancement end in destruction, which are followed by gradual rebirth and subsequent destruction once again. Humanity's attempts to break through to an advanced state of being, the mystical Fourth Mansion of St. Theresa of Avila, have been stopped by a conspiracy. There is a group of personalities, known as the Returnees, who return, life after life. They try to prevent the advancement to the Fourth Mansion because they want to keep the world as it is for their own pleasure. They are opposed by the Harvesters, who want humanity to advance.

Freddy Foley is a reporter who learns about the conspiracy of the Returnees. The Harvesters have joined in a mental link, which they call brainweaving, allowing them to influence the minds of others toward humanity's advancement. Foley, brushed by this power, can sense what is happening in distant locations and see the patterns of the conspiracy. He becomes aware that the time of peace, prosperity and achievement is about to end. When he learns too much about the Returnees who are causing the decline, they capture him and attempt to replace Foley's mind with the mind of a new Returnee. Because Foley has been touched by the power of the brainweaving, he is changed into something unforeseen, a mixture of the powers of both groups. The result of this combination of the Harvesters and the Returnees is a mystery. It may enable humanity to go on the Fourth Mansion, or it may cause another cycle of destruction.

On one level, *Fourth Mansions* is the story of a reporter's investigation of an implausible conspiracy involving kidnapping, false identities and war. The reader is swept up in the swiftly moving plot by Lafferty's unique style. His writing is vivid, colorful, and extravagant. His characters are endowed with a passionate desire to live life to the limits. *Fourth Mansions*, like all of Lafferty's work, has multiple levels of meaning. It is a meditation about the war between good and evil, with an ambiguous ending that reflects Lafferty's view of the cyclical nature of existence.

Past Master. Astrobe is a former Earth colony that has surpassed its mother world and become the central planet of human civilization. It is a world without poverty or misery, with the arts open to all, without physical or mental illness. It seems to be a utopia, but there are grave problems. Millions of people have deserted this perfect life, either through suicide in comfortable, neat Termination booths, or by moving into one of the new and terrible slums. Cathead is the largest of these slum cities, larger than any other city on the planet. It is a teeming, polluted place where work is very dangerous, where dead bodies are stacked in the streets, and where there is grinding misery and poverty. The rulers of Astrobe want to find a leader to save the colony. They do not feel that any of their contemporaries are qualified and turn to humanity's past for their candidate. They decide to bring back Sir Thomas More because of his popularity and leadership, and because he did have one moment of true honesty, which is more than most people have had.

More, transported to the future, is shocked by the misery and savagery of Cathead, but also disturbed that the structure he created in *Utopia* as a satire has been used as the basis for Astrobe civilization. His distrust of the ease of Astrobe and concern about Cathead lead More to doubt the validity of the philosophy behind the existence of Astrobe. This makes him a threat to the Astrobe Dream, and a target for the mechanical men who can read minds and are programmed to kill anyone who is a danger to the dream. Their initial efforts to kill More are unsuccessful, and they eventually stop as More appears to accept the dream. More is selected president, never realizing that his mind is being controlled by a group of Programmed Men. These Men are mechanical creations and worship Ouden, the great Nothingness. They intend to use More to outlaw all remnants of belief in an afterlife as part of their plan to eliminate everything and return the universe to nothingness. As in his earlier life on Earth, when he would not swear obedience to Henry VIII as head of the church, More faces an ultimate choice; he refuses to sign the bill that forbids belief in the "beyond" in any form. After vetoing it three times, More is sentenced to death by beheading. More's followers and the men who had him brought to Astrobe believe that his death will be the yeast that will trigger the rebirth of their world. They hope that More's death and the rebellion that follows will be sufficient to allow a new cycle to begin.

Past Master is an allegory of good versus evil and of belief versus nothingness. Lafferty's characters live life to the fullest, denouncing those who are unwilling to experience emotion. On Astrobe, millions leave a life without love or hate for the pain and misery of the slums simply to be able to feel something. Lafferty uses Christian symbolism, with More as a king whose death may be the salvation of his people, betrayed into execution by a friend and companion. As with most of Lafferty's work, there is no conclusion. Everything waits to see if More's sacrifice was sufficient to cause a new cycle to begin for humanity. *Past Master* is an analysis of the utopian dream and of the nature of humanity.

The Reefs of Earth. Earth has a very poor reputation. Its people are hostile and unconcerned with their environment. The Puca are an alien race with unusual powers; they can make verses that can kill, talk with ghosts, and foresee the future. Puca are allergic to the fearful, alienated Earth; if they remain on Earth, they die. Two Puca brothers and their wives have come to Earth to see if anything can be done to save the planet. Their children, born on Earth, are immune to the sickness that quickly kills the adults. One of the women dies swiftly of the Earth allergy. The brothers, murdered by a local sheriff and his men, are avenged by one of the Puca children and an Indian woman. The remaining Puca adult, dying of the allergy, advises the children that Earth is now theirs to remake as they wish. They may want to kill off all humans, and indeed some deaths may be necesssary to make Earth adapt to them, but they may also want to leave some humans alive. Nothing stands between the Puca children and the future of Earth.

The Reefs of Earth is full of unique, sometimes absurd, details, such as the car with an automatic pilot that includes a factor for determining which direction a pig in the middle of the road will run at night, or the Indian burial mound that is so full that its inhabitants refuse to accept any new burials. The novel is full of black humor, with numerous bloody deaths described in ironical verse. It is also about transformations. The Puca aliens will change Earth, for better or worse. The Puca are primitive and powerful, but whether or not they will redeem or destroy human-ity remains unresolved.

Biographical/Bibliographical Readings

Chris Drumm, *An R. A. Lafferty Checklist: A Bibliographic Chronology* (Chris Drumm, 1983). Patricia Ower, "R. A. Lafferty," in *Twentieth-Century American Science-Fiction Writers* (Gale, 1981), v.1, p.250-55. "R. A. Lafferty," in *Speaking of Science Fiction: The Paul Walker Interviews* (Luna Publications, 1978), p.11-23. [Linda K. Lewis]

LAKE, DAVID J.

Life and Works

David Lake was born in India on March 26, 1929, of British parents. He was educated at St. Xavier's School in Calcutta and Dauntsey's in Wiltshire. From there he attended Trinity College Cambridge, graduating in 1952. He added to his B.A. a diploma in education and one in linguistics from the University College of North Wales.

Before emigrating to Australia and becoming a naturalized citizen in 1975, he lectured extensively in several countries in the Orient, including Thailand and Vietnam. He held a position at the University of Queensland, Brisbane, Australia, as a lecturer and completed his Ph.D. there in 1974.

Lake's critical work on H. G. Wells ("The White Sphinx and the Whitened Lemur: Images of Death in *The Time Machine*,") was published in *Science Fiction Studies* (v. 6, 1979) and indicates both his interest in the genre and his love of Wells. He has written two stories drawing on *The Time Machine*. "The Man Who Loved Mor-locks" (1981) is a sequel to Wells's work, and his short story, "Re-deem the Time," is a retelling of *The Time Machine*.

Walkers on the Sky (1976) was followed by the Breakout se-ries--*The Right Hand of Dextra* (1977) and *The Wildwings of Westron* (1977) being the first two volumes. In 1980, Lake published *The Fourth Hemisphere*, and his most recent work is *The Ring of Truth*, published in 1986.

Many of Lake's novels were published in Australia and are not readily available in the United States. His short stories can be found in Australian anthology collections published by Void, Out-back, and Quartet.

In addition to his science fiction, Lake has an interesting collection of published work. He published a book of verse, *Horn-pipes and Funerals*, which reveals both his sense of humor and his pessimism. He has also written on John Milton's *Paradise Lost*, Greek tragedy, and Thomas Middleton's plays.

Themes and Style

The major stylistic element linking Australian writers is the clarity of the alien worlds that they create. Lake has said that when he first flew over Australia the desert made him think he was over a distant planet. This is reflected in his novel, *Walkers on the Sky*. His creations of alien beings, planets, and sensibilities are a major strength in his work, and his ideas are also drawn from his Asian experience.

Thematically, Lake's work centers around the experience of colonists sent to far distant planets and their encounters with alien beings. Lake acknowledges elements of Blake and Lewis in his science fiction; this is particularly evident in *The Right Hand of Dextra* and *The Wildings of Westron*. In the Dextra books, the colonists are puritanical as they incorporate the aliens, but it is the Dextrons who are the innocents. One of Lake's major themes is the reflection of the colonial situation with aliens corresponding to Asians.

Lake's pessimism is balanced by his humor. He does not foresee a particularly good future for humanity in regard to human relationships with aliens. He veils his seriousness with a thin veneer of humor as he makes fun of politics, religion, sex, and the progress of the human race.

Plot Summaries of Major Works

The Fourth Hemisphere. Earth has been destroyed, but survivors have colonized other planets, managing to retain a cold war mentality. Andrew Adams is sent to 54 Piscium, an Earth-type planet, on a mission to convert the inhabitants to capitalism before the communists reach them. He finds a renaissance world of slavery and sexism, strange inventions, and legends. Living as a steward brings him to preach against the system. This necessitates his leaving, and he ends up on an expeditionary voyage to find New America. He has resolved to save the Piscians from the same mistakes his own ancestors made. The New Americans are very different from his expectations. They eventually leave him with decisions to be made concerning his new Eden.

The world Lake creates is like Earth, but with strange trappings and the evolution of a higher humanity. Lake has indulged in the creation of marvelous new societies, customs, physiologies, and mental attitudes. It carries traits of the medieval visualizations of the new world. Like Gulliver, Adams is in the position to examine and be party to all the political, religious and sexual institutions of a new society. Lake's central idea is the initial motivation of the capitalist message and its implication in New America. The novel also embodies his ideas on colonization, with his cameo of the European arrival in America. His revelations of the utopia to be found still adhere to his overall pessimism and his comments on the nature of humanity. He tells the tale with great humor, however, and his descriptions of flora and fauna are clear and intriguing. Lake definitely writes science fiction in an older, referential style, taking a random exploratory plot and turning it into a sharp satire of contemporary fears and the mores that form them.

Walkers on the Sky. Signi Sigmison signs on as a guard on a spaceship and travels to many varied and different lands. The planet Melior was terraformed by Earth colonist 10,000 years before. The original crew made themselves immortal through advanced medicine and are known as the "Gods." The terraforming of the planet was achieved by encircling it with a series of three concentric forcefields; the inhabitants live under the outermost forcefield sphere. Beneath them lies the middle world, a realm of classical and medieval kingdoms. The cities are built on mountains or islands of soil resting on the forcefields. Between these kingdoms, sailing ships skate along on top of the forcefield. Signi's ship is attacked by pirates and he escapes to a vaguely Roman society based on slave labor. Signi escapes and manages to break through the actual surface of Melior to the netherworld. This is populated by very primitive peoples, including a group who have the means to fly. Signi organizes the netherworlders to fight the society he escaped from, who plan to enslave them.

The central theme of the novel is how people are shaped by their culture and environment. The Gods have designed the various cultures after Earth models ranging from Viking to Etruscan. The Gods control their creations by forbidding technology in an effort to avoid the problems of high technology experienced on Earth. Signi acts as a pawn and, like chess, power and powerlessness are also themes of the book. The power actually rests not in the hands of the slavers, but in those who have direct control of society. The hierarchical structure of Melior reflects its social system, with the Gods on top and the primitive inhabitants below. The societies that are utopian are thus only because they were designed on utopian lines rather than the development of a perfect society. The Gods themselves are not even free from their own cultural upbringing, which affects their ability to effectively create new forms or possess absolute creative license.

Biographical/Bibliographical Readings

John Clute, "David J. Lake," in *The Science Fiction Encyclopedia*, ed. Peter Nicholls (Doubleday, 1979), p.340. "David J. Lake," in *Contemporary Authors New Revision Series* (Gale, 1983), v.10, p.280. Michael J. Tolley, "David J. Lake," in *Twentieth-Century Science-Fiction Writers*, ed. Curtis C. Smith (St. James, 1986), p.418-20. [Nickianne Moody]

LAUMER, KEITH

Life and Works

Keith Laumer was born on June 9, 1925, in Syracuse, New York. He entered the U.S. Army at the age of eighteen and served from 1943 to 1946 in the European theater during World War II. He attended the University of Illinois from 1946 to 1949, studying architecture. A year at the University of Stockholm earned Laumer a science degree, followed by a second bachelor's degree in architecture from the University of Illinois in 1952. After graduation, Laumer went back into the armed forces, serving as a lieutenant in the Air Force from 1953 to 1956. From 1956 to 1958, he was in the U.S. Foreign Service in Rangoon, Burma. Reentering the Air Force yet again, Laumer held the rank of captain from 1960 to 1965. Since 1965, he has been a full-time writer.

Laumer's first science fiction story, "Greylorn," appeared in 1959 in *Amazing Stories*. Since then, he has turned out over forty science fiction short stories, fifty books, and thirty articles on model airplanes. His major critical acclaim began with a Nebula award nomination in 1965 for *A Plague of Demons*. He has received other Nebula nominations: for best novel--*Earthblood* (1966); for a serialization--"Seeds of Gonyl" (1970); for best novelette--"The Body Builder" (1966), "Once There Was a Giant" (1968), and "The Plague" (1970); for best short story--"Prototaph" (1966), "The Right to Revolt" and "The Right to Resist" (both in 1971), "In the Queue" 1971 (which also received a Hugo nomination); and for best novella--*The Day before Forever* (1968) and *The Wonderful Secret* (1977), also a Hugo nominee. Laumer has never won the top prizes for science fiction writing, but his many nominations indicate the steady quality of his work. Several collections of his short stories have been published--*Nine by Laumer* (1967), *Greylorn* (1968), *It's a Mad, Mad Galaxy* (1968), *The Best of Keith Laumer* (1977), and *The Galaxy Builder* (1984).

Themes and Style

Laumer is a prolific author who has mastered a variety of science fiction forms. He developed three series, plus a large number of unrelated individual books. His basic theme, apparent in nearly all of his books, is a straightforward "good triumphs over evil" story. This end is often accomplished by a superhero who single-handedly defeats seemingly overwhelming odds to whip the foe and/or win the fair maiden. Laumer's treatment of the fair maiden is usually shallow; her body is well developed but her character is not. The superhero concept appears in *A Plague of Demons* (1965), *Glory Game* (1973), *Infinite Cage* (1972), *The Long Twilight* (1969), *Star Treasure* (1971), *Ultimax Man* (1978), and even *Bolo* (1977), where the superhero is a supertank with a conscience.

One of Laumer's most profitable series involves the adventures of J. Retief, interstellar diplomat and trouble shooter extraordinaire. Through at least ten volumes, Retief travels to alien worlds and ignores bureaucracy to negotiate for his superiors in the Corps Diplomatique Terrestrienne. This series does not exemplify Laumer's best writing, but the stories are fast-moving, sometimes humorous (albeit somewhat cutesy), and may remind the reader of real Terran diplomatic bloopers. The Lafayette O'Leary series--*Time Bender* (1966), *World Shuffler* (1970), and *Shape Changer* (1972)--are written in a broad comic style that is not particularly effective. Better by far is the *World of the Imperium* (1962) and its sequels--*The Other Side of Time* (1965), *Assignment in Nowhere* (1968), and *Beyond the Imperium* (1981)--which are particularly successful in the development of parallel worlds. An important theme in this series and in several of Laumer's other works is the manipulation of time as in *Dinosaur Beach* (1971), *The Day before Forever* (1967), and *Night of Delusions* (1973). Laumer handles this complex and intricate concept with grace and intelligence. Laumer at his best is imaginative, unpredictable, and very literate.

Plot Summaries of Major Works

The Day before Forever. Steve Dravak wakes up in a world he has never known--the city is different, the language not quite the same. After being in a brutal fight, a little man named Jess finds Steve bleeding to death, and patches him up for a price. Jess wants Steve to help him break into ETORP, Eternity Incorporated, the cryonic center which controls birth permits, organ transplants, cosmetic surgery, and longevity treatments. ETORP controls life itself, and distributes it to all who can afford the exorbitant prices. Steve discovers that he is not the middle-aged man his memories tell him he should be; he is quite young. Strange memories from his past float to the surface, assisting in his search for answers. Steve and Jess make it to an underground vault beneath ETORP, where they find a corpse holding a clue in his mummified hand. Steve has a feeling of deja vu and realizes that he has been here before and has worked with the dead man in the battle against ETORP. Security forces discover Steve and Jess, chase them through the underground labyrinth, and Jess is killed. The clues, plus Steve's own memories, lead him to a cabin in the wilderness of Wisconsin, where he discovers a little girl frozen in a tank, and then to a castle where he comes face to face with the man he seeks. The man who runs ETORP is Steve Dravak. The last pieces of the puzzle fall into place; the little girl is his daughter, Duna, who has been electrocuted in an accident and frozen to await medical treatment. The original Steve had cloned himself several times and then frozen himself so as to be alive when medicine had evolved to the point that Duna could be saved. His clones have manipulated ETORP into a powerful and inhumane operation. He has Duna revived, and together they run ETORP in a much more humanitarian way. All does not end well, however, as Steve discovers one day that yet another Steve Dravak (Number 8) has awakened somewhere, and is on his way.

The Day before Forever has a very intricate plot line, a kind of serial character development. It is like a big jigsaw puzzle, with each successive Steve clone adding another piece to the puzzle. This theme, along with parallel worlds and time travel, is intellectually demanding and fascinating. Steve is typical of the larger-than-life hero in Laumer's stories. The fate of the world depends on him because he is battling a corporation which has power over life and death, even immortality. Although he uses violent means, his humanitarian goals justify them.

A Plague of Demons. When Superspy John Bravais is hired to find out what is happening to the war dead, he does not realize what he is getting into. He observes an unearthly creature, resembling a canine species gone mad, removing the brain from a casualty of a Middle Eastern war and, when he tries to report it, finds himself fighting with a superhuman general, mortal but enhanced with powers such as Johnny has never seen before. His contact, Felix, helps Johnny become powerful, too, and builds defenses into his body--he can lift over 2000 pounds, visualize things in the ultraviolet range, increase the acuity of his hearing, and various other feats. The dog creatures kill Felix, but before he dies, he tells Johnny of a safe place in America. Johnny stows away on a submarine and makes his escape to America, but after several battles, the hounds from hell finally corner and kill him. His brain awakes encased in a huge war machine, a gigantic tank engaged in an endless war against other war machines, directed by human brains taken from eons of wars in dozens of star systems. Johnny has to fight to gain conscious control of his brain and remember his human past, but once free, he learns how to free some of the other brains and persuades them to join him in a mad fight for freedom. They are able to defeat some brigades by being able to think creatively, as humans, and to defeat others by freeing some of the mechanized warriors. Finally, Johnny and a few staunch allies break into the seat of power and Johnny defeats the Overmind and demons that defend it. Many of the victorious war machines choose to go back to Earth and find bodies for their brains to live in, but Johnny decides to stay on in the outposts of civilization, protecting humanity in its reach for the stars.

Leave it to Keith Laumer to provide a totally unexpected twist. Whoever heard of a superhero dying halfway through an adventure story? But die he does; superhero John Bravais has to meet the supreme challenge of regaining his status without his body. The first part of this novel reads like a James Bond episode with supergadgets developed to help Johnny fight the extraterrestrial creatures. In the second half, he has the huge tank as the biggest gadget of all. As always, the values embodied by Laumer's superheroes are present: loyalty, justice, bravery, integrity, and a dedication to an idealized, cooperative, democratic society.

Ultimax Man. Dammy Montgomerie is about to be killed by some of his underworld colleagues in criminal Chicago when he is rescued by Zorielle, who steps in and transports Dammy to another place. Zorielle appears to be an elderly, kind little old man, interested only in helping Dammy to recover his strength and learn some new skills. The old charlatan has some incredible teaching machines which instruct Dammy in karate, cribbage, basket-weaving, and intergalactic travel. Being a suspicious, small-time Chicago hood, Dammy learns more than his tutor intends. Zorielle has been merely experimenting with Dammy, and intends to exterminate him; Dammy steals a spaceship and escapes. In his ensuing adventures, the full range of Dammy's incredible education is used to elude threatening creatures on other planets. The ability to manipulate matter using only his brainpower enables Dammy to change poisonous alien plants into edible food which he can teleport directly into his stomach, to rearrange his own molecules to escape from a variety of prisons, and to master the art of levitation. Finally Dammy meets a nearly two million-year-old man whose skills rival his own. Together the two explore life, death, and human potential.

Laumer's writing often involves a superhero, and Dammy is no exception. He is, in fact, the ultimate superhero. The difference is that the adventures are secondary to the development of Dammy's character and value system. The interrelationship of the two supermen and their eventual concentration on developing human potential on Earth is a "good triumphs over evil" theme familiar in Laumer's work, but the action takes place inside Dammy's character, rather than on a battlefield.

Biographical/Bibliographical Readings

"Keith Laumer," in *Speaking of Science Fiction: The Paul Walker Interviews* (Luna Pubs., 1978), p.101-06. Charles Platt, "Keith Laumer," in *Dream Makers* (Berkley, 1983), v.2, p.113-22. Hugh M. Ruppersburg, "Keith Laumer," in *Twentieth-Century*

American Science-Fiction Writers (Gale, 1981), v.1, p.255-63. [Kay Jones]

LE GUIN, URSULA K.

Life and Works

Ursula Kroeber Le Guin was born on October 21, 1929, to an academic family, and has been associated with the academic life ever since.   Her parents, Alfred Louis, anthropologist, and Theodora Kracaw Brown Kroeber, writer, introduced her to the intercultural sympathy and empathy so evident in much of her writing.   Le Guin has two older brothers, Theodore Charles and Karl, as well as an older half brother, Clifton, from her mother's earlier marriage to Clifton S. Brown, who died in 1923.   Her father's work with Native Americans and his sharing of their mythology laid the foundation for the lyric mythology in *The Dispossessed: An Ambiguous Utopia* (1974), *The Word for World Is Forest* (1977), *The Eye of the Heron*, and other novels.   Her mother's book, *Ishi in Two Worlds* (1961), is an ethnological classic.

Le Guin's education did not follow the anthropological trail blazed by her father, however.   Her B.A. degree from Radcliffe in 1951 showed her interest in French and Italian Renaissance literature.   She then completed an M.A. at Columbia University and began doctoral studies.   She was awarded a Fulbright scholarship to study a French poet, but met Charles Le Guin and married him in France on December 25, 1953.   She worked while Charles was completing his doctoral training and turned to full-time writing after he began teaching.   Daughter Elisabeth was born in 1957, Caroline in 1959, and son Theodore in 1964.   Much of Le Guin's writing during this period was poetry, some of which appeared in little magazines.   During the 1950s, she wrote five unpublished novels and several short stories.   Her first publication was the short story, "An die Musik," which appeared in *Western Humanities Review* (Summer, 1961).

Although her first published works were short stories, many of them contained the seeds of later novels.   "The Word of Unbinding" and "The Rule of Names" both contributed to the Earthsea trilogy, and "Semley's Necklace" was the first of many Hainish stories.   "Winter's King" set the stage for the classic *The Left Hand of Darkness* (1969).   Much of her early critical acclaim was due to her lyric, poetic style offered as an alternative to the macho, technological tone of much of the science fiction of the current time.   In 1966, Le Guin's first two novels appeared: *Rocannon's World* and *Planet of Exile*.   These were the first installments in what came to be called the Hainish cycle.   The entire cycle covers approximately 2500 years and relates many aspects of the race of people from Hain who colonized planets across the galaxy. The novels did not appear in chronological order: *Rocannon's World* is set in League Years 250-350, while *Planet of Exile* takes place in League Year 1405. The next Hainish novel to appear is *City of Illusions* (1967), which adds another story to the lives of the people in *Planet of Exile* some seven hundred years later. *The Left Hand of Darkness* (1969) is the next novel to appear in the Hainish cycle and is considered Le Guin's best book, winning both the Hugo and Nebula awards. Her novella, *The Word for World Is Forest*, received a Hugo award in 1973. The most recent Hainish novel, *The Dispossessed: An Ambiguous Utopia*, was published in 1974 and won the Hugo, Nebula, and Jupiter awards for best novel. A duality is created by two worlds which circle each other and have a common sun. A brilliant physicist, Shevek, travels between them and finds flaws in both. The descriptive beauty of Le Guin's treatment of both the vastly different scenery and the political and cultural systems is unparalleled in modern science fiction writing.

Intertwined with the writing of Hainish cycle was the creation of the Earthsea trilogy. Ostensibly written for children, but delightful and magical for readers of all ages, this series began with *A Wizard of Earthsea* (1968), a novel about the coming of age of Ged, the protagonist. It is followed by *The Tombs of Atuan* (1971), in which Ged discovers sexual love. The final volume, *The Farthest Shore* (1972), follows Ged to maturity and his heritage as king of Earthsea. All three of these novels won awards for children's literature.

Le Guin has been nominated for approximately two dozen major awards and, as has been noted, has won several. *The Lathe of Heaven* (1971) was nominated for both the Hugo and Nebula awards. This novel deals with the ability to dream and make the world over through dreams, and is a superb example of character development. George Orr, the gentle hero, and his companion, Heather LeLache, struggle against the "mad scientist," psychologist William Haber. Orr wants to be cured of the "gift of dreams" and Haber wants to use it for his own ends.

Themes and Style

Rocannon's World developed a theme which appeared in many of Le Guin's later works, that of a sympathetic, open meeting of different sentient races. The ability to accept beings different from oneself is apparent throughout the Hainish cycle and is probably grounded in Le Guins's acquaintance with anthropology. The use of mental telepathy or "mindspeak" also plays a role in her novels. Although the quest for the true self is a theme frequently used in science fiction, Le Guin's Falk in *Planet of Exile* is unusually complex and well developed. In *The Left Hand of*

Darkness, the confrontation between two vastly different cultures reaches a dramatic high point in an incredible journey across a vast glacier. Estraven and Ai must wrestle with each one's essential "Otherness," and the result is a sensitive brotherhood across what appeared to be a vast alien gulf. The androgynous people of Gethen provide a fascinating look at at the roles of humans in a genderless world. *The Word for World Is Forest* is a very specific condemnation of exploitive colonization. This is the flip side of her usual sympathetic approach. In this moving short novel, Le Guin points out the dangers of not recognizing the worth of a planet's indigenous inhabitants.

Ursula Le Guin has exerted a major influence on science fiction writing by providing a successful model for a more descriptive, lyric narrative style and showing alternatives to more technocratic themes. Her contemplative prose is beautifully crafted and stands up to the rigors of academic interpretation as well as the test of pure enjoyment.

Plot Summaries of Major Works

The Dispossessed. Annares is the moon, the twin planet and reflection of Urras. Settled by anarchists from rich, lush Urras, the landscape of Annares is arid and poor. Shevek grew up on Annares but never fit in. In a society committed to cooperation, Shevek is unique, a brilliant physicist. Gradually Shevek realizes that his theories are being exploited by his mentor, Sabul, and that his home planet is not interested in what he has to offer. He and his partner, Takver, are separated when he no longer cooperates with Sabul, and they are forced to live apart for four years. When they do get back together, Shevek finds that Takver and their friends have all suffered because of their relationship with him. Consequently, he flees to Urras, where he is welcomed royally. Shevek finds the cultural differences confusing: the conspicuous consumption evident in allowing the female half of society to be idle, the wasteful nature of a society rich in resources. It becomes apparent that the scientists on Urras want to exploit Shevek's theories for commercial gain. He would have given all he had freely, but rebels when they try to force his knowledge from him. When he tries to help the revolutionary classes, Shevek finds himself on the run again. Finally, through the intervention of Terran ambassadors, Shevek returns to Anarres with a renewed enthusiasm for a culture that allows freedom and cooperation and with a dedication to the vigilance required to keep it free.

The Dispossessed is both more political and more scientific than Le Guin's usual style. She makes it clear that the political is closely intertwined with the personal, both on Annares and on Urras. Shevek's theories of Simultaneity and Sequency make possible great scientific advances, such as the ansible (a communication device allowing instantaneous tranmission of sound) and faster-than-light travel. The ansible appears in several of Le Guin's works and has become a standard science fiction device. Shevek's crowning achievement, his General Temporal Theory, is not possible without the use of of an ancient Terran theory, that of Einstein, called the Theory of Relativity. This points out the superiority of cooperation, rather than competition, as a cultural mode. *The Dispossessed* is subtitled *An Ambiguous Utopia*, and the ambiguity is constantly demonstrated. One example of Shevek's realization is that the obstacles placed in his way are both societally inspired and societally prohibited. Then, too, is the extreme poverty of Anarres contrasted with the lushness of Urras. Le Guin's skill with description makes the landscape of the two contrasting planets come alive. Her development of the character of Shevek creates a man too strong to be crushed by the conflicting pressures he experiences in both worlds. Some critics purport that this novel is the finest science fiction book ever written.

The Lathe of Heaven. George Orr is reported for taking more amphetamines and barbiturates than he is entitled to and is sentenced to Voluntary Therapeutic Treatment. The psychiatrist to whom George is assigned, Dr. William Haber, is at first skeptical of George's claims to "effective dreaming" which influences the reality around him. When George demonstrates, Faber realizes the potential of controlling the world through George's dreams. Beginning with relatively insignificant changes, such as modifying the picture on his wall, Haber concocts plans to make the world a better place. He induces a dream of his own promotion, one step at a time, to the directorship of a huge research institute. George's dreams are not entirely controllable, however. When he is told to dream away the overpopulation problems, he dreams that a terrible plague wipes out billions of people. When he awakes, it has happened and his dream has altered the past for everyone alive. He enlists the aid of an aggressive, black woman lawyer, Heather LeLache, to try to get Haber to quit using his dreams, but it does not work. When Haber tells George to dream that humans no longer fight wars with humans, George dreams up an alien threat to unify the world. The aliens take up residence on the moon. George tries to escape to his cabin in the woods. Heather finds him there and hypnotizes him to help him rid himself of his dreams; she also suggests that the aliens are no longer on the moon. When George awakens, the aliens are invading Earth! When George dreams that everyone is at peace with everyone else, everyone turns gray, literally. Even Heather is now gray, and becomes George's wife. In a last attempt, Heather hypnotizes George once more with a suggestion that his dreams are no longer effective. However, Haber has discovered a way to hook himself up to a machine, the Augmentor, so that he can have the same power of making his dreams become reality. Already teetering on instability, this experience drives Haber quite mad. His insane dreams nearly wreck the Earth. George manages to unhook Haber from the machine and Earth begins to return to normal.

Le Guin provides a terrifying look at humanitarianism running amok. The character of George Orr is gentle and humane, unwilling to tamper with reality consciously, wanting only to be cured of his ability to dream effectively. Haber, on the other hand, starts out wanting to improve things, but develops into a megalomaniac when he is seduced by the power he can control. Heather is an unusual heroine, stronger, more aggresive, and more real than many science fiction heroines. Le Guin has a fine hand at developing real and believable people. The overall theme of the novel is hopeful for humanity because, no matter what mess George dreams up, humans seem able to adjust and make the best of it.

The Left Hand of Darkness. On the planet Gethen, called Winter, envoy Genly Ai has two purposes: to learn as much as he can about the people of Gethen and to persuade them to join the Ekumen of Known Worlds. Prime Minister Estraven has the ear of the king and tries to gain an audience for Ai. When the king dismisses Ai as an unimportant imposter, Estraven is banished from the kingdom of Karhide. Ai travels to the next country, Orgoreyn, to introduce to them his message of peace and brotherhood. He is received no more warmly there; in fact, he is placed in custody on a "Voluntary Farm" for further questioning. On the farm, he is drugged with something dangerous to his alien chemistry and nearly dies, but Estraven rescues him. Knowing they will be hunted down on the main roads, Estraven and Ai flee across the great glacier, the Gobrin. In the eighty days it takes them to cross the glacier, Ai learns a great deal about the people of Gethen. He knew in an academic way that the people were neither male nor female, but both. On the ice, he learns the subtle changes, the feminization, that takes place periodically when a person goes into "kemmer." He learns that Estraven has sacrificed his prestige and position in the interest of gaining what Ai wants, the entry of Gethen into the brotherhood of the Ekumen. As they struggle together against the elements, the pair become like brothers, learning to speak telepathically, understanding the alienness of each other. Once the terrible ordeal ends, Ai learns just how much Estraven is willing to give up. Returning to Karhide while under banishment is punishable by death, and with his death, Estraven is able to prove the importance of serving humanity, rather than one nation on one world.

Le Guin uses a reporting narrative style very effectively in *The Left Hand of Darkness*. Ostensibly the report of Genly Ai on his experience on Winter, the story is interrupted with mythical accounts, anthropological surveys, and sections of Estraven's journal. The description of the political machinations of both countries makes the people of Gethen seem very human and real, in spite of their androgynous sexual nature. The culture and the people are so appealing that Genly Ai finds himself more changed by the contact than he expected to be, more in tune with the aliens than he ever dreamed possible. When Ai and Estraven build a friendship, even brotherhood, where fear and distrust existed before, it is an intensely moving scene. Le Guin's beautiful prose style is warm and descriptive, perfectly crafted. In this novel, she is at her elegant and eloquent best. As always concerned with the anthropology and psychology of her characters, Le Guin's work is thoughtful and uses philosophical themes which happen to be set in other times and places.

Biographical/Bibliographical Readings

Brian Attebury, "Ursula K. Le Guin," in *Twentieth-Century American Science-Fiction Writers* (Gale, 1981), v.1, p.263-81. Elizabeth Cummins Cozell, *Ursula K. Le Guin: A Primary and Secondary Bibliography* (G. K. Hall, 1983). Daniel N. Samuelson, "Ursula K. Le Guin," in *Science Fiction Writers*, ed. E. F. Bleiler (Scribner's, 1982), p.409-18. George Edgar Slusser, *The Farthest Shores of Ursula K. Le Guin* (Borgo Press, 1976). Susan Wood, "Discovering Worlds: The Fiction of Ursula K. Le Guin," in *Voices For the Future*, ed. Thomas D. Clareson (Bowling Green University Popular Press, 1979), v.2, p.154-79. [Kay Jones]

LEIBER, FRITZ, JR.

Life and Works

The year 1910 was marked by a visit from Halley's comet, the death of Mark Twain, and the birth of Fritz Leiber, Jr., in Chicago on Christmas Eve. With these portents during his birth year, and hearing his actor father recite Shakespeare during his first years of life, it is no surprise that Fritz Leiber became a literate writer equally at home in science fiction and fantasy.

Leiber spent his childhood touring with his parents' repertory company. In his teens, he read the works of Wells, Verne, Lovecraft, and Burroughs. During his college years at the University of Chicago, it had been assumed that he would act in his father's Shakespearean company. Instead, after graduation in 1932, he traveled to New York to attend the General Theological Seminary. While at school, he served as a lay reader and minister to two New Jersey Episcopal churches. Leiber returned to the University of Chicago in 1933 to study philosophy. Involvement in the theater did come to pass; in 1934 the young Leiber began touring with his father's road company. In 1936, Leiber married Jonquil

Stephens and the two were together thirty-three years, until her death in the fall of 1969. Justin Leiber, their only child, was born in 1938. Whether from heredity, environment, or both, he has also become a writer of science fiction.

The year 1941 found Fritz Leiber working as an instructor in speech and drama at Occidental College in Los Angeles. After Pearl Harbor, he was able to participate in the war despite his pacifism, by being a precision inspector at the Douglas Aircraft plant in Santa Monica. Near the end of World War II, the Leibers returned to Chicago, where the writer became an editor at *Science Digest*. After twelve years on the editorial staff, Leiber left in 1956 to devote himself to writing full-time. Soon thereafter, the family returned to California. With Jonquil's death in 1969, he moved north to San Francisco, where he now lives.

From his first published story in 1939 ("Two Sought Adventure" in *Unknown*) to the present spans a writing career of nearly half a century. Though perhaps not so prolific in words as Asimov, due to Leiber's concentration on short fiction, he has written over 200 stories, more than a dozen novels, many essays and articles, and two volumes of poetry. Fritz Leiber has won Hugo awards for *The Big Time* in 1958, *The Wanderer* in 1965, "Gonna Roll the Bones" in 1968, "Ship of Shadows" in 1970, "Ill Met in Lankhmar" in 1971, and "Catch That Zeppelin" in 1976. He has been awarded Nebula Awards for "Gonna Roll the Bones" in 1967, "Ill Met in Lankhmar" in 1970, and "Catch That Zeppelin" in 1975, as well as a Grand Master Nebula in 1981. For fantasy, Leiber has received the Ann Radcliffe award for *Conjure Wife* in 1970, the Gandalf award in 1975, the August Derleth award for "Belsen Express" in 1976, and World Fantasy Awards in 1976 for "Belsen Express" and in 1978 for "Our Lady of Darkness." He has been the World Science Fiction Convention Guest of Honor in 1951 and in 1979.

Themes and Style

Throughout his career, Fritz Leiber has been consistently ahead of his time. *The Wanderer* (1964) was the first disaster novel to describe the cataclysm by its effects on multiple characters; he was a champion of sexual freedom at least a decade before it became acceptable. This theme was combined with the idea of parallel worlds in "Nice Girl with Five Husbands" (1951), which antedates the current enthusiasm for alternate universes by three decades.

The relationship between fantasy and reality is integral to all of Leiber's work. Indeed, his stories and novels meld these elements, embodying his fascination with their relationship. Many do not fit nicely into a box labeled "fantasy" or "science fiction"; for example, his fantasy story "Ill Met in Lankhmar" (1970) won both Hugo and Nebula awards as best science fiction story. His masterful command of language makes his writing a joy to read, and it has allowed him to be a consummate parodist in several major pieces. His early immersion in the theater shows in many works; the novel *The Big Time* (1961) could be staged almost as written. His description of theater in freefall and three dimensions in *A Specter Is Haunting Texas* (1969) defines a world later elaborated by Spider Robinson in *Stardance*. Leiber's works form a series of explorations of the human mind as it reacts to change, sometimes internal, sometimes external. From another perspective, his experiments resemble those of a psychologist, who changes conditions and observes subsequent behavior. Leiber's championship of the individual, and his antiwar sentiments, are fundamental to several important works. Characters in *The Big Time*, all low-level participants in a cosmic war, lament the impossibility of their ever understanding the conduct, progress, and reasons for the war from their participation in minor skirmishes. Worse, they have no way even to tell if they are on the "right" side. Nonetheless, their actions during the crisis in the temporal way station do have an effect, especially on each other. In *The Wanderer*, a single person mitigates the damage done to Earth by the presence of the alien planetoid by shaming the felinoid Tigerishka into admitting she is afraid of her pursuers. The aliens, by callously bringing their war into the Solar System, are shown to be no more advanced in morals or ethics than humans, even though they control a much more powerful technology.

Elements which appear frequently in Leiber's writings are cats portrayed as equal to or better than people--it's the humans who seem to be the pets in "Cat's Cradle" (1974); chess--"The 64-Square Madhouse" (1962) explores the philosophic implications of gaming with a machine; and monsters--human, like the sadistic wrestler Little Zirk in "Coming Attraction" (1950); robotic, like the mechanical "angels" in *Gather, Darkness* (1950); and alien, like the shapeshifting moll in "The Night He Cried" (1953). Leiber is indeed an author who defines "the right stuff" in his field.

Plot Summaries of Major Works

The Big Time. All the action in *The Big Time* occurs in the Place, a rest-and-recuperation center for combatants in the Change War, a cosmic conflict between the Spiders and the Snakes. Unlike many change-the-past, change-the-future stories, this universe has temporal inertia, and requires major disruption of the past to alter the course of time. Into this way station, already occupied by its personnel (an innkeeper, a doctor, and entertainers), come soldiers fresh from battle. The second such group to arrive, which includes two nonhumans, brings with it a tactical nuclear weapon. In an effort to isolate their haven from the War, the hostess Lili inverts (twists out of space and time) the Place. Erich, a Nazi-era German colonel, responds by triggering a thirty-minute countdown for the bomb. Greta Forzane ("twenty-nine and a party girl") solves the mystery of the Inversion device, and the bomb is disarmed in time.

Fritz Leiber says that *The Big Time* was written in a hundred days, at the end of one of his dry spells in 1956. It is perhaps the finest example of his commitment to literature as theater. All of the devices of the stage are here: a single setting, clear-cut entrances and exits, stage directions for movement about the set, multiple subplots evolving within the larger scheme, and a violent crisis near the end. The cast is characterized by distinctive dialogue, including monologues. Sid Lessingham speaks Elizabethan, as if he had stepped out of a Shakespearean play; the Cretan warrior describes her battles in poetic meter; Greta's language is rich in twentieth-century slang; there are even delightful mixtures, such as "Thou saidst it!"

In this novel, populated by characters recruited from disparate times and places by snatching them just before death, Leiber explores the effects of war on individuals. Bruce Marchant, a poet-soldier from World War I, laments the permanent loss of human masterpieces, and of entire cultures (whether from altering the timestream or from bombs is unimportant). He and Erich von Hohenwald debate the validity of participation in the war. It is clear that questioning the necessity of the war, and whether we are on the "right" side, is essential to remain human. Blind participation in the name of military obedience is uncivilized behavior. In the end, speaking as the octopoid Ilhilihis, Leiber puts forth his view that war is necessary to the evolution of any species. Without conflict, there cannot be progress. Within this larger context, people must refuse to be degraded by the horrors of war. Instead, these events must be used as a maturing force, for the individual and for society.

Gather, Darkness. One of Fritz Leiber's earlier novels, *Gather, Darkness*, presents a world ruled by the theocratic Hierarchy, descendants of scientists who survived a nuclear holocaust. The populace is controlled by imposed educational and de facto poverty, as in the Middle Ages. The novel begins with Brother Jarles preaching sedition to a group of commoners. Unbeknownst to him, higher priests are watching; they permit his incitement to revolution in hopes of identifying more rebels. Jarles is introduced to the opposition Witchcraft by Sharlson Naurya, a woman who refuses to become a forced prostitute for the priesthood. He is offered a chance to join the rebels by the leader, known as the Black Man. After refusing, he is expelled and arrested by the priestly Gestapo. After brainwashing by the sadistic Brother Dhomas, Jarles becomes a double agent, and indirectly responsible for the death of Asmodeus, the Witchcraft's secret member of the

Hierarchy's Apex Council. Meanwhile, the Black Man has been captured, but is rescued by his cloned "familiar," Dickon. Ultimately the Witchcraft vanquishes the Hierarchy, as the World Hierarch is revealed as a commoner who has risen through the ranks of the priesthood under false pretenses.

Leiber's fascination with language again is apparent: the capital city's name, Megatheopolis, invokes its purpose in a single world. The chief Enforcer for the priests is named Cousin Deth. The Hierarchy, described as the most perfect form of government the world has ever known, is portrayed as repressive, hypocritical, and autocratic. Violations of secular law are punished as religious transgressions.

Gather, Darkness is built on the ironic concept that all of its seeming supernatural phenomena are based on advanced technology. The death rays of the Great God are lasers, the Angels are aircraft, priestly omniscience is made possible by teleholography, and a priest's robes contain both offensive and defensive weapons. Within this context is the message of the book: that it is dangerous to restrict either knowledge or power to an elite, which will certainly be corrupted by it. Limiting science to the upper levels of the ruling class stifles research and progress, and denies the people the laborsaving fruits of technology. Even so, a note of pessimism is evident in the end: the Black Man predicts that the commoners will expect the Witchcraft to establish a religion to replace the Hierarchy, complete with statues of Sathanas in the churches. In other words, freedom cannot be total; there must be some structure in society.

A Pail of Air. This collection of short stories, most written in the fifties, is as close to pure science fiction as Fritz Leiber comes. The title story, "A Pail of Air" (1951), describes a family surviving in a world without a sun. Earth has been captured by a dark star, and these people live in a Nest, blanket-walled to hold in heat and thawed-out oxygen. When "rescued" by a team from atomic-powered Los Alamos, they are ambivalent about leaving their home. Fats Jordan, in "The Beat Cluster" (1961), is an overweight musician and spokesman for a group of dropouts ("drifters and dreamers") living in space, in castoff habitats. When faced with eviction by a housecleaning new administrator, their fans on Earth and at Research Satellite One realize the services these rejects provide, and successfully lobby for cancellation of their expulsion. "The Foxholes of Mars" (1952) is a grim tale of a soldier in a far future war. He sees the futility of the war, and is more angry with his own species for being in it than with the alien enemy. The anger makes him kill one of his comrades-in-arms, a gung-ho soldier (perhaps the first instance of Vietnam-era "fragging"). Back home during a truce, a streetcorner harangue brings the realization that leaders must be murderers to win. "The 64-Square Madhouse" (1962) pits the first chess playing computer against an assembly of international grandmasters. The machine, programmed by a chess master, nearly wins the tournament. The humans prevail only when they realize they are playing against the programmer, and develop strategies to defeat him. In "Nice Girl with Five Husbands" (1951), the artist Tom Dorset is unknowingly blown a century into the future. When he encounters a group marriage with frighteningly intelligent children, he tries to explain puzzling events by bending them to fit his time. When told that he is in 2050, he is so distressed that he hardly notices being whirled back to his own time by the reversed time wind. The penultimate story, "Coming Attraction" (1950), depicts a post-World War III New York, where women mask their faces but not their breasts, and wrestle men. An English visitor rescues a woman from a street attack, and she entreats him to help her escape her life as the battered girlfriend of the male TV wrestler, Little Zirk. The denouement shows her to be a masochist, who reminds the visiting Briton of a "slimy white grub" beneath an overturned rock.

No setting, character, or theme is common to these stories. They nonetheless showcase Leiber's art: his powerful visual imagery makes the environment real, whether it is orbiting plastic bubbles or a chess tournament. The message of the stories is in the reaction of the human mind to the stress of changed circumstances. The soldier strikes out blindly against the senseless waste of war, and though his action does not affect the outcome of the battle, his mind is expanded. The family in its snug Nest is uncertain whether a return to civilization is best; perhaps living in constant danger is a more important stimulant for growth. Some of the chess masters are threatened by the computer's prowess. Instead, Leiber says we should form a partnership, a synergism, and augment our ability. "Coming Attraction" is a truly chilling story, in much the same way as Ellison's "A Boy and His Dog". A way of life repugnant to the reader is presented as unquestioningly accepted by the inhabitants of the story. Rather than being stimulated to grow by adversity, the characters have adapted by espousing the new rules--this is the dark side of the human mind, which cannot be ignored. Ever inventive, pushing back the boundaries of the possible, these stories are the essence of literate science fiction.

The Wanderer. A lunar eclipse begins *The Wanderer*; this is followed by the sudden appearance of a new planet near the moon, whose initial silhouette resembles a yin-yang figure. This body, actually a planetsized spaceship, causes devastating (eighty times normal) tides on Earth. By means of rapid changes in point of view from one individual or group to another, the nature of the intruder is gradually illuminated. We learn from an astronaut who escapes from a lunar base that the planetoid is breaking up the moon to use as fuel. The astronomer, Paul Hagbolt, is levitated (along with a cat) into a shuttlecraft by a female alien,

Tigerishka. During his captivity, Paul prevails upon this humanoid cat to acknowledge humans as an intelligent species, and she later explains that the inhabitants of the invader are rebels. Fleeing from the galactic police, they are accused of violations against the conservative government. In periodic flashes back to Earth, exaggerated tides impact upon a solo transatlantic sailor, a group of flying saucer enthusiasts in California, a bibulous poet in England, a dying Florida millionaire, American military leaders, and a fortune hunter in the South China Sea. The grand finale consists of the arrival of a second planetoid (the cops), and a trial in which Paul is coerced to testify in favor of Tigerishka's "people." A final battle with laser beams, reminiscent of *Star Wars*, ends with the escape of the *Wanderer* into hyperspace, whence it came.

Science fiction has a long tradition of disaster stories, from Wells' *The War of the Worlds*, through J. G. Ballard's various ends of the world, to Niven and Pournelle's *Lucifer's Hammer*. Leiber's novel was the first to delineate the effects of a cataclysmic event through the reactions of a series of ordinary people. This device, seeing the invasion/inferno/comet strike through the eyes of multiple characters, has since become a standard in this subgenre. Here again in *The Wanderer* is Leiber's empathy for the individual at the mercy of a greater power--and there are wheels within wheels. The *Wanderer's* crew are both ravagers and ravaged. They callously cause major damage on Earth, and wield powerful weapons against which humanity has no defense. In turn, they are the underdogs in their flight from the galactic authorities, and the author deliberately creates sympathy for these Wild Ones, the rebel aliens. In the final pages of the book is a discussion of the effects of war on the individual. The technologically advanced aliens are noted to be as warlike (immature), as is humanity--and as contrite as we would hope to be when the damage they cause is pointed out. It is suggested that the only cure for war must come from little nothing guys. Perhaps war is inevitable, and a necessary part of evolution; but individuals can choose whether and how to participate, even though some choices may be painful, or even fatal.

Biographical/Bibliographical Readings

Norman L. Hills, "Fritz Leiber," in *Twentieth-Century American Science-Fiction Writers* (Gale, 1981), v.1, p.281-90. Fritz Leiber, *The Book of Fritz Leiber, Vols. I and II* (Gregg Press, 1980). Judith Merril, "Fritz Leiber," in *The Magazine of Fantasy and Science Fiction* 37:1 (July 1969), p.44-61. Sam Moskowitz, "Fritz Leiber," in *Seekers of Tomorrow* (Ballantine, 1966), p.283-302. Brian Stableford, "Fritz Leiber," in *Science Fiction Writers*, ed. E. F. Bleiler

(Scribner's, 1982), p.419-24. Tom Staicar, *Fritz Leiber* (Frederick Ungar, 1983). **[David L. Starbuck]**

LEINSTER, MURRAY

Life and Works

Born William Fitzgerald Jenkins in 1896 in Norfolk, Virginia, Murray Leinster wrote science fiction for nearly fifty years. Schooled in public and private schools in Norfolk, Leinster's formal education ceased during eighth grade. He began writing in his early teens, and an essay on Robert E. Lee in *Virginian Pilot* was his first publication. Leinster served on the Army's Committee of Public Information during World War I, and then was briefly employed by the Prudential Insurance Company in Newark, New Jersey. He was writing full-time by the time he was twenty-one, and his first science fiction story, "The Runaway Skyscraper," was published in *Argosy* in 1919. Leinster married Mary Mandola in 1921.

During his first fifteen years of writing, his stories appeared in many magazines, both popular and science fiction. A truly professional writer, a substantial portion of his output in the 1930s was mysteries and westerns. After a stint in the Office of War Information in World War II, Leinster returned to primarily writing science fiction. He was astonishingly prolific during the postwar years, publishing many of his best stories: "First Contact," "The Ethical Educations," "Pipeline to Pluto," "The Power," "A Logic Named Joe," and "The Strange Case of John Kingman." Many of his stories are collected in *The Best of Murray Leinster* (1976, Ballantine) and *The Best of Murray Leinster* (1978, Corgi). His best known series, the Med series, includes four novels and one story--*The Mutant Weapon* (1959), *This World Is Taboo* (1961), *Doctor to the Stars* (1964), *S.O.S. from Three Worlds* (1966), and "Quarantine World" (1966). His best pure space opera novel was *The Pirates of Zan* (1959). He received the Hugo award for "Exploration Team" in 1956, and was guest of honor at the twenty-first World Science Fiction Convention in 1963.

Leinster began writing before the "Golden Age," continued through it, and was still writing in the final decade of his life. Sometimes writing as Will F. Jenkins, Leinster had well over one thousand stories published. His pen name, pronounced "Lenster," was taken from the Irish county of his ancestors. Known as "The Dean of Science Fiction" in his later years, Leinster was a craftsman as well as a writer. He defined the scientific problem story as an important part of the genre. He also wrote the first story of parallel worlds. He was an inventor and maintained a private laboratory throughout his life. His Jenkins System was used by the movie industry to project background scenes behind actors on the screen. Stories written by Leinster in the early 1930s predicted combat methods used in World War II, such as landing tanks from ships and high-altitude precision bombing. During his last years, Leinster continued to be productive (he produced the final Med Service chronicle, "Quarantine World," in *Astounding/Analog* in 1966), while living at his home "Ardudwy" in Gloucester, Virginia. Murray Leinster died in June of 1975.

Themes and Style

By the end of the first page, the reader can tell the book is by Leinster--his dialogue is distinctive. His language is spare, often terse, and ordinary; never pretentious, seldom poetic. Ideas of importance, especially philosophical ideas, are put forth in short, declarative sentences, punctuated by exclamation points.

Leinster championed rationality--the heroes in his adventures exemplify the use of the scientific method to solve problems. They form a hypothesis, consider alternatives to prove or refute it, and arrive at an answer which restores order to the world. His problem-solvers are not computers, nor are they plodding, second-rate experimenters. They operate like the best scientists. Not that Leinster's protagonists do not have human qualities--they are fallible, irrational at times, and sometimes baffled by events. The tension between human needs and rationality is often the crux of a story. In "Exploration Team," Huyghens expostulates to his antagonist Bordman that a wholly rational entity is a rational animal, not a human. What sets humans apart is their synthesis of logic and emotion. These define humanity for Leinster.

Leinster's heroes are never high in the official hierarchy; they are always fieldmen, junior officers, or slightly disreputable characters. The implication is that being at the top of either a civilian or military bureaucracy stultifies, stifles creativity, and disqualifies a person from being able to solve problems. The freedom and autonomy of a Med Service person is carefully contrasted to the impediments embodied in civil servants of all types. Whether consciously or not, a parallel is drawn between the original American pioneer "can-do" spirit and the increasing postwar devotion to maintaining the status quo coincident to the rise of bureaucracies. Leinster despises unthinking functionaries.

The theme of stability is important in Leinster's writing. Many stories are set against a framework of galactic society which has many common elements--every planet has a Port City, spaceships are launched by a ionosphere-powered landing grid, and are propelled by the FTL Lawlor Drive. Though different regimes hold sway on various planets, because of the enormous times and distances involved, there can be no central interplanetary government. Instead, the fabric of humanity's domain is held together by a network of agencies--the Med Service, the Colonial Survey. A common plot device is to apply a usually malign stress to a part of the system. The protagonist, in defeating the crisis with science, restores the system to normalcy.

Advanced technology is very much a part of the setting, rather than the focus, of Leinster's fiction. Although its basis is often plausibly explained, only rarely does it form the central point, or the solution to the posed problem (as in "Critical Difference," where improving the landing grid saves the planet). "A Logic Named Joe" predicts the current Information Age, in which "logics" (read personal computers") take over and criminalize many of society's functions. It is a forerunner of the recent spate of cybernetic intelligence stories, such as William Gibson's "Neuromancer." Technology is often reduced to the mundane, people-driven spaceships much like speedboats with little concern for the requirements of orbital mechanics. When necessary to the plot, technology even regresses (in *Tallien Three*, in which the spaceship has plywood floors).

Some important Leinster stories portray encounters between humans and aliens--"First Contact" is the most famous. Seldom are the aliens inimical monsters; almost never are they truly alien, with foreign rules of society and conduct. More often they are anthropomorphic, with human weaknesses and drives, thus rendering them as humanity's cousins who just look different. The Plumies in "The Aliens," or even the sentient plants in "Proxima Centauri," seem motivated by very human principles. Even the aquatic Shadi in "De Profundis" are ruled by a scientific bureaucracy which cannot accept new ideas.

Never as poetic as Sturgeon or Bradbury, many Leinster works contrast humanity's petty endeavors with the immensity of the cosmos by means of almost lyrical passages. There is a dry humor in Leinster. Each chapter in the Med series novel *The Mutant Weapon* begins with an aphoristic quotation from Fitzgerald's *Probability and Human Conduct*. Despite the fact that Fitzgerald was Leinster's middle name, denoting that this was a made-up reference, some readers wrote to obtain a copy of the work.

Leinster's stories and novels have been described as westerns set in outer space, and as space opera, as if these epithets somehow denote second-rate work. We should not forget that without the seminal work of this and other science fiction pioneers, the genre would not now be so strong. Without this tradition and the following it developed, there would be too few to read the more "literate" science fiction of the present.

Plot Summaries of Major Works

"Exploration Team." Huyghens, officially a criminal on his home planet, is the sole human member of an illegal Kodius Company outpost on the planet Loren Two. His companions are four mutated Kodiak bears and a trained eagle. Their isolation is suddenly violated by the unexpected arrival of Colonial Survey Officer Bordman, who has come to check on the progress of an authorized colony, far from Huyghen's location. Bordman's presence creates instant tension, as he is charged with enforcing the law which Huyghens and his company have broken. As the two duel, we learn that a colony of a few men and many robots was landed months ago and has not been heard from since.

Primitive signals are detected from the site of the colony, indicating possible survivors. The two men and the bears trek toward the source of the transmission in a rescue attempt. As they near the Sere Plateau, a camera carried by the eagle shows herds of sphexes migrating up its sides. The team fights its way through streams of the carnivorous monsters; it is learned that the herds are returning to their spawning grounds. When they reach the colony, three men are found barricaded in a mine. Their robot defenders have proven useless against an onslaught of determined sphexes. The men sterilize the sphex eggs, thus paving the way for the future successes of human endeavors on Loren Two.

The sheer ferocity of the sphexes, and the intelligence and cooperation of the bears, makes a striking setting for these events. The crux of the story is the definition of the essence of humanity: fundamentally rational, but with the flexibility to change as circumstances dictate. The demise of the colony demonstrates that robots, mechanical versions of rational animals, cannot substitute for humans.

"Exploration Team" is probably Leinster's best definition of what makes humans unique--the ability to handle the unexpected. Always within the rubric of scientific analysis, his characters field whatever nature throws at them. No robot, no animal that operates on a purely rational basis, can do as well. This celebration of the human spirit is a central theme of all of Leinster's work.

"**First Contact.**" The survey ship *Llanvabon* meets a foreign starship in the Crab Nebula. A junior officer, Tommy Dort, achieves communication with the aliens. The two species feel each other out, each searching for a nondestructive way to allow the other to depart without revealing their home planet. The aliens, although gill-breathing, bald, and telepathic, are almost human and "likable cusses." They even share off-color jokes with Dort. Here again, in typical Leinsterian fashion, it is not the captains of the ships who solve the problem. Tommy suggests that the two cultures swap spaceships, after precautionary destruction of starmaps to return home, each bearing evidence of the other's existence, and allowing for safe meetings in the future. This is one of the best tales of humanity's first encounter with another civilization and has appeared in many science fiction anthologies.

The Med series. *The Mutant Weapon* (1959); *This World Is Taboo* (1961); *Doctor to the Stars; The Grandfathers' War; Med Ship Man; Tallien Three* (1964); *S.O.S. from Three Worlds* (1966); and "Quarantine World" (1966) form Leinster's major series. Written in the last decade of his career, the books are among his most mature works. The setting is the Leinsterian universe. Told from the perspective of Calhoun, an Interstellar Med Service field man, the stories form a chronicle of solutions to problems ostensibly of public health. Populations are menaced by malnutrition (*The Grandfathers' War, This World Is Taboo*), plagues (*Tallien Three, The Mutant Weapon*), and a ground-induction field in *Med Ship Man*. These threats are usually instigated by an evil person or persons, often from off-planet, whose goal is planetary subjugation. In all, cures for the various pestilences are incidental--it is the solution to the uncivilized human beings that tells the story of the human colonies throughout the galaxy whose civilization does not go beyond the use of tools. Calhoun is a fixer rather than an innovator; the end result of his labors is always a return to stability and normality.

Calhoun has a complete biomedical laboratory in a compartment of his ship, the *Aesclipus Twenty*. In addition, he is provided with a living laboratory in the form of the tormal, Murgatroyd. This lemurian animal, invulnerable to all infectious diseases, is an instant antibody factory and cuddly and lovable to boot. Written at the beginning of the modern explosion of immunology, this monosyllabic ("Chee!) animal predicts capabilities that are at the forefront of high-tech medical science in the 1980s. Calhoun's solutions to the societal problems in these novels tend to be swashbuckling, even Draconian. Famine is relieved by the temporary theft of grain stores in orbiting spaceships, missiles and landing grids are destroyed by rocket flames, a city is set on fire. As in other works, any problem, whether scientific or social, yields to simple, common sense evaluation and analysis.

There are strong parallels to the western movie here. Calhoun is very much the Lone Ranger, winning against formidable adversaries. Although women appear in Med Service stories, they are always victims to be rescued, not lovers. In the end, Calhoun leaves the woman (somewhat wistfully), as he drives his spaceship off to the next crisis.

The Pirates of Zan. Bron Haddan, native of Zan and an inventor, is falsely accused of murder on the planet Walden. This society cannot tolerate change; lives of extreme boredom are lived with the help of tranquilizers. Bron's power receptor represents a challenge to the status quo and is rejected. Hadden escapes to Darth with the help of an Interstellar Ambassador, whose philosophy sets the stage for the novel--government suppresses adventure and rebels are to be cherished.

On Darth, Bron is immediately embroiled in the fate of Lady Fani. The daughter of Don Loris, she has refused to marry Lord Ghek, who in turn has kidnapped her (a successful public abduction is a legal marriage on Darth). The newcomer rescues Fani, returns her to her father, and is forced to flee by the arrival of pursuers from Walden. In space in a stolen ship, he encounters refugees from Colin. These unfortunates have embarked on a migration to the planet Thetis, having traded their homes for spaceships and agricultural machinery. During their voyage, the machines have been found to be worthless fakes.

The hero becomes a pirate, in the family tradition. He hijacks a space merchant's ship, sells its cargo, and by a series of Machiavellian maneuvers, gets enough money to refurbish the Colin's fleet. He also becomes rich. After raiding Walden, he returns to Darth with his crew of impressed soldiers and Nedda, his former girlfriend. His archpirate grandfather appears, and approves of his grandson's development. Nedda is matched with Lord Ghek, Bron Haddan is urged to marry Lady Fani by her father, and the soporific Walden is jolted out of its torpor--all because one man dared to be different.

This novel is one of the very best examples of pure space opera. Set in the Leinster universe, complete with landing grids and spaceships, it is a hero who vanquishes the enemy (not, interestingly, the pirates), rights the wrongs, and gets the girl in the end. In case we miss the point that this is space opera, much of the action takes place on the feudal planet Darth, complete with lords, ladies, and sword-wielding soldiers.

Leinster is having fun in this book, but his trademark of problem-solving by analysis remains the foundation. Bron Hadden solves problems by thinking them through, or with an invention. There is no magic here.

Biographical/Bibliographical Readings

John Clute, "Murray Leinster," in *Twentieth-Century Science Fiction Writers*, ed. Curtis C. Smith (St. James Press, 1986), p.111-17. Donald Hassler, "Murray Leinster," in *Science Fiction Writers*, ed. E. F. Bleiler (Scribner's, 1982), p.434-36. Sam Moskowitz, "Murray Leinster," in *Seekers of Tomorrow* (World, 1966), p.47-65. [David L. Starbuck]

LEM, STANISLAW

Life and Works

Stanislaw Lem was born on September 12, 1921, in Lvov, Poland, which is now a part of the Soviet Union. He was the only child of a family wealthy enough to employ a French governess. Though he considered himself somewhat spoiled, he performed well as a student. As a child, he enjoyed solitude and his game of inventing official papers and documents is a technique he still uses when creating new settings for his books. Like his father, mother, and uncle, he studied medicine but was interrupted by World War II. Since he is Jewish, his family was in danger but his father was able to acquire false papers to protect his immediate family. However, some of his relatives were murdered during the occupation. During the war, Lem worked as a garage mechanic for a German business and occasionally participated in underground activities.

In 1946, he moved with his parents to Krakow, Poland, where he resumed his medical studies and began his writing career with short stories, poetry, and novellas. In 1947, he became a junior research assistant for the Circle for the Science of Science at Jagellonian University. This organization was a clearinghouse for scientific literature from the United States for all Polish universities and gave him access to the latest developments in the various sciences. From 1947-49, he was the editor of a monthly magazine, *Zycie Nauki* (The Life of Science), and published several articles in the journal. He gave up his medical studies without receiving his diploma. In 1948, he wrote his first novel, *The Hospital of Transfiguration*, which was not published until 1955 because of political reasons. Since 1949, Lem's profession has been writing. He won a prize given by the city of Krakow for his fiction work, *The Errors of Dr. Stephan T.* In 1953, he married and now resides in Kliny, Poland. He and his wife have one son.

Lem is cofounder and member of the Polish Astronautical Society and a member of the Polish Cybernetics Association. He has received several awards from his country for his literary achievements. In 1965 and 1973, he received recognition from the Polish Ministry of Culture and in 1976 he received the Polish State Prize for literature. In 1973, he received a special honorary Nebula award for his science fiction works, but it was rescinded in 1977 amid controversy concerning articles that he wrote that were critical of science fiction as legitimate literature. *Microworlds: Writings on Science Fiction and Fantasy* (1984) contains several of these controversial articles.

Lem's work has spanned five decades and includes science fiction and detective novels, short stories, plays, teleplays, screenplays, and articles for magazines. His works have been translated into more than thirty languages and except for his science fiction, which is read in the United States, most of his writing has not been translated into English. Some novels now available in English are *The Star Diaries* (1957), *Memoirs Found in a Bathtub* (1961), *Return from the Stars* (1961), *Solaris* (1961), *The Invincible* (1964), *Tales of Prix the Pilot* (1968), *The Futurological Congress*

(1971), *A Perfect Vacuum* (1971), *Memoirs of a Space Traveler: Further Reminiscences of Ijon Tichy* (1982), *More Tales of Prix the Pilot* (1982), *One Human Minute* (1985), and *Fiasco* (1986).

In an autobiographical essay Lem states that he feels that the most important parts of his life are his intellectual struggles. This attitude is reflected in the intellectual struggles encountered when searching for accurate information about Lem's life and works. Lem prefers to have his ideas studied, rather than his biography. For example, sources disagree on details surrounding films made of his novels. One source states that *The Planet of Death* was filmed in East Germany under the title *The Silent Star*; another source states that *The Astronauts* (1951) was filmed as *The Planet of Death*. It is refreshing, however, to note that both sources agree that *Solaris* was made into a Russian film in 1972 under the same name.

Themes and Style

Three major themes dominate Lem's works--the use of artificial controls to manipulate and maintain the masses in a society where reality is often buried beneath layers of deceit; the natural desire of human beings to dominate other worlds, often destroying that which they do not understand in preference to abandoning their own egotistical viewpoint; and the role of man in deciding his own destiny and how much that role depends on chance.

The Futurological Congress and *Memoirs Found in a Bathtub* are the best illustrations of manipulation of the individual by artificial controls issued by the government and the Church. In *Congress*, the entire novel unfolds layer after layer of deceit. There are so many layers revealed that the reader is unsure by the end of the story what is the truth or if all layers are versions of the truth. Drugs and chemicals of all types are used to manipulate the public. Chemicals initially control the revolutionaries, are later used to help society, and finally used to cover up the deplorable world condition. *Memoirs* posits the deception of the individual by both government and organized religion. The controlling grip of the Catholic Church manifests itself in the character of at least one priest in many works. Lem does not portray the Church or Christianity in a charitable light; religion adds to the deceit of life. Religion of any kind takes on a sinister tone. In *Fiasco*, the machine Deus (reminiscent of Zeus) becomes a diety in its own right, a religion of science and mathematics that manipulates the crew of the *Hermes* into tragedy.

Lem addresses his themes clearly and repeatedly. Control by government, religion, environment, machine, and chemicals destroys the human spirit. Stagnation, decay, and finally death occur, but not before everything is destroyed. Be it capitalism, the

Church, or science, too much control of the individual is detrimental. Yet Lem offers no alternatives to these devices of society.

Several of Lem's works deal with the natural inclination of humankind to destroy that which they do not understand. In *The Invincible*, an Earth crew encounters a foreign and hostile life form. The first instinct is to fight and destroy the cloud, but this fails. The Earthmen cannot just leave the planet and the cloud as they are. The same theme appears in *Fiasco*.

There is a fine line between what is ordered and what is chance in Lem's works; how people react to crisis, the choices they make and where luck fits into the situation are other favorite themes of Lem's. *Being, Inc.*, a novel reviewed in *A Perfect Vacuum*, is about various companies that use computers to arrange or rearrange peoples' lives for a fee. But the buyers do not know which parts of their lives are affected by chance and which are ordered by the computer. Prix, the pilot, on the other hand, seems to have control of his life. He somehow manages to reason out problems and solve mysteries. Lem's works involving mystery can always be solved because there is no phenomenon that cannot be explained by logical reasoning. Yet beyond the reasoning is always an element of luck. The dual existence of logic and luck stems from Lem's solid science background and the luck that touched his own life during World War II.

Lem's idea that science fiction should deal with the whole race or species and not just specific individuals is readily apparent in his characterizations. The majority of his characters are never fully developed. Background characters all tend to be shallow; a few are only introduced by name. Often it seems they are just present to fill out the setting. Lem does some interesting things with his characters, however. He changes names back and forth, merges two people into one, and even ressurects them from the dead. There are no children in his works and his female characters are extremes and doll-like. The two best developed characters are Prix the Pilot and Ijon Tichy, who could be taken as Everyman. These are likable fellows just trying to get by, cynical of life and in their way arrogant about the superiority they secretly feel over the rest of humanity. They cope with life's daily problems and although they appear as bumblers, they always manage to get through their crises. Even death is not the end for Prix. He is killed only to be re-created in the form of Mark Tempe in *Fiasco*.

Lifeless characterization reflects Lem's sterile, cold settings. Regis III in *The Invincible* is a desert planet but the reader does not feel heat, only a frigid world. Solaris is a magnificent planet orbiting a white dwarf star and a red star. The effect of these two stars on the planet is beautiful and extreme yet the laboratory in which Kris Kelvin works out his dilemma is cold and sterile.

Near the end of *The Futurological Congress*, Ijon is shown the Earth in its true state and it is cheerless and wintry.

When describing machinery, scientific theories, or other technological instruments, Lem is just the opposite. He envisions and believes in the most creative ideas of mechanization. He has no such enthusiasm when it comes to humanity. His belief in the perfection and stability of sciences outweighs the frailty of humans and their institutions. In *Fiasco*, the love of the machine becomes an entity of its own, a diety that has a religious following. Mistreated or abandoned robots often act more humanely than do humans. Robots tend to be anti-heroes, underdogs, and are mistreated and taken advantage of by humans.

Lem attempts to keep the reader off balance in deciding what his point of view really is, perhaps because he is also confused by it. He criticizes capitalism as manipulative and controlling, yet describes socialism in much the same way. His style is a product of his conflicting philosophies--the emotional insecurity of his young adult years and his scientific background. Writing is his escape, just as suicide is often used as an escape in his works.

Perhaps the the most dominant aspect of his work is his pessimistic view of humans and society. Humans are responsible for the decaying condition of the world. They have the power to make the world better, but Lem does not feel that the Earth is heading that way. Technologically, man may reach great heights, but humanity will never evolve mentally or spiritually beyond the desire to explore and conquer. Medically, man may become almost immortal, but never enlightened. Lem uses satire, irony and black humor to expand on his philosophies. The humor is funny, but sad at the same time. Lem asks humanity to consider whether or not it is foolish.

Plot Summaries of Major Works

Fiasco. The story is set in two time periods. Parvis, a young and aggressive pilot, has been trained by Prix. Parvis sets down on Saturn's moon, Titan, during a routine supply dump and finds the ground crew under stress. Four able-bodied, alert, large machine operators have disappeared during a ground transport from the Depression to the outpost of Grail. Prix was lost when he went to rescue the others. Hearing the news about his old instructor, Parvis puts on the necessary gear for taking cargo to Grail in one of the large Diglas. The Diglas are huge machines made of metal, powerful but clumsy, and they take a great deal of experience to maneuver. Parvis successfully takes the Digla into the Birnam Wood, a wood of geysers that erupt instantly and without warning, causing ground instability. Almost clear of the Wood, Parvis is unexpectedly thrown off balance by an eruption. Debris falls around him, his Digla collapses and he fears that he will die.

Before he loses consciousness, he activates the quick freeze vitri-faxe process and freezes his body.

Centuries later, six frozen bodies are found in the Depression on Titan and are brought aboard the space ship *Eurydice*, in orbit and bound for a deep mission in space. Doctors on the space ship decide that only two bodies are in good enough condition to save and, of the two, the vital organs must be shared. Therefore, only one body can be returned to life. The computer records of the missing men are in disorder and the two that will be combined are only known to have a name that begins with the letter "P." Prix and Parvis are merged together and the resulting human calls himself Mark Tempe. Mark has sustained neurological damage in the freezing process and has no memory of Prix or Parvis, so he joins the crew of the *Eurydice* as it sets off an expedition to the planet Quinta.

For centuries, humans have lived in the hope of finding other life forms in the universe. A credible theory is that there are other intelligent beings, but that humanity has not been able to make contact because the aliens have either been too immature or too advanced to understand the radio signals. A window on time is created--a window that can calculate an alien civilization's point of maturity at the time when a ship with humans can be sent and communication will be understood by both species. *Eurydice*'s mission is to make contact with the aliens and Mark Tempe is chosen to be part of the small contact force on the smaller ship, the *Hermes*. The small landing crew will investigate all phenomena and establish the communication link which fulfills the mission. The crew is unprepared for what they find on the planet Quinta. The Quintans are at war and the expedition is attacked. The crew of *Hermes* retaliates and the mission becomes one of communication at any price. After many retaliations, the planet gives in to Earth's demands and Tempe is sent to meet the aliens. What Tempe finds on Quinta gives new meaning to the word "fiasco" and imparts a different meaning to the motives and philosophies of human exploration of the universe.

All of Earth's resources have gone into the project to make contact with the alien life on Quinta. Communication becomes the prime objective of the Earthmen as they refuse to take no for an answer to their probings. The Earthmen threaten and attack the planet until they ultimately destroy the world they desired to contact.

The Futurological Congress. *The Futurological Congress (from the Memoirs of Ijon Tichy)* tells of the adventures of the world renowned cosmonaut, Ijon Tichy. He attends the Eighth Annual Meeting of the Futurological Congress held at at the Hilton in Nounas, Costa Rica. The meeting is being held to deal with the population explosion and possible ways to check it. Ijon attends one session in which the Japanese plan to deal with population growth and the Americans want to propose fertilization as a felony when the hotel is attacked by revolutionaries. Ijon and some of his friends head for the sewers under the Hilton.

Ijon begins to hallucinate while in the sewer. At first he thinks that his body was destroyed and his brain transplanted into a black woman's body. He awakes from his dream and is shot by the revolutionaries, but since he believes he is still hallucinating, he is vitrified (frozen in liquid nitrogen) until a cure is discovered. He is revived in the year 2039, and finds himself in a new society that uses psychem drugs. Knowledge is acquired by way of the stomach since books are no longer read but eaten. When Ijon takes algebrine capsules, he gains a higher knowledge of mathematics. He is later told that everyone takes pills to fantasize evil because evil no longer exists.

Ijon has problems with the new society and cannot understand why people seem to pant for no reason. His friend, Professor Trottelreiner, lets Ijon see the world as it really is--overcrowded, with no animals and enormous food shortages. To be able to see the truth, Ijon is given yet another drug. The layers of deception are peeled away for Ijon and finally he finds out why everyone pants. Fortunately for Ijon, this turns out to be yet another hallucination.

Ijon Tichy is also a major character in *The Star Diaries* and *Memoirs of a Space Traveler*. Both chronicle his adventures in space as the human representative from Earth. Various escapades within the two novels describe his experience with time travel, how he participated in and fouled up the creation of Earth, his description of how washing machines turn into criminals, and his viewing of his own personal possessions on exhibit in a museum of the future.

The Invincible. The *Invincible* is a rocketship on a mission to the desert planet Regis III to find out what happened to the *Condor*, another rocketship that landed on Regis III a year before. Rohan, the navigator, is the narrator and his thoughts reflect the philosophies of Lem. After landing, the crew discovers very old metal ruins which are thought at first to be a city, but later prove to be a machine. The crew concludes that something has prevented life from being established on the land and that the marine life has a magnetic detector capability.

When they finally locate the *Condor*, mummified bodies are found inside and skeletons outside. The crew had died of dehydration and starvation. The outside hull of the *Condor* is corroded, and on the inside materials have been destroyed and thrown about. When the *Invincible* is later attacked by a black cloud of tiny metallic particles, some of the crew develop amnesia due to a magnetic shock. A few of the magnetic crystals are captured and tested. After several experiments, the scientists discover that in the individual state the crystal cannot or will not defend itself unless joined by other crystals. An automated machine, *Cyclops*, is sent out to retrieve other specimens. A battle takes place between the *Cyclops* and the black cloud and the machine turns on the *Invincible*. The remainder of the crew destroys the *Cyclops* with an atomic bomb.

From their research on the magnetic cloud, the scientists believe that the cloud is the evolved inorganic life of machines left over from an earlier civilization. There is a debate as to whether to destroy the cloud or leave it alone.

Memoirs Found in a Bathtub. The novel opens with an alien Hisonostors' archaeological view of what life was like in the Neogene period of Ammer-ka (America) and focuses on the worship of Kap-eh-taahl (capital). This worship, to which the citizens of this lost race were devoted, is believed by the aliens to have led to the final downfall of civilization on Earth. One manuscript that is found especially typifies the flaws of the lost race. The memoirs are discovered deep inside the Rocky Mountains, and trace the activities of a spy sent to the Third Pentagon to take up his mission for the protection of his country. In the spy's attempts to contact his superiors, he falls into bureaucratic dodging, intrigue, subterfuge, paranoia and murder. Caught up in a labyrinth of lies, bizarre situations, and unusual characters, the spy is unable to escape or to find a solution to his dilemna. He finally commits suicide, his only way out.

Lem's novel builds a jungle of deception perpetrated by government and organized religion. The spy is lost in a web of intrigue and lies so much that he eventually has no sane basis in reality. He has the choice of becoming a character in the charade of espionage, or refusing to play, which in his case means death. The Church plays a large part in *Memoirs* as it does in many of Lem's works.

Solaris. Kris Kelvin is sent to join an established scientific study team on Solaris. After ten years of preparation and anxious to begin work, he is bewildered when no one meets him on arrival. Investigating the problem, Kelvin stumbles upon Dr. Snow, one of three scientists assigned to the station. Snow talks like a man gone mad and never really tells Kelvin what has happened, only that he must be prepared for the unexpected. Kelvin first experiences a strange phenomenon in the appearance of a large, black Amazonlike woman. He follows her to the frozen corpse of Dr. Gibarian, his mentor in earlier years. Kelvin then begins to seek out all that is known about Solaris.

Solaris is a planet dominated by a large ocean--a living, moving, reactive body of water. Earlier scientists had quickly established evidence that the ocean was filled with (or was, within itself) an intelligent life form. All attempts at communication were unsuccessful. Kelvin discovers a replica of his wife, Rheya, beside him. He had driven her to suicide ten years before. Frightened and disgusted by the morose replica, he tries to learn what he can from her, but she does not know where she came from or why she exists, only that she cannot leave Kelvin's side. Kelvin discovers that each of the three resident scientists have Phi-creatures like Rheya, unique creations of their own psyche. Kelvin tries to piece together the mysterious appearances of the Phi-creatures, linking them to the ocean's attempt to communicate or possibly being a gift of the ocean. In the end, Kelvin believes that the ocean is able to retrieve memories from the deep recesses of the human mind and create replicas. This is the only way that the ocean can make contact. Direct communication cannot be established because of the physiological differences in each species.

Solaris reinforces Lem's belief that humans do not desire space exploration to uncover mysteries, but to expand Earth's values and control on a universal scale. The alien life form, the ocean, is never identified by the humans as a superior being in its evolutionary development, but it is so beautifully different and awesome in its power and thinking that the reader can ascertain its sophistication. Humanity has no way of relating to it because there is no common communication link. The human scientists become increasingly unstable because they cannot relate to the ocean. When faced with what cannot be understood, humans eventually experience a kind of insanity and soon attempt to destroy what is different.

Tales of Prix the Pilot and **More Tales of Prix the Pilot.** In the first novel, Lem introduces the funny, unpredictable, and very fallible cadet, Prix. Prix is a bungler who has the uncanny ability to survive any predicament he is thrown into, and triumph over predicaments throughout the vast reaches of space. Each short tale (nine stories in all) deals with a mystery or event that cannot be solved until Prix unwillingly becomes a part of the adventure and uses a variety of skill, smarts, and uncanny luck to survive.

In *More Tales of Prix the Pilot*, Prix is older and less awkward as a navigator and heavy machine operator. He is wiser and less cocky than in his previous adventures, but he still manages to bungle a situation and then triumph over it. More sure of himself, more cynical of life and his fellow humans, Prix reveals more of his philosophy of life, humans, and the great unknown. "The Accident" and "The Hunt" especially end on a sad note by making robots unsung heroes, and more deserving of survival and praise than the humans around them. The ineptitude of government and those in authority is dealt with in a cynical fashion that is hardly humorous. Prix shows less of his previous character and more of the woes of Stanislaw Lem.

The tales of Prix the Pilot exemplify the ineptitude of humans due to bureaucratic control and control of environments. Lem addresses these themes clearly and repeatedly. Stagnation, decay, and finally death occur, but not before everything is de-

stroyed. Be it capitalism, the Church, or science, too much control
of the individual is detrimental and yet Lem offers no alternatives for society.

Biographical/Bibliographical Readings

"Stanislaw Lem," in *Contemporary Authors* (Gale, 1982), v.105,
p. 279-82. "Stanislaw Lem," in *Contemporary Authors Autobiography
Series* (Gale, 1984), v.1, p.255-66. "Stanislaw Lem," in *Contemporary Literary Criticism* (Gale, 1986), v.3, p.343-45. Darko Suvin,
"The Open-Ended Parables of Stanislaw Lem and *Solaris*," in *Solaris* (Walker, 1970), p.205-16. Richard E. Ziegfield, *Stanislaw Lem*
(Ungar, 1985). [Twyla Reinig and Illene Renfro]

L'ENGLE, MADELEINE

Life and Works

Madeleine L'Engle Camp was born on November 29, 1918 to
Charles Wadsworth, author and playwright, and Madeleine
(Barnett) Camp, in New York City. Not wanting to trade on her
father's well-known name, she uses L'Engle for her writings. Her
early schooling took place in the United States and Switzerland.
A graduate of Smith College, Northhampton, Massachusetts, in
1941 with an A.B. with honors, she also did graduate work at the
New School for Social Research in 1941-42 and Columbia University in 1960-61. During a brief stint in the theater she met her
husband Hugh Franklin; she says that she met him in "The Cherry
Orchard" and married him in "The Joyous Season." Their marriage
took place on the 26th of January, 1946. Franklin died in
September of 1986. For a while, they kept a small-town general
store in Connecticut before returning to New York City. They
had three children. L'Engle has taught at St. Hilda's and St.
Hugh's School, which her children attended. During the summers
she has been a member of the faculty, University of Indiana,
Bloomington in 1965-66 and in 1971; writer-in-residence, Ohio
State University, 1970; the University of Rochester, 1972; and
Wheaton College, Illinois, 1976. She has been librarian at the
Cathedral of St. John the Divine in New York.
Among her other activities, she has served as a member of
the Board of Directors, Authors League Foundation, and as presi-
dent of the Authors Guild of America. Among the many awards
and honors she has received are the A.L.A Newbery Medal for
Children's Books, 1963; the Sequoyah Award, 1965; and the Lewis
Carroll Shelf, 1965 for *A Wrinkle in Time*; the University of Southern Mississippi award, 1978, for outstanding contributions in the
field of children's books; the American Book Award (paperback),

1980, for *A Swiftly Tilting Planet*; the Logos Award for nonfiction, 1981; and the Catholic Library Association Regina Medal, 1984. Collections of her manuscripts can be found at Wheaton College, Illinois, in the Kerlan Collection; at the University of Minnesota, Minneapolis, in the de Grummond Collection; and at the University of Southern Mississippi, in Hattiesburg.

L'Engle has written many different types of works, fiction and nonfiction, for adults and for children. In this essay, emphasis will be on her works which can be considered science fiction. Her most admired novels are found in the Time trilogy, which consists of *A Wrinkle in Time* (1962), *A Wind in the Door* (1972), and *A Swiftly Tilting Planet*, (1978).

Themes and Style

In his 1969 article about his wife, Hugh Franklin commented that how much of Madeleine there is in her adolescent heroines, only she knows. But he does know that she has put a lot of herself into the mother characters. Somehow she manages to juggle being wife, mother, and writer. Perhaps one reason she can write so well for children, is that she still has much of the child in her; for example, she relishes Christmas as few people do.

In her articles that have appeared in *The Horn Book Magazine*, L'Engle talks about the writing process, the importance of creativity, and communication. One reason she likes to write for children is that they still understand the universal language found in fairy tales. This fact opens up a way of communicating not always available when writing for adults. The creative process cannot be analyzed. A writer has a need to be very curious about people and life, yet when writing about them, the writer needs to be objective. The impulse to write is a compulsion, which must be controlled by the writer. L'Engle feels there is no such thing as a nonreligious subject. For her, the great theologians and modern mystics are found in the great scientists such as Einstein. The writer must look at the chaos of the universe and try to find some order in it; most important is to look at the pattern in terms of love and joy. Guadior, whose name means great joy, expresses this sentiment in *A Swiftly Tilting Planet*.

Time travel is a theme common to the Time trilogy. In *A Wrinkle in Time*, Mr. Murry gets into trouble when he experiments with tessering, which uses the fifth dimension for time travel. In *A Swiftly Tilting Planet*, Charles Wallace Murry travels back in time to save the world from a nuclear war. Of the three, *A Wind in the Door* has the least to do with time travel, but rather deals with the ability to change in size. In order to save Charles Wallace, his sister Meg and the others need to become small so that they can talk to his farandolae (found in human cells). These works are also listed as examples of high fantasy. Some feel that the awarding of the Newbery Medal (1963) to *A Wrinkle in Time* signaled a coming of age for this type of literature.

Her latest work, *Many Waters* (1986), returns to this series; actually, in time sequence it falls between *A Wind in the Door* and *A Swiftly Tilting Planet*. The main characters are the twins, Sandy and Dennys, who previously have not been featured. Although they do not possess the scientific minds or intuition of others in the family, they have picked up some knowledge about tessering, which does come in handy. In *A Wind in the Door*, one of the main characters is a cherubim; seraphim and nephilim are added to the human characters. Besides the tessering, the story primarily focuses on how the twins handle themselves, first in an unknown time and place, and then in a story whose ending they know. They are aware that they must not change history.

In her children's works, there are two main series, one dealing with the Austin family and the other with the Murry/O'Keefe family, which is the family present in the Time trilogy. Characters from these two series move back and forth, which can make it confusing if a reader is not familiar with both sets. Science, as distinct from science fiction, is present in both series. In *The Young Unicorns* (1962), a villainous scientist has a laser device which he plans to use for evil. Practically the entire Murry/O'Keefe clan are scientists. Experiments by Dr. O'Keefe with the regenerative powers of starfish and the desire for this information by an enemy form the plot for *The Arm of a Starfish* (1965).

Most of her works contain a strong sense of the importance of family life. The characters gain the strength from their families to see them through an ordeal. A common theme is the constant battle between good and evil. In the Time trilogy, evil is first personified by IT, a computer trying to control a whole planet. Although there is the battle between good and evil, her characters are not personifications of either, but real people. A good example of this, from the Time trilogy, is Mr. Jenkins, who appears in the first two books. Both Meg Murry and Charles Wallace Murry, because of their high intelligence and descent from a family of scientists, have difficulty adjusting to school. Mr. Jenkins is first shown as he tries to get Meg to work up to her potential. She is always being sent to his office, because her schoolwork, especially in areas other than mathematics, is not up to par. Even in mathematics, Meg can do the work, but not in the way the teacher wants it done. One of Meg's tests is to identify the real Mr. Jenkins from his two look-alikes, which are really projections. Meg finds it difficult, but she does remember something nice about him. The battle between good and evil contains religious elements. The elements are not overt, but are present in the philosophical elements and use of love of others to help get through a crisis.

In two of her works, Biblical characters, cherubim and seraphim, are presented as real creatures. She uses mythical creatures such as unicorns, of which there seem to be two different types. Gaudior, in *A Swiftly Tilting Planet*, is a time traveling unicorn. The unnamed unicorns in *Many Waters* do not speak and appear to be different from Gaudior's species.

Madeleine L'Engle is a prolific writer. Her works for young people are considered to be well-told stories which keep the reader's interest. Science, science fiction, and fantasy play roles in many of these works. She is able to present real people facing difficult decisions about issues which affect all of us. At times, the personal situation reflects the world around us, with the outer world reflected in the inner world. At other times, the heroes and heroines are responsible for saving the world. Because of the philosophical issues presented, her works for young people are also of interest to adults.

Plot Summaries of Major Works

The Time trilogy

A Wrinkle in Time. The first novel in the Time trilogy introduces us to the Murry family, living in a small New England town. Both parents are scientists and as the story opens, Mr. Murry has been missing for some time. The heroine, Meg Murry, the eldest child, is going through a difficult adolescence. Next come twin boys, Sandy and Dennys, who are described at one point as being run-of-the-mill. The youngest is Charles Wallace, not yet in school, but able to read and write beyond his years. He also "knows" things intuitively. He and Meg have a rapport with each other. Calvin O'Keefe befriends Meg and is welcomed into the Murry family. Charles Wallace meets Mrs. Whatsit and her companions, Mrs. Who and Mrs. Which. These three ladies help Meg, Charles Wallace, and Calvin to find and rescue Mr. Murry on the planet of Comazotz. Evil, or the Black Thing, is spreading across the universe, taking over planet after planet, turning them dark. One manifestation is IT, a giant brain that controls the life of everyone on Comazotz in order to create total conformity. Mr. Murry was working on the fifth dimension, or tesseract, when he ended up on Comazotz. The tesseract is a form of travel across space and time. While rescuing Mr. Murry, Charles Wallace is trapped by IT and in order to save him, Meg must use the one thing IT does not have, love.

This Newbery Medal winner combines elements of science fiction, fantasy, and real life. It has the theme of good versus evil, so prevalent in L'Engle's work. Here the Mrs. Ws represent the forces of good which work through the children to combat evil in the form of IT. The whole idea of time and space travel using the fifth dimension is presented as a just-discovered science fact. The explanation of how it works is given in a comprehensible way. The protagonists visit several different planets and meet aliens on Ixchel. These aliens are interesting; they don't have eyes, but use their other senses to gain a picture of the world, although without color. The villain is a giant brain, or computer, called IT, which captures Charles Wallace when he tries to outwit IT. IT's weak point is a lack of emotions, so that Meg defeats it with love. Some of the traditional fantasy elements include the giving of gifts by the Mrs. Ws as they send the children off to Comazotz. References to freak weather as the story begins link the elements to the effects of the spread of evil. The novel also is the story of a young girl learning to cope with adolesence and trying to fit into a small town, when her family is anything but ordinary. This work is an interesting blend of different elements which make it an attractive book for readers with different interests, including adults.

A Wind in the Door. The second book in the Time trilogy is *A Wind in the Door*. Barely a year has passed since the adventures of Meg, Charles Wallace, and Calvin in *A Wrinkle in Time*. Although the children rescued Mr. Murry in the first book, evil is still trying to take over the world, this time by causing mitochondritis, a disease which occurs when the farandolae refuse to deepen. Mrs. Murry, a biologist, is just about to prove the existence of farandolae, when Charles Wallace is striken by the disease. Farandolae inhabit the mitochondria which is part of each cell. Meg and Calvin, with the help of a cherubim named Proginoskes, must save him. The problem is being caused by the Echthroi, or the un-Namers. Proginoskes is a Namer, as is Meg. To save Charles Wallace, Meg must pass three tests. The first is to pick out the real Mr. Jenkins from the two fake ones created by the Echthroi. Mr. Jenkins was the principal when Meg had problems in school and is now principal at Charles Wallace's school. Again she must use her love to identify the real Mr. Jenkins. Mr. Jenkins joins the group who travel to Metron Ariston, where they meet Sporos, a young Farandola. Blajeny, the Teacher, has taken them there since on Metron Ariston, size is irrelevant and they can get over the problem they have of trying to imagine something as small as a farandola. The second test for Meg is to get Sporos and the other farandolae to deepen. The Echthroi have convinced them that they can remain free and pleasure-seeking. Calvin and Meg join the dance, and it is Mr. Jenkins who saves her when she is sucked into the ring. But then he is surrounded by Echthroi who try to kill him by creating a void. Proginoskes saves Mr. Jenkins by entering the void. Meanwhile the farandolae start to deepen. Meg names the un-Named and thus defeats the Echthroi. Meg, Calvin, and Mr. Jenkins find themselves in Charles Wallace's room where they learn that he is recovering.

Again the world is being threatened and again it is up to the Murry children, with the help of Calvin O'Keefe, Proginoskes, and

the unlikely Mr. Jenkins, to save it. The threat has changed from
one which controls and destroys planets from the outside to one
which destroys people from the inside. Again the interrelatedness
of everything is emphasized. There is the combination of the everyday, with Charles Wallace's problem of adapting to school,
alongside the cosmic battle being fought within his body.   The
fantasy elements include the concept of Naming. As long as something can be named, it exists. Although a star might be destroyed,
as long as Proginoskes remembers its name, it is not totally lost.
For this reason, the Echthroi work on trying to un-Name things.
The plot is a complex one, expecially during the second and third
of Meg's tests, which flow from one into the other. Proginoskes,
the cherubim, is a real creature, rather than the Biblical concept
of cherubim as angels, and brings a delightful new character to
literature. He explains that he is not related to cherubs, those fat
little creatures with tiny wings. Again L'Engle has created an interesting mix of science, the discovery of mitochondria and farandolae, and fiction, how to cure mitochonditis by stopping
Echthroi.

   A Swiftly Tilting Planet. The third book in the Time trilogy
is *A Swiftly Tilting Planet*. Nine years have passed since *A Wind in
the Door*. Meg Murry has married Calvin O'Keefe and is expecting
their first baby. Charles Wallace is now fifteen, though small for
his age. The entire story takes place on Thanksgiving Day. Mr.
Murry receives a phone call from the president, which informs
him that Madog Branzillo, dictator of Vespugia, will start a nuclear war with the United States within twenty-four hours.
Vespugia is located on the far tip of South America, close to
Patagonia. The conversation which follows the phone call stirs a
memory in Mrs. O'Keefe. First she remember a rune that her
grandmother taught her. The rune is essential to the story, not
only because Charles Wallace uses it to ward off danger while he
tries to find the Might-Have-Been that will stop the war, but also
because the verses of the rune become the titles for the chapters
of the book, helping to frame the story. Mrs. O'Keefe also thinks
that there is something familiar about the name Madog Brazillo.
As the story goes on, the reader learns that Mrs. O'Keefe is dis-
tantly related to the dictator. Gaudior, a time traveling unicorn,
comes to help Charles Wallace in his quest to find the Might-Have-
Been who can save the world.

   The first important stop in Charles Wallace's travels in time
reveals the story of the two Welsh brothers, Madoc and Gwydyr,
who come to the new world long before any other white men.
Madoc, a seventh son, marries Zyll, princess of the People of the
Wind. He can only do this after defeating his evil brother,
Gwydyr, who also wants to marry her so that he can unite two local tribes and become their ruler. After his defeat, Gwydyr goes
to South America--to Vespugia, to be exact. This confrontation

between good and evil repeats itself through history, culminating in the story of the twin brothers Matthew and Bran Maddox. Bran Maddox goes to Vespugia along with settlers from Wales. There they discover Indians with blue eyes, descendants of Gwydyr. Gwen, sister to Bran and Matthew, also travels to Vespugia and is courted by Geder, one of Gwydyr's descendants. Geder is killed by a fall over a cliff. The Might-Have-Been has been changed so that at the end of the story, the ruler of Vespugia is famous as a man of peace. Problems for Charles Wallace and Gaudior were caused by the Echthroi (first encountered in *A Wind in the Door*), who keep sending Projections to confuse the time travelers.

As with her other works, this book is a mixture of fantasy and science fiction. The Echthroi are still trying to take over the universe and turn it into a place of evil. But as long as there are people who remember the Old Music, the harmony of the universe, it can be saved. Mrs. O'Keefe is one of these people. Her rune is Irish; Madoc and his brother, Gwydyr, and their descendants are Welsh; and reference is made to an ancient British queen, Brandwen. All these elements from the British Isles become interconnected in the story. Besides the main theme of good versus evil, there is also the theme of how everything in the universe is interconnected. One discussion dwells on what effect the destruction of the planet Earth could have on the solar system and beyond. Time travel with its connection to theories of the relativity of time and space, and the need for the leaders to be descended from the good brother are elements of science fiction. Many other elements are straight from fairy tales, such as a unicorn and a magic rune.

Biographical/Bibliographical Readings

Hugh Franklin, "Madeleine L'Engle," *The Horn Book Magazine*, 39:4 (1963), p.356-60. Madeleine L'Engle, "The Centipede and the Creative Spirit," *The Horn Book Magazine*, 45:4 (1969), p.373-77. Idem, "The Expanding Universe: Newbery Acceptance Speech," *The Horn Book Magazine*, 39:4 (1963), p.351-55. Idem, "What Is Real?" *Language Arts*, 55:4 (1978), p.447-51. Pat Pflieger, "Madeleine L'Engle," in *Reference Guide to Modern Fantasy for Children* (Greenwood, 1964), p.304-07. **[Mina Jane Grothey]**

LESSING, DORIS

Life and Works

Born on October 22, 1919, in Kermanshah, Persia (Iran), Doris May Lessing was the first child of Alfred Cook Tayler and Emily

Maude McVeagh Tayler, both British citizens. In 1924, the Taylers emigrated to Southern Rhodesia (Zimbabwe) to take up farming, where they lived a life of poverty and hardship. She received no formal education after age fourteen, but pursued a course of reading of her own choosing. Between the years 1939 and 1949, Lessing married and divorced twice and bore three children. She was active in a Rhodesian Marxist group until 1949, when she emigrated to London, where she currently lives. Since 1956, when she officially resigned from the British Communist Party, she has become progressively more apolitical, although she has marched for nuclear disarmament and campaigned for civil defense. Distrusting collective ideologies, religious and political, she has chosen to remain outside such groupings.

Her first novel, *The Grass Is Singing*, was successfully published in England in 1950. During the ensuing thirty-five years, Lessing has published twenty novels, six plays, eight volumes of short stories, one book of poems, and numerous essays. She has received three major awards: the Somerset Maugham Award (1954) for *Five: Short Novels* (1976), the French Prix Medici for foreign literature (1976), the German Shakespeare Prize (1982), and the Austrian State Prize for European Literature (1982). Her novels have been translated into more than twenty languages, and over thirty-five dissertations have been written on her work.

Lessing's landmark work, *The Golden Notebook* (1962), brought her worldwide recognition. *The Four-Gated City* (1969), part of her five volume series, *Children of Violence*, was a crucial step in Lessing's advance toward the genre of science fiction. Feeling that she had exhausted the possibilities of the experimental mainstream novel, Lessing turned to more science fiction with the publication of *Re: Colonized Planet 5, Shikasta* (1979), the first volume of her Canopus in Argos: Archives series. *Shikasta* was quickly followed by *The Marriages between Zones Three, Four, and Five* (1980), *The Sirian Experiments* (1981), *The Making of the Representative for Planet 8* (1982), and *Documents Relating to the Sentimental Agents in the Volyen Empire* (1983).

Themes and Style

Doris Lessing, an intellectual writer who draws from her own political background and experience, displays a wide range of knowledge and interest in such topics as racial injustice, the colonial hypocrisy of empires, psychology, mysticism, and the lives of contemporary women. Although she has been called a communist, a feminist, and a radical, she rejects labels and demands the freedom to explore and experiment in her writing and to use whatever styles and techniques will suit her purpose. Lessing began as a writer in the realist mode, soon gaining a reputation for experimenting with structure. As her work progressed, her primary themes centered around collectivism, the individual and the whole, to be distinguished from the pseudowhole presented by collective ideologies, such as religious, educational, and nationalistic institutions. The relationship between the white colonial collective and the individual is explored in her early works, and later the hypocrisy of imperial colonial expansion is central to *The Sirian Experiments*. From an intergalactic perspective, the Canopus in Argos novels have continued Lessing's exploration of social and psychological processes and the relationship of the individual to the whole.

Although critics and fans were surprised when Lessing officially entered the realm of science fiction, this was a natural development in the continued expansion of her themes, for a writer describing entire universes, alternate realities, and distant futures is free to experiment with structure and to explore infinite possibilities. Lessing sees science fiction as an opportunity to raise readers' abilities to transcend the thought conventions of their particular historical moment and situation. Lessing prefers "space fiction" as a description of her work, for she extrapolates from present sociological conditions to future realities, downplaying scientific technologies, while emphazing the mystical, drawing from mythology and sacred literatures.

Lessing uses the fictional convention of presented selected reports, letters, texts, and journals taken from the archives of the Canopean Empire, which provides a detached, impartial perspective for commenting on the human condition. The life forms on the planets in Lessing's cosmos are growing and transforming toward a perfect interaction and cooperation with each other and the universe. To develop this central theme, she defines three galactic empires: Canopus, represeting goodness and lawfulness according to certain indefinable laws of nature; Sirius, the naive, the self-deceiving, the ignorant; and Shammat, representing chaos, evil, and power misued. The basic tension in the series derives from these opposing rivalries.

The novels themselves are loosely connected. They are archival reports which can be read at random. Each novel follows a different structure and narrative form. Lessing has said that *Shikasta* is the Bible rewritten as science fiction, using textbook excerpts, reports from Canopean agents on Earth, and the journal of a young woman, creating a diverse and intricate narrative texture. *Shikasta* is the long drama of Earth's history viewed from a cosmic perspective. *The Marriages between Zones Three, Four, and Five* is an allegory of spiritual progress built around a love story. *The Sirian Experiments* is written in the words of Ambien II, a female bureaucrat high in the colonial goverment of the Sirian empire. Ambien describes the millenia-long evolution of her own consciousness and the development and decline of the Earth, seen from the disinterested eyes of an extraterrestrial visitor. *The*

Making of the Representative for Planet 8 is a relentless funereal dirge, told from the viewpoint of an inhabitant of Planet 8, which is entering an ice age leading to the inevitable deaths of all the inhabitants. *The Sentimental Agents* is a not entirely successful satire on the effects of rhetoric used for social and political exploitation. The archival reports and letters are are written in a candid and humorous manner.

Lessing uses many science fiction conventions to advance her central theme. The intervention of extraterrestrials is most fully explored in *Shikasta* and *The Sirian Experiments*. The rise and fall of galactic empires is outlined in *Sirian* and *Sentimental Agents*. Cosmic disasters cause ineradicable problems in *Shikasta* and *Planet 8*. An alternate reality is the explanation for the existence of the zones in *Marriages*. Described as panoramic, visionary, and utopian, the Canopus novels effectively utilize the vastness of time and space. The force of evolution, physical and psychological, the process of constant change within the cosmos, and the place of human beings in it, all foundations of cosmic science fiction, are integral to the Canopus series.

Plot Summaries of Major Works

Canopus in Argos: Archives (series)
    Re: Colonized Planet 5, Shikasta. Generally referred to as *Shikasta*, this novel is the first in Lessing's series, and documents the history of Earth and its inhabitants. Originally called Rohanda, Earth was recognized by the Canopeans as a place of pristine beauty and great evolutionary potential. The work of the Canopeans--whose purpose is to help various galactic species evolve onto ever higher levels of existence--proceeds according to plan for thousands of years on Rohanda. However, due to sudden shifts in the cosmic balance, the natural forces of Rohanda are disrupted and the atmosphere is poisoned, leading to a degeneration of the physical, intellectual, and spiritual development of Earth's inhabitants. The Canopeans now call Earth "Shikasta," meaning the hurt, the damaged, for it has become a vale of tears, a place of cruelty, bigotry, ignorance and suffering, a place susceptible to evil and disharmony.

The agents of Shammat, an empire antagonistic to Canopus, are quick to infiltrate Shikasta, encouraging chaos and corruption. Johor and Taufiq are Canopean agents assigned to support and maintain what little harmony and goodness remain on Shikasta, as well as to help resist the influences of Shammat. Throughout the history of Earth, the agents appear to humans on different occasions in angel-like guises, similar to the angels in the Old Testament. At other times, they incarnate and live the usual lifespan of human beings. Toward the end of the book, Johor and Taufiq act as contrasting characters. Both are agents of Canopus, but

Taufiq succumbs to the disease of Shikasta, forgetting his mission. Meanwhile, Johor incarnates as George Sherban, a messianic figure, who is instrumental in leading the humans who survive after the catastrophic wars of the twentieth century to a return to harmony and oneness. The book culminates with a trial of the white race for crimes against other races, which broadens into an indictment against all the inhumane behaviors of the past, regardless of race. The stage is then set for the return to Rohanda's original purity as the cosmic imbalance readjusts itself.

Shikasta embodies in some respect all of the themes which concern Lessing throughout the series a whole. Her description of present and future conditions--pollution, starvation, near-extinction--relate directly to her concerns about human inhumanity, racial injustice, and the self-deception and inherent evilness of dictatorial empires whether they be socialist, democratic, or communist. The spiritual evolution of the collective unconscious and of individuals is the reason-for-being advanced by Lessing, and what began so hopefully and fortuitously in the early days of Rohanda, and was so disastrously interrupted by cosmic disturbances and the evil influences of Shammat, is finally resolved in an optimistic scenario of humans and animals once again progressing together on utopian Rohanda.

Lessing presents *Shikasta* as a collectiion of archival documents, including factual historical reports by Canopean agents, dry synopses of Shikastian conditions by Canopean officials, sociological descriptions of types of individuals, and the personal journal of a young woman. The varying styles and viewpoints of these pieces provide the reader with a comprehensive, panoramic description of Shikasta's long history. Lessing uses science fiction and its conventions of extraterrestrial intervention and space and time travel as a framework on which to display her philosophical beliefs.

The Marriages between Zones Three, Four, and Five. The original book, *Shikasta*, explains that surrounding the Earth are six metaphysical zones, each representing a level of ascending spiritual progression. The inhabitants of the zones answer to "laws" they receive from unseen beings called the "Providers," presumed to be the Canopeans.

Al Ith, the queen of Zone Three, is commanded to marry Ben Ata, the king of Zone Four. Zone Three, a place of beauty, peace, and plenty, bases its matriarchal society on love and equality among all individuals. In contrast, Zone Four is a paternal, militaristic society, wherein women are subordinate to men and there are specific class levels and rankings. Al Ith and Ben Ata progress from an antithetical relationship to one of binding love, as they learn new ways of perceiving and of loving, sexually and spiritually. The union causes Ben Ata to institute changes in Zone Four's society. There is less emphasis on martial abilities and more on cultivating the land and crafts. Women begin to gain status and men begin to develop nonmilitary strengths. The Providers then command Al Ith to return to Zone Three and Ben Ata to marry the queen of Zone Five. Al Ith has been replaced as ruler and is no longer recognizable to her own people. She settles by herself near the upper border, and people begin to gather near her to talk, to learn, and to turn their eyes toward Zone Two. Ben Ata's new marriage causes an exchange of influences between Zones Four and Five, and gradually throughout the no-longer complacent zones, individuals begin to look upward and strive to enter the next zone, as Al Ith eventually enters Zone Two.

This second book in the Canopus series is an allegorical, evolutionary fable in which Lessing elucidates her mystical vision of the cosmos. Of the five books in the series, *Marriages* is the most tenuously connected to the science fiction genre and to Lessing's Canopean empire.

Marriages illustrates Lessing's belief that individuals must evolve and that societies must remain open to exchanges with others in order to encourage that evolution. The zones themselves represent stages of consciousness along a mystical path. On another level, the novel explores the interplay of dominance and need between men and women. On a personal, emotional level, the tale of Ben Ata and Al Ith is a passionate, deeply moving love story between a man and a woman.

Lessing includes the novel in the Archives of Canopus by using the fictional convention that it is a history narrated by the Chroniclers of Zone Three. Beautifully written in the manner of a medieval romance, Lessing unfurls her fable as though it were displayed in a series of brilliantly woven tapestries in the gallery of an ancient castle.

The Sirian Experiments. The central character in the third novel in the Canopus series is Ambien II, one of Five who rule the Sirian Empire. During a galactic conference, the Canopeans offer the Sirians a portion of the planet Shikasta (Earth) to use for research purposes. Dedicated to the expansion of its empire and to the full utilization of the resources on its many planets, the Sirian government rationalizes the exploitation of its subject peoples as being necessary for the greater good. They use their base on Shikasta as a laboratory for genetic and social manipulation of some of their more primitive subjects. Ambien II is assigned the responsibility for the experiments. During the ensuing millenia, a near immortal because of advanced biological techology, Ambien II is slowly transformed by her contact with two Canopean agents, Klorathy and Nasar. She eventually accepts the enlightened Canopean wisdom and returns to Sirius, advocating the Canopean message that the care and nurturing of people, animals, and planets--none of whom must be exploited or oppressed--is of primary importance, not the fulfillment of arbitrary colonial policies. For voicing such convictions, she is expelled from Sirius.

The Sirian Experiments is included in the Canopean Archives as the personal narrative of Ambien II, written during her exile. Covering an enormous time span in Shikasta's history, Lessing concentrates on Earth's fabled past as she presents Ambien's recollections and observations of prehistorical dwarves and giants, the beautiful society of Atlantis, the depravity of Sodom and Gomorrah, and the oppressive, bloody cruelty of the Aztec and Mongol empires. Because Lessing presents the panorama of human history through the eyes of a long-lived, galactic wayfarer, Ambien, we are able to view the planet Earth from the perspective of a vast, unlimited universe. Through Ambien's various experiences on Shikasta, Lessing is able to comment on such social issues as human inhumanity, the suppression of women and minorities, and the rise and fall of societies. On one level, the novel offers a classic struggle between good and evil. On another level, the book's purpose is to describe the raising of Ambien's consciousness about herself, her empire, her universe, and the relationship among the three. Here, Lessing returns to her exploration of the evolution of the individual, the hyprocisy of colonial empires, and the universality of collective consciousness. In the novel, as in most didactic literature, ideas are emphasized; events support them.

The Making of the Representative for Planet 8. The fourth novel in the series is narrated by Doeg, a poet-singer on Planet 8 in the Canopean empire. Planet 8, once a utopia, is entering an ice age which will destroy all life on the planet. The Canopeans have planned to space lift Doeg's people to Shikasta, but it is no longer suitable, because of the cosmic disaster which befell it. With no alternative available, the inhabitants of Planet 8 will suffer and die. Johor, an agent of Canopus, arrives to counsel and encourage Doeg and his people. Through dialogues with Doeg, Johor teaches the people to accept the cosmic plan and to learn to transcend matter, as the few survivors do just before their deaths when their spirits rise above the planet and combine to form a collective consciousness, the final representative of Planet 8.

The novel itself is a grim, relentless narration of suffering and despair. The most didactic novel in the series, *Planet 8* addresses the universal question of why must there be suffering and evil? And, in such circumstances, what is the point of enduring, if it leads only to death? Johor provides little in the way of concrete answers for, in the way of mystics, he is unable to put his Canopean truths into words that the uninitiated can comprehend. However, a partial answer is suggested by the final ability of Doeg's people to transcend their physical bodies, after enduring so much. Whereas Lessing explored the evolution of the individual in previous books, here she is concerned with spiritual evolution on a far greater scale. For along with the message that Death is another name for the Collective Consciousness, Lessing posits that in the scheme of mystical wisdom, all suffering is a part of cosmic evolution.

Documents Relating to the Sentimental Agents in the Volyen Empire. Three neighboring planets, on the borders of the declining Sirian Empire, will soon unite to become the Volyen Empire. Into this hotbed of political contention arrive the antagonistic agents of Shammat, an empire dedicated to achieving absolute power through disharmony and chaos, the agents of Canopus, an empire committed to the beneficial evolution of all life; and finally the Sirian agents, a colonial empire in its waning stages. Shammat's primary weapon is the use of "Rhetoric," the use of language selectively chosen to appeal to the deepest emotions and so to adversely sway an unsuspecting populace. So powerful is this weapon, Canopean allies have established a Hospital for Rhetorical Diseases for those unfortunate enough to succumb to attacks of "rhetoric." However, there are many people that the hospital cannot reach, and these people, inspired by grandiose words, are manipulated into agitation and revolt. Klorathy, a Canopean agent, has been sent by his superior, Johor, to deprogram Incent, a young agent who has fallen prey to the emotional sentimental propaganda of Krolgul, an agent of Shammat.

The documents in the title are the letters that Klorathy sends to Johor describing political and social scenes and his attempts to cure Incent of his susceptibility to sentimental rhetoric. Lessing allows Klorathy--who appeared in *The Sirian Experiment*--to display a broad sense of humor, although an underlying seriousness is always apparent. She creates Incent (perhaps a play on the word "innocent"), the naive, well-meaning fool, to demonstrate the adverse effects of human susceptibility to rhetorical manipulation. The entire novel is Lessing's vehicle for commenting on the destructive effects of sentimental propaganda. The people of the developing Voylen Empire, having been conditioned to respond in emotional ways to certain words and phrases, often called inspirational language, are manipulated and victimized by the political and religious institutions of Shammat and Sirius. Although Lessing has criticized collective institutions and ideologies earlier in the series, here she approaches the problem from the perspective of the social hypocrisy apparent in the rhetorical processes by which collectives become powerful. *The Sentimental Agents*, because of its variation from the austerity of the other Canopus novels, enriches the series as a whole. However, the book is good social commentary rather than good science fiction, and, as a satire, it is not entirely successful; as always, however, Lessing commands attention and stimulates thought.

Biographical/Bibliographical Readings

Harold Bloom, *Doris Lessing* (Chelsea House, 1986). Betsy Draine, *Substance under Pressure: Artistic Coherence and Evolving Form in the Novels of Doris Lessing* (University of Wisconsin Press, 1983). Mona Knapp, *Doris Lessing* (Knopf, 1984). Dee Seligman, *Doris Lessing: An Annotated Bibliography of Criticism* (Greenwood, 1981). Jenny Taylor, ed., *Notebooks/Memoirs/Archives: Reading and Rereading Doris Lessing* (Routledge & Kegan Paul, 1982). [Dianne P. Varnon]

LONGYEAR, BARRY BROOKES

Life and Works

Born in 1942 in Harrisburg, Pennsylvania, Longyear attended Staunton Military Academy in Virginia and later, for a brief time, the Pittsburgh Institute of Art. After joining the army and serving as a missile technician on Okinawa and in Key West, Florida, he left the service and attended Wayne State University for two years, majoring in social studies. While in Detroit, Longyear became a microfilm production manager, a position which eventually led to a career as ghostwriter and publisher in Philadelphia. Still later, Longyear moved to Fornington, Maine, to run a printing firm, where he and his wife, Jean, presently live.

Longyear began writing science fiction in 1978, his first story appearing in *Isaac Asimov's Science Fiction Magazine* in that same year. Remarkably, Longyear was awarded both the Nebula in 1979 and the Hugo in 1980 for best novella of the year with his story, "Enemy Mine." This novella has since been developed into the full length novel, *Manifest Destiny*, and in 1985 into the film of the original name, *Enemy Mine*. Longyear has also created a series dealing with a traveling space circus, which includes the titles *Circus World* (1981) and *Elephant Walk* (1983). He has at various times used the pseudonym Fredrick Longbeard. Longyear is very interested in developing the talents of young writers and has compiled an outstanding writers' guide called *Science Fiction Writer's Workshop I* (1980). His brilliant start also brought him the John W. Campbell award for best new author in 1980.

Themes and Style

Longyear's works have alternately been praised and vilified by the critics. After his awards in 1979 and 1980, Longyear's works have decreased in popularity with some critics. There is general agreement that "Enemy Mine" and his other works about human/alien interactions show genuine talent and a great flair for suspense, particularly when Longyear draws upon his own military background to provide the solid foundation of his work--a talent that is yet to be fulfilled as Longyear matures in his writing.

While critics find fault with Longyear's lack of interest in technological gimmickery, the readers find his Circus World series both entertaining and heart wrenching. The three volumes--*City of Baraboo*, *Elephant Walk*, and *Circus World*--demonstrate a genuine humor and ability to involve the reader. Even if this talent is never fully realized, Longyear's *Science Fiction Writer's Workshop* will certainly constitute a major contribution to the field of professional writing.

Plot Summaries of Major Works

Circus World series

City of Baraboo. Set in the early twenty-first century, this novel deals with the death of the circus on Earth, its migration to the stars, and its colonization on Momus, the Circus World. The *City of Baraboo* is a circus spaceship named for Baraboo, Wisconsin, where Ringling Brothers/Barnum and Bailey originated. John J. O'Hara is "the governor," owner and operator of the O'Hara circus, which has been forced to leave Earth because of repressive environmental laws forbidding shipment of wild animals from district to district. Building a spaceship capable of carrying a circus and financing the operation brings the governor to the edge of bankruptcy and at the mercy of Karl Arnheim, the principal villain, who is O'Hara's main competition. Using various classic scams that prey upon Arnheim's weaknesses and greed, O'Hara manages to successfully launch the circus ship before the animals can be destroyed. Once in space, the circus rapidly adjusts to the changes necessary for the survival of the circus. Advance men are sent ahead to advertise; the "Patch," a legal fixer, manipulates the local authorities to surmount local regulations; and new acts are added from various worlds visited. But O'Hara cannot escape the terrible twisted vengeance of Karl Arnheim. In the end, the ship is sabotaged and the passengers forced to colonize on an isolated planet in order to survive.

Both amusing and rich in circus lore, the novel holds together very well, despite its patchwork origins as previously published material. The reader becomes immersed in a sea of circus detail and language, entering the world of fantasy and illusion that is at the heart of any circus. The characterizations in this book are designed to tug at the heartstrings, as a series of memorable circus figures such as the Patch, Warts, the alien route man, and little Tyli, the Moss-Headed Girl, parade across the pages of the novel. Most surprising is the humorous quality of this novel and how well the elaborate scams show up that ancient saying: You can't cheat an honest man--or alien!

Elephant Walk. The spaceship *City of Baraboo* has crash landed on an unknown planet. The great cats are dead, the elephants goring and trampling the handlers in their pain and terror, Arnheim the villain is dead, and the great O'Hara as well. But the circus has known many fires and many terrible tragic deaths, and will hopefully survive this apocalyptic landing as well. With O'Hara dead, the power and mystery of the circus evolves upon the handlers and the surviving elephants, or bulls. Realizing that they lack the technical knowledge to escape from Momus, the circus performers are forced to colonize the world, sacrificing the great elephants in road and bridge building. The novel concentrates on Little Willy, the daughter of Bullhook Willy, who died saving the bull elephants from the fiery crash, and of Lady, who killed her great cats and then herself when the suffering cats were dying aboard the damaged ship. Little Willy is determined to save the few remaining elephants, for in them the colonists see the spirit and hope of the circus. Regretfully, all the elephants are female. As each year and each tragedy takes its toll of the great bulls, the colony becomes less a circus and more a struggle for simple survival. As the colonists become further removed from their circus origins, they begin to adopt the old bizarre ways to the new planet. No one is to rule, no laws can be made without the agreement of the whole, and the only punishment is that of "outcast" or "black-balling." By the conclusion of the novel, Little Willy, her son Johnjay, and granddaughter Girl have adjusted to the deaths of the bulls, and the reader senses that the circus will continue.

This is the most emotionally wrenching and grimmest of the three Circus World volumes. The first novel was lightly humorous and followed the classic sting operations of the circus as we know it. The third novel is also upbeat, dealing with the resurrection of the circus. But this middle novel deals with the love and sacrifice the animal handlers must make for their charges, and with the suffering and death of both the handlers and the elephants. The characterizations are well drawn. Willy, her ethereal daughter May, and her rebellious telepathic son Johnjay all become close to the reader. The plot is clear with a few light touches to relieve the constant, looming tragedy, such as the selection of the circus flags to form the new uniforms designating each group--the fortune tellers, the magicians, and the bull handlers. Certain technical details necessary to successful science fiction are not present however. Where does the food come from to feed all those elephants? Where are all the other details of colony life, the need for food crops and farming? Longyear ignores these technical elements and instead concentrates on the human element. A very readable and absorbing novel that stands alone without the other two volumes, it will send the reader scrambling to find out what happened before and after.

Circus World. Several generations have passed since the circus spaceship crash landed on Momus, a planet named for the ancient Earth god of ridicule. The planet lies between the warring Ninth and Tenth Quandrants, and is a jewel that each would like to add to their crown. To this end, the Ninth Quandrant sends Lord Allenby, a young ambassador, to set up relations and treaty negotiations with the Momus government. After a series of amazing and ridiculous failures, Allenby begins to realize the difficulty of his task. Momus has no government--and how can he make a treaty with a world that has but one one law--that no law can be made without petition of 50,000 of the population, and the agreement of the majority? As a result of this one law, no other law has ever been passed, and no other form of government considered--a reaction to the terrible laws that drove the circus from Earth centuries ago. Allenby finds that in order for his case to be presented, he must have "an act that plays" and an audience willing to pay to hear. The remainder of the novel details, in howling good humor, Allenby's attempts to be heard, his apprenticeship in the magic arts, and his eventual founding of a new "flying circus" in space. Interspersed with this amusing story is the more serious tale of war, evil magicians, and abortive coups, as the Tenth Quadrant attempts its own plan of conquest.

Longyear has a talent for revealing that beyond the evil and plotting of any empire are beings that may be well intentioned or may be quite evil. In this novel, he demonstrates that individuals of good intention exist within all organizations and, despite the organization, that evil thrives within the structure of the organization. Momus has a good magician, such as Fyx, and an evil one, Fyx's brother, Rogor. The Tenth Quadrant has an evil scientist--Short the Vorilian--and Naavon, the mercenary with the heart of gold. The principal flaw of *Circus World* is its uneven construction. Formed by a series of previously published short stories, the reader must work hard to maintain interest in characters that appear and disappear within a few pages. Longyear's writing style, which is strong on characterizations, suffers when subjected to this fairly typical arrangement. The reader should care as deeply at the end of *Circus World* as they wept for Little Willie and Reg, the last elephant, in the previous volume, *Elephant Walk*, but the uneven, artificial construction prevents this necessary involvement.

Manifest Destiny. In the twenty-first and twenty-second centuries, humanity is expanding outward, conquering and seizing worlds, until more than 200 planets are under human control. In a series of four stories, three previously published, this outward conquest highlights the continuing expansionist and colonial policies that seem inherent in the human condition. The four stories are tied together by a series of short extracts from the Earth's Legislative Assembly minutes, as through the years it considers various motions and treaties regarding this "manifest destiny." The first story, "The Jaren," is placed early in humanity's outward expansion. The tale opens with a human safari sometime after the conquest of the Shikazu, a primitive warrior people who controlled nine planets. Eeola, a native bearer, chief cook and bottle washer, relates the story of his Jaren and of the dedicated military society within the Shikazu. The Jaren is a grouping of five males or females formed in early life during various rites of passage and bound together by some strange energy force from within the planet. Raised and trained in military and warrior skills, they provide the backbone of the Shikazu infantry. In telling of the deaths of the Jaren and eventual tragic defeat of the Shikazu, Longyear highlights that which is cruelest and most disturbing within the human nature--the urge to conquer.

The second story, "Enemy Mine," is perhaps the best known due to the movie of the same name. Willis Davidge is a fighter pilot brought down on an isolated, miserable planet by an enemy ace, called Jeriba, who also crashes. The two characters continue the war on the ground, eventually gaining mutual respect for each other. Jeriba is a Drac, a hermaphroditic reptilian race with a strong philosophical and moral code. As the pair struggles to survive the harsh environment, an eventual truce is called. Jeriba dies giving birth to a baby, Zammis, which Davidge agrees to raise in the Drac traditions. In the process of learning the philosophy and lineage of the Dracs, Davidge comes to realize the senselessness of the hatred and bigotry in humanity's expansion to other planets. He resolves to return Zammis to its family. The remainder of the story reflects this uphill battle once they are rescued and the terrible price that Zammis pays as an outcast in the Dracon society.

The next story, "Savage Planet," concerns a third alien race, the Benda, and their human teacher, Michael Fellman. Set twenty years after the tale of Davidge and Zammis, the human expansion and exploitation continues. The plot is more terrible and sinister as the mining companies design a systematic program of genocide. Human professors are hired to carry out the teaching of the Benda in such a way that the structure of the society, based upon a biological necessity, is destroyed. Fellman begins to realize that his teachings are literally destroying the Benda society and reproductive patterns. He begins a systematic campaign to teach his charges the true meaning of freedom and equality in such a way that the race can survive.

The final story, "USE Planet," is a story which reflects the most likely result of human expansion, a human civil war between the colonialists and the pacifists, called "Ronnies," after the planet Rhana. The story deals with the trainee, David Merit--or "DeMerit," as he is called by his drill instructor, Murdo. Following David through boot camp to his eventual capture and escape from the enemy, the tale is the most harrowing and savage of the four stories. Body parts, the smell of burning flesh, and the up-close-and-personal senseless tragedy of civil war join in a strong statement regarding the human capacity for violence.

The style of the four stories varies considerably, but reflects the gradual evolution of the human race from an expansionist to a maturing race worthy of consideration for a full partnership in the Ninth Quadrant Federation of Habitable Planets. Written within two years of each other, the style of the stories has not evolved, but the writing is moving and effective. The finest of the stories is clearly the Nebula and Hugo award winning "Enemy Mine," which highlights the best in the human condition against a backdrop of interplanetary war. The well-developed characters, their motivations and sensitivities are beautifully drawn, forming an unforgettable portrait. The least flawed of the remaining three stories is "Savage Planet." The characters are once again believable. Less so is the "Jaren," which requires too much willing suspension of disbelief. The mysterious unexplained blue fire that gives the Jaren its power, and the clearly primitive warrior society that adapts immediately to the technological advances of the Shikazu off-world society, strains credulity. The author seems to make his point, that expansionism is at the price of native cultural genocide. The least successful and most brutal story, perhaps because of the savagery of the human civil conflict, "USE Planet," seems a thinly disguised war story that just happens to be set in the twenty-second century. Longyear shows a wide range of writing talents and fine sensitivity in all four stories, however. The rich fabric of alien cultures revealed in "Enemy Mine" deserves recognition and the anticipation that Longyear will at some point produce another such jewel.

Biographical/Bibliographical Readings

Barry Longyear, *Science Fiction Writers Workshop-I: An Introduction to Fiction Mechanics* (Owlswick Press, 1980). Shawna McCarthy, "Interview with Barry Longyear," in *The Berkley Showcase* (Berkley, 1980), v.2, p.193-200. Darrell Schweitzer, "Barry Longyear," *Rigel Science Fiction*, (Summer 1983), p.38-43. Idem, "Barry Longyear," in *Twentieth-Century Science-Fiction Writers*, ed. Curtis C. Smith (St. James, 1986), p.458-59. [Colleen Power]

LOVECRAFT, H. P.

Life and Works

Howard Phillips Lovecraft was born in Providence, Rhode Island, on August 20, 1890. He was a child prodigy, reading at the age of three and writing at four. Because of his father's early death, Lovecraft was brought up by his mother, whose possessive and smothering influence made him a recluse for most of his life. He spent his entire existence in Providence except for short trips and for the brief period of his marriage to Sonia Haft Greene in 1924, which ended in separation and was childless. This reclusiveness was accentuated by intermittent poor health, an early period of which prevented his completing high school, but Lovecraft was highly intelligent and intellectually curious, and continued a self-directed education until the year he died.

Among his early interests were science and mythical and horror fiction. From the latter derives his own early fantasy fiction, which deals with conventional themes and is imitative of Edgar Allen Poe and Lord Dunsany, as well as his scholarly study, *Supernatural Horror in Literature* (1927). His interest in science led to his first published work, a series of articles on astronomy in local newspapers and his later science fiction. After this he studied chemistry and maintained a home laboratory (1909-12), but this vocation foundered due to his continued poor health and the realization of the hard work under the discipline's surface glamour.

Despite illness, which continued to keep him from any regular employment, he remained an omnivorous reader and a letter-writer to popular periodicals. This correspondence introduced him to amateur journalism and publishing, to which he devoted much time from 1914 on, and to the occupation of ghost writer, revisionist, and regional author. On the sparse proceeds of this occupation, supplemented by a small income from a family inheritance, Lovecraft lived a frugal but apparently not unhappy existence until his death from cancer on March 15, 1937.

Lovecraft incorporated science fiction elements into his stories gradually and sporadically. At first, as in "Beyond the Wall of Sleep (written in 1919) and "From Beyond" (1920), their appearance was minor. Over the next decade their role became increasingly important, and in "The Dunwhich Horror" (1928) and "The Whisperer in Darkness" (1930), they are major and intrinsic. In his masterpieces, "The Colour out of Space" (1927) and "The Shadow out of Time" (1934-35), they dominate the story wholly, as they do in *At the Mountains of Madness* (1931). This last title and *The Case of Charles Dexter Ward* (1927-28) are full-length novels; all of Lovecraft's other works are technically classifiable as short stories, though his later works stretch that definition by running to as many as 30,000 words, and are usually referred to as novelettes. Out of some fifty stories that were published under Lovecraft's own name, at least a dozen used scientific elements pivotally enough to be labeled science fiction.

During his lifetime, Lovecraft's work appeared either in pulp magazines of low and specialized circulation or in the amateur press, to which the public had no access. Often years would elapse between the composition of the stories and their publication. They received little general acclaim, although applauded by a small coterie whose enthusiasm encouraged their first appearance in book form in 1939 in *The Outsider and Others*. As science (and later science fiction itself) became an ever-increasing part of everyday knowledge and familiarity, Lovecraft's stature grew, and two generations after his death his fiction is not only kept constantly in print, but in popular pocket book form has sold in the millions of copies and has been translated into five languages.

Lovecraft wrote considerable verse cast in the forms and styles that echo his beloved eighteenth century. He was also a first-class essayist and an indefatigable and perennially interesting letter-writer. Indeed, it is from publication of his letters, which so impressed his correspondents that most preserved them, that we know as much as we do about the man's personal life, characteristics, and beliefs.

Themes and Style

From boyhood, Lovecraft was an agnostic; throughout his life he remained a rationalist and a materialist. He had an immoderate love for the eighteenth century, where mechanistic materialism held sway, and often expressed the wish of having been born during that time. But he also had an ineradicable love for the weird and the fantastic. His most important contribution to literature was reconciling these conflicting elements. This he accomplished by substituting science for religion and tradition, making the inexplicable supernatural into the explainable supernormal. In so doing, he necessarily placed his stories into the category of science fiction. Lovecraft took an outsider's view of the universe--humanity and its doings were evanescent on a cosmic time span; other civilizations, both on this planet and elsewhere, preceded humanity and would follow it. The climaxes of his stories strike notes of fear and horror through making this concept immediate and believable to their characters, most of whom have lived their lives in the comfortable assumption of humanity's innate superiority and ascendancy. Lovecraft manages this through a meticulous attention to circumstantial, scientific detail which makes it impossible for readers to escape the conclusion to which they have been led. Lovecraft also attempted, less successfully, to substitute for existing tradition a new one of his own invention. This took the form of quotations from imaginary books (he coined, for example, *The Necronomicon*) and references to nonhuman beings with unpronounceable names (this has become known as the "Cthulhu mythos," though Lovecraft never used that phrase). These two devices were seized upon and added to by fellow writers to authenticate their own work. The spreading surfeit not only defeated the original purpose of increasing verisimilitude but, in mistaking shadow for substance, has since obscured Lovecraft's first and major accomplishment in the genre.

Lovecraft's prose style is not as forward looking as his themes, being unduly influenced by Poe and writers who fluorished two centuries earlier. Even after the thematic orientation toward science helped purge its more florid excesses, it remains ornate and Johnsonian, richer in adjectives than we are accustomed to today--or, even, than one finds in most fiction of the 1920s and 1930s. The sentences are long, and often bristle with unusual and multisyllabic words. But there is a fine-tuned precision about it, and a clear crescendo accompanies the storyline. Critics have praised Lovecraft's use of anaphora and metonymy.

Plot Summaries of Major Works

"The Colour out of Space." A strange meteor falls on a New England farm and has profound effects on all of the life forms in the area. The story is narrated in the first person by a surveyor who comes to the area years later to plan for a reservoir that will cover the region. The surveyor encounters at the site an area of gray, powdery desolation where nothing will grow, locally termed "the blasted heath." He is curious about its origin and finally learns through an elderly inhabitant the story of how an alien life-form in the meteorite poisoned the soil and eventually destroyed the crops, farm animals, and the family living there. Its effects on human beings was mental as well as physical, and involved possession of the victims' minds by the alien intelligence.

Lovecraft judged *The Colour out of Space* to be his best tale. Lovecraft's style here is more sober, down-to-earth and self-effacing than usual, and the narration is enlivened and underscored by conversation in the colloquial speech of the region. The inspiration for the setting is known to be the Quabbin Reservoir in north-central Massachusetts, whose construction actually began the year he wrote the story. The pacing follows a careful crescendo, and the descriptions, imagery, and choice of atmospheric and prosaic detail are handled with great care and skill. There is no mention of *The Necronomicon* or invented mythological figures to detract from the overall sombre mood, which exemplifies Lovecraft's cosmic view at its purist. Originally published in *Amazing Stories* (September, 1927), the story received honorable mention in Edward J. O'Brien's *Best American Short Stories* of 1927, and has been widely antholgized since its original appearance.

"The Shadow out of Time." A race of extraterrestrial beings with a highly advanced civilization establishes a colony on this planet in the distant, prehistoric past. These beings have developed the ability to project their psyches through time, displacing those of chosen living beings in other ages and civilizations. The Great Race (as it is called) does this to assemble firsthand historical records of all other cultures in the universe which ever existed or will exist. While the invading psyche occupies the body of a stranger and scans the world to bring back information, the displaced psyche occupies the original body of the invader back in our prehistoric past, and is occupied in personally recording further data from its own memories into the Great Race's records. After these tasks have been completed, both psyches are restored to their original bodies. To protect the sanity of the being who has been so used, all memories of the period are expunged from the conscious mind; the person will seem to himself or herself and to others simply to have recovered from a period of amnesia.

All of this is gradually and tantalizing revealed by the narrator, Nathaniel Peaslee, a college professor who has been a victim of such a mind exchange. Peaslee is able to describe the process because the imposition of amnesia on him is imperfect; he is subject in dreams--and ultimately in waking hours--to remembrances of what occurred. He investigates his own reported actions while his body was possessed and simultaneously institutes a study of other recorded cases of amnesia, finding that in some of them recollections exactly paralleling his own have surfaced. The climax of the story comes when Peaslee is led to the very spot on the planet where the Great Ones lived--now a ruin--and with quickening memory explores its hauntingly familiar innermost recesses.

"The Shadow out of Time" is the most detailed and emotionally compelling picture we have of Lovecraft's bleak view of the cosmos and of humanity's ultimate insignificance. Its complex plot is developed rationally; the descriptions are vivid and the labyrinthine supporting details never rob the story line of forceful clarity. On its original magazine publication (*Astounding Stories*, June, 1936), it received a mixed critical reception, but is now regarded as one of Lovecraft's most powerful and compelling pieces of science fiction.

Biographical/Bibliographical Readings

Donald R. Burleson, *H. P. Lovecraft: A Critical Study* (Greenwood Press, 1983). L. S. DeCamp, *Lovecraft: A Biography* (Doubleday, 1975). S. T. Joshi, *H. P. Lovecraft* (Starmont House, 1982). Idem, *H. P. Lovecraft and Lovecraft Criticism* (Kent State University Press, 1981). Frank Belknap Long, *Howard Phillips Lovecraft: Dreamer on the Nightside* (Arkham House, 1975). H. P. Lovecraft, *Selected Letters*, 5v., ed. August Derleth, Donald Wandrei, and James Turner (Arkham House, 1965-76). [A. Langley Searles]

MACLEAN, KATHERINE ANNE

Life and Works

Katherine MacLean was born in Glen Ridge, New Jersey, on January 22, 1925. Her father was a chemical engineer, which perhaps encouraged her high school interest in science and math. She earned a B.A. in economics from Barnard College in 1950 and an M.A. in psychology from Goddard College in 1977. Her education has continued in many fields. She has had training as a nurse assistant and advanced Red Cross emergency first aid coursework. She went on to study medical nutrition for her Ph.D. MacLean has earned a Doctor of Divinity degree from the Universal Life Church. She has been married three times and has one son, Christopher Dennis Mason, born in 1957.

Her work experience has been extremely varied. She has worked as a nurse's aide, EKG technician, food analyst, laboratory technician, quality control biochemist, editor, book reviewer, public relations and publicity worker, photographer, office manager, payroll bookkeeper, and college English teacher.

She won a Nebula Award for "Missing Man" (1971), from the Science Fiction Writers of America. She was one of the organizers of the Free University of Portland, and she has taught creative writing and literature (including science fiction) there as well as at the University of Maine and elsewhere. She is also a recent president of the Science Fiction Writers of America.

The first collection of MacLean's short fiction, *The Diploids and Other Flights of Fancy* (1962), contains eight short stories which are some of her best work from the 1950s. These stories originally appeared in *Galaxy*, *Astounding Science Fiction*, and *Thrilling Wonder Stories*. Another collection, *The Trouble with You Earth People*, was published in 1980 and contains the novella, "Missing Man."

Over the years, MacLean has collaborated with several different people. She worked with Harry Harrison to write *Web of the Worlds* in 1955 and with Charles V. DeVet in 1962 on *Cosmic Checkmate*. In 1975, she collaborated with Tom Condit on *Trouble with Treaties*, then wrote two novels with Carl West, *The Man in the Birdcage* (1971) and *Dark Wing* (1979). She has written under the pseudonyms Charles Dye and G. A. Morris.

Themes and Style

There were few women in science fiction in the 1950s when MacLean won the respect of her predominantly male readers and colleagues through her excellent knowledge of science and extremely competent storytelling skills. Though her most productive writing period was in the 1950s, she has continued to write science fiction stories based upon sound scientific principles and excellent logic.

MacLean writes science fiction out of a belief that this fiction works as a "popular education" to illustrate possible future disasters extrapolated from logically predicted events. Therefore, most of her fiction deals with the near future and science's effects on the individual and society.

With early stories such as "The Pyramid in the Desert" and "The Diploid," MacLean indicated a strong interest in medical themes and used medical professionals as main characters. One of her best stories dealing with medical themes is "Contagion" where colonists, in order to survive a plague on their new world, become look-alikes. Suddenly the relationship between personality and outward appearance is at issue. A neurosurgeon in "The Origin of the Species" destroys the best parts of his patients' minds so they can adapt in society. Another litte story, "Gimmick," shows the use of a virus as a weapon.

MacLean's two novels written with husband Carl West, *The Man in the Birdcage* and *Dark Wing*, are weaker, less successful works. *Dark Wing* presents a future where practicing medicine is illegal, yet a teenager with old medical kits from an ambulance performs complicated operations. It is not as believable as her earlier works, but it is in keeping with her medical theme and use of medical people as main characters.

MacLean's short stories continue to be her strong point where innovation and elegance compete with strong characterization and sensitive depictions of the personal element in humanity's future.

Plot Summaries of Major Works

The Diploids and Other Flights of Fancy. The first four stories of the *Diploids* collection deal with psychology, particularly defense mechanisms humans create to allow us to function. MacLean used that term, "Defense Mechanism" (1949), for her first published story and the lead entry in the collection. In it, she proposes that infants have psi perception, but adults do not because they block it as a defense mechanism against the information explosion that forces specialization and limits communication when they are presented with a new communication form, such as musical language. In "The Pyramid in the Desert" (1950), endocrinologist Helen Berent needs a defense against her fear of injury or death after using a process of cell rejuvenation that makes her immortal. She finds her defense mechanism in the knowledge that the process increases the rate of mutation, thus the inevitability of death by cancer; thereafter she is able to enjoy life without the need to protect herself from any possible accident.

While the fourth story deals more with a sociological theme, "Feedback" (1951) also presents a defense mechanism, this one against conformity. William Dunner's attempts to teach individualism are a defense against peer pressure to conform, yet his students use conformity as a defense against what is alien or different.

"Pictures Don't Lie" (1951) deals with a computer programmer's misguided efforts to make his machines conform with his reality rather than factual reality; the truth is that the alien space ship he has contacted is microscopic. A rather humorous look at social programming is found in "The Snowball Effect" (1952), where a sociologist's defensive demonstration results in an unstoppable organization because he failed to include any mechanism against unlimited growth.

MacLean shows what can happen when scientific defense mechanisms are circumvented in the title story, "The Diploids" (1953). Genetically designed embryos are smuggled from a lab, allowed to mature, and then begin organizing and preparing to reproduce their own "superior" kind. "Games" (1953), the final story of the collection, depicts the use of telepathy as a defense against political oppression. A scientist who refuses to give his knowledge to the government for military use does give it to a small boy whose adult political attitudes are thus influenced by the scientist.

Missing Man. George Sanford has a talent for finding people. Ahmed, his childood gang leader, now a member of New York's Rescue Squad, works with George to find people in trouble or ones giving off bad vibes that influence the general populace negatively. George becomes better with each rescue, even rescuing an important city engineer computer operator. However, George is intrigued by the youthful gang leader who had kidnapped the computer operator. But when George seeks him out, the teenager uses George's talents against the city. George's escape and coming to terms with his talent conclude this fast-paced novel on a satisfying note.

This novel is the combined result of three earlier short stories: "Fear Hound (1968), "Rescue Squad for Ahmed" (1970), and her Nebula Award-winning novella "Missing Man" (1971). Typical of all of MacLean's works, this novel uses good hard science and logic to study the culture of New York in the future. The psychological and scientific details of the story are quite accurate, but the development is rather uneven in spots, even though the plot has obviously been carefully planned. As in all her stories, MacLean's characterization here is excellent.

MacLean's most common themes are all evident in this novel. She has always dealt with ethical questions of medical and scientific experimentation. Here, she addresses the ethical question of using brainwipe for the criminal elements in society. She has also had a long fascination with psi powers, particulary telepathy, which is the talent that makes George so valuable in *Missing Man*. Finally, this novel is perhaps most representative of MacLean's novels in its display of her marvelous talent to explore the future's possibilities.

The Trouble with You Earth People. This collection is a mixture of stories from the 1950s, 1960s, and 1970s. One frequently anthologized story, "Unhuman Sacrifice" (1958), deals with a missionary's misguided efforts to save an alien teenager from what the missionary believes are pagan religious rites of the boy's world. What the missionary actually succeeds in doing is allowing the teenager to evolve beyond his sentient stage to a nonsentient weed stage, which the alien's practices normally prevented. "Syndrome Johnny" depicts an ever-young man who lets loose a devastating plague every generation or so in order to speed up evolution and strengthen the race. Other stories in this collection, though perhaps not as memorable, do typify the humanistic elements so common in MacLean's works throughout this period.

The most important story included in this collecion is the novella "Missing Man" (1971), for which MacLean received a Nebula. MacLean used this novella, combined with two earlier short stories, "Fear Hound" (1968) and "Rescue Squad for Ahmed" (1970), to create her novel *Missing Man*, published in 1975. The story is very strong in characterization and as a psychological and sociological study of a none-too-distant New York City, when it is divided into ethnic, political, or religiously oriented communes.

Two of the works MacLean wrote in collaboration represent her venture into the space opera genre. She originally wrote "Second Game" (1958) with Charles V. DeVet, and then expanded it into the novel *Cosmic Checkmate*. Even here her attention to detail is evident. Robert Lang plays the Veldian version of our chess to discover why Velda's people won't peacefully join Earth's federation. He purposefully loses the first game to discover their weaknesses, and then wins the second with the insights he has gained. He plies this same strategy to let the Veldians win the war while the federation truly wins the second game by assimilating the conquerors into its cultures. In the second space opera, "Trouble with Treaties" (1959, republished as a novel under the same title in 1975), humor is rampant in this farce about an adaptable Earth crew in a game of bluff with a rigidly strict alien culture.

Biographical/Bibliographical Readings

Judith E. Boss, "Katherine Anne MacLean," in *Twentieth-Century American Science-Fiction Writers* (Gale, 1981) p.5-8. Katherine MacLean, "The Expanding Mind," in *Fantastic Lives: Autobiographical Essays by Notable SF Writers*, ed. Martin H. Greenberg (Southern Illinois University Press, 1981), p.79-101. **[Barbara Ann Luther]**

MALZBERG, BARRY N.

Life and Works

Barry Norman Malzberg was born on July 24, 1939, in New York City. From an early age, he displayed literary leanings and claims to have always known that he wanted to be a writer. He graduated from Syracuse University in 1960, served in the U.S. Army, and held a job with the New York City Department of Welfare before being awarded a Schubert Foundation playwriting fellowship in 1964. The fellowship did not result in any published plays. Malzberg admired the careers of Norman Mailer and Philip Roth, particularly Roth's short stories, and he aimed for a similar career path. When this did not materialize, Malzberg realistically chose new directions.

While working at the Scott Meredith Literary Agency, he became familiar with the various commercial markets and decided he could produce work as good as or better than that which was being published. From 1968 to 1976, he wrote extensively, prolifically publishing both novels and short stories. The bulk of his output was science fiction, pornography, and suspense novels, and he used many pseudonyms, including Mike Berry, Claudine Dumas, M. L. Johnson, Howard Lee, Lee W. Mason, Francine di Natale, K. M. O'Donnell, and Gerrold Watkins. During this early stage of his writing career, he also served as editor for *Amazing*, *Fantastic*, and as managing editor for *Escapade*.

Beyond Apollo (1972) is Malzberg's best known science fiction novel, having won the John W. Campbell Award for best book of 1972. It was the subject of both high acclaim and bitter controversy. Its detractors often claimed that it was insulting to Campbell's memory to recognize such a book in his name. Another of his better known novels is *Herovit's World* (1973). Critics have attacked *Herovit's World* as not being science fiction at all, and it has been suggested that at least some of the events related in the novel parallel Malzberg's own life. *Galaxies* appeared in 1975, expanded from the novelette "A Galaxy Called Rome."

Malzberg has been a prolific writer of short stories which have been collected in *Out from Ganymede* (1974), *The Many Worlds of Barry N. Malzberg* (1975), *Down Here in the Dream Quarter* (1976), *Malzberg at Large* (1979), and *The Man Who Loved the Midnight Lady* (1980).

Except for the collections of his short stories, Malzberg abandoned the science fiction genre in 1976. Since then he has published *Chorale* (1978) and *The Remaking of Sigmund Freud* (1985). To date, he has published over 200 novels and short stories, of which about one third are science fiction. Most recently he has been writing mystery and suspense tales, as well as coediting several collections of short science fiction and supernatural fiction.

Themes and Style

In *Beyond Apollo, Galaxies*, and *Herovit's World*, Malzberg employs the scenario of a novel within a novel. The main characters are science fiction authors: Harry Evans is a writer approaching insanity in *Beyond Apollo*; Lena Thomas is a down and out science fiction author in *Galaxies*; and Jonathan Herovit is a prolific science fiction writer in *Herovit's World*. Malzberg is playing games with his readers throughout *Beyond Apollo*. His extensive use of bridge and chess problems, mordant humor, cryptograms, and anagrams are the obvious games. The not-so-obvious ones are the mental puzzles that must be worked with to try to sort the narrated events into some type of comprehensible form. The theme of a novel within a novel seems to work well for Malzberg, giving the perspective and points of view from two different sources rather than the usual single point of view or personal narrative.

There seems to be no middle ground in the appraisal and appreciation of Barry Malzberg's science fiction. His writing has usually aroused strong responses among critics, academics, and fans. He often explores anxiety states in both the hard and soft sciences and seldom supplies solutions for any given situations. His characters often gripe, grumble, and complain their way through stories in which compromise and negativity render them unsympathetic. Malzberg himself became disillusioned with his contributions to the genre and called a halt to his science fiction writing in 1976.

Plot Summaries of Major Works

Beyond Apollo. The major character, Harry Evans, has returned alone from a two-person NASA mission. He is insane, and Dr. Forest is trying to find out what happened. Throughout their interaction, Evans maintains that he will write a book, called *Beyond Apollo*, detailing the events surrounding a failed mission to Venus. Dr. Forest probes his mind, trying to determine what happened to Captain Jack Josephson, who theoretically should not have been able to disappear from the self-contained and sealed spacecraft. Evans' responses are contradictory and illogical, and Dr. Forest takes full advantage of Evans' belief that *Beyond Apollo* is a novel to be written and not a real past event. He coaxes, cajoles, and intimidates Evans, trying to get to the truth. The relationship between Evans and Josephson is discovered to have become homosexual. Neither character in the proposed novel is identified as gay; however, they do have sex in a rather violent sex scene and Evans is quite clearly in love with his captain.

The scheme of a novel-within-a-novel allows for action and evidence to appear subtly, cryptically, symbolically, and enigmatically. The story contains graphic violence and explicitly sexual passages and requires an effort on the part of the reader. Because of the novel's confusing structure, the reader is challenged to determine exactly what is going on. Harry Evans' insanity, coupled with an unstructured and not easily defined plot, make this a difficult task. Most of the novel is related by Evans in the first person as he describes his projected novel. The reader can be forgiven for considering whether Evans was really on a mission to Venus or whether he is merely an insane writer fabricating fantasies. The book closes with an epilogue containing a letter from a publisher accepting Evans' manuscript for publication.

Galaxies. The main character in this book is a worn-out science fiction author, Lena Thomas, who is contemplating writing a story about an astronaut who enters a black hole. The novel itself cannot be written, but only perceived through the eyes of the fortieth-century era. As the astronaut is the only conscious being on her spaceship, she must experience the black hole alone and be solely responsible for her actions. Everything she experiences is filtered through the perceptions of an Earthbound, disillusioned, current-day author. It contains long sequences discussing black holes, neutron stars, and technology and science in general. These discourses compliment the quandries faced by Lena Thomas in trying to overcome the circumstances created by entering the black hole. Lena's situation is never resolved. In the beginning the black hole is artificial--something created as a test by the decadent and bureaucratic government on Lena's home world. The second possible ending sees Lena frozen into an eternal state of nonexistence. In the third alternative, the ship is destroyed; and the fourth option has Lena and her shipmates arrive in present-day New Jersey where the citizens become the unknowing bodily hosts to the time travelers.

Malzberg disclaimed any pretense of the story being a novel at all in the original novelette, "A Galaxy Called Rome." He has said that he shares a personal relationship with the fictional author who represents his own desires, fears, and attitudes. Despite its nontraditional approach, *Galaxies* is quite definitely a work of hard science fiction. The long descriptions of the black hole and the use of science and technology in the far future are more defined here than in other novels. The theme of a fictional novelist in an impossible situation permeates Malzberg's major novels. The blend of science fiction extrapolations with psychological themes appeals to some readers, but not to others.

Biographical/Bibliographical Readings

Barry N. Malzberg, ". . . And A Chaser," in *Fantastic Lives*, ed. Martin H. Greenburg (Southern Illinois University Press, 1981), p.102-17. Michael W. McClintock, "The Contemporaniety of Barry N. Malzberg," *Extrapolation*, 23:2 (Summer 1982), p.138-49. Charles

Platt, "Barry N. Malzberg," in *Dream Makers* (New English Library, 1980), p.77-86. Brian Stableford, "Insoluble Problems: Barry Malzberg's Career in Science Fiction," *Foundation* 11/12 (1977), p.135-41. [John Dunham]

MARTIN, GEORGE R. R.

Life and Works

George R. R. Martin was born in Bayonne, New Jersey, on September 20, 1948. He received bachelor's and master's degrees from the Medill School of Journalism at Northwestern University. After college he worked for two years for the Cook County Legal Assistance Foundation for VISTA (1972-74). Martin's first novel, *Dying of the Light* (1977), was preceded in 1975 by the novella *A Song for Lya*, for which he received a Hugo Award. In 1980 he received Hugo awards for the novella *Sandkings* and the short story "The Way of Cross and Dragon." *Sandkings* was also awarded a Nebula in 1979. His more recent science fiction works include *Windhaven* (1981) and *Tuf Voyaging* (1986). Nonscience fiction novels of Martin's include *Fevre Dream* (1983) and *The Armageddon Rag* (1983). He has recently been associated as producer with the television series "Beauty and the Beast."

Themes and Style

Beginnning with his first novel, *Dying of the Light*, Martin has built a series of detailed worlds in which human beings are strangely lost and out of place, and must struggle to know themselves and others, and to understand the environment around them. *Dying of the Light*, a futuristic fantasy set on an isolated world spinning its way slowly into a cycle of darkness, examines traditions and the clash of cultures. The old feudalistic culture of High Kavalan, transplanted to the dying planet Worlorn, is richly imagined and quite logical, if barbaric.

Both *A Song for Lya* and "The Way of Cross and Dragon" deal with religion and its place in modern culture. *A Song for Lya* tells of Lya's conversion, despite the opposition of her lover, Robb, to an alien cult, the Joined. The Joined are a happy cult, having found an ecstatic union that gives each convert a profound sense of love, with the drawback being that this loving feeling is caused by a parasite which slowly but inevitably destroys its host. "The Way of Cross and Dragon" debates whether religion should bring happiness or truth, the two being far from synonymous; an interstellar inquisitor examines a heretical movement that canonizes Judas, and finds his own faith in doubt.

Sandkings is a horror story about a cruel and amorally vicious man who abuses his insectlike pets (Sandkings). By seeking revenge upon their owner, the Sandkings begin to change into something strikingly like their hated owner.

Martin often deals with lonely, alienated characters who are believably human. They question themselves and are confronted with difficult situations, but almost always find strength to overcome difficulties, and in the course of their struggles come to new understandings of themselves and their worlds. *Windhaven* (1981), written in collaboration with Lisa Tuttle, is a novel about a young woman who challenges tradition and changes the world to suit herself, and spends the rest of her life dealing with the ramifications of her action. Martin's latest novel, *Tuf Voyaging*, shows another lonely protagonist, one who learns that to play God and change the ecology of planets is a risky business.

Plot Summaries of Major Works

Sandkings. Simon Kress, a rich and sadistic man, keeps "pets" who entertain him by fighting. In pursuit of new diversions, he purchases a colony of Sandkings, antlike alien life forms which fight wars and worship the one who feeds them. At first delighted with his new toys, Kress becomes impatient and begins starving the Sandkings to make them fight more frequently and more fiercely. Soon this also palls, and Kress pits the creatures against other animals. Disgusted by Kress's obsession, his former lover Cath M'Lane attempts to destroy the Sandkings, which only gets her killed and fed to them. The Sandkings manage to escape from Kress's abuse; and they imprison and eventually kill him.

Martin's novella, which won both Hugo and Nebula awards, is a cautionary tale about the self-indulgent tendencies of modern humanity. Kress's search for entertainment leads him to take actions which eventually destroy his life, and the results of his cruelty may ruin the entire planet. The Sandkings, although they hate Kress and his sadistic torture of them, appear to be evolving into creatures very like their former owner/god. Simon Kress taught his children well, and they will grow up to surpass him in cruelty and destructiveness.

A Song for Lya. Robb and Lya, a pair of psi-talents, have been hired by the planetary administrator of Shkea to discover why humans are converting to the Shkeen religion, the Cult of the Joined. While religious conversions would not ordinarily be a source of concern, in this case conversion means a submission to the Greeshka, a mindless parasite that eventually destroys its host. During the process of destruction, however, the Joined, as those infested with the parasite are known, feel delirious waves of love which transcend all other emotions. Lya, fearful of aloneness and seeking a deeper love than can be found in any human relationship, achieves union with the Greeshka and joins an overmind of undying consciousness.

Martin tells *A Song for Lya* from Robb's point of view and details his pain in losing Lya. Robb, an empath, had loved Lya to the full extent of his power, and had joined with her in a far closer bond than "normals" (nonpsi-talented) could achieve. But to Lya, unless love was a total knowledge and acceptance of the loved one, it was futile. Martin often deals with characters who are, as most humans, lost and adrift, and details their quest for self-knowledge. Lya finds peace and happiness, and Robb comes, if not to approve, at least to accept her decision, and to understand that her choice is not one that he can make. Perhaps it may be true, as Lya says, that we can never truly know one another, but, as Robb discovers, we can keep trying.

Tuf Voyaging. Centuries before Haviland Tuf acquired it, the Ecological Engineering Corps had abandoned one of its biowar seedships around an obscure planet named Hro B'rana. The seedship is a traveling biogenetic laboratory, stocked with cells from millions of lifeforms from various planets--everything from viruses to dinosaurs, ready to be cloned and disseminated. Haviland Tuf, an obese and eccentric small-time trader and lover of cats, hired to provide transport for a group determined to reclaim the seedship, instead claims it himself and sets up a business as a biological engineer. He specializes in providing miracles, for a price. Among his first clients are the people of S'uthlam, a race rapidly breeding themselves beyond the meager capabilities of their planet, but who refuse to consider any means of population control. Tuf, working with Tolly Mune, the elderly administrator of the S'uthlamese orbiting docking bay, manages to produce a series of plants and lifeforms to alleviate the food crisis, and to escape with his ship, which the government of the planet had planned to confiscate. Five years and many successful assignments later, Tuf returns to S'uthlam to make a payment on the loan used to finance repairs to his ship and finds that the situation has not really changed, although he and Tolly Mune have passed into S'uthlamese folklore as a pair of star-crossed lovers, much to his surprise. The S'uthlamese have responded to the increased food production of their planet by multiplying at an even greater rate, and now need a second helping of Tuf's "loaves and fishes." Tuf again comes through with a set of varied lifeforms to feed them, but delivers these with a warning that they must change their way of life or face famine again. In the last section of the book, Tuf returns a third time to S'uthlam, and finds that once again his solution has failed. The S'uthlamese, for all their beliefs in the sanctity of life, are preparing to wage an expansionist war in order to find new worlds that can feed and house their multitudes. Tolly Mune, now the head of state, challenges Tuf to find a solution that will have permanent effects. Forced to play god, he creates a food plant that will inhibit reproduction, and Tolly Mune, seeing that there is no other alternative to war and famine, is forced to go along with what she views as a monstrous violation of her people's free will.

Tuf Voyaging takes a hard look at the nature and corrupting influence of power. Haviland Tuf learns in his travels how dangerous it is to tamper with the ecological balance of any system, yet finds himself compelled to do so over and over again. At first content to provide what he is asked for, he soon comes to regard his views as more valid and usually more benevolent than those of his clients, and proceeds to solve their problems in ways they do not appreciate. To the reader, surveying the circumstances from the outside, Tuf's actions and attitudes may seem justified. Yet the question remains--what right has anyone to interfere with the workings of nature in such a fashion, and what side effects might such interference create? The novel displays a sensitivity to the questions of ecological balance that it raises, with obvious applications to contemporary society. The biowar seedship is first described as a plague star, and although renamed the *Ark*, it nevertheless continues to bring destruction. Martin's novel points out that destruction disguised as benevolence may be the most dangerous of all.

Windhaven. Coauthored with Lisa Tuttle, Windhaven is a planet of small islands set in vast seas on which a lost human colony has developed its own civilization; and the major method of communication between the storm-tossed islands are the flyers, a heriditary guild soaring through the skies on wings of metallic fabric scavenged centuries ago from their ancestors' spaceship. When Maris of Amberly, foster child of a flyer, finds her wings are to be taken from her and given to her foster father's son, a boy who has no interest in flight, she rebels, and wins over the flyers to accept her radical idea of awarding wings on the basis of merit. Academies are formed to teach those who wish to learn to fly, but as time goes on, the born flyers and the Onewings, as the newcomers are nicknamed, find themselves bitterly split. Maris, the girl who changed the world to suit herself, finds that she must face the consequences of that change to unify the flyers of Windhaven again. In the epilogue to the novel, Maris comes to realize that sometimes legends hold more truth than reality, and accepts the mantle of legend in her death.

Windhaven is, in setting and theme, not unlike Anne McCaffrey's *Pern* books, or Ursula LeGuin's *Earthsea*. Martin and Tuttle are not content just to tell a standard story of an adolescent girl overcoming societal disapproval and earning her right to an occupation previously closed to her for whatever reason. They realize that social change of the sort Maria effects must be followed by far-reaching consequences. In this case, the opening of a hereditary guild brings into the flyers group those who, raised outside the flyer tradition, question the old values. A crisis erupts some thirty years after Maris wins her wings, when a young Onewing chooses not to follow the tradition of carrying any message without regard to content and alters messages in order to prevent a war. Discovery of the Onewing's actions not only costs her life, but threatens to destroy the long-held prerogatives of the flyers to live above the dictates of the landbound, who live under a feudal system. Maris is able to find a nonviolent solution to the crisis, but it is evident that only time will truly heal the split between flyers and Onewings. *Windhaven* does not offer easy solutions to the questions it raises, and in the character of Maris, gives readers a very human protagonist who makes mistakes and works out ways of dealing with them. She had not envisioned the changes her quest for wings would cause, but is farsighted enough to realize that the changes, made inevitable by her actions, must be dealt with in a way that will bring Windhaven forward.

Biographical/Bibliographical Readings

"George R. R. Martin," in *Contemporary Authors* (Gale, 1979), v.81-84, p.360-61. Rose Flores Harris, "George R. R. Martin," in *Twentieth-Century Science-Fiction Writers* (St. James, 1986), p.485-86. [Candace R. Benefiel]

MAY, JULIAN

Life and Works

Julian May was born on July 10, 1932, in Chicago, Illinois. In her youth, she remembers reading Andrew Lang fairy tales, cutting out Buck Rogers comic strip panels, and collecting Wonder Women comic books. In 1947, when she was a teenager, she discovered science fiction pulp magazines, a discovery that inaugurated the first phase of her involvement with the genre. She founded a fan group called "Science Fiction International" (with members in the United States, Canada, England, and Australia) and edited the group's fanzine, "Interim Newsletter." While at Rosary College in Chicago, she published her first science fiction story, "Dune Roller," in the December, 1951 issue of *Astounding*. (This story has been anthologized frequently and made into television shows and a movie.) During this period, she also published one other science fiction story, "Star of Wonder," and went to several science fiction conventions. In fact, she met her future husband at a convention in 1951, and she chaired the 1952 Chicago World Science Fiction Convention. In 1953, she married Ted Dikty, a publisher and science fiction fan.

When she realized that she could not make a living writing science fiction, May worked from 1953 to 1957 for a Chicago encyclopedia publisher as a science editor, writing some 7,000 encyclopedia articles on science, technology, and natural history. Late in the 1950s, she lost interest in science fiction, since it was becoming more experimental and less traditional. From 1957 to 1978 she wrote about 250 nonfiction books: juveniles, sports, biographies, and natural histories. The second phase of her involvement with science fiction began in 1976 when she attended her first science fiction convention in more than two decades, dressed in a diamond-festooned costume. Gradually, by thinking about what kind of person would wear such an outfit, she gathered material for and outlined the "Milieu Trilogy," a work which May has not yet written. However, this same research and thinking lies behind a tetralogy that she has written--her immensely popular The Saga of the Pliocene Exile, set later in time than the "Milieu Trilogy." The four parts of this tetralogy are *The Many-Colored Land* (1981), *The Golden Torc* (1982), *The Nonborn King* (1983), and *The Adversary* (1984).

Themes and Style

May writes for two audiences. Her first audience is anyone wanting to be entertained. An experienced book marketer, interested in producing books that sell, she consciously decided to write not for the typical science fiction reader but for a wider audience. So, on one level, her work is straightforward adventure stories, tales akin to the British thrillers and mysteries that she likes to read in her spare time--though, she admits, more bloodthirsty, rambunctious, humorous, and sexy. Clearly, her marketing strategy is paying off, for her Pliocene Saga novels have sold well. May's second audience is academic readers--interested in something more than adventure stories. For them, she has consciously included a deeper level, drawn from Celtic and Norse mythology, the legends of King Arthur, Irish and German fairy tales, folklore, cultural anthropology, Jungian psychology, nineteenth-century romanticism, and even theology (especially that of Pierre Teilhard de Chardin).

One of the most striking aspects of the Pliocene Saga is May's success at characterization. Again, this is conscious, a reaction to the idea-oriented science fiction of the 1970s and a return to what she sees as the "people orientation" of Golden Age science fiction. In any case, most readers find her characters real, plausibly motivated, complex, and sympathetic. Interestingly this is somewhat paradoxical, given the fact that she admits basing many of her characters on mythic and/or Jungian archetypes, such as the Trickster (Aiken Drum), the Flying Dutchman (Richard Voorhees, a failed man redeemed by a woman's love), or the Narcissist

(Brian Grenfell, a lover destroyed by his passion). However, the seeming paradox is easily resolved. Her characters are multi-faceted individuals first, and archetypes second.

Despite May's insistence on the existence of a deeper level in her work, scholars have yet to write much on the Pliocene Saga. May herself has written *A Pliocene Companion* (1984), a useful compendium of information about the saga which also includes a list of books that influenced her.

Plot Summaries of Major Works

The Saga of the Pliocene Exile
The Many-Colored Land. At the beginning of the twenty-first century, humanity is admitted to the Cadunate Galactic Milieu, a group of five metaphysic races. A century later, aided by these races, humanity has spread to nearly 800 planets and achieved peace and prosperity. But not everyone fits into the new, highly civilized Human Polity. And the worst of the misfits must choose among prison, psychological reorientation, euthanasia--or Exile. Exile is possible because in 2034, Professor Theophils Guderian had invented a fixed-focus, one-way time gate: its terminus is the Rhone River valley of Western Europe in the Pliocene Epoch, six million years in Earth's past. The journey is one way, because any living thing retrieved from that past disintegrates when it arrives in the present. Group Green consists of eight people who pass through the time gate at the end of August, 2110. All have good reasons for choosing Exile. Bryan Grenfell, an anthropologist, is following his lover, Mercy Lamballe, who chose Exile earlier. Stein Oleson is an atavistic warrior who cannot find release even in a dangerous twenty-second century job. The xenophobic Richard Voorhees is a spacegoing trader who refused to aid a Poltroyan ship. Felice Landrey, a seventeen year old, has been barred from the sport of ring-hockey. Elizabeth Orme has lost her husband in an accident. Aiken Drum has been declared an ir-reclaimable criminal. Sister Annamaria Roccaro wishes to become an Anchorite, impossible in the religious climate of the Milieu. And Claude Majewski, a 133 year old exopaleontologist, has just lost his wife.

Although schooled in survival techniques and well equipped, Group Green is unprepared for what awaits them in the past. The Pliocene era is ruled by two alien groups--the Tanu, technologically advanced and who use golden torcs (worn around their necks) to energize their latencies, and the Firvulag, operant metapsychics, adept at far-sensing, psychokinesis, and coercion. Tanu and Firvulag are deadly enemies who reenact annually the highly ritualized Grand Combat. The Tanu control the time gate terminus and Group Green falls under their sway. The Tanus separate the group--Elizabeth, Bryan, Aiken and Stein, are sent to

Muriah, the Tanu capitol in the south where they are treated well due to their individual capabilities. The others--Claude, Richard, Felice, and Annamaria, are sent to Finiah in the north, where the women will serve by bearing Tanu children (Tanu women are nearly all barren) and the men will practice a suitable trade. After Felice engineers an escape, her group joins the Lowlives, a small band of human rebels led by the widow of Professor Guderian. Madame Guderian has formed an alliance with the Tanu's ancestral foes, the Firvulag. The novel ends with the success of the first stage of her plan to free humanity from the exotics (the two groups of aliens).

The Golden Torc. Aiken Drum, Stein Oleson, Bryan Grenfell, and Elizabeth Orme arrive in Muriah, where they discover a complicated political situation. Thagdal is the Tanu High King by virtue of his excellent germ plasm: he has sired over 11,000 children. His children all successfully adapt to the golden torc that brings their latent metafunctions to operancy (usually, a small percentage of Tanu children die after getting their torcs). Thagdal is prohuman, interested in human innovation, and favoring human-Tanu interaction. Nontusvel is his queen and mother of the host, her 242 children by the king. The host, led by Nodonn Battlemaster (eldest son of the king and queen), is antihuman, wary of human innovation, and demanding a return to the days before the human advent. Finally, the Peace faction works toward ending the Tanu/Firvulag battle-religion and the Grand Combat, which the Tanu, having adopted human tactics, have won for the last forty years.

Soon Group Green is embroiled in Tanu politics. Mayvar Kingmaker chooses Aiken as her candidate to replace Thagdal as king. Thagdal recruits Bryan to do an anthropolgical study of human-Tanu interaction. And Brede Shipspouse (her mate was the ship that died bringing the exotics to Earth centuries earlier), guardian of both halves of the dimorphic race, wishes Elizabeth to help her people achieve metapsychic unity. Meanwhile, three other members of Group Green, having escaped, are with Madame Guderian and her band of human rebels, fighting to end the Tanu domination. Felice Landry and Sister Annamaria join a strike force aimed at the torc factory in Muriah. Claude Majewski goes to the time gate with Madame Guderian--they plan to close the gate by telling the twenty-second century operators about the enslavement of the time travelers.

The Golden Torc blends plausible details about Pliocene topography, flora, and fauna with fast pacing, well-developed characters, numerous subplots, gripping suspense, and a surprise ending. Although the novel is grand scale space opera, intended mainly to entertain, it also stimulates thinking about such things as ambition, love, duty, courage, guilt, insanity, pacifism, and cross-cultural problems.

The Nonborn King. Decimated by a catastrophe, the Tanu are so weakened that Aiken Drum, a human, successfully aspires to the Tanu kingship. Aiken is the nonborn king because, in Earth's future, he was born as a test-tube baby. Although young, he has formidable metapsychic powers, fertility, charm, and political genius. Several of the more pragmatic Tanu leaders follow Aiken to Goriah, once the seat of Nodonn Battlemaster (heir apparent to Thagdal)--now presumed lost. Aiken's allies include Culluket the Interrogator, Aluteyn Craftsmaster, Alberonn Mindeater, Bleyn the Champion, and even Mercy-Rosmar, formerly Nodonn's wife.

Aiken faces three challenges as he tries to consolidate his position as ruler of the Many-Colored Land. One is Felice Landry, a metapsychic even more powerful than he, dangerous because she is sadomasochistic, hopelessly insane, and obdurately opposed to the Tanu. Another threat is the Tanu conservatives, antihuman traditionalists ruled by Nodonn Battlemaster (who did not perish after all). The third problem for Aiken is the Firvulag, who now outnumber the Tanu four to one. The Firvulag comonarchs, Sharne-Mes and Ayfa, his wife, believe they can annihilate the Tanu once and for all.

Aiken's Machiavellian machinations are complicated by three other factors--Howlers (mutant Firvulag), Lowlives (human freedom fighters), and Elizabeth (a Grandmaster Redactor who heals Felice, and later Aiken himself). But the real surprise is the reemergence of the operant human beings who had come through the time-gate twenty-seven years earlier, crossed the Atlantic, and settled in Florida. Led by Mark Remillard, these humans are the survivors of a group who in 2083 rebelled against and nearly defeated the entire Galactic Milieu. Marc and several of his group are metapsychic Grand Master Magnates, much more powerful than the nonoperant Tanu. The children of the rebels are restless, unsatisfied with their Pliocene exile and planning to construct a time gate to return to the twenty-second century. Marc is forced to turn his attention from his star search (he is looking for a metapsychic race to rescue them) and toward Europe. Aiken has met some of his original challenges: the Firvulag Great Ones fail to kill him, and both Felice and Nodonn are dead. His complications await him in the final novel of the tetraology.

The Adversary. Although his victory over Nodonn consolidates Aiken's position as Tanu King, his personal and political troubles are just beginning. Aiken had ended the fight with Nodonn by assimilating Nodonn's primary metafunctions. Unfortunately, Aiken cannot use these powers right away, but must forge new neural pathways in a hurry, before the unchanneled metafunctions destroy him.

The Firvulag still outnumber their brother race and ancient enemies, the Tanu. Moreover, the Firvulag rulers have reinterpreted the Nightfall myth of the Tanu-Firvulag battle-religion:

they think that Nightfall will not be a fight to the death, but a conflict the Firvulag can win and survive. Aiken takes the rebel children of Marc Remillard under his wing and sets up an inevitable confrontation with Marc. The leaders of the Peace Faction, which opposes the battle-religion, utilizes Elizabeth Orme who tries her best to be a Pliocene ombudsman by negotiating amongst the various groups. Aiken aids the Rebel Children as they work on the time gate and resist Marc's overtures. The Howlers surreptitiously join Aiken's High Table, pledging to work against Nightfall in return for Aiken's help in changing their horribly deformed bodies. The main conflicts are resolved at the Grand Tournament that concludes *The Adversary*, but the conclusion is open-ended, leaving the possibility of a sequel to the Saga of the Pliocene Exile as well as a prequel (already in process).

Much of May's Pliocene Saga stems from two sources. The first source is the 50,000 or so nonfiction books she read from 1953 to 1978 as research for her own articles and books. Biography, folklore, geology, history (especially English history), mythology, paleontology, political science, and sociology--these subjects, among many others, she knows, remembers, and uses in her fiction. Thus, May's work is encyclopedic, chock full of both real and plausibly imagined facts. The other great influence on the Pliocene Saga is Golden Age science fiction, especially the work of E. E. "Doc" Smith, whom May calls her literary grandfather. May shares with "Doc" Smith immense vision, galactic scope, tempestuousness, and above all, love for action-filled science fiction.

Generically, the Pliocene Saga is classic space opera. First, like other space operas, it is a hodgepodge of almost every major science fiction theme--faster-than-light travel, time travel, first contact, metapsychics (May prefers this more elegant-sounding European term to the Americanisms "esp" and "parapsychology"), teleportation, and advanced technology. Second, it is not pure fantasy but fiction erected on a scientific base--May claims that her physics, earth sciences, and genetics are either accurate or plausible. Third, May borrows her narrative techniques not from novels but from drama--and proudly proclaims that the Pliocene Saga is melodrama worthy of Puccini. Fourth, May is an opera fan and has said that she had Wagner's *Ring* in mind while she was "composing" the Pliocene Saga--as well as Debussy, Faure, Dvorak, Rachmaninoff, Stravinsky, and the *Carmina Burana*.

Finally, as the list of composers above suggests (and May admits), the Pliocene Saga is romantic. All eight members of Group Green (protagonists of the saga) are in love or fall in love. May fills her pages with the medievalism favored by Romantic authors--ladies in beautiful costumes, knights in colorful armor, ritual pageantry, sumptuous banquets, exciting trysts, shining castles, caparisoned steeds, valued weapons, and glorious tournaments. May's descriptions are frequently overwrought, tending toward the "purple prose" favored by many romantic novelists and poets. In Marc Remillard, she creates a character similar to Milton's Satan as interpreted by romantics like Shelley (i.e., the gloriously doomed rebel). She yokes four quintessential romantic themes--love (as stated earlier), exile (in one way or another all the characters in Pliocene Europe are exiles), evolutionary teleology (all consciousness is evolving toward "coadunation," i.e., Unity), and optimism (the protagonists win, even when they die).

Biographical/Bibliographical Readings

T. E. Dikty and R. Reginald, *The Work of Julian May: An Annotated Bibliography and Guide* (Borgo Press, 1985). "Julian May," in *Something about the Author* (Gale, 1977), v.11, p.175-78. May S. Weinkauf, "Julian May," in *Twentieth-Century Science-Fiction Writers*, ed. Curtis C. Smith (St. James, 1986), p.488-89. [Todd H. Sammons]

MCCAFFREY, ANNE

Life and Works

Anne Inez McCaffrey, who was born in Cambridge, Massachusetts, in 1926, regards her April Fool's birthday as an auspicious sign for a writer. She attended Radcliffe College, majoring in Slavic language and literature; her senior thesis was on Yevgeny Zamiatin's *We*. After graduating cum laude, she worked as a copywriter and stage manager, and studied voice and theater. She married E. Wright Johnson in 1950; they were divorced in 1970.

McCaffrey began writing in the 1950s because new stories did not appear quickly enough to satisfy her reading appetite. In 1959, she published "The Lady in the Tower," the story she prefers to acknowledge as her first science fiction story. In 1967, *Restoree*, a satire of science fiction and gothic romances, was published. Her next works were the first of the Pern books, *Dragonflight* (1968) and *The Ship Who Sang* (1969) about McCaffrey's alter ego, Helva.

Although the books about Pern and Helva are McCaffrey's most popular works, she has created several other worlds. *To Ride Pegasus* (1973) is a collection of stories chronicling the discovery of a scientific method of detecting psychic activities and the subsequent efforts to obtain professional status and legal protection for those with psychic talents. *Get off the Unicorn* (1977) is another collection of stories, including the Charity series. *Decision at Doona* (1969) involves the simultaneous colonization of Doona by humans and Hrruba, a catlike race. Both groups fear the possibil-

ity of racial conflict, but are equally afraid of being forced to return to their home planets. *Dinosaur Planet* (1978) and *Dinosaur
Planet Survivors* (1984) tell of the exploration of a world which
presents numerous contradictions, including the presence of dinosaurs and other species that may have originated on several different planets.

In addition to her science fiction stories and novels, McCaffrey has edited a cookbook of recipes from science fiction au-
thors--*The out of This World Cookbook* (1973)--and has written romantic mysteries.

McCaffrey was the first woman to win both the Nebula
and Hugo awards. In 1968, she won the Hugo award for "Weyr
Search" and the Nebula award for "Dragonrider." *White Dragon*
won the Gandalf award and the Australian Ditmar award in 1979.

Themes and Style

McCaffrey's major theme has always been the emotional
relationships between her characters. She regards love and sex as
integral parts of life and of her work. In "A Womanly Talent,"
she wrote the first sex scene to appear in *Analog*. Her use of
strong emotions has led her work to be criticized as overly sentimental. Some of the criticism comes from a failure to recognize
the humor and satire prevalent in her work. *Restoree* was written
as a combined satire of the science fiction and gothic genres. In
To Ride Pegasus (1974), criticized for its traditional women's roles
as wives and mothers, the women are the ones who achieve the
goals of the organization. Traditionally science fiction has not
been noted for strong emotions; their presence in McCaffrey's
work has brought both praise and criticism.

McCaffrey has said that she does believe in the goals of the
women's movement, although she does not consider herself a feminist. Her belief shows clearly in her creation of strong women
characters. They include students, artists, and leaders, each willing to struggle to achieve her goals. Some are generous and self-
sacrificing, others are selfish and vengeful. They are all complex,
skillfully portrayed individuals.

McCaffrey's most common metaphor comes from the arts. Her
background in theater and music is reflected in most of her works.
Killashandra, in the Killashandra series, was a voice student before becoming a crystal singer. Helva, in *The Ship Who Sang*, sings
and performs in Shakespearean drama. On Pern, the traditions are
taught and opinions are shaped by music and songs.

McCaffrey's strength lies in her ability to create believable
characters, both human and alien, in realistically portrayed settings. Her stories tell of survival and courage in overcoming injustice and adversity.

Plot Summaries of Major Works

The Dragonriders of Pern series. Pern, with its flame-breathing dragons and their riders, is McCaffrey's most popular world. *Nerikla's Story* and *Moreta: Dragonlady of Pern*, set during the early years of Pern's development, tell of the struggle to survive a lethal flu epidemic. The following six books (*Dragonflight*, *Dragonquest*, *The White Dragon*, *Dragonsong*, *Dragonsinger*, and *Dragondrums*) are set in later periods, when dragonriders under the leadership of F'lar and Lessa must rebuild the power of the dragonriders to save Pern and create a new future for themselves.

Pern's neighboring planet has an irregular orbit. When it approaches Pern, it casts spores, or threads, onto Pern, that destroy all life they touch. The dragons, who can communicate telepathically with their riders, are bred to fight the threads by destroying them as they fall. After many years, the society on Pern becomes highly structured. The general population lives in Holds, governed by Lord Holders. The craftspeople are governed by Guilds, without any loyalty to a specific lord outside of the Guild. Dragonriders live in weyrs, protected specific areas. The Holds provide the weyrs with food and supplies in exchange for protection from the threads. As generations pass, the inhabitants of Pern forget that the planet was originally colonized by humans, and have lost much of the technology of their ancestors. The threads, which have fallen at regular intervals, suddenly stop. After decades without threadfall, the Holds come to believe that the dragonriders are no longer needed. There is only one weyr left, which receives very little support from any of the Holds. Lessa and F'lar, leaders of the weyr, believe that the threads will return. They work with some of the Guilds to restore the influence of the dragonriders and unite Pern to fight the threads. They help rediscover the origins and technology of the original colonists and help begin a renaissance in music, society, technology, and government. Lessa and F'lar hope to make the weyrs and Holds self-sufficient, beginning a new way of life on Pern.

Pern is a carefully created, consistent world. The social structure economy, legends, culture, geography, and biology are depicted in convincing detail. The characters are multifaceted. Some are generous and loving; others are selfish and vindictive. They can be jealous, possessive, demanding, gentle, compassionate, and tender. Many of the people and dragons of Pern are among McCaffrey's most memorable creations. Lessa is a stubborn, caring, mischievous, brave woman who grows from a servant girl to a rider of a queen dragon. Menolly, forbidden to sing by her family, becomes a valued member in the Harper's Guild. The dragonriders and their dragons may be the most enduring of McCaffrey's creations.

McCaffrey's major theme in the Pern series is the ability of the human spirit to survive and prevail against seemingly overwhelming difficulties. Some endure the loss of family and friends; others are severely injured. They discover ways to rebuild their lives and continue working toward their goals. The people of Pern learn to adapt to new methods, rediscover old techniques and accept changes, if their society is to survive. Some resist the changes, but most realize the necessity of redirecting the society of Pern without destroying its traditional values.

The Killashandra series. Killashandra is the protagonist of two books, *Crystal Singer* and *Killashandra.* Intergalactic communication and travel depend on crystals mined only on Ballybran by crystal singers. The miners must have perfect pitch to locate and cut the crystals. Anyone who remains on Ballybran becomes infected with a symbiote that changes body chemistry; it prolongs life, speeds healing, and increases sensory perceptions, but there are serious disadvantages. It also creates sterility and memory loss, and forces the singers to return to Ballybran regularly to avoid illness and convulsions.

Killashandra is a music student obsessed with achieving a first class career. When her teachers finally tell her that she can never reach the heights that she desires, she is deeply depressed and leaves school. She meets a crystal singer at a space port, seemingly by accident. Impressed by his wealth and status, Killashandra decides to apply for membership in his guild. She passes all the entrance tests, adapting easily to the symbiote, and discovers an affinity for the very valuable black crystal. Her first attempt at locating crystal results in a large strike of black crystal. After cutting the crystals, Killashandra installs them in a planetary communications system in a solo performance far beyond any of her previous ambitions. Her initial success does not continue for long. Storms destroy her site of black crystal, and Killashandra has difficulty finding a new site. Eventually, she discovers some white crystal, a type needed to repair a special multisense organ on Optheria. She is eager to get away from Ballybran and welcomes the assignment to replace the crystals. Her trip involves her in a conspiracy to expose the subliminal manipulation of the Optherian government. The government maintains a very restrictive society, ruling by sensory manipulation that is achieved by using the organ which Killashandra was sent to repair. She is kidnapped by a group working against the government, but manages to escape. During the escape, she meets the young man who had kidnapped her, but he does not recognize her. They become friends, then lovers. As she learns about his plans, she decides to join him in attempting to overthrow the government. Together they expose the manipulation of the leaders and bring new freedom to Optheria.

Killashandra is talented, intelligent, loving, arrogant, manipulative, and obsessed with success. Her concern for people is less compelling than her desire for fame and fortune. She is continually being manipulated by people and events, particularly by the crystal singer's guild and its guild master. The Killashandra series is the most musical of McCaffrey's works. In addition to Killashandra's training and the requirements of crystal singing, music is pervasive on Optheria. McCaffrey uses music throughout both books to advance and reinforce her plot lines.

The Ship Who Sang. Helva was born with normal intelligence and severe physical handicaps. The technology of the Center Worlds can enclose such a person in a shell with sensors, making a useful life possible. These shell people receive their education and training from the government and then work for Center Worlds until the costs of the initial surgery and education are repaid. Helva can see, hear, speak, and manipulate objects. She is placed in a spaceship, becoming part of the ship. Such scout ships are called brains, and their human partners are called brawns. Although some ships regard their brawns as nuisances, Helva enjoys companionship and wants a permanent brawn. Helva falls in love with Jennan, her first brawn, but he is killed. She grieves for him, but recovers from the loss. Her love, grief, and healing are reinforced by her assignments and passengers. She helps a passenger, Theoda, overcome her own grief by helping a planet recover from a disastrous plague. When her ship is hijacked, Helva shows more compassion, humanity, and courage than her temporary brawn. As Helva helps her temporary brawns to solve their problems, she also resolves her own problems. Her most important functions become physical and emotional healing.

Helva, as the title indicates, does sing. She can also vary her voice to assume any role in a drama. McCaffrey uses the arts to a great extent--music, drama, poetry, and dance--to show her characters' emotions. In many of the stories, music and drama are integral parts of the plot.

The Ship Who Sang has been criticized for being episodic and overly sentimental. It was originally published as separate short stories, and although there is thematic unity in the work, it remains more a collection of stories than a novel. The themes of loving and healing are by definition emotional, but McCaffrey remains in control of the sentiment. She makes subtle use of irony and humor to insure that an incident does not become cloyingly sentimental. The book is noteworthy for its combination of the arts, love, and healing within a cybernetic situation. Helva is a clearly drawn character, a compassionate woman who can be angry or sad or happy, and who also happens to be a spaceship.

Biographical/Bibliographical Readings

Rosemarie Arbur, *Leigh Brackett, Marion Zimmer Bradley, Anne McCaffrey: A Primary and Secondary Bibliography* (G. K. Hall, 1982). Edra C. Bogle, "Anne McCaffrey," in *Twentieth-Century American Science-Fiction Writers* (Gale, 1981), v.2, p.14-19. Mary T. Brizzi, *Anne McCaffrey* (Starmont House, 1986). [Linda K. Lewis]

MCINTYRE, VONDA N.

Life and Works

Vonda N. McIntyre was born on August 18, 1948, in Kentucky. She attended the University of Washington, graduating in 1970 with a degree in biology. Her graduate study was in genetics. In 1970, she attended the Clarion Science Fiction Writers' Workshop. Her first published story, "Of Mist, and Grass, and Sand," won the Nebula award for best novelette in 1973. In 1976, she and Susan Janice Anderson coedited a collection of feminist science fiction stories, *Aurora: Beyond Equality*. Her expansion of "Of Mist, and Grass, and Sand," became the novel, *Dreamsnake*. It was published in 1978 and won both the Hugo and Nebula awards. In 1979, *Fireflood and Other Stories*, a collection of her short fiction, was published. *Superluminal*, an expansion of her novelette "Aztecs," was published in 1983. McIntyre has also written several novels set in the "Star Trek" universe; she did the novelizations for three of the movies as well as two original novels.

Themes and Style

Much of McIntyre's work reflects her education and continuing interest in biology and genetics. A frequent theme concerns genetic manipulation for specialized purposes. In *Dreamsnake*, the snakes are altered to make their venom a means of healing. The protagonist of "Fireflood" has been altered to travel through rocks, water, or air in order to explore other planets. The divers of *Superluminal* can live underwater and refer to whales as their cousins. In some cases, these genetic alterations result in alienation and isolation when those altered are denied the opportunity to develop fully their new abilities.

McIntyre has said that she began writing science fiction because it was a field that would let her characters develop as far as their abilities would allow. The need to be free, to be able to grow and develop, is a continuing theme in her work. In *Superluminal*, Laenea is willing to do whatever she must in order to become a pilot of the faster-than-light space ships, including having her heart replaced with an artificial pump and leaving the man she loves. McIntyre portrays the suppression of natural abilities as

painful and evil. In *Dreamsnake*, Melissa and Gabriel both have
great potential that has been suppressed by others. They begin to
use their talents after Snake's intervention in their lives.

McIntyre is a feminist. Most of her protagonists are independent and strong women. They can be tender and vulnerable as
well as tough and ruthless, depending upon the circumstances.
They are multidimensional people who work toward their goals
and are able to acknowledge their own mistakes. Her female
characters accept responsibility for their own lives and for their
influence upon the lives of others.

McIntyre combines the technical and psychological areas of
science fiction in her explorations of the emotional effects of genetic alteration. Her works are about human potential, whether
she is writing about individuals or societies. Her style and language are lyrical, creating vivid moods through her descriptions.
All of these elements combine to add depth to her exciting adventure stories. Critics have called her one of the best new science
fiction writers of the 1970s.

Plot Summaries of Major Works

Dreamsnake. The world is recovering from a nuclear war
whose causes are long forgotten. There are nomadic camps and
small towns, and a city named Center, enclosed in a dome, which
has a high level of technology. The people of Center have dealt
with people from other planets who brought the dreamsnakes to
this world. Center refuses to help the healers get more dreamsnakes and the healers have been unsuccesful in breeding or
cloning dreamsnakes, which are used to ease pain and provide an
easy death. Their scarcity limits the number of healers that can
be sent out. The healers have learned techniques of genetic manipulation to alter some snakes whose venoms can cure many ill-
nesses. Snake is a young woman in her first year as a healer. Her
major means of healing involves the use of three snakes: Sand, a
diamondback rattlesnake; Mist, an albino cobra; and Grass, a
dreamsnake.

Snake is treating a young boy in a desert village. His parents
see Grass beside the child, become frightened and kill the dreamsnake. Snake blames herself for not making them understand that
Grass would not have harmed the child. Since she cannot be a
healer without her dreamsnake, she will have to return to her
teachers and explain her failure. There are no more dreamsnakes
available for her; she will have to stop working as a healer. One
of the group, Aravin, wants to return with her to help explain
that it was not her fault, but she refuses his offer.

On the way back, she is asked to help an injured woman.
Jesse has fallen and broken her back, an injury Snake cannot cure.
Jesse is from Center; if Snake can get her back to the city, she

may be able to get help. Unfortunately, Jesse dies of radiation illness before the journey even begins--her fall had been into an old bomb crater and the radiation, not the fall, had killed her. She had already told Snake that her family in Center would help her; they might even be able to get her another dreamsnake. Snake realizes that even though she could not save Jesse, she still wants to be a healer.

Snake's possessions have been searched and destroyed while she was helping Jesse, probably by one of the crazies who roam the desert. She climbs the horse Jesse gave her and rides to Center. She feels as though she is being followed, but she never sees anyone. Along the way, she stops at a small village and meets a young girl, Melissa, who has been abused physically and sexually by her guardian. Snake adopts Melissa and offers her a chance to escape and build her own life.

When Snake and Melissa reach Center, Snake tries to get help, but she is rejected because the citizens react with horror to the healers who practice genetic manipulation. The two travelers head back and are captured by the crazy who had been following them. He takes them to a dome, where they are imprisoned by North, who puts Melissa and Snake in a very cold pit with numerous dreamsnakes. Melissa becomes unconscious as a result of their bites, but Snake is less affected. After being bitten innumerable times, Snake goes into a semiconscious state, where she realizes that there are a great many dreamsnakes of all sizes and stages of maturity. When she sees three of them breeding, she realizes that the dreamsnakes are triploid, requiring three to breed and also that intense cold is necessary for maturity and breeding. The healers had been overprotective, which had prohibited and slowed down maturation and reproduction.

Snake and Melissa manage to escape from the pit with some of the mature dreamsnakes in a sack and a new hatchling in a pocket. They are free, but Melissa is in shock and Snake is close to total exhaustion. Arevin finds them (he felt responsible that his family had killed her dreamsnake and had followed her across the desert). Together they revive Melissa. Snake finally resolves her feeling of guilt over Grass's death, realizing that otherwise she would not have met Melissa and discovered the dreamsnakes and their secrets. Snake and Arevin have repaid their debts to one another and they may now have time to get know each other better.

Dreamsnake, expanded from the story "Of Mist, and Grass, and Sand," is a Hugo and Nebula award winning novel that contains most of McIntyre's major themes. The snakes are the results of genetic manipulation, reflecting her interest in biology. Her feminism shows in most of the women in the novel; they are strong, self-sufficient, tough, vulnerable, caring, and ruthless. The women are multifaceted individuals, skillfully portrayed. The characters in this novel challenge the limits seemingly imposed by their societies, stretching to reach the extent of their abilities. *Dreamsnake* is a well-written novel, with vividly created societies and memorable characters. It is also an adventure story about the search for the rare dreamsnakes. It succeeds in combining feminism, psychology, and biology in an absorbing manner.

Biographical/Bibliographical Readings

Melissa J. Gaiownik, "Vonda N. McIntyre," in *Contemporary Authors New Revision Series* (Gale, 1986), v.17, p.305-07. Geraldine Morse, "Vonda N. McIntyre: An Interview," *Galileo* 15 (Nov. 1979), p.8-11. Natalie M. Rosinsky, "Vonda N. McIntyre," in *Twentieth-Century Science-Fiction Writers*, ed. Curtis C. Smith (St. James, 1986), p.497-98. [Linda K. Lewis]

MERRIL, JUDITH

Life and Works

Judith Merril was born in New York City on January 21, 1923. Her given name was Josephine Judith Grossman and evolved into Judith Merril after the end of her first marriage, which resulted in the birth of a daughter, Merril Zissman. Early in her writing career, she was a member of the Futurians along with her second husband, Frederik Pohl, whom she married in 1949 and divorced in 1953. Merril married a third time, to Daniel W. P. Surgrus in 1960, and was divorced in 1975. In the 1960s, Merril migrated to Canada out of opposition to the Vietnam War and a distaste for the institutional violence which it brought about both in the United States and other countries. She presently resides in Toronto and has the distinction of having donated her private collection to the Toronto Public Library, where it became the basis for a special "Spaced Out Library" dedicated to science fiction and fantasy literature. She was a ghostwriter, historian's assistant and writer's assistant before selling her first stories and articles in magazines in the 1940s and 1950s. Merril has authored two novels, *Shadow on the Hearth* (1953) and *The Tomorrow People* (1960) and collaborated with Cyril Kornbluth on two others, *Gunner Cade* (1952) and *Outpost Mars* (1951). She has also published three novellas collected in *Daughters of Earth* (1952) and many short stories in single author collections, as well as multiple author anthologies. Merril has used the pseudonyms of Rose Sharon, Ernest Hamilton, and Eric Thorstein, and, with Cyril Kornbluth, as Cyril Judd. Her latest collection was *The Best of Judith Merril* (1976), which includes one of her finest stories, "Daughters of Earth," covering six generations of pioneer women. She has been director of the Milford Science Fiction Writers Conference (1956-

61). An active participant in the science fiction critical community, she taught science fiction writing classes and workshops for the Port Jervis, New York, Adult Education Program in 1963-64, the University of Toronto (1971-72), Sir George Williams University (1972), and Trent University (1983). Between 1965 and 1969, she published a book review column in the *Magazine of Fantasy and Science Fiction*. Her career as an editor of anthologies of science is significant and of long standing, beginning in 1950 and continuing into the present with her twentieth anthology, *Tesseracts: Canadian Science Fiction* (1985). She edited thirteen volumes of *The Year's Best SF* (with varying titles) from 1956 to 1970. Merril's honorary degrees and awards include: a B.A. degree from Rochdale College, 1970; the Science Fiction and Fantasy Award (1983); and Canada Senior Arts Grant, 1984-85.

Themes and Style

Because of her perceptive abilities to choose unusual and ground-breaking stories, Merril has been one of the first American champions of the New Wave science fiction, an attempt to meld science fictional interests in the effects of technology on humans with literary experimentation in narrative form. Merril has edited anthologies that introduced many new science fiction writers and the more unusual stories from established writers. *Beyond Human Ken* (1952), twenty-one stories about alien lifeforms, combines technological science fiction and fantasy by such stylistically dissimilar authors as Murray Leinster and Stephen Vincent Benet. *England Swings SF* (1968) brought many English New Wave writers to the attention of American science fiction readers, an effort for which she was as much criticized as praised. Her most recent *Tesseracts* provides the same service in relation to Canadian writers, especially as she includes stories that were originally published in French.

In her own writings, Merril's concern for the survival of the human race is manifest. She attacks our disregard of the environment, the proliferation of nuclear power and weapons without adequate safeguards, and the privileging of political intrigue over humanitarian values. The importance of community and family relationships, in the best senses of those social institutions, is often a central theme in her fiction. Merril was one of the first women writers in the 1950s to create female characterizations of strong women's cultures in which women were more active than passive in the plot lines. This is especially reflected in *Daughters of Earth*. Women become equals and power figures in many of her short stories, and Merril is credited with establishing a new women's perspective during this period.

Plot Summaries of Major Works

Daughters of Earth. This book is a collection of three novellas, "Project Nursemaid" (1954), "Homecalling" (1956), and "Daughters of Earth" (1952).

"Project Nursemaid." This story is narrated from the perspective of a young colonel who has been assigned to find young women who will give up their babies to be raised in the lighter gravity of the moon, so they will have a good chance of surviving as long-term inhabitants. The colonel must be sensitive to the needs of the prospective mothers, cognizant of project agendas, and aware of the political side of his endeavors, which would be viewed with a jaundiced eye by the American public. However, his dedication to the success of the project and its necessity are never in question.

"Homecalling." This story explores the other end of the narrational spectrum, alternating between the perspectives of a young girl shipwrecked on an alien planet and the matriarchal alien female with psionic abilties who adopts her. In this story, both narrators are unreliable--each thinks they know what they are doing, and the reader is held in suspense about the nature of their misunderstanding.

"Daughters of Earth." This novella is the best known of the three. It is lyrical, establishing virtual cantos out of mother-daughter stories that span the future centuries of space exploration, each ending with the refrain, "Darling, aren't you afraid?" There is a bit of wistfulness in this story also, for it begins with a woman who never leaves Earth and her daughter Joan, the one who goes into space. Joan is the first of the daughters upon whose efforts space exploration and colonization depend. The narrative is written by a mother for her daughter, Carla, the sixth daughter and third explorer in the line. Letter and diary excerpts from their ancestors cast a historical tale in several narrative voices. None of the mothers or daughters are portrayed as stereotypical, faceless wives and mothers, which at once gives them depth as characters and denies the truth of such stereotypes.

For stories originally published in the science fiction magazines of the 1950s, this is a remarkable collection of stories and perhaps one of the reasons Merril was praised for introducing the women's perspective into the science fiction of the time. The mere fact that women are acknowledged as active rather than passsive partners in space exploration set many of her stories apart from her contemporaries. In these tales, their visions, heroism, and plain hard work is placed at center stage. Even aside from these considerations, the collection is compellingly human. Especially in "Daughters of Earth," one thirsts after more details from each of these women's lives that are all the more enticing because they are elusive. Merril's strength as a writer is best displayed in her shorter works, where this quality of suggestion can be exploited to the fullest.

Outpost Mars. Set entirely on the planet Mars, this novel deals with a colony called Sun Lake, consisting of second and third generation Earth settlers. The atmosphere is very thin, but a pill has been developed which makes it possible for normal humans to survive on the surface of Mars. The Sun Lake colonists are not quite independent of Earth, because they cannot produce this substance, but they eventually hope to be able to do so. The lines are clearly drawn between those who wish to exploit the natural resources of the planet, represented by the very rich Mr. Brenner of Brenner Pharmaceuticals, and those who see Mars as the last clean place where human beings can hope to continue the race. Brenner is also, incidentally, a known drug trafficker and, just to increase the tension of this uneven opposition, has in his pay the Earth government's representative, Commissioner Bell. The colony's livelihood is imperiled by Brenner, who threatens to impound its off-planet shipments while he searches for drugs he claims to have been stolen from him. In the process of investigating the claims, the colonists discover the existence of another race living in the caverns near Sun Lake. These survivors are of human origin, children of the first colonists who have mutated to the point where conditions of life on Mars are more natural to them than Earth. They also possess psionic powers. Thus the Sun Lakers struggle as much with those who would turn Mars into a mirror of the dying, overpolluted, and overpopulated Earth as they do with the harsh realities of of life on an alien planet.

Outpost Mars opposes the forces of imperialistic capitalism with those of independence-seeking colonists; the lines between the bad and the good guys are clearly drawn. The novel contains the brave, self-sacrificing heroes of both sexes who always loom large in frontier stories. These include the always-present pioneer doctor, here Dr. Hellman, and the brave colonists, male and female, who labor for a dream they do not expect to see realized in their lifetimes. In many ways, the novel is typical of the 1950s adventure science fiction, with the added depth that much of Merril's writing acquires through a close examination of monolithic political systems and their negative effects on the lives of individuals. The political skepticism is unusual for the gung-ho patriotic science fiction of the period.

Shadow on the Hearth. This novel is an account of the aftermath of a massive nuclear attack. The focal character is a thirty-seven-year-old mother of two, who generally goes about her business while worrying about her daughters' possible radiation sickness and the absence of her husband. She is also bothered by the unwanted attentions of a neighbor who has been in charge of their area of town, and the marauding bands of vandals, and attempts of government agents to scapegoat two of her friends. Mrs.

Mitchell's facade of calm is made necessary by her attempts to protect her children both from the radiation and from the government. Underlying her fears is a belief that the government cannot be trusted to provide the public with full and accurate information.

The horror of nuclear radiation is not the only factor that makes this novel into a timeless and sobering tale, but also the very real threat that, like the hapless Eastern and Western Europeans who suffered from Chernobyl, the Indians injured by the chemical leaks in Bhopal, and the many Americans genetically injured by the nuclear industry at Love Canal, our leaders may be attempting to protect themselves from public outrage by simply withholding pertinent information. The relationship between mother and child and the effects of nuclear radiation incorporate all of a mother's strengths, loves, and fears for the security and future of her children. The novel is similar to the mother in Merril's most anthologized story, "Daughters of Earth," in which a young wife fears that her unborn baby will be deformed because its father was exposed to high levels of radiation. Both the novel and the story are still read and appreciated by members of the antinuclear movement. Whether nuclear accident or nuclear bomb, the results are, sadly, the same.

The Tomorrow People. A disturbed survivor of the first Mars landing, Johnny Wendt, tries, with the help of his girlfriend, Lisa Trovi, to remember what happened to his missing fellow travelers. Johnny's increasing inability to live with his nonmemories of the Mars visit drives Lisa away. She flees to the moon base to do research on the virus that Johnny brought back in his body, and which she is probably carrying in his baby. The moon-based researchers have begun to act in strange ways, living in closer harmony and interpersonal congress than can be expected in a small, intellectual community such as exists on the moon. This becomes the problem of the psychiatrist who had tried to help Lisa with Johnny. Phil Kutler, the psychiatrist, thinks that Johnny knows more than he is telling and that this somehow relates to the rapidly growing Mars-virus colony which now exists on the moon base. On the political level, problems of convincing a skeptical Earth that the research should be supported to a reasonable conclusion and the interference of opposing political candidates who wish to make it an isue of their campaign becomes the problem of Pete Christensen, the moon base administrator. He must defend the reported immorality of his researchers as well as the importance of their work. All of these problems are solved by a couple of babies not yet born. Through prenatal, nonjudgmental minds of Lisa and a Russian woman's babies, the virus entity is finally able to communicate with humans. Through their link, Johnny discovers the source of his suppressed memories of his partner, as well as his partner's accidental death. Phil solves the problem of the moon researchers' affections for one another, and Pete is finally able to explain the significance of their research as the means for further exploring human communication.

The plot here is more complex than the *Shadow on the Hearth* or either of Merril's collaborations. It involves first contact with mind-reading Martians in nonhuman form, psychological insecurities brought about by this contact, and sensitive negotiations for government research funding for projects designed to determine the nature of the aliens. This clever extrapolation of a telepathic, virus-based entity which itself is only gradually discovering the fragile nature of human life is played out through the personal, political, and psychological levels of human interaction. Although some of the characters are shadowy and the motivations, especially on the part of Earth politicians, not always clear, *The Tomorrow People* is ultimately satisfying as science fiction that explores with some depth the wonders of human-alien communication. Of the four novels Merril has produced either soley or in collaboration, this is undoubtedly the best.

Biographical/Bibliographical Readings

Chris Morgan, "Judith Merril," in *Science Fiction Writers*, ed. E. F. Bleiler (Scribner's 1982), p.433-40. N. M. Rosinsky, "Judith Merril," in *American Women Writers* (Ungar, 1982), v.3, p.164-66. Jean W. Ross, "Judith Merril," in *Contemporary Authors New Revision Series* (Gale, 1985), v.15, p.316-19. Brian Stableford, "Judith Merril," in *The Science Fiction Encyclopedia*, ed. Peter Nicholls (Doubleday, 1979), p.393-94. **[Janice M. Bogstad]**

MILLER, WALTER M., JR.

Life and Works

Walter M. Miller, Jr. was born on January 23, 1923, in New Smyrna Beach, Florida, the son of Walter, Sr., and Ruth Adrian Jones. He attended the University of Tennessee from 1940 to 1942, at which point he enlisted in the U.S. Army Air Corps. He flew some fifty-three combat missions, including one in 1944 in the bombing of Cassino, Italy. This was the site of the famous Monte Cassino monastery, which the Germans were using as an artillery spotting post, and the monastery itself was very heavily damaged. Whether or not this influenced Miller's later conversion to Roman Catholicism is not clear. However, he did become a Catholic in 1947. It was also in 1947 that he began attending the University of Texas to study engineering. Sources differ as to whether or not he ever finished his degree.

In 1950, Miller began writing and by 1957 had published forty-one stories. He also wrote television scripts for the early "Captain Video" series. In the period from 1955 to 1957, he published the novellas which were to become *A Canticle for Leibowitz* in 1960. These were published in three consecutive parts in Anthony Boucher's *Magazine of Fantasy and Science Fiction.* After its reworking and novel form in 1960, the novel won a Hugo award in 1961. With *A Canticle for Leibowitz*, his public writing career ended, although several collections of his short fiction appeared in the early 1960s. These include *Conditionally Human* (1962) and *The View from the Stars* (1964). These were later combined into *The Short Stories of Walter M. Miller, Jr.* (1978). "Darfsteller" is clearly the best of Miller's stories and was awarded a Hugo in 1955 for best novelette.

Although Miller's *A Canticle for Leibowitz* is one of the best known and best read science fiction novels of the modern age, not very much is known about Miller himself. He has virtually disappeared from the scene since the novel was published and has not produced any material since that time. Yet his popularity has been maintained through this one outstanding novel.

Themes and Style

The themes which Miller uses are to some extent limited and appear in his few works. Of prominent importance is the theme of faith and religion. One sees this in many of his short stories, from "Conditionally Human" (1952) and "Crucifixux Etiam" (1953) to *Canticle*. His other major theme is that of technological change. In some of his stories, the focus is biological--"The Will" (1954), "Blood Bank" (1952), or "Conditionally Human." In others, "Darfsteller" (1955) being the major example, Miller's focus is more clearly on pure technology and the influence it has on society.

Although Miller's literary output was not substantial, he has succeeded where more prolific writers have not. He has been acknowledged as a model to others writers of science fiction, having been able to make the quantum leap from genre writing to mainstream, with his one great work, *A Canticle for Leibowitz*. Miller has, according to Norman Spinrad's introduction to the 1975 Gregg Press publication of *A Canticle for Leibowitz*, achieved a level of art where most have failed and has "created one of those lovely pinnacles of literature that touches the writer's life and our own with a rare moment of greatness . . . ."

Plot Summaries of Major Works

A Canticle for Leibowitz. The first part of the novel, "Fiat Homo," takes place in the New Dark Ages after a nuclear holocaust some six hundred years earlier. During the holocaust, Isaac Edward Leibowitz had been a minor technician who survived the nuclear bombing. In the aftermath, in a period when scientists and indeed all learned people were attacked and killed by the masses, Leibowitz lived long enough to find refuge in the Catholic Church and to establish his own abbey, with the intent of protecting what little knowledge he could. Leibowitz was killed by a mob when it was discovered that he had been a weapons specialist before the Deluge. His monastery survived, and "Fiat Homo" tells of the discovery of further relics of Leibowitz and of his canonization. Brother Francis Girard is the novice who finds the relics in the remains of an old bomb shelter. They include a delicatessen shopping list, a memo book, and, most important, a blueprint for "Transistorized Control System for Unit Six-B." This latter item becomes the lifework of Brother Francis, who spends his time producing a gold-illuminated manuscript which is to be taken to New Rome for the canonization process. In the intervening years, however, Brother Francis is plagued by the head of the abbey, Dom Arkos, who fears that the discovery of the relics will be seen as grandstanding by those in New Rome and might ruin the chances for Leibowitz to become a saint. Although the canonization is successful, Brother Francis is killed by a roving band of robbers as he returns from New Rome.

Part 2, "Fiat Lux," takes place in 3174 A.D. in what has become the new Renaissance. Science has been on the rise, as has a more sophisticated political system, with Hannegan, a powerful lord, attempting to consolidate the fiefdoms in North America. With the consolidation comes the constant threat of war, and the monks of the abbey are dismayed when Thon Taddeo, a secular scholar who wishes to use the materials that have been preserved, comes to the abbey. Even the monastery is not free from the advances of science, for Brother Kornherr has successfully created a foot-powered dynamo which produces light. Hannegan pronounces that he is the only rightful ruler and that the church will heed him in all things, thereby defining the policy that science and the state have regained power.

"Fiat Voluntas Tua" is the third part of the novel and brings the abbey to year 3781 A.D., a new nuclear age. The order has been forced to deal with the lost power of the church and is preparing itself for the next holocaust which they know will surely come. Consequently, the monks have prepared a spaceship which will transport several members of the order as well as the Memorabilia of Saint Leibowitz into space in the hopes that their mission of preserving knowledge will be saved for future generations. Soon nuclear radiation is poisoning the population and the current abbot, Dom Zerhchi, is faced with a death camp for homeless victims which has been placed outside the abbey. Zerchi himself is fatally injured by an atomic blast. As he attempts to maintain consciousness so that he can experience the suffering that he has seen in others, he is offered a communion wafer by a nuclear mutant. As he dies in the desert, the spaceship is being loaded and is launched towards Centauri, and the world faces its second holocaust.

Although Miller wrote on a theme popular in the 1950s, postnuclear war destruction, his treatment of the subject is extremely complex, for he has woven into it the constant struggle between church and state and many of the attendant issues. Each segment of the novel handles a series of different conflicts analogous to the development of the Roman Catholic Church and our own civilization. "Fiat Homo" and "Fiat Lux" portray the church in its traditional role as preserver of knowledge, as in our own Dark Ages, and its decline in the Renaissance. There are definite parallels with the development of science as well. Miller's question appears to be whether the human moral character will allow humanity to overcome the temptations offered by science. Will humans have the ability to choose and save themselves and civilization, having learned from mistakes in the past? At the end of the novel, Miller has answered this question with a resounding "No," but he continues to offer hope for future civilizations as the spaceship leaves the Earth on its mission of preservation of knowledge and faith.

The themes in Miller's novel reflect the duality of his thinking. The basic approach is the development of technology, good or bad. Although Brother Kornherr's dynamo provides the abbey with substantial light for the first time, it is also the beginning of the modern development leading to the next nuclear age. Is this good or evil? This is a question which Miller leaves unresolved, since the nuclear power provides not only the destruction of the world but also provides the mechanism by which the spaceship can leave. The rise of the new technological civilization, with its attendant increase in the power of the state, leads to the decline of the church. Yet it is the church which will survive to pioneer a new life for humanity. From its death comes a new rebirth.

"The Darfsteller." Ryan Thornier was once a famous actor. Now he is a janitor in the New Empire Theater, the actors having been supplanted by automated dolls run by a mechanical director, the Maestro. Resentful of his replacement by a machine and still proud of his former reputation, Thornier goes about plotting his one final performance and, he thinks, his suicide. He sabotages one of the actor-tapes and plans to replace the doll in the performance of the play, one which he had rehearsed as his last professional performance. The plot works all too well; the producer, Jade Ferne, and even his former leading lady, Mela Stone, become involved in helping him deal with the automated actors on stage. What Thornier does not take into consideration, however, is that he will also become involved with outwitting the Maestro, who ac-

commodates for the "unusual" performance. At the end of the
play, Thornier barely avoids being killed by a real bullet placed
in the gun by the Maestro. The story ends with Thornier's realization that the theater will not die, even though the form has
changed. He accepts, on a limited basis, human use of technology
and with it, humanity's function as the specialist for creating new
specialties.

The tension in the story derives from the extensive plotting
that Thornier must do in order to replace the actor-doll. Constantly in fear that his substitution will be discovered, Thornier
evokes admiration, pity, and even respect as he justifies his actions to himself. "Darfsteller" is not only a story of the conflict
between humans and increasing technology; Miller has also written
a loving story of the theater, of the actor devoted to his or her
craft, the "darfsteller." Thornier himself says he is no
"schauspieler," an actor who is there merely to try to please the
audience. The conclusion of the story, with Thornier's acceptance
of technology balanced by his acceptance that he can transcend
the technology, provides an emotionally satisfying ending for the
reader.

Biographical/Bibliographical Readings

David Cowart, "Walter M. Miller, Jr.," in *Twentieth-Century
American Science-Fiction Writers* (Gale, 1981), v.2, p.19-29. David
M. Samuelson, "Introduction," in *The Science Fiction Stories of Wal-
ter M. Miller, Jr.* (Gregg, 1978), p.vii-xxv. Idem, "Walter M. Miller,
Jr.," in *Twentieth-Century Science-Fiction Writers*, ed. Curtis C. Smith
(St. James, 1986), p.513-15. **[Jeanne M. Sohn]**

MOORCOCK, MICHAEL

Life and Works

Michael John Moorcock is a British author and editor who
also has experience as a book designer, reporter, reviewer, and musician. He was born near London on December 18, 1939, and his
work is often set in or near London. His early education was er-
ratic--he changed schools often and quit as soon as he could at the
age of fifteen. His earliest vocational interests were in journalism, beginning with a handmade magazine called *Outlaw's Own* in
1951, followed by the editorship of *Tarzan's Adventures* in the late
1950s. From 1958 to 1961, Moorcock edited for the Sexton Blake
Library, a publisher of pulp thrillers. It was during this period
that he began to submit stories to the British science fiction and
fantasy magazines. Most of his earlier stories were heroic fantasy

rather than science fiction; his first Elric story appeared in *Science Fantasy* in 1961.

The 1960s were a decade of change for Moorcock. In 1962, he married Hilary Bailey and they had two daughters in rapid succession. In 1964, he began editing *New Worlds*, building a reputation as a strong, creative, and brave leader of what came to be known as the British New Wave in science fiction. His willingness to experiment and allow freedom of expression uncovered important new authors who had been boycotted by more traditional editors. Although he is considered to have had a liberating influence on science fiction, Moorcock made very little money from editing. He began to write in order to support his family, turning out fantasy epics, science fiction, and one nonscience fiction novel, *Caribbean Crisis* (1962). Two well-known fantasy works are *The Stealer of Souls* (1963) and *Stormbringer* (1965). Three works appeared in 1965, *Warriors of Mars*, *Blades of Mars*, and *The Barbarians of Mars*, which clearly showed the early influence of Edgar Rice Burroughs. His science fiction novels of this period show the unmistakable signs of his youth and his push to write quickly.

His maturity and experience began to appear in *The Sundered Worlds* (1965), in which he introduced the multiverse, a concept which appears in almost all of Moorcock's work to the present. In 1966, Moorcock published *Behold the Man*, one of his most noteworthy novellas, which won the Nebula award. During the late 1960s and 1970s, Moorcock wrote the novels for the four-volume Cornelius Chronicles, which had its beginnings in *New Worlds*. The four volumes in the series are: *The Final Programme* (1968), *A Cure for Cancer* (1971), *The English Assassin* (1972), and *The Condition of Muzak* (1977). During this decade, he also published the Dancers at the End of Time trilogy, which consists of *An Alien Heat* (1972), *The Hollow Lands* (1974), and *The End of All Songs* (1976).

In 1978, Moorcock and his wife were divorced. That same year appeared *Gloriana: The Unfulfill'd Queen*, a predictably antifeminist novel which was nominated for both a Hugo and a Gandalf award and which was awarded the Campbell World Fantasy award in 1979.

Themes and Style

Michael Moorcock has been both precocious and prolific, is equally comfortable in fantasy and science fiction, and is as complex and mysterious in his real life as in his writing. He hides his real self behind opera cloaks, full beards, and music. Although themes and characters reappear in much of his work, his treatments in various series are so different that they seem to have been written by different writers. In this way, Moorcock is a good representative of his own multiverse concept.

His multiverse consists of multiple universes, alternate realities coexisting in parallel time lines. Some of the same people and events are repeated with variations on the theme. Many of the same characters appear in Moorcock's novels, with either the same name or with the same initials. Jherek Carnelian and Jerry Cornelius are two of his favorites. In the Cornelius Chronicles, Jerry Cornelius lives and moves as hero, antihero, scholar, assassin, and spy. Psychedelic treatment of time and space make up one theme of this series; entropy is the other. The manic freewheeling of Cornelius in and out of reality contrasts with the depressive psychosis of encroaching rust, decay, holocaust, and other unpleasant disassociations into nothingness. This is not a series for those who like tidy answers and neat plot lines.

Moorcock's skill with characterization is readily apparent in his treatment of Karl Glogauer in *Behold the Man* as a neurotic, even psychotic time traveler who lives out the Christ legend. The haunting and tortured presence of Glogauer may not be pleasant, but it is undeniably memorable.

Much more fun is the Dancers at the End of Time trilogy. The hero, Jherek Carnelian, is the darling of the remnant of civilization at the End of Time, where entropy is about to result in the ultimate disappearance of everything. His frivolous attitude is changed through time travel. Although some critics consider this trilogy rather fluffy, it does contain one of the few hopeful stories in Moorcock's science fiction work.

Plot Summaries of Major Works

Behold the Man. As a boy, Karl Glogauer is fascinated with the story of Jesus. He and his friends play a game in which Karl is tied to the schoolyard fence in the position of crucifixion. His boyhood prayers are a mixture of blessings, sorries, and thank yous. He has a sad childhood, impoverished because his mother is distant and manipulating. The first time he tries to kill himself is when he is fifteen. He joins a church club to meet girls and to immerse himself even more thoroughly in the Christian theology; sex and religion became inextricably linked in his mind; girls are silver crucifixes and boys wooden crosses. At the age of twenty-two, he begins an affair with Monica, an older woman who enjoys arguing religion and mythology with Karl. She tries to tell him that religion is dead. In order to prove that it is real and historical, Karl travels in a time machine to Palestine in 28 A.D. His machine crashes and he is rescued and tended by John the Baptist and his band of Essenes. He becomes comfortable with John and his group and allows John to baptize him. Karl becomes more obsessed with finding Jesus. Finally, he leaves the safety of John's camp and goes to Nazareth. When he finds the poor home of Joseph, the carpenter, and his wife, Mary, he is devastated to find out that Jesus is a hunchback, a congenital idiot, whose entire vocabulary consists of his name. Mary is promiscuous and cheap; she invites Karl to return when her husband is gone.

He is mortified and seeks shelter in the synagogue; the rabbis mistake him for a holy man. Well, why not, he thinks. Monica has told him that he has a messiah complex, and this is his chance to prove it. He preaches to the people, he heals some believers of hysterical blindness and other psychosomatic disorders, and he begins to develop a following. Here is a role he can really get into and he plays it as close to the historical record as he can. He builds his band of twelve disciples, searching until he finds the ones he knows should be in the group. He rides into Jerusalem on a little donkey. For the first time in his life, Karl is not alone and not afraid. He lives the life of Christ and he dies on the cross.

Behold the Man is an expansion of the novella Nebula winner. It is shocking, but that is its intention. The story is told in a fascinating format. Life in 28 A.D. is interspersed with little vignettes from Karl's life as a child, adolescent, and young adult. Questions asked in the present past are answered in the past present. Creativity is one of Moorcock's strongest features and this novel is no exception. He develops the character of Karl very carefully, neurosis by neurosis. The reader sympathizes with Karl, even if Karl really is crazy.

Dancers at the End of Time trilogy

An Alien Heat. As the trilogy begins, there are not many people left at the end of time on Earth. Those who still live spend all their time amusing themselves and the others. Jherek Carnelian is considered one of the most creative and amusing people left on Earth. His mother, the Iron Orchid, applauds many of Jherek's creations and games and is especially intrigued by his passion for the long past nineteenth century. Jherek and his mother--indeed, all of the people--have unlimited power available to them through rings which create anything the wearer can imagine. In a trip back in time, Jherek meets and becomes obsessed with a time traveler from England in the late nineteenth century, Mrs. Amelia Underwood. In a time when love is no longer practiced, he falls in love with her. She rejects him, partly because there is a solid, although boring, Mr. Underwood back in 1896. When he returns to the end of time, the resident mad scientist, Brannart Morphail, assures Jherek that time will assert itself and return Mrs. Underwood to him.

The Hollow Lands. In the second novel in the trilogy, Mrs. Underwood still has not appeared, and Jherek goes back to Bromley, England, to find her. Enroute he encounters a Mr. Wells, who is most interested and skeptical of Jherek's tales of time travel. Jherek finds both Mr. and Mrs. Underwood at home and explains to Mr. Underwood that he wishes to take Mrs. Underwood back to the end of time with him. At first, Underwood thinks Jherek mad; then he is persuaded that Mrs. Underwood has been unfaithful to him and throws them both out. Jherek and Mrs. Underwood get into the time machine which unfortunately malfunctions, and the romantic pair either goes back to the Paleozoic age, or bypasses the end of time and arrives back at the beginning.

The End of All Songs. In the third volume, another time traveler shows up at the beginning of time. A Time Centre had been set up in this early period because it would have little effect on the order of things. Consequently, time tolerates its presence there. At the Time Centre, a time capsule is set up to take Jherek and Mrs. Underwood back to his time. They are enthusiastically welcomed back with a huge party based on the theme "1896." Amelia Underwood is the belle of the ball. The party is somewhat spoiled when two time travelers return from an assessment of the fate of the universe to pronounce the imminence of the end of the world. Amelia has just found herself adapting to life at the end of time, learning to use power rings to create fairy-tale castles, and warming to Jherek's attentions. Mr. Underwood arrives in due time in the company of several English constables. Before they can capture the lovers, the world begins self-destructing all around them. Lord Jagged arrives and admits his role in manipulating events for his own ends. He is Jherek's father, and had deliberately passed on his genes to enable a son to found a race that could survive and go on living in another time after this time line had ended. He then finds Amelia Underwood, and puts her in the position of the new Eve for Jherek's Adam. Jherek and Amelia will travel beyond the end of time to a new beginning.

Reading just the first two novels in this trilogy would leave the reader with the sense of frivolous fun and incredible amusements. It is not until the third volume that any sense of purpose emerges. Jherek and the other dancers at the end of time are, at first, interested only in their own amusement and create elaborate entertainments for themselves. When Amelia Underwood judges their culture by the rigid standards of nineteenth-century England, she seems slightly hysterical. Yet, she has a reality and solidity which makes Jherek and his friends unsubstantial and amorphous by comparison. It is the blending of the two cultures which makes a balanced whole.

The world created by Moorcock for the end of time is fantastic. His characters have limitless imaginations when it comes to creating intricate worlds or changing their appearance. The lavish parties they create and the flowery language they use indicates the value they place on being amused. The appearance of Lord Jagged as creator and manipulator puts him in the role of a god who is about to begin human life all over again, with his son and new daughter-in-law as the new Adam and Eve.

Biographical/Bibliographical Readings

Peter Caracciolo, "Michael Moorcock," in *Twentieth-Century Science-Fiction Writers*, ed. Curtis C. Smith (St. James, 1986), p.519-22. Colin Greenland, *The Entropy Exhibition: Michael Moorcock and the British New Wave in Science Fiction* (Routledge, 1983). Peter Nicholls, "Michael Moorcock," in *Science Fiction Writers*, ed. E. F. Bleiler (Scribner's, 1982), p.449-58. [Kay Jones]

MOORE, C. L.

Life and Works

Catherine Lucille Moore was born on January 25, 1911, in Indianapolis, Indiana. Raised on an early diet of Edgar Rice Burroughs and Lewis Carroll's *Alice in Wonderland*, Moore's first contact with science fiction was as an adult, when she bought a copy of *Amazing Stories* at the newsstand across from the bank where she worked. Almost immediately she wrote and submitted to *Weird Tales* the short story "Shambleau," which critics now regard as one of the pivotal points in the history of twentieth-century science fiction. This most influential of early women science fiction writers used the initials "C. L." because of her fear of losing her job at the bank at the height of the Great Depression, rather than due to any prejudice in science fiction against women authors.

Upon marrying Henry Kuttner in 1940, Moore quit her bank position and began one of the most famous collaborations in the history of science fiction literature. Under some seventeen pseudonyms, Moore and Kuttner wrote many science fiction short stories, among them two Science Fiction Hall of Fame stories, including the entertaining "Mimsy Were the Borogroves," published originally in 1943 under their best known pen name of Lewis Padgett. The other title, attributed mainly to Moore rather than Kuttner, is the moody, mysterious "Vintage Season" under the name of Lawrence O'Donnell. Other often used pseudonuyms include Keith Hammond, C. H. Liddell, Woodrow Wilson Smith, Paul Edmonds, Kalvin Kent, and Hudson Hastings.

Moore's educational background, interrupted by the Depression, included a year and a half at Indiana University. Beginning in the early 1950s, Moore and Kuttner attended the University of Southern California, Moore attaining her bachelor's degree in English in 1958. Her significant career as a science fiction writer was drawing to a close, with her last novel being *Doomsday Morning*, published in 1958. In that year Kuttner died, and Moore assumed full responsibility for teaching their joint course on science fiction writing at USC. As Moore's science fiction writing career declined, her writing in other fields burgeoned. Becoming a prolific script writer, she produced many plots for television and movies, including "Sugarfoot" and "Maverick." In 1963, Moore completed her master's in English and married Thomas Reggie. While she continued her script writing, her only further science fiction writing was organizing her Jirel stories into a single *Jirel of Joiry* novel in 1969. In 1980, Moore began her autobiography which never appeared. C. L. Moore died of Altzheimer's disease on April 4, 1987, having received virtually every award available in both science fiction and fantasy. Moore has been honored additionally by the naming of a star located in the constellation Cepheus, as "C. L. Moore."

Themes and Style

The concentration on character development, on alien thought patterns, and the introduction of classic literary techniques such as the use of myths that shape human behavior are now recognized as major innovations that can be credited to Moore. These themes are quite apparent in her early writing, and were part of the success for the short story "Shambleau," in which the reader is drawn to the alien fleeing the vengeful mob. These themes recur in such later stories as "No Woman Born," in which a terribly burned dancer is fitted with an android body which results in her gradual alienation from the rest of humankind. This story was one of the first appearances of a cyborg in science fiction.

Moore's early stories are noted for the sensitively drawn characterizations and sexuality. Both elements were innovations with far-reaching repercussions for the entire science fiction genre. Many psychological and sociological science fiction novels of the the 1960s and 1970s owe their stylistic origins to their initial use in Moore's writings.

Moore stresses the importance of human decisions and human errors in judgment as determining factors in the fate of humankind. In Moore's later works, such as "Judgment Night," circumstances are not allowed to dominate the fate of her characters. Both of Moore's strongest female characters, Jirel of Joiry and Juille of Ericon, are assigned the responsiblity for their own mistakes in judgment, giving the stories a dark, poignant tone.

These strong female characters found a surprisingly strong following among the predominately male readership prevalent in the science fiction of the 1930s. The sensitive and sensual nuance of these feminine role models was unique in an era of bug-eyed monsters and high technology, and has drawn praise from feminist critics of the 1980s, who have begun to recognize this writer so far ahead of her time.

The evocative and sensual, almost decadent, mood created by Moore in many of her stories reaches a high in "Vintage Season," in which mysterious visitors from a strange "other place" gather on

Earth to experience a vintage year, much to the puzzlement of the local residents. In this story, Moore shows herself capable not only of creating outstanding mood and ambiance, but also of sustaining a mystery which involves and grips the reader. While this and many of Moore's other short stories were coauthored by Henry Kuttner, critics generally recognize that Moore's principal contributions were the creation of ambiance and characterizations which rendered depth to so many of their stories.

Primarily identified as a writer of short stories, Moore was noted as a writer of extremely long stories, often exceeding 10,000 words in length. This characteristic has caused some difficulties for anthologizers attempting to include her stories in their collections.

Plot Summaries of Major Works

"The Black God's Kiss." Jirel of Joiry, a fifteenth-century warrior queen created by Moore, balances the fierce strength of a warrior with the sensual regal beauty of a woman. In this short story, Jirel's citadel is captured by Guillaume, a magnificent giant of a man. Jirel is stripped and then brutalized by Guillaume. Vowing revenge, Jirel enters an enchanted, distorted world in which the black statue of a god gives her the weapon for her ultimate revenge.

Richly sensual in description and in mood, this is a tale of very strong protagonists attracted sexually to each other, even against their own best judgment. With both protagonists able to decide their own fates, they are nonetheless drawn into mutually destructive acts by their own sensuality and passion. Most critics regard this first Jirel story as the finest of the series.

Doomsday Morning. Written in the late 1950s, this novel supposes a future United States in which personal freedom has been submerged into the will of a totalitarian regime. Utilizing a mass communications network, forced labor camps, and mass relocation, the government finds itself involved with a rebellion against these restrictions. Howard Rohan, a great actor in a traumatic decline following his famous wife's infidelity and tragic death, is manipulated by Ted Nye, secretary of communications for the United States. COMUS, as the Department of Communications is called, wants Rohan to find the principals in the rebellion. As the novel progresses, Rohan finds himself drawn into the center of the controversy, and joins the rebels.

Told from a first-person perspective and without a strong female figure, the novel lacks much of the characteristic moody description and sensuality that characterizes most of Moore's previous work. Concentrating instead upon the implications of the communications revolution, Moore develops a world which is being gradually oppressed and eventually choked to death by its government-controlled communications. Typical with Moore, the story evolves on the effects of personal decisions and the far reaching importance that one person's decisions can make, creating a web of personal and impersonal destruction.

Judgment Night. This is a classic novella of the decline of a galactic empire, and the courage of its rulers in their attempt to defend the empire from the barbarian horde--the H'vanni. The complex plot includes at least five separate protagonistic cultures, each attempting to insure the fall of the other civilizations and thus their own survival. The principle characters are Juille of Ericon, the daughter of the emperor, and Ediger, the hereditary ruler of the H'vanni.

In Juille of Ericon, Moore has created a strong, emotionally controlled woman who must submerge her own basic sexual drives in her attempt to defend the Lyonese Empire. In defending this empire, Juille has been warned by the oracle that only one of her decisions can result in the survival of her civilization, and has been given a weapon that can only be fired once, and irrevocably. The same oracle has issued a similar warning to Ediger, leading both of the principals to assume that their race will conquer. Their judgments of what will bring survival for their people are obscured by the deep sexual bond that develops early in the story. These judgments pale into insignificance in a final and unexpected twist to this complex, multilayered story.

Assassination, seduction, and betrayal provide a rich tapestry against which the decline of empire is acted out. With many parallels to Greek and Roman civilization, including the use of oracles and the cycle of historical decline, this tale typifies the sensuous, seductive atmosphere of some of Moore's previous work. Utilizing two successful themes--the passionate female warrior princess, and responsibility for personal decisions--Moore manages to personalize the decline of empire.

"No Woman Born." This often-reprinted short story is one of the first treatments of "cyborgs" in science fiction literature. The beautiful dancer and entertainer, Dierdre, is burned in a terrible theater fire. In a Frankensteinian twist, a scientist manages to restore her still-conscious brain into a beautiful golden but inhuman body. A woman once worshipped by millions for her sensual and elegant voice and body must now find a new role for herself in a world that still wants to remember her as she was.

In this strongly written plot, one senses the trap that many women admired for their beauty are trying to escape. The world wants to imagine its heroes and heroines as indestructible, unapproachable, and unchanging. Moore presents the consequences of having a woman actually achieve this pinnacle. Whether, as a cyborg, she will become gradually isolated and distant from humanity is hinted at in its conclusion. Nonetheless, the story's description of a woman and her friends trapped by their decisions into a taut cycle of personal tragedy is overwhelming in its sadness.

"Shambleau." This first published story by Moore appeared in *Weird Tales* in 1934, and was an immediate sensation. Introducing Northwest Smith, an adventurer who would reappear in other Moore stories, the plot evolves around the growing obsession of Smith with a seductive alien who combines the sexuality of a woman with the sensual attractiveness of the unknown. As Smith becomes increasingly drawn to the caresses of the alien, he becomes aware that her sexual attraction is a deadly addiction, one he is unable to break.

Intertwining the myth of the Medusa and the vampire with richly sexual interplay, Moore creates an alien who is at once strongly feminine and terrifyingly vulnerable. By combining the allure of the alien with a delicate female form, and assigning her to the protection of the tall, tanned, handsome adventurer who rescues her from the mob, Moore then plays out the age-old tragedy of the virile male and the unattainable myth woman, the fabled woman who can grant a man every ecstasy, but at a tragic cost.

Biographical/Bibliographical Readings

Jeffrey Elliot, "C. L. Moore," in *Science Fiction Voices*, no.6 (1983), p.45-51. Damon Knight, "Genius to Order: Kuttner and Moore," in *In Search of Wonder* (Advent, 1967), p.139-45. Sam Moskowitz, "C. L. Moore," in *Seekers of Tomorrow* (Hyperion, 1966), p.303-18. Natalie M. Rosinsky, "C. L. Moore," in *Selected Proceedings of the 1978 Science Fiction Research Association National Conference* (1979), p.68-74. Fredrick Shroyer, "C. L. Moore and Henry Kuttner," in *Science Fiction Writers*, ed. E. F. Bleiler (Scribner's, 1982), p.161-70. [Colleen Power]

NIVEN, LARRY

Life and Works

Laurence Van Cott Niven was born on April 30, 1938, in Los Angeles, California. He uses the pen name Larry Niven. Niven started college at the California Institute of Technology in 1956, but he dropped out a year and a half later because of poor grades. While at C.I.T., he fell under the spell of science fiction. In 1962, he successfully graduated from Washburn University (Kansas) with a B.A. in mathematics. Niven attended graduate school for one year at the University of California, Los Angeles, before he decided to drop out in order to devote full time to writing.

Niven has the distinction of perfecting his writing during his first year. His great-grandfather left him a trust fund on which he survived while he was writing. After a solid year of rejection slips, his short story "The Coldest Place" was published by *Worlds of If* magazine in 1964. "World of Ptavvs" appeared the next year in short story form and was quickly followed by "The Warriors" (1966) and "Neutron Star" (1966). Niven became a rising star in science fiction literature when "Neutron Star" won the 1967 Hugo award.

All of Niven's earlier short stories became the basis of what is Niven's most popular creation--the Known Space series. Known Space is a series of stories and novels, with a time span ranging from the present day to the thirty-first century. The stories trace the human colonization of space and its hazards. The series has dominated Niven's career. The most famous novel in it is *Ringworld* (1970), which won the Nebula and Hugo awards in 1970 and 1971. The 1976 Hugo award-winning novelette, *The Borderland of Sol*, is also part of the series. Other popular works in the Known Space series are *Protector* (1973) and *The Ringworld Engineers* (1980).

Niven has written two other short stories that became Hugo award winners. "Inconstant Moon" won in 1972 and "The Hole Man" won in 1975. Niven wrote what many consider to be his best work in 1983. *The Integral Trees* is a highly imaginative narrative which involves a human colony living in a gas torus that rotates around a neutron star. A sequel, *The Smoke Ring*, was published in 1987.

In 1974, Niven coauthored a book with his good friend Jerry Pournelle. The result was the highly acclaimed first contact novel, *The Mote in God's Eye*. The pair have collaborated frequently since then, producing *Inferno* (1976), *Lucifer's Hammer* (1977), *Oath of Fealty* (1980), and *Footfall* (1985). Niven also collaborated with David Gerrold on *The Flying Sorcerers* (1971) and with Steven Barnes on *Dream Park* (1981).

Themes and Style

Science and technology dominate most of Niven's works. He is a hard-core science fiction writer in the tradition of Asimov, Clarke, and Heinlein. Niven's heroes are almost always loners. They either cannot or will not conform to society. They usually possess some expertise or knowledge that society needs. While Niven's heroes are not disdainful of society, they do their best to avoid human interaction. This antisocial characteristic underlies most of Niven's writing, but there is concurrently a feeling of hope and optimism. Part of the optimism lies in Niven's belief in science and technology as solutions to most of the problems that arise in his storylines. Niven prefers the us-against-them attitude when he develops a plot and, invariably, this is expressed as the technologically advanced overcoming the technologically weak. History is written in favor of the victors, and in Niven's case, his victors are always morally correct because they have more scientific knowledge. Ignorance is frowned upon in Niven's universe and is a definite liability.

Niven's works are action-oriented and rarely do his characters experience any moral conflicts within themselves. Inner conflict is generally straightforward and easily resolved. Niven prefers an adversarial approach to life with simple answers to complex questions.

Plot Summaries of Major Works

The Integral Trees. The crew of the cyborg-controlled Earth spaceship *Discipline* mutiny and escape to a binary star system known as T3. The T3 star system consists of a G0 star, which orbits a neutron star. Surrounding the neutron star is a breathable gas torus, which is inhabited by various kinds of free-fall life forms. The mutineers settle on the life forms known as integral trees, so named because they resemble the mathematical integral sign. Five hundred years pass and the mutineers forget that they came from Earth or that there is a spaceship called *Discipline* still in orbit around the neutron star, which has come to be called Levoy's star. The mutineers have physically adapted to life in the gas torus by becoming very tall and weak. Some are physically handicapped because the genetic pool was very small and mutations have occurred.

The Quinn clan is just one of several clans that have developed within the gas torus, called the Smoke Ring. The Quinn clan members find that they must leave the tree they are living on, because the tree is dying. In a search for food on their dying tree, they meet the Dalton clan. The two clans reluctantly join forces to search for a new tree and discover other, more advanced, clans. One of the advanced clans, the Carthers, enslaves the Quinn and Dalton clans. The Quinns and Daltons escape using a Cargo and Repair Model (CARM), that is left over from the mutineers' escape from the *Discipline*. The CARM enables the Quinn-Dalton clans to settle into a new tree and become part of the well-organized London Tree clan. All of the activities of the various clans are kept under close surveillance by the cyborg intelligence aboard the *Discipline*.

The plot lines of mutiny, clans, and colonization of an unexplored region in *The Integral Trees* are rather classic and mundane. What heightens the plot is the free-fall life forms found in the Smoke Ring, the mutation of Earthmen to survive in free-fall, and the omnipotence of the cyborg intelligence on the spaceship *Discipline*. Even the spaceship's name evokes a question of whether or not the mutineers are really in charge of their own actions. Is the cyborg merely an observer, or is it a manipulator?

Lucifer's Hammer. Civilization as we know it ends when a gigantic comet strikes the Earth. Timothy Hamner is an amateur California astronomer who first discovers the comet while it is still far out in space. When the comet passes behind the sun, it fragments and changes its orbit directly toward Earth. Initially, humanity does not believe that the comet will strike the Earth, but when it becomes apparent that it will, everyone is caught unprepared.

The comet strikes Earth and sets off earthquakes and tidal waves which throw tons of water into the atmosphere, causing a perpetual rain. Survivors form small groups within what is left of society. Every type of social and political structure evolves, including anarchy, religious fanaticism, dictatorships, even cannibalism. Timothy Hamner is one of the survivors, and he becomes a member of a somewhat civilized colony that is headed by a former senator.

Senator Jellison's colony battles to maintain some sort of government through laws and the preservation of human technology. A fanatical, antitechnology mob opposes the senator's group and has focused itself upon the destruction of the sole remaining nuclear power plant in California. The battle is eventually won by the protechnology Jellison group with the use of mustard gas. The nuclear power plant is saved and with it, the future of humanity.

Lucifer's Hammer was successfully coauthored with Jerry Pournelle. It was published in the mid-1970s when disaster novels and movies were in vogue. Niven's favorite theme of the advantages of science and technology is quite evident in the novel. The protechnology group are the heroes; the nuclear power plant is humanity's saviour.

The Mote in God's Eye. The Moties are the first alien intelligence encountered by humans. They live in the region of space known as the Coal Sack. The year is 3017 and constitutes the Second Empire of Man. At first, the Motie civilization appears highly advanced and peaceful. Each individual Motie has developed a specialized function and lives within a specialized group. Unfortunately, the groups are in constant war with each other and are pressured to breed frequently in order to maintain a numeric advantage over the other. Frequent breeding leads to overpopulation and the overtaxing of the limited resources of their solar system. The Motie civilization eventually collapses into a Dark Ages cycle and must start over again. The Motie civilization has gone through thousands of these cycles.

Humans have unwittingly provided the Moties with a solution to their problems. The Moties have not been able to advance sufficiently to develop a working knowledge of hyperspace. Humans give the Moties the essential knowledge which enables them to leave their own solar system. Now the Moties can colonize any world in the universe with their excess population. Having opened a Pandora's box, humanity must choose between war with the Moties or extinction.

Ringworld. A civilization of aliens called puppeteers discovers that the core of the Milky Way has exploded and the resulting radiation will soon make the galaxy uninhabitable. The puppeteers, a mild-mannered and non-confrontational race, decide that the best thing to do is to leave the galaxy. On their way to the Magellanic clouds, they discover a strange ring-like object in orbit around a distant star and decide to explore it. Being cowardly, they contract the exploration to a couple of humans and a cat-like kzin. The Ringworld is a large ring that is one million miles wide and 600 million miles long. The Ringworld is in an orbit of ninety-three million miles center about a G2 star. It has over three million times the area of Earth.

Louis Wu and Teela Brown are the humans hired for the expedition. Louis Wu is almost two hundred years old and has lived a very full life. He accepts the challenge of exploring the Ringworld because he is tired of human society. Teela Brown is a young woman who accompanies Wu because her luck has been genetically inbred. A savage warrior kzin, called "Speaker-to-Animals," is recruited for protection. The head of the expedition is an insane puppeteer named Nessus. Nessus is considered insane because courage seems to be one of the normally cowardly puppeteer's attributes.

Ringworld tells the story of the team's landing, exploration, and escape from the magnificent world. The novel is a showcase for the technological possibilities of Ringworld. The interaction of the societies of Ringworld with its explorers is very entertaining. Annoying to some is the abundance of unanswered questions concerning the origin and fate of the wondrous Ringworld. The novel is the most popular of Niven's Known Space series.

The Ringworld Engineers. Twenty years after its discovery, Louis Wu and the kzin, "Speaker-to-Animals," return to Ringworld with the recently deposed puppeteer leader known as The Hindmost. They discover that the orbit of Ringworld has become unstable, and it will be destroyed within months if nothing is done. The control center of Ringworld must be found in order to correct the orbit. After several adventures with alien societies, the control center is found by Wu, the kzin, and the puppeteer. They find Teela Brown in the control center. She has been there for twenty years, trying to correct the orbit. Teela has been transformed into a "Pak protector," since she ate from the tree-of-life root. The Paks are the builders of Ringworld. Teela cannot allow the intruders to touch the control center because she is a protector. However, she must allow them to repair the center. Teela dies protecting the center, but she gives the threesome the knowledge necessary to make the repairs. Louis Wu, the Hindmost, and "Speaker-to-Animals" are able to complete the repairs, but they remain stranded on Ringworld.

The sequel to *Ringworld* answers many of the questions that arose in the first novel. *Ringworld*, *The Ringworld Engineers*, and the other stories and novels in the Known Space series reflect Niven's themes of the wonders of scientific and technological innovations. The protagonists make up a team consisting of humans and aliens who must work together to accomplish their goals.

Biographical/Bibliographical Readings

Richard Finholt and John Carr, "Larry Niven," in *Science Fiction Writers*, ed. E. F. Bleiler (Scribner's, 1982), p.459-65. Donald L. Lawler, "Larry Niven," in *Twentieth-Century Science-Fiction Writers*, ed. Curtis C. Smith (St. James, 1986), p.537-39. Thomas Wiloch, "Larry Niven," in *Contemporary Authors New Revision Series* (Gale, 1985), v.14, p.355-60. Raymond J. Wilson III, "Larry Niven," in *Twentieth-Century American Science-Fiction Writers* (Gale, 1981), v.2, p.37-41. **[Eric Nuddell]**

NORTON, ANDRE

Life and Works

Alice Mary Norton was born on February 17, 1912, in Cleveland, Ohio. She attended Western Reserve University from 1930 to 1931. From 1932 to 1950, she worked at the Cleveland Public Library as a children's librarian, except for a brief period during World War II, when she worked at the Library of Congress. She was an editor at Gnome Press from 1950 until 1958. In 1967, she moved to Florida, where she continues to live and write.

Norton began writing historical fiction and adventure stories in the 1930s, changing her name to "Andre" because the field was still dominated by male writers. When she first started writing science fiction, she used the pseudonym Andrew North. Her first science fiction novel, *Starman's Son: 2250 AD* (variant title, *Daybreak--2250 AD*) was published in 1952. She quickly became one of the most prolific and best-selling authors in science fiction and fantasy. Norton's science fiction books have an appeal to all ages, from children to adults.

Norton wrote many titles in series--among which are The Forerunner series (*Forerunner* [1981] and *Forerunner: The Second Venture* [1985]), The Solar Queen series (*Sargasso of Space* [1955], *Plague Ship* [1956], *Voodoo Planet* [1959], and *Postmarked the Stars* [1969]), The Time Traders series (*Time Traders* [1958], *Galactic*

Derelict [1959], *Defiant Agents* [1962], and *Key Out of Time* [1963]), and The Warlock series (*Storm Over Warlock* [1960] and *Ordeal in Otherwhere* [1964]).

Themes and Style

Norton's most frequently used theme is that of an outsider who overcomes difficulties and ultimately finds a place to belong. It is an archetypal pattern that occurs in legends and tales of many cultures. Most of her protagonists are young people, without close family or friends, who must struggle to survive. Some have grown up alone in slums or have seen their only relatives die, as does Charis in *Ordeal in Otherwhere*. Other characters are afraid of trust due to previous betrayals. Some characters, such as Simsa in the Forerunners series, have been outcast because of their unusual appearance or powers. Using their intelligence and skills, they mature into valuable members of a group. As in many classic tales, they first must pass through an initiation, in which they discover new abilities or powers which enable them to save their new friends. Throughout their maturation, they find friends, beliefs, and a place where they are accepted.

Norton often uses psychic abilities in her stories, both fantasy and science fiction. Some of her aliens have the ability to control minds, to teleport, or to summon memories from a stranger's past, as do the Wyverns in the Warlock series. There is often a conflict between those attempting to impose the will of their group upon others and those struggling to maintain individual will. Many of her heroes and heroines develop telepathic rapport with animal companions, as Dane does in the Solar Queen series. The animals are allies, with desires and wishes of their own, yet are willing to work with the humans. The human-animal relationships reinforce Norton's theme of the necessity of cooperation, with each contributing special talents.

Norton has said that she is antimachine, that she believes that reliance on technology can be a source of frustration. While technology in various forms, from spaceships to weapons, is present in her work, it is never the major element in a story. Rather, Norton concentrates on the emotions and relationships of her characters, even in her space operas. The lifeless worlds left by the wars of the ancient unknown race called the Forerunners serve as her warning of the dangers of the abuse of technology. This concern about technological dependence is a continuing theme in her work.

Many of Norton's stories share a common universe even though they are not part of a series. The main legal force in her works is the Patrol; Survey Teams handle the exploration of new planets; interstellar business is done by Trading Companies and Free Traders. The common features give the reader a sense of familiarity, providing a known background for the new races and worlds she creates.

In a genre not known for its use of ethnic characters, Norton has often created black and American Indian characters, ranging from an Apache in *Defiant Agents* to a young black girl in *Star Ka'at* (1976). In the 1960s, Norton began using women as her protagonists despite her publisher's initial reluctance. Most of her work since that time features women characters who are as strong, adventurous, and determined as her earlier male characters were. Many women now writing science fiction and fantasy have said that Norton and her female characters inspired them to begin writing.

Norton is a storyteller who creates a sense of wonder in her readers. Her vivid worlds, fascinating aliens, and sympathetic characters are places and people that her readers want to meet again. Norton's adventure stories are built around relationships, growth, and friendship.

Plot Summaries of Major Works

The Forerunner series. *Forerunner* and *Forerunner: The Second Venture* tell the story of Simsa, an outcast in the Burrows of Kuxortal because of her black skin and silver hair. While selling artifacts, she meets a space man, Yun Thom. Simsa and her hunting companion, a birdlike animal, travel with Thom and discover the ancient ruins of a Forerunner city in which a temple statue looks exactly like Simsa. Simsa, drawn to the figure, discovers that she is descended from the Forerunners, a people who vanished long ago. Since she now contains two identities, Simsa of the Burrows and the elder Simsa of the Forerunners, her memories and emotions are overlapping and very confusing. Simsa and Thom realize that the city contains ancient ships and weapons, and summon the Patrol to stop the pirates from stealing them. Thom then arranges for Simsa to go to the Zacathans' planet where the unique knowledge of the Elder Simsa will be valued, but those taking her there plan to use her talents for their own profit. She escapes by crashing the ship's lifecraft on an unknown desert world. The inhabitants help her to survive, and hide her from search parties. When Thom tries to find her, the natives force his ship to crash, but Simsa convinces the natives to help him. Even though she feels that he betrayed her by turning her over to those who wanted to use her, he had saved her from the Burrows, and she cannot let him die. Simsa creates a false memory of her death in Thom's memory to keep him from hunting her. She goes to the ruins of another city where she undergoes a ritual initiation that unites her divided identities. Realizing that she has created a division in Thom that could be as painful as her dual identity has become, she decides to correct her actions.

Thom's memory has already been corrected by the Zacathan and she is offered a place of refuge as the last of her people. Simsa and Thom have saved each other's lives, and now have a chance to start over as equals.

Simsa, like many of Norton's women, finds her true identity. She reconciles her contradictory feelings about Thom and unites her dual identities. The main adventure is Simsa's journey to her own indentity, reflecting Norton's interest in people rather than machines.

The Solar Queen series. This series consists of four novels, *Sargasso of Space*, *Plague Ship*, *Voodoo Planet*, and *Postmarked the Stars*. As the series begins, Dane Thorson is waiting to discover what his first space assignment will be. While most of his fellow students have been assigned to ships belonging to one of the major trading companies that dominate interstellar trade, Dane is shocked to be assigned as an apprentice cargo master on the *Solar Queen*, a free trader. The Free Traders are small, independent ships with very low status. On the planet Limbo, the crew discovers a Forerunner complex being used by pirates. Their success in dealing with this problem wins them valuable trading rights on Sargol, a source of perfumes and gems. Trade goods from Sargol conceal an alien creature whose attacks cause most of the crew to fall ill. The *Solar Queen* is identified as a plague ship, carrying an unknown disease; she is to be destroyed on sight. Dane and the few who have not become ill manage to save the ship by destroying the alien creature. The *Queen*'s next adventure is on Khatka, a hunting resort where the chief priest is using magic and illusions to conceal an interstellar poaching conspiracy. Dane, his captain, and the ship's doctor work with a Ranger to expose the scheme, using some illusions of their own. The *Queen*'s next assignment takes them to a planet that is the target of a plot to drive the colonists away by creating mutant monsters. The planet has a mineral that increases telepathic powers; if the colonists leave, the mineral could be exploited secretly. Dane develops telepathic communication with a brach (an animal whose intelligence has been increased so much by the mineral that it has become an intelligent species). Dane, a Ranger, and the brach work together to defeat the conspiracy. The *Solar Queen* buys the conspirators' ship at auction, and Dane, who began as a very reluctant apprentice cargo master, will become the cargo master of the *Queen*'s new consort ship.

Dane's journey from newly assigned apprentice to cargo master on the new consort ship follows Norton's pattern of a young person's growth to maturity. The series is especially notable for its varied races, such as the feline Salarik of Sargol who are fascinated by natural spices, and the vivid worlds such as the deserted Limbo. These backgrounds and alien lifeforms give depth to the adventures of Dane and his shipmates.

The Time Traders series. Four novels comprise this series: *Time Traders*, *Galactic Derelict*, *Defiant Agents*, and *Key out of Time*. The main characters are Gordon Ashe, Ross Murdoch, and Travis Fox, agents working on Operation Retrograde, a time travel project. Ashe is an archaeologist whose knowledge helps him assume the role of a trader in Earth's distant past and on alien planets. Ross Murdock has had a history of arrests before being offered a choice of rehabilitation or volunteering for a secret military project; he opts for the project and matures into a responsible member of the team. Travis Fox, an Apache who feels that the white world has rejected him because he is Indian and that he can no longer accept the traditional Apache beliefs, discovers Ashe and Murdoch looking for an alien spaceship and is asked to join their expedition.

In *Time Traders*, United States agents believe that the Russians have discovered an alien space ship that crashed in Earth's past. The United States has created Operation Retrograde to find the ship and prevent the Russians from using the weapons they have stolen from the ship. Murdock finds the alien ship, and accidentally enables the aliens, who still exist, to trace the wreck. They destroy their ship and the Russian bases connected to it. Murdoch and his colleagues escape with tapes that show that other wrecks exist in United States territory, ships that may hold the secrets of space travel.

In *Galactic Derelict*, Ashe, Murdoch, and Fox discover one of the alien ships in the prehistoric past of the Southwest. An attempt to bring it forward to their present is complicated by an earthquake that triggers the ship's launching, following programmed flight instructions. The men visit strange worlds, from a robot refueling stop to a planet with beautiful ruins and a tribe of winged humanoids. After experimenting with tapes obtained from the humanoids, they finally reverse the course program and return home, bringing with them tapes and records of many new worlds.

In *Defiant Agents*, the tapes of the new planets brought back by Ashe's team have been shared among the nations of Earth. The United States and Russia have developed experimental techniques that help people remember ancestral abilities and may thus help them to survive on frontier planets. The United States hopes to settle the world Topaz with Apaches, but the team led by Travis Fox discovers that the Russians have stolen the tape and have already put a Mongol colony on the planet. Fox and the Mongols form a reluctant alliance to defeat the Russian authority on Topaz. The Apaches and the Mongols were both raiders, hunters, horsemen, and fighters; they will work together in their new world.

In the final novel, *Key out of Time*, Ashe, Murdoch, and Karara, a Polynesian with two dolphin companions, must discover why the planet Hawaika has changed so dramatically from the records on the alien tapes. They are swept back into the past of Hawaika, and find themselves in the middle of a war between two local groups. They discover that the aliens who made the tapes are attempting to take over the planet by causing conflict between the native races. Ashe and his associates convince the groups that they must work together to defeat the alien attack. Ashe and his team do not know if they have succeeded in change Hawaika's future, but they will build their lives in this time, hoping that the aliens will not return.

This series has most of Norton's characteristic themes. Murdoch and Fox are outsiders who change and mature, finding places where they belong. Fox and Karara have telepathic rapport with the dolphins. The dislike of technology is more directly expressed in this series than it is in much of Norton's work--in *Galactic Derelict* some of the characters wonder if their voyage in a ship they cannot control may be a punishment for attempting to discover hidden secrets. The series also exemplifies Norton's ability to create and describe worlds, ranging from prehistoric Earth, to a robot world, to a world of tropical islands like Hawaika. These elements all combine to create a vivid background for the exciting adventures of a group of sympathetic people.

The Warlock series. The planet Warlock and its rulers, the Wyverns, are the subject of two books, *Storm over Warlock* and *Ordeal in Otherwhere*. Most of the survey reports about Warlock indicate a planet ideally suited for colonization, and a Survey Team is sent to prepare for the arrival of a colony ship. The team is attacked by Throgs, aliens resembling beetles, and only two members of the team survive. Ragnar Thorvald is a survey officer who had believed that Warlock needed further exploration. Shann Lantee had been hired to care for the animals, including two wolverines that have a rapport with him. Ragnar and Shann discover that Warlock is inhabited by a race whose women have psychic abilities. These women, called Wyverns by Ragnar, are very surprised when Ragnar and Shann show psychic talents of their own, since most of the men of Warlock do not have any such abilities. The Wyvern and the humans work together to prevent the Throgs from conquering the planet. Shann remains on Warlock with Ragnar as part of the official delegation.

Charis Nordholm is brought to Warlock by a trader who needs a spokeswoman to deal with the Wyverns, who refuse to deal with most men. She is drawn from the colony of humans by strange dreams. In the wilderness, she meets Shann and his wolverines. They discover that one of the large Trading Companies is operating on Warlock illegally, using the males of Warlock in an attempt to discover the secrets of the Wyvern powers. The company has developed a mental shield, and some of the males are now free of the Wyvern control. The males will fight to keep their new freedom, which exists only within the range of the company shield.

Shann, Charis and the wolverines unite to create a mental power of a type unknown on Warlock, trying to persuade the males and the Wyverns that there are alternatives to civil war. They offer examples of new ways that may allow the males and females of Warlock to work more equally. In the sequel *Forerunner Foray*, which does not take place on Warlock, one of the main characters is Ris Lantee, who identifies himself as a Wyvern-trained son of mind-linked liaison officers, indicating that Shann and Charis remained together on Warlock.

Both Shann and Charis are outsiders who must build new lives in new worlds, following Norton's dominant theme of the outcast reaching maturity. *Ordeal in Otherwhere* is one of the first times that Norton uses a woman as protagonist. Charis is as strong and as capable as Shann, which is unusual for the early 1960s when the book was written.

Biographical/Bibliographical Readings

"Andre Norton," in *Speaking of Science Fiction, the Paul Walker Interviews* (Luna Publications, 1978), p.263-70. Charles Platt, "Andre Norton," in *Dream Makers* (Berkley Books, 1983), v.2, p.95-102. Roger C. Schlobin, *Andre Norton: A Primary and Secondary Bibliography* (G. K. Hall, 1980). **[Linda K. Lewis]**

OLIVER, CHAD

Life and Works

Symmes Chadwick Oliver was born on March 30, 1928, in Cincinnati, Ohio, the son of Winona Newman--a professional nurse and noted artist, and Symmes Francis Oliver--a surgeon. As a young boy, he was an avid reader of detective and spy thrillers, but a serious bout with rheumatic fever gave him the opportunity to discover science fiction magazines which he read exhaustively; he wrote numerous letters to the editors as critic and enthusiastic reader. His family moved to Texas where Oliver attended high school in Crystal City (a prototype for the Jefferson City of *Shadows in the Sun*, 1954). He became an unabashed permanent settler in Texas. His attempts at publishing in science fiction were finally realized in 1950 when he sold two short stories: "The Boy next Door" (*Magazine of Fantasy and Science Fiction*) and "Land of the Lost Content" (*Super Science Stories*). Attending the University of Texas at Austin, he majored in English with a minor in anthropology, and in 1952 received his M.A. in English with his graduate thesis "They Builded a Tower," a discourse on the history of science fiction. He met his wife, Beje (Betty Jane Jenkins) at Austin, and they married during his Ph.D. studies at UCLA where he received a doctorate in anthropology. He was well known enough in the science fiction world by this time so that their wedding was attended by such notables as Ray Bradbury, A. E. VanVogt, and Rog Phillips. During this period he published his first novel, *Mists of Dawn* (1952) for the juvenile audience, followed by his first adult novel, *Shadows in the Sun* (1954). His short stories were regularly appearing in numerous anthologies and on the Judith Merril honor role. After completing his doctorate in 1961, he spent a year with his wife and daughter in Kenya doing field research before returning to Texas, where he became a member of the faculty of the anthropology department at the University of Texas, Austin. The year in Kenya provided the setting and material for *The Shores of Another Sea* (1971).

Although his career in anthropology took much time away from his science fiction writing, he progressed significantly in his academic field, becoming head of the anthropology department from 1967 to 1971. He branched out in 1967 to write a western historical novel, *The Wolf Is My Brother*, which won the coveted Spur award. He is currently still on the faculty at the University of Texas.

Themes and Style

Oliver's science fiction features the elements of anthropological approaches to the observation of humans and aliens. The anthropologist is often the hero or much-relied-upon specialist on a space expedition or scientific project, as in *Unearthly Neighbors* (1960) and *The Winds of Time* (1957). A recurring concept is the premise that humans are not unique to the planet Earth but rather a common occurrence throughout the universe. In *The Shores of Another Sea*, one group of scientists, alien and ironically baboon-shaped, studies human samples in the Kenya Primate Research Station. Observing other planet's cultures or alien cultures is done with the careful scrutiny and analysis offered by the sciences of anthropology and sociology.

There is an alluring value to the primitive. In *Mists of Dawn*, there are some basic good values projected onto Cro-Magnons that allow Mark Nye and his youthful counterpart to become close friends in spite of extreme cultural differences. *Giants in the Dust* (1976) proposes that civilizations may die from apathy and it is the challenge of survival that can put new life into a culture. Humans are the animal with endless questions--people who worry about nations will discover galaxies. Oliver's writings make us think, examine, and probe as if we were on scientific expeditions. Time past as well as time future offers the material to examine cultural development and think carefully of our own progress.

Plot Summaries of Major Works

Giants in the Dust. A civilization may advance to a point where its members have no more challenges; they then settle into a state of apathy which threatens to decay the lifeforms of the civilization itself, eventually leading to extinction. If the governing authority has insight and a scientific sophistication of sorts, it can attempt to devise an experimental solution. On this planet, a government project is proposed which will take samples of the living members of the current society and transport them to a compatible planet, strip them of their cultural memories and allow them, in small and scattered colonies, to begin the survival and developmental process all over again. Their lives will spin out like some form of drama visible to the citizens left in the advanced, yet decaying, culture, and if the experiment is successful, it may be repeated, offering an alternative life style to those who would choose to live a high risk life of survival similar to that of their primitive ancestors. Varnum, a disgruntled but superior misfit in the current society, is given the opportunity for leadership in the experiment. While his cultural memories will also be stripped, they will return after a time, allowing him more control over the experiment, and allowing him to choose the fate of the civilization to be created. Varnum's choice is inevitable and at the end of the experimental time frame, the new society will hide itself from the old to continue their existence unmolested by the observers.

Oliver values the drama of survival and the life force it manifests. Moving an advanced civilization back to the time of ancestral roots renews the spirit and introduces the long lost passion for existence that comes from risk and danger. Basic values are recaptured, and life in its simplest form seems to be the best. Oliver draws on current theories of the life-style of primitive humans with which to describe the experiences of Varnum and his fellow survivors.

Shadows in the Sun. The setting is Jefferson City, Texas, in the 1950s. Paul Ellery is a student of cultures, trained in scientific observation techniques. He remembers a mission statement of his discipline--that one must look at the small towns of America as objectively as one would look at a primitive tribe. What Ellery discovers is the beginnings of colonization by an alien race. Not aliens of the ominous, hostile sort, but rather a gentle, sophisticated species whose history is so extended that Earth's history is only a miniscule fraction of theirs. Ellery senses intuitively that the bizarre is at work in this small Texas town. The situation of the galaxy shows an overflow of population from a myriad of planets--the common problems of ineffective birth control, ironically, that sets other forms of people adrift, looking for less developed planets on which to settle their excess populations. Ellery's astuteness is recognized by the aliens and he is afforded the special treatment of explanation--their method of removing the prying observer without harm, by providing the answers so that the observer leaves in peace.

This is Oliver's first adult science fiction novel and one in which he sets out many of his theories of humanity's place in galactic development. The aliens look identical to Earth dwellers, since humans are a rather common animal in the galaxy. The aliens mean no harm to humanity. They sidle in and drive the native inhabitants of the town to the cities by means of unconscious persuasion. They offer Ellery the opportunity to become one of them, and in a struggle down to mere minutes, he wrestles with his values as a member of American society and youth. Oliver has claimed a fondness for this novel as having biographical significance in his own development. Ellery and Oliver may had much in common while in their twenties.

The Shores of Another Sea. The setting for this novel is Kenya, East Africa, at the Kikumbuliu Primate Research Station where Boyce Crawford and his family have relocated from Texas to undertake specialized research on baboons. The baboonery is ordinary as research stations go, and trappings and studies continue as usual, until disappearances and ominous forbodings make it clear that something dangerous and bizarre is occurring. The death of a long time British settler and the kidnapping of Crawford's daughter builds into an hysteria that finally reveals the presence of extraterrestrial creatures who take on the appearance of baboons, and who are also in the process of collecting and performing experiments on human subjects. Thus, at this research area where Crawford and his coworkers had, with limited concerns, gathered their animal subjects, they are now sought after for the same purposes, subjected to scrutiny by the aliens. There is no verbal contact between species, but essential feelings transcend the situation when each group finds it has trapped a significant member of the other group. Pain, worry, fear, and intense heroism penetrate the lack of technical language and, on a basic level, there is intellectual contact leading to recognition and compassion for both kinds of beings. The aliens retreat and Crawford and his family head back to Texas.

There is a premise that no matter what form it takes, the scientific mind and attitude has a commonality of ethics and recognition that allows dissimilar beings to feel a kinship. This work stands apart from Oliver's other novels in that it is less scientifically analytical and more infused with primitive intuition basic to the primeval setting of the African landscape. The landscape is described with sensitive detail, a result of Oliver's own research experience in Kenya in the early 1960s. The irony exists in the duality of the scientific experiments and proposes that each race, human and alien, feels the inherent need to explore and investigate new worlds and new lifeforms.

Unearthly Neighbors. The first sighting of a planet with human beings is followed up with an expedition of scientists and their families to make contact with the humans and discover the nature of their civilization. Their behavior, as captured by pictures from the space probe, is studied and analyzed ruthlessly, but the conclusions are meaningless until the actual immersion of the expedition into the environment. The expedition is staffed with a physical anthropologist, a cultural anthropologist, a linguist, a psychologist, and an archaeologist--a medley of scientists with which to completely investigate the makeup and system of this newly found group of humanoids. All the specialists of Earth's society cannot quickly decipher the society on Sirius Nine. The inhabitants of Sirius Nine are remote, detached, accompanied by doglike animals, and eventually they massacre the investigators leaving only two survivors. Charlie Jenkins and Monte Stewart are left to decipher the society of Merdosi of Walonka. When Monte finally returns to Earth years later, and Charlie has long since died, the language barrier has been broken and a peaceful meeting of the two societies is possible.

In this novel, Oliver again proposes the idea that the existence of people, or humanoids, throughout the universe is a strong possibility. What appears to have happened is that a divergence of evolution has occurred with this species, so that instead of mechanical and technological development, they have focused on powers of the mind. Their appearance is that of primitive, tree-dwelling humans, but their powers to control the sanity of the two investigators, to control the animals and plants around them, and to use dreams and thoughts as communication equalizes whatever measures of civilized advancement are used. Motives of kindness and compassion are evident in both species. This is a first contact story that leaves the reader with a good dose of anthropological theory to create an entirely plausible situation.

The Winds of Time. Twentieth-century Weston Chase, an American sportsman on a fishing trip in the Colorado mountains, finds himself caught up in the drama of others who came from another place and another time in the galaxy, seeking, on a space expedition, other humans from parallel cultures that may have advanced more technologically and culturally and yet who have still managed to escape total devastation. It is a mission of hope. Chase is caught in threatening weather and finds himself in a cave as the crew of aliens comes to, after a drug-induced sleep of thousands of years. Since their scientific and linguistic techniques are so far advanced, they can quickly absorb the language structure of Chase's dialect and communicate their tale of purpose and survival. Camaraderie between the aliens and the American grows, and Chase is commandeered into assisting the crew in solving the problem of their malfunctioning spaceship. The bond that Chase may have had with his own civilization weakens as his loyalty to Arvon, Nseline, and the others grows--particularly as his marriage has disintegrated in his absence. Chase decides to join his new friends in their quest and return with them to their planet, Lortas.

A basic idea of this novel is that humans are not so unique as to occur in time and space only once, but can appear over and over throughout the universe--and thus can seek to contact others, looking for the results of civilization in many locations and throughout many times in order to find success in reaching a technological mastery of the environment without devastation. Before the landing on Earth, the anthropologist is fatally wounded, but through his scientific knowledge provides the key to understanding the alien planet Earth and predicts the cultural development and location of the living human forms at the time the ship lands. The anthropologist of the crew, though he dies, is a titled member of the team with the command of a science that may well hold the key for eventual survival of humans among other humans.

Biographical/Bibliographical Readings

H. W. Hall, *Chad Oliver: A Preliminary Bibliography* (Dellwood Press, 1985). William F. Nolan, "The Worlds of Chad Oliver: A Biographical Introduction," in *The Edge of Forever* (Sherbourne, 1971). Gary K. Wolfe, "Chad Oliver," in *Twentieth-Century Science-Fiction Writers*, ed. Curtis C. Smith (St. James, 1986), p.551-52. Idem, "The Known and the Unknown," in *Many Futures, Many Worlds*, ed. T. D. Clareson (Kent State University Press, 1979), p.94-116. **[Lorraine E. Lester]**

ORWELL, GEORGE

Life and Works

George Orwell is a pseudonym used by Eric Arthur Blair. He was born on June 25, 1903, to British parents in Motihari, Bengal, India, where he remained until he was returned to England for his education. He stayed in England until 1922, having attended Henley-on-Thames Convent School, St. Cypian's, Wellington School, and Eton College. Returning to India, Orwell held several police jobs, including a stint at the Police Training School in Rangoon. He held the position of assistant superintendent in several cities. He returned to Europe in 1927 and lived in both London and Paris.

This period of his life was rich with varied experiences, which he skillfully reproduced in his writing. Notable among his early work is the essay, "Shooting an Elephant," in which he vividly recalled his obligation as a police officer in India to kill an elephant. The autobiographical work, *Down and Out in Paris and London* (1933), masterfully recounts his experiences living in the lower social orders of those cities. With deep conviction, Orwell served with the United Marxist Workers' Party Militia in Spain, and his *Homage to Catalonia* (1938) is an often-praised result.

Orwell was wounded in Spain and returned to England where he continued free-lance journalism, worked with the Home Guard, and contributed his writing skill to the British war effort. He was a prolific writer under both his real and pen names and contributed regularly to *New English Weekly*, *Time and Tide*, *Observer*, *Manchester Evening News*, and *Partisan Review*. He also served as editor with Secker and Warburg publishers. His output included essays, articles, poetry, radio broadcasts, fiction, news, and book reviews. His best remembered novel is his only science fiction novel, *1984*, published in 1948. He is also remembered for *Animal Farm* (1945), a political satire. His keen observances and insights, coupled with his journalistic and literary expertise, gave Orwell the ability to produce the quality of writing to which many authors aspire. He died January 21, 1950, at his remote home on Jura, a part of the Hebrides Islands, Scotland.

Themes and Style

Orwell's writing was powerful and effective, employing words in their utmost economy. He was an acknowledged social commentator, keenly aware of world affairs and, with the publication of *Animal Farm*, his international reputation was firmly established. This brilliant satire of Soviet politics reflected Orwell's disillusionment with the evolution of that system, as well as offering a warning of the dangers of European fascism. Although *1984* was his only work of science fiction, it is so powerful and so widely recognized that "Orwellian," "dystopian social order," and "Nineteen Eighty-Four" have become universally synonymous. As with much of his writing, Orwell based the story on what he experienced and saw around him. Wartime life, disillusioned citizenry, and powerful bureaucratic governments easily lent themselves to his extrapolations.

Plot Summaries of Major Works

1984. The setting is London after World War III, in a world where the three superpowers continue warring. The world of 1984 is authoritarian, repressive, violent, unrewarding, fearful, homogenized, and without hope. Winston Smith's job within the Ministry of Truth (Minitrue) is to rewrite history. This process utilizes "Newspeak," the official party language. The party uses many techniques for emotional control: "doublethink" is the ability to simultaneously hold and believe two contradictory views; "thoughtcrime" and "facecrimes" are punishable offenses. Big Brother oversees all and dictates that "War Is Peace," "Freedom Is Slavery," and "Ignorance Is Strength." Winston Smith's world is bleak. He and everyone risk becoming "unpersons" for having a private life or not absorbing and appreciating the daily two minutes of hate. In his one attempt to form a relationship with a woman, he finds happiness, but it is too brief and too fleeting as they are both arrested by the authorities. He is imprisoned, tortured, and finally is made mindless so that he will accept his life as the bureaucracy wants it to be.

1984 is often compared with Huxley's *Brave New World* and Zamiatin's *We.* Each approaches differently a potential world future. Zamiatin's is rationalized and painless, Huxley's is the reverse of Big Brother, while in *1984* Orwell is preoccupied with the state control of emotions, physical pleasure, and thought. Orwell's war work with the British Broadcasting Corporation gave him a broad perspective of then current world conditions and he expanded and extrapolated them. "Newspeak" can be directly attributed to his personal experiences with Basic English and official censorship. Similarly, it is no coincidence that "thoughtcrime" corresponds to the Nazi law forbidding homosexual thoughts, or that the description of the portraits of Big Brother could also be of Stalin. Actual political maneuvering and shifting military and economic alliances both before and during World War II can be compared to the state of affairs between "Oceania," "Australasia," and "Eastasia." Though the book is admittedly a satire, it represents a frightening possibility for a future world. The novel has become a classic of modern science fiction.

Biographical/Bibliographical Readings

Bernard Crick, *George Orwell, A Life* (Secker and Warburg, 1980). T. R. Fyvel, *George Orwell: A Personal Memoir* (Weidenfeld and Nicholson, 1982). Irving Howe, *Orwell's Nineteen Eighty-Four* (Harcourt Brace, 1963). Robert E. Lee, *Orwell's Fiction* (Notre Dame University Press, 1969). Christopher Small, *The Road to Miniluv* (University of Pittsburgh Press, 1975). William Steinhoff, *George Orwell and the Origins of 1984* (University of Michigan Press, 1975). Edward M. Thomas, *Orwell* (Oliver and Boyd, 1965).
[John Dunham]

PANGBORN, EDGAR

Life and Works

Edgar Pangborn was born in New York City in 1909 and educated at the Brooklyn Friends School, from which he graduated in 1924. He attended Harvard University for two years, the New England Conservatory of Music, and was a farmer from 1939-42 in Maine. After serving in the army from 1942-45 he settled in Voorheesville, New York, with his sister Mary, with whom he lived until his death. His first novel was a mystery, *A-100*, published by Dutton in 1930 under the name of Bruce Harrison. However, he considered that his literary career started with his first science fiction story, "Angel's Egg," first published in *Galaxy* in 1951 and collected in *Good Neighbors and Other Strangers* (1972). In 1954, he published his first novel, *West of the Sun*. *A Mirror for Observers* (1955), part of the Davy series, published in 1955, was the winner of the British International Fantasy Award. *Davy* (1966) was nominated for both the Hugo and Nebula awards and *The Company of Glory* (1975) was nominated in 1974 for the Jupiter. Both *Davy* and *A Mirror for Observers* made the final list on the 1972 Locus poll of best all-time novel. The other book in the postholocaust Davy series is *The Judgment of Eve* (1968). Pangborn died in 1976. The seven stories collected in *And Still I Persist in Wondering* were assembled and retyped by Pangborn himself as part of the Davy cycle and published posthumously in 1978. His last novel, *The Atlantean Nights Entertainment*, was also published after his death in 1980.

Themes and Style

Pangborn has been rightly called the master of empathy. He is an extremely sharp and sensitive observer of people, their motives, their loves and tragedies, their hopes and their failures. He is moving, funny, witty; his characters grow and develop before us and are unforgettable. One is unlikely to forget Davy in the novel of the same name--a robust, witty humorous philosopher, nor the three men in *The Judgement of Eve*. While many of his stories and novels take place in a postholocaust world, he is totally unconcerned with depicting the horrors of that world or the technology that has been lost. His interests lie with the valiant attempts of loving men and women to bring a new, more ethical world out of the ashes. He ponders on the ethical choices people make, and on a person's own moral worth and integrity. If humanity has failed in the past and destroyed parts of its world, Pangborn is optimistic that humans will succeed in the future. His works sing of the beauty and joy of the world and reflect in sorrow on its flaws. Pangborn is reported to have said that love is not an event or a condition but a country we are privileged to visit. To read Pangborn is to be privileged to share that sorrowful, joyous, and much-loved country.

Plot Summaries of Major Works

Davy. Some 300 years after Earth's old civilization has been destroyed by nuclear war and plagues, the population lives in small farming communities within several small nation states in the area which was New England. The people of this time are ruled by the Murcan Church which keeps them uneducated and ignorant, banning old books and old ideas. The story is told in retrospect by Davy, writing his autobiography aboard the schooner *Morning Star* which sails east searching for a new continent.

Beginning with his birth in a whorehouse and his upbringing in a state orphanage, Davy skillfully weaves the story of his life. At age nine, he is bonded out to the Bull and Iron Tavern where a few years later, as a lusty young redheaded adolescent, he has the first of many sexual adventures. He leaves the small village and on the road, he meets three other travelers (Sam, Jed, and Vilet), who join him on their way north. Some marvelous adventures take place along the road, among which is the theft of clothes by Davy from a fake medium, the death of Jed by a tiger, and the conversion of Vilet from a hotblooded camp follower to a nun. Davy continues on the road with Sam who, it appears, may have been his father.

Davy and Sam meet up with Rumley's Ramblers, a caravan of philosophizing, free living entertainers who accept Davy for his musical talent, and Sam for his skill in selling Mother Spinkton's Home Remedy. During the four years they wander with the Ramblers, Davy learns to read and write, which makes him only that much more certain of the ignorance perpetuated by the church. When Sam dies, Davy leaves the Ramblers and meets his future wife, Nickie, who readily persuades him to join the Society of Heretics. Meanwhile, the *Morning Star* has located an island. The heretics aboard ship have been involved in an attempted reform of the church which has resulted in a victory for the old guard and the departure of forty freemen on the schooner. After Nickie dies in childbirth on the island, Davy and a small company sail on to continue their quest.

Davy is one of Pangborn's most well-known stories. Davy is a memorable, warm, witty character and the novel is lifted by the marvelous dialog reminiscent of Huckleberry Finn along with Twain's type o homespun wisdom and philosophizing. His dialog has the unmistakable twang of the cracker barrel philosopher along with the ability to tell a tall tale to make his point and a proper skepticism about the world. With the homespun dialogue of rural America, Pangborn combines the bawdy adventures and lusty language of the seventeenth century, reminding one of Fielding's *Tom Jones*. He also has a great talent for pulling from institutions of the past and extrapolating them into the future, such as the Murcan church. Some of the symbols repeated in others of his works are seen here: the tiger who executes judgment, the new settlement Neanarchos, a new place which rejects the old law, similar to Delphi or Adelphi in his other stories. While the story may be taken as simply a picaresque novel of a young boy growing up in a hard world, on another level it is the story of an individual's search for freedom and ethics in a world gone awry. Pangborn, through Davy, rejects the dogma of his age and demands that the individual seek a rational, free existence where he can learn and grow. This is not a story of a grim postcatastrophe world, but a world where people of courage and kindness still search for good and have hope of overcoming evil.

The Judgment of Eve. This short novel is a retelling of the legend of Eve by an unknown scholar trying to reconstruct the legend, which has grown up many years later about her. The beautious Eve Newman and her blind Mother Alma live with only the mutated and ugly Caliban, isolated from the world somewhere in New England after a one-day war has devastated much of the world. To their isolated dwelling come three men, Kenneth Bellamy, Ethan Nye, and Claudius Gardiner. Ken, charming, urbane, and nearsighted, with a love of learning; Ethan, young, massive, redheaded, a wilderness hunter with a feeling for the land but no words with which to express himself; Claudius, middle aged, once a renowned violinist, whose left arm was destroyed during the one-day war. Eve sends the three suitors off to return when the leaves turn and tell her the meaning of love, at which time she will make her choice.

Ken and Claudius set out to the ruins of Redfield where Ken finds some eyeglasses, and meets mad Grace Silver who lives in an unreal world foraging in the dead town, bringing back jewels and eating from old tins of food. Ken allows her to believe that he is her dead lover, steals her diamond necklace, and leaves, only to encounter a tiger. He trails the tiger back to Redfield to warn Grace only to find that she has killed herself. After he buries her, he sets up camp in the public library and settles down to explore through the shelves and shelves of books. Claudius wanders off to East Redfield where he meets Dr. Stuyvesant who persists in playing the violin badly. Stuyvesant contends that Claudius could never have been a violinist and that he should go into psychoanalysis. Claudius, too, sights the tiger and begins to track it. Ethan journeys North to the White Mountains where he fancies he will meet Gods. He is caught by the residents of Hampshire Grants, a fight ensues, and the governor dies of a heart attack leaving Ethan free to climb to the summit of the mountain where he too sees the tiger. The three eventually return to the house of

Eve, each having found something within themselves that makes them understand love. And Eve's choice? Pangborn's solution is just right--why spoil it by telling?

The Judgment of Eve is part of the Davy series, which takes place in various years from the time of the nuclear holocaust to some 300 years thereafter. The novel, while set in a ruined world, nevertheless does not deal with the horrors and degradation of the time but with the beauty and strength of individual human beings who, in spite of adversity, behave in an ethical manner. The legend is a bit of Grimm, where the princess sends her suitors off on a quest, and much of Frank Stockton's "The Lady and the Tiger," including the tiger. In this short novel, each of the men confronts the part of himself which rejects love and overcomes it. The tiger, which appears symbolically in other Pangborn stories, also stalks each of them through this novel. Grace and Dr. Stuyvesant are symbols of those who either stagnate or die because they cannot come to terms with the realities of the present or the future. Ken, who with spectacles can suddenly see all the beauty that has always been around him, is symbolic of humanity, which will awaken to the beauty within itself. Eve is the story of a beginning. She is the mythic Mother of a new world encompassing all in her love.

A Mirror for Observers. The Martians have come to Earth over 30,000 years ago and have hidden themselves in underground cities while taking the role of observers. They await humanity's ethical evolution, which will make it possible for Martian and human to form a union. But among the Martians are those like Namir, who believe that union will never come and whose aim is to destroy all humanity. Namir has found Angelo, a twelve-year-old boy of enormous moral potential, whom he intends to subvert. While the Martian law forbids harming Angelo unless he does positive harm, the Martian High command sends an observer, Drozma, to observe and assist in Angelo's development. We are told the story of Angelo by Drozma (alias Benedict Miles) in reports to the director of the North American Martian Missions. Miles takes a room in the boarding house which Angelo's mother has run since the death of Angelo's father.

Angelo is a small, lame, adolescent. He is interested in the study of philosophy, particularly ethics, and is an unusually gifted painter. Miles returns from a walk and finds that Namir has broken into his room, stolen his Martian scent destroyer, and killed Angelo's dog, Bella. Billy Kell (who later turns out to be Namir's son) lures Angelo into an initiation ritual with a youthful gang called Mudhawks and Angelo is deceived into knifing another boy whom he believes has killed Bella. The Mudhawks and the Diggers meet in a gang war and in the ensuing battle, Angelo is caught. His mother dies of a heart attack and Angelo disappears.

Nine years later Drozma has a new face in New York and is still searching for Angelo. Billy Kell and Namir have convinced Angelo (alias Abraham Brown) to follow the infamous Joseph Max, head of the Organic United Party which preaches nationalist and dictatorial policies. The party has also seduced into its fold Jason Hodding, expert on virus mutations. When one of the Organic Unity Party workers leaps off the party penthouse taking with him a vial of Hodding's new airborne virus, Angelo renounces his party ties. In the pandemic that follows the spread of the mutated virus, the Organic United Party is destroyed and Namir killed, but Angelo survives.

A Mirror for Observers takes its name from the ancient mirror that Drozma shows to Angelo which allows one to see one's future. Some of the same images that appear in Pangborn's other novels are seen here. The image of the tiger appears here both as a fleeting shadow of evil on the landscape and in one of Angelo's paintings as a wounded creature succored by the giant hand of God. The idea of a new state to be called Delphi (the place where truth may be found) is also repeated here. The characterizations are some of Pangborn's best, both the sympathetic portrayal of the Martians waiting for the world to grow up and ever so slightly assisting in its moral development, and the conflict of Angelo in expressing the moral principles which so much of the world has discarded. The story represents the age-old confrontation of Satan and God for the soul of the good person. Drozma, representing the side of God, as does Angelo or Abraham, is aptly named either angel or the father of Judaic/Christian ethics. Namir represents Satan, who will assist in the fall of the Angel because humans are inherently cruel and evil. This novel is probably Pangborn's clearest enunciation of belief in the potential good inherent in the human race. Even the name of the Martians, Salvayans in their language, is an allusion to the salvation of the human race. In Pangborn's final vision goodness will prevail; the world has suffered a great blow but it will heal itself.

West of the Sun. After eleven years on the spaceship *Argo*, in the year 2056, five explorers sight what appears to be a habitable planet. They land safely on Lucifer, but *Argo* is lost. The party consists of Dorothy Leeds, pregnant with her first child; Paul Mason, who loves Dorothy; Dr. Christopher Wright, anthrolopologist; Ed Spearman, ship's pilot; Sears Oliphant, biologist; and Ann Bryan. To the dismay of Spearman, Wright is declared leader of the party. The explorers' first contact with any being is an eight foot tall, furry gray and white creature. The gentle giant Mijok, as he is called, is taught human speech and becomes their friend. They then encounter a tribe of pygmies led by Queen Abro Pakriaa, who believe that the explorers are gods. On a visit to Pakriaa's village, they find that the only important males are medicine men who are in charge of the ceremonies related to their female idol, Ismar, to whom human sacrifices are made. In the midst of an important village ceremony, Spearman falls asleep and begins to snore. His actions are taken as an insult to the gods and he is dragged away to be sacrificed to Ismar. The party makes a hasty escape with the help of the giant Mijok.

The explorers have discovered an island ten miles offshore, free from the dangers of carnivorous flying and burrowing animals, where they have established a settlement called Adelphi. On the mainland, the thirty-mile-long settlement of pygmies is ruled by Lantis, self-named Queen of the World, who is about to attack Pakriaa's villages. The explorers are prepared to aid Pakriaa's soldiers against Lantis. Paul and Spearman vie for leadership and in a close vote, Paul is elected. Paul, Mijok, and Pakriaa lead the advance to the south. Spearman is to follow in the lifeboat and if necessary fly them to Adelphi for safety, but he deserts and joins the Lantis forces. The expected bloodbath comes, Sears is killed, and some thirty survivors including pygmies, giants and, explorers retreat to Adelphi.

The survivors on Delphi have lived in harmony with one another. They find Ann, wandering out of her wits, having fled from Spearman, who, during the pygmy battle, had lured her to Vestoiaa, the capital of Lantis. Using pygmy slaves, Spearman has mined the iron under the deadly Kaksma Hills, conquered Vestoiaa, and made himself god. Ann, who originally loved Spearman, has borne him twins but has begun to hate him for the degradation of all their moral principles. A party of giants, pygmies, and explorers leaves for Vestoiaa to rescue Ann's children. As Paul tries to reason with a crazed Spearman, a spaceship appears in the sky. This is the last interstellar ship to be funded by the Federation until proof is brought back that interstellar travel is feasible. Spearman steals the spaceship; unable to understand its new technology, he plunges into the sea, and the story ends.

The earliest of Pangborn's science fiction novels, *West of the Sun* explores the possibility of various races living in harmony. But this space saga is flawed and the characters are often stilted and unreal. Nevertheless, it is interesting because it presages many of the ideas that Pangborn was to develop later. Here, as in *A Mirror for Observers*, we have the idea of a new state of good people to be called Adelphi, the place where truth might eventually be known. Here the benevolent philosophy of the main body of explorers is set against the degradation of Spearman who succumbs to evil and corruption. The ideas of love, acceptance, courage, and generosity laying the foundation of a new society is a pervasive theme which continues in Pangborn's more mature works.

Biographical/Bibliographical Readings

Peter Beagle, "Edgar Pangborn: An Appreciation," *Locus* (9:4) 1976, p.186. Patricia Bizzell, "Edgar Pangborn," in *Twentieth-Century American Science-Fiction Writers*, (Gale, 1981), v.2, p.65-67. John Clute, "Edgar Pangborn," in *The Science Fiction Encyclopedia* (Doubleday, 1979) p.446. **[Judith R. Bernstein]**

PANSHIN, ALEXEI

Life and Works

Alexei Panshin was born on August 14, 1940, the son of a Russian immigrant father, in Lansing, Michigan. He attended the University of Michigan for two years (1958-60), where he began writing seriously. After spending the next two years in the U.S. Army, serving in Texas and Korea, he returned to college at Michigan State University in East Lansing. He received a B.A. in 1965 and promptly entered graduate school at the University of Chicago, leaving with an M.A. in 1966.

In the meantime, Panshin had begun publishing professionally. His first sale, in 1963, was the story "Down to the Worlds of Men," to *If* magazine. By 1966, he had published a few other short stories in *Amazing* and *Analog*, such as "The Sons of Prometheus."

While working for the Brooklyn Public Library in 1966-67, Panshin created the work that would first earn him the serious attention of the science fiction community. His critical writing earned him a 1967 Hugo award for Best Fan Writer. His first novel, *Rite of Passage*, appeared in 1968, winning a Nebula award. The year 1968 was an energetic one for Panshin--indeed, it has proven the most productive of his career. Now a full-time author, Panshin also published a well-received study, *Heinlein in Dimension: A Critical Analysis* (1968), in which he views the inconsistent ideology presented in Heinlein's fiction and public pronouncements as subjective products of Heinlein's psychological development. Two more novels appeared in 1968--*Star Well* and *The Thurb Revolution*, both featuring the character Anthony Villiers and his furry, six-foot, froglike companion, Torve the Trog.

In 1969, Alexei Panshin married Cory Seidman and they began writing as a team. Despite this doubling of efforts, Panshin's productivity fell off in the 1970s. His next book was a collection, *Farewell to Yesterday's Tomorrow*, which appeared as a 1975 hardbound followed by an augmented 1976 paperback. It consists largely of short stories from the mid-1960s on, including "The Sons of Prometheus" and "When the Vertical becomes the Horizontal," first published in *Universe 4*. The latter concerns Woody Asenion, a man terrified of getting wet, who suddenly grows from self-confinement into joyful liberation when caught in a rainstorm.

With Cory, Panshin moved increasingly in the direction of literary and social criticism, and in 1976 they published together *SF in Dimension: A Book of Explorations*, much of it consisting of earlier reviews and essays. In 1978, they published a book of essays in Italian, *Mondi Interiori*, and their first novel together, *Earth Magic*. The Panshins have published only one more book, a collection of fiction and nonfiction entitled *Transmutations: A Book of Personal Alchemy*, available only in a 1982 small press edition.

Themes and Style

"The Sons of Prometheus" introduces a fictional set-up Panshin would use with great success: an overcrowded, war-ravaged Earth has sent a seed population into space to perpetuate the best of terrestrial civilization. The spaceships have managed to colonize dozens of planets, but, subsequently, human populations have divided fairly strictly into Ship-dwellers and planet-dweller Colonials. The former control technology, often much to the resentment of the rugged if more primitive pioneers on the various worlds. In this tale, one Philip Tansman, a Ship-dweller, is drafted into the Sons of Prometheus group, which secretly oversees the technological advancement of the Colonials. Tansman shares a common prejudice against the Colonials, but risks much to help fight a planetary plague in a sudden conversion to commitment. Ironically, the very Colonial he helps threatens to betray him to the suspicious pioneers, and Tansman must take the Colonial's life. The act only enhances his commitment, however. This story provides the best early example of Panshin's favorite themes: the maturation of the individual and the development of social progress within an orderly social context. The world of Ships and Colonials and the themes of maturation and social commitment are further developed in *Rite of Passage*. This "rite of passage," which all Ship inhabitants must endure, consists of being set down on one of the pioneer worlds, there to struggle for a month with local conditions and local inhabitants. Those who survive the ordeal, and many do not, return to the Ships to take up their lives as adults.

The Villiers novels (*Star Well* and *The Thurb Revolution*) suggest in manner the mock romances of eighteenth century novelists like Laurence Sterne and Tobias Smollett. Villiers himself is a young, aristocratic adventurer who, though cool and cynical about life and society, takes an active part in righting wrongs. In *Star Well*, for instance, Villiers defeats a gang of body smugglers, or "thumbrunners," while at the same time convincing the daughter of a criminal figure to continue her unexciting education, as her father wishes, so she can rise to better things. In *The Thurb Revolution*, Villiers performs a similar function in persuading a young man to accept his familial and social responsibilities, even as Villiers and Torve promote a small cultural revolution against a Puritanical bureaucracy. A darker hint that Villiers is the intended target of assassination carries from this novel to the next in the series, the 1969 *Masque World*. Here Villiers must avoid his assassin while circumventing his powerful and self-centered uncle, Lord Semichastny. Many readers have found *Masque World* less interesting--in characterization, plotting, and tone--than the earlier works in the series. It proved to be the last Villiers novel.

"How Can We Sink When We Can Fly?" and "Farewell to Yesterday's Tomorrow," are both essaylike critiques of society's inflexibility in the face of the need for change and the short-sightedness of the answers given by contemporary progressive thought. Panshin himself maintains that the future will be better, though he is less clear, given the above-noted problems, how human advancement will be achieved.

Plot Summaries of Major Works

Rite of Passage. The human species has abandoned its overcrowded, war- and pollution-ravaged Earth and taken to the stars. There, what is left of humanity has split into two general groups: the inhabatants of the Ships, who preserve human history and technology, and the Colonists, who are populating various worlds in primitive conditions reminiscent of the American frontier. A good deal of ill feeling, prejudice, and outright hostility exists between the two groups. Given the limited environments of the Ships, the elites who inhabit them have devised a harsh method for keeping their populations small and elite, via the Trial. This is a rite of passage that each individual must undergo at the age of fourteen, in which he or she is dropped on a pioneer planet for thirty days of struggling for survival against the depravations of climate, native life, and hostile Colonists. Those who live through the Trial return to the Ship to life as full adults. Mia Havero, a twelve-year-old girl of narrow mind but great potential, is the narrator. She guides us through the years immediately preceding her rite of passage, through her relationships with peers and authority figures, through her training for the Trial, and through the ordeal itself. She emerges as a young adult who has gained a wisdom and compassion lacking even in her society.

Given Panshin's critical interest in the work of Robert Heinlein, it is not surprising that Panshin's realm of ships and Colonists extrapolates to some extent from Heinlein's works. The hierarchy among the elites of the Ships and the rough Colonials corresponds to Heinlein's division of humanity into mathematicians, peasants, and animals. Heinlein's social Darwinism is also evident in the practice of the Trial and in the violently competitive environment of the frontier planets. Panshin departs from Heinlein's more libertarian technology in favor of a liberal acceptance of the intellectual elite's obligation to serve and assist those elsewhere in the hierarchy. Part of Panshin's thematic emphasis of maturation is his belief in the individual's responsibility for others. *Rite of Passage* remains his best statement of this position.

The Thurb Revolution. Anthony Villiers, Lord Charteris, a young aristocrat, cooly cynical but not at all unkind, lives in a far future. He travels from planet to planet in a somewhat decadent search for amusement, accompanied by Torve the Trog, an inscrutable but harmless alien who resembles a furry, six-foot frog. In the process Villiers blithely intervenes in the lives that touch his, assisting in his courtly way to see that the deserving get their just desserts, for better or worse. As Villers and Torve prepare to leave the planet Shiawassee, they fall into the company of a discontented student and some "yagoots," a local variety of hippielike free spirits. After amusing himself with this group, Villiers is on his way to the rural planet Duden, to escape someone following him in a galactic version of tag. Villiers and Torve soon reach Duden, followed by Fred the student and Ralph the yagoot, who are enchanted with the young viscount and the Trog. The young men are pursued in turn by Admiral Beagle, Ralph's puritanical, authoritarian, and ludicrously bombastic uncle, and by David, a quiet youth who is actually Gillian U., an heiress in love with the well-born Fred. Bringing up the end of the trail is Kuukkinen, who has been crossing the galaxy in his tag game with Villiers. There are many madcap efforts as the groups try to find or avoid each other, while a growing community of students and yagoots gravitates to Villers and Torve. Ultimately Villiers defuses the sundry situations in classical comic form--with the help of Torve and a pink cloud that crankily insists it is God--dealing out comic humiliation to the obnoxious Beagle and the rewards of order restored to the rest. The cloud is also the catalyst to the future marriage of Fred and Gillian, which will assure Fred's mature acceptance of his leadership role in planetary society.

Panshin's serious themes of passage to adulthood and social commitment show their comic faces in *The Thurb Revolution*. The plot is frivolously complicated and subordinate to the confrontations between the characters. The style of the prose is mannered and droll, with much authorial commentary, on the whole reminiscent of the parodic tone of the mock romances of an earlier century. A light book, it is a whimsical companion to his more earnest *Rite of Passage*.

Biographical/Bibliographical Readings

John Clute, "Alexei Panshin," in *The Science Fiction Encyclopedia* (Doubleday, 1979), p.447. Alexei and Cory Panshin, "Science Fiction, New Trends and Old," in *Science Fiction, Today and Tomorrow*, ed. Reginald Bretnor (Harper & Row, 1974), p. 217-34. Amelia A. Rutledge, "Alexei Panshin," in *Twentieth-Century American Science-Fiction Writers* (Gale, 1981), v.2, p.67-70. Darrell Schweitzer, "Interview with Alexei and Cory Panshin," *Thrust* 13 (Fall 1979), p.33-35. **[Stephen W. Potts]**

PIPER, H. BEAM

Life and Works

Henry Beam Piper was born in Altoona, Pennsylvania, in 1904. Very little is known about his early years, although he lived almost his entire life in the Williamsport, Pennsylvania, area. While writing science fiction, he was employed on the engineering staff for the Pennsylvania Railroad. On the 11th of November, 1964, he committed suicide. This was attributed to the break-up of his marriage, indebtedness, and a feeling that his career as a writer was over. His death was a tragic loss, as his last works show a depth in style altogether missing from his earlier works.

Shortly after World War II, during the Golden Age of science fiction, Piper began his career as a writer. His first sale, "Time and Time Again," was to *Astounding* (April, 1947). During the next twenty years, he published more than twenty short stories, most of which were published in *Astounding*. The majority of his stories were part of his two series: the Terra-Human Future History and Paratime. Ace collected and republished most of the stories in four volumes--*Federation* (1981), *Empire* (1981), *Paratime* (1981), and *The Worlds of H. Beam Piper* (1983).

A few of Piper's stories were later expanded into novels, and a number of his novels were serialized in the magazines. A notable exception was *Uller Uprising* (1952), which was first published in a hardbound edition and serialized the following year. In 1953, *Murder in the Gunroom* was published. This was Piper's only nonscience fiction novel. With the exception of *Lord Kalvan of Otherwhen* (1965), a Paratime novel, and *Murder in the Gunroom*, his other novels all belong to his various series.

Piper's "Fuzzies" are one of the most popular extraterrestrial characters ever created. After the initial publication of *Little Fuzzy* in 1962, their popularity was cause for two sequels to be written. *The Other Human Race* (also published as *Fuzzy Sapiens*) was published in 1964. The second sequel was presumed lost for twenty years before being published in 1984 with the title *Fuzzies and Other People.* Fuzzies are rabbitlike animals with golden fur, a round head, big ears, and a humanoid face with a little snub nose.

Themes and Style

Piper's major creation is his Future History series involving more than 5000 years of Terran future. Piper once thought to create one work for each century; he only completed nine novels and ten stories. They present a complex tapestry of things to come. Piper devises many new and exotic worlds. Although technology is important, the plots have some basis in human history. All of the stories take place on distant planets. The only exception is "The Edge of the Knife," which is, chronologically, the first story in the series and introduces a history professor at a small college in the Midwest who has visions of future events.

The Paratime series has for its settings some parallel time-line to Earth in which a civilization is based on Mars. The Martians are descendants of terran colonists who have had to survive after a nuclear war destroys Earth. The survivors discover the "Ghaldron-Hesthor Transposition Field" which facilitates travel between parallel time lines (hence the name para-time, or para-time). This leaves a lot of room for playing "what if" history, in which Piper shows himself to be an expert, recombining historical events and coming up with new and fascinating variations of what might have happened if. . . .

Whether a story is part of the Paratime or Future History series, Piper's plots rely on the self-sufficient human. This type of person, nearly always male, uses inner strength to pull through situations that weaker persons cannot survive. The self-sufficient individual does not back down although an unpleasant decision must be made. Piper includes a character that fits this description in nearly every story. Character development, however, is not a factor in the novel *First Cycle* (1982), since it recounts the entire cycle of planetary life.

Plot Summaries of Major Works

The Cosmic Computer. The Systems States War ended not too long ago. It is now early into the ninth century A.E. (Atomic Era) and the planet Poictesme, the former headquarters of the Third Terran Force (TTF), is barely surviving. The Federation has spent trillions readying for war on Poictesme, and then without warning, the rebellion ends and peace comes to Poictesme. Many of those who remain find a living by scavenging the leavings of the TTF. When Conn Maxwell returns to Poictesme after a six-year absence on Earth, he finds almost universal desperation. The known locations of Federation bases are almost empty and their one export commodity is controlled by crooks. Conn has a plan to revitalize the planet. It involves partially exploiting the almost religious belief in a supercomputer, Merlin, supposedly used by the Federation to win the war. Merlin cannot be located, although it was rumored to be somewhere on the planet. During his research to locate Merlin, Conn also finds in the official records of the planetary system the locations for many undiscovered treasure troves. He plans on using this information for building Poictesme's own interplanetary and interstellar spaceships so that the planet can become successful again. He is almost defeated by the too fervent belief in Merlin and the ruthless people who turn this belief against him, until Merlin is finally found--then disaster strikes, or it could be hope, depending on one's point of view.

The original title, *Junkyard Planet*, in some ways more accurately describes the novel. Until Merlin is found, the story is more one of economic revitalization and sociopolitical unrest than one of mystical technology. Individual and collective justice and self-reliance are central themes. A short story version, "Graveyard of Dreams," is substantially different in plot details, but expresses the same ideas. This is the last mention of the Terran Federations in Piper's Future History series.

First Cycle. Although humans and the Terran Federation have a small role in the introductory and final chapters, the entire story centers around a nonhuman planetary system: a yellow star (Elektra), a red dwarf star (Rubra), and eight planets. Two of the planets are born out of the destruction of a methane giant when the two stars join together; one is arid and called Hetaira, the other is watery and is called Thalassa. Each of the planets develop life culminating in intelligent forms. In alternating vignettes, the development of life, then the creation of race, society, religion, culture, and technology are traced until a time when the two can finally meet. Their meeting results in conflicts which are ultimately resolved.

Unfinished at the time of his death, this is possibly Piper's least well known and most important novel. In this novel Piper/Kurland reveal a deep understanding of human developments and history. Granted that nonhuman life may not react anything at all like what is described here, the reactions between these two civilizations, in human terms, are precisely described by historical accounts. Piper/Kurland's main question in the novel is: Why? Why must different cultures react with violence when confronting each other? Unfortunately, he does not answer this question.

The Fuzzies books

Little Fuzzy. In the seventh century A.E. (Atomic Era), the Chartered Zarathustra Company exploits their property, a class III uninhabited planet it calls Zarathustra. Jack Holloway, a sunstone miner on Zarathustra, meets the first "Fuzzy" to which he pins the moniker, "Little Fuzzy." With their discovery, the company tries many ways both fair and foul to have the Fuzzies declared legally nonsapient. Through Jack Holloway's persistence and much help from friends, the Fuzzies are declared sapient, and Zarathustra becomes a class II inhabited planet, and the company loses it charter.

The main question posed by Piper is the definition of sapience. Without a definition the Fuzzies cannot retain the claims for their planet. Many theories are postulated, incorporating much of the psychology known by Piper. Corporate cruelty and greed versus Federation fairness and individual good are also themes of this novel.

The Other Human Race. The now charterless Zarathustra Company is coming to realize just what effect losing their charter means. Fuzzies are intelligent life forms, extraordinarily trusting and sensitive, which need human protection. Victor Griego, president of ZC, has a change of heart concerning the Fuzzies after being adopted by one, but other, more ruthless humans still seek to exploit them. A plot is uncovered to sell Fuzzies into slavery or trick them into breaking the law. With the company's help, the criminal are brought to justice.

Exploitation is the central theme in this second novel: what types of exploitation are acceptable, what types are not, and to whom. There is also the ethical dilemma of whether to help the Fuzzies when it is discovered that their evolution took a wrong turn and their population is dwindling. The solutions presented here are definitely in the direction of progress as Piper saw it.

Fuzzies and Other People. In this final novel, the Fuzzies finally have an adventure of their own without major human intervention. Now that the company and the planetary government are on good terms and the sunstone mines on the Fuzzy reservation are operating well for all parties, Little Fuzzy is allowed to go visiting. On his visit to the mine, he is accidentally separated from his friends and swept down an underground river. His errant navigation leads him to discover a small band of Fuzzies not yet cognizant of humans. Through a series of trials (a forest fire for one), the band unites to save itself and is finally found by the worried humans. Parallel to Little Fuzzy's adventures, the humans are again engaged in a legal battle over the Fuzzies' future.

The ability to lie as a determinant of maturity is posed in this story, as is the question of education versus ignorance. Primitives (as the Fuzzies are considered to be) must be educated to a state of self-reliance or they will not be able to survive without intervention. This final novel was published twenty years after Piper's death.

Uller Uprising. In the fourth century A.E. (Atomic Era), the Chartered Uller Company is allowed by the Terran Federation to exploit the planet Uller if it also exploits the planet Niflheim. Uller is a silicon-based planet and Niflheim is a flourine-based gaseous ball without a solid surface. Human life on Uller needs help. On Niflheim all life forms not indigenous must be completely protected to survive, even sunlight is deadly. The Ulleran population's social structure is similar to the feudal societies of Earth's sixteenth or seventeenth centuries, and is in varying states of war between rulers. Since the company, as it is commonly referred to, and Terrans have come, some Ullerans have found it politically expedient to make their ouster a common cause. Utilizing a religious movement and political intrigue, one kingdom attempts to oust the Terran population. Although the natives are numerically superior, the Terrans, with the help of rival kings and another race of Ullerans, manage to quell the revolt. The Terrans are commanded by Carlos von Schlichten (a Nazi descendant). Due to his military status, he receives little argument and proceeds to end the uprising. The Ulleran population must be made to understand that company exploitation will be beneficial to their society.

In addition to the given physical characteristics of the Ullers, Piper's plot is primarily derived from the Sepoy mutiny which took place in British-colonized India. The characters are somewhat thinly developed, possibly because so much of the tale is closely detailed military action. Piper places great store in individual self-reliance; the man or woman who will make things happen without conferences or committees. The moral conflict arises between the so-called benevolent exploitation of the Ullerans and their rights to exist and live their lives without intervention. In the eyes of the commander of the Terran military, an individual death is of little consequence, when the greater good--future membership in the Terran Federation--is recognized.

Biographical/Bibliographical Readings

Gordon Benson, Jr., *H. Beam Piper* (Galactic Central, 1985). John Clute, "H. Beam Piper," in *The Science Fiction Encyclopedia* (Doubleday, 1979), p.462. John L. Espley, "H. Beam Piper: An Annotated Bibliography," *Extrapolation* 21:2 (Summer, 1980), p.172-81. William B. Thesing, "H. Beam Piper," in *Twentieth-Century American Science-Fiction Writers* (Gale, 1981), v.2, p.70-73. **[Richard Page]**

PISERCHIA, DORIS

Life and Works

Doris Elaine Piserchia was born on October 11, 1928, in Fairmont, West Virginia. She attended Fairmont State College before joining the U.S. Navy in 1950. She married Joseph John Piserchia in 1953 and left the Navy in 1954, after the birth of her first child. She is the mother of two sons and three daughters. From 1963 to 1965, she undertook graduate studies in educational psychology at the University of Utah. Her first professional science fiction sale was the short story "Rocket to Gehenna" which appeared in *Fantastic Stories* in 1966. The bulk of her short story output appeared in the early to mid-1970s. To date Piserchia has published thirteen novels using both her own name and the pseudonym Curt Selby. Her novels include *Mr. Justice* (1973), *A Billion Days of Earth* (1976), *Earth Child* (1979), *The Fluger* (1980), *The Spinner* (1980), *Earth in Twilight* (1981), *Doomtime* (1981), and *Blood Country* (1981).

Themes and Style

Female characters are featured throughout much of her writing, and their adventures are often set in colorful and well-defined environments. Piserchia has displayed an interest in the paranormal and the pseudosciences throughout her short fiction and novels. Telepathy, teleportation, intelligent animals, mutating plants, zombies, and vampires all make appearances in her work. She has been noted for her skill in blending elements of other genres (i.e., horror and fantasy elements) within a science fiction framework. She has also been criticized for developing plot and setting at the expense of characterization. Indeed, her human characters are often secondary and/or subservient to their surroundings to the extent that external forces become the central concern of her tales. This is most apparent in *Earth Child* and *Doomtime*, where vegetation is battling for control of Earth. *The Fluger* and *The Spinner* both feature alien monsters. Her work often reflects major sociological and psychological concerns. Despite her talents and ever-expanding development as an insightful social critic of social systems and loss of ethics in a technological society, Piserchia has not received much notice from literary critics.

Plot Summaries of Major Works

"Rocket to Gehenna." The story concerns an official who utilizes a disposal system to eliminate corpses on a supposedly vacant, uninhabited planet. To the official's surprise, the planet is indeed inhabited by a weird, comical lifeform with particular approaches to certain topics. This short story reveals a humorous side of Piserchia rarely observed in her other works. Often reprinted in anthologies, this unusual story reveals Piserchia's life-long concern with the theme of social systems out of control. It is well written with a keen sense of existential irony.

The Spinner. Long buried in its bubble until unearthed, the alien creature is very cunning, highly intelligent, and is named Mordak. The alien who came to Earth at some point in the past is in the form of a large blue spider with a nasty disposition. The spider comes into direct and violent conflict with a city and its human inhabitants. The confrontation is destructive, and the alien creature spins a web of death for all humans that it encounters. Grayish-blue in appearance, this creature with long, stringy hair on its head has a lean, humanlike form and large blue eyes. The underlying social problems on Earth are as equal a destructive and terrifying threat to human survival as is the presence of Mordak, who serves both the role of outcast and outsider.

The Spinner is one of Piserchia's most enduring and popular novels in which the elements of horror, mystery, and fantasy are blended with science fiction to create a grim statement on a technological society. The novel displays the author's skills at imagery, irony, concern for social problems, and concern for ethics within a technological world. Within a host of characters and a complex plot, Piserchia reveals the terrifying conflict of alien creature versus human environment; Mordak's threat is compounded by the social problems eating away at the structure of human society.

Biographical/Bibliographical Readings

John Clute, "Doris Piserchia," in *The Encyclopedia of Science Fiction* (Doubleday, 1979), p.462. "Doris Piserchia," in *A Reader's Guide to Science Fiction* (Facts on File, 1979), p.117. J. A. Salmonson, "Hero as Hedonist: The Early Novels of Doris Piserchia," in *Critical Encounters II*, ed. Tom Staicar (Ungar, 1982), p.15-22. [John Dunham]

POHL, FREDERIK

Life and Works

Born in Brooklyn, New York, on November 26, 1919, Frederik Pohl was a high school dropout who entered the world of science fiction as a fan. He admits to having devoured science fiction as a youth and was a founding father of the Futurians in 1937. Some of his more successful collaborations in writing were with the people he met through the Futurians. Pohl's professional science fiction career began at age nineteen as an editor of two magazines, *Astonishing Stories* and *Super Science Stories*. He married Doris Baumgardt in 1940; they were divorced in 1942 just before Pohl went overseas with the armed services in the war. In 1945, while overseas, he married Dorothy LesTina. After the war, he worked as a literary agent, claiming to represent about seventy percent of the top science fiction authors of the 1950s. He and Dorothy were divorced in 1947 and he married author Judith Merril in 1948. They had a daughter, Anne, born in 1950, about a year before her parents divorced. In 1952, Pohl married Carol Metcalf Ulf with whom he had three children, one of whom died in infancy.

Pohl was writing regularly during the 1950s and also edited several anthologies. He worked for several years in the field of advertising, an experience which contributed to several of his works, such as *The Space Merchants* (1953) and its sequel, *Merchants' War* (1984), and the short stories later collected in *Midas World* (1983). The best known of his works is *The Space Merchants*, which Pohl wrote in collaboration with C. M. Kornbluth. Also in collaboration with Kornbluth were *Search the Sky* (1954), *Gladiator-at-Large* (1955), and *Wolfbane* (1959). His collaboration with Jack Williamson produced several juvenile adventure works, and the Starchild trilogy (1977), consisting of *The Reefs of Space* (1964), *Starchild* (1965), and *Rogue Star* (1969). Many of his shorter works have been collected in *The Frederik Pohl Omnibus* (1966), *The Best of Frederik Pohl* (1975), and *The Early Pohl* (1976). He has used many pseudonyms, among which are James Mac-Creigh, Warren F. Howard, Paul Flehr, Ernst Mason, Charles Satterfield, and Edson McCann.

From 1960 through 1969, Pohl edited two more magazines, *Galaxy* and *If*, an assignment he termed the hardest and best job he ever had in his life. For this effort, he was awarded the Hugo award for Best Professional Magazine for *If* in 1966, 1967, and 1968. When the magazines were sold, Pohl turned to full-time writing. Since that time, he has been nominated for at least fifteen awards and received a Hugo for best short story in 1973 for "The Meeting" (with C. M. Kornbluth), a Nebula for *Man Plus* in 1976, and the Nebula, Hugo, and John W. Campbell awards in 1978 for *Gateway*. The Gateway novels, called the Heechee saga, consist of three novels--*Gateway* (1977), *Beyond the Blue Event Horizon* (1908), and *Heechee Rendezvous* (1984). Pohl served as president of the Science Fiction Writers of America from 1974 to 1976.

Frederik Pohl has been nearly everything that one can be in the field of science fiction and most of those jobs he has done very well. His development as a writer is clear and his stature in the field is undeniable.

Themes and Style

Although Pohl uses traditional science fiction devices, such as parallel worlds in *The Coming of the Quantum Cats* (1986), space explorations in *Starburst* (1982), *Black Star Rising* (1985), and *Jem* (1978), and the technological advances in *The Year of the City*

(1984), it is probably for his sense of poetic irony and for character development that Frederik Pohl is best known. Very few of
Pohl's works are completely serious; *Man Plus* probably comes the
closest to straight, nonhumorous situations. It is also in *Man Plus*
that Pohl's skill with developing complex characters can be seen.
The increasing humanity of Roger Torraway as he becomes a cyborg, part man and part machine, is a beautiful piece of craftsmanship. Robin Broadhead, the hero of *Gateway* and the rest of
the Heechee saga, is a skillful blending of the two elements, humor and characterization. Robin is a very complex character,
ranging from definitely chicken-hearted in his aversion to space
exploration to guilt-ridden at his ill-gotten gains. But the
predicaments Robin finds himself in range from amusing to hilarious.

Plot Summaries of Major Works

The Heechee saga

Gateway. Alternating between discussions between Robin
Broadhead and his computer shrink via flashbacks to the events in
his past, the tale of the discovery of Heechee civilization and
space travel, made possible by the exploration of abandoned
Heechee ships, unfolds. Robin has escaped from a food mine by
winning a lottery and has used his prize money to travel to
Gateway to become a prospector. Traveling on Heechee ships programmed to travel to Gateway and return, with no possibility of
control by the human pilot, brings vast riches to some and death
to others. Robin discovers that he is afraid to go out into space
and makes friends with a woman, Klara, who feels the same way.
Finally, they go out on a Five, a ship designed for a five person
crew, but come back empty-handed. After a fight with Klara,
Robin takes out a One and cancels the program, when he discovers
that it is merely going to Gateway 2 not to a planet. No one has
ever lived after cancelling a program, so Robin receives praise instead of blame for tampering with the controls. After studying
the tapes of the trip, Gateway Corporation decides to send two
ships to the same destination. Robin and Klara volunteer to go.
What they discover is a huge black hole. After being sucked in,
the crew uses the thrust of both ships to throw one free, but the
one that gets out is the one with just Robin aboard. He is credited with a valuable scientific discovery, but is devastated with
guilt at having left his love trapped in the black hole, like a fly
in amber. His discoveries pay off handsomely, and he is able to
enjoy his guilt in style.

Beyond the Blue Event Horizon. In this sequel to *Gateway*,
Robin commissions a trip to an Heechee artifact, which turns out
to be a food factory, capable of converting carbon, nitrogen, hydrogen, and oxygen into edible foodstuffs in sufficient quantities

to feed the starving billions on Earth. The crew on the little ship discovers that they are not alone on the food factory when they meet Wan, the orphaned descendant of a Gateway prospector couple. He has survived on another planet, nicknamed Heechee Heaven, and makes regular trips to the Food Factory on a cargo ship. Other inhabitants of Heechee Heaven are descendants of captured Australopithecines from Africa and their baby-sitting machine. When the crew visits Heechee Heaven, they are captured, and the Oldest One (the machine) pens them up for further study. Robin steals a huge computer and a ship to rescue the crew and finds the central computer, which unlocks all the secrets of Heechee navigation and other technological advances. The scientific awards for these discoveries make Robin the richest person in the whole solar system.

Heechee Rendezvous. In the final installment, an old friend of Robin's, Audee Walthers, makes a startling discovery. He puts his mind into contact with the hidden, elusive Heechee. When Audee reports his experience to Robin, Robin decides to go out in search of the Heechee. Robin and his science program, nicknamed Albert Einstein, decide that the Heechee are hiding in a black hole. If they can come and go from one black hole to another, their secret can be used to rescue the long-trapped Klara. In the meantime, Wan, the youth discovered living alone on Heechee Heaven, has grown up and is rich because of his claims to the Heechee artifact. He seduces Audee's wife, Dolly, and sets off in search of his long-lost father, whom he believes to be captured in a black hole. His poking around near black holes alerts the Heechee fleet, living in time-reduced security in the largest black hole. Wan does discover a trapped ship, but it contains Klara, still alive. Because of the time-slowing effects of the black hole, Klara thinks she has been trapped for hours instead of years. Tampering with the black hole is too much for the Heechee; they come out of their hiding place and capture Wan and Klara. Their purpose is peaceful, however, and brings a warning that a race of Assassins is coming to wipe out life in the solar system. Robin, racing toward a rendezvous with the long sought Heechee, suffers a fatal heart seizure; his personality is captured on a computer program so that he can live on indefinitely. Klara delivers the Heechee message to the world, whose governments at first interpret it as a threat of war. Then, with Robin's help, they understand that both races should work together to be ready to face the threat of the Assassins.

The first of the three novels, *Gateway*, is one of Pohl's best and best-known works. The development of the character of Robin Broadhead is central to *Gateway*'s theme and is extremely well done. Robin emerges as a complex, troubled man, whose guilt at profiting at the great expense of his partner and lover, Klara, blocks his full enjoyment of his wealth. Pohl's message is that the capitalistic corporation controlling Heechee exploration, the ineffective governments of Earth who allow the vast overpopulation to expand, and the efforts of a flawed hero are all weak straws on which to lean. The sequels are not as effective from a technical standpoint, but offer relatively satisfying conclusions to puzzles posed in *Gateway*. The adventures are fast-paced and the technological inventions are creative. Although Robin's reduction to a mere computer program by the end of the last volume makes it unlikely that he will continue as an active hero, it may be necessary for another sequel to deal with the Assassins.

Jem. When Danny Dalehouse, professor of exobiology at Michigan State University, first hears about Kung's Star, he thinks of grants and exploration and exciting discoveries in exobiology. The Earth is divided into three power blocs representing the primary resources of People, Fuel, and Food. Each bloc seeks planets to colonize for their own uses. When Danny's friend Marge Menninger, boss lady of funds distribution for the Space Exploration, Research, and Development Commission, makes a trip to "Son of Kung" (the planet Jem) and includes Danny, his dream comes true. The only disappointment is that a manned ship from the "Peeps" beats them into space by a week.

When Danny's ship lands, the crew discovers that the Peeps camp has been attacked by shelled creatures who resembled two-hundred-pound crabs. The other life form which exists on the planet, helium-filled balloons floating in the sky and singing to each other, release an aphrodisiac fluid when startled. Danny learns to communicate with them while floating beneath a net of balloons. Representatives of the Fuel bloc countries arrive, set up their own camp, and begin exploring for oil. They discover a third race of sentient creatures, who burrow beneath the ground and are sensitive to light. The "Greasies" begin using the underground creatures in raids on the other camps; the "Fats" begin using the gasbags to spy on other camps; and the "Peeps" use the crablike Krinpits for transportation. The planet Jem has become an armed and subtly hostile environment, a microcosm of the hostilities escalating on Earth.

When five more ships come to reinforce and resupply the Food Camp (Danny's camp), the first person off the ship is Marge Menninger. She is a major and in command of the arriving troops. The news from Earth is bad--riots, martial law in Los Angeles, ships sunk, and terrorism. The ships Marge arrives in are not fitted for a return trip; the intent is to colonize Jem with the people already present and to expect no more supplies. The war on Jem is escalating, too. The Fuel bloc launches an attack with machine guns and flame-throwers. The Krinpits turn on the last survivors of the People bloc and kill them. Marge commands a force through underground tunnels to set off a nuclear explosion on a Fuel bloc base. When the dust settles, Danny and the few survivors of the remaining two camps realize the folly of further fighting and settle down to colonize a world.

Human short-sightedness is clearly depicted by Frederik Pohl's political blocs on Jem, replications of the same factions on Earth. Danny is the most well-rounded character Pohl has created in this adventure; he is intelligent, passionate, humane, and, in the end, wise enough to stop the fighting. The hostilities between the human blocs and the native species on Jem indicate the despair Pohl feels for humanity; the meager "happy ending" is too little and too late. When Earth wipes itself out, Jem's colonies are the last hope for the survival of the human race and seem a pretty puny effort at that.

Man Plus. Roger Torraway, experienced astronaut, heroic rescuer of Russian cosmonauts in trouble, is playing third banana in the race to place a modified human on Mars. The president of the United States is putting a great deal of pressure on Roger's team to complete the cyborg, adapted to live independent of life support systems, in the hostile environment of the Martian plains. When the nearly completed human-machine, Willy Hartnett, dies of sensory overload, and the second-in-line man has been removed by presidential order, Roger is left with the honor of being adapted for Martian life, of becoming "more of a man." And less. His eyes are replaced with superior instruments for visual perception; his genitals are removed because they become unnecessary; his limbs are replaced with better devices. He is a meld of human and machine, superior to both. And inferior as well. As he is changed, Roger struggles to deal with the changes. As he is rendered impotent, he becomes aware of his wife's infidelity. In a deliberate ploy, Nurse Sulie Carpenter has also been modified, but only with hair coloring and contact lenses, to look like Roger's wife. Sulie exhibits more sensitivity to Roger's emotional state than did his wife, Dorrie. Sulie brings him a guitar and teaches him how to use his computer-enhanced skills to master it. She listens to and understands his fears. When Roger flees the compound to face Dorrie with his anger, she turns down his plea for fidelity, and Sulie soothes him to sleep upon his return. Finally, Roger, priest-scientist Don Kayman, and communications expert Alexander Bradley travel to Mars. The two unadapted humans must wear space suits. The exploration of the surface holds some surprises, such as the crystalline plants growing in the sand. The team starts some plantings under a dome of artificial atmosphere and carries out experiments; Roger's mechanical adaptations are working well. However, Roger finds himself less and less interested in the problems of his more human companions, until he runs into some mechanical difficulties and they help put him right again. Sulie joins him on Mars with the intent of staying there with him to help set up the colony. The species which will colonize Mars consists of the cyborgs, of which Roger is the first, the unadapted humans like Sulie, and, in the end, the artificial intelligences that have engineered the whole plan. The computers have banded together and decided that humans are going to wipe out Earth, so they plan and execute the project to put human, cyborg, and machine in the security of Mars for safekeeping.

Pohl exerts a great deal of effort on the emotions and fears that Roger Torraway develops as he is changed from human to human/machine. Since the anonymous narrator of the story turns out to be totally mechanistic, it is perhaps natural that Roger's emotional upheavals would be fascinating to a computer. The logic of the computer network is inescapable; if the machines are to survive, some way must be developed to have humans survive as well. The computers play a major role in the action and motivation of the characters, but are hidden and manipulative. Pohl is expressing his distrust of humanity's own control over the future, a theme recurrent in several of his works.

Biographical/Bibliographical Readings

Stephen H. Goldman, "Frederik Pohl," in *Twentieth-Century American Science-Fiction Writers* (Gale, 1981), v.2, p.73-85. Frederik Pohl, "The Publishing of Science Fiction," in *Science Fiction, Today and Tomorrow*, ed. Reginald Bretnor (Harper & Row, 1974), p.17-45. Idem, "Ragged Claws," in *Hell's Cartographers*, ed. by Brian W. Aldiss and Harry Harrison (Weidenfeld and Nicolson, 1975), p.144-72. David N. Samuelson, "Critical Mass: The Science Fiction of Frederik Pohl," in *Voices for the Future*, ed. Thomas D. Clareson and Thomas L. Wymer (Bowling Green University Popular Press, 1984), v.3, p.106-26. Idem, "Frederik Pohl," in *Science Fiction Writers*, ed. E. F. Bleiler (Scribner's, 1982), p.475-83. **[Kay Jones]**

POURNELLE, JERRY

Life and Works

Jerry Eugene Pournelle was born in Shreveport, Louisiana, on August 7, 1933. Pournelle grew up in the South, and at the age of seventeen entered the U.S. Army during the Korean War. Released from the army in 1952, he attended the University of Iowa for two years before moving on to Seattle. In 1955, he completed his bachelor's degree at the University of Washington followed in short order by a master's degree in statistics and systems engineering. Pournelle completed two doctorates, one in psychology in 1960, and a second in political science. While at the University of Washington, Pournelle worked as a research assistant in the medical school and later as a psychologist at Boeing. In 1964, just before the Boeing "bubble" burst, Pournelle moved to Southern California to work for Aerospace Corporation. This was followed by a stint at American Rockwell, three years as a professor at Pepperdine, and one year as executive assistant to Sam Yorty, then mayor of Los Angeles. His first professional novel was published in 1969, *Red Heroin*, under the pseudonym Wade Curtis. In 1970, he left his position with Yorty to begin writing full-time with his second novel, *Red Dragon* (1971), also using the Curtis name. Since then Pournelle has written more than a dozen novels and several works of nonfiction. Now using his own name, Pournelle frequently writes in collaboration with Larry Niven on the Second Empire Co-Dominium series, set in the twenty-first through the thirtieth centuries. The first novel in their collaboration was the highly successful first-contact novel, *The Mote in God's Eye* (1974). This was followed later by *Lucifer's Hammer* (1977), which has become the most popular comet-hits-the-Earth disaster novel in this decade. Pournelle and Niven's most experimental work is *Inferno* (1976), a modern Dante in hell.

As a single author, Pournelle's best known and most memorable character is the Co-Dominium Marine officer, John Christian Falkenburg, in a series of military science fiction. He also singly wrote *King David's Spaceship* (1980), based on a story published in *Analog* in 1972, *The Mercenary, West of Honor* (1976) and *Janissaries* (1979) followed by its sequel, *Clan and Crown*.

Themes and Style

One of the best educated of modern science fiction writers, Pournelle has written the science column for *Galaxy* magazine, and admits that his novels have such a solid scientific basis because his column required him to keep up with the leading edge of new technology. Pournelle brings to science fiction an edge of realism, often writing about the cyclic nature of history against a grim backdrop of perpetual war. Not strong on female characterization, most of his women characters assume very secondary and traditional roles. Even his heroines (such as Glenda Ruth Horton in *The Mercenary*) long for the strong arm of a man to protect them. His Falkenburg novels concentrate on taut, but romantic, militarism on savage worlds that allow little room for love or permanency.

Whether writing with Niven or alone, Pournelle works are fast action adventure stories. Pournelle delights in his role as a storyteller and reveals himself as a major talent in the field of traditional science fiction. The principal criticisms leveled against Pournelle are the strong voice of his conservative views on social justice and reform and the glamorization of militarism. His worlds of the Co-Dominium are an uneasy alliance of American and Russian interests. The Co-Dominium is gradually being dismantled by greed, intrigue, and political self-interest. As colony worlds become the dumping ground for Earth's burgeoning welfare poor, the original hard-working settlers are threatened by the influx of immigrants who seem generally to be looking for a free lunch. Using the cold, calculated slaughter of these welfare reformists by Falkenburg in *The Mercenary*, the world's poor are made to be slightly less than human, wreaking incalculable harm upon the first settlers, ravaging and torturing young girls, as in *West of Honor*. Falkenburg and his officers are the noble warriors, complete with bagpipes, fighting a losing battle against the combined forces of politics and reduced military budgets.

Pournelle is an exciting writer, catching up the reader with his contrasts, the nobility and loneliness of command, and intricate warfare tactics. This excitement has brought considerable popularity to his works, and resulted in several awards, including the John W. Campbell award in 1973, and the presidency of the Science Fiction Writers of America in 1974.

Plot Summaries of Major Works

Janissaries. The action begins on a hillside in twentieth-century Africa. CIA special forces are in a losing battle when suddenly the fighting men are whisked away by a group of aliens. The aliens are in the market for mercenaries to fight their battles, although they are willing to return the soldiers afterward to fulfill their glorious destinies. When offered the choice to go with the aliens or be killed, the mercenaries choose to live. Led by Rick Galloway, the soldiers eventually end up fighting a primitive culture on Tran, a world with a drug-supported economy. Comprised of previously captured earlier Earth cultures including Native Americans and Romans, Tran is a world of confusing cultural contrasts, ripe for consolidation under one ruler. Rick Galloway and his forces, with their superior knowledge of technology and tactics, lead the movement.

A very fast-moving story, *Janissaries* reflects Pournelle's great interest in the role of technology in societal development and his relatively conservative economic views. Utilizing the strengths of a militaristic society, Pournelle weaves an exciting tale of intrigue, political infighting and battlefield tactics to create a richly textured novel. Those who enjoy militaristic science fiction will also appreciate the sequel, *Clan and Crown*.

King David's Spaceship. Prince Samuel's world is a lost colony reverted to barbarism in the fall of the First Human Empire. With the rise of the Second Human Empire, the Imperial Navy rather handily overcomes the colony forces to reestablish the control of the empire. Into this situation strides Colonel Nathan MacKinnie and his soldiers, losers to the might of the Imperial Navy. Recruited by the local King David's secret police to join traders on the first off-world venture, MacKinnie is to acquire the knowledge necessary to raise the planet from its role as a subject colony to that of a participating member in the empire. MacKinnie's awareness of the changing values of his world and of the disappearance of his buccaneer style of fighting form the basis for an entertaining story.

King David's Spaceship is based on an earlier story which appeared in *Analog* in 1972. As with many stories expanded from an earlier concept, there are some rough edges and even rougher transitions, as the pace will change considerably when the original story concept is pursued. However, Pournelle has never let such details get in the way of an exciting military science fiction novel, and this one is no exception. As with his Falkenburg novels, this one concentrates on the role of technology and the isolation of the command officers. Yet, unlike earlier works, there is a great deal of fun and comedic action present, as the characterization of an essentially nineteenth-century military genius is inserted into a space-going civilization. One is not quite certain how the Second Empire will be prepared to deal with Colonel McKinnie and his troops.

The Mercenary. Consisting of three shorter pieces, the novel parallels the development of the career of John Christian Falkenburg, a Co-Dominium Marine officer, and the retrenchment of humanity's first great expansion into the hundred colony worlds that comprise the Co-Dominium. Senator John Rogers Grand and Grand Admiral Lermantov are striving against all odds to put out the brush fires around the Co-Dominium. John Falkenburg is the principal weapon in their arsenal. Falkenburg is a mercenary colonel with a cashiered batallion of Marines who go first to the planet Hadley and then to Tanith. Hadley is an idyllic planet that has become the dumping ground for the poor of Earth's cities. Lacking basic skills and education, these welfare recipients are demanding that the colony support them. Manufacturing a revolution to take over the government, the highly ambitious vice-president, Bradford, helps to bring in Falkenburg's Mercenary Legion, then uses them to arouse the suspicion of the government, the technological branch of the local citizenry, and the rebels. In one incredible scene, Falkenburg turns a mass constitutional rally into a bloodbath, effectively executing the majority of the fifty thousand assembled and thus solving Hadley's problem with welfare recipients. From this grim, unforgettable episode, Falkenburg gains a reputation as a leader willing to take on long odds and win. On Tanith, Falkenburg meets his match in Glenda Ruth Horton, a young wisp of a girl leading a losing fight on New Washington, an agrarian society, against the Confederacy, a technologically superior force from off-world. As the story progresses, the reader realizes that this planet will be where Falkenburg either fights his last battle or settles in for good.

The final action scene and the political machinations of the conclusion are predictable, but uneven. In the attempt to combine three stories into one novel, the differences in style and shift in focus are confusing. While Falkenburg stands out as the principal character, the occasional disappearance and reappearance of the Co-Dominium's politicians are used as the mortar to bind the layers of the story together in a rather uneven amalgam. Despite this flaw in form, the three stories are thought-provoking on their own merits. Glorifying the loneliness of command and the military tradition, the stories form the basis for necessary reading as background for other Co-Dominium stories.

West of Honor. In a prequel to *The Mercenary*, Falkenburg is a young captain in the Royal Marines. The colony of Arrarat, a planet settled by the World Federation of Churches, is being abandoned by the Co-Dominium as a backward agricultural planet. In the process of this abandonment, the populace is saddled with a flood of convicts and tranports from Earth's slums. Into the bloody battle for control between the farmers and the gangs, the few Royal Marines fight a rear-guard action reminiscent of the Roman's retreat from their colonies.

Pournelle manages to demonstrate in this novel an outstanding talent for storytelling. The action is fast-paced and the characterizations are minimal, while the battles glorious and bloody. On Arrarat, Pournelle reveals the tightrope walked by many writers, exposing all the sides in the conflict as complex issues without facile resolution. And yet Pournelle suggests, with his basic optimism, a belief in humanity's intrinsic honor and in technology to act as a force for good. At the same time, he misses the opportunity to develop some outstanding and memorable personalities such as Kathryn, a colony farm leader raped and tortured by the gangs, who is attempting to restore her shattered private life. Pournelle's action scenes would be considerably strengthened by adding richness and depth to his principal characters. Despite these weaknesse, *West of Honor* is a novel intended for those preferring straight science fiction with a technology base and lots of military action.

Biographical/Bibliographical Readings

Richard D. Ehrlich, "Niven and Pournelle's *Oath of Fealty*: A Case of Improvement?" *Foundation* 27 (1983), p.64-70. Jeffrey Elliot, "Jerry Pournelle: From Space Program to Space Opera," *Science Fiction Voices* 3 (1980), p.53-64. Charles Platt, "Jerry Pournelle," in *Dream Makers* (Berkley, 1983), p.1-14. Madison A. Sowell, "The Niven-Pournelle Dante: A Twentieth Century Odyssey Through Hell," *Studies in Medievalism* 2 (Summer 1983), p.75-78. [Colleen Power]

PRIEST, CHRISTOPHER

Life and Works

Christopher Priest was born in Cheadle, Cheshire, in the north of England, on July 14, 1943. He was educated in Manchester and currently divides his time between part-time lecturing at the University of London and writing.

Priest has been involved in the British Science Fiction Association; he has been vice-president of the association and reviews editor for its magazine, *Foundation*. He has also written the introduction for a collection of Australian short stories, *Envisaged Worlds* (1978). He was awarded a Ditmar award for *The Perfect Lover* (1977). He received the British Science Fiction Association award in 1974 and again in 1979.

Priest first published in the 1970s and is associated with the British New Wave. He published short stories in Moorcock's *New Worlds* and also in the American magazine *Quark*. His short stories have been collected in two volumes--*The Real Time World* (1974) and *An Infinite Summer* (1979). He has also edited *Anticipations* (1978) and an anthology of British science fiction, *Stars of Albion* (1979). His first novel, *Indoctrinaire*, was published in 1970. Priest's second novel, *Darkening Island*, did not appear until 1972. *The Inverted World* was published in 1974. In 1976, his novel *The Space Machine* was published. He made moves toward and is accepted by British mainstream fiction, but returned to science fiction with *The Glamour* in 1984.

Themes and Style

In his first novel, *Indoctrinaire* (1970), Priest showed his first exploration of realities, shifts, and their perspective. The protagonist, Dr. Wentik, is researching an experimental drug and is imprisoned by a government agent. By trying to make sense of his situation, Priest's characters in this and other novels are often faced with intense situations where they must survive or maintain their sanity. Wentik discovers that he is a bridge between his present and the future two centuries away. He has no control over his experience of the future and cannot work out what either time period wants from him. Priest returns to this theme in *The Glamour*. From these realizations, the characters attempt to establish the nature of freedom and whether they or their captors possess it.

Priest works in the same way as Wells, taking a paradox or expression and working it out to its logical conclusion. This approach has sometimes been to the detriment of character and plot, but he is progressing toward a rectification of this with novels like *The Perfect Lover* and *The Glamour*. Like Brian Aldiss, Priest pays his tribute to H. G. Wells in *The Space Machine*. A traveling salesperson meets the time traveler's niece and is drawn into the narrative of *The War of the Worlds* and *The Time Machine*. This is an often humorous pastiche of the two novels. They have been reworked so that we are able to view the attack of Mars and expand Wells' conceptions of both his realist and science fiction literature.

Darkening Island (British title: *Fugue for a Darkening Island*) reflects much more on British culture and is expressive of the problems first perceived in the 1970s. Priest uses a backdrop of near-future Britain for his plot in this and other works. A war in Africa causes an influx of refugees to Britain, and the resulting tension leads to civil war. Priest uses a variable viewpoint to concentrate on a man and his family as they experience the turbulence.

His shorter pieces also hinge on paradoxes and his main interest is in the conflicting perspectives of a character's perception of reality. Quite often he is dealing with time travel, experimentation, or novel aspects of relationships.

Plot Summaries of Major Works

The Glamour. Richard Grey is a cameraman who finds himself in a nursing home, a hero after he has been blown apart by a terrorist car bomb. Although he attains physical well-being, he is troubled by amnesia. The main thing that he cannot recall during this time is the nature of his relationship with Susan, who comes to the hospital to help him restore his memory. Events are wandering and confused due to his amnesia. Grey discovers that his ability in film making was due to his unconscious operation of the glamour. Susan herself is glamourous and was attracted to him because of it. This attraction brings Grey into competition with Niall. Niall is Susan's previous lover and is enmeshed in the subculture of the glamourous, who exist but are invisible to the rest of society. The tension arises between Susan and Richard as she tries to explain their relationship to him. In doing so, she must face a large number of inconsistencies in how she views the world and those around her.

Priest is dealing with the conflict of fantasy and reality in a direct narrative. He draws upon the theme of possession with the same type of relationship which destroys other of his dreamworlds. *The Glamour* is a challenging paradox. The changes in viewpoint examine the ultimate themes of identity and security. Through writing in this manner, Priest manages to create an alternate world. Getting to the truth of the matter is a theme prevalent in contemporary British fiction; Priest allows science fiction to make its contribution as well.

The Inverted World. Howard Mann comes of age in the City of Earth and joins the mysterious guilds. He is gradually initiated in the work of the guild members, the nature of his work, and his world. His city is actually a construction which is perpetually moving forward. It is the guild's purpose to enable the city to do this by continually relaying a track, along which the city is winched. The city is in eternal pursuit of the optimum and this is the priority of the guild members, but they cannot explain it to the city dwellers. The optimum is the place where the environmental conditions are like that of the home world. If they do not keep moving, the outside members know that they are subject to the distortions of time and place.

The novel starts out from the initial premise of a hyperbolic world and is well executed. It suggests Abbot's *Flatland* in its adherence to geometry. Idea is central to the story and in the foreground of character development. There is a world-within-a-world theme which grows greater as Helward questions and strives toward an understanding of his world and its reality. Priest cases the conflict of opinion and belief within Helward's marriage and coming of age. Apart from sustaining the idea and accounting for paradooxes in the inverted world, Priest is dealing with how people adapt and respond to paradigms.

The Perfect Lover (British title: A Dream of Wessex). This novel is set against the background of the near future in Britain as the country experiences terrorism. Julia Stretton is returning from the Ridpath project, her few day break having been ruined by the chance meeting with Paul, a past lover. She works as part of an experiment which combines the subconscious of forty scientists in an attempt to create a projected world of the future. From their observations of the future world, it is hoped that the participants will be able to solve current world problems.

Before she resumes her alternate personality in Wessex (the dream world), Julia is given the task of finding David Harkman. He has been in the dream world for too long a time and appears to have lost his awareness of the real world. Within the dream world, Julia and David embark on a relationship which holds over when Paul, Julia's previous lover, enters the experiment and drastically changes the world. As Julia and David proceed in the new Wessex, they begin to experiece difficulty in identifying and choosing between the real and dream worlds.

The Perfect Lover takes up the perception of the future and the dream worlds in order to return to the present that was initiated in *Indoctrinaire*. The growing relationship between David Harkman and Julie is handled with precision and conviction by Priest. The central themes of the novel are Julia's relationship with Paul, her exertion of her own identity, and the eventual comparisons of the two worlds. Their worlds are being shaped by their concerns and desires as well as their ignorance of the actual nature of Wessex. Priest's extrapolation of the future Britain and the scientists' conception adds to the atmosphere of the book.

Biographical/Bibliographical Readings

"Christopher Priest," in *A Reader's Guide to Science Fiction*, ed. Baird Searles et al. (Facts on File, 1979), p.120. Charles Platt, "Christopher Priest," in *Dream Makers* (Berkley, 1983), v.2, p.25-33. [Nickianne Moody]

RANDALL, MARTA

Life and Works

Marta Randall was born in Mexico City on April 26, 1948, then moved with her family to San Francisco when she was two years old. She attended Berkeley High School and went on to San Francisco State College from 1966 to 1972. While married to Robert H. Bergstresser, Randall had one son. She also published one story under the name Marta Bergstresser: "Smack Run," published in *New Worlds 5* in 1973. She divorced in 1973, but married again in 1983, to Christopher E. Conley. Since 1968, she has been office manager for H. Zimmerman in Oakland, California.

Her first two novels, *Islands* and *A City in the North*, were published in 1976, followed by *Journey* (1978) and *Dangerous Games* (1980). Other novels include *The Sword of Winter* and *Those Who Favor Fire* (1984). Randall taught at the Clarion Science Fiction Writers Workshop in 1982, then at workshops at Portland State University in 1983 and the University of California, Berkeley, in 1984 and 1985. During this same time, she was active in the Science Fiction Writers Association, acting as vice-president in 1981-82 and president from 1982 to 1984.

As a writer, Marta Randall has shown her versatility by experimenting in the short story, novella, and novel forms. She also tried her hand at editing with Robert Silverberg for *Dimension 11* and *12* and alone on *Nebula Awards 19*.

Themes and Style

Randall comes out of the 1970s feminist movement in science fiction, in that her stories are far more concerned with the people than the science of her future worlds. Many characteristics found in Randall's works are typical of feminist science fiction. Her stories portray strong females as well as nurturing males. These characters are sexually uninhibited as their worlds are free of sexual taboos. Randall's worlds are vividly described and imaginatively created, yet the social order--for most Terran groups at least--remains much as we know it today.

Randall's stories all move briskly, yet when one begins to enumerate the action in them, one realizes that her stories move primarily through thoughts, dialogue, and changes within people more than through drastic and numerous actions. Two of her early stories, "A Scarab in the City of Time" (1975) and "Megan's World" (1976), deal with strong females who, when thrust into situations not of their choosing, still work toward the good of their fellows at the expense of their own happiness. The nameless female narrator in "Scarab" has the thankless task of an unpopular prophet leading people back into the world from their tiny encapsulated city. Megan, in "Megan's World," has fled from people because of her artificial "modifications," yet she accepts first a role as mediator between Terrans and aliens and finally a most undesired role as the aliens' new goddess who can lead them toward peace and progress.

Randall's short stories to the present continue to depict women in difficult circumstances who struggle to come to terms with their worlds and themselves. It is not always a successful attempt. In "The View from Endless Scarp" (1979), the woman Markowitz fights a harsh environment and the laughter of its inhabitants to a realization that she is like them and will remain on their world. The female in "Sea Changes" (1985), however, does not understand the transformation she is undergoing as she and an alien shift to the other's persona, and she becomes even less capable of comprehending by the story's end.

As in her short stories, Randall predominantly depicts female protagonists in her novels. One of her first two novels, *Islands*, portrays an aging female archaeologist living in a world of immortals. It is perhaps Randall's strongest work to date, as it explores humanity's fear and courtship of death. *A City in the North* has two complex females and an enigmatic alien. This novel uses a journalistic style similar to William Faulkner's in *As I Lay Dying* to allow the reader more insight and understanding into the character and the situation. Here Randall points out that exploitation can go both ways; no one way may necessarily be ennobled through persecution.

Randall experimented with a different type of novel when she wrote *Journey* (1978) and *Dangerous Games* (1980). In these long novels, she follows the Kennerin family through their settling and prospering in a frontier world. The novels have been classified as family sagas of the future. They read like complex historical novels, full of passion and intrigue. Primarily, though, the novels are about the people and their interactions both within and without the family unit. As for strength of character, however, the women are still stronger in these works.

Randall's work primarily revolves around pioneers looking to make a home and coming to grips with personal and physical challenges. One of her strengths is that she depicts men and women as equals even though she typically writes from the feminine viewpoint. Another strength in her works is the depiction of children and the elderly as valuable, influential participants in shaping society. In each of her imaginatively drawn settings, Randall has woven together engaging personal triumphs and insightful visions to create strong tales of the pioneering human spirit.

Plot Summaries of Major Works

A City in the North. Toyon is a wealthy businessman pursuing his childhood dream of visiting an ancient city on a distant, backwater planet called Hoep-Hanninah. He and his estranged wife have come to visit, hoping to reestablish their love. Alin Kennerin, Toyon's wife, is a woman of many talents, including ethnology. She comes to study the natives, but she ultimately gives more than she learns. The human establishment on Hoep-Hanninah is meager. The governor is suspicious of any visitors who might report his ineptness to govern, but others in the colony are the truly vicious ones. They have learned that the pollen from a native prayer plant, when mixed with hydrochloric acid, makes a very addictive, hallucinatory drug for Terrans. The planet's company manager has learned of this and is selling the drug off-world while subjecting Terrans working for him to addiction to the drug. The Hanninah natives have been forced to help provide the pollen, and discover that, when Terrans are given the drugs in their presence, they are able to see into the Terrans' minds. The natives give the drug to Alin without her knowledge. She appears to be uniting with the natives when, in actuality, she is becoming addicted and is being used to teach the Hanninah more of Terran culture and thought.

Quellan is a hard-working woman, street-wise yet sensitive and sensible. It is Quellan who guides Toyon and Alin into the wilderness to help them find the ancient city. By the time Quellan, Toyon, Alin, and other natives reach the ruins of the ancient city, the governor has discovered the treachery of the plant manager, subdued him, and set out to find the evil Terrans. He kills them, but is himself mortally wounded. Alin, addicted and by now discarded by the Hanninah, is cured of her addiction and she and Toyon turn for home.

The alien Hanninah are beautifully portrayed in the novel, not as innocents or victims, but as oppressed aliens who have no compulsions about using Terrans for their needs. The novel is written in journal fashion, which allows for a steady revealing of the complex characters. Toyon and Alin show themselves to be frustrated and perplexed about their relationship. The journals depict their courage as they struggle in the alien world. Their entries are sprinkled with entries from Quellan who brooks no nonsense and the governor's entries, whose meek blindness and then horror of the situation lends insight and excellent variation. Pacing throughout the novel is smooth and the shifting point of view lends depth. There are many beautiful descriptive passages, and Randall's theme on the need to deal carefully with other people and other worlds is effectively presented.

Islands. Aging Tia Hamley regrets her decision to invite her lover from fifty years ago, Paul, and his new lover to join her aboard the *Ilium* as she explores one of the submerged Hawaiian islands. Paul and Jenny, his current love, are immortals seeking pleasure and new experiences. Their reactions to Tia are typical of what she has experienced all her life. Paul, fascinated with death, is enamored of her and again becomes her lover, but this time it is death he is making love to, not Tia. Jenny, on the other hand, is repulsed by Tia, then curious, and only later on is she able to see Tia as more than an aging body.

Tia believes that she is the only living mortal and indulges in self-pity and self-hatred. She has never come to terms with her mortality and views her sixty-seven-year-old body as an awful, decaying shell. However, in the submerged ruins of the island, she finds an intact building which houses the knowledge she needs to become immortal. Tia descends to the building, believing that her angry words caused a crew member's death. Another shipmate tries to kill her, claiming she is jinxed. He leaves her beneath the water believing she is dead. When she reappears before the crew member, he stalks her in a crazed frenzy and Tia kills him in self-defense, only to learn that he is mortal like her; it is his self-hatred and fear of growing old like Tia that caused his apparent hatred of her, but she had never recognized it.

Probably Randall's strongest science fiction novel, *Islands* focuses on the emotions of a heroine who cannot biologically achieve immortality in a world of immortals. Yet through this aging freak, Randall is able to delve into the psychology, morality, and phobias of a perpetually youthful society. Tia discovers in the ancient ruins from the twenty-first century her own kind of immortality and ultimately moves to a higher level of consciousness, which allows her to become one with the universe. The heroine of *Islands* is very strong and well developed, as are most of Randall's female characters. Emotions are powerfully presented, and Randall creates a fascinating psychological study of immortals who fear death above all else. Typical of the feminist science fiction of the 1970s, Randall explores sexual taboos and alternatives within this society. With excellent use of detail, flowing poetic prose, and fast-paced action, Randall portrays characters seeking to belong and coming to terms with their humanity.

The Kinnerin Family saga

Journey. *Journey* and *Dangerous Games* form a two-volume family saga involving the Kennerin family. Jason and Mish have been outlawed from Earth because Jason's aristocratic family found commoner Mish an unacceptable mate for him. The young couple buy the planet Aerie and go there to build a home. They have three children, Jes, Quilla, and Hart, and Jason also brings in over 200 refugees from another world that was suffering political violence before its sun went nova. The child Hart cannot accept the newcomers, tries to set fire to one of their homes, and then is caught and blackmailed by a bitter refugee biologist.

Quilla grows up quickly, taking on much responsibility in running the family planet. Young Jes lives a space adventure when he saves the Aerites from the political nasties coming to take their refugees back. He begins training in space.

On Aerie, the intelligent six-armed marsupials, called Kasirene, are cooperative and friendly, yet the humans and aliens grope for a common ground. The children find it in a game they develop together, which enables individual friendships between humans and Kasirene to develop and deepen. Then seventeen-year-old Hart is caught after killing several young Kasirene. The event is hushed and Hart is shipped off the planet to a university. He returns ten years later, a surgeon, wanting to help his father who has been crippled in an accident. However, Hart's new companion, an evil, aging millionaire, causes Jason's death, and Hart leaves again. This time he has been wrongly accused and misunderstood. On another planet, he uses his skills to further the ruling class's power in order to save his son--a son cloned from his own body. After he and his son, Spider, escape that world, Hart realizes how much love a parent has for a child. When he learns that his brother is looking for him, Hart and Spider go home.

This is a novel of world building, but it is far more a story of people, and particularly family. Randall not only creates a society but also a community of aliens and humans. And she studies one pioneering family as it establishes itself on a distant world. The females of this family are especially well drawn. Mish is many-talented, as is her daughter Quilla. Mish's other daughter, Meya, is no less capable or complex. The aliens are fascinating in their early aloofness and in their alien nature and appearance. They are ignored by the Kennerins only when it comes to protecting their son for the wrong he had committed against them. This long family saga is gripping despite its lack of violence. It is truly about the daily lives of a pioneer family creating a home, community and society.

Dangerous Games. The Kennerin family saga begun in *Journey* continues in this novel. Sandro Marquez signs on with now spaceship captain Jes Kennerin. Sandros's family had been in competition with the Kennerins before the giant Parallax gained control. Now Sandro hires on, looking for revenge. Jes brings home a stray from Gensco Station where his repair jockey had been a Santa Theresan named Tatha. The furred Theresans had been created to adapt better to their home world, but most humans saw them as cats and predators. They were poorly treated as a rule. Tatha manipulates Jes into helping her find and regain her child from Gensco, then he takes her back to Aerie as a good place to raise her child. Jes grows to love Tatha, though he will not admit it. The Kennerin family sees the need to have a predator among them because they realize their own ineptness at handling something as huge and treacherous as the Parallax.

Hart Kennerin's son, Spider, is growing up quickly and is telepathic. Hart is extremely dependent on his son, almost living through him. His sister, Meya, has a daughter of her own, literally, having asked Hart to clone her baby Alin as he had cloned Spider. Baby Alin is also telepathic and depends on Spider to communicate for her from her very birth.

The native Kasirene have grown distrustful of the humans, and one finally calls for retribution for Hart's youthful killing of several young Kasirene twenty years earlier. The punishment is to be that the entire Kennerin family will be informed of what Hart did; then the Kasirene will take his son Spider from him to be raised by the Kasirene. This almost destroys Hart, but Spider accepts it and spends a year alone with the Kasirene. Unrest among the Kasirene grows so that when a Parallax ship stops in their space station for repairs, the Kasirene leader buys the captain's story that Parallax would be better for them than the Kennerins. Tatha has been busy playing side against side, and she takes many risks to save Aerie.

This novel plays a small family business against a giant, faceless corporation which eats worlds without notice. The political intrigue primarily takes place on Aerie, where the simple farming community is easily set up and agitated. The Kennerins continue to be fair-minded and good to the people on Aerie while the natives appear more complex as they realize the implications of the changes in their world. Because the intrigue occurs in an agrarian world, it seems simplistic, and the danger is resolved a little too easily. There is very little bloodshed, and given the extremely high stakes this seems unrealistic. The novel is very long, the cast of characters almost requires the reader to keep a list to keep them straight. The novel is whole by itself, but the story is best appreciated as a continuation of *Journey*, where we learn of Hart's youthful actions. The varied point of view adds spice, but most of all the female characters' spirited efforts to save their world and their families is what makes this a good piece of science fiction.

Biographical/Bibliographical Readings

Lester del Rey, "The Reference Library," *Analog Science Fiction/Science Fact* 98 (Nov. 1978), p. 170-71. Hoda M. Zaki, "Marta Randall," in *Twentieth-Century Science-Fiction Writers*, ed. Curtis C. Smith (St. James, 1986), p.592. **[Barbara Ann Luther]**

ROBINSON, SPIDER

Life and Works

Spider Robinson was born in New York City in November of 1948. He received a B.A. from SUNY Stony Brook in 1972. He also attended the New York State University College in Platts-burgh and Lemoyne College in Syracuse. Robinson began his ca-reer as a science fiction reviewer, winning the 1977 Locus poll as best science fiction critic. He reportedly felt that he could write better stories than many of those he reviewed. Thus, while Robin-son worked nights as a watchman on a sewer project in Babylon, New York, he spent his days reading and writing science fiction. Ben Bova published Robinson's first story, "The Guy with the Eyes," in *Analog*, and it was the first of a series that became a collection of short stories, *Callahan's Crosstime Saloon* (1977). In 1975, he married Jeanne Corrigan, who began collaborating with him on his science fiction works.

Robinson has been the recipient of several science fiction awards: John W. Campbell Award for Best New Science Fiction Writer of the Year in 1974; Hugo award in 1977 for "By Any Other Name" (later expanded and published as *Telempath*); and the Hugo and Nebula awards in 1977 and 1978 for the novella, *Star-dance* (1977), coauthored with Jeanne Robinson. *Stardance* was expanded and republished as a novel in 1979. Other works by Robinson include *Mindkiller* (1982) and *Night of Power* (1985).

Themes and Style

The setting for *Callahan's Crosstime Saloon* is an Irish-Ameri-can bar in Suffolk County, New York. The stories are told by the clientele. A common theme of Robinson's is a coming together of a group of people who have been spiritually, morally, and physi-cally hurt by a hostile, violent, and corrupt society. The setting for this and other works is the near future on Earth. Life has been complicated by pollution of the atmosphere, "police action" wars in third world countries, and a society beset by rampant crime.

In *Callahan's*, *Telempath*, and *Stardance*, the narrators are spir-itually and physically wounded people who are redeemed by their ability to share joy with others. Robinson is a product of the 1960s, and though disillusioned by much of the violence and moral corruption of that era, he also reflects the beauty and joy of the communal spirit that came from the "Hippie" philosophy and the poetry and music of that same period.

Nowhere in his books is society more in danger of destruction (and rebirth) than in *Night of Power*, a powerful story in which New York City is in the throes of a racial war, and in *Mindkiller*, in which Robinson tells a story of human degradation through addiction to brain stimulation. Again, his belief in the salvation of humanity through the joy of community and love ends these novels with a hopeful note.

Plot Summaries of Major Works

Callahan's Crosstime Saloon. In Callahan's saloon, the price of any drink is fifty cents. Only one dollar bills are accepted, and the drinker has a choice of taking fifty cents in change from a box by the door as he or she leaves, or standing up, making a toast, and throwing the glass into the fireplace; a lot of glass is found in Callahan's fireplace. The clientele of the saloon are broken people (not always human) who come to Callahan's for spiritual repair. They find not only solace and sympathy here, but a communal spirit and empathy, for all have suffered and no one is better or worse than the other.

The joy of joking and sharing is told in stories or contests, the most prevalent being the ritual of topping each other's sometimes abominable puns on "Punday" (after Sunday and Monday comes Punday). In one story several of the clients find themselves in a sort of mindmeld, helping a new client, a telepath, reach his catatonic brother through telepathic means. In another story the group takes an alien into their fold when he asks for sanctuary because he no longer wishes to carry out his terrible task on Earth. A female who has lived for centuries and is childless is the recipient of sympathy and comradeship after her story is told to the regulars at Callahan's.

Not all of the stories are strictly science fiction, yet all are uplifting in the end because the people in Callahan's act as one and accept each new member's fears and foibles while helping the newcomers to gain strength. The book has many similarities to Arthur C. Clarke's *Tales from the White Hart* in its style. "Anything can happen at Callahan's" is the theme of this collection, but the regulars all act predictably once we know that they empathize so strongly with the joys and sorrows of others. In the last story, we get a clue as to why Callahan's (and Callahan himself) offers sanctuary and community for others; the reason is one of hope for the destiny of humanity.

Mindkiller. In 1999, Joe Templeton has lost his memory of the past four years, and Norman Kent has lost his sister. When the sister is found, so is Joe's memory. Joe is a burglar who uses computers to tell him when someone is away from home. He breaks into an apartment one night to find that the tenant, Karen, is committing suicide by "wireheading," directing electrical stimulation to the pleasure center of the brain. This addiction to ecstasy becomes a cause; Karen is saved and joins Joe to find the source of wirehead apparatus and eradicate it.

Norman is a professor rescued from a suicide attempt by a man who subsequently robs him. Norman returns to his apartment and finds his sister, Maddy, waiting for him. She comforts him, but then disappears. Norman embarks on an investigation to find her. In the many ironic twists and turns which follow, it turns out that Norman and Joe are the same person. Karen takes a woman as lover, who turns out to be Norman's former wife; she recognizes that Joe is Norman. When the mastermind of the wireheading industry is found, he turns out to be the boyfriend of Norman's sister, Maddy.

Mindkiller is an exciting mystery, with a Heinlein-like theme of mind control but ending with a different twist when Joe/Norman, Karen, Maddy and the mindkiller come together for the ultimate in mindblending. The joy of sharing and becoming as one is part of Robinson's hope for humanity.

Night of Power. At a time when racial tension is at a breaking point in the not-too-distant future of New York City, the Grant family comes to New York so that the wife, a black dancer named Dena, can dance with a ballet company. Dena's husband, Russell, and his daughter from a previous marriage, Jennifer, are white. The city erupts into violence when it is taken over by black revolutionaries in one night of riots and mayhem, and the racially mixed family becomes the focal point for a theme of separation and unity. The black leader of the armed revolution, Michael, saves the Grants from an altercation with some street thugs and later helps them escape the violence of the night of power. Russell learns of a plot by some of the revolutionaries to assassinate Michael and warns him. Jennifer and her Hispanic boyfriend, who are at a concert when the rioting erupts, spend the first night fighting to survive. Jennifer is coming of age and later that night, in hiding with her boyfriend, makes love for the first time.

Interwoven into the story of racial separatism is the story of the family's struggle to remain united. The wife/stepmother is black, the father and daughter are white, the boyfriend is Hispanic. Dena meets a former lover who is also a dancer and a black, and tension develops between Dena and her husband. This novel has a lot of brutality, sexuality, and violence, necessitated by the theme of the intense struggle for unity and community and love. Robinson's theme of total empathy and unity being the answer for the salvation of humanity is told by emphasizing the antithesis of hatred and prejudice.

Stardance. This near-future story is narrated by a man, Charlie Armstead, who is a former dancer, unable to dance anymore due to a bullet injury to his hip. He is embittered and cynical and works as a video specialist for dancers. Charlie becomes the video man for Shara Drummond, a very talented dancer, but one whose large size prevents her from becoming a great dancer.

Shara develops a new dance form: free-fall dancing in space. Shara, her sister Norrey, Charlie, and others in the free-fall dance troop become famous. The handicaps that restricted dancing on Earth are gone--Charlie's injury and Shara's size. Plasmoids, angel-like aliens from outer space, appear at the space station and for some time simply watch the dancers. Shara studies their movements and then dances for them. Shara dies from unknown causes, but her dance has opened communication with the aliens. The remaining members of the troop have an opportunity to dance for the aliens and they learn from the Plasmoids about a higher plane of unity and love. The dancers relate this knowledge to the rest of the world and the dancers attain a state they call "Homo caelestis."

Like Robinson's other stories, the world is polluted, ecologically and morally. However, he believes that there is hope for humanity through love and complete unity--a way out of the morass of corruption. The dancing troop develops a communal closeness, a love that transcends the bitterness and competition of life on Earth. They come together as "Homo caelestis," and share with the aliens through the poetic communication of the dance. Coauthored with his wife, Jeanne, *Stardance* won both the Hugo and Nebula awards as a novella in 1977 and 1978.

Biographical/Bibliographical Readings

B. A. Beatie, "Narrative Technique in *Stardance*," *Extrapolation* 23:2 (1982), p.175-84. John P. Brennan, "Spider Robinson," in *Twentieth-Century Science-Fiction Writers*, ed. Curtis C. Smith (St. James, 1986), p.609-11. John Clute, "Spider Robinson," in *The Encyclopedia of Science Fiction*, ed. Peter Nicholls (Doubleday, 1979), p.502. [Janet E. Frederick]

RUSS, JOANNA

Life and Works

Born In New York City on February 22, 1937, Joanna Russ was the daughter of two teachers. She was raised and educated in New York City. Russ's interest in science fiction arose through her early educational background, having attended the Bronx High School of Science and winning the Westinghouse talent search her senior year. Graduating in 1957 with distinction from Cornell University, where she studied under Vladimar Nabakov, she sold her first science fiction short story "Nor Custom Stale" to the *Magazine of Fantasy and Science Fiction* in 1959. By 1960, Russ had finished Yale University's Master of Fine Arts program, specializing in playwriting and dramatic literature. She then accepted a lecturer position at Queensborough Community College. In 1963, she married Albert Mateau, divorcing him in 1967. In that year she became a lecturer in English at Cornell, with subsequent positions at SUNY, Binghamton, the University of Colorado, and most recently as professor of English at the University of Washington.

Russ's first novel, *Picnic on Paradise*, originally a separate 1968 Ace novel, has been sandwiched into a collection of other Alyx stories called *The Adventures of Alyx* (1983). Her second novel was *And Chaos Died* (1970). Her third novel appeared in 1975, *The Female Man*. *Kittatinny: A Tale of Magic* (1978) and *On Strike against God* (1980) are later works published by small presses. Some of her short stories are collected in *The Zanzibar Cat* (1984). Russ's list of honors include the 1968 Nebula award finalist for *Picnic on Paradise*, the 1971 Nebula finalist for "Poor Man, Beggar Man," the Nebula award for Best Short Story, 1972, for "When It Changed," and the 1983 Nebula and Hugo novella awards for "Souls."

Themes and Style

Beautifully written and yet very torturous, Russ's style reflects her strong literary training. Most of her novels, such as *Alyx*, are written in the classic *Gulliver's Travels* mode, in which a stranger is thrust into a society that both challenges conventional ethos and pokes sly, startling, satirical fun at traditional female-male relationships. Yet her humor is bitter, full of savage raw anger, picking away the crusty scabs of sexual inequality, exposing the festering wounds at the heart of feminist literature. Often the societies she creates, such as Whileaway, are optimistic feminist utopias, freed of the sexual agressiveness and paternalistic chauvinism identified with male dominated cultures. Yet her women heroines, especially Alyx, the transtemporal agent of *Picnic on Paradise*, and Janet Evason, of "When It Changed" and *The Female Man*, are wonderfully alive, full of wry humor and equanimity. Yet Russ does not limit her principal characters to female roles, for in *And Chaos Died* the homosexual Earthman, Jai Vedh, is thrust into a society of telepaths. Beneath all of Russ's writing lies a core of feminism. At a Modern Languages Association meeting in 1975, Russ revealed that a passage in her first novel describing the heroine's nightmarish wallflower attendance at a dance was snubbed by her professor at Cornell, in deference to the work of a fellow male student describing a gritty, savage husband-wife rape. She recognized at that time that because of her feminist attitudes, she was barred from consideration as a serious mainstream writer. Despite this discouragement, Russ has been a tremendous influence on science fiction writing. Her near-stream-of-consciousness writing sets a rich tone for the reader. Often written in a second-person narrative, as in *The Two of Us*, Joanna Russ highlights the finest writings of the modern science fiction trend toward humanism rather than technology. Needless to say, her highly controversial and extraordinary variations from the traditional narrative style and her optimistic femminist message have earned her both vilification from some reviewers and deification from her many fans.

Plot Summaries of Major Works

And Chaos Died. This satirical portrait of a telepathic versus seemingly normal society is set in the distant future. A spaceliner is destroyed, leaving two survivors, the captain and his confined insane passenger, Jai Vedh. The ship's survival module lands on a planet peopled with a lost colony of telepaths. The seeming randomness, disorder, and anarchy of the telepathic society cannot fit the captain's rigid mode; however the insane, uninhibited homosexual Jai has found a home. Evne, an exotic paranormal member of the colony, gradually leads Jai to a mental wholeness, healing his damaged mind. As the realization grows that Jai's entire civilization suffers from similar disorders, the telepaths expand outward to mend the torn fabric of Terran societies.

The incredibly vivid sensual nature of living in a truly open paranormal society sets the tone for this harsh indictment of Terran society. The rigid rules and laws that society imposes on the individual twists and contorts their nature, Russ seems to be saying in true Rousseau-like fashion; this necessitates letting down the barriers, releasing the hurt and anger, to help us cope with everyday living. Using the tehcnique of an outsider thrust into an alien society, Russ provides a mirror for humanity's wounded souls. And yet this is not altogether a hopeful, upbeat message, for the telepaths have been tampered with and have killed their mentors. The tone of savage sensuality and mockery provides the reader with a sense that Russ may not be pointing to an intrinsic good in humans, but instead to a natural amorality, an expression of her own existential philosophy. The stream-of-consciousness style present in most of Russ's work is ideally suited for highlighting the nature of a paranormal society. An exciting and mind-expanding novel that improves with rereading, it is not easy or light entertainment, but is beautifully crafted and original.

The Female Man. Written with four female principals, Janet, Jael, Joanna, and Jeanine, the novel is a cross-time and alternate realities dialog between four women. Jeanine Didier is struggling with her feminine role on a present day Earth, one that never came out of the Great Depression and never experienced the social upheavals of a Second World War. Her main concerns are pleasing her lover Cal, her cat Mr. Frosty, and wondering where she can get her next pair of nylons. Janet Evason (who also appears in

"When It Changed") is a resident of Whileaway, the female utopian world many centuries in the future. Joanna is a familiar feminist product of our contemporary society, a melding of the other characters. Jael, also called Alice Reasoner, is an assassin, a product of a future literal war of the sexes. The four alternately disgust, horrify, and amuse each other as each narrates and reveals their secret dreams and most erotic vices.

The dizzying internal dialog that sets the uneasy, disturbing tone for the reader, enhances the free-wheeling feminist style, with alternate passionate sexuality and exquisite humor. The humor rests mostly in the earlier passages, those which reveal the thoughts and hopes of Jeanine and Janet. In the latter half of the book, more layers have been stripped away, with Joanna and Jael revealing a deep core of violence and anger expressed in graphic sexual passages and raw flaring dialog. The book is an uneasy amalgam of humor and anger, leaving the reader fascinated, but not lightly entertained. The critics have found little common ground in their criticism, with most male reviewers patronizingly disappointed and most female reviewers sympathetically amused. The novel is an outstanding and extraordinary work of literature certain to enhance and enlighten with each rereading.

Picnic on Paradise. Alyx is a thief. Thrown into the Grecian Seas some four thousand years in the past for stealing, she is accidentally scooped up more dead than alive with other ancient Tyrean samples by a group of archaeologists from the Trans-Temporal Center. An agency located in Earth's far distant future, the Trans-Temporal Center never seems to quite be able to get things right. Alyx is recruited for her elemental nature and primitive survival skills. As the novel opens, she has been sent to Paradise, a resort planet, to try and rescue a group of stranded tourists caught in the middle of a commercial war turned very bloody. She regards this war as something of a picnic, and herself as the only adult, herding a group of overgrown children. As the group moves across the surface of the world, the situation becomes progressively more grim. Losing members of her party to the brutal weather and the hunters, Alyx finally loses touch with reality, retreating into a fantasy world, forcing the other survivors to cope with the present without her aid. But the tourists are too much a product of their highly technological society; they cannot discipline themselves to live in the present, concerned instead with their trappings of civilization, accouterments that may doom them.

This Nebula award nominee is the most tightly plotted and constructed of Russ's works. With a clear beginning, development, and ending, Russ clearly states in her vivid narrative style her powerful messages regarding the nature of the human condition and the nature of our technological society that has left us a crippled group of nonsurvivors. Once again, Russ's heroine is a stranger, an alien observer, moving across a hostile landscape, placing her looking glass up to the cracked and warped characters that surround her. The first of Russ's novels, this work is the least experimental and easiest to read, but lacks the full force of her later, more powerful indictments of modern society.

We Who Are about to . . . Eight human passengers of a wrecked spaceliner attempt to survive on a deserted world. The female narrator is a maverick, a cynical antisurvivalist. The other passengers are all optimistic that they will survive to form a thriving "lost world" colony. But the narrator tells a grim tale of reality. These are the civilized products of a highly technological society, one far ahead of even twentieth-century Earth. They lack survival skills, an adequate gene pool, or sufficient supplies. They do have a murderous narrator, who eventually drives herself to execute each of the other survivors. The final part of the novel is like a madwoman's soliloquy, as she tries to regain control of herself.

This grim rejoinder to survivalist fiction is less successful than most of Russ's other works. The mesmerizing vision of the berserk narrator as she sets out on her bloody foray is gradually replaced by 100 pages of meandering thoughts on feministic philosophies, existentialism, and self-revelation. The words are beautifully crafted, the tone is merciless. There is, however, an essential optimism lacking that one has come to expect from Russ. This is not so much a tale of survival as a polemic tract. She raises questions that have no easy answers and challenges the conventional science fiction wisdom that relies on hope and the human will to survive.

The Zanzibar Cat. This 1984 collection of short stories is most notable for its inclusion of Russ's 1968 Nebula award winning "When It Changed," various vampire fantasy stories, and one final Alyx story. "When It Changed" is a wonderfully written story well worth the purchase price of the entire volume. Russ creates the world of Whileaway, a female Utopian lost colony, devastated ten generations before by a plague which killed off all the men. Learning to artificially fertilize ova, the society is able to continue its generations, gradually adjusting to the lack of male domination. Janet Evason and her wife, Katy, live on a farm with their three children. When the first men in ten generations land on their farm, Janet is forced to deal with her increasingly hostile reactions to the men's patronizing pity for their plight. The story brings home joltingly the sense of powerlessness and rage that is felt when all that you honor and have fought to obtain is so casually dismissed. The vampire stories deal with female vampires in the Victorian age. The Alyx story, "A Game of Vlet," is situated in ancient Tyre, prior to Alyx' accidental recruitment into the Trans-Temporal Agents ranks. Admittedly inspired by an Avram Davidson tale, Russ creates a satirical yet terrifying story of magic gone awry. An elaborate and cursed gaming board provides some thieves with a key to the governor's palace. Alyx is irreverent and irrepresible as she bloodily manipulates her opponents. Like the other Alyx stories, the tone is savage, although the style less didactic than in her other works. However, Russ indicates that this is her final Alyx story. Two very fine jewels are reprinted here in all their humor--"Dragons and Dimwits" is a fantastic take-off on all those hideous magic tales, while "Useful Phrase for the Tourist" is a riotous Earth/alien phrase book. The full range of Russ's talents are demonstrated in this collection, showcasing her evolution from the early tentative fragile feminist voice of the 1960s to the confident spirit of the 1980s.

Biographical/Bibliographical Readings

Beverly Friend, "The Female Man," in *Survey of Science Fiction Literature*, ed. Frank Magill (Salem, 1979), v.2, p.766-69. Marilyn Holt, "Joanna Russ," in *Science Fiction Writers*, ed. E. F. Bleiler (Scribner's, 1982), p.483-90. Charles Platt, "Joanna Russ," in *Dream Makers* (Berkley, 1983), v.2, p.191-201. Natalie Rosinsky, "A Female Man? The 'Medusan' Humor of Joanna Russ," *Extrapolation* 23:1, p.31-36. Joanna Russ, "Toward an Aesthetic of Science Fiction," *Science Fiction Studies* 2 (1975), p.112-19. [Colleen Power]

RUSSELL, ERIC FRANK

Life and Works

Eric Frank Russell was born in 1905 in Sandhurst, England, into a military family. He spent most of his youth living in Egypt and the Sudan while his father served as an army instructor. Russell, himself, served in the King's Regiment from 1922 to 1926, and once again during World War II in the Royal Air Force. At the age of thirty-two, his first science fiction story was published, "The Saga of Pelican West" (1937), and from that point on, he became a regular contributor to *Astounding*. Russell's first novel, *Sinister Barrier* (1948), is reported to have spurred on the inaugural publication of the American science fiction magazine, *Unknown*. His other novels include: *Dreadful Sanctuary* (1951), *Three to Conquer* (1956), *Wasp* (1957), *The Great Explosion* (1962), and *The Mindwarpers* (1965). He was a contemporary of Olaf Stapledon and somewhat influenced by Stapledon's metaphysical views and projections of the spiritual awakening of humanity, which is particularly evidenced in *Sentinels from Space* (1954). Russell reputedly introduced Stapledon to the phenomenon of science fiction magazines--a phenomenon which seems to have astounded Stapledon by pointing out the number of writers contributing to that genre and of which Stapledon seemed virtually unaware. There are several collections of Russell's stories, some of which are: *The Best of Eric Frank Russell* (1978), *Deep Space* (1956), *Six Worlds to Conquer* (1958), *Far Stars* (1961), and *Like Nothing on Earth* (1975). Russell died in 1978, nearly fourteen years after he stopped contributing to science fiction.

Themes and Style

Many of Russell's novels reflect a familiarity with the military and strategic intelligence installations, due to his father's military career and his own involvement. He describes very vividly the immense bureaucratic complexities involved with government operations and draws a sardonic picture of the classic military personalities. Russell's novels for the most part reflect the writing style inherent in the fast-paced cloak and dagger espionage adventure. Although the settings are quite futuristic and the warring sides are forces from different planets, the action and analysis are quite similar to twentieth century military tactics. In yet another vein, Russell has published a series of short stories that feature a space crew of mixed lineage--Martian and Earth types--and characterized by the presence of a well-liked robot of large proportions named Jay Score. The comraderie of the crew, and the interaction of their personalities, gives this series of stories, collected in *Men, Martians and Machines* (1958) a quite different aspect from his other novels. There is a great deal of humor in Russell's story writing, and a delicacy and sensitivity that is emphasized in many of his short stories. He particularly portrays the tentacled Martians as amiable if somewhat different characters. The Jay Score Martians are fanatic chess players and capable of doing several things at once with equal concentration. They are somewhat offended by human body scents, and carry around bottles of hooloo scent to dim the effect. At the same time, they can exhibit childlike excitement that makes their tentacles quiver, and vague shades of color to radiate from their bodies like animated strobe lights. Jay Score is an unusual robot in that one quickly forgets his mechanistic heritage and sees him capable of feeling human emotions. Many of the themes of Russell's stories and novels deal with awareness of the futility of war and warlike behavior in favor of the peaceful recognition of the value of the basic warm emotions of friendship, love and tolerance for the differences and varieties of lifeforms everywhere.

Plot Summaries of Major Works

Dreadful Sanctuary. The plot is set in 1972, when rocket probes are setting out for Venus and meeting with unexplained self-destruction. Along with the abortion of space missions, various key scientists and engineers mysteriously die or disappear, and the unraveling of these events becomes the task of John J. Armstrong, a trusted agent, Hansen, and a number of other allies. They discover a secret but politically powerful organization known as the Norman Club, meaning "nor-man" versus "hu-man." The history of Earth beings is described as beginning with the aboriginal yellow-skinned races of Terra, which are added to by human types that originated on Mars (white-skinned), Venus (brown-skinned), and Mercury (black-skinned). Many thousands of years ago, the aborigines of Earth were by far the most primitive compared to their extraplanetary counterparts who had managed to devise equipment that could measure sanity, and who defined insanity as a characteristic of those marked with an innate ability to wage war among themselves and therefore contribute to their self-destruction. The sane, peaceful sorts were left on their home planets, but Earth was designated as a repository for the insane. The Martian, Venusian, and Mercurian rejects were shipped to Earth and bred among the native Terrans (many of whom were sane, but still developmentally far behind), and the Earth's population evolved into its current form. Meanwhile, the Norman Club has become a self-appointed guardian group of life among the planets, determined to thwart ongoing space exploration of primitive minds until their morality catches up to their technology.

The ominous suggestion of the superbeing and moral judgment of others reflects a sensitivity to the war calamities of the 1940s. The view of humanity as having evolved from a conglomeration of insane Martians, Venusians, and Mercurians is quite funny in a way. In another way, it is perhaps an excuse for evolving human warlike conditions. It is the faced-paced adventure and risk and violence characteristic of many detective novels that defines Russell's style.

The Mindwarpers. An enemy plot, attributed to foreign governmental powers, is exposed that attempts to weaken the defense base of the United States by thinning out the scientific and engineering professional pool. Top secret government engineers and scientists begin to resign from their positions, or disappear from their families, or even die. The rate of attrition is not so noticeable at first as to create panic, but does attract the attention of United States investigative forces. Richard Bransome is a metallurgist in a government security installation which is reminiscent of many such top secret laboratories. Bransome suddenly becomes aware that evidence has turned up which is connected to a crime he himself committed years before. His fear of being discovered is so overwhelming that he is obsessed with his predicament, takes an unscheduled leave, and returns to the alleged scene of his guilt. He is followed by an investigator who sees him as yet another mysterious professional dropout. Bransome's panic intensifies, once he is aware of being followed, and he goes through a series of chases and strategic escapes before he realizes the reasons underlying his feelings of guilt.

Russell often bestows telepathic powers or other evolved mind skills on his characters throughout his writing, as his prediction of the developments of the future both technologically and biologically. The explanation for the disappearances of America's top scientists is a form of hypnosis--so advanced and effective is the imposed guilt for nonexistent but deeply believed events that the victims escape from their jobs and their lives rather than risk self-exposure. It is the scientific inquiry mind set that overrides caution in the case of Bransome, and thus reveals the unknown enemy's plan. Action, along with telepathy and psychology, are the main qualities of this novel, rather than intricate, futuristic projections.

Sentinels from Space. The novel offers a description of the future situation of humanity after space travel is practical and colonization has occurred. At the point in time of the novel's setting, Mars, Venus, and Earth are populated by humans who began on Earth. Mars and Venus are colonies repeating an old historical pattern of wanting political independence from their mother source, and feeling the active resistance of Earth to give it to them. Thus there is unofficial warfare, sabotage, and a need for unofficial defense and interversion. The inhabitants of the colonies differ from Earthbound humans in that they have evolved unique characteristics. The long-term space travel necessary to reach Mars or Venus, in addition to the rather thin atmosphere of Mars, particularly, has subjected the colonies to prolonged cosmic ray bombardment which in turn stimulates mutational occurrences evidenced in an assortment of special abilities. Thus, there are hypnotics, teleporters, telepaths, facial mimics, pyrotics, and many other variations of futuristic talents. Genetic laws dictate that only the dominant strain survive, resulting in one special talent usually evidenced in an individual. When individuals appear with an array of special abilities, they are highly suspect as possible aliens, or ominous freaks. David Raven and his wife, Leina, are two such unusual individuals on Earth--as are Charles and Mavis on Venus, and Horst and Karin on Mars. The World Council (the main security arm of Earth government) has identified Raven as an individual with a uniqueness that qualifies him to intervene as an undercover agent in the escalating hostility between the colonies and the Earth. While these threesomes fill their roles in the Earth colonies' struggle, there is, for them, a sense of immunity from death. In the final moments, their true purpose is revealed--that of guardians of humanity in the forms it takes on its planets, for humans are in a grublike form, analogous to larvae awaiting metamorphosis into the equivalent of a winged spirit. The structure of the political situation produces the inevitable political dishonesty and disloyalty along with bombastic and pompous power holders.

This early novel may well show an influence of Olaf Stapledon's writings on Russell's thought lines. It is certainly the most metaphysical of the Russell novels suggesting an optimistic existence yet in store for humanity. Spy thriller action abounds, with the use of special talents giving at least colorful variety. However, there is also a second story line coexisting throughout the fast-paced plot: the story that explains the existence of such characters as David Raven, Leina, Charles, Mavis, Karin, and Horst. They apparently lack fear, no matter what the risk, and exhibit a calm acceptance of the inevitable. In contrast to the typical Russell adventure plot, the proposal of life after death, along with its delicate symbolism, ends the novel with a startling poetic finish.

Wasp. James Mowry is assigned to infiltrate a war zone on the planet Jaimac (ninety-fourth planet of the Sirian Empire) and sabotage the politically fueled Sirian attack against the Terran civilization. Although the Sirian combine has been held at bay for years and at the expense of many deaths, the Terran approach is now to inject within the Sirian borders adventurers who revel in risk-taking and who will undermine the war mentality of the citizens of the enemy civilization through subtle propaganda techniques, well-placed assassinations, and anything else it takes to create a mental reversal of the populous. There are not great numbers of these adventurers--in fact, only one "wasp" per planet--and singularly, but as effective as the small but painful insect namesake, the strategy may prove as effective as sending great hordes of armies to achieve a weakening of Sirian power.

Once Mowry is situated on Jaimac, the novel proceeds with the style of a war adventure--fast-paced, violent, and stealthy. The science fiction angle of the plot is nearly absent, save for the unfamiliar place names and terminology. There is the addition of a little device called a "periboob," an amusing fake device resembling a periscope in the water, with the ability to duck under water level at the approach of a ship, genuinely mimicking the behavior of an authentic submarine periscope. The effects of social and mob psychology are exploited throughout the novel. This work is probably the least science fictional of Russell's novels in the science fiction genre.

Biographical/Bibliographical Readings

Malcolm Edwards, "Eric Frank Russell," in *Science Fiction Writers*, ed. E. F. Bleiler (Scribner's, 1982), p.197-203. Sam Moskowitz, "Eric Frank Russell," in *Seekers of Tomorrow* (Hyperion, 1966), p.133-50. **[Lorraine E. Lester]**

SABERHAGEN, FRED

Life and Works

Fred Thomas Saberhagen was born in Chicago, Illinois, on May 18, 1930. After attending parochial school in Lombard, Illinois, and public school in Byron, Illinois, he graduated from Lane Tech High School in Chicago. He then served as an enlisted man in the U.S. Air Force from 1951 to 1955, operating electronics gear aboard B-36 aircraft. In 1956, he returned to Chicago, enrolled at Wright Junior College, and started work as an electronics technician for Motorola, Inc. In 1957, he received a two-year degree from Wright. In 1962--after publishing his first science fiction story, "Volume PAA-PYX," in the February, 1961 issue of *Galaxy*--he left Motorola to become a free-lance writer. From 1967 to 1973, Saberhagen worked as an assistant editor for *Encyclopaedia Britannica*. Since 1973, he has been writing science fiction full-time.

Unlike many other commercially successful science fiction writers, Saberhagen sold his first story relatively late--when he was in his early thirties. Since then, however, he has produced dozens of short stories, around two dozen novels (one novel, *Coils* [1982]) is a collaboration with Roger Zelazny), and five collections of short fiction. He has also edited two thematic science fiction anthologies: *A Spadeful of Spacetime* (1981), stories about time travel without time machines; and *Pawn to Infinity* (1982), science fiction stories based on the game of chess.

Saberhagen favors series writing. In fact, he is best known for the Berserker series, in which humanity struggles for thousands of years against killer machines (called Berserkers) whose primary programming is to seek out life and destroy it wherever they find it. To date, Saberhagen has written four Berserker novels and more than twenty Berserker stories. The four novels are *Brother Assassin* (1969), *Berserker's Planet* (1975), *Berserker Man* (1979), and *Berserker: Blue Death* (1985). Saberhagen's short story collections that contain only Berserker stories are *Berserker* (1967), *The Ultimate Enemy* (1979), and *The Berserker Wars* (1981). In addition, a few Berserker stories may be found in Saberhagen's two other collections: *The Book of Saberhagen* (1975) and *Earth Descended* (1972).

The Berserker series is barely half of Saberhagen's science fiction output; much of the other half is also series writing. He retells the tale of Count Dracula in a loosely connected series of four novels: *The Dracula Tape* (1975), *The Holmes-Dracula File* (1978), *An Old Friend of the Family* (1979), and *Thorn* (1980). Dracula also appears briefly in *Dominion* (1982). In each of these novels, Saberhagen rationlizes the count's powers and makes him sympathetic, thus correcting the "bad public image" given to Dracula by the vile Bram Stoker. Interestingly, Saberhagen also retells Mary Shelley's *Frankenstein* in *The Frankenstein Papers* (1986). Saberhagen's trilogy--*The Broken Lands* (1968), *The Black Mountains* (1971), and *Changeling Earth* (1973)--are about a postholocaust world where machines have become animate and where magic works. After thoroughly revising all three of these novels, Saberhagen published them together in 1979 under the title *Empire of the East*, which is now the definitive edition of this trilogy.

Themes and Style

In his nonseries work, Saberhagen varies tried-and-true science fiction themes. His first novel, *Golden People* (1964; revised 1984), uses an idea he returns to in *Empire of the East*--a force field negates all high technology within it. *Water of Thought* (1965; revised 1981) presents a newly colonized alien world and a potent liquid drug. *Specimens* (1976) is a science fiction horror story about an interstellar probe and possession by an alien. Two of his nonseries novels are alternate history stories: *Mask of the Sun* (1979), in which twentieth-century soldiers of fortune fight during the early 1500s alongside the Incas against Pizarro's Spaniards, and *A Century of Progress* (1983), in which a man from 1984 travels back to Depression era Chicago in order to insure the demise of the Nazi Third Reich. *Love Conquers All* (1979) uses the science fiction technique of inversion--casual sex is the norm, chastity is sinful, and men go to brothels in order to look at the stars and philosophize with fully clothed women. In *Octagon* (1981), a young boy convinces a Los Alamos supercomputer that the game they are playing is real--with results as interesting as those in the 1985 movie, *Wargames*, which uses the same theme. *The Veils of Azlaroc* (1978), Saberhagen's most original novel, converts time into a physical substance--a veil that falls yearly on the star planet Azlaroc, covering everything and eventually isolating old-timers from the newly arrived.

Saberhagen believes that science fiction is helping to define what humanity and the universe are all about. More specifically, his work, especially the Berserker series, deals with life's war against death and with the differences between organic and mechanical consciousness. His strongest work also blends straightforward adventure with historical, literary, or mythic allusions. For instance, Johann Karlsen, the hero of "Stone Place" in *Berserker*, reminds us of Washington, Lincoln, and even Jesus Christ; *Brother Assassin* has characters similar to Leif Ericsson, St. Francis of Assisi, and Galileo; "In the Temple of Mars" and "Masque of the Red Shift" (both in *Berserker*) allude to Chaucer's "Knight's Tale" and Poe's "Masque of the Red Death;" "Starsong" (reprinted in *The Book of Saberhagen*) reprises the myth of Orpheus and Eurydice; and details in *Berserker Man* recall the Arthurian quest for the Holy Grail.

Critics fault Saberhagen for a sometimes awkward style that is, at its best, merely workmanlike; for plots that are sometimes overly schematic or mechanical; for flat characterizations; for indulgence in the quasioccult; for unconvincing villains (most of whom are simply evil); and for disappointing endings. Nonetheless, his stories sell, mainly because he has a natural feel for narration, a sound scientific imagination, the ability to make the unfamiliar convincing, and a flair for seeing possibilities in time-worn science fiction or fantasy conventions. Also, despite his gritty realism and insistence on the universal presence of evil, Saberhagen is an optimist--it is often a close thing, but in his stories life always triumphs over death.

Plot Summaries of Major Works

Berserker. The eleven stories in this collection first appeared in *Galaxy* between 1963 and 1966. All eleven stories form part of Saberhagen's Berserker cycle, a series of tales about a war between humanity and gargantuan killing machines known as berserkers because of their monomaniacal ferocity. Created by a race now long extinct for a conflict long ago settled, the cybernetic machines have survived their creators, but continue to obey their original programming--searching the galaxy for life and destroying it whenever they find it. Inevitably, the berserkers meet the human race, now space-going.

Six of the stories stand alone, although each vignette explores an aspect of the human berserker war. In "Without a Thought," Del Murray foils a berserker mind beam (which causes temporary amnesia and insanity in humans) by figuring out how to make his not-very-smart aiyan (half-dog, half-ape) mimic a human being learning a simple board game. In "Good Life," the title character discovers that his berserker master had lied to him--with fatal results to the berserker. As the berserkers gather in "Patrons of the Arts" for a concerted attack on Earth, Piers Herron, the world's greatest living artist, accompanies a museum ship carrying artistic treasures to safety. Herron is a cynical, antilife aesthete, but after being captured and then released by a berserker, he discovers that he loves living and humanity after all. Carr, the pacifist protagonist of "The Peacemaker," fools a berserker into curing his cancer. "Mr. Jester" pairs a berserker confused about its purpose with a human being who tries to bring laughter to a planet ruled by fun-hating bureaucrats. Finally, "Sign of the Wolf" shows a cautious berserker lured to its death at the hands of a planetary defense system ignorantly worshipped by primitive people unaware of its real function.

The other five stories in the collection focus on Johann Karlsen, hero of the first major human victory over the berserkers. Other important characters in these stories are Mitchell Spain, a Martian poet; Hemphill, a man determined to punish the berserkers for killing his family; and Felipe Nogara, Karlsen's brother, the ruthless ruler of the Esteel empire. "Stone Place" tells how Karlsen, high commander of Sol's defenses, heals the tensions threatening to divide his fleet just in time to triumph over the berserkers--and lose his fiancee. In "What T and I Did," the man who betrayed Karlsen's fiancee to a berserker finds love, and through love, the ability to control his evilness. Based on "The Masque of the Red Death" by Poe, "Masque of the Red Shift" examines Nogara's decadent court, which, as in Poe's story, welcomes its own destroyer--a berserker machine disguised as a brainwashed rebel. "In the Temple of Mars" borrows its central idea--the temples of Venus, Diana, and Mars--from Chaucer's "The Knight's Tale." Jor, a gladiator, has been programmed by Katsulos, one of Nogara's police and secretly a berserker-worshiper, to assassinate Hemphill, who is now a high admiral. The plot fails when Lucinda frees Jor, whom she loves, from his martial programming. And in "The Face of the Deep," Karlsen, orbiting a hypermass (a black hole), saves himself when he discovers how to distinguish between berserkers and humans.

Berserker Man. Years, possibly centuries, after humanity nearly defeated the berserkers in an epic battle, the berserkers have recouped and are stronger than ever. In a desperate attempt to fend off extermination, Tupelov, the Terran Secretary of Defense, has overseen the development of a new weapons system, code-named Lancelot. Constructed of force fields, Lancelot confers on its wearer super powers, including sensory acuity, faster-than-light speed, near invulnerability, and titanic strength. Unfortunately, Lancelot requires a human brain as an active component--and most humans are not strong enough physically to make use of the weapon. Tupelov searches among humanity's one hundred billions for someone capable of wearing Lancelot.

Humanity's savior turns out to be Michel Geulincx, an eleven-year-old wood-working artist growing up on the distant planet of Alpine. Michel's adoptive parents, whom he thinks are his bioparents, are Sixtus and Carmen Geulincx. Michel's bioparents are actually Elly Temesvar and Frank Marcus, who conceived him while they were under berserker attack just before they entered a mysterious region near the Galactic Core--the Taj. Tupelov brings Micel and Carmen to the Terran solar system, where Michel is soon caught up in the problems of learning how to master Lancelot. As Michel matures, he masters Lancelot, is captured by a berserker sneak attack but manages to escape. He learns of his real mother and father and roams the galaxy in search of them.

He eventually takes his place as the human representative among the humans who form a mysterious community in the Taj.

The novel illustrates Saberhagen's tendency toward mythologizing in the Berserker stories. Here the myth is clearly the Arthurian quest for the Holy Grail, with Michel as the pure, potent child-hero, Galahad; Marcus as Lancelot, Galahad's father, unable to do what his son can do; and the Taj as the Grail castle, sheltering the magnificent Grail Company. But despite the mythological underpinnings, despite the familiar details of the Berserker series, and despite Saberhagen's craftsmanship, *Berserker Man* is not totally successful, mainly because in the last third of the novel Saberhagen rushes through Michel's development. Nonetheless, Saberhagen breaks new ground here, for Michel and the Lancelot weapons system evolve into something unique--a human/machine symbiosis transcending the cast-iron distinctions between life and nonlife, so important to the berserker mentality. One wonders what will happen should Michel, in a future story, emerge from the Taj.

Empire of the East. This novel is made up of three previously published novels, *The Broken Lands*, *The Black Mountains*, and *Changeling Earth*. Thousands of years ago, nuclear war had broken out on Earth. However, moments before most of the deadly missiles hit their targets, a defense computer had initiated a process, called the Change, calculated to revise subatomic reality and make nuclear explosions impossible. This Change was supposed to be temporary, but slight miscalculations and a second, unforeseen Change issuing from the other side made it nearly permanent. The result, millenia later, is that the North American continent is enthralled to an empire ruling in the East. Magic reigns and "Old World" technology is all but forgotten, but feared and distrusted when it is remembered.

Rolf, a young farmer, joins the Free Folk (guerilla forces of the West) after Eastern soldiers butcher his parents and kidnap his sister, Lisa. Chief among the Free Folk are its leader, Thomas; its wizard, Loford; and its best warrior, Mewick. The local Eastern authority is Satrap Ekuman, whose beautiful and evil daughter, Charmian, is about to marry Lord Chup of the Northern Provinces. Both West and East are searching for a mysterious old world object called Elephant, which turns out to be a nuclear-powered tank. And, indeed, Elephant plays a large part in Ekuman's defeat, as do two magical objects: the Thunderstone (which causes a storm whenever it changes owners) and the Stone of Freedom (whose bearer cannot be imprisoned).

After her father's defeat, Charmian has fled to the viceroy of the East (Som) in the Black Mountains. Aided by the wizard Hann and a handsome young soldier, Charmain plans to overthrow Som. Lord Chup reveals Charmian's plans to Som and is promised the leadership of Som's elite guard if he will sacrifice Charmian to the the demons serving Som. The demons are nuclear explosions transmuted by the Change into conscious and evil survivors of the East. Before the sacrifice, the Demon/Lord sallies forth to battle the Western Army.

John Ominor is emperor of the East and his great demon is called Orcus. Prince Duncan of Islandia is the leader of all the Western Forces. Ominor is worried about a mysterious being calling itself Ardneh, which has surreptitiously helping the West. Ardneh leads a group from the West to its cave which houses the heart of a hydrogen fusion power lamp, and Ardneh is revealed as the Automatic Restoration Director-National Executive Headquarters. In other words, Ardneh is an old world computer capable of changing the world back, when it deems the time is propitious.

Empire of the East blends sword and sorcery with technology. On the one hand, the novel contains bloody swordplay, beautiful women, exotic and dangerous flora, sentient animals (flying reptiles and large diurnal birds), magical objects, good and bad sorcerers, demons, vicious villains, and virtuous heroes. On the other hand, it has nuclear-powered tanks, fire extinguishers, medical evacuation helicopters, rejuvenation centers, and geothermal heat exchangers. But until the final section, Saberhagen inverts the usual relationship between these two aspects. In our technological world, scientists scoff at magic; in Saberhagen's magical world, sorcerers scoff at technology. The novel also blends two different styles. It is both a straightforward adventure story and a didactic tale cautioning against overreliance on technology.

The Veils of Azlaroc. Azlaroc, a star-planet, forms a three-body system with a pulsar and a moderate-sized black hole. As the system sweeps along, it gathers interstellar matter until, about once a year, it deposits that matter--reconsituted by the unimaginable forces of the pulsar and the black hole--on Azlaroc. This annual event is called veilfall and once an object is enveloped by a veil, it becomes more and more isolated from objects existing in the present. Other important concomitants of veiling are that veiled objects cannot leave Azlaroc, that time passes slowly for objects within veils, and that for a veiled object the planet's topography remains the same as it was at the time of veiling.

Three groups of humans are on Azlaroc: explorers, settlers, and tourists. Four hundred years earlier, the explorers had been caught by a veilfall, thus becoming Yeargroup One (all humans veiled during a particular veilfall are called a yeargroup). Gradually, as news of Azlaroc's uniqueness spreads, other human beings decide to settle on the star planet. Finally, still others just come to visit, leaving well before veilfall, which by now is accurately predictable. As Sorokin and the immensely wealthy Ramachandra, both settlers of Yeargroup 410, attempt to leave Azlaroc, a tourist, Leodas Ditmars, has been hired to retrieve a book written by one of the Yeargroup poets. Another tourist is seeking to find a woman caught in Yeargroup 365. An explorer from Yeargroup 1, Chang Timmins, aware that veilfall will be unprecendently early this year, tries to warn the tourists, but is too late.

This novel is composed from four short stories with Azlaroc furnishing the setting and motif. Saberhagen knows how to embroider on a basic concept and in this novel we learn about interpenetration (when a tourist and an explorer, for example, cohabit the same space), quantum seeding (the method Azlarocean plant life uses to propogate), and "diving" apparatus (diving apparatus spreads the veils, thus improving communications between people separated by many veils). The novel seems fragmented and yet the brilliance of the concept overwhelms both character development and the metaphoric, philosophical, and psychological possibilities of the veiling idea. The daring idea of a place where hundreds of time frames coexist simultaneously is truly original and his treatment of Azlaroc is a testament to Saberhagen's fecund sense of wonder.

Biographical/Bibliographical Readings

Leonard G. Heldreth, "In Search of the Ultimate Weapon: The Fighting Machine in Science Fiction Novels and Films" in *The Mechanical God: Machines in Science Fiction*, ed. Thomas P. Dunn and Richard D. Erlich (Greenwood Press, 1982), p.129-52. Alfred D. Stewart, "Fred Saberhagen," in *Twentieth-Century American Science-Fiction Writers* (Gale, 1981), v.2, p.94-96. Idem, "Fred Saberhagen: Cybernetic Psychologist," *Extrapolation* 18 (1976), p.42-51. [Todd H. Sammons]

ST. CLAIR, MARGARET

Life and Works

Margaret St. Clair was born on February 17, 1911, in Hutchinson, Kansas. She has spent most of her life in California, including her college years at the University of California, Berkeley, where she received her M.A. in 1933 (Phi Beta Kappa). Her maiden name was Neeley. She married Eric St. Clair in 1932. From 1938-41 she helped him as horticulturist at the St. Clair Rare Bulb Gardens in El Sobrante, California. Since 1945, she has been a full-time writer. Her husband Eric has also published in *Magazine of Fantasy and Science Fiction* and has written some children's books.

St. Clair began publishing science fiction with "Rocket to Limbo" for *Fantastic Adventures* in 1946, at a time when her detective and other fiction was being rejected. Her best known pseudonym was Idris Seabright when writing for *Magazine of*

Fantasy and Science Fiction. Her first story under the Seabright name was "The Listening Child," which was chosen by Martha Foley as a distinguised short story of 1950. For several years, Idris Seabright was as well known as Margaret St. Clair and perhaps more highly regarded. She has since become one of the more noted women in the field. In the late 1940s, St. Clair wrote the Oona and Jiks series which appeared in *Startling Stories.* St. Clair feels that she has been far more successful as a writer abroad than in the United States. She has had about 150 stories published. Many of her best short stories appear in *The Best of Margaret St. Clair* (1985). There are twenty stories in this collection, with publications ranging from 1949 to 1980. Other collections of her stories are in *Three Worlds of Futurity* (1964) and *Change the Sky and Other Stories* (1974).

Her first novel was *Agent of the Unknown* (1956), which originally appeared as "Vulcan's Dolls" (1952) in *Startling Stories.* Other novels include *The Green Queen* (1956), *The Games of Neith* (1960), *Sign of the Labrys* (1963), *Message from the Eocene* (1964), *The Dolphins of Altair* (1967), *The Shadow People* (1969), and *The Dancers of Noyo* (1973).

Themes and Style

St. Clair was a woman writer who did not have to disguise her sex in order to be successful as a writer in a male-dominated field. Her earlier work is rather more subtle than the contemporary pulp fiction of the time. She was able to write in a natural female voice at a time when some women writers of science fiction were outdoing the men in tough-flavored style. Margaret St. Clair had a penchant for tackling conservative themes and for using gadgetry and environments symbolically. For example, her short story "Idris' Pig" (1949) is an adventure comedy set on Mars. Her earlier works introduced some sensitive characterizations, including portrayals of housewives, single mothers, and young children, into a field which was highly technologically oriented. Her earlier tales also had a larger fantasy element than her later works. St. Clair's best work is tightly written short fiction. Her novels are not as consistently well crafted as her shorter work. While some of her longer works suffer from overambitious exploration of diverse themes, the best of her novels are those most concerned with the individual's experience with the extraordinary, or a group's commitment to a visionary future as in *The Dolphins of Altair.* Two of her novels, *The Green Queen* and *The Games of Neith,* feature heroines as active characters who are either chosen to lead or inspire their respective societies toward change. In *Neith,* the female protagonist is an early example of a woman working equally with a man against evil forces. St. Clair chooses to write science fiction because of her feeling that it develops a global consciousness, not only to humanity, but to the other inhabitants of this world as well.

Plot Summaries of Major Works

The Best of Margaret St. Clair. There are twenty stories in this collection. The collection shows the range of writing and St. Clair's development as a writer. Only those stories considered science fiction have been summarized here--the others are horror and/or fantasy.

In "Child of Void" (1949), things are not right in Hidden Valley. Eddie, the narrator, is a ham radio operator, but has problems getting his radio to work properly. Other strange things happen and Eddie and his brother discover a luminous egg which presents them with alluring visions of those things they most desire. Whatever is in the egg has come to Earth to colonize it and needs the juice from electricity to hatch. It can also use the energy from anger, so it creates situations which lead to anger. Eddie tries to blow up himself and the egg, but starts an earthquake instead, which sends the egg into outerspace, except for Ischeevar, who now lives in Eddie's big toe. "Hathor's Pets" was first published in 1949. Hathor was the Egyptian sky goddess, personification of the sky in which the sun rises and sets, which is how the Hathor of this story appears to her pets. Except that these pets are humans, passengers on a stratoliner which got into trouble and came to Hathor's planet in a lifeboat ship after their stratoliner crashed. They try several different schemes to get Hathor to let them go home, but they are only punished for their efforts. The story puts the humans in the role of pets, a reversal of Earth roles, and strengthens St. Clair's theme of kindness toward all inhabitants, be they plant or animal. "Idris' Pig" (1949) was originally entitled "The Sacred Martian Pig." The pig is a sort of Martian cult figure and everyone on Mars wants to possess it. As the pig is traveling from Earth to Mars, George Baker, the shipboard psychiatrist, is talked into delivering the pig to a patient. George has many adventures as he tries to fulfill his mission. The story is a mixture of adventure, romance, and comedy.

In "Brightness Falls from the Air" (1951), the Ngayir, or bird people, live on a planet colonized by Earth. The last remaining Ngayir put on aerial fights for the delight of humans. Kerr tries to help them and is attracted to one of the Ngayir, Rhysha. Rhysha participates in an aerial fight to get money for food and is killed. The problems of intergalactic sociology are incisively extrapolated in this brief study of a culture uneasily propped up by "bread and circuses." For all the luminous beauty of her storytelling, it is a poignant picture of a once-creative citizenry using its triumphs to gratify a lust for vicarious bloodletting. The story "New Ritual" (1953) features a female protagonist and gives a fu-

turistic twist to the plight of the dissatisfied housewife, as a deep
freezer turns everything from apricots to an inattentive husband
into more desirable items. "Prott" (1953) takes place on the edge
of an asteroid belt, where a diary attached to a signal rocket is
found. The diary tells how its writer went out to learn more
about the prott, which is a nonprotoplasmic form of life. They
try to communicate with the writer using telepathy. The prott
seek an active listener. Rather than lead them back to Earth, the
writer never returns but stays in space. He does send back the
original signal rocket and the reader learns that the prott followed
the rocket and found Earth anyway. They are pestering everyone
to listen to them. "Short in the Chest" (1954) features Marine Major Sonya Briggs and a philosophical robot called a "huxley."
When Major Briggs is sent out to find out why newborn pigs will
not nurse, she finds no answer. She goes to the huxley, who unfortunately has a short circuit and and tells her to shoot her next
sexual partner. This story is remarkable for its portrayal of
women and its grappling with questions of sexuality. In the future time, relations between the armed forces are not very good.
To relieve interservice tensions, sexual relations between members
of the different services is ordered. The triviality of the newborn
pigs, plus the dysfunction of the robot, make for a hilarious story.

"The Nuse Man" (1960) is a salesman, or Nuse Man, who sells
mysterious powers originating on the far side of the year 3000.
The salesman tells his story to a woman who never buys from him,
but does listen to his stories. He had sold an ipsissifex, a type of
matter duplicator, to the king of Ur who used it make bricks to
build temples. After the king's death, the son had a problem with
the brickmakers, who have been put out of work by the machine,
and the bricklayers, who have too much work to do. When the
salesman returns for his money, all the old temples have been torn
down and life is back to normal. In "The Old Fashioned Bird
Christmas," (1961), the bird referred to in the title is not a turkey
or even a goose, but a raven. Reverend Clem Adelburg preaches
against the excessive use of lights at Christmas. This theme does
not make him popular with the PE&G, a subsidiary of Nous, the
Infinite, which supplies power. In a state of siege by the bird
emissaries of the power company, Adelburg uses prayer for escape.
Mazda, his wife, uses magic to help him; when the two forces converge with the power source from the future, the result is a transfer to an alternate world of Neo-Druidism. "The Wines of Earth"
(1967) tells of John da Volara, a sixty-five-year old grower of
premium wine grapes in the Napa Valley. He lives alone and likes
a glass of wine while he works on his books. When Joe is visited
by aliens who are doing a wine tour of the galaxy, Joe offers
them his best wine which they politely taste, but they are not impressed. They take Joe to their ship where he tastes their wine,
and it is superb. The visitors leave one of their bottles of wine

with him. "Is this how Dionysius came to the Greeks?" wonders Joe, as he puts away the very special bottle of wine.

"Wryneck, Draw Me" (1980) is the most recent story in the collection. The reader never knows who the narrator is, partly because the narrator, "I," does not know itself. "I" appears to be the sole surviving independent personality within "Jake." Jake is a computer into which many people elected to be stored when the world was dying from pollution. "I" knows that it hates humanity because of the destruction that humans caused to the world. Jake has fallen in love with itself. It builds a superpenis and vaginal tunnel, but even this does not satisfy Jake, and it goes quiet. In the end, creatures invade the tunnel. "I" feels not hands, but paws, and "I" feels secure knowing the Earth is in good hands--oops, paws.

St. Clair's progression from 1949 to 1980 reveals her great concern for preserving the planet and its inhabitants. Most of the stories contain a good deal of wry humor and irony in addition to the didactic aspect. Women treated as equals and sexuality are the themes in several of the stories. St. Clair enjoys writing the stories and also makes them fun for the reader.

The Dancers of Noyo. The setting is California after a series of earthquakes, followed by plagues, have decimated the population. Sam MacGregor, a Pomo Indian, is training to be a medicine man. Much of the population that survived is American Indian. The tribal societies are divided between the Mandarins, the older generation, and the young people. Dancers are clones who force the young people to dance by using whips. Criminals are given chemicals to control their violence. Sam has leadership potential and is seen as a threat to the Mandarins and the Dancers, so he is sent on a a vision trip, sort of a quest for the Grail, by the Dancer of Noyo, his settlement. Sam is given a natural drug to stimulate visions. On his trip Sam meets Franny O'Hare, daughter of the scientist who created the Dancers, and saves her life when her community commits mass suicide. They hide in her father's laboratory and there they discover where the Dancers are grown and destroy the embryonic ones. When Sam reaches Gualala, the destination of his Grail trip, he is put on trial. He manages to escape and kill the master dancer. All the other Dancers die at the same time and their spell is broken. Life will change as the younger generation demands more input and control.

The story relies upon a male protagonist to hold together a tale of the future. His quest for personal identity is set against a world dominated by powerful androids, the Dancers. The rural life is extrapolated from the communal movement so prevalent in America in the 1960s. Drugs play an important part in this world and it shows what could happen if the drug culture remains strong. The ultimate happy ending rests with the ability of the young people to rebuild a new society.

The Dolphins of Altair. The narrator is the dolphin Amtor, who is also the dolphin historian. Amtor is physically deformed with a rudimentary hand on his left side, just one effect of pumping radiation into the oceans. Madaline "Maddy" Paxton, who is also called Moonlight or Sosa (after a dolphin heroine) is a secretary at the Naval Research Station, receiving telepathic communications from the dolphins as they seek humans to help them in their cause. These dolphins are not ordinary dolphins, but the descendants of an alien race which came to Earth from the planet Altair. Many of the dolphins are held captive by the Naval Research Project. The original aliens were amphibians, but in order to live on Earth, they divided themselves into humanoids, who interbred with the humans, while others became dolphins. Maddy is unsure about the communications from the dolphins and seeks the aid of Dr. Ted Lawrence, a psychiatrist. Meanwhile the dolphins also contact Sven Erikson, an explosives expert. After the dolphins are freed from the research stations, work begins on the project to melt the polar ice caps to cleanse the oceans and save the dolphins. The ice caps are melted with assistance from Altair, and the oceans rise about a hundred feet, destroying many coastal population centers.

This work presents a cogent argument for the full sentience of dolphins, and makes some frightening suppositions about the repercussions of capturing and treating intelligent animals as beasts. It is a moving work critical of humanity's disregard for the ecosystems of Earth.

Biographical/Bibliographical Readings

John Clute, "Margaret St. Clair," in *Science Fiction Writers*, ed. E. F. Bleiler (Scribner's, 1982), p.491-95. Margaret St. Clair, "Introduction: Thoughts from My Seventies," in *The Best of Margaret St. Clair*, ed. Martin H. Greenberg (Academy, 1985). Idem, "Wight in Space: An Autobiographical Sketch," in *Fantastic Lives*, ed. Martin H. Greenberg (Southern Illinois University Press, 1981), p.144-56. **[Mina Jane Grothey]**

SCHMITZ, JAMES H.

Life and Works

James Henry Schmitz was born on October 15, 1911, in Germany. The son of an American businessman, he spent his early life in Germany except for a year at business school in Chicago. While serving in the U.S. Air Force during World War II, he began writing science fiction, publishing "Greenface" in 1943 in *Unknown*. He did not become a full-time writer until the 1960s. He married Betty Mae Chapman in 1957. Schmitz died on March 18, 1981.

His first collection of stories, *Agent of Vega*, published in 1960, chronicles the adventures of the Zone Agents of the Vegan Confederacy. They are stories of adventure, alien invasions, and galactic conquest, all done with a touch of humor. Schmitz's stories have been collected in *A Nice Day for Screaming and Other Tales of the Hub* (1965) and *A Pride of Monsters* (1970).

Two of Schmitz's novels combine strong women characters, alien invasion, and a humorous touch. In *The Demon Breed* (1968), a powerful invasion force is terrified into a complete retreat when Dr. Nile Etland, a scientist, convinces them that she is a Tuvela, a supernatural guardian of humanity. Etland has assitance from three mutant otters who delight in tricking the alien invaders. *The Witches of Karres* (1966) follows Captain Pausert and three girls with unusual psychic powers through a series of adventures. They escape from pirates, travel through time, become involved in imperial politics, and ultimately save the universe. Pausert is both helped and hindered by a giant vatch, an energy entity which believes that Pausert and all of his adventures are part of the vatch's dream until the vatch discovers that it can be captured by Pausert.

Themes and Style

Like much of Schmitz's best work, *The Witches of Karres* mixes psychic powers, romance, adventure, and humor. Most of Schmitz's work concerns the efforts of an individual or small group to deal with a dangerous threat to humanity or one of the characters. It may be a galactic problem, such as Danestar's efforts to stop an alien signal in "The Searcher," or a more personal problem, such as Telzey's efforts to save her pet crest cat in *The Universe against Her* (1964). In either case, the successful resolution is usually achieved by the intelligence, resourcefulness and stubbornness of the protagonist.

Schmitz has two main series characters, both of whom are adventurous women. Trigger Argee, introduced in *A Tale of Two Clocks* (1962), is a government agent who discovers that she has a latent telepathic affinity for alien life forms. Telzey Amberdon is the heroine in *The Universe against Her*, *The Lion Game* (1973), and *The Telzey Toy* (1973). Telzey is a young law student who uses her considerable telepathic abilities to help her friends and the Federation. Trigger and Telzey work together in "The Symbiotes" (1972) and "Compulsion."

Schmitz's characters frequently have extrasensory powers. Telzey is a telepath whose talents develop more fully as the character matures. In *The Witches of Karres*, the people of Karres have a wide range of psychic powers. Psychic abilities are an accepted

tool of governments and private security agencies throughout
Schmitz's Federation stories.

Schmitz's work is notable for his use of women as main characters. In a time when women rarely appeared in most science
fiction, Schmitz was unique in making them the protagonists of
his space adventure stories. The women in his works range in age
from young girls to grannies; they are capable, efficient, and intelligent, with a sense of humor about themselves and the universe.

Plot Summaries of Major Works

The Demon Breed. The Parahuans believe that the Federation
is protected by a secret race, the Tuvelas, who are responsible for
the Parahuan defeat in an earlier war. The Parahuans have decided to test their theory and the Federation defenses by invading
the planet Nandy-Cline. Dr. Cay, a scientist, is captured but manages to leave information about the invasion and the belief in the
Tuvelas for Dr. Nile Etland. Although Dr. Etland is a biologist,
not a government agent, she uses the resources of the area, such as
plants that release acid bombs, to terrify the Parahuans into believing that she is a Tuvela, frightening them into abandoning the
invasion. The Federation council must consider the galactic implications of the defeat and the best means of taking advantage of
this second defeat of the Parahuans. In a final shift, there is an
analysis of the invasion by a third group which had been considering attacking the Federation. Their debate about the possible
existence of Tuvelas leads to an analysis of the dangerous nature
of the Federation, with or without Tuvelas.

Nile is not a Tuvela; she is an intelligent, capable and skilled
human who uses her environment to survive and provide tools.
She is not overconfident, however; she knows the risks and is
afraid, but will not allow her fear to keep her from taking action.
The Demon Breed shows Schmitz's ability to tell an interesting adventure story with a heroine who uses her knowledge to overcome
her opponents.

The Universe against Her. Telzey Amberdon is a fifteen-
year-old law student, daughter of a member of the Federation
Council. She is vacationing on the planet Jontarou when she is
informed by a government agent that her pet is a crest cat, a
species believed to be extinct, and must be taken to the Federation
Life Bank. Humans had hunted crest cats for sport, but hunting
them became very dangerous--for every crest cat that was killed, a
hunter also died. After humans began hunting the crest cats from
aircars, the crest cats apparently became extinct. Telzey's crest
cat communicates with her telepathically, telling her that the crest
cats are still on Jontarou and that their council wants Telzey to
help them meet with the human government. The crest cats, who

are intelligent, telepathic, and capable of invisibility, had considered the early hunts a challenging sport, but when humans used unfair advantages such as aircars, the crest cats went into hiding. They now want official Federation recognition as an intelligent species, or they will declare war on the humans. The planet administrator is initially reluctant to believe Talzey's report, but quickly changes his mind when the crest cat council becomes visible in his office. Telzey helps arrange the treaty, and sadly leaves her former pet on Jontarou.

The Psychology Service on Earth, which tries to monitor those persons with psychic abilities and to recruit some of them for government service to insure that their powers are not misused, discovers Telzey's powers. The service plants a psychic warning in Telzey's mind, causing her to become aware of a disapproving police officer who is always around when she uses her psychic abilities. Since she is uncertain about the motives of the service, she tries to find ways to work around the warnings. Back at law school, Telzey uses her developing abilities to save a classmate, Gonwil, from being killed. Telzey alters the memories of her classmate's dog, proving to a court that Gonwil was the innocent victim of a conspiracy. The Psychology Service reluctantly agrees that Telzey's solution was the best choice, given the personalities involved. When Telzey at last manages to make her psychic police officer vanish, she discovers that the service put it there as test to see if she had the ability to remove it.

The novel combines many of Schmitz's favorite elements: a strong heroine, psychic powers, sentient aliens, and swiftly moving adventure and humor. The feline crest cats demand admiration and respect in their efforts to become recognized as legitimate forms, which then will allow them to function as individual lifeforms rather than as pets. Telzey's psychic abilities enable her to help both sentient aliens and other members of her own human race. Not only does she show strength, but also a great deal of compassion toward all living beings.

The Witches of Karres. Captain Pausert from Nikkeldepain had been on a very long and succesful trading expedition and was looking forward to returning home to his fiancee after his final stop on Porlumma. Being a kind man, he could not stand idly by as a young female slave was beaten, even if his only solution was to purchase her and her two sisters. The girls are from Karres, a legendary planet whose inhabitants have a wide range of psychic abilities. After visiting Karres and working with the girls, Pausert begins to develop psychic abilities of his own. Pausert and the witches face many dangers, including pirates of the Agandar, energy entities, war robots, and an invasion of aliens from another universe. They do save the universe in an interdimensional confrontation, triumphant at last, even if the crisis seems to have been ignored by the rest of the Empire. When

Pausert and the witches visit the Empress of Karres, most of the court appears ungrateful and even unaware of the many battles fought by Pausert and the witches to save their planet.

The Witches of Karres is full of exotic settings, unusual creatures, and interesting characters. There are continual problems for Pausert--just when he believes that the situation is under control, something else goes wrong. The episodes are very similar to the serial "Perils of Pauline" as the group moves from one adventure to another. As in much of Schmitz's writing, the women characters are strong characters with psychic abilities, there are unusual plot twists, strange adventures, and unusual aliens, and all are treated with a sense of humor.

Biographical/Bibliographical Readings

"James H. Schmitz," in *Speaking of Science Fiction: The Paul Walker Interviews* (Luna Publications, 1978), p.85-100. Mark Owings, *James H. Schmitz: A Bibliography* (Croatan House, 1973). Amelia A. Rutledge, "James H. Schmitz," in *Twentieth-Century American Science-Fiction Writers* (Gale, 1981), v.2, p.100-102. [Linda K. Lewis]

SCORTIA, THOMAS N.

Life and Works

Thomas Nicholas Scortia was born on August 29, 1926, in Alton, Illinois. Scortia believes that the early loss of his father provided a critical influence over his later development. His mother managed to hold together the family's business interests and encouraged Scortia's eclectic scientific interests. Encountering his first science fiction magazine, *Astounding Stories*, at a local drugstore in 1939, Scortia became an instant addict. With stints in the military during World War II and after, Scortia completed his chemistry degree in 1949 at George Washington University. He began writing science fiction in college, submitting his first story, "The Prodigy," to *Science Fiction Adventures* in 1953. The magazine ceased publication and never paid Scortia but, encouraged by his first sale, Scortia began a successful career. Scortia's sound scientific knowledge comes from his training as a physical chemist. After working in several companies including Celanese Corporation and United Technology, Scortia rather bitterly parted ways over management disputes. Since 1970, he has been a full-time writer, known best for his disaster novels. *The Glass Inferno* (1974), coauthored with Frank Robinson, was adapted as the movie *The Towering Inferno*. His most significant and timely novel to date, also coauthored with Robinson, is *The Prometheus Crisis*

(1975), which deals with a severe nuclear plant meltdown. Yet another collaboration with Robinson, *The Nightmare Factor* (1978), deals with biological warfare. *Artery of Fire* (1972) is one of the few science fiction novels to use a handicapped person as the hero. His early short stories are collected in *Caution! Inflammable!* (1975).

Themes and Style

Thomas Scortia's work is characterized by fast action, suspense, and solid science. Concentrating on the near future, most of Scortia's novels deal with the aerospace and nuclear energy industries. Often designed as a disaster theme, Scortia constructs dark satires when dealing with the industrial complexes. His heroes are often technicians within an industry who pay the price for the disasters arising from incompetent management. The pessimistic tone of Scortia's novels is often offset by the essential optimism lurking beneath Scortia's despair, creating complex and dramatic appeals to the reader's intellect.

Plot Summaries of Major Works

Artery of Fire. Norman Bayerd is a principal scientist working on the new power grid located in space. He suffers from a crippling disease known as Cushing's syndrome. On Earth, he would be disabled, but in space, Bayerd is able to live a fairly normal, if painful, existence with the help of remotely controlled androids. The power grid from the outer planets to Earth is badly needed to provide the fissionable materials the planet needs to survive, but someone is trying to sabotage the work before it is finished.

With quick switches from exotic, oriental locales on Earth to the eerie glow of the power grid, Scortia's first science fiction novel reveals the strength and coherency that reaches fruition in Scortia's later collaborations. Drawing on his knowledge of aerospace technology, the author reveals a fine grasp of the need for suspense and action to keep the novel moving quickly. This is one of the few science fiction novels to use a handicapped person as the hero of the tale. The novel also stresses a familiar theme with Scortia, the role of the scientist in a civilization that maintains a delicate balance between the political necessities of upper management and the reality of what technology pushed beyond reasonable limits can wreak on the civilization.

The Nightmare Factor. Dr. Calvin Doohan is a British epidemiologist working for the World Health Organization. Called in on a mysterious outbreak of a Legionnaire-like disease with a startling one hundred percent mortality rate, Doohan finds himself quickly embroiled in the political machinations between the federal and local government agents. The mysterious epidemic is eventually revealed as part of a right wing plot within the federal government to establish an effective biological warfare weapon. The weapon itself proves to be doubly dangerous because of an extremely complex mode of transmission and frighteningly long-term genetic disturbances. The rapid fire sequence of events as the various scientists are eliminated and their investigations obliterated produces a novel that is hard to put down. Biological warfare may be a humane weapon, compared to nuclear warfare--it can also be readily manufactured at low cost with even primitive equipment.

Coauthored with Frank Robinson, the theme is that of near future terrorism through biological warfare. The suspense in the novel is sustained to the very end. One puzzling pattern that appears in this novel, as well as in other Scortia-Robinson collaborations, is the development of two major characters, and the now predictable death of one of those characters by the conclusion. Despite this flaw, which tends to restrict the reader's involvement, this novel is well written and timely.

The Prometheus Crisis. Begun in the style of testimony given before a select committee hearing on the meltdown of the Prometheus One nuclear reactor in California, the committee discovers a terrifying sequence of nuclear construction design flaws, corporate mismanagement, and bad luck. The plant's manager, Greg Parks, and assitant manager, Barney Lerner, become victims of the political machinations that surround the tightly interwoven relationship between the federal government and the nuclear industry. The reader is led from the meltdown itself to the consequences on the local population, on agriculture, and on major metropolitan problems.

Coauthored with Frank Robinson, this is the original "China Syndrome" novel about the meltdown of a nuclear reactor and the consequences of such a disaster. This novel has been both prophetic and dwarfed by the events at Chernobyl. Scortia attempts to demonstrate the lengths to which a government desperate to provide nuclear power will go to cover up the culpability of those involved. As with later Scortia novels, the scientists and middle managers will pay the full price for both their own miscalculations as well as those of the more distant corporate managers and politicians. *The Prometheus Crisis* is a grim, fast-moving novel with minimal characterization. It is a very realistic science fiction nightmare of the near future that reflects an almost unbelievable reality surrounding a nuclear power conspiracy.

Biographical/Bibliographical Readings

Thomas Scortia, "Science Fiction as the Imaginary Experiment," in *Science Fiction Today and Tomorrow*, ed. Reginald Bretnor (Harper & Row, 1974), p.135-48. "Thomas Scortia" in *A Reader's Guide to Science Fiction*, ed. Baird Searles et al. (Facts on File, 1979), p.128-29. George Zebrowski, "Thomas Scortia," in *Twentieth-Century Science-Fiction Writers*, ed. Curtis C. Smith (St. James, 1986), p.635-36. **[Colleen Power]**

SHECKLEY, ROBERT

Life and Works

Robert Sheckley was born in New York City on July 16, 1928, but grew up in Maplewood, New Jersey. Upon graduation from high school, he moved to California and performed a variety of odd jobs until joining the army in 1946. He served with the occupation forces in Korea until 1948 when he moved back to New York City and enrolled at New York University. In 1951, he graduated with a B.A., and the same year he sold his first story, "Final Examination," to *Imagination* magazine. He sold ten stories in 1952 and nearly fifty in 1953, allowing him to devote his full time to writing and to satisfy his lifelong love for world travel.

Many of these stories went to the newly founded *Galaxy* magazine under the editorship of Horace L. Gold. Science fiction was undergoing a major change in those days, moving away from the nuts and bolts space operas and starting to explore the possibilities in the soft sciences, such as psychology, sociology, and anthropology. *Galaxy* was, for Sheckley, a godsend for those who could not understand physics, mathematics, or numerology. During this period, Friday night poker games were held regularly in Gold's apartment, and the regulars included, besides Sheckley, such luminaries as Isaac Asimov, Jerome Bixby, Algis Budrys, Frederik Pohl, and William Tenn. Sheckley credits his voluminous output of short stories during the early and middle 1950s both to Gold's relentless prodding and to the fact that he felt very comfortable with that length of work. Perhaps due to this exposure, many of his works that were considered classics were, if not dismissed, at least not fully appreciated at the time. It is remarkable and lamentable that none of his works has recieved a Hugo or Nebula award. He published three collections of short stories, *Untouched by Human Hands* (1954), *Citizen in Space* (1955), and *Pilgrimage to Earth* (1957) before writing his first novel, *Immortality Delivered* (1958), later revised as *Immortality, Inc.* (1959).

While tapering off in his production of short stories, he has continued to publish novels at irregular intervals. Most of these are either expanded stories of earlier stories or use central themes previously developed. His novels include *The Status Civilization* (1960) about a society populated entirely by criminals with strictly enforced rules of conduct, including killing another human being before one is allowed to become a "free" citizen. *Journey beyond Tomorrow* (1962) shows how an observer from the far future might misinterpret our time due to incomplete and distorted records. *The Tenth Victim* (1966) is a novelization of the screenplay he wrote for the film of the same name based on his earlier short story, "Seventh Victim" (1953). *Mindswap* (1966) concerns a man whose body has been swindled from him. Travel through various alternate worlds is the theme of *Dimension of Miracles* (1968). In the 1970s, Sheckley published *Options* (1975) and *Compton Divided* (1978). From January of 1980 until September of 1981, Robert Sheckley served as fiction editor for *Omni* magazine and upon stepping down remained as contributing editor. In *Dramocles* (1983), Sheckley takes his shot as sword and sorcery with, as usual, humorous results. *Victim Prime* (1986) is the long-awaited sequel to *The Tenth Victim* and *Hunter/Victim* (1987) and continues his vision of a world where legalized murder is a way of life.

Themes and Style

Sharp, piercing satire laced with more than a touch of humor characterizes most of Sheckley's work. He has managed to spear most of society's sacred cows at one time or another and has not hesitated to parody science fiction itself. The ultimate space adventure lampoon may indeed be "Zirn Left Unguarded, the Jenghik Palace in Flames, Jon Westerly Dead," collected in *Nova 2* (1972). Sheckley's humor runs the gamut from broad slapstick and visual humor as in the AAA Ace Planetary Decontamination (and Transportation) Service stories written in the 1950s, to the macabre, such as "Watchbird" (1953), detailing a technological solution to an an age old problem that goes horribly awry. Sheckley's matter-of-fact style serves to disguise the fact that his tongue is often firmly in cheek, and it is difficult to discern when he is being serious and when he is setting us up for the surprise ending. Also apparent is his disdain for the urban metropolis which he usually portrays as either a desolate wasteland or free-for-all combat zone inhabited by con artists, small-time hoods, and assorted other misfits.

A major theme created by Sheckley is the idea of the "hunt," first seen in "Seventh Victim," in which, due to various societal pressures, murder has become legalized with its own rigidly codified rules and regulations. This idea and variations play important roles in many of Sheckley's works, including *Immortality, Inc.*, and is the primary theme in his latest novels, *Victim Prime* and *Hunter/Victim*. Another recurring theme utilized by Sheckley is the mind having the ability to migrate to a different body. The ramifications of this migration furnish the plot lines for *Immortality, Inc.* and *Mindswap*, and the theme is also used to a lesser extent in other novels and stories.

Sheckley's protagonists are generally rather ordinary young or middle-aged individuals thrust into extraordinary circumstances. They are likely to be naive, even bumbling, and to be swept along by the flow of events instead of being in control. Cool, jut-jawed heroes will not be found in his stories except for purely satirical purposes. Particularly in his short stories, characterization is relegated to a secondary role, the extrapolation of a particular event or situation to its logical conclusion being the primary focus. This is a successful formula for Sheckley and when he deviates from it, as he does in some of his later novels, mixing straight narrative adventure with deep metaphysical introspection, the results are not as satisfactory. One of his greatest strengths is his ability to convey, usually with a great deal of wit, that we live, basically, in a very hostile universe that was not designed with human comfort in mind. Our role in the grand scheme of things may not be reordained as rulers of the galaxy, but is more apt to be along the lines of suckers or cosmic victims, barely scraping to get by. His numerous stories of contact with alien cultures invariably involves some key misunderstanding or lack of knowledge on the part of humans leading to either disastrous or humorous results.

Plot Summaries of Major Works

Citizen in Space. In the title story, the main character has developed an inferiority complex because the government does not pay enough attention to him. Everyone is entitled to constant surveillance and merits his own spy, but his is decidedly second-rate and causes him much embarrassment with his friends. Dissatisfied, he emigrates to a distant planet. Along the way he encounters, first, a stowaway, then a young boy stranded in space, and finally, various other characters whose true purpose is to spy on him and each other. Alas, the spies are also incompetent and he must both rescue them and pretend that he is not aware of their duties. He becomes ruler of his own planet, but now everyone on Earth wants to defect there and he cannot get anyone to spy for him.

In "A Ticket to Tranai," the hero books passage to a planet that appears to be the perfect utopia--no war, crime, or poverty, with a stable economy that does not resort to socialistic, communistic, fascist, or bureaucratic practices. There is a catch, of course, and the hero learns of it barely in time to escape with his life. "Hunting Problem" concerns the difficulties an alien boy scout has in earning a merit badge. He must procure a pelt of the elusive Mirash in order that it may be affixed to the scout flagstaff. Unfortunately, Mirash is their term for human and a landing ship from Earth has just arrived. It appears bleak for the humans, but all ends happily as the alien boy scout proudly displays his bounty--zippers, tubes, buttons, and holsters flashing in the sunshine.

Humankind receives a harsh lesson in "The Mountain without a Name." Humanity has expanded to other planets and is treating the planets much as Earth was treated, taking the resources and minerals without regard to the environmental or ecological consequences. This time, however, the planet fights back, causing mysterious accidents among the work crew that is trying to raze a mountain. What is more, this is the final straw and the whole universe decides to object to the presence of humanity. In "The Accountant," nine-year-old Morton Dee is failing in school. Instead of being a dutiful son and learning the family trade of wizardry and casting spells, he insists on studying to be a C.P.A. In desperation, his father conjures up representatives of the Dark One to try to scare some sense into the boy, but Morton deftly turns the table and we are given some insight into what ultimate evil might become.

"The Battle" presents an interesting scenario for the end of the world. Suppose in the final Armageddon that the forces of good are represented by a modern, mechanized military force. Who might be raised from the dead on Judgment Day if humans were not actually involved in the fateful battle? This collection of twelve short stories contains several of Sheckley's finer early works. The stories range from space opera to fantasy and include such themes as alien encounters with humans, ecological and environmental concerns, and humanity's search for utopia on other planets. As usual, humankind does not come out too well as an explorer and emigrant to other worlds, intimating that we certainly cannot succeed on other worlds considering the mess that has been made of Earth.

Immortality, Inc. The hero of this tale is Thomas Blaine, a dull, distinctly nonambitious junior yacht designer who awakes one morning realizing that his most recent memories concern his involvement in an auto accident that caused his death. His mind has been snatched from 1958 and transported to 2110, where it takes up residence in a new body, or "receptacle." This is all part of an advertising campaign by the Rex Corporation, a huge conglomerate that manufactures reincarnation machines, hereafter drivers, and the like. Blaine, instead of being grateful for his reprieve from death, immediately starts finding faults with his new body, even though it is clear that it is superior to his previous one. Blaine explores the twenty-second century and tries to relate it to his twentieth-century viewpoint. If you were wealthy and could afford "Hereafter Insurance," then, according to the Suicide Act of 2102, you could become one of the "Hunted," with professional killers willing to give you the ultimate thrill. Blaine's gullibility allows him to be conned immediately. Along the way, he meets some very odd characters and receives quite plausible explanations for such phenomena as ghosts, zombies, and spirit world contact. Blaine almost loses his life permanently, but his trials as he learns to cope with his new life force a maturity on him and he finds a fulfillment that he had not obtained in his previous life.

Originally serialized in *Galaxy*, this was Sheckley's first novel. The future world that he paints is, on the surface, dissimilar to our own, but in reality is still driven by the same human strengths and weaknesses that have been prevalent throughout human history. This future is predicated on the assumption that the death of the body and the death of the mind do not necessarily coincide. This is probably Sheckley's most seminal work, for here he either introduces or amplifies many of the ideas that appear in his later works. He has a very cynical view of this future, but the action moves at such a rapid pace and there are so many surprising twists that one does not really have time to dwell on the bleakness. The ultimate excitement, of being pursued and killed by professional murderers, is alleviated only by the reincarnation possibility which assures immortality and a second chance.

The Tenth Victim. The time is after the fourth world war, and it has been decided that there must never be another one. But the people who have engineered the peace have come to the regrettable conclusion that there is a need for violence in a large percentage of humanity. The scientists have the scientific knowledge to breed this violent aspect from the race, but instead decide that this trait is necessary for the survival of the species. Thus, they decide to legalize murder--strictly voluntarily and governed by strict rules. Once a person signs up, he or she is given two weeks to kill the assigned victim. If successful, the killer then becomes a victim. If the killer survives by killing the hunter, then the person can either quit or start the cycle over again. Within ten years, a third of the world has signed up for at least one kill, and the number eventually settles to a fourth of the population. The Emotional Catharsis Board is the government body set up to regulate and supervise the hunt. The names of the victims are chosen completely at random--the hunter is given only a name, address, and description and must use a standard caliber pistol to kill the prey. The victim is informed of the selection a week before the hunter is given the victim's name.

A range of new services springs up to accommodate this new wrinkle in society. A victim could wear his or her choice of armor, preferably a Protec-Suit with its built-in, guaranteed, no-bulge gun pocket. A victim could also hire spotters, specifically trained to detect the presence of a hunter on the prowl. Hunters, too, have their aides. Ambushes, traps--anything is legal as long as the Hunter does the killing personally, one on one. The penalties for wounding or killing the wrong victim are severe, and to kill for profit or personal animosity is punishable by death. The potential rewards, in addition to the emotional satisfaction, are great. If one hunts successfully ten times, one becomes eligible for the Ten Club, the most elite group on Earth. Members of the Ten Club are granted unlimited wealth, power, and sex. Stanton Frelaine has made six kills and is anxiously awaiting notification of his seventh victim. He has used all types of chicanery and deception to achieve his present status, posing at times as a bill collector or milkman. He had to chase one victim throughout the Sierra Nevada and was wounded before he bagged him. He has read all the standard works on the subject including *Development of the Ambush* and *Tactics for Hunting Humans*. This time, Stanton draws a woman as his prey. The game is open to anyone, of course, but Stanton has never considered a woman as a possible victim. This has always been a "man's" sport. What is worse, the woman, Janet Patzig, does not seem to be taking even rudimentary precautions in defending herself. She has not hired any spotters and appears in public without any protection. The line between hunter and hunted blurs, and Stanton begins to feel as though he is the victim.

This is a classic, lively adventure whose basic premise has been imitated many times. Whether or not the legalization of murder provides an acceptable moral substitute for war is not answered, but is rather presented as an alternative--war, in and of itself, is legalized murder. The novel presents a fascinating and frightening view of the Earth's future.

Untouched by Human Hands. In "The Cost of Living," Sheckley postulates what may happen if the current trends in our credit-based economy are continued. Sheckley's keen eye saw, more than thirty years ago, exactly what is happening in our society. The trend is always to acquire the fanciest new gadgets and the most modern amenities as long as they can be bought on credit. But, with meaningful employment being eliminated by automation, more flexible terms must be arranged, such as mortgaging your children's or even your own grandchildren's future income. They won't mind--after all, it is being done for their own good. "Specialist" postulates a confederation known as "Galactic Cooperation," whose members are bred to have but one function. An organic spaceship composed of sentient beings lands on Earth after one of its propulsion units malfunctions. A soldier is kidnapped, and it is explained to him by the ship's crew that the original purpose of human beings is to serve as "Pushers." The "Pushers" have the ability, when used in conjunction with other parts of the ship, to propel it at velocities in excess of the speed of light. Long ago, a colony of these "Pushers" had been stranded on Earth and, lacking the shipmates needed to fulfill their original purpose, had grown bored and developed such things as civilization. They had become unspecialized, and were not now realizing their true destiny, else why would they be almost continuously at war?

"The Demons" is a comic tale making light of all the pacts with the devil by adding several new twists. In this version, Neelsebub, great-grandson of Beelzebub, conjures up what he thinks is a demon and demands he be given great amounts of gold. Unfortunately, in this case, the demon is Arthur Gammet, an insurance salesman who has no idea what is going on. Searching for a way to placate Neelsebub, Gammet conjures another demon. This one turns out to be an insurance salesman like himself, albeit from another planet, and together they conspire to bottle up Neelsebub while they discuss their common profession.

This first collection of stories secured Sheckley's place as one of the sharpest and wittiest observers of the human condition. The stories were published in 1952 and 1953 in science fiction magazines, primarily in *Galaxy*. That he achieved such maturity and poignancy within two years of publishing his first story is quite an amazing feat. Interstellar travel, the rather mundane insurance salesmen, the mortgaging of children and grandchildren, and the idea that humanity is basically a "propellant" for alien space ships are humorous, yet thought-provoking stories of future Earth.

Biographical/Bibliographical Readings

Malcolm Kiniry, "Robert Sheckley," in *Twentieth-Century American Science-Fiction Writers* (Gale, 1981), v.2, p.102-06. Chris Morgan, "Robert Sheckley," in *Twentieth-Century Science-Fiction Writers*, ed. E. F. Bleiler (Scribner's, 1982), p.497-504. Charles Platt, "Robert Sheckley," in *Dream Makers* (Berkley, 1980), p.19-26. Darrell Schweitzer, "Robert Sheckley: An Interview," *Science Fiction Review* 10:3 (Aug. 1981), p 7-9. **[Bill Trousdale]**

SILVERBERG, ROBERT

Life and Works

Born in Brooklyn, New York, on January 15, 1935, Robert Silverberg was entranced with science fiction when he was still a young boy. While still in his early teens, he was not only writing science fiction stories, but was submitting them to magazines for publication. Although he was not successful in his early attempts at publication, this lack of success did not prevent him from going on to become one of the most prolific science fiction writers and editors of our time. He began serious efforts at publication when he was still a student at Columbia University and with no little success. Many of his efforts were collaborations with magazine writer Randall Garrett, but many were published as solo works.

His first published story was "Gorgon Planet" (1954) and his first novel was for juveniles--*Revolt on Alpha C* (1955).

By September, 1956, recently graduated from Columbia and just married, Silverberg was voted a Hugo award as the year's most promising new writer. Until 1959, Silverberg continued to produce massive amounts of science fiction but then abandoned it for some time, feeling that his artistic abilities would be more highly rewarded financially in other media, e.g., nonfiction books for young readers, biography and other general nonfiction. However, by 1966, he considered himself back into the science fiction mode, although nonfiction continued to involve him. "Hawksbill Station," first published in novella form in 1966, was a turning point for Silverberg's reputation. Nominated for a Hugo as well as a Nebula award, it served to show that Silverberg could turn out material of quality. "Passengers" appeared in 1967, and for this Silverberg won a Nebula. By 1968, he was definitely considered successful in his field. *Nightwings* won a Hugo award in 1969. In addition to "Passengers," Silverberg also won Nebula awards for "Good News from the Vatican" (1970), "Born with the Dead" (1974) and for the novel, *A Time of Changes* (1971). His novella, "The Feast of St. Dionysus," won a Jupiter award in 1972 and *Nightwings* won the 1976 French Prix Apollo award. During his early years, he used many pseudonyms; the most frequently used were Calvin M. Knox, David Osborne, and Ivar Jorgenson.

Silverberg had been living since 1961 in a very large house in New York City formerly belonging to Mayor Fiorello La Guardia. In February, 1968, a major fire broke out in the attic of the house and destroyed most of the house along with many of his materials. Silverberg admits that he was very affected by this event, so much so that it altered his approach to writing. No longer able to produce the prodigious amounts of material that he had earlier in his career, he also began to take a more reflective, visionary tone.

Silverberg continued to write through the mid-1970s; he produced such novels as *Tower of Glass* (1970), *A Time of Changes* (1971), *The World Inside* (1971), and *The Stochastic Man* (1975). Suddenly, after writing *Shadrach in the Furnace* (1976), he announced his retirement from writing science fiction; he was once again disillusioned with the field. Fortunately for his fans, his retirement lasted only a few years, and by 1980 he was publishing again. *Lord Valentine's Castle* (1980) was the first to appear, followed by *Majipoor Chronicles* in 1981. Although different from his earlier introspective works of the early 1970s, Silverberg continues to produce considerable material for the science fiction reader.

It should be noted for the record that Silverberg's enormous production over the years includes many volumes of science fiction anthologies which he has edited, some of which are collections of his own stories, the most recent being *Beyond the Safe*

Zone (1985). These anthologies continue to appear, as do novels and short stories. Although his returns to the world of science fiction have brought changes of theme as well as subject, the returns have been welcome ones.

Themes and Style

Certainly Robert Silverberg must be considered a writer of great technical merit. His early works, turned out with such rapidity, would not have sold without the recognition of a major talent lying beneath. However, it was only when Silverberg began to examine intrinsically more important themes that his talents came to the fore. By the 1960s, he began to explore the more serious ideas that will stay with him as he matures as a writer. A short story, "To See the Invisible Man," handles the theme of alienation, one which reemerges in one of his best novels, *Hawksbill Station* (1967). Both works deal with the pain that accompanies alienation, and within each is the absolution that arises with the main character's understanding of the situation. Likewise the stories "Passengers," "Flies," and "Sundance" evidence the exploration that Silverberg makes into these two very basic themes.

Much of Silverberg's work has little hard-core science, although there is frequently a setting placed in some future time, or a little high technology thrown in. Silverberg's works deal more with introspective characters or political implications than with space travel or bug-eyed monsters. He uses his alien creatures as metaphors for the alienation of humanity. He also uses them as ideals to which humans should strive in terms of their attitudes about life, toward each other and the world. In some writings, the alien world is one which has achieved a much higher spiritual plain than our own. It is not infrequent in Silverberg's works to discover that his alien beings have achieved the ability for rebirth and renewal, as in *Downward to the Earth* (1970) and *The Book of Skulls*.

All the while, Silverberg is experimenting with different literary techniques in his acknowledged attempt to bring science fiction more in line with the techniques of mainstream fiction. He develops different points of view within the same novel (*The Book of Skulls*); he frequently uses present tense narration for the immediacy it provides ("Passengers"); in one of his best and most complex stories, "Sundance," Silverberg uses multiple narrations as well as present and past tense in an effective tale of ambiguity and illusion.

Plot Summaries of Major Works

The Best of Robert Silverberg. In 1976, Silverberg compiled and published this book, which gathers together short stories from his then-twenty-year career, complete with his own introductions to each story. The stories summarized here are representative of Silverberg's short science fiction and clearly demonstrate the changes in style and theme from 1954 to 1971.

"Road to Nightfall" (1958, written in 1954) is set in New York in 2054 after a devastating nuclear war. Humanity has degraded to its lowest form, cannibalism. Paul Katterson has been able to scrounge enough food to keep himself alive. When it is revealed that all food supplies have been cut off from New York, the people resort to capturing other humans for food. Although the story is a very simple one, Silverberg skillfully builds the suspense. One hopes for respite that never comes, and Silverberg's implication of survival outweighing humanity is the final message.

In "Warm Man," Davis Hallinan is the warm man, one who soaks up the troubles of the residents of New Brewster like a sponge. The residents are drawn to Hallinan and reveal to him all their darkest troubles--their adulteries, terrors, secret dreams. After being confronted by a troubled child, Hallinan dies from "overload." Silverberg mocks people and plays on their selfishness. Ironically, Hallinan, who seems like a kindly man helping those who are in need of relieving some of their psychological burdens, is himself not completely selfless; he needs to soak up their troubles for his own self-worth. His final words before dying are, "I. . . was. . . a. . . leech. . . ."

The first two stories were from the 1950s. By 1962, when Silverberg was reentering the science fiction field, he had a new approach. In "To See the Invisible Man" (1962), Silverberg begins to handle the theme of alienation which will reappear in many of his later works. The year is 2104 and the main character has been sentenced to one year of invisibility for the crime of coldness to his fellow humans. He is condemned to wear a mark on his forehead which symbolizes that he is an outcast from society. At first fascinated with his abilities to get away with petty crimes, he soon realizes that invisibility is a curse, for without human intercourse life has no meaning. The year finally ends and, no longer invisible, the man slowly makes his way back into society. He sees another invisible person, feels compassion for him, and is arrested for speaking to him. The cycle begins again.

In "Flies" (1965), the man Cassiday has been rebuilt by the "golden ones" after a space accident. He is returned to Earth in the middle of the twenty-fourth century with only a minor change--he has been made more sensitive to the feelings of his fellows so that he can transmit to the "golden ones" the raw emotions felt by Earthlings. However, it does not work quite as expected. Cassiday returns without a conscience and simply experiments cruelly with the emotions of others. The golden ones realize their error, return him to their planet and alter him once again, this time turning his perceptions inward. Davis Hallinan is then destroyed by the sufferings of other Earthlings. The cannibalism in this story is psychic, rather than physical.

The aliens of "Passenger" (1967) participate in a direct takeover of the bodies of their victims. During the time a person has been taken over, he or she has no memory of what has occurred. In future New York, Charles Roth has just awakened from being "ridden" by a passenger. In an effort to make a connection with his real self, he approaches a young woman, Helen Martin, whom he suddenly realizes that he knew in his ridden state. They attempt to form a relationship, but Charles is taken over by a passenger and, instead of Helen, walks away with an attractive young man. The story is told in the first person and present tense, which gives the story an immediacy and an intensity of feeling. In this case, human alienation has been created by aliens.

"Sundance" (1968) tells the story of Tom Two Ribbons, a biologist with a team of scientists on an alien planet. Ostensibly the task is to eliminate the herds of "Eaters" which destroy the oxygen-producing plants on the planet. Tom's psychological state is such that he begins to confuse the extermination of the Eaters with the extermination of the American Indian and bison on the Great Plains. He drifts back and forth in a dreamlike state. "Sundance" is one of Silverberg's stylistically experimental stories. In an attempt to explore different levels of ambiguity, he uses several different viewpoints and both present and past tenses. Silverberg's stylistic changes shift as Tom's psychic state shifts.

In "Good News from the Vatican" (1971), the Vatican computer has had a hand in the selection of the next pope and the potential pope (a robot) has already promised an agreement with the computers of the Dalai Lama and the Greek Orthodox Church. Six persons sit around a cafe table in Rome and discuss the coming selection; and no one is surprised when a robot is confirmed as Pope Sisto Settimo, or Sistus the Seventh. The whole story is done tongue-in-cheek and is a delightful way of handling the takeover of the world by robots and computers.

These selected stories from *The Best of Robert Silverberg* show the range of Silverberg's work, his technical development, his experiments with different themes and styles, and to some extent, his development as a serious writer. In some ways science fiction has less meaning to Silverberg than the communication of his basic ideas. These stories were written when Silverberg felt that the world was troubled and bewildered, and they are an expression of that belief.

Downward to the Earth. Set in the twenty-third century, the main character, Edmund Gundersen, returns to a planet which had once been colonized by Earth, but has since been returned to its own intelligent life forms. The planet Belzagor, formerly called Holman's world by the colonists, is a primitive world, inhabited by two closely intertwined species, the elephantlike nildoro who

seem the more intelligent of the two species, and the apelike suli-
doror. Gundersen has returned to make his own act of contrition.
While he had been colonial administrator, he had kept seven of
the nildoror from making a pilgrimage of rebirth and had inter-
fered with an inviolable religious rite. Becoming fascinated with
the process of rebirth as well as feeling intense guilt over his actions, Gundersen wants to seek his own rebirth and redemption.

Gundersen journeys to the Mist Country, from the jungles
where the nildoror live to the icy mountains where rebirth takes
place. Gundersen encounters a number of his former acquaintances from the time he was colonial administrator. Each in his
or her own way has used or abused the planet. He meets Van
Beneker, who was once Gundersen's clerk, but now operates a
tourist service escorting world weary groups across the planets. At
Paradise Falls, he reencounters Seena, a former mistress now married to Kurtz, a former colonist who has now assumed a monstrous
form as punishment for abusing the snake serum used by the nildoror in their ceremony. Kurtz had instead used it as an hallo-
cinogen and when he attempted his own rebirth, his shape mir-
rored the monstrous part of his soul. Gundersen eventually
reaches the Mist Country, undergoes rebirth, and becomes unified
with those few humans who have undergone this process before.
Gundersen has become immortal.

Silverberg himself has acknowledged his indebtedness to
Joseph Conrad's *Heart of Darkness* in this novel. The former, a
journey to the interior of primitive Africa upon which the evils
of the civilized world have been imposed, is indeed partially reflected in the primitive world of Belzagor. Silverberg's character
is very aware of the evil imposed by the colonists, but particularly
by himself, as he yearns for atonement. The encounter with alien
intelligence, comparable to African tribes, who are used as slaves
by the colonists, seems an all too familiar theme in our current
world. As with *Nightwings*, alienation and redemption are major
themes to which Silverberg keeps returning.

Hawksbill Station. The Station, a prison for political prisoners from the twenty-first century, exists in the Cambrian era, a
time when the Earth was only ocean and rock. The Hammer, a
time machine which transports everything to the Station, is glow-
ing, but instead of the anticipated food or equipment, a new prisoner arrives. The prisoner is Lew Hahn, and the other prisoners
suspect that he is some sort of spy. Since the Hammer can transmit in only one direction, i.e., from the future to the past, no one
can understand Hahn's purpose. Barrett, the uncrowned king of
the Station, is finally able to confront Hahn and discovers that
reverse transporting is now possible. Hahn has been charged with
making exploratory trips to see if humans still exist in the Station
and if they are sufficiently socialized to return. Barrett offers to

stay so that scientists may come to study the Station and learn what they can about the development of the world.

Hawksbill Station has been written in two forms. The first, a novella published in *Galaxy* in August of 1967, focuses solely on the occurrences at the Hawksbill Station itself and the people who have been banished there. In the novel, the setting is expanded to include the New York City of the future as well as all of the political activity which occurred there and which resulted in Barrett's being banished. The novel introduces the eponymous Hawksbill, inventor of the time machine. The novel shifts back and forth between twenty-first century New York and the Cambrian era in a somewhat uncomfortable way.

The three basic themes found within *Hawksbill Station* are time travel, political injustice, and the infernal struggles of humans with their fate. Barrett is one of the few psychologically stable people left at the Station, and even he is beginning to deteriorate emotionally as he attempts to deal with his increasing age and physical disabilities. As frequently occurs in Silverberg's work, the actual scientific aspects of the novel take a subsidiary role to the development of the characters. The grey sea and a few textbook trilobites generally suffice to set the scene of the Cambrian period. Yet Silverberg accomplishes the sense of utter desolation, of despair and loneliness that makes the Hawksbill Station seem real, a prison for the mind and soul as well as for the body.

Nightwings. In the far distant future of Earth, three people are traveling to the city of Roum. The leader is a Watcher, a member of a guild whose function it is to watch for the prophesied invasion by aliens from outer space. The second traveler is Avluela, a young girl who, because of her butterfly-type wings, is able to fly through air, but only at night. The third, a mysterious "changing," called Gormon, is also a part of the group. As they travel to Roum, they find that the civilization on Earth has degenerated into a Third Cycle from the technological magnificence of its Second Cycle. The city still makes use of some of the relics, but civilization is past its prime. Society is made up of carefully regulated guilds and is ruled by an evil Dominator class.

The Watcher is rejected by the guild, which has become disillusioned by the long years of watching for invaders who never come. Homeless, the three appeal to the Prince of Ruom, who becomes enamored of Avluela. Gormon, who has been her lover, is possessed with rage and vows vengeance on the Prince. As the three tour the city, Gormon announces that he is the alien and has been spying on the Earthlings. He tells the Watcher that indeed an invasion is coming soon. When it does, Earth is easily conquered. Gormon and Avluela fly away together. The Watcher decides to go to Perris in hopes of joining the Rememberers, chroniclers of Earth's history.

Tomis, formerly the Watcher, becomes a Rememberer and finds an image recording showing how the invaders were treated in the Second Cycle of Earth. Tomis travels to Jorslem in the hope of becoming rejuvenated by the guild of the Renewers, a process which allows humans to be reunited through entering one another's spirit. Tomis is successful in the Renewal. The healing process becomes complete and the invasion of the Earth becomes unimportant as all people become as one.

Nightwings was published first as a novella. It originally covered the journey of the three travelers and the arrival in Roum. Although *Nightwings* has a strong mythological background, it can still be considered within the bounds of science fiction. The focus is on the world of the future, one that passed beyond its technological superiority into a world of decadence and decay. Redemption can be accomplished when humans become one spirit. Alienation within one's self, a standard Silverberg theme, is dominant, as is the political issue of dominance by cruel leadership. The lack of understanding of other cultures and the focus on humanity becoming united are presented as themes which continue to emerge in Silverberg's works.

Biographical/Bibliographical Readings

Thomas D. Clareson, "The Fictions of Robert Silverberg," in *Voices for the Future*, ed. Thomas D. Clareson (Bowling Green University Popular Press, 1979), v.2, p.1-33. Idem, *Robert Silverberg: A Primary and Secondary Bibliography* (G. K. Hall, 1983). Robert Silverberg, "Sounding Brass, Tinkling Cymbal," in *Hell's Cartographers*, ed. Brian Aldiss and Harry Harrison (Weidenfeld and Nicolson, 1975), p.7-45. **[Jeanne M. Sohn]**

SIMAK, CLIFFORD D.

Life and Works

Clifford D. Simak was born on his grandfather's farm in Millville, Wisconsin, on August 3, 1904. His respect for the cultural values and rural life of the American Midwest are apparent in his writing throughout his life. Educated at the University of Wisconsin, Simak worked as a newspaperman at several midwestern newspapers for over forty-nine years. His first real job was as a reporter for a paper in Michigan. Afterwards, he also worked on newspapers in Iowa, Minnesota, Missouri, and North Dakota until he joined the *Minneapolis Star*, where he worked as a copy desk editor, news editor, and science columnist until his retirement in the mid-1970s. His wife, Agnes, whom he married in

1929, worked with Simak as critic and typist throughout his career.

At the annual Nebula Awards dinner in April, 1977, Clifford D. Simak was honored with the Grand Master Award in recognition of his outstanding contributions made to the field of science fiction. Not so much for any individual story or novel, this award recognized the entire body of his work as consistently high and worthy of acclaim. Early in his writing career, it seemed unlikely that such a pinnacle of recognition would ever come. He wrote a half dozen short stories (the first being "The World of the Red Sun" in 1931) and one novelette in the early 1930s, but became discouraged with the quality of pulp science fiction magazines and/or the lack of critical recognition his work had received. Whatever the reasons, he stopped writing for several years. When John Campbell assumed the editorship of *Astounding Science Fiction*, he asked Simak to resume writing. Campbell encouraged Simak to write a piece, originally published in 1939, which eventually was published as *Cosmic Engineers* (1950).

One of Simak's best early works began with the appearance of "City," a short story published in 1944, in which the obsolete human institution of living closely together in large groups gives way to rural estates for the wealthy and to primitive tribalism for the have-nots. A series of related stories developed the dangers of machine-dominated cultures and the superiority of more pacificistic, psychically oriented species. In the society of "City," the doggish culture supersedes humanity and institutes the brotherhood of the animals to replace the failed brotherhood of humanity. Eventually, eight stories were gathered together and related through the ingenious device of a canine editor, complete with doggish scholars debating the relative merits and demerits of ancient theories. In the book form, *City* (1952) won the International Fantasy Award in 1953. In 1958, his story "The Big Front Yard" was a Hugo winner. Simak's *Way Station* (1963) won the Hugo award and *A Heritage of Stars* (1977) was a Jupiter award winner.

A prolific writer, Simak published many novels over the years, including: *Time Is the Simplest Thing* (1961), *All Flesh Is Grass* (1965), *A Choice of Gods* (1972), *Destiny Doll* (1971), *Cemetery World* (1973), *Project Pope* (1981), *Shakespeare's Planet* (1976), *The Visitors* (1980), and *Highway of Eternity* (1986). Some of his stories have been collected in *The Worlds of Clifford Simak* (1960) and *Best SF Stories of Clifford Simak* (1967)

Themes and Style

With *Cosmic Engineers*, Simak's theme of questioning the omnipotence of humanity appeared--a theme not in keeping with the optimistic "manifest destiny" theme so apparent in the works of many writers of the 1930s. Campbell is credited with providing

Simak the opportunity to voice these doubts and personal convictions, thus opening the door to others who wished to explore humanity's flaws.

Technology, according to Simak, tends to inhibit humanity's abilities to develop fully. This theme is fully developed in *A Choice of Gods*, in which billions of humans are whisked away from Earth, leaving a pastoral society consisting of a few farmers with their robot staff, plus a few hundred Indians. The people left behind are free to develop their minds and learn to transport themselves to the stars telepathically. The robots, on the other hand, retire to a monastery and contemplate the nature of God. The piety and religious nature of robots is also developed in *Project Pope*, in which a society of robots spend a millenium trying to build an infallible computer at Vatican 17. The mystical and contemplative nature of Simak's work is especially apparent in *The Fellowship of the Talisman* (1978) and *Way Station*.

Simak tends to find a successful device and use it over and over again. Friendly wolves appear in a half dozen of his novels. *Highway of Eternity* and *The Visitors* both have newspaper reporters as protagonists. Simak recognized the increased visibility of women characters in science fiction by making the reporter female in *The Visitors*, whereas *City* had no female inhabitants at all.

One theme which appears quite frequently is that of the benign alien, as in *Highway of Eternity*, *Cemetery World*, *A Choice of Gods*, and *A Heritage of Stars*, among others. Especially is this true in *Way Station*, which is a veritable menagerie of friendly folk from other planets. Incorporeal beings, such as ghosts and spirits, abound in Simak's rural landscapes, along with traditional little people such as gnomes, elves, and goblins. Simak's worlds are peopled by species, including robots, who can work together for the good of all; the message is that brotherhood is not the province of humanity alone.

Plot Summaries of Major Works

A Choice of Gods. Early twenty-second-century Earth was highly technological, complex and crowded, numbering more than eight billion humans worldwide. Then, one day, most of humanity disappears, leaving the Whitney family, their 67 house guests, some 300 Indians, and uncounted robots, to carry on. Left alone, the Earth reverts to a wild and natural state, the only cultivated land being the acres surrounding the Whitney estates. Left without technology, the Whitneys and their house guests develop mental powers to compensate. For example, they learn the art of teleportation, even throughout the star systems. Jason and Martha Whitney stay home to cultivate the gardens of Earth with their robot staff. Other robots build monasteries and study humanity's religions, trying to figure out the role of robots in theology. Still other robots busily work on The Project. The Indians return to nature, reviving their old relationship with the Earth. Jason's twin, John, returns home from star-hopping with two startling revelations: a great force, The Principle, exists at the center of the universe and exerts great power over everything; and the people who had been taken away from Earth have been found and some of their representatives are coming back. When the vanguard of the people arrives, the two cultures, the mental and the technological, seem incompatible. The robots working on The Project reported that The Principle has communicated with The Project and forbidden the travellers to come back to Earth. Realizing that they are in the middle of a controlled experiment with awesome power backing it up, the two segments of humanity agree to go their separate ways.

Simak's contention, that technology interferes with humanity's full development as a spiritual and mental being, is readily apparent in *A Choice of Gods*. The value of rural life, the inner strength derived from the land, the awesome power hidden in the human mind, and the potential for kinship between widely divergent beings are familiar themes which Simak has wrestled with throughout his nearly sixty years of writing. Can a robot or an alien have a soul? Is there a Priniciple or, perhaps, a God, controlling human destiny? Simak may not be a mystic, because he does not answer these questions, but in posing them, he takes on the role of a spiritual and sensitive philosopher.

City. The canine species has become the dominant form of life on Earth. In an effort to examine the "Man Myth" thoroughly, this collection of tales has been assembled. It is difficult for dogs to fully comprehend how the human mind might have functioned, so the readers are cautioned against taking the tales too seriously. "City" is a large collection of humans living under crowded conditions in one place; life is difficult under these circumstances. Cars have become obsolete because of personal helicopters and families have moved to the country. Cheap labor is supplied by robots on family estates in the country. John J. Webster, a former City official, argues that the City has failed and the world is better off for that failure. As people live in the country, however, they become afraid to leave their estates. This is dramatically revealed when a Webster, four generations later, finds himself physically unable to leave his home to save the life of his friend, the Martian philosopher, Juwain. His robot, Jenkins, protects Webster from being forced out of his manor house and condemns him to a life of guilt. Bruce Webster, great-grandson of Jerome, develops a strain of sentient dogs to spy on the mutants living in the hills, descendants of the City dwellers who escaped to primitivism after the exodus. The dogs learn to work with Jenkins and other robots and become the dominant species when humanity deserts Earth for a Jovian paradise in transformed bodies. Only Tyler Webster and a few other humans remain, living in Geneva, seat of world government. The few humans seek various forms of amusements, hobbies, and diversions until Jon Webster returns to the old estate and discovers the developing dogs. Jon fears human intervention in the dog's progress and returns to Geneva, then encloses the City in a secure metallic dome. The dogs develop psychically, and Jenkins helps them discover other parallel worlds. The tales end with the peaceful brotherhood of animals strictly forbidding killing of any kind, even of the ants whose developing civilization threatens canine survival.

City won the International Fantasy Award in 1953. It is possible, Simak contends, that humanity has been spoiled by technology. When the cities decay, man (and Simak refers almost exclusively to the male of the human species) hides out on great estates, aided by friendly robots and sentient dogs. The ridge runners, who revert to a totally primitive life-style, develop mental powers through mutation. Simak's familiar search for brotherhood finds humans left out in *City*; the brotherhood develops between dogs and other animals and robots. The irony Simak introduces is that even the superior canine race can be threatened by another culture, that of the ants. To Simak's way of thinking, civilization and technology definitely impede human development.

Way Station. Enoch Wallace is in charge of the Way Station, and he has been in charge for nearly a hundred years. He had been selected for the job just after the American Civil War. For the most part, his responsibilities consist of providing safe shelter for travelers. And what an interesting lot these travelers are. Take the alien from Thuban VI, for example--he requires a tank with a certain solution in it to be able to breathe, and he communicates with a series of clicks, like a telegraph. Enoch keeps files on all his visitors so that he can improve his hospitality if repeat visitors should return. It is a quiet but interesting life until the outside world begins to intrude. First comes the Watcher, who spies on Enoch, tries to break into the station, and finally steals the body of the unfortunate Hazer who had died while visiting Enoch. Then there is Lucy, the beautiful deaf mute from the poor family down the road. Lucy and Enoch have established a gentle communication about the wild life and woodlands surrounding them. One night, Lucy is savagely beaten by her superstitious father who fears her strange healing powers. Lucy flees to Enoch's cabin for sanctuary. A visitor from the stars recognizes Lucy's talents as a truly spectacular gift that can be used for peace. Enoch's Watcher is persuaded to return the body of the Hazer which calms the criticism of Enoch by the Galactic Center, and Lucy calms the mob of backwoodsmen who threaten Enoch's security. Because of the importance of Lucy's gift to world peace, Enoch is accepted into the Galactic Center's association of worlds.

Way Station won a coveted Hugo award in 1964. The ability of aliens with very different forms and habits to cooperate and coexist is clearly demonstrated by the character, Enoch. Communication, tolerance, and understanding is necessary to establish good relationships betweeen individuals and worlds. Simak clearly feels that the spiritual and psychic power of humans, in this novel depicted by the sensitive deaf mute, Lucy, can be developed only in a rural setting, undistracted by techology and civilization.

Biographical/Bibliographical Readings

Thomas D. Clareson, "Clifford D. Simak: The Inhabited Universe," in *Voices for the Future*, ed. Thomas D. Clareson (Bowling Green University Popular Press, 1976), v.1, p.64-87. Sam Moskowitz, "Clifford D. Simak," in *Seekers of Tomorrow* (Hyperion, 1966), p.266-82. Roald D. Tweet, "Clifford D. Simak," in *Science Fiction Writers*, ed. E. F. Bleiler (Scribner's, 1982), p.513-18. Donald A. Wollheim, "Toward Galactic Maturity," in *The Universe Makers* (Harper & Row, 1971), p.90-93. [Kay Jones]

SMITH, E. E. "DOC"

Life and Works

Edward Elmer Smith was born on May 1, 1890, in Sheboygan, Wisconsin. Smith's family later moved to Idaho. Working as a carpenter, a lumberjack, a miner, and a surveyor, Smith managed to earn enough money to complete his degree in chemical engineering at the University of Idaho in 1914. Smith was hired as a food chemist by the U.S. government in 1915, and moved to Washington, D.C., where he obtained a Ph.D. in food chemistry from George Washington University in 1919. In that year, he began to write his remarkable *Skylark of Space* (1928), with the assistance of Ms. Lee Garvey. With great persistence, Smith submitted *Skylark* to various magazines throughout the 1920s. Finally, Gernsback at *Amazing Stories* agreed to serialize it in 1928. Over the next forty years, Smith continued his Skylark series--*Skylark of Space* was followed by *Skylark Three* (1943), *Skylark of Valeron* (1948), and *Skylark DuQuesne*(1966)--and developed an even greater rival in popularity, the Lensman series. The first volume of the Lensman series, *Galactic Patrol*, was published as a serial in *Astounding* in 1937 and as a novel in 1950. Other Lensman stories were serialized in science fiction magazines in the late 1930s and early 1940s, then severely reworked into novels by the early 1950s. The next three volumes were *Gray Lensman* (1951), *Second-Stage Lensman* (1953), and *Children of the Lens* (1954). He wrote two additional volumes, *Triplanetary* (1948) and *First Lensman* (1950), to provide historical background. In 1957, Smith retired from his career as a chemist, and continued writing until his death in 1965.

Critics are divided on the subject of Smith's importance, with Donald Wollheim's *The Universe Makers* containing a single oblique reference to Smith. On the other hand, some have referred to him as the "colossus of American science fiction" and his importance as difficult if not impossible to overestimate. Despite the disagreement from the experts, "Doc" Smith's popularity with fans continued until his death in 1965, earning him numerous awards including a place in the Science Fiction Fans' *Hall of Fame* in 1964. In the years after his death, Smith's work surged in popularity with readers, and remains today perenially popular with the *Star Wars* crowd.

Themes and Style

"Doc" Smith is regarded as the father of space opera and credited with expanding the scope of science fiction from the limits of the solar system to the unlimited expanse of the universe. With clear-cut, handsome heros and dark villains, his work is reminiscent of the western dime novels that preceded them. And yet, his work is complex and immense in scope. It is believed, for instance, that the Lensmen's four central novels were conceived of as a complete universe in a single 400,000 word work, then broken down to simplify publication. Smith painted his stories on an immense canvas, portraying the future with a breadth and energy that far exceeded his contemporaries. Yet his work has its weaknesses and has not easily withstood the ravages of modern science fiction critics. There is an uneasiness felt by modern readers in the heroes and heroines who tend to be physically perfect and very fair, and villains whose evil seems to have a basis in their darker complexions or deformities. Additionally, the stories often become bogged down because of their complexities, forcing the reader to try and muddle through the structural difficulties. Yet, the energy and excitement, the magic that Smith projects in his expanding vision, cannot be underestimated when one remembers that when Smith began writing, Einstein had not yet been awarded the Nobel prize for his work in relativity, and the scientific proof of the movement of distant galaxies was less than ten years old.

Plot Summaries of Major Works

The Lensman series
Galactic Patrol. Placed hundreds of years in the future, and against a backdrop of multiple galaxies, wars rage between the Galactic Patrol and its enemies. Kimball Kennison, a young Earthman and recent Academy graduate, is swept up in this con-

flict between the forces of good and evil. Backing the patrol are mysterious Arisians who provide the telepathic psionic "Lens" with which each qualified patrolman is equipped. In a battle for control, the pirates of Boskone are threatening the security of the galactic civilization. Kennison and his alien allies become the key players in invading the Boskone's Grand Base, in a scene vaguely reminiscent of *Star Wars*. The battle extends beyond the individual star systems into an ultimate battle for control between two immortal enemy forces, Arisia and Eddore. The Lensmen are a great eugenic experiment by the Arisians to provide the final weapon in their ultimate conflict with the utterly enimical Eddoreans.

In 1937, Smith began the Lensmen series with this first key volume, *Galactic Patrol*, appearing as a serial in *Astounding Science Fiction*. The next three volumes, *Gray Lensman*, *Second-Stage Lensman*, and *Children of the Lens* were soon to follow and may be considered as a unified concept. In fact, some evidence exists that the four were originally one immense novel that Smith broke down into publishable form. When Smith regrouped the series for publication as novels during the 1950s, he wrote two additional volumes, *Triplanetary* and *First Lensman*, to provide historical background for the central core of the tetralogy. Smith's incredible scope in this series has perhaps never been surpassed by another writer. He manages to combine five separate serials into one coherent whole. The fact that he successfully did so may reflect both his maturity as a writer, but also the magnitude of his vision. The concept of two ultimate forces, in existence and in conflict from the beginning of the universe, and using race upon race, generation upon generation, as weapons, has seldom been as successfully received by the reader, or vilified by the critics. The critics may have complained about Smith's simplistic concepts, muddling scientific ideas, and embarrassingly primitive characterizations, but the fans loved him. Twenty years after his death, the mass popularity of the Lensman with the youth of America cannot be denied. The power, the moral "rightness," and immense scope are most appealing to a youthful audience. The central volume, *Galactic Patrol*, is regarded as the finest of the Lensman series.

The Skylark series

Skylark of Space. Richard Seaton is the larger-than-life hero and Blackie DuQuesne the matchless villain that confronts him in this first of the great space operas. Set in the twentieth century, Seaton is a scientist who discovers a mode of travel that allows him and his friends to explore the reaches of the galaxy. Pursuing his rival DuQuesne, who has acquired Seaton's formula and kidnapped his fiancee, Dorothy Vaneman, the Earthmen encounter a galaxy peopled with bizarre races, mile-long spaceships and embroiled in vast expansive wars. Seaton and DuQuesne become locked in their own personal duel that extends over the length of the galaxy and three subsequent novels.

Today, much of the Skylark series seems painfully dated in its concepts. Dorothy Vaneman is the classic fainting heroine of romantic dime novels, although she does mature considerably in the last volume of the series, *Skylark DuQuesne*. The hero is pure, motivated by good intentions. The villain is an unrelieved personification of evil. The characters are cardboard cutouts that have little depth and few options. And yet, the scope and sweep of this novel must be recognized for its remarkable impact on readers. The spirit of adventure is uplifting, the morals are impeccable and the suspense is sustained. The novel is extremely far-ranging in its scope, creating a universe that had only been hinted at by other writers. The excitement generated by this novel continues to draw generations of new, young readers, who will delight in the light-hearted romanticism and power fantasies portrayed in the Skylark series. *Skylark of Space* was followed by *Skylark Three*, *Skylark of Valeron*, and *Skylark DuQuesne*. All were first serialized in *Amazing Stories* and *Astounding Science Fiction*. *Skylark of Valeron* has been regarded as the most stylistically sound of the four volumes.

Biographical/Bibliographical Readings

John Clute, "E. E. Smith," in *Science Fiction Writers*, ed. E. F. Bleiler (Scribner's, 1982), p.125-30. Ron Ellik and Bill Evans, *The Universes of E. E. Smith* (Advent, 1966). Sam Moskowitz, "E. E. Smith," in *Seekers of Tomorrow* (World, 1966), p.9-26. Jane B. Weedman, "E. E. Smith," in *Twentieth-Century American Science-Fiction Writers* (Gale, 1981), v.2, p.132-36. [Colleen Power]

SPINRAD, NORMAN

Life and Works

Norman Richard Spinrad was born in New York City on September 15, 1940. He received his entire education in New York, graduating from the City College of New York in 1961 with a B.S. in prelaw. He worked as a welfare investigator and a literary agent before publishing his first short story, "The Last of the Romany," in *Analog* in 1963. Other than a stint as a radio talk show host, he has been a full-time writer ever since.

Spinrad's first novel, *The Solarians*, appeared in 1966, followed the next year by *Agent of Chaos* (1967) and *The Men in the Jungle* (1967). All three contain more elements of traditional science fiction, even space opera, than do his short stories, though they share the same broad concerns and moral ambivalence. *The Solarians* pits humankind against a more powerful adversary in interstellar warfare, but the ultimate destruction of Earth proves liberating for the few humans who remain. In *Agent of Chaos*, the authoritarian Hegemony rules the solar system, with the acquiescence of most of humanity. Two competing groups strive to overthrow the regime; again, a suicidal act of destruction provides the key for doing so. Of these early novels, *The Men in the Jungle* is the darkest and most grotesque. The hero, another revolutionary trying to topple a brutal regime, aids and abets sadism and cannibalism to achieve his goal, only to have the planet thus freed degenerate into further violence.

In the late 1960s, Spinrad moved to London, there to participate in the expansion of the science fiction New Wave sponsored by Michael Moorcock's *New Worlds* magazine. It was there that Spinrad's novel, *Bug Jack Barron*, first appeared in serialization. Published in book form in 1969, it was quickly picked up on both sides of the Atlantic as a model creation of the New Wave--experimental in language, critical of our political and media institutions, philosophically dark, and ambivalent about the future.

In *The Iron Dream* (1972), Spinrad headed off in a new experimental and controversial direction. The novel consists of a standard pulp-era sword and science fantasy entitled *Lord of the Swastika*, written by one Adolf Hitler, who, in an alternate universe, migrated to the United States after World War I to become a science fiction illustrator and writer. The pseudonovel, along with fictional forewords and afterwords, presents a criticism of the fascistic tendencies underlying this kind of science fiction and its fandom as well as of the world that made a Hitler possible.

The rest of Spinrad's publishing output in the 1970s showed much variety. His short stories appeared in three collections: *The Last Hurrah of the Golden Horde* (1970), *No Direction Home* (1975), and *The Star-Spangled Future* (1979). He also turned out two nonfiction collections and the science fiction novella, *Riding the Torch*, which won the 1974 Jupiter award. Spinrad edited two science fiction anthologies in this decade, *The New Tomorrows* (1971) and *Modern Science Fiction* (1974).

A new phase of his fiction career commenced in 1979 with the publication of the novel *A World Between*, the first of four recent novels that posit a triumph of 1960s values, politics, and philosophies in the future. The other novels to date in this phase are *Songs from the Stars* (1980), *The Void Captain's Table* (1983), and *Child of Fortune* (1985).

In addition to his other work, Spinrad wrote a well-remembered episode of "Star Trek"--"The Doomsday Machine"--and served successively as vice-president and president of the Science Fiction Writers of America. He has been nominated for a total of ten

Nebula and Hugo awards, as well as a National Book Award for *The Iron Dream*, which took the French Prix Apollo. One of his recent publications is *Stayin' Alive: A Writer's Guide* (1983), a collection of his columns for the trade publication *Locus*.

Themes and Style

Spinrad's early short stories have been compared to Ray Bradbury's. Like Bradbury's, they tend to emphasize human values over technological ones and frequently suggest that the future may not be the positive experience dominant in the Golden Age science fiction tradition. Unlike Bradbury, Spinrad does not take refuge in simple horror or protective sentiment, however. Very much a writer formed in the 1960s, he shoves his characters--and readers--up against the existential void and challenges them to find meaning in the universe. And he investigates the many means for doing so in the modern world--particularly religion, politics, drugs, and the electronic media. In the title story of the collection *No Direction Home*, for instance, he delineates in serial anecdotes a future in which everyone commonly uses psychotropic drugs, under force of law and social custom. When one experimental soul foregoes chemicals, he finds the cold emptiness of reality a "bummer." The story suggests that we need our illusions to protect us from the fact of our insignificance in the cosmos. Here, as in most of Spinrad's work, the reader is left with an uneasy ambivalence; Spinrad rarely offers easy choices or clear-cut good and evil.

Among his later works, *A World Between* focuses on his motif of the influence of mass media on the masses, amid a war for the goal of a peaceful, well-adjusted planet. Utopia is also threatened in *Songs from the Stars*. Here, nuclear destruction has left hippiedome in charge of what is left of America, while the old technocracy hangs on as an underground sect. High tech and holistic thought find they need each other, however, in order to reach out for the wisdom offered by the intelligent races of other stars. Ironically, it is the hippies, and not the scientists, who are better equipped to receive the cosmic messages.

High tech and holistic thought also come together in the fictive universe of *The Void Captain's Tale* and *Child of Fortune*. Both treat Spinrad's favorite theme of humanity's search for meaning within the void. Space itself exemplifies the inherent emptiness of reality. In these novels, humanity has peopled many worlds; it is the Second Starfaring Age, and void ships jump the light years. Using a language built of many languages and a dominant world view constructed of 1960s' Eastern-oriented mysticism, Spinrad sends his void captain into an erotic entanglement with the void. The heroine of *Child of Fortune* seeks her identity during a socially approved *wanderjahr* that carries her from planet to planet and into adventures that are erotic, psychedelic, metaphysical, and perilous. Though Spinrad's novels of the eighties still possess ambivalence and dark moments, they offer a more positive, even comic vision, of the future. They may be taken as Spinrad's leap of faith, following the existentialist angst of his earlier work.

Plot Summaries of Major Works

Bug Jack Barron. Jack Barron is a Berkeley radical turned TV talk-show host. While he has sold out to the system to some extent, he uses his public power in populist causes. He invites his audience to call in with whatever is bugging them and to "bug Jack Barron." What bugs Barron is powerful multimillionaire Benedict Howards, who is leading a controversial research effort into immortality and wants Barron's media influence on his side. The skeptical, arrogant Barron begins a cat-and-mouse game with the death-obsessed capitalist, trying to dig out the dark--and, as it turns out, grotesque--secret that Howards is trying to hide. He discovers that achieving immortality involves a Faustian bargain: one can live forever, but at a terrible cost.

This novel appeared at the crest of the science fiction New Wave and is still considered a prime example of the movement. Originally serialized in Moorcock's *New Worlds*, it earned Spinrad considerable notoriety, and even condemnation in the British parliament for its gritty naturalism. True to the New Wave, the novel is noteworthy not only for its naturalistic handling of human psychology, sexuality, moral dilemmas, social institutions, and the fear of death, but for its innovative use of language. The narrative's blend of slang and prose poetry is comparable to the experiments of the 1950s Beats and the 1960s new journalists. The novel remains a heady, challenging reading experience.

Child of Fortune. Sunshine (born Moussa) Shasta, a bright and attractive young woman, has been raised by typically enlightened parents on the comfortable planet Glade. She sets out on her *wanderjahr*, the standard conclusion to everyone's education. For an indefinite period, each young person quests among the settled worlds, to find his or her own way around, freely experience life, and finally choose a first name (or "freenom") that expresses his or her identity. Sunshine's search for adventure and purpose begins on the chaotic carnival world of Edoku, where she seduces the hippie King Peter Pan. Under his influence, she learns to follow the free path of the Yellow Brick Road, in the footsteps of wandering minstrels, gypsies, hippies, and free spirits of every era. From there she takes off with the drug-obsessed hedonist seeker Guy Blad Boca, who leads her to the planet Belshazaar. This is the home of the Bloomenveldt, a giant forest full of huge, alien flowers that psychotropically ensnare anyone who comes within reach of their perfume. Only her will and wisdom allow Sunshine to escape the seductive control of Bloomenveldt's blooms. Her self-discovery and self-assertion allows her to find herself and her freedom.

The universe of *Child of Fortune* is so full of interesting folk, varied planets, and philosophical options that Spinrad's void (an empty, meaningless universe) remains well hidden. There are answers to be found, or invented, and a good deal of meaning in the cosmos if one lives creatively enough to produce it from the raw materials. This novel seems to represent an end to Spinrad's own existential quest: a la Camus, after the void comes the choice. If life and the universe lack inherent meaning, it is up to the thinking beings to give it meaning by liberating human spirits and exercising freedom of choice.

The Iron Dream. This is a novel within a novel. Opening the novel, one finds the title *Lord of the Swastika* by Adolph Hitler, complete with laudatory blurbs, a biographical note tracing Hitler's career in the United States as an immigrant illustrator turned science fiction writer, and a list of other Hitler novels including *The Master Race* and *The Triumph of the Will*. The internal novel, *Lord of the Swastika*, is a science fantasy in pulp mode, with all the fascistic wish-fulfillment characteristics of the subgenre. It traces the Wagnerian career of Feric Jaggar, who returns from exile to the country of Heldon to claim his birthright as a perfect human genotype in a world peopled by grotesque mutants and threatened by a giant conspiracy between the monolithic regime of Zind and a small but ubiquitous racial minority known as the Dominators. Once he has claimed, in Arthurian fashion, a phallic iron fist called the Great Truncheon, he wields it over an evermounting procession of fervent rallies, marches, purges, and gory battles. Ultimately, he sends his seed by rocket to the stars.

This novel is more than a dark parody of Nazism. Spinrad's irony extends to the science-fantasy realm we know as recent history and--closer yet to home--to the world of science fiction fandom, where Hitlerian ideas are much in favor, when disguised as pulp power fantasies. *The Iron Dream* deftly dramatizes Spinrad's concerns regarding the dangers of mass psychology, whether exemplified by the political rally or the fan convention. The mass mind, Spinrad pointedly reminds us, is easily warped by charismatic leaders and media manipulation.

Songs from the Stars. In a postholocaust Earth, what is left of the American West has become Aquaria, a loosely bound society rooted in the hippie values of the late 1960s. High tech is regarded as black sorcery, in large part being responsible for the holocaust. Long-range travel takes place by pedaled glider, long-range communication by messenger relay networks. When Clear Blue Lou, hippie sage, judge, and "natural man," is called to a mountain commune to settle a tribal dispute over a black market in forbidden items, he meets Sunshine Sue, a leader of the Word-of-Mouth circuit. They find themselves hauled into a conspiracy by the Spacers, an underground group of Technocrats who want to use the broad influence of Lou and Sue to force their suspicious constituency to accept space travel again. Ironically, when Spacer Arnold Harker finally gets Lou and Sue to accompany him to the orbiting space station where communications from other stars have already been received, it is the hippies, with their holistic cosmic view, and not the scientists, who can accept the sensual chaos of the void and its intelligences.

While much of Spinrad's earlier work was haunted by the specter of an empty, meaningless universe, too reminiscent of death and existential void, this novel provides an antidote to the previous gloom by offering up a cosmos full of joy, wisdom and belonging--of intelligence that successfully creates its own meaning in the face of the ultimate annihilation of not only the individual but of the universe itself. Though Spinrad shows his usual ambivalence regarding human nature and the moral issues it confronts--particularly during a three-way battle of wills on the space station--the novel ends on a far more positive note than the work of Spinrad's first phase. He also develops here his depiction of flawed utopias begun in *A World Between*; his Aquaria is described in loving detail, sensuously, sympathetically, and humorously, and here Spinrad's penchant for ambivalence shows forth once more, without slighting its blemishes.

The Void Captain's Table. The future of humankind has colonized the planets of many stars, which are connected by the great void ships of the Second Starfaring Age. Genro Kane Gupta is captain of one of the void ships. In order to jump the light years from star to star, the ship's engines are biomechanically hooked into the pilot (in this case, Dominique Alia Wu), who must always be a sexually maladjusted female. The void ship jumps only when she is stimulated by the ship's propulsion system into an instantaneous orgasm of cosmic proportions. Pilots, not surprisingly, grow addicted to the experience, though it inevitably leads to physical debilitation and premature death. Because of her wasted state, and her unique erotic relationships with the void, the pilot remains persona non grata among the crew and the honored passengers, the bevy of decadent interstellar jet-setters who fill time and space with hedonistic indulgence. Captain Gupta finds himself in trouble when he threatens the ship's delicate social balance, and the lives of all, by becoming infatuated with his pilot, Dominique. Through her he develops an erotic association with the void; with her, he experiences, albeit briefly at second hand, the eternal ecstacy the void can offer. Dominique is using the captain; she wants him to cut her loose during jump, though this would mean her death and the marooning of the ship in deep space. Given this hard decision, Genro finally opts for the metaphysical leap, though he sacrifices much to do so.

In the microcosm of the void ship, Spinrad returns to one of his favorite themes, the means used by human beings as individuals and as societies--to come to terms with the ultimate emptiness that surrounds us. As in his other works, his future society is meticulously and delightfully depicted--in its mannered, multilingual speech, in its moral libertarianism, and in its hippie-style fondness for the mystical and sensual aspects of Oriental metaphysics. The brightness of this vision tempers the perennial darkness of the Void.

A World Between. The world of the title is Pacifica, a physically congenial planet that has allowed its colonists to evolve a nearly utopian civilization, free of violence, authoritarianism, and inequality. Presiding over social organization is an enlightened government and an intricate and efficient media network that keeps the citizenry well informed. The government is led by Carlotta Madigan and the media is regulated by Royce Lindblad. These leaders and their world face a crisis when the Pink and Blue War catches up to them. This is a war between the sexes and very different, if equally strident, world-views. One side is the Femocracy, a hegemony of radical lesbian-feminists who control Earth among other planets; opposing them are the Transcendental Scientists, a cold-blooded, male chauvinistic technocracy. Both groups gain ready access to Pacifica's wide open media system. The war of propaganda for the control of Pacifica endangers the world's equilibrium and comes close to ruining its pure institutions. Only defections from women on both sides of the conflict allow Pacifica's independent survival. In the meantime, the Pacificans learn that the ideal balance of society and of the sexes requires constant effort; it is not self-perpetuating.

Here Spinrad not only tackles the power of the media and the political influence welded thereby on the mass mind, he also projects the yet-current debate over sex roles and society into the future. His usual studied ambivalence turns into an argument for moderation, for "dynamic stability" between the extremes that forever threaten the mass mind and the political systems.

Biographical/Bibliographical Readings

Thomas D. Bacig, "Norman Spinrad," in *Twentieth-Century Science-Fiction Writers*, ed. Curtis C. Smith (St. James, 1986), p.688-89. Patrice Duvic, *Le Livre D'Or de Norman Spinrad* (Paris, Presses Pocket, n.d.). Ira Rae Hark, "Norman Spinrad," in *Twentieth-Century American Science-Fiction Writers* (Gale, 1981), v.2, p.139-48. Norman Spinrad, "A Prince from Another Land," in *Fantastic Lives*, ed. Martin H. Greenberg (Southern Illinois University Press, 1981), p.157-74. [Stephen W. Potts]

STAPLEDON, WILLIAM OLAF

Life and Works

Stapledon was born on May 10, 1886, at Wallasey (Merseyside) Cheshire, England, to Emmeline Miller and William Clibbett Stapledon. Stapledon's father worked for a shipping firm at Port Said, where Stapledon spent the first five years of his life. As an only child, his experiences were focused on his parents and he was greatly influenced by their love of great literature and their academic values. He completed his B.A. and M.A. degrees in history at Balliol College, Oxford, and attempted to follow a vocation with the shipping industry, but quickly returned to the academic environment where he taught at Manchester Grammar School and lectured at evening courses in the subjects of industrial history, literature, and psychology. He eventually became an adjunct to the faculty of the University of Liverpool. In 1919, he married Agnes Zena Miller. Their two children, Mary Sydney and John David, were born in 1920 and 1923.

World War II and the development of the atomic bomb clarified Stapledon's political philosophy. He personally sheltered an Austrian student during the Hitler invasions. He was decidedly socialist and committed to world peace. His epic writings of humanity's future reveal the poignant trial and error and close evasions of total annihilation. At the Cultural and Scientific Conference for Peace in New York in 1949, he spoke against the continued development and use of nuclear weapons. In 1950, he died at home of a sudden heart attack.

He really did not begin his writing career until late in life. At the age of forty-two, Stapledon was publishing in the *Journal of Philosophical Studies*, which was then serving as the leading forum for such authors as Bertrand Russell, Julian Huxley, and Alfred North Whitehead. Stapledon was not really aware of the science fiction genre as an evolving literture. He was amazed at the existence of science fiction magazines and their contributors when he was introduced to them in the 1930s while dabbling in philosophical fiction. His first monumental work of science fiction was *Last and First Men* (1930). During the next two decades, he wrote and published *Last Men in London* (1932), *Odd John: A Story between Jest and Earnest* (1935), *Star Maker* (1937), *Darkness and the Light* (1942), *Old Man in the New World* (1944), *Sirius: A Fantasy of Love and Discord* (1944), *Death into Life* (1946), *The Flames* (1947), and *A Man Divided* (1950). Among his posthumously published work was *The Opening of the Eyes* (1954) and the collection *Far Future Calling; Uncollected Science Fiction and Fantasies of Olaf Stapledon* (1979), edited by Sam Moskowitz.

Themes and Style

While writing for philosophical journals, the definitions and interrelationships of reality and perception drew Stapledon's attention. In a short story, posthumously published, entitled "The Man Who became a Tree," a very intense exploration into the feeling/perceptive process of metamorphosis is achieved. Aspects of his monumental work, *Last and First Men*, examines perception and reality as well. In the novel, the scope of two billion years of human history is described by the last survivor, and the recital takes the reader through an extensive assortment of philosophical theories of society, exploring political and social hypotheses. Another exploration into perception is recorded in *Odd John*, a novel which poses the situation of a human mutation of superior intelligence and mental talents who finds himself amidst the masses. *Sirius* examines the predicament of a product of genetic experimentation--a dog with superhuman intelligence who still maintains a tie to primal instinct. *Star Maker* extends the imaginative hypotheses of human history of *Last and First Men* to a history of the entire universe.

Plot Summaries of Major Works

Last and First Men. The format is that of a history text, rather than a novel. The history is astounding in its scope and imagination, as it treats the course of humanity from its very beginnings, over a range of two billion years, to its final termination. The source of the information is the telepathic invasion of the last survivor into the mind of the current writer. The writer himself experiences the creativity of a typical fantasy writer and in fact considers the content of the work his own. Only at the end of the saga is the true source revealed and the ultimate tragedy felt in its total impact.

In this account, humanity evolves through eighteen separate species, a myriad of mental and physical metamorphoses, and plays out many dramas of political and social theory and religious philosophies. There is raw survival against elements and aliens. There is an evolved consciousness bordering on the divine. And there is everything in between. The lessons of humanity are learned and then forgotten. Trials are repeated in many patterns, and Stapledon's ability to spin out solutions and test them philosophically is staggering. Throughout the saga, a poetic flow takes shape in attempt to give cosmic meaning to the odyssey.

Odd John: A Story between Jest and Earnest. Odd John is a superintelligent human who represents a giant step in the evolution of the intellect, and even the physical evolution of humankind. John is a lone but superior misfit, and his story is told with his permission by a very ordinary but perceptive and sympathetic family friend. The signs of John's uniqueness are noted early and manifested in the slowly developmental schedule of the infant John. Even the pregnancy itself is drawn out eleven months, resulting in a fetus born prematurely. John feels the loneliness of being unique, but from an unexplainable drive and through his telepathic skills, he is able to contact others like himself. All of these beings are long-lived, with life expectancies encompassing hundreds of years. They attempt to form a utopian colony in solitude on a hidden island, but their eventual discovery and danger of exploitation by the world powers leads to their ultimate destruction.

Stapledon allows superior intelligence to become the vehicle through which to theorize about the evolution of cultural values and mores, and through which to critique history and political science issues. There is even a permissible suspension of the moral system of the times, in the name of a greater goal, to enable a higher-level being to survive. John continually reveals his mental prowess as evidenced in accelerated comprehension of both physical and philosophical issues, in inventions of advanced technological apparatus, and eventually in the development of telepathic skills. There are many discourses in the novel on John's thoughts about politics, social history, and meaning of sexuality from the vantage point of the higher intelligence.

Sirius: A Fantasy of Love and Discord. The dog, Sirius, is the product of a series of breeding experiments, undertaken by a British experimenter, which embodies a high level of intelligence approaching, and in some cases, exceeding that of human mentality. There is a very poignant sensitivity expressed by the genius dog as he develops artistically and with great passion, bound in an unusual but deeply felt relationship with the human daughter of his breeder, Plaxy. The puppy and the child are raised together, and mature in the way of their species, but intellectually and telepathically they share a closeness that transcends mortality. Sirius, though intelligent, is never entirely free of the primal dog instinct and exhibits this instinct in sheepherding and eventually sheep- and human-killing.

Stapledon repeats a theme similar to that of Odd John--that of a mutated member of a species with attributes that make him unique among his kind, and therefore a misfit struggling to discover and retain a solid identity. Stapledon's existentialistic writing is well developed in this novel. The tragic flaw of the experiment and the relationship is that Sirius' bestial part remains and fluctuates out of his or anyone else's control while the deeply moving and sensitive spirit struggles for sanity.

The Star Maker. This novel is a historical account of the entire universe over a period of 50 billion years, is related from the inward perspective of a man on a hillside, who is whisked off in a dream to view the entire spectacle and to to come face to face with himself and the ultimate creator, the star maker. Systems of planets form and destruct as natural phenomena. Suns are born and burn out. Sanity and insanity present the basic political struggles--the mad United Empires and the sane League. Planets/worlds maneuver like fleets of ships. Religious or spiritual quests have basic significance in the evolving system of worlds that approaches the mind-encompassing all. When the traveler returns to his hillside, having absorbed all the magnitude of time and space, he reflects that it is all the more urgent for the struggle for sanity among this tiny human race.

Although the scope is much broader than that of *Last and First Men*, the novel is actually much shorter, and therefore the history unfolds at a breathless pace. The saga is a metaphor for humanity's quest for God and particularly for an understanding of God. The immensity of the story offers the frame for the immensity of the higher being.

Biographical/Bibliographical Readings

Leslie A. Fiedler, *Olaf Stapledon: A Man Divided* (Oxford University Press, 1983). John Kinnaird, "Olaf Stapledon," in *Twentieth-Century Science-Fiction Writers*, ed. Curtis C. Smith (St. James, 1986), p.693-96. Sam Moskowitz, "Olaf Stapledon: Cosmic Philosopher," in *Explorers of the Infinite* (World, 1963), p.261-77. Idem, "Olaf Stapledon: The Man behind the Works," in *Far Future Calling: Uncollected Science Fiction and Fantasies of Olaf Stapledon* (Oswald Train, 1979), p.15-69. **[Lorraine E. Lester]**

STRUGATSKY, ARKADY AND BORIS STRUGATSKY

Life and Works

Of the many living practitioners of the rich tradition of Russian science fiction, none are better known in the West than the brothers Strugatsky. Arkady, born in 1925, served in World War II before going on to the Moscow Foreign Languages Institute. There he specialized in Japanese language, literature, and folklore, while developing expertise as well in English. Boris, born in 1933, took his professional credentials from the faculty of mechanics and mathematics at Leningrad University, after which he became a research worker in astrophysics at Pulkovo Observatory. Their combined backgrounds in comparative literature and space science show in the fiction they have always composed together.

Their earliest work appeared on the heels of a general broadening in Soviet science fiction that came after the twentieth Party Congress of 1956 officially renounced Stalinism. In addition, the launching of Sputnik created a new interest in the Soviet reading public for more visionary tales of technology and the future.

Their longer pieces--"Land of Crimson Clouds," "Destination: Amaltheia" (1960), *Space Apprentice* (1981)--have a juvenile flavor, and seem at times openly didactic on the value of human beings and the inevitability of scientific advance and the triumph of socialism. All are set in a single fictive universe with the same future history. From this context also come the short stories collected as *Noon: 22nd Century* (1962).

Throughout the 1960s, the Strugatskys' deeply rooted humanism increasingly showed signs of skepticism and doubt. *Predatory Things of Our Time* (1965), published in English as *The Final Circle of Paradise* (1976), borrows a character from their early universe and sets him in a decadent capitalist outpost on Earth to criticize some of humanity's less attractive characteristics. The novel was criticized in turn by a number of the Soviet establishment's more conservative critics who did not find the book uplifting enough.

Their novel *Hard to Be a God* (1964), published about the same time, had a much better reception. For a time the most popular science fiction novel in the Soviet Union, it cast the Strugatskys' concerns about human improvability in a sword and sorcery mode. Other works published in the 1960s include: *Monday Begins on Saturday* (1965), *The Tale of the Troika* (1968), *The Second Martian Invasion* (1968), and *The Snail on the Slope* (1966-68). The 1970s brought forth *Prisoners of Power* (1971), *The Ugly Swans* (1972), *Roadside Picnic* (1977), and *Definitely Maybe* (1976-77).

Themes and Style

From their earlier juvenile fiction and the swashbuckling heroes of *Hard to Be a God*, the Strugatskys' vision darkened and they turned away from future extrapolation toward more metaphorical and fabulist forms, many with an openly satirical edge. The lightest of these works is *Monday Begins on Saturday*, about an institute for scientific magic; it is crammed with motifs from Russian folklore and the tradition of science fiction. In its sequel, *The Tale of the Troika*, the authors create a humorously Kafkaesque attack on the inanities of bureaucracy, which they see as one of the major barriers faced by humanity in its quest of scientific and social advance.

Other satirical fantasies are *The Second Martian Invasion*, which has humanity yielding its independence to subtle alien invaders, out of selfish, stupid, short-range goals, and the surreal *The Snail on the Slope*. The latter is actually two interwoven novellas, tracing the counterpoint quests of Kandid, who is trying to escape a grotesque forest, and Pepper, who is trying to escape the impossible bureaucracy assigned to explore and exploit the forest. Both contend fruitlessly with entropy; all the progress each makes only brings him full circle, so that he is more trapped at the end than at the beginning. A similar, if qualified, pessimism is found in *Prisoners of Power*, a science fantasy set on a world much resembling our own, torn with political and ideological rivalries, always on the brink of war. Like the hero of *Hard to Be a God*, the protagonist here--an innocent from a Utopian Earth--finds himself swept up in the social ills of the planet, and even gives in to them on occasion until he develops a modicum of wisdom.

With the publication of *The Ugly Swans* in 1972, it became clear how far the Strugatskys had come from the sunny optimism of their early juveniles. It takes place entirely in a community in some unspecific European country, in the vicinity of a "leper" colony. The colony is in fact inhabited by a group of human mutants, highly intelligent and ultimately quite powerful. Despite their sinister appearance and behavior, it appears that these "slimies" represent a new advance in human evolution, though one that will mean the destruction of humanity as we know it.

Human progress also finds itself altered or stalled by outside forces in *Roadside Picnic* and *Definitely Maybe*. With the former, a short novel, the Strugatskys reached a zenith of sorts--in its economic and effective descriptions of the horror and corruption that follows an alien visitation, the haunting depiction of one such "Zone" filled with the leavings of the visitation, and the human suffering of the very believable characters whose lives have been effected. *Definitely Maybe*, if lighter in tone, has a group of creative people suddenly stopped short by what appears to be a natural law. The universe, in fact, acts like a sort of police state, pressuring these people to give up their research and holding human progress in check.

The fiction of the Strugatskys belies many of the assumptions common in the West about Soviet literature. Though their earliest work adopted the Soviet line regarding humanity's socialist future, as their career progressed they grew increasingly critical of human institutions and human perfectability. Fundamentally, however, if their optimism later waned, they remained, as of their last work, humanists, skeptical only because humankind fails to live up to its potential.

Plot Summaries of Major Works

Definitely Maybe. The tale is set entirely in a modern apartment building in Leningrad, and told wholly in fragments from the viewpoint of Malianov, an astrophysicist on the verge of a theoretical breakthrough. He suddenly finds he is unable to continue his work, however, because of a series of bizarre events--annoying phone calls, a mysterious package, strange visitors. Malianov soon discovers that his friends, all approaching

major breakthroughs in their own sundry fields, are suffering similar distractions, and even warnings. At first they appear to be
the victims of police harassment; as the obstacles to their progress
continue, one of the men comes up with the theory of the Homeo-
static Universe, which suggests that there may be a natural law
preventing intelligent life from learning too much and thus upsetting the balance of the cosmos.

The question is left unresolved, and the Western reader cannot
help noticing the parallels between the behavior of the Homeo-
static Universe and a police state. But whether one sees the state
or the cosmos as the barrier to progress, it is clear that the Strugatskys have come far from the unlimited horizons of *Noon: 22nd
Century*. As one of the brothers' last novels, it remains their last
word on the subject of human potential. The struggle, indeed,
would seem hopeless, but that one ray of hope lingers: it is a billion years or so to the end of the world, one character notes, and
who knows what humankind may yet be capable of achieving?
But it is not likely that great progress will be made in our lifetimes, or even by the twenty-second century. The Russian title of
this novel, which translates as *A Billion Years before the End of the
World*, gives a better idea of its scope than the arbitrary English
title. But then the story itself only hints at the possible issues involved.

Far Rainbow. Rainbow is a colonized planet orbiting a distant star, a world given over largely to physics research. Scientists
unleash a wave of "zero-energy" that threatens to wipe out all life
on Rainbow. The rest of the novel shows the many ways that the
characters attempt to handle the crisis, publicly and privately.
There are two characters in separate subplots: the ship captain,
Leonid Gorbovsky, and a young, headstrong technician named
Robert Sklyarov. After it becomes clear that the wave will not
stop until it has destroyed the planet, Sklyarov single-mindedly
struggles to get his girlfriend to the equatorial port city and into
space, throwing away the lives of others, including children, in
the process. The selfless Gorbovsky, on the other hand, proposes
to send all the children off-planet in his starship, though that
means sacrificing all the products of Rainbow's scientific and
artistic community--not to mention the lives of all the adults.

Gorbovsky's decision marks the Strugatskys' main concern
here, the value of human life, and especially that of children, who
represent the future, over everything else. The catastrophe caused
by experimentation with "zero-energy" suggests the more dangerous
technologies of our own time, such as nuclear weaponry. Scientists must expand human knowledge--say the Strugatskys--but not
by putting humanity itself at risk. Scientific concerns are subordinate to ethical ones. Despite this thematic emphasis, this novel
lacks the didacticism found in some of their earlier fiction. The
complexity of the characters and their moral dilemmas carry much

of the plot. This work is a prime example of what Soviet critics call "optimistic tragedy"; its conclusion is bittersweet, blending the pathos of imminent death with continued hope for the future and faith in human strength.

Hard to Be a God. Don Rumata, a sword-wielding aristocrat, dwells on an alien planet called Arkanar, locked in a battle between feudalism and fascism. In reality, he and his colleagues are agents sent from Earth to intervene in the conflict and set the society on the proper path to social progress. Rumata, however (his real name is Anton), makes the mistake of falling in love with his flawed, adopted land and with a native woman named Kyra. Gradually, he actually becomes this lout of noble birth named Rumata, and finds himself seduced by the violent ways of his milieu.

Central to this work, as to much of the fiction of the Strugatskys' middle period, is the idea of the importance of education and proper social institutions toward the development of ethical individuals. The animal part of human nature can never be wholly erased--as Rumata/Anton comes to recognize--but a society that encourages and celebrates the best in people can keep the beast in check. A culture like this of medieval Arkanar, dominated by a Hitlerian tyranny, stormtroopers, a militant church, and assorted bandits, can only bring out the worst, even in an enlightened individual like Anton.

This novel is the first by the Strugatskys to show an element of real skepticism regarding human potential. In conversations with a pair of defeated progressives, one a fugitive intellectual, the other a revolutionary, Rumata rounds out his doubts about the possibility of positive change on this world, finally noting that the enemy one must fight for liberation is within oneself. In *Hard to Be a God*, the Strugatskys created a powerful, popular mix of action and ideas. The novel quickly became their most popular novel in their native country, and remained so. It combines swashbuckling heroes and a fast-moving plot with their favorite social concerns.

Noon: 22nd Century. This book, the Strugatskys' first, brings together twenty short stories published circa 1960. Set in the near-future universe of their earliest fiction, the stories cover two centuries of humanity's scientific and social progress. Though some of the stories seem naive in their faith in a sunny Marxist future, the total effect of the volume is charming in its optimism. And all is not wholly well. The most interesting of the characters that reappear throughout the stories, in fact, are those with problems of adjustment. Kondratev and Slavin are two twentieth-century cosmonauts marooned in the twenty-second century by relativistic space travel; Kondratev in particular has trouble finding a place for himself in the world of his great-grandchildren. Even natives of this future time have their poignant moments, their

failures. Pol Gnedykh and "Athos" Sidorv are romantics whose
spirits yearn for more than any society can offer, and thus must
always remain dissatisfied. Another character, Leonid Gorbovsky,
appears in the ironic "Pilgrims and Wanderers," which contrasts
human space exploration with the out-of-water wanderings of a
newly discovered cephalopod. Other tales examine the favorite
concerns of the Strugatskys' early fiction: the value of scientific
progress, the great value of human life, the worth of useful work
for the betterment of humankind, and the unlimited potential for
the species.

Following the standard Soviet line of the time, the authors
delineate an Earth united by the peaceful triumph of enlightened
communism. With the final touches being put on utopia on Earth,
humanity reaches out to the other planets in the solar system, and
beyond, pushing forward the frontiers of knowledge. Much of the
positive tone of this work can be ascribed to the youth market for
which the book was intended.

Prisoners of Power. Maxim is an innocent with superhuman
powers from a utopian Earth. He crash lands on a planet populated by human beings recovering from nuclear war, though they
continue their hostilities in Cold War fashion. Maxim finds himself in the Land of the All-Powerful Creators, ruled by a Nazi-
style oligarchy who controls the population by radio waves
beamed directly into the brain. Maxim stumbles naively through
one adventure after another, from joining the fascistic Legion to
joining the underground that is trying to overthrow the oppressive
regime. Slowly Maxim acquires some insight and political wisdom,
even as he begins to give in to the inevitable violence of this
world. By the climactic section of the novel, ironically labelled
"Earthling," Maxim is single-handedly and single-mindedly carrying on a fierce campaign against the center of power, sparing no
one who gets in his way. Maxim discovers, in the end, that fellow
Earthmen are behind the oligarchy of the All-Powerful Creators,
their intent being to set the planet on the path to progress. Maxim
wishes to join the effort, though only if the manipulators abandon
some of their more abusive methods, such as the radio waves. But
Maxim receives no promises, and although the push for social
progress will continue, we are left wondering how anything could
succeed on this vicious world.

As an extended moral fable, *Prisoners of Power* lacks the complex characters of the Strugatskys' more realistic fiction. Maxim
in particular seems a cipher, subject to the influence of those immediately around him. One wonders what sort of a utopia could
have produced a being so lacking in judgment. But we are not to
take the characters literally, given the work's darkly satirical
edge. *Prisoners of Power* handles a theme similar to that of *Hard
to Be a God*: the importance of good institutions for the social and
ethical health of the individual. The novel shows a sophisticated

skepticism far different from the naive optimism of their earlier fiction.

Roadside Picnic. Alien starships visited the Earth, but departed without making contact. They did leave behind them, however, a good deal of alien trash, scattered over five zones in various areas of the world. Despite strict security measures, an entire blackmarket subculture has sprouted around the zones. At the leading edge of this underworld are the Stalkers, who risk their lives and much more to sneak items from the zone and into the hands of scientists, the military, and entrepreneurs. Human beings are caught between the pressures of their less-than-ethical society and the disturbing if seductive alienness of the zone and the artifacts it contains. Stalker Red Schuhart lives in Harmont, Canada. Red sees his colleagues killed and horribly maimed in their search for the alien trash. He himself spends time in jail and fathers a mutant child. As the story progresses, the deleterious physical effects of the zone increase. More awful still is the ethical degeneration of the hero, as he learns survival at all costs in his selfish, short-sighted milieu.

Roadside Picnic effectively brings together a number of the Strugatskys' favorite themes, without once lapsing into moralizing and didacticism. As in other works, we see the influence of society on the individual, opportunities for scientific progress lost by the weaknesses in human nature, and in a motif evident in their later works, we see humanity almost wholly unequipped to deal with the truly alien. This short novel represents a high point in the Strugatskys' career, perhaps their highest point.

Biographical/Bibliographical Readings

V. Gakov, "A Test of Humanity," *Soviet Literature* (1982, no. 1). Stephen W. Potts, *The Second Marxian Invasion: The Dialectical Fables of Arkady and Boris Strugatsky* (Borgo Press, 1986). Darko Suvin, "Criticism of the Strugatskii Brothers' Work," *Canadian-American Slavic Studies* (Summer 1982), p.286-307. Idem, "The Literary Opus of the Strugatskii Brothers," *Canadian-American Slavic Studies* (Fall 1974), p.454-63. [Stephen W. Potts]

STURGEON, THEODORE

Life and Works

Theodore Sturgeon was born Edward Hamilton Waldo on February 26, 1918. In 1929, his name was legally changed to Theodore Hamilton Sturgeon when his stepfather adopted him. He worked as a salesman, a copy editor, a seaman, a story editor, a literary agent, a bulldozer operator, and a resort hotel manager before becoming a free-lance writer. He began writing short stories in 1937 for the McClure syndicate. Two years later he started writing science fiction and fantasy for John W. Campbell's magazines, *Unknown* and *Astounding*. His first published science fiction story was "Ether Breather" in *Astounding* in 1939. Sturgeon became one of the contributors to Campbell's Golden Age of science fiction, though his works were not nearly so technologically oriented as some of the other authors.

For nearly fifty years, he alternated periods of prolific writing with times of severe writer's block. Some of the pseudonyms used by Sturgeon include E. Hunter Waldo, E. Waldo Hunter, and Frederick R. Ewing. He published several novels and over 150 short stories. His short fiction has been often anthologized and his works have been collected numerous times. Several collections of Sturgeon's short stories are: *Without Sorcery* (1948), *E Pluribus Unicorn* (1953), *A Touch of Strange* (1958), *Sturgeon in Orbit* (1964), *Starshine* (1966), *The Worlds of Theodore Sturgeon* (1972), *Sturgeon Is Alive and Well* (1971), and *Case and the Dreamer* (1974). In addition to science fiction, Sturgeon wrote mysteries, westerns, and scripts for television including two popular episodes of "Star Trek--"Shore Leave" and "Amok Time." He is credited with developing the "prime directive" of "Star Trek," the policy of noninterference with developing cultures. As a critic, he wrote numerous book reviews and articles about science fiction. Sturgeon died on May 8, 1985.

Sturgeon's awards include the *Argosy* prize in 1947 for "Bianca's Hands," and the International Fantasy Award for *More Than Human* (1953) in 1954. "Slow Sculpture" won the Nebula award in 1970 and the Hugo award in 1971.

Sturgeon is one of the few science fiction authors to have a proverbial law named for him. While attending a science fiction convention, someone read numerous examples of poorly written science fiction and stated that most of it was trash. Sturgeon's response, that ninety percent of everything is trash, became identified as Sturgeon's Law. It was a quick response, and far less characteristic than his motto, "Ask the next question." He believed that this motto, symbolized by an arrow through the letter Q, was indicative of continuing curiosity, of the need to challenge prejudice and custom to find new answers and further questions.

Themes and Style

Sturgeon's most dominant themes have involved emotion. He has explored the nature of love, particularly as a solution to loneliness and a method of emotional healing. His work seldom involved technology; he concentrated on psychology and philosophy. Many of his works, most notably *The Dreaming Jewels* (1950) and *More Than Human*, consider the true meaning of humanity. Sturgeon used science fiction as a means to discuss the struggle between good and evil and the process of a person's maturing into a responsible, ethical adult. His protagonists, such as the people in "Slow Sculpture," are often outcasts, alienated from society, who find comfort and an end to their isolation through love and begin as well to grow toward ethical and psychological maturity. Sturgeon repeatedly stressed the need for tolerance and understanding of people and attitudes that may have differed from society's norms.

Sturgeon also used his work to attack political, social and sexual taboos. In "Thunder and Roses", he warned of the dangers of nuclear war. "Mr. Costello, Hero" was an attack on the hysteria of the McCarthy era. Several works, such as "Microcosmic God," addressed the ease with which individuals can abuse power. Much of his work has been controversial because of its sexual content. "The World Well Lost" is one of several pieces involving homosexuality, and "If All Men Were Brothers, Would You Want One to Marry Your Sister?" deals with incest.

Sturgeon was a master of literary style. His tone varies from story to story; each character has a distinctive voice. *Godbody* (1986) is written in separate sections, each part about a different character and with its own clearly recognizable tone. Sturgeon's humor shows in his language, especially through the use of puns, and in his subjects. "It Was Nothing--Really!" describes a defensive shield made of nothing; the inventor, observing that perforated items always tear everywhere except along the perforations, realizes that nothing is stronger than something.

Sturgeon is a powerful writer who makes his readers feel the emotions of his characters and who evokes strong reactions toward his characters. His style and emotional content make him one of science fiction's most compelling and admired writers.

Plot Summaries of Major Works

The Dreaming Jewels. Horton "Horty" Bluett had been adopted by Tonta and Armand because Armand thought the adoption might help him win an election. Horty's childhood is difficult because of Armand's cruelty. When Armand tries to lock him in a closet, three fingers on Horty's left hand are severed.

Horty runs away and is found by some people from a traveling carnival. Zena, a lovely midget, decides to protect Horty. She disguises him as a girl, introduces him as her cousin, and trains him to join her musical act. Pierre Monetre, owner of the carnival, treats Horty's hand. He had been a doctor, but was forced to resign because the hospital needed a scapegoat for a patient's death. He has become a misanthrope whose obsession is a form of crystal life. They are jewellike cells with faceted walls that have the power to create life as part of their dreams. Monetre believes that the freaks, incomplete or misformed animals and people, are the result of the incomplete dreams of these crystal cells. He is seeking an intermediary whom he can use to control the crystals. He has learned to use the crystals to control the individuals thus created, and often uses Zena's crystal to summon her. As the carnival moves from place to place, Monetre hides crystals with bacilli or disease-bearing insects near them; when the crystals dream, the evil will be altered into new forms, and humanity will suffer.

Horty spends several years at the carnival, finding friendship with Zena and the other carnies and a place where he belongs. He remembers his home occasionally, thinking of his fear and hatred of Armand and his affection for Kay Hallowell, a neighbor girl who was kind to him. Horty has not grown; he appears to be a midget. Monetre at last remembers Horty's old injuries and wants to examine the hand. Zena realizes that Horty must leave before Monetre discovers that Horty is a creature of the crystals, regardless of how afraid he is of leaving the security of the carnival.

Horty, now a grown man, is performing as a musician in the town where he grew up. He overhears Armand attempting to blackmail Kay into having an affair with him. Horty gives Kay enough money to leave town and tells her to mislead Armand by arranging a meeting for the following evening. Kay does not recognize Horty, but agrees to do as he says because of her fear of Armand. Horty alters his appearance to become Kay and meets Armand. Horty demands to know if Armand had been cruel to anyone, and then cuts off Armand's three left fingers. Armand comes to talk with Monetre about freaks and regeneration, telling him about Horty and Kay. Neither realizes that it was Horty, disguised as Kay, who cut off the fingers. Monetre wants to find Kay, believing she is the one who can regenerate and therefore is the one who can talk to the jewels. He has her kidnapped and brought to the carnival.

Horty goes to the carnival to rescue Kay and confront Monetre. In a desperate struggle, Horty follows Zena's suggestion and asks the crystals how to destroy their dream-things. Zena knows that it will destroy her, but believes that it will also destroy Monetre. Knowing Zena is dead, Horty still struggles to defeat Monetre. He attacks Monetre and succeeds in killing him even though Monetre crushes the crystals that once controlled Horty.

Zena and Armand are dead; they were the only crystal dream creations in the room except for Horty. Horty believes that he survived because his crystals had completed their work with him. Horty communicates with the crystals to plead for Zena's life, but seems unsuccessful. Armand's death will be explained as a heart attack. Kay's memory of the recent days will be erased; she does not belong with the carnival or with the synthetic person that Horty now knows himself to be. Horty will assume Monetre's identity and retrace the route of the carnival, attempting to repair the damage Monetre had done. Horty becomes aware of a hunger for ants, or for the formic acid that they contain; he needs it after his crystals have been active.

The Dreaming Jewels, Sturgeon's first novel, contains many of the themes that would pervade his work. It is about love, evil, and the true nature of humanity. Zena's love for Horty cannot be returned until he learns who he actually is. Both Armand and Monetre are obsessed with power and will use it to achieve their goals. The power of the crystals, as with much power, is a neutral force that may be used for good or evil. Horty and Zena are outcasts, synthetic creations who are isolated from normal society, yet their compassion and love make them more human than Monetre, who is human but evil. Some critics have said that *The Dreaming Jewels* is flawed by some unconvincing characters and by the author's belief that tragedy, as exemplified by Zena's death, is "bad art." In spite of these problems, *The Dreaming Jewels* is a spellbinding story as well as an exploration of the meaning of love and the nature of humanity.

"Microcosmic God." James Kidder is a biochemist who lives on his island inventing a wide range of things from paint remover to new methods of farming. His inventions make him, his bank, and his banker, Conant, very wealthy. Kidder's only contact with the outside world is by phone to Conant. Kidder has not been the actual inventor for most of the things that had made them wealthy, however; the items were created by a new race, the Neoterics--a small, extremely intelligent race created by Kidder in his laboratories for adaptability, creativity, and brilliance. They are about three inches high, exist in an ammonia atmosphere, and live at a much faster speed than humanity. In less than a year they have equaled humanity's technological development. Kidder, whom they consider their God, communicates with them through teletype machines.

The Neoterics invent a new kind of energy, involving beamed power from a transmitter to a receiver. When Kidder refuses to give Conant the entire design, Conant arrives on the island with troops and takes it. Conant uses the power to blackmail the United States president to agree that Conant will become the power secretly controlling the presidency. Conant plans to kill Kidder and the workers who build the power plant when the president agrees to his terms. Kidder discovers the plan and tells his Neoterics to develop an impenetrable shield. Kidder and Conant's chief engineer, Johansen, survive the bombing of the island ordered by Conant because the Neoterics invent a shield that protects the entire island. Kidder and Johansen continue their research together in isolation inside the shield. The power transmitter is blocked by the shield, leaving Conant powerless, broken, and insane. The Neoterics are continuing to develop, and may emerge someday.

"Microcosmic God," one of Sturgeon's earlier stories, is a study of obsessions. Kidder cares only about knowledge; his Neoterics are things to be used, not a race with feeling and emotions. Conant wants money and power; he is as ruthless with people as Kidder is with the Neoterics. "Microcosmic God" show the dangers of intellect and obsession which do not have the balancing influence of compassion and conscience. It is an inventive, tightly paced story. Even though Sturgeon later said that the literary style was somewhat weak, its plot has made it a favorite among readers.

More than Human. *More Than Human* is the story of the maturation of a different kind of life form, "Homo Gestalt," which is made up of several different individuals who communicate telepathically. Baby, a Mongoloid infant, is the computerlike brain; Bonnie and Beanie are black twins who can teleport; Janie, an unloved girl, is a telekineticist. They are brought together by Lone; when he dies, Gerry becomes the central control.

Gerry will do anything he believes necessary to protect the gestalt. When he realizes that the existence of this new entity is endangered by the security and love that each individual has found with an acquaintance of Lone's, he kills her. When Gerry fears that the investigations of a antigravity device made by Lone will lead back to him and the others, he discredits the Air Force officer involved, nearly driving him to suicide.

Janie, unable to accept Gerry's growing cruelty, helps the officer, Hip Barrows, recover his health and memory. Barrows forces Gerry to realize that Homo Gestalt must develop a conscience, a sense of ethics. The gestalt is alone now, but since each segment can be replaced, it is immortal and must build for the future of both Homo Sapiens and Homo Gestalt. Barrows becomes part of the gestalt, as its ethical voice. As Gerry accepts the validity of Barrows' lesson on ethics, he becomes ashamed of his earlier actions. When he realizes the necessity of an ethical code, he hears voices welcoming him into the community of Homo Gestalt. There are many other similar entities who have existed for centuries. They had hoped that the gestalt Gerry led would develop a conscience and mature sufficiently to join their community, which is also a part of human society.

More Than Human is Sturgeon's major novel, and one of the most influential science fiction novels. When it was written, it was unusual because of its literary stylistic devices which were then more common in mainstream fiction. It also differed from most science fiction of the period in its emphasis on psychological rather than technological development. The novel deals with issues of morality, alienation, maturity, love, and the nature of humanity. The children, who are all outcasts, find a sense of belong-

ing in a new identity, which must then find its own role and
ethics. Homo Gestalt is composed of individuals, but its composite
identity exists separately. The individual children and the gestalt
must mature into responsible adults, developing an ethical code
even though the moral codes of human society may or may not
apply to a gestalt society. *More Than Human* is a novel of considerable emotional power that has remained influential since its
publication in 1953.

Slow Sculpture. She is a young woman, panic-stricken by the
discovery of a lump in her breast. She goes to his orchard and
tells him she is dying. He invites her into his home, telling her
that he will fix the lump. In the atrium of his home is a fifteen
foot bonsai which he has nurtured for half of his life. Bonsai are
the result of slow, careful attention; some of the most interesting
begin with damaged plants which develop character. It almost
seems as though the growth becomes a matter of negotiation and
compromise between the person and the plant. He treats her with
a process involving a massive electrical charge. When he identifies her lump as a very malignant cancer, she collapses. When she
recovers from shock three days later, she admits that she had
never seen a doctor. She had retreated when he put her fears into
words. She is still afraid in spite of his assurance that she is
cured. She starts to thank him but he assumes she is about to lec-
ture him about the need to share the cure with humanity. In his
experience, most people who say that mean that they could make
money from it. He does not want to be involved with humanity
or with her; he just wants to be left alone. She tells him that all
she wanted to do was thank him. He does not believe that she can
be grateful until her cure is confirmed; to thank him now would
be an act of faith, which is almost nonexistent.

The next morning she appears to have gone, but he finds her
contemplating the bonsai. She wanted him to have one act of
faith in his life and wants him to believe that she will not go to a
doctor to have the cure confirmed. Before she leaves, however,
she does want to know why he is so angry and frightened. He
tells her that he is an engineer and a lawyer who has always tried
to ask the next question, to discover not simply why something
happens but what follows and might happen. As a result, he has
invented an exhaust system that would reduce pollution and use
cheaper fuel, which was bought and suppressed by an automobile
company. He is angry because people are selfish and stupid. She
responds that people are like bonsai--if he asks the next question
correctly, if he treats them with consideration and respect, they
will respond. She is now afraid to ask her next question, of why
he is frightened, so he answers it for her. He is afraid of close
personal relationships because he does not know what to do. She
tells him that they must be treated gently, as you treat any living

thing, bonsai, or person. She wonders if two twisted trees ever made bonsai of one another. He asks her name.

Slow Sculpture, which won both the Hugo and Nebula awards, is about two frightened people who find the possibility of love and peace together. Its themes, as in most of Sturgeon's work, are love, compassion, and understanding. The bonsai serves as a metaphor for the need for patience and for negotiation and compromise. The two protagonists, whose names are never given, may build a healthy relationship together, with patience and love.

"Thunder and Roses." There has been a devastating nuclear war. Sergeant Pete Mawser is looking forward to a concert by Starr Anthem, a very famous singer who is visiting his base. It is the only thing to look forward to in an insane world that is disintegrating around him. His barracks, built to hold three hundred men, now has three dozen. In a research laboratory, Pete and his friend Sonny discover a hidden room with relays, switches, and a Geiger counter. In the concert, Starr sings about humanity and life, and talks about the effects of the war. She tells them that no one on their continent can survive, and that those overseas will not escape unharmed. If what remains of the United States retaliates, then all humanity will die. If they do not strike back, humanity may live.

Pete meets Starr after her concert. She has traveled from base to base with her message, hoping to find the last of the master firing keys for the missiles in order to prevent the missiles from being fired. She tells Pete that his town of 900 people is the largest one left, and that if the missiles are fired, the Earth will be destroyed. Pete sees in her a hope for humanity and promises the master key will be destroyed. Starr, who had been near one of the first bomb blasts, dies in his arms.

Sonny, listening to a recording of Starr's performance, realizes that the secret room holds the means of retaliation. Infuriated by her death, Sonny prepares to fire the missiles. Pete follows him and kills him rather that let him launch the missiles. Pete destroys the mechanism, hoping that humanity makes the best of its last chance to survive.

Thunder and Roses is a compassionate story about the attempt to preserve humanity after a nuclear holocaust. Sturgeon contrasts Pete's fears with Sonny's hatred and Starr's compassion. As with most of Sturgeon's best work, the emphasis is on the need for love, forgiveness, and understanding, especially when circumstances make those qualities most difficult to achieve. The story, written in 1947, remains a powerful denunciation of the dangers of nuclear warfare.

Biographical/Bibliographical Readings

Lahna F. Diskin, *Theodore Sturgeon* (Starmont House, 1981). Idem, *Theodore Sturgeon: A Primary and Secondary Bibliography* (G.K. Hall, 1980). Donald L. Lawler, "Theodore Sturgeon," in *Twentieth-Century American Science-Fiction Writers* (Gale, 1981), v.2, p.150-64. Lucy Menger, *Theodore Sturgeon* (Ungar, 1981). Sam Moskowitz, "Theodore Sturgeon," in *Seekers of Tomorrow* (Hyperion, 1966), p.229-48. **[Linda K. Lewis]**

TENN, WILLIAM

Life and Works

William Tenn and Kenneth Putnam are both pseudonyms used by Philip Klass. Born a genuine cockney in London on May 9, 1920, Tenn was raised in Brooklyn where his family moved in 1922. Tenn completed public school in Brooklyn's Abraham Lincoln High School, then attended several colleges and universities (including City College and Columbia). Tenn never received a college degree, although he accumulated sufficient course hours from various schools to graduate. During the Second World War, Tenn served in the U.S. Army. Immediately after the war, Tenn held a variety of jobs while selling stories to *Galaxy Science Fiction*, *The Magazine of Fantasy and Science Fiction*, and various other popular science fiction magazines. In the 1950s, Tenn worked full time as a freelance writer and editor; from time to time he waited tables and held other odd jobs to maintain contact with people and society. In the early 1960s, Tenn worked for two years as a copywriter and account executive for an advertising firm. Though extremely successful in advertising, Tenn left the job to avoid being trapped in a non-science fiction profession. Tenn became assistant professor of English at Pennsylvania State University in 1966, where he established the second oldest regularly offered class in science fiction in the United States.

Tenn began his literary career with a number of stories in the late 1940s. Since then, he has had over fifty stories in print, as well as two novels. Three collections of Tenn's stories were published in the 1950s: *Of All Possible Worlds* (1955), *The Human Angle* (1958), and *Time in Advance* (1958). In 1968, these (except for *Time in Advance*) were reissued with three additional collections: *The Seven Sexes*, *The Square Root of Man*, and *The Wooden Star*. The concurrent publication of his novel, *Of Men and Monsters* (1968), provided a uniform edition of all Tenn's major works through 1968. Tenn's first novel, *A Lamp for Medusa* (1951), was not included among the 1968 reprints. In the years since, Tenn has published a few short stories, most notably "On Venus Have

We Got a Rabbi" (1976) and his most recent story, "There Were People on Bikini, There Were People on Attu" (1983).

Best known for his humorous stories, Tenn pioneered the use of science fiction as a vehicle for political satire in the late 1940s. Sci-fi publishers at the time, however, were averse to printing politically controversial satire. Tenn had great difficulty finding a publisher for "The Brooklyn Bridge Project" (1948), a story satirizing the House Committee on Un-American Activities. "Null-P" (1950), possibly Tenn's most renowned short story, was also rejected by several editors before being accepted for publication.

Aside from writing, Tenn has served as consulting editor for science fiction periodicals and for a science fiction anthology, and has published several critical essays under his actual name, Philip Klass. In 1957, Tenn acted as interim editor for three issues of *Magazine of Fantasy and Science Fiction*. In 1968, he was invited to be consulting editor of *MFSF*, this time editing a special issue that focused on science fiction in the university. Tenn compiled what is reputed to be the first thematic science fiction anthology, *Children of Wonder* (1953), in which all of the stories focus on the theme of childhood. *Children of Wonder* was the first monthly Science Fiction Book Club selection. Tenn's critical essays include: "On the Fiction of Science Fiction" (1954); "Jazz Then, Musicology Now" (1972); "An Innocent in Time: Mark Twain in King Arthur's Court" (1974); and "Wells, Welles, and the Martians" (1988).

Retiring from the Pennsylvania State University faculty in June of 1988, Tenn is now professor emeritus of English and Comparative Literature. He has two novels in the works: one in the same satirical mode of his earlier fiction, the second a serious piece only vaguely associated with science fiction.

Themes and Style

Tenn contributed a keen twist of humor to science fiction literature of the post-World War II era. While staged in fairly standard settings (time travel, encounters with aliens, etc.), Tenn's fiction employed satire, ironic reversal, and wit to address major social, political, and scientific issues of the 1940s to the 1960s. At times, such as in "The Flateyed Monster" (1955), Tenn produced pure slapstick, a welcome addition to the science fiction literature of the post-war decade. In all Tenn stories, whether through humor, drama, or occasionally romance, readers are exposed to penetrating insights into basic human feelings and motivations.

A theme Tenn derived directly from the mind set of the cold war was the impact of nuclear war upon society, i.e., what comes after the nuclear deluge. "Null-P" portrays a post nuclear war Earth in which absolute mediocrity is worshipped and people become so lulled into apathy that they are easily overrun and domesticated by intelligent dogs. "Generation of Noah" (1950),

"Eastward Ho!" (1958), and "Will You Walk a Little Faster?" (1951) are other Tenn stories depicting post-nuclear war societies. The witch hunt fanaticism of the 1940s and 1950s is a second recurrent theme in Tenn's writings. The central action in *Of Men and Monsters* is precipitated by a witch hunt. Tenn returns to the witch hunt theme in "Firewater" (1952), one of his longer stories, in which xenophobic Firsters zealously demand the expulsion of all aliens from Earth. Two time travel stories, "Sanctuary" (1957) and "Winthrop Was Stubborn" (1957), also portray societies intolerant of unorthodox beliefs and behavior. Tenn occasionally turned to yet another theme, pacifism, not from any personal conviction, but rather in tribute to his father, an inveterate pacifist. "The Deserter" (1953) is the most notable of Tenn's pacifist stories.

Tenn's most persistent theme--a theme heavily imbued with ironic reversal--is that of humanity (or whatever happens to be Tenn's choice of intelligent creature) confronting beings of significantly superior intellect and technology. Tenn provides his audience with a taste of what it's like to be on the receiving end of colonization. This theme is most poignantly presented in "Eastward Ho!," a story in which Seminole, Sioux, and other Indian tribes gradually push the Anglos back into the Atlantic Ocean. The theme is also present in *Of Men and Monsters* and "The Liberation of Earth" (1953). An interesting twist is introduced in "Venus Is a Man's World" (1951), a future world in which men are dominated by women. In his essay, "Wells, Welles, and the Martians," Tenn posits that switching positions between conqueror and conquered has been a key theme since the earliest days of science fiction.

Tenn perceives science fiction as a literary genre limited only by the imagination of its authors and the credulity of its readers. With this in mind, Tenn has reeled off stories that place people (and other creatures) in sometimes bizarre and usually humorous situations that purposefully stretch the imagination. Tenn narrates his stories in a precise, unpretentious prose which succeeds in drawing readers into the central action of each story, frequently startling the reader with sudden ironic twists that derive logically though unexpectedly from the plot. Most every Tenn story forces the reader to think, and then to think again. This skill in combining humor and wit with serious issues places Tenn in company with Swift, Voltaire, and other past masters of satire. His empathetic depiction of compelling human experience, gleaned from Theodore Sturgeon, guarantees Tenn a place in the realm of science fiction.

Plot Summaries of Major Works

"Eastward Ho!" Jerry Franklin follows the New Jersey turnpike south from New York City to Trenton, New Jersey. As am-

bassador from the United States of America, his instructions are
to deal with the Indian tribe that has crossed the Delaware River
(presumably the Seminoles) to grab land from United States terri-
tories.   Presenting his credentials from the Great White Father,
Jerry discovers that a Sioux tribe under Chief Three Hydrogen
Bombs is occupying the Trenton area.   The high level of Sioux
technology amazes Jerry: oil lamps, firearms, even microscopes,
all technologies long lost to white men.   Though intimidated by
the obvious supremacy of the Indians, Jerry informs them that,
according to treaty, the Sioux had agreed to take no United State
land east of the Susquehanna River.   Chief Three Hydrogen
Bombs replies that population pressure is pushing the Sioux and
that United States residents do not use most of the land they occupy.   Besides, if not taken by the Sioux, the lands would be
stolen by the Seminoles.   Before returning to New York City, Jerry
learns that the entire east coast has fallen to Ojibwa-Cree-Mon-
taignais tribes.   Brandishing the revolver given to him by Chief
Three Hydrogen Bombs, Jerry flees for Asbury Park where the
Tenth Fleet of the U.S. Navy is stationed.   With Jerry in charge as
the highest living official of the United States, the fleet sails for
Europe to rediscover the heritage of the white man.

Grounded in blatantly humorous, forceful use of ironic reversal, "Eastward Ho!" amuses at the same time it saddens.   Tenn's
straightforward   narrative--generously   spiced   with   biting   hu-
mor--excels in this story, ensuring the acceptance of the otherwise
unbelievable Indian-white man role reversal.   The powerful use of
irony also ensures appreciation of the plight of the American Indian (and other oppressed groups) through the course of modern
history, a major objective of many Tenn pieces.

"Firewater."   Algernon Hebster, president of Hebster Securi-
ties, is one of the few humans who deals with Primeys--humans
who have lost most of their human characteristics (including personal hygiene) after leaving human society to live and work in areas reserved for the virtually unknown aliens.   A keen businessman, Hebster has created a financial empire in illegal dealings
with the Primeys involving the trade of human artifacts for alien
technological wonders which he sells in his chain of retail stores.
The government's Special Investigating Commission (SIC), unable
to catch Hebster in the act of his illegal dealings with Primeys, is
equally unable to undermine the propaganda of the Firsters, a
powerful xenophobic movement whose goal is to reestablish human
dominance on Earth by expelling the aliens and their Primey
goons.   Espousing slogans such as "Humanity First" and "Shop Humanitarian," the Firsters assume a religious zeal in targeting Hebster and others who deal with Primeys as sacrilegious traitors.
Fueling the Firsters is the total inability of humans, including
academic researchers, to understand the aliens or their motives.
All interaction with the aliens is done indirectly through Primeys.

Researchers who seek to comprehend alien ways "go Primey," thereby losing most capabilities of human communication. As Firster propaganda reaches fever pitch, the government is on the verge of collapse. The SIC convinces Hebster that he, owing to his ties with the Primeys, represents the last chance to open communications with the aliens and thereby avert political chaos. Hebster succeeds and reveals that the apparently superior aliens are actually awed by the humans who they think are technically superior to themselves.

One of Tenn's more serious works, "Firewater" is also among his best first contact stories. The belief by rational characters--Hebster and the SIC men--that communication with the aliens will relieve tensions within human society is central to the story. Tenn juxtaposes this rational approach to interplanetary relations with the Firsters' zealous mistrust of aliens. In "Firewater," Tenn turns his favorite theme on its head, allowing an apparently inferior human society to get the better of the invaders.

"The Liberation of Earth." A distant future elder on Earth, whose environment has become virtually uninhabitable owing to a series of catastrophic wars, narrates to his people the story of Earth's liberation. The first Dendi arrived in spaceships and, after language problems were worked out, informed representatives of the United Nations that they had come to Earth to protect the Galactic Federation from the treacherous Troxxt, an authoritarian, wormlike organism. The Dendi staked out several locations needed for defense installations (which involves relocating the United States capitol to Denver), and then recruited human volunteers to help with construction. When the Troxxt attacked, flack from the incredible weapons of the Dendi and Troxxt killed thousands of humans. The eventual defeat of the Dendi and landing of the Troxxt began the second liberation of Earth. The Troxxt explained that they were in fact the true liberators of the universe, freeing worlds from the tyrannical rule of the Dendi. After executing Earth leaders who had assisted the Dendi, the Troxxt proceeded to construct defensive sites in anticipation of renewed Dendi efforts to subjugate humanity. Liberation follows liberation, resulting in a ruined environment and the near annihilation of humanity--the ultimate liberation.

Told in the first person narrative, this is a provocative tale. The theme of Earthlings as innocent dupes for the Dendi and Troxxt strongly resembles the cold war maneuvering which occurred during the 1950s. The ruin of the Earth resembles the destruction of Korea, which was underway in 1953. Furthering the themes of cold war politics is Tenn's use of shallow, rhetorical statements by the liberators--which are similar to the self-serving propaganda of the cold war liberators of the 1950s.

Of Men and Monsters. On an Earth where giant alien monsters have replaced miniscule people as the predominant species,

Eric the Only encounters a variety of unusual circumstances as he prepares for his initiation into manhood. Living in tunnels that honeycomb the insulation of alien houses, humans manage physical sustenance by raiding alien larders; ideological support is provided by a religion that recalls the past greatness of humanity and foretells a resurrection of human dominance through adherence to human technology. To the aliens, humans are nothing but vermin to be exterminated. Eric becomes involved with a group of heretics who believe that humans must adopt alien science to defeat the monsters. When tribal leaders begin a witch hunt to eliminate heretics, Eric and a few others barely escape execution and flee into the vast rooms of the alien houses. In a variety of adventures, including captivity by alien scientists researching ways to exterminate people, Eric finally links up with a tribe of humans unknown to his people. This tribe, philosophically tied neither to human nor alien science, reveals to Eric its pragmatic plan for evading the increasingly effective pesticides and vermin traps of the aliens. The plan is to infest the insulation of alien spacecraft to evade extermination. The consequence is that the aliens unknowingly spread the human race throughout the universe.

Tenn's best full-length novel--originally published as the short story "The Men in the Walls"--*Of Men and Monsters* is a hero-myth epic. The novel concentrates on the myth-making process as future humanity, displaced as masters of the universe, struggles to create a mythical-intellectual paradigm that can sustain its physiological existence and support its psychological needs. The persecution of alien scientists is an example of Tenn's use of witch hunts of the 1950s as a theme. Tenn throws in an interesting twist: neither the traditionalists nor the revisionists present a viable world view. The eventual answer to humanity's place, colonizing space by infesting the insulation of alien space craft, is as unexpected as it is undeniable. Though humorous on the surface, *Of Men and Monsters* is a compelling statement of human adaptability and will to survive.

"Venus Is a Man's World." The Male Desuffrage Act, a cornerstone of the maternal revolution following the Third Atomic War, has generated a unified Earth upon which women are in charge. With the male population decimated by warfare and many surviving males sexually impotent owing to radioactive contamination, women interested in fruitful marriages are forced to seek mates elsewhere. Venus, a rugged planet in the process of frontier settlement, is one of the few places where males outnumber females. As a male minor bound to the will of his older sister, Ferdinand Starling is involuntarily a passenger on the spacecraft *Eleanor Roosevelt*. His sister and three hundred other females are destined for Venus in search of available males. On board, Ferdinand meets Butt Lee Jones, a rough frontiersman who has stowed away on the *Eleanor Roosevelt* after a calamitous visit to Earth.

Spending much of the journey engrossed in Jones's tall frontier tales, Ferdinand (Butt Lee calls him Ford as it is more masculine) learns that men can be other than the submissive companions of dominant females. Male raw physical strength and daring, Ferdinand learns, are necessary in taming the wilderness environment of Venus. When Ferdinand's sister and the ship's authorities discover Butt Lee Jones, events and negotiations lead to an unexpected conclusion, an ending very satisfying to Ferdinand.

One of Tenn's more ironic tales, "Venus" employs one of Tenn's preponderant themes--the social, political, environmental situation of Earth following a series of nuclear wars. The role reversal of men and women is intended not to aggrandize one sex at the expense of the other, but rather as a plausible (and rather humorous) reaction of society to the ravages of war. Those wars, given the socio-political milieu of the 1950s, were necessarily the product of untamed male aggressiveness. Tenn also encourages the envisionment of a world in which the traditional dominator is dominated.

Biographical/Bibliographical Readings

Malcolm Edwards, "William Tenn," in *Science Fiction Writers*, ed. E. F. Bleiler (Scribner's, 1982), p. 525-30. Charles Hackenberry, "Painter at the Keyboard," *Extrapolation* 26(1) (Spring 1985), p.50-55. Idem, Interview with a Time Traveler," *Pennsylvania English* 10(2) (Spring 1984), p.5-13. Brian Stableford, "The Short Fiction of William Tenn," in *Survey of Science Fiction Literature*, ed. Frank N. McGill (Salem Press, 1979), v.5, p.2065-69. **[Duncan M. Aldrich]**

TIPTREE, JAMES, JR.

Life and Works

James Tiptree, Jr., is the major pseudonym of Alice Hastings Bradley Sheldon, born in Chicago in 1915. She also wrote under the name Raccoona Sheldon. In "Everything but the Signature Is Me," Sheldon says that she spent her time from age three to age twenty-six being a painter. For a short time she was the *Chicago Sun*'s art editor.

After enlisting in the United States Army, she was the first woman ever put through Air Force Intelligence School at Harrisburg, became a photo-intelligence officer and started work at the Pentagon. After leaving the C.I.A, she earned her Ph.D. in experimental psychology. It was at this time that she began to write science fiction; she was already a maverick in the psychology departments. In order to retain her respectability she took the name Tiptree from a marmalade jar and added James. Her husband,

Huntington Sheldon, added the "Jr." for whimsy's sake. As a very private person, she also felt that a male name would be a good camouflage and that a male name would slip by less observed. It was not until 1977 that she revealed herself to be Alice Sheldon.

She published her first short story in *Analog* in 1967, the year after she received her Ph.D. From 1968 to 1974, she published many stories in *Galaxy, Analog, Amazing* and *The Magazine of Fantasy & Science Fiction*. She became known in the science fiction community in part as the author of a series of articles, begun in 1971, largely about adventures in foreign lands.

Tiptree was best known as a short story writer, although she wrote three novels, *Up the Walls of the World* (1979), *Brightness Falls from the Air* (1982), and *Starry Rift* (1986). Her last novel, *Starry Rift*, is actually three stories loosely gathered into a novel. *Ten Thousand Light Years from Home* (1973) was Tiptree's first short story collection, followed in 1975 by *Warm Worlds* and *Otherwise*. Robert Silverberg, in the introduction to this collection, discusses the reasons Tiptree could not possibly be a woman, finding something ineluctably masculine about her writing. One of the stories, "The Women Men Don't See," was nominated for the 1974 Nebula, but Tiptree withdrew it from consideration. It is believed that she did not wish to gain a prize for a feminist story which had been widely praised as a sympathetic portrayal of women by a male author. On May 19, 1987, Tiptree committed suicide at the age of 71, after killing her husband, Huntington Sheldon, in their suburban home in Washington, D.C.

Themes and Style

The main focus of Tiptree's writing is an exploration of the psychology of beings, whether these beings be human or alien. Her concern is not with the technology of the future but with morals and motives. Her characterizations are memorable because she builds the entire biological, cultural, and psychological environment in which a race operates. While her aliens often behave in ways we might think of as very human, her humans are often misfits, dreamers, alienated, and powerless. Some stories are set on an Earth on which sociopolitical trends are extrapolated into the future. Others, like "Up the Walls of the World," are set in a complex interaction of human and alien worlds. Her narrative is sparse, fast-paced, using jazzy idiomatic words, and often there is a complex story within a story. She has a witty and often acerbic humor as in the ending of "Houston, Houston, Do You Read?," winner of the Nebula and Hugo awards. Her stories may be shrouded in mystery and suspense until the last line, as in the "Screwfly Solution." Tiptree comments that her basic narrative instinct is to start from the end, preferably 5,000 feet underground on a dark day.

Tiptree's focus is the striving of the personna, whether alien or human, for completeness which requires transcendence from the biological imperative. But humans are biologically limited beings, subject to powerful sociobiological drives. These drives are so compelling that in Tiptree's work, sexuality, the perpetuation of the species, is often connected with violence and death. The most powerful statement of the biological imperative is found in "Love Is the Plan, the Plan Is Death." Moggadeet revels in the love of his mate, even as she devours him in order to feed her young. "Love Is the Plan. . ." also elucidates another prominent theme of Tiptree's, that the survival of humanity as now constituted may not last without a major reordering of drives.

In many of Tiptree's stories, love and sex are such powerful drives that they threaten the very existence of the race. In "A Momentary Taste of Being," humans are merely the spermatoza used to fertilize an alien ova in a greater master plan. "Your Haploid Heart" defines the highest human ideal as freedom from the sexual drive and yet it must lead to annihilation of the race. Aliens manipulate the agressive aspect of human sexuality in the award-winning "The Screwfly Solution" for the purpose of destroying all humankind. Tiptree's consistent message is that reproduction is a catastrophe, but that humanity cannot exist without it. She presents us with the ambiguity that without sexual drives the human race is incomplete, even though the sexual drive leads to pain, suffering, and death. Love is most successful in Tiptree's stories when it is divorced from the sexual drive. In "Up the Walls of the World" and "With Delicate Mad Hands," the highest form of love is that of shielding the beloved from pain.

In the overpowering biological drive among humans, women are the powerless victims. Tiptree's extraordinary ability to portray women as victims has led many critics to call Tiptree a radical feminist writer. The women in her stories often go to extreme lengths to improve their status. In her 1974 Hugo award winning "The Girl Who Was Plugged In," a deformed young woman allows her mind to be plugged into a beautiful cyborg in order to experience some happiness. In "With Delicate Mad Hands," Carol flees in the starship. In "The Women Men Don't See" Ruth and Althea leave the planet with unknown aliens because they hope for a better world elsewhere. Carrying this theme further in "Houston, Houston, Do You Read?," Tiptree gives us an an immortal feminist community where male intruders must be killed to protect society. The devastating conclusion of "Your Faces, O My Sisters" only makes more invidious the comparison between the peaceful society of women and the brutal society of men. Tiptree is antiromantic and pessimistic. She explores the attitudes supporting a sexist society and finds few acceptable solutions to the male/female problem.

Plot Summaries of Major Works

"Houston, Houston, Do You Read?" Three male astronauts, Lorimer, Davis, and Geirr, are thrown 300 years into the far future. The men are rescued by the spaceship *Gloria*, piloted by women. They gradually learn that Earth is now populated entirely by women who reproduce by cloning. All males died centuries ago of a plague and all live births since have been female. The three men fantasize about the importance of being the only three males alive and putting women in their traditional roles. Geirr, expecting to be valued for his sexual prowess, rapes one of the women. Davis tries to take over the ship and become the paternalistic religious father who will provide sons to rule over the women. Lorimer, playing the role of the chivalrous protector, attempts to defend the others with the argument that everyone has aggressive fantasies. He is informed by the women that only in a society of males are there aggressive fantasies. In this new society, the male is an alien. He has no useful role to play and his aggressive behavior is dangerous. The story ends with the clear understanding that the three men must be destroyed.

This is Tiptree's most radically femininist story published in the feminist collection, *Aurora, beyond Equality*. Its title implies a pervasive male world of the national space program. She has an opportunity to explore the future of human potential in an all-female society and finds that world pursuing peaceful interests with its focus on nurturing the young. She has solved the problem of sex and violence by eliminating one part of humanity. However, while Tiptree makes clear her perception of males as aggressive and violent, she also indicates the incompleteness of the all-female society, which has a limited gene pool and thus a limited variety of individuals. One of the results is the paucity of new creations. Tiptree concentrates in this story on showing us the shocked emotions of the three men as they discover their insignificance--a total role reversal for them. She contrasts that with the matter-of-fact manner in which the women assume that males will display their latent agressive tendencies. The ending is a classic Tiptree twist.

"Love Is the Plan, the Plan Is Death." In this short story, an alien insectoid life form, Moggadeet, grows to maturity escaping the jaws of his mother. As he grows up from a small golden-furred baby to a large black thing, he is thrown out of the cave by his mother. While he is growing through the winter, instinct (the plan) leads him and he does not have to think. In his wanderings he comes across an old black one who miraculously has survived and who unlike other black ones is able to tell him about the plan and the cold which is increasing and killing the forest. At winter's end, Moggadeet finds that he has become a huge black monster. While in his subconscious he remembers his brother

Frim, he rips him apart in the struggle for supremacy over the small red female, "Lilliloo." His special hands appear, special juices flow from his jaw and he binds her with silken threads. During all the warm period that follows, he feeds her and tends her until she is big enough for mating. Moggadeet continues to struggle to escape the plan's imperatives even as his lover, perhaps his sister, grows bigger and stronger. Finally he rips away the silken threads that bind her and she has become a mother. With their last food gone and winter coming, she devours him to feed her young on his body. As he dies he savors the ecstacy of his love and accepts his death as part of the plan.

Tiptree's characterization of the young Moggadeet growing to maturity and dedicating himself to escaping the biological plan, is a skilled and charming presentation of the huge, lovable furry creature singing love songs. Yet Moggadeet's attempt to assert free will is important, for he is one of the few of his race that realizes that if Lilliloo, so caught up in the necessity of motherhood, does not pass on his warning that the climate is changing, the entire race may perish. Yet biological imperatives in most cases are deadly--Moggadeet dies happily, as did his brothers before him, because the biological imperative is too strong to resist. But Tiptree warns us, if there is not change, the whole race may die too.

"The Screwfly Solution." The story opens with Alan in Colombia, South America, setting up a biological pest control program while his wife writes him a series of letters, each more alarming than the former, about the increasing murder of women. Included in her letters are notes from his friend Barney, who is engaged in a program to destroy the spruce budworm moth. Both are concerned with finding the vulnerable link in the behavioral chain in order to destroy harmful insects. Alan, frightened for Ann, leaves for Michigan but becomes infected with a virus and kills his daughter. Prominent church officials, meanwhile, affirm the view that women are nowhere defined as human, but are merely a transitional expedient. As the killings become epidemic, Public Health teams call it mass mania while biologists note the relation of the killing to geography and wind conditions. A Glasgow professor notes the close linkage between the behavioral expression of aggression/predation and sexual reproduction in the male. He speculates that some viral substance has affected the failure of the switching function from aggression to copulatory behavior. As women disappear from the Earth, Ann, dressed as a boy, is in hiding; the story ends on an astounding but believable note.

The award-winning "Screwfly Solution" is Tiptree's most bitter and pessimistic indictment of male sexuality. She has said that males at their extreme are totally focused on the aggressive or provocative vulnerability that is promoted by genital contact. It is this aggression that ultimately destroys the race. Women are characterized by Ann as hypnotized rabbits--a toothless race, the victims in the pattern of human sexuality. She also indicates that women are the victims because only extreme circumstances will lead them to take cooperative action with other females and by then it is probably too late.

Up The Walls of the World. Tiptree's first novel creates a full-blown space opera in three complex interwoven settings. There is the "Destroyer," an enormous deranged stellar being inwardly anguished and lonely, destroying all suns in its path. The second setting is a secret government parapsychology research project on Earth which is using alienated telepaths. Among the telepaths is Winona, an aging housewife no longer leading a useful life; Daniel Dann, the group's physician, crippled by guilt over his inability to prevent the death of his family; and Margaret Omali, a computer technician who has been scarred psychically and emotionally. The final setting is Tyree, a planet inhabited by giant winged telepathic creatures, which lies directly in the Destroyer's path and will soon be incinerated. The Tyreenni, in a desperate attempt to save their race, construct an energy beam which allows some of them to transfer their minds into the bodies of members of the parapsychic project on Earth, whose minds are then transferred to Tyree. Daniel finds that on Tyree he can be very valuable because he has the psychic power to absorb another's pain, and to alleviate the pain of the Tyreenni, who are being burned in the wake of the Destroyer. Winona gains status on Tyree where "fathering" is a sacred duty, because she has "fathered" four children. Other alienated parapsychics are made whole by the friendly atmosphere of Tyree. Margaret is drawn into the Destroyer to become its computer operator and to lead it to understand its mission of creating a "firebreak" to contain a conflagration started by exploding stars in the center of the galaxy. Eventually the Destroyer becomes a rescue craft for survivors of the destroyed planets, with its first passengers being the surviving Tyreenni and parapsychics.

Consistent with Tiptree's concern with nurturing, on Tyree child rearing is the race's primary duty, a sacred function reserved for the males, who accordingly have higher status than females. Tiptree portrays positive attitudes towards child bearing and nurturing, although she has satirically noted that because it is carried on by women in human society it has little status. On the planet Tyree males nurture the children and this gives them the most important role in society. Tiptree's solutions to the question of sex and violence raised in so many of her works is answered in this novel. Because sex has only symbolized violence to Margaret, when she becomes bodiless in the Destroyer she finds peace. This is a depiction of both the destruction of a world, the Tyree, and the creation of a new world through combined efforts of humans and aliens, without sexual characteristics to get in the way. Shorn

of their bodies, Dr. Dann and Omali can help each other carry out
the great tasks of the universe with the Destroyer, which is also a
great bodiless form. Finally with all these various bodiless humans and Tyreenni in the "Destroyer," Tiptree posits the need for
life forms to maintain their pluralistic behavioral structures.
Some Tyreenni leave the Destroyer to enter new bodies and continue to train their young. Other humans and Tyreenni continue
to explore the stars and the future. This is a vast theme concerned
with questions of being and nonbeing, love and pain, the continu-
ance of the race. Frequent shifts of point of view and changes in
temporality require a concerted effort on the part of the reader,
but it is well rewarded.

"With Delicate Mad Hands." The protagonist of this short
story is Carol Page, another of Tiptree's alienated characters
whose face is spoiled by a huge, fleshy, obscene, pugged nose. Orphaned and ugly, she grows up with an inner "Voice" which calls
to her and propels her with an unquenchable desire to go among
the stars. She completes the space training program and is chosen
for longterm space work not because of her ability but because, as
a woman, she is considered a "human waste can" and will not
cause any competitive problems among the men while satisfying
all their needs. Sexually abused by the crew, she acquires the
nickname Cold Pig because she can feel no real desire for the abusive males whom she serves. She is assigned to the ship *Calgary* on
an extremely long-range mission beyond Uranus. Four of the
ship's five scout ships are out on long flights with only the captain and the injured fifth scout pilot in the ship. Carol requests
permission to fly the fifth ship and the captain denies her request
because she is a female. He rapes her brutally, and, in a fit of
madness (or sanity), she poisons him. Alone and happy to be free
of her servitors, she takes control of the *Calgary* and heads toward
outer space. A highly radioactive starlike planet appears before
her and she lands. There she meets the owner of her mysterious
voice, an alien named Cavana, who to his people has the defect of
having floppy, piglike ears. Cavana is a star caller who must give
up all for love of the stars and the person with whom he makes
contact. Carol and Cavanna communicate from the ship until her
oxygen is gone and she must go onto the planet's surface. The
planet's radiation kills her within days, but Cavana and Carol
share an intense, nonphysical love before she dies.

Carol is perhaps the most well defined of Tiptree's women
who seek to escape their role as submissive victim in a male-dominated world; a world where women are used by men for their own
sexual pleasure without any concern for their partner. In an act
uncharacteristic for Tiptree, the males are killed by the victim,
who flees to another planet. Here she discovers that, devoid of
sexual overtones, she and Cavanna can develop an intense and loving relationship in which love is most sublime when the loved

one's pain can be removed, even if it causes death. It is significant that in the final words of the story we discover that Cavanna, whom Carol had thought of as male, is female.

"Your Haploid Heart." An interplanetary biological investigator discovers a race of sapient people who possess two distinct and alternating modes of reproduction. One generation is large, long-lived, asexual and reproduces by budding. The next generation (their offspring) is small, short-lived, and reproduces sexually (giving birth to the asexual form). The sexually produced Flenni have half as many chromosomes as the asexual Esthaans; they are living gametes in whom every genetic imperfection is expressed and weeded out by the individual's death. But the incompleteness of the Flenni is not only a weakness and a selection mechanism, it is also the source of an incomparable beauty. They are beings who are literally all male or all female. The most virile man, the most seductive woman, is in fact a blend. But the Flenni are the pure expression of one sex alone and overwhelmingly irresistible. The asexual Esthaans have formed the notion that sex and reproduction are revolting, unspeakable things and in what they see as a struggle for higher civiliation, they are eliminating the Flenni on whom their existence depends.

The question of gender is central to much of Tiptree's work. Humanity is linked to sexuality and to fixed gender roles. These roles make humanity incomplete and are destructive. Just as the Esthaans are intent on destroying the Flenni, upon whom their existence depends, males are constantly destroying females upon whom their civilization depends. Sexuality itself is confining but the struggle to transcend its limits is to annihilate oneself. The unresolved conflict of humanity's desire to transcend biological limits and yet to perpetuate the race is most clearly expressed in "Your Haploid Heart."

Biographical/Bibliographical Readings

Virginia Bemis, "James Tiptree, Jr.," in *Twentieth-Century American Science-Fiction Writers* (Gale, 1981), v.2, p.167-71. Charles Platt, "James Tiptree, Jr.," in *Dream Makers: The Uncommon Men and Women Who Write Science Fiction* (Berkley, 1983), p.257-72. James Tiptree, Jr., "Everything but the Name Is Me," *Starship* 16 (Fall 1979), p.31-34. Susan Wood, "James Tiptree, Jr." in *Twentieth-Century Science Fiction-Writers*, ed. Curtis C. Smith (Macmillan, 1981), p.531-41. **[Judith R. Bernstein]**

TUCKER, WILSON

Life and Works

Arthur Wilson Tucker was born at Deer Creek, Illinois, on November 23, 1914. Tucker received his education in Illinois and was employed as a film projectionist and electrician at the University of Illinois and 20th Century Fox for nearly forty years. A devoted family man (one daughter and four sons), he was known among his friends for his sense of humor, kindness, storytelling abilities, and was respected for his skills as an editor. Winner of both the Hugo award in 1970 as best science fiction fan writer and the John W. Campbell Memorial Award (retrospectively, for *The Year of the Quiet Sun* in 1973) Tucker was also honored as Guest of Honor at the twenty-fifth World Science Fiction Convention in 1967.

A stylist who is also research-oriented, Tucker often revises his own work for republication, usually expanding a given work into a more detailed creation. He published his first fanzine, *The Planetoid*, in 1932. His first story, "Interstellar Way Station," written as Bob Tucker, appeared in *Super Science Novels* in 1941. During his long writing career, he remained friends with many American authors, and was a lifelong friend of novelist Robert Bloch.

His short fiction appears in *The Best of Wilson Tucker* (1982). He is best known to science fiction readers for his science fiction novels *The City in the Sea* (1951), *The Lincoln Hunters* (1958), *The Year of the Quiet Sun* (1970), *The Time Masters* (1953, revised in 1971), *Ice and Iron* (1974, expanded 1975), and *Resurrection Days* (1981).

Themes and Style

Long interested in film techniques, Tucker's fiction reflects a polished, cinematic approach to scenes, characterizations, and dialogue. Major motifs in his fiction include the use of the time travel theme, social history, and religious and philosophical concerns interwoven with the concepts of honor, moral stance, individuality, mercy, and outsider versus insider.

Plot Summaries of Major Works

Ice and Iron. Fisher Yann Highsmith is a scientist on the edge of an ice field in the near future Earth, accompanied by several colleagues including a librarian named Jeanmarie. Locked in a New Ice Age, they are investigating its spreading impact when weird items and bodies start materializing in the ice-covered landscape. These objects appear to come from a warm climate. In the distant future, a battle for control of the environment and possession of people is underway. Through weapons, and a warp in time related to these weapons, the future is dropping its dead into Highsmith's present.

The novel is fast-paced science fiction laced with elements of mystery which create an entertaining puzzle for readers to unravel. A well-crafted plot allows the reader to move from one time era to the other, and through subtle characterization, contrast the struggles of Highsmith and his group with those of the warriors and hunters of the future as the novel builds to an unusual climax.

The Lincoln Hunters. In the distant future, Amos Peabody, a collector of historical items, wants to locate the lost speech given in 1856 by President Abraham Lincoln. Peabody calls on the services of Time Researchers to assist in finding the speech, which means going back into time across a postnuclear era that eliminated much of humanity's historical archives and artifacts. In the current time period, Time Researchers are often hired to locate and retrieve past documents and realia. Benjamin Steward is selected to do the job. Evelyn Kung monitors and makes commentaries on Steward's travels into the past.

A time-travel novel with a complex plot and a host of intriguing characters including "Bobby Bloch" (the personna of Robert Bloch, a close friend of Tucker's), the novel reads like a historical documentary with touches of ironic humor. Evelyn serves as the feminine gemstone in this novel as she portrays the anchor of strength in a story dealing with ideas, humanity, and the durability of the human spirit.

Resurrection Days. A journeyman carpenter named Owen Hall was killed at a railroad crossing in 1943. Several thousand years later, he is resurrected in a world controlled completely by women; he is the only free man in a world where men are less than second-class citizens. The men in his future are androidlike in the sense that they do function as men physically, but they have no spark of independence or soul within them. Owen Hall cannot tolerate these men who are men in name and physical functioning only, nor can he accept what he perceives as a dangerous world where women control everything in all ways, manners, and approaches. Within a short time, Hall commences to upset, confuse, and disintegrate this futuristic, feminine-controlled world by exerting his rights in a thinking struggle-to-the-death approach for freedom to be an individual, capable man.

Thrown into the future society, a man from the twentieth century, with that century's male attitudes, is seen as an anachronism. Sexual roles are reversed and rather than giving in to the situation, Owen Hall upsets the society by attempting to reestablish himself (and ultimately other men). Whether or not female-controlled society is any better than male-controlled society is not the issue. The pathetic note to this novel is that equality among individuals of both sexes seems to be impossible, and that humanity may indeed keep switching back and forth between mastery of the two genders rather than working together to establish a reasonable, equitable society where all work together for the sake of the race.

The Time Masters. A top-secret project called "Ridgerunner" is threatened by the appearance of an unusual man named Gilbert Nash, who is apparently a man without a past. Government agents seek to discover the true identity of Gilbert Nash and what his plans are. An agent's secretary, Shirley Hoffman, comes into direct contact with Nash and discovers that Nash is Gilgamesh, the immortal hero of Ancient Assyria, and that Gilgamesh, in reality, is a marooned and lonely extraterrestrial seeking to escape his fate with the aid of the secret government project.

This is one of Tucker's most popular novels and deals with individuality, outcasts, outsider versus insider, and the loss of innocence. The search for happiness is also apparent. A well-crafted novel, filled with suspense, *The Time Masters* touches on some of Tucker's major concerns and serves as an excellent introduction to his works.

The Year of the Quiet Sun. Time travel takes us to Will County, Illinois, in the year 2000. The United States faces Armageddon with China and the U.S.S.R. at war; and America has undergone a debilitating black revolution. The five major characters have individual choices and decisions which will shape history--Brian Chaney, William Moresby, Arthur Saltus, Gilbert Seabrooke, and the intelligent and compassionate Katrina van Hise. Through Katrina's eyes and visions, the reader comes to understand the social awareness that permeates the novel, which in subtle fashion reflects some definite concerns of Tucker as he saw them in the turbulent decade of the 1960s in the United States.

One of Tucker's most enduring science fiction novels, *The Year of the Quiet Sun* also reflects a major motif: to exist, to struggle, to function and learn is a journey through time, from birth to death, and the final destination will come as it comes, whether we expect it to be that way or not. A fast-paced work, with Biblical symbols in abundance, it is a study of human beings involved in existential aloneness, a struggle for survival, and the need to establish meaning out of chaos. This award-winning novel is considered by some critics to be among the classics of contemporary science fiction.

Biographical/Bibliographical Readings

John Clute and Peter Nicholls, "Arthur Wilson Tucker," in *The Science Fiction Encyclopedia*, ed. Peter Nicholls (Doubleday, 1979), p.614-15. "Wilson Tucker," in *Speaking of Science Fiction: The Paul Walker Interviews* (Luna Pubs., 1978), p.340-60. **[Harold Lee Prosser]**

VANCE, JACK

Life and Works

Jack Vance is perhaps the least well-known master in the field of science fiction. Winner of two Hugos and a Nebula, arguably the most distinctive stylist in the field and the finest creator of alien ambiances, he remains unknown to many readers, simply because he has no interest in publicizing himself at all. Vance is reluctant to discuss biographical details. He was born John Holbrook Vance in San Francisco, California--a birth date of August 28, 1920, is often cited--into a family with deep roots in California. Vance says his great-great-grandfather arrived before the Gold Rush. He attended the University of California, Berkeley, studied physics and journalism, and graduated with a B.A. in 1942. He worked as a merchant seaman, a carpenter, and a jazz horn player. He decided to become a freelance writer toward the end of his college career and slowly won a reputation after a long apprenticeship publishing in pulp fantasy magazines like *Thrilling Wonder Stories* and *Amazing*. In 1950, his first novel, *The Dying Earth*, was published. It is a series of loosely connected tales taking place on Earth in the infinitely distant future during Earth's dying moments before the sun burns out. Vance's dying Earth is poignant, febrile, melancholy; every rock is gravid with the past. As always with Vance, the focus is on the ambiance rather than the action, and the technology is magical and organic rather than scientific.

In 1963, Vance won his first Hugo for *The Dragon Masters*. On an alien planet, descendants of men fight an ancient war with off-world aliens, each side using mutants bred from captured enemies as their warriors. In 1963, he also published *The Star King*, the first of five novels in the Demon Princes series. Other novels in the series include *The Killing Machine* (1964), *The Palace of Love* (1967), *The Face* (1974), and *The Book of Dreams* (1981).

In 1965, Vance wrote *The Eyes of the Overworld*, the black-comedy adventures of Cugel the Clever, Vance's greatest anti-hero, an unscrupulous rogue with a heart of brass in a world populated entirely by hucksters and montebanks. In 1966, he published *The Last Castle*, which won both the Hugo and Nebula awards, in which a claustrophobic race of effete nobles is destroyed by Neanderthal drones. In 1969, he published *Emphyrio*.

Vance's major short stories include "The Men Return," "The Miracle Workers," "The New Prime," and "The Moon Moth." His short stories have been collected in *The Best of Jack Vance* (1976) and *The Moon Moth and Other Stories* (1975). Among his other notable novels are *Big Planet* (1957) and the Tschai tetralogy, *The Blue World* (1966) and *Showboat World* (1975). His latest novel is *Araminta Station* (1987), the first book of the Cadwal chronicles.

He writes mystery fiction under his given name of John Holbrook Vance and won the Edgar Allen Poe award for *The Man in the Cage* (1960). In 1984, he was voted a Life Achievement Award at the World Fantasy Convention, and he has been Guest of Honor at major science fiction conventions.

Vance does not see his work as belonging to any genre or category, and he claims no mentors or models. He says he never reads science fiction and shows no interest in the science fiction establishment. He has lived in the same house for thirty years and has been married to his wife Norma for over forty years.

Themes and Style

Almost all of Vance's work addresses a central science fiction question: how to solve the tug of war between antithetical, equally attractive ideals: tradition versus progress, individualism versus society and culture, freedom versus social order, heroism versus static beauty, emotion versus reason, fantasy and magic versus science and realism. In the Vance mythos, the two sides of the tug of war are represented by the hero and the culture.

The hero is a solitary rationalist problem-solver, homeless, contemptuous of all religions and ideologies, independent, cynical, and goal-oriented. Culture is depicted as rigid, repressive, claustrophobic, ossified, effete, moribund, compulsive, and tied to dogma and ritual. For Vance, a culture is inherently arbitrary--any set of social rules works as well as any other, and the society over the next ridge will worship the left nostril or condemn to death anyone who uses fricatives in speech; absolutist--disobedience results in immediate banishment or death; intricate--often requiring a lifetime of practice to master; and illusory--based on a lie, usually spread by the "haves" to keep the "have nots" deluded and productive. These types of heroes and cultures are illustrated in *The Blue World*, *The Last Castle*, *The Dragon Masters*, *Emphyrio*, "Miracle Workers," and others.

Vance's hero is free, but spiritually barren; the culture is enslaved, but emotively and culturally rich, with all the things that the hero lacks--home, past, blood, community, family, religion, faith, answers. At his worst, the hero is a soulless despoiler of ancient grandeur; at its worst, the culture is a stagnant pavane danced by automata and supported by the toil of slaves.

The hero and the culture struggle for supremacy in two paradigmatic Vance plots, each reworked in several of his works. In the first, the "myth of the outsider" (*Big Planet*, *Showboat World*, and the Tschai tetralogy), a stranger on a linear quest wends his way through a picaresque series of bizarrely idiosyncratic cultural enclaves. Each encounter poses the basic Vance question: which is more powerful, individualistic freedom or community? The stranger is powerful because he is a relativist, unbound by ethnocentrism or belief. But he is ignorant of local custom, so he is constantly in danger of spitting on the flag--unintentionally violating local taboos he cannot see. He is hobbled by not knowing the rules of the game, yet he is also free not to obey them. If the plot of the novel is dramatic, the stranger will win, and exploit the society to further his quest; if the plot is comic, he will lose, and suffer some hilariously ghastly punishment for his breach of etiquette.

In the second Vance myth, the "myth of the iconoclast" (*Emphyrio*, *The Blue World*, *The Last Castle*, *To Live Forever*, *The Dragon Masters*), a shy, "fey" loner, raised in a repressive, claustrophobic society but a spiritual outsider, is driven by inner questions which he cannot silence and which force him to think unconventional thoughts. The thoughts lead him almost against his will to the truth, some unforgivable skeleton in the society's closet which, once revealed, destroys the social fabric, bringing freedom, anarchy, bloodshed, and destroying the ancient beauty--an inherently tragic pattern. Vance's best examples of his use of myths are found in his short stories rather than in his award-winning novels.

In both Vance myths, the culture's richness is symbolized by a totem, a magnificent, ancient communal creation. The hero's needs--the quest or the need for answers--destroys the totem. The questor tramples it thoughtlessly; the iconoclast reluctantly concludes that it obstructs growth and regretfully destroys it.

Vance's early heroes are conventional linear questors (*Big Planet*, *Five Gold Bands* [1950]); their lack of ethnocentricism is seen simply as a virtue, and the ethnocentric aliens they encounter and exploit are inferiors. In the middle of his career, Vance's heroes begin to have doubts (Demon Prince series, *Emphyrio*); they may devote their lives to questing, but they agonize over what they must give up to do it--homes, families, feelings, roots--and they often are not even sure of what they are trying to accomplish or why. Their accomplishments are as much losses as gains. In the third stage of Vance's career, the protagonists have largely given up questing (*Trullion: Alastor 2262* [1973], *Maske: Thaery* [1976], and *Wyst: Alastor 1716* [1978]). They have nowhere to go, and they sit tranquilly, contemplate the rich, emotive, alien ambiance, and treasure their heritages. Vance chooses static cultural values. His early heroes blast off to far-flung stars and new adventures; his late heroes defend their ancestral homes.

Vance's style is legendary, as unique, quirky, and idiosyncratic as his alien cultures. Vance claims to have learned it from no one, and it reads like it. Its primary qualities are amplitude and dry wit, a refreshing alternative to the conventional workmanlike prose of traditional science fiction. This verbal profligacy is an exact parallel to the fabled profligacy of Vance's imagination: where another writer might invent a curious, emotionally pungent alien society or two per novel, Vance creates dozens, and constantly lets the reader catch glimpses of dozens more in the background, never explained but merely implied in asides and throw-away lines. The style also makes Vance the premier creator of alien ambiances. Vance seeks to allow the reader to catch a whiff of alien senses. To do this he writes in a language of his own creation, with a shadow of alienness in it. Vance's style is also funny, with an ascerbic, tragicomic, satirical edge that springs from his misanthropy and finds expression in extreme latinity, nominalization, and circumlocution.

Plot Summaries of Major Works

Demon Prince series

The Star King. In the opening of the first novel of the five novel series, a young Kirth Gersen watches his entire community become enslaved by raiders of the five Demon Princes, the most dire criminals in the universe. Gersen dedicates his life to tracking down the five and wreaking vengeance, dispatching one Demon Prince per volume. Gersen first pursues Malagate the Woe, a man-like representative of a race called Star Kings. Malagate seeks the coordinates of an Eden-like, weirdly beautiful planet with a complex plant and animal ecology. Gersen takes three suspects to the planet and forces Malagate to reveal himself. Malagate dives underground; he treasures the planet because it approximates his lost home world. His motives seem more noble than evil, and we sense his own loss as much as his villainy. He is killed by a grazing autochthon and enters the ecologic cycle. The planet is despoiled; paradise is lost. A year later, Gersen returns to the planet and uproots a seedling that is Malagate reborn.

The Killing Machine. Gersen seeks Kokkor Hekkus, called "the killing machine." Hekkus is desperately amassing a vast sum of money--why? He is in love with the divinely beautiful Alusz, princess of the mythical planet of Thamber, who has staged her own kidnapping and placing herself under ransom to avoid his touch. Gersen finds a way to pay Alusz's ransom and she leads him to Thamber, a fantasy world out of time, with sword-wielding knights and grand battles between Good and Evil. Kekkus plays the evil prince, at war with Sion Trumble, golden-haired force for good and Alusz's betrothed. At Trumble's court, Gersen reveals that Trumble, Hekkus, and several other players in the drama are all Kokkor Hekkus, who is a hormagaunt, a creature who can change faces. Thamber is Hekkus's Disneyland, where he can act out any emotionally excessive melodrama, casting himself in all the good parts. Gersen kills Hekkus. Thamber then loses its fantasy quality and becomes part of the drab commercial galaxy. Again Gersen has destroyed something precious. Alusz realizes that the new Thamber is no place for fairy princesses and leaves with Gersen. This novel is considered to be one of Vance's best-constructed plots.

The Palace of Love. This is the richest and subtlest in emotional timbre of the five volumes and Vance's personal favorite. Gersen seeks Viole Falusche, who has cast himself in the role of the galaxy's foremost cultivator and scientist of pleasure (and by necessity, its obverse, pain). Gersen, posing as a journalist, researches Falusche's past and discovers that Falusche is a more pathetic victim than egomaniacal villain. Jheral Tinzy, the high school flirt, enticed, rejected, and mocked the pimply young Falusche; Falusche has been attempting to punish and win over substitute Jherals ever since. Gersen is invited to Falusche's legendary palace of love, a hidden Xanadu where guests come to take part in Falusche's ongoing experiments in the limits of pleasure. The best part of the book is the guests' languid, moody voyage by aircar, boat, wagon and foot to the palace, meticulously choreographed by Falusche. Gersen destroys Falusche, but by then the secret of the palace has been revealed; Falusche kidnapped Jheral and has been cloning her cells, producing an endless series of Jherals in hope of eventually breeding one that will love him. But each new Jheral takes an instant dislike to him. Jheral seems the real villain, and Gersen seems to punish the wrong person. Again an Eden is destroyed by Gersen's "success"--the Palace of Love is dismantled, and its Eloi-like inhabitants are forced to enter a harsh real world for which they are unprepared.

The Face. In this novel, Gersen stalks Lens Larque, the ugly, mad prankster. For some reason, Larque is busily buying up the mining rights to Shanitra, the moon in the sky above the neighborhood of the socially prominent Methlens. It turns out that Larque tried to buy a house in the neighborhood and was refused by the next-door owner, who said he did not want to look at Larque's ugly, boorish face. Larque in retaliation has mined the moon with explosives that will reshape the moon's face to match his own, so the Methlens can gaze on it forever. Gersen kills Larque, but by then Gersen has been spurned by the neighbor's daughter because of class differences--Gersen and Larque now share the grudge. Gersen decides to finish Larque's prank, and he detonates the explosives.

The Book of Dreams. Gersen's last foe, Howard Alan Treesong, is even less worthy of grandiose hatred, and the inevitable vengeance seems even less satisfying. Gersen discovers a photograph of ten unknown people at a dinner, one of whom is Treesong; he runs a publicity contest in a galactic magazine offering prizes to anyone who can identify the ten. One contestant is Treesong's father, who identifies Treesong as Howard Hardoah, son of conventional parents on a quiet Amish-like backwater planet called Moundervelt. He is, in fact, due home shortly for a high school reunion. Gersen attends the reunion, where Treesong hands out embarrassing punishments to those who shamed, mocked, or insulted him as a boy. Gersen attempts to kill Treesong, but fails.

On Moundervelt, Gersen discovers the Book of Dreams, a sort of diary kept by Howard in his youth and since lost. It reveals a complex imaginary world peopled by a band of adventurers called the Palladins. Gersen uses it to trap Treesong. He enlists the aid of the Cleadoes, a Ma and Pa Kettle couple, whose son Nimpy was murdered by the young Hardoah out of spite and who now work as custodians in a large nature preserve. He publicizes the fact that the Cleadoes have the book. When Treesong comes for it, the Cleadoes casually lock Gersen in a room while they smoothly dispatch Treesong by "marmelizing" (stuffing) him, since Mr. Cleadoe is a collector of animal species in the preserve. The galactic emperor of crime is made a fool of by two rubes, while our hero fumes helplessly and looks on. As Treesong dies, the Palladins, multiple heroic personalities within him, are heard forsaking him--again, a king of imaginative greatness dies. Gersen, his life's work accomplished, feels deflated rather than elated now that his quest is done.

The books in the Demon Prince Series offer many rewards. Gersen is a complex character, carrying on a never-ending internal debate on the wisdom of heroic quests. The logistics of outmaneuvering the five villains involve some of Vance's best plotting. Each quest takes Gersen through various quirky, alien cultures. Each of the Demon Princes has his own unique psychosis, so each novel is permeated by a distinct aura of playful horror--whimsical, grandiose, fantastic. Since the five books cover Vance's best years (1964-81), they summarize his growing disenchantment with science fiction's myth of questing, progressive heroes.

Emphyrio. Ghyl Tarvoke lives in Ambroy in the planet Aume, a world ruled by fastidious, supercilious Lords who live in eyries in the clouds. The citizens devote their lives to making magnificent, flawless artworks by hand--any form of duplication or mechanical production is taboo. The society is puritanical, ossified, joyless, impoverished. The Lords are assumed to live in sybaritic self-indulgence. As a boy, Tarvoke is told he is fated to accomplish great things, and he feels a strange kinship with the ancient tale of Emphyrio, a vague figure from an ancient myth who tried to free the human race from warring monsters by speaking "the truth." Only the first half of the myth is known. Tarvoke begins to wonder about things, and is instantly labeled a troublemaker. The planet offers no opportunities for questing, and Tarvoke marks time with aimless musing. He falls pointlessly in love with one of the Ladies, and discovers that the lives of the Lords are curiously bland.

Tarvoke makes his way to a distant world, where he discovers that Ambroy crafts are museum pieces beyond price. If the craftsmen are paid a pittance, the Guild takes a small cut, and the Lords live simply, where are the profits of the Ambroy craftsmen going? Tarvoke returns to Ambroy to break the Guilds' monopoly, but the Guilds reject the idea of change. He journeys to Earth and learns the second half of the Emphyrio legend: Emphyrio preached peace to the monsters and was killed for it, but the monsters mused on his message and embraced a life of tranquillity. Earth historians explain the myth. The monsters came from Damar, the moon above Aume. The Damarans, unable to breed puppet-like automata, mistakenly sent the monsters to Aume; Emphyrio converted the creatures to peace, then departed for Damar. Tarvoke discovers the dusty tomb of Emphyrio, is overwhelmed with anticlimax, and intuitively discovers the tragi-comic secret behind the society of Aume. The Lords are literally puppets, created by the Damaran puppet-makers to justify and disguise their plunder of the craftsmen of Aume. The eyries are stage fronts. The men of Aume have slaved for two thousand years in service to simulacra. Tarvoke reveals the secret to all of Aume. The craftsmen of Ambroy slaughter their overseers and enslave the Damarans.

The craftsmen of Ambroy are now free--but the grandeur of the illusion is lost, and, it is assumed, there will be no more splendid artifacts. Truth has prevailed, but truth is always pedestrian. *Emphyrio* is Vance's subtlest use of the iconoclast myth.

"Miracle Workers." On the planet Pangborn, descendants of earthmen have created a feudal society where magic is the prevailing science and magicians--the jinxmen--are the engineers. Magic is called logic; empiricism, the ancient and largely forgotten way, is derided as mysticism and magic. The ancient scientists are considered "miracle workers." Mild-mannered apprentice jinxman Sam Salazar finds himself compelled to ask iconoclastic questions. He does things just to see what will happen and is considered witless. Lord Faide of Faide Keep attacks and takes Ballant Keep in a battle. At a victory banquet, the master jinxmen summon their demons to provide sport, and jinxman Hein Huss, sensing the future, predicts that jinxmanship shall decline from that moment. He takes Sam Salazar into his service.

Returning home, Faide's party is attacked by the First Folk, a race of apparently mindless subhumans driven off the land by the arriving earthmen sixteen centuries earlier. The First Folk have bred organic weapons by adopting the methods of the first earthmen--the ways of random experimentation and mechanistic empiricism. The First Folk attack with plantings of impenetrable forests, thorns, pit traps, poisonous plants, snares, wasps projected from blowpipes, sacks of stinging mites. Faide's troops are slaughtered. The jinxmen are powerless, since magic only works on human psychologies. Salazar devises a rough but effective plan and burns a path to the keep with oil.

Faide Keep is vast, supposedly impervious. The First Folk lay seige. They belch a hardening foam from their gills until the keep is engulfed--suffocation is imminent. Man's only hope is Salazar, who simply "tries things" without reason and sees what happens. He discovers by random experimentation that vinegar dissolves the foam; knights armed with vinegar clear a path through the foam and sue for peace. The First Folk agree. Sam Salazar decides to continue his experimentation. Others will join him. The jinxmen gloomily foresee a future of intellectual anarchy, cogs, and gears. A thousand years of magic wanes; presumably a thousand years of mechanism begins. Vance's eternal pendulum between antithetical absolutes has begun to swing again.

"The Moon Moth." Edwer Thissell has the unenviable post of Consular Representative on the planet of Sirene. The notorious assassin Haxo Angmark has landed on Sirene and disappeared; Thissell must find him, but this involves talking to the Sirenese, a formidable task. Communication on Sirene demands mastery of a terrifyingly complex linguistic, symbolic, and musical system. The Sirenese value only "strakh," social status. Strakh is determined in ways too subtle for off-worlders to divine, but it is manifested by one's facial mask. Going maskless is an unforgivable sin. All statements on Sirene must be ornately and indirectly phrased; Sirenese literally cannot comprehend things said simply. All statements must be accompanied by the appropriate music played by the speaker on the appropriate instruments. The instruments are fiendishly hard to play and each instrument has different tuning, modes, and tonalities. Choice of instrument, mode, scale, and ornamentation all suggest subtle shades of meaning, offering delicate counterpoint of amplification to any verbal message, and that metamessage must match perfectly with one's strakh and the strakh of the addressee. The Sirenese kill anyone who fails to conform to the dictates of strakh.

Thissell plunges into the Sirenese culture, where his every attempt to talk to the natives is a social blunder. It is Vance high comedy as he fumbles with the ponderous instruments and steps on toes with each inappropriate glissando and ill-chosen chord. The Sirenese are driven to murderous rage. Angmark captures Thissell, takes Thissell's Moon Moth mask for himself, and parades the bare-faced Thissell before the horrified Sirenese, telling them that Thissell is Angmark. But Angmark has miscalculated the Sirenese mentality. The Sirenese are indifferent to Angmark's crimes; for them the only crime is gaucheness, and Moon Moth, now on Angmark's face, is the criminal. They kill Angmark. Thissell convinces them that he is the bravest among them, since he bore the society's greatest shame in order to bring the criminal Moon Moth to justice. His strakh is now unassailable, and his place in society secure. This is one of Vance's best "spitting on the flag" stories and is often anthologized.

Biographical/Bibliographical Readings

Terry Dowling, "Kirth Gersen: the Other Demon Prince," *Science Fiction* 2:11, p.55-56. Daniel Levak and Tim Underwood, *Fantasms: A Bibliography of the Literature of Jack Vance* (Underwood-Miller, 1978). Jack Rawlins, "Linear Man: Jack Vance and the Value of Plot in Science Fiction," *Extrapolation* (Winter, 1983), p.356-69. Idem, *Demon Prince: The Dissonant Worlds of Jack Vance* (Borgo Press, 1986). Tim Underwood and Chuck Miller, eds., *Jack Vance* (Taplinger, 1980). **[Jack Rawlins]**

VAN VOGT, A. E.

Life and Works

Born Alfred Elton Van Vogt on April 26, 1912, in Manitoba, Canada, Van Vogt indicates that his mother takes full credit for his becoming a writer. While he does not really believe in her attempts to influence his prenatal development by reading mystery stories, he does acknowledge that there was probably considerable postnatal reinforcement of her desire. After an early accident that resulted in unconsciousness, fantasies, and strange images, Van Vogt turned in later life to Dianetics in an attempt to reduce this early childhood trauma. In 1926, he bought his first science fiction magazine, *Amazing Stories*, and became an instant fan. Van Vogt made his first sale to *True Story* in 1932, and then moved on to writing radio plays. By 1938, he decided to submit "Vault of the Beast" to Campbell at *Amazing Stories*. Van Vogt became a prolific writer of science fiction, with *Slan* appearing in 1946, *The World of Null-A* in 1948, *The Voyage of the Space Beagle* in 1950, and the *The Weapon Shops of Isher* in 1951. Then began a hiatus from creative science fiction writing as Van Vogt became involved with Ron Hubbard and the Dianetics movement, becoming a "dianetics auditor." By 1964, Van Vogt had split from Hubbard and began to write *The Silkie*, which appeared in novel form in 1969, soon followed by other science fiction novels. Van Vogt has been honored as co-guest of honor at the fourth World Science Fiction Convention in 1946, received the Manuscripters Literature Award in 1948, and other awards including the Ann Radcliffe Literature Award and the award of the Count Dracula Society.

Many authors, noted for exciting adventure stories, such as Thomas Scortia, credit Van Vogt as their mentor and model in first writing science fiction. Others, such as Damon Knight, vilify Van Vogt, describing him as a "regiphil" and "cosmic jerrybuilder." Regardless of these labels, Van Vogt has maintained a steady band of devoted readers, those who can enjoy a fast-paced, romantic adventure yarn, and who can forgive the weaknesses in plot.

Van Vogt's most recent works, such as *The Silkie*, *Renaissance*, and *Quest for the Future*, reveal his continuing ability to grow and improve as a writer.

Themes and Style

Van Vogt's fiction consists of fast-paced action with complex interwoven plots. The principal weakness in his work is the tendency to confuse the reader with specious inventions, such as the "roboplane" in *The World of Null-A*, to resolve a critical cliffhanger. While his science is weak and his storylines are unpredictable, Van Vogt has a devoted following because of his larger-than-life romantic heroes and the taut, galloping suspense of his stories. Van Vogt tugs at the reader's heartstrings with his images, such as the small, terrified boy at the start of *Slan* clinging to his mother's hand as she is about to sacrifice herself to the hunters to save her child. Van Vogt is not concerned with "everyperson," but with the "Right Person." He is consumed with the hero from extraordinary circumstances, the hereditary sovereign. The small orphan boy will predictably turn out to be the son of a martyred hero, and his sweetheart the daughter of another regent, as in *Slan*. Clane, the mutant in *Empire of the Atom*, eventually rules a kingdom modeled after Tiberian Rome.

Plot Summaries of Major Works

Renaissance. A world in which men wear rose-colored glasses and are dominated by women forms the questionable premise upon which this latest Van Vogt novel is based. The alien Utt arrived on Earth forty years before and had traced the destructiveness of the human race to the human male. Now human males are required to take drugs that cause near-sightedness and to wear special rose-colored lenses to prevent further stimulation of the optic nerve. Unfortunately Grayson, hero of the novel, breaks his glasses and begins to experience unusually male-dominating traits. Grayson's misadventures are relayed in quick-moving dialogue and in very humorous scenes, as he gradually tries to come to grips with his new-found freedom, discovering along the way, of course, that no one is completely freed from their inhibitions. In the final scenes of the novel, the author succeeds in poking holes in monogamy, organized religion, and even in the alien conspiracy.

With a certain amusement and a definite satirical look at male-female relationships, Van Vogt uses the vehicle of human versus alien to highlight his satire. Maintaining his usual choppy style of writing, he manages to produce an enjoyable novel quite different in tone from most of his serious darker dramas that highlight the human potential for destruction. The characterizations are also far more complete than in his previous novels, allowing his characters to vacillate and prevaricate in a very natural mode. This novel reveals Van Vogt capable of growing in stature as a writer. Though he may lose some of his appeal to his previous audience, this novel should help him gain a much wider acceptance.

The Silkie. The legend of the merman is explored in this, one of Van Vogt's moodier and more mystical science fiction works. The novel opens with Marie Lederle and her father attempting to get clients to keep their sea cruiser financially afloat. On one of their trips, Marie meets and falls in love with a mysterious stranger who, it turns out, is the first genetically engineered silkie. Marie becomes the mother of the first silkie-human child. The novel then moves on into the future of humans in space, now with an extensive silkie population, comprised of the full telepathic silkie and the more aberrant variants called 'V's. These 'V's have identified an extraordinary young boy, sufficiently aberrant to warrant destruction. Camp, a dominant silkie male sent to evaluate the child's potential, becomes involved in an elaborate plot that pits humans, silkies, and variants against each other for eventual control. Ultimately the story turns on the boy, Tem, who is part of an alien plan to conquer the solar system and Camp, who has been manipulated by Tem to believe he is the child's father.

Van Vogt has returned to the exciting, fast-paced stories so welcomed by readers in the 1950s. Using the familiar theme of humans fighting hostile, inimical aliens, he manages to introduce in rapid order three human-originated races, juggling the intricate plots for control between these three subspecies. Van Vogt writes each episode in the novel in short scenes that heighten and sustain the excitement. Unfortunately, this also causes a certain amount of discontinuity and unavoidable unevenness. The novel is extremely complex with continuous hints that each plot and subplot is a facade for a deeper conspiracy, leaving the reader hurrying through to the conclusion to help puzzle out the contradictions. This novel, published in 1969, is certainly proof that Van Vogt has managed to return to his earlier popularity, despite his new darker vision of human destiny.

Slan. Mutants with superhuman abilities named after S. Lann, their human discoverer, the slan were once in control of Earth, but have now been overthrown and are victims of genocide. Jom Cross is a young slan boy who grows up free, but is being constantly hunted by his intended executioners. Kathleen, another young slan, is a prisoner of the state, kept as an experiment in the ruler's palace and constantly threatened by the political maneuverings of her human captors. Inevitably the two meet and fall in love, but are tragically separated when the enemy locates their hiding place. Gradually the novel exposes several plots, some by human, some by slan, and others by a mysterious almost-slan element, each fighting for control of Earth and human destiny.

While the technology is dated, the strength of this novel is in its fast-paced, yet poignant scenes typical of Van Vogt's work. The layers of political maneuvering, with plots, intentions, and cautious self-interest, are Byzantine in their complexity.   Piling betrayal upon betrayal, the author creates a nightmarish world in which the principals struggle to achieve a modicum of peace and happiness. The hero is cast in the classic mode of the compassionate and sensitive man confronted by desperate savage enemies. Van Vogt is one of the first science fiction writers to portray mutants as positive, useful beings, evolved rather than warped by their struggles to overcome prejudice and achieve a normal life. This author reaches within his characters to find their own salvations, revealing his views that life is at once grim and full of promise. This is an exciting novel, despite the dated technology.

The Weapon Shops of Isher. Situated on Earth, the weapon shops of Isher have been established to provide power, in the form of defensive weapons, to the everyday person. The shops are intended to provide a balance, a court of last resort against the growing power of the state. Although the novel opens in present day Earth with the accidental appearance in a local neighborhood of a weapon shop, the novel, and the shop, quickly returns to Earth thousands of years in the future, where the Empress Innelda is involved in a final confrontation with the power of the shops. The weapon shop had been accidentally thrown back in time by Innelda's government project that was attempting to neutralize the force field that surrounds the shop. Chris McAllister, a twentieth-century reporter, enters the shop and moves forward with it as it returns to its own time. McAllister brings a buildup of time energy with him that can destroy the city of Isher if released all at once. The weapon shop staff realizes this and dresses him up in a specially treated suit. But McAllister has become the fulcrum in a balance with government project-building, becoming a seesaw, thrown forward and backward in time at increasingly great intervals. Accumulating additional energy, McAllister becomes first a hazard to the safety of Earth, and eventually of the solar system. Against this backdrop another story is going on--that of Cayle Clark, a rebellious youth with an extremely high potential for trouble. Because of his potential, the weapon shops, controlled by Robert Hedrock, begin to use Clark as a weapon in their conflict with Innelda's corrupt government. Hedrock in turn is actually an immortal named Walter S. deLany, the founder of the weapon shops. The various story elements eventually resolve in the final chapters.

Originally written in 1951, the novel depends upon fast action and complexities of plot to hold the reader's interest. Van Vogt does not stop to explain how the time project works, why special suits are so readily available, or why the all-knowing weapon shops are unaware of Hedrock's true identity. The unusual respect Van Vogt has for hereditary sovereigns is revealed by the careful separation of Innelda from responsibility for the actions of her generals, and the indication that assassinations in the past have dealt with the imperial family's officers, never of the family members. In Cayle Clark, Van Vogt displays his fascination in his concept of the "Right Person" theory, that a particular special individual becomes the principal motive force in a particular era. With the layers of political maneuvering, complexities, and conspiracies, and at least three separate principal male characters, Van Vogt still manages to juggle the pieces in a fashion that has not lost any of its excitement in the thirty-five years since first publication. Critics and fans regard this and *The World of Null-A* as among Van Vogt's best.

The World of Null-A. Gilbert Gosseyn has come to the city of the Machine to compete in the games that will determine his future wealth and position in society. But something goes desperately wrong. Is he who he thinks he is, or is he a double, with an identical set of memories as the original? Null-A refers to non-Aristotelianism, one of three concepts upon which the games are based, the other two being Null-N, or non-Newtonianism, and Null-E, non-Euclidianism. The ultimate winners of the Machine's games have totally integrated personalities and are qualified to emigrate to Venus. The supposedly incorruptible Machine, however, appears to be under the control of the humanlike Erna, aliens who are gradually gaining control of the judiciary and police services. The mystery of Gosseyn's death and rebirth, the layers of political betrayal, and the concept of an ordered society in which some can reach their full potential culminates in the final chapters, as most elements are resolved.

The novel contains strong clues to the awe which writers of the thirties and forties had for atomic energy. A flashlight is not simply a flashlight, it is an "atomic flashlight," a beacon is an "atomic beacon." Other than the occasional use of such terminology, the novel reflects a distant future in which thugs still smoke cigarettes, slug gagged captives, and drive around in long dark chauffered limousines. The novel is also flawed in certain of its assumptions, such as the mysterious Professor "X," crippled and hideously deformed, who is readily identifiable as Larvisseur, mentioned in chapter two; if the reader can make these connections, so should the brilliantly integrated mind of Gosseyn. Some of the conversations are mere games and appear to make little sense. At one point, Gosseyn confronts President Hardie who, like a genie in a fairy tale, agrees to answer three questions in exchange for information, then refuses to answer some of the questions. Still the mysteries, the complexities of plot, with its compelling convolutions, capture the reader's imagination. This story with its concept of the totally sane, integrated personality which can reach its full personal potential may reflect Van Vogt's personal belief in humanity which drew him ten years later into the Dianetics movement. This first Van Vogt novel reflects this perennial popularity with the science fiction public, who are willing to forgive the weaknesses and to remember his strengths--excitement, scope, optimism and imagination.

Biographical/Bibliographical Readings

Jeffrey M. Elliot, "A. E. Van Vogt: A Writer with a Winning Formula," *Science Fiction Voices*, no.2 (1979), p.30-40. Damon Knight, "Cosmic Jerrybuilder: A. E. Van Vogt," in *In Search of Wonder: Essays on Modern Science Fiction* (Advent, 1967). Sam Moskowitz, "A. E. Van Vogt," in *Seekers of Tomorrow* (World, 1966), p.213-28. A. E. Van Vogt, "My Life Was My Best Science Fiction Story," in *Fantastic Lives*, ed. Martin H. Greenberg (Southern Illinois University Press, 1981), p.215. Idem, *Reflections of A. E. Van Vogt: The Autobiography of a Science Fiction Giant, with a Complete Bibliography* (Fictioneer Books, 1975). Colin Wilson, "A. E. Van Vogt," in *Science Fiction Writers*, ed. E. F. Bleiler (Scribner's, 1982), p.209-18. Donald A. Wollheim, "Of Men like Gods," in *The Universe Makers* (Harper & Row, 1971), p.45-49. [Colleen Power]

VARLEY, JOHN

Life and Works

John Varley was born in 1947 in Austin, Texas. He spent his precollege years in Texas, interested in science (especially aviation) and science fiction. Planning to study physics and astronomy, he enrolled at Michigan State University in 1965. However, for the first time in his life, he had to work hard for his grades, and decided to switch majors. His interest in film and science fiction prompted him to try English, but he soon discovered that it had nothing to offer him. He then dropped out of college, traveled for a while, stayed in San Francisco for about nine years, and, after marrying Anet Mconel and having three sons, moved to Oregon in 1975 because it was a good place to raise a family. In 1973, Varley began writing science fiction. His impact was immediate--he was selling stories the next year, and soon he was being hailed as among the best of the new young writers. His first novel was *The Ophiuchi Hotline* (1977). A popular author, Varley has received critical accolades for his work, including the Hugo and Nebula awards for best novella of 1978 ("The Persistence of Vision") and for the best novel of 1979 (*Titan*). *The Persistence of Vision* (1978) includes some of his other short fiction, as does *The Barbie Murders* (1980). Three novels compose the Gaean trilogy: *Titan* (1979), *Wizard* (1980), and *Demon* (1984).

Themes and Style

Varley remembers the first science fiction book he read --Robert A. Heinlein's *Red Planet*, which Varley read when he was in the seventh grade. He credits Heinlein for instilling in him (via an editorial in *Analog*) a no-nonsense approach to writing--begin stories, finish them, send them off, and keep sending them off until they sell. Varley's science fiction emulates many of the characteristics in Heinlein's science fiction; strong plots, solid extrapolations, complex backgrounds taken for granted by the characters in the story, juvenile or adolescent protagonists (often female), a focus on ideas, aphorisms (in *Demon*, Varley's Cirocco Jones sounds at times like Heinlein's Lazarus Long), and, above all, adventure stories. Indeed, reviewers frequently call Varley "the new Heinlein." But Heinlein's clear influence on Varley should not blind us to Varley's originality, most notably in his settings and central theme.

Most of Varley's fiction takes place in one of two differently imagined futures. Most of his short fiction and his first novel, *The Ophiuchi Hotline*, consist of what is called his Eight Worlds future, and are based on a future where aliens immensely superior to human beings invade the Earth. Natives of a gaseous giant planet, these aliens are first-order intelligences. When they arrive in the solar system, they are really interested in communing with the Jovians, but they also effortlessly destroy all human artifacts on Earth in order to free second-order intelligences (sperm whales, killer whales, and bottle-nosed dolphins) from the human threat (humans are classed as third-order intelligences, along with such things as bees and coral). After the invasion, the human race is reduced to a marginal existence on Luna, from which it spreads, painstakingly, to every inhabitable niche in the solar system--except for the interdicted Earth. Varley explores a different future in the Gaean trilogy. Here, a NASA mission to Saturn discovers a twelfth moon, which turns out to be an artifact shaped like a giant inner tube. After their ship is destroyed and they spend six months in an unconscious state, the crew members awaken inside the wheel world to find that its governing sentience--Gaea--is capricious, callous, and nearly omnipotent. It is obvious that Varley does not agree wholly with Heinlein's dictum that the human race is the toughest in the universe, destined to sweep all before it. And while humans eventually defeat Gaea in the trilogy, they almost fail--and the novels stress the near-hope-lessness of puny humans challenging the World/Goddess.

Varley also differs from Heinlein about the effect of techno-logical change on human beings. No matter what external changes occur in a Heinlein work, his characters rarely exhibit internal changes. Varley, on the other hand, believes that different tech-nologies change the way human beings act and think. Indeed, human malleability is Varley's central theme; it also governs many of his subsidiary concerns.

Change figures prominently in Varley's ideas about sex. In the Eight Worlds stories, changing your sex is as common as going to the dentist is today. Few people are what Varley calls male or female "stable," so most people switch back and forth several times during their lives. Two corollaries result from the near-universal-ity of frequent sex changes. First, sexual experimentation is the norm, which explains the variety of sexual modes depicted in Varley's fictions--homosexuality, heterosexuality, bisexuality, pan-sexuality, and incest. And, second, technical knowledge always has ethical repercussions. For example, in Varley's "Retrograde Summer" (in *The Persistence of Vision*), the protagonist has a diffi-cult time understanding the nuclear family, a concept he feels is certainly wrong.

A final elaboration of Varley's concern with change is his in-sistence on human possibilities. One might almost say that Varley structures his futures as arenas where anything imaginable goes. In the Eight Worlds stories, humans swim in a quicksilver lake on Mercury, find blast crystals in a Venusian desert, sculpt the weather in a huge "Disneyland" carved out under the surface of the moon, experience being an African lioness, compose music while living among Saturn's rings, fall in love (via holographic projections) out beyond Pluto, and set off for Alpha Centauri in an asteroid starship. Varley's work exhibits perfectly his defini-tion of heroism--adapting to and surviving in a dangerous uni-verse while at the same time living life to the fullest.

Varley's insistence on human change sets him against certain limiting activities. Specifically, in *Demon*, Varley satirizes various rigid, imperialistic human institutions: the military, political bu-reaucracies, religions, corporations, and even Hollywood. Varley also abhors racism and sexism.

Although change is Varley's central theme, he is also aware of certain permanent universal principles, such as the impossibility of travel faster than the speed of light, the tremendous tidal forces of even a small black hole, and the basic needs of a living organism. He writes in a format closer to hard science fiction than to fantasy. His techologies startle us, but no more than per-sonal computers would an engineer in the mid-1950s. Moreover, Varley believes that no one can predict exactly how the future will differ from the present. His work explores two possible futures--and inculcates attitudes that might help humanity to live through the shocks (whatever they may be) of the "real" future.

Plot Summaries of Major Works

The Gaean trilogy

Titan. *Titan*, Varley's second novel, is the first novel of the Gaean trilogy and is continued by *Wizard* and *Demon*. *Titan* opens in 2025 A.D. aboard the deep space vehicle *Ringmaster*, whose seven-member NASA crew includes Cirocco (Rocky) Jones, the female captain; Gaby Plauget, an astronomer; Calvin Green, a doctor and the expedition's biologist and ecologist; April 15/02 Polo and August 3/02 Polo, physicists and clone sisters; Eugene (Gene) Springfield, the pilot; and Bill, the chief engineer. Nearing Saturn, their destination, they discover that the planet has an hitherto unnoticed twelfth satellite. Further observations establish that it is a huge torus, 1300 km in diameter, 250 km wide, 175 km from top to bottom, and six-spoked with a central hub. After they orbit the object, a large tentacled arm suddenly shoots out, shreds their ship, and begins wrapping parts of itself around the crew members, who lose consciousness. Six months later, they wake up inside the torus, separated and changed by the preawakening experiences. Cirocco and Gene can understand the song-speech of the Titanides, a half-human, half-horse race which looks like the centaurs of classical mythology. Calvin understands much about where they are, including the object's name (Gaea) and the whistle-speech of the sky-giants--benign, sentient blimps. And August has lost April, who is now Ariel of the Eagle clan of angels, avian humanoids at war with the Titanides. After Cirocco meets up with Gaby, then Calvin, and then Bill and August, she decides to find out what is going on by climbing to the hub via one of the spokes (a difficult but not impossible act in Gaea's low gravity).

At first, *Titan* seems derivative, a conflation of Niven's *Ringworld*, Clarke's *Rendezvous with Rama*, and Farmer's Riverworld novels. But Gaea turns out to be not an artificial world, but a self-aware being--a female Titan with a life span of three million years, relatives scattered throughout the galaxy, daughter-Titans orbiting Uranus, an infant daughter Titan growing up on Iapetus (one of Saturn's moons), and an insatiable appetite for Earth's pop culture (she has seen *The Wizard of Oz*, *2001*, and *Dune*). And while Varley does use well-known science fiction themes (including one of the oldest--an alien impregnating a human female), he also packs his picaresque novel with an original mix of well-drawn characters, rousing adventure, broad humor, varied sex (free-fall, promiscuous, bisexual, heterosexual, lesbian, incestuous, and even involuntary, i.e. rape), startling props (the Titans use organic radios), and unusual settings (after their heroic climb, Cirocco and Gaby meet Gaea in a room modeled after the room

David Bowman dies in at the end of *2001*.) But Gaea is 3,001,266 years old: her body is decaying, some of her twelve satellite brains are rebelling, and she herself is slipping toward senility. Although *Titan* ends happily, such things hint at the much more sombre sequel, *Wizard*.

Wizard. Seventy-five years have passed since the end of *Titan*. Shadowed in her orbit around Saturn by a terrestrial ship ready to annihilate her if she makes one false move, Gaea, the aging but still crafty Titan, becomes essential to humanity by offering miraculous cures for irremediable diseases. To earn a cure, ailing humans must (a) pass the somewhat capricious screening on Earth, and (b) prove themselves heroic on Gaea--according to Gaea's definition. Two youngsters are among the forty humans annually granted an audience with Gaea and made "pilgrims"--seekers of heroic opportunities. One is Chris'fer Minor (renamed Chris Major) who suffers from a rare disorder that periodically loosens his sense of reality and often turns him into a barbarian interested only in fighting and fornicating. The other youngster is Robin the nine-fingered, a nineteen-year-old epileptic who has grown up in an all-female space colony (the Coven) and who once deliberately cut off a finger while trying to forestall a seizure.

Chris and Robin are recruited by Cirocco Jones and Gaby Plauget for a dangerous journey around Gaea's rim. Cirocco is now Gaea's Wizard (Gaea's representative on the rim); Gaby is a free-lance troubleshooter, with plenty to do, since Gaea's ancient body needs a lot of repair work. Both receive the same reward: near immortality. However, there are hidden costs, naturally, given Gaea's fey despotism. Gaea has made Cirocco responsible for perpetuating the race of Titanides, beautiful half-human, half-equine beings whom Cirocco loves. At a carnival held every myriarev (420 terrestrial days), Cirocco must choose the few Titanides who will be allowed to have children (Gaea's whimsical joke--a Titanide egg can be fertilized only by being placed in Cirocco's mouth). The grief Cirocco causes by being unable to choose them all has driven her into annual alcoholic binges. Gaea upsets Gaby by setting up various interesting ways to watch pilgrims die while trying to become heroes. Gaby decides that Gaea is not a goddess but City Hall--and vows to overcome her, or die trying.

Accompanied by four Titanides, the four human beings set off to circumnavigate the twelve regions that make up the interior of Gaea's body. Gaby's idea is to sound out the satellite brains that control each region and see if they would join a rebellion against Gaea. When Gaea figures out what they are up to, she sends Gene and a squadron of buzz bombs (Gaea's latest abomination--organic ramjets capable of spearing a human being) to kill Gaby. The novel ends, and sets up its sequel, *Demon*, when Cirocco confronts Gaea and declares herself Wizard no longer, but Demon, Gaea's sworn enemy.

Although similar to *Titan* in being an adventure tale that uses the quest motif, *Wizard* is darker than *Titan*, more interested in grim survival than in the picaresque. But *Wizard* also balances grimness with joy--primarily through Chris and Robin, who overcome their physical and mental maiming and discover love and friendship. Chris finds love with Valiha, a young female Titanide. And Robin finds that not all men want to rape her--her preconceptions do not include men like Chris, who soon becomes her friend. Unlike the eternal child their first names suggest (Christopher Robin), Chris and Robin do grow up. And in *Wizard*, Varley exhibits explicitly a tendency present in much of his work toward the genre of *Bildungsroman*.

Demon. The concluding volume of the Gaean trilogy opens twenty years after the end of *Wizard*. Gaea, the three-million-year old Titan whose enormous body orbits Saturn, has become demented. Obsessed with twentieth-century Hollywood movies, she genetically engineers a traveling movie-making crew--locations scouts, advance party, production crew (camera creatures called bolexes, arriflexes, panaflexes), with their producers, whose excretion is developed film. The star of everything they shoot is Gaea, naturally, who has become an enormous Marilyn Monroe, fifteen meters tall ("fifty foot two, eyes of blue"). Gaea's ultimate goal is to make an epic film about her war with Cirocco Jones, once Gaea's Wizard and now her implacable foe. Toward that goal, Gaea builds Pandemonium, her studio-fortress, in Hyperion (one of the twelve regions that form Gaea's toroidal body). The epic movie has five short subjects, three features, and a fadeout. In the short subjects, World War V begins and continues, until very few humans remain alive; Conal Rey--great-great-grandson of Eugene Springfield (a crew member on the original ship which discovered Gaea)--comes to Gaea seeking revenge for the mistreatment of his ancestor; Robin of the Coven returns to Gaea with her daughter, Nova, and her infant son, Adam; Cirocco is visited by Gaby Plauget, whose body dies at the end of *Wizard*, but whose soul lives on, dedicated to killing Gaea; and Cirocco travels to Chris's treehouse in Dione (Chris is the father of Nova and Adam and he is also gradually turning into a centauroid Titanide).

In the First Feature, Gaea kidnaps Adam to force Cirocco (who has become very good at surviving after twenty years of Gaea's hunting for her) into a showdown. In the Second Feature, Cirocco prepares for the showdown--mainly by civilizing Bellinzona, a wicked city where Gaea has been dumping the miserable dregs she has been "rescuing" from the dying Earth. In the Third Feature, Cirocco marches her army halfway around the rim to beseige Pandemonium, then distracts Gaea while Gaby does the real job of killing her. And in the Fadeout, a resurrected Gaby (still hopelessly in love with Cirocco) fails to interest Cirocco in helping to govern the wheel-world.

Obviously, *Demon* is Varley's most cinematic novel to date, borrowing heavily from individual movies, such as *King Kong*, *The Wizard of Oz*, and *Star Wars* and from types of movies, such as horror movies, gangster movies, and war movies. It is also Varley's most satirical work to date, showing (often comically) the lunacy of politics, religion, militarism (and patriotism), corporations, urban civilization, racism, sexism, anthropocentrism, human nature in general, television, and Hollywood itself. The ending symbolically presents one of Varley's major themes. Freed from her need to live for others (i.e., the Titanides), Cirocco dives down the Hyperion spoke, not knowing whether she will survive the 600 km fall, but reveling in the risks, uncertainties, and possibilities of being human.

The Ophiuchi Hotline. In 2050 A.D., two asteroid-sized spaceships arrive in the solar system. The ships are piolted by natives of a gas giant planet, who are at the apex of the universe's three-tier intelligence hierarchy. One of the ships lands on Jupiter, seeking Jovians, who are also first-order intelligences. The other ship lands on Earth, where the aliens (soon called simply Invaders) rescue sperm whales, killer whales and dolphins (second-order intelligence) from human beings who are ranked in the third order along with birds, bees, beavers, ants, and corals, by the simple expedient of destroying all human artifacts. Two years later, ten billion people have starved to death. The human survivors gather on Luna and endure, until many decades later they have spread throughout the solar system--to everywhere, in fact, but Earth, which the Invaders have made off limits. Humanity receives a huge boost when, out beyond Plato's orbit, it discovers information being beamed in from the direction of the star 70 Ophiuchi. Information gleaned from this "hotline" revolutionizes human technology. Cloning and memory recording become routine, so that a clone can be awakened with the proper memories should the original person die--thus creating a kind of immortality. Small black holes are found and made the center of orbital power plants. Vegetable entities called symbs (from "symbionts") pair with human beings and live in Saturn's Rings. Finally, small nullfield generators that replace a lung allow human beings to survive in space or on nonterrestrial planets like Mercury, Venus, and Mars. In 560 O.E. (after the Occupation of Earth), Lilo-Alexander-Calypso, a genetic engineer, has been sentenced to permanent death (all records of her genotype will be destroyed so that she cannot be cloned) for experimenting with human DNA, considered a "Crime against Humanity." She is saved by Boss Tweed, former president of the Luna government and leader of the Free Earth movement, who needs her help in his war against the Invaders. (Like his namesake, Tweed is ruthless. For one thing, he has made his own child into a batallion of killer-clones, all named Vaffa). Lilo is cloned many times. The fourth clone, Lilo-4, is taken to

Poseidon, the smallest moon of Jupiter, on which Tweed has set up an observation station. Lilo-4 begins an escape, but winds up encountering an Invader and being translated to Earth several thousand years in the future. Lilo-5 is sent to Pluto to investigate a strange message from the Ophiuchites--payment is due on 400 years of information. And Parameter/Solstice, a human-symb pair, awakens a clone hidden by the original Lilo. Accompanied by the clone of a disbarred teacher who has also fallen into Tweed's clutches, this Lilo takes over Poseidon and helps it head for Alpha Centauri.

Varley's first novel, *The Ophiuchi Hotline* is part of his Eight Worlds future history, which also provides the setting for most of his short fiction. Although fairly short, the novel includes a wide variety of science fiction motifs--cloning, black holes, symbiosis, genetic engineering, space colonies, invasion by aliens, time travel, prospecting in space, interstellar travel, first contact, faster-than-light travel, and singularities. The novel is not perfect--its ending is abrupt and some readers have trouble keeping track of all the clones. But it does illustrate Varley's strengths--his fertile imagination, his ability to fuse traditional elements into a fast-paced adventure story, his skill in subordinating technical information to character development and plot, and his awareness that life seven centuries in the future will be different from life now--though it will not seem odd to people living then. Like Heinlein, with whom he has been compared, Varley convinces us that the future he creates would work.

The Persistence of Vision. This collection reprints nine short pieces first published between 1975 and 1978. Five appeared in *The Magazine of Fantasy and Science Fiction*, three in *Galaxy*, and one in *Isaac Asimov's Science Fiction Magazine*. Six were nominated for various awards and the title story won both the Hugo and Nebula awards for best novella.

The collection opens with "The Phantom of Kansas," a mystery story with an unusually determined murderer and a murder victim who can be reborn through cloning and memory recording. In "Air Raid," the basis for Varley's novel *Millenium*, time travelers from the far-distant future rescue passengers from a doomed airliner and offer them a chance to colonize a planet orbiting Alpha Centauri. "Retrograde Summer" records how a young man raised on Mercury discovers his past when he meets his Lunar-clone sister and they are trapped by a quake in an achingly beautiful quicksilver grotto. "The Black Hole Passes" depicts a man and a woman, separated by four million miles of space, who experience a frustrating, unconsummated love, until a passing black hole solves their problem. Nine days after arriving "In the Hall of the Martian Kings," the first manned expedition to Mars is reduced to five people; twelve years later the second expedition is startled to find the survivors alive and thriving. "In the Bowl" joins Kiku, an amateur geologist from Mars vacationing on Venus, and Ember, a young Venusian who wants desperately to get off her planet. In "Gotta Sing, Gotta Dance," Barnum and Bailey, a human-symb pair (the vegetable symb allows humans to live in space), come to Janus, a moon of Saturn, to sell a symphony they have written. After a relaxing vacation spent in the Kenya "Disneyland" as an African lionness, the narrator of "Overdrawn at the Bank" finds his consciousness hooked up to a computer for a year, because somehow the Disneyland has misplaced his body. And in the title story, Varley tells how a permanently displaced man in a stainless steel society hitchhikes out of Chicago, eventually comes across a community of blind and deaf people in New Mexico, leaves them after despairing of mastering their five languages (handtalk, shorthand, bodytalk, Touch, and ***), but returns to the community soon after New Year's, in the year 2000--where his special friend, Pink, makes him one of them by giving him the gift of blindness and deafness.

Most of the stories are part of Varley's Eight Worlds future history, in which humanity--having been expelled from Earth by the Invaders, lives scattered throughout the Solar System, aided by technology derived from laser-propelled information pouring in from the direction of the planetary system 70 Ophiuchi. The remaining stories are set in the near future, before the end of the twentieth century. All the stories exhibit inventive thinking, plausible extrapolation, clearly drawn characters, strong women, fast-paced storytelling, competent style, and painstakingly detailed backgrounds.

Biographical/Bibliographical Readings

Melissa E. Barth, "John Varley," in *Twentieth-Century Science-Fiction Writers*, ed. Curtis C. Smith (St. James, 1986), p.748-49. Daniel Deprez, "An Interview with John Varley," *Science Fiction Review* 6 (Aug. 1977), p.8-14. **[Todd H. Sammons]**

VINGE, JOAN D.

Life and Works

Joan D. Vinge was born Joan Carol Dennison on April 2, 1948 in Baltimore, Maryland. When she was eight her father moved to Southern California, where she grew up. She claims that Andre Norton directly or indirectly influenced most of the major choices in her life. While in junior high school, she read her first Andre Norton novel and started writing science fiction stories and drawing. Hoping to be an illustrator, she entered San Diego State University as an art major, transferring to archaeology and anthropology in which she received her B.A. in 1971. Vernor Vinge, her first husband, a science fiction writer and mathematician, encouraged her to take her science fiction writing seriously. She divorced Vinge and later remarried and settled in Chappaqua, New York. In 1974, she published her first novelette, "Tin Soldier," followed in 1976 by *The Crystal Ship: Three Original Novellas of Science Fiction*. *Outcasts of Heaven Belt* (1978) was her first novel, followed by her novella, *Legacy* (1980), which continued in the same world. Both her "Eyes of Amber" novelette in 1977 and her novel, *The Snow Queen* (1981) won Hugos. *World's End*, a psychological science fiction novel which continued *The Snow Queen*, was published in 1984. *Psion*, published in 1982, was her first young adult novel and was chosen as a Best Book for Young Adults by the American Library Association. Her latest collection of stories is *Phoenix in the Ashes* (1985). Vinge is a contributor to *Analog*, *Galileo*, and *Issac Asimov's Science Fiction Magazine*. In addition to her original writings, she has very successfully adapted as a children's book *Return of the Jedi Storybook* (1983) from the movie of the same name and has done several other movie tie-ins, among them *Ladyhawke*, *Return to Oz*, *Mad Max beyond Thunderdome*, and in 1984, *The Dune Storybook*.

Themes and Style

Vinge comments that she likes to write anthropological science fiction with an emphasis on the interaction of different cultures and peoples to their surroundings. She believes that science fiction is the anthropology of the future. She does an ethnography for the society she creates; laying out the physical setting, the economic base, the resources, religion, beliefs, etc., and makes them real and recognizable. Her characters are simple, believable people alienated within their society, as Chaim and Mythili in *Legacy*, or displaced from their society, as Betha in *Outcasts of Heaven Belt*. In *The Snow Queen*, one finds Moon as an outsider.

In order to emphasize the degraded and unhealthy values of society which foster alienation, Vinge's stories are often set in a very primitive area or a future Earth which has been destroyed by disaster. *Outcasts of Heaven Belt* is a civilization destroyed by civil war; *Mother and Child* takes place on a planet decimated by plague where hearing and sight are impaired and speech has been lost; and the planet Tiamat of *The Snow Queen* survives in an era centuries after the collapse of the higher civilization of the Old Empire.

Her characters, very often female, pass through a period of alienation accompanied by pain and suffering but ultimately achieve an understanding of self. Vinge sees alienation as a normal process which is transcended through understanding and communication. Thus she dwells in most of her stories on the dif-

ficulties of communication, and we see communication in many
forms.   In "Eyes of Amber," T'uupieh communicates through a
space probe to the Earthling Shannon, whom she never sees.   In
Psion and *The Snow Queen*, the characters communicate through
telepathy.   Love is seen as the most perfect form of communication.   Vinge's forte, therefore, is the romance.   Her stories often
derive their plots from myth and fairy tale.   Her characters struggle against evil and dispair before achieving a lasting love.   And
like fairy tales, her stories have an uplifting moral, a faith in the
future.   Her lovers survive in worlds which are often ugly and
harsh, but there is hope that having learned to improve their self
image and have compassion and love for others, they have the potential for improving their society.

Plot Summaries of Major Works

Eyes of Amber.   An Earth probe is sent to Titan around 2000,
but it malfunctions and is found by the winged Lady T'uupieh, a
noblewoman who, dispossessed of her lands, has become the leader
of a band of outlaws and a hired assassin.   T'uupieh believes that
the probe is her personal demon which will give her great power.
Earth musician and linguist Shannon Wyler, on the Titan project
in Oregon, uses a synthesizer to speak to T'uupieh through the
probe in her language of musical chords.   The lord Chwiul has
hired T'uupieh to kill his brother Klovhiri and his brother's wife
Ahtseet who, incidentally, is T'uupieh's sister.   T'uupieh is quite
willing to kill both Klovhiri who took her lands, and her sister
whom she condemns for marrying him.   In return she hopes to
have her lands returned by Chwiul.   Shannon, however, believes
that T'uupieh's killing is evil and he is encouraged by his mother
to dissuade her.   But T'uupieh believes that a mere mortal can
make no change in the normal order of things and she challenges
the Demon (probe) to twist fate, something only it can do.
    Shannon tells T'uupieh his name, which in her superstitious
mind convinces her that he is her lover and then he uses the electrical defense system of the probe to warn Klovkiri of the trap.
Chwiul, infuriated at having his plot thwarted, attempts to kill
T'uupieh but the probe strikes Chwuil dead, saving T'uupieh's life
and that of her sister Ahtseet.   T'uupieh allows herself the
thought that perhaps, just perhaps, she is not displeased that her
sister is saved and that with Chwuil dead, Klovhiri will be in her
debt.   Shannon has some hope that his actions have changed
T'uupieh's values.
    In this Hugo award winning novelette, Vinge displays her
craftsmanship in creating a world and the memorable character of
T'uupieh, who exemplifies its culture and mores.   Like many of
her tales, it has all the elements of a fairy tale, with the benevolent mother, the rivalry of siblings and the ultimate triumph of

the heroine, T'uupieh. Titan is a typical Vinge primitive society where superstition prevails, the ability to rob and murder are necessary for survival, and our winged heroine survives by being more cunning and ruthless than others. T'uupieh is another of Vinge's alienated characters who, after learning to communicate with what to her is her lover, the Demon space probe, begins if ever so slightly to change her values about society and its requirements for survival. It is also likely that the anthropologist Vinge expresses her ambivalence over the desire of the Earthman Shannon to impose human value structures on other species and cultures.

Legacy. This novella takes place in the same environment as *Outcasts of Heaven Belt*. Heaven Belt is an asteroid belt once populated by a human colony that was virtually destroyed by civil war. The Demarchy survived in a tiny pocket of planetoids where existence depends entirely on an artificial ecosystem. Everything that is vital for life--air, water, food--has to be processed in the Demarchy's partially destroyed distilleries. What is left is barely adequate for survival and the war has destroyed the technological knowledge that would enable production of replacement parts. So the Demarchy constantly searches for artifacts of the old civilization which it uses to repair the factories and preserve its fragile existence.

Chaim Dartagnan and Mythili Fukinuki are thrown together with the Demarch Siamang as a spaceship prepares to rescue a prospector stranded on Planet Two. Dartagnan is a mediaman who has traded his integrity for the public relations job of reporting on the rescue operation. In a society where nuclear radiation is so high that one of the most valued resources are women who can bear healthy children, Mythili has had herself sterilized so that she could become a pilot. The ship lands on Planet Two; the unscrupulous Siamang kills the survivor, Sekka-Olefin, in order to keep the valuable salvage for himself and prepares to kill Mythili. Unknown to Mythili, the planet has a thin atmosphere into which Chaim shoves her, hoping she will survive while he and Siamang head back to the Demarchy. On their arrival, Chaim, who has fallen in love with Mythili, denounces Siamang for murder, losing all possibility of being rewarded for his part in the salvage operations. Mythili does escape, with the unlikely assistance of a Demarchy policeman, Wadi Abdhiamal. Mythili and Chaim are permitted to use Sekka-Olefin's ship to bring in salvage. Mythili, having no other choice, joins Dartagnan, still embittered at what she thinks is his betrayal on Planet Two. They eventually discover a planetoid with an abandoned factory and equipment which is salvageable.

The primary focus of *Legacy* is the relationship between Chaim and Mythili as they realize that they are mutually dependent and must form a partnership in order to survive. Both are typical of Vinge's characters, lonely and alienated, who must learn to communicate with each other. They are aptly named, Dartagnan after the swashbuckling hero in *The Three Musketeers* and Fukinuki, pronounced as you like. As in many fairy tales they do indeed find a "treasure" and while perhaps not living luxuriously ever after, they learn to adapt and survive in their world. Vinge's stories are always filled with hope for the future, a hope based on a loving relationship. As in many of Vinge's stories the alienated characters conquer loneliness and alienation by learning to communicate and love. But love is not a panacea. Their world will not improve, but they will survive within it. Vinge projects the emotions of her characters with considerable skill, making this simple, accessible story of a maturing love and understanding a very good read.

Outcasts of Heaven Belt. Bethe Torgusson and members of her family travel light years from the planet Morningside on the starship *Ranger* to find the fabled treasures of Heaven Belt and trade with its people. The need to enlarge a small and vulnerable population has forced Morningside into the security of extended families and multiple marriages. Mutual aid for survival is the foundation of its society. Contrasted to this is Heaven Belt, which was an entirely self-sufficient colony in which everything had to be processed or manufactured. A disastrous civil war has caused the loss of the technological knowledge necessary to maintain the manufacturing process. Radiation has caused genetic mutations, sterility, and few normal births and the world is slowly dying. The two groups of Heaven Belt survivors, the Demarchy and the Grand Harmony of the Ringers, compete with each other for scarce resources.

When the starship *Ranger* appears, it is mistaken for a ship of the Demarchy and attacked by the Ringers. Unable to leave without refueling, it continues on to Lansing the capital of the Demarchy. Meanwhile, the Demarchy has sent Wadi Abdhiamal, chief negotiator, to Lansing to intercept the *Ranger* and at any costs to take the ship whose fusion reactor is a prize both governments seek. Not to be outmanuevered, the Ringer navy is in hot pursuit. As the *Ranger* makes for Lansing, it is sighted by Shadow Jack and Bird Alyn, pirates from Lansing. The pirates are captured by the *Ranger* which proceeds with them towards Lansing. Unaware that both the Demarchy and Ringers are closing in, Bethe, the ship's female captain, agrees to slip into Mecca, the main distillery headquarters for the Demarchy, and trade their cat Rusty, an exceedingly rare commodity, for fuel. They escape the attempted capture but fail to refuel, taking Wadi Abdhamial as hostage and head for the Ringers where they now plan to steal the fuel. Wadi concludes that if either side takes the ship, war will ensue destroying what is left of the Demarchy, and so agrees to help Betha escape from Heaven Belt. He succeeds in getting fuel from the Ringers and also saves Betha's life. The Demarchy and Ringers both move into position around Lansing and threaten to blow up the ship rather than let the other side capture it. At the last instant, Wadi and Bethe convince both sides that their only chance of survival is to become trading partners.

Outcasts of Heaven Belt has aspects of both a science fiction space opera and elements of mythology, with the characters in search of a hoped-for treasure in another world. The plot is well developed, as is the world in which Heaven Belt is set. The landscape is bleak, living is difficult, and frightened people are unable to cooperate for their own survival. The characters are well drawn and believable and we remain interested in their efforts to live with and understand each other's worlds. Bethe Torgusson is the strong female protagonist, displaced from her planet Morningside by her decision to volunteer for this mission and further isolated by the loss of her extended family. Wadi, offended by the idea of a society with multiple husbands and wives, comes to appreciate the need for creative solutions for survival and falls in love with her. In this harsh world, Vinge shows us that only through mutual cooperation can inhabitants survive. From a beginning of distrust they learn to cooperate in order to save what little they have.

Psion. Our hero, Cat, is an adolescent orphan, half Hydran and half human, who lives in the subterranean slums of Oldcity situated under the leaking sewage of the beautiful city of Quarro. Cat lives in a dreamworld of drugs in which he escapes from the underworld, whose inhabitants are used as a source of slave labor. The Federation government survives only as a regulatory agency that controls the planetoid Cinder, the source of the telhassium crystals which make interstellar travel possible. Cat is caught by the Federation guards and slated for slave labor when he is identified as a potential "psi" and is sent to the Sakaffe Research Institute to participate in a psi research project. He antagonizes the director, Dr. Siebeling, but is befriended by an empath, Jule. An argument with Siebeling causes him to be driven out of the institute and shipped to Cinder, where the Telhassium crystals are mined. Enslaved among others who are dying of harmful radiation, Cat is rescued by the Hydrans, naturally telepathic aliens, who are hiding on Cinder. They awaken within him his enormous latent psi powers. Meanwhile Rubiy, the psion criminal that Cat was originally trained to combat, offers Cat and Cat's friend Jule wealth, independence, and enormous power to join him in taking over the world by controlling Cinder and interstellar travel. Out of love for Jule, Cat refuses. Ultimately Cat must challenge Rubiy and kill him, but in doing so he sacrifices his psi powers.

Psion, Vinge's first young adult novel, is a gripping, accessible, suspense story as we anxiously await to see if Cat will develop his psi powers and survive all the adventures that lie ahead. It is also a space opera which, through a series of exciting episodes, shows

us the development of a young person's character and values and like other picaresque novels, it is the account of a young person's adventures through adversity. Cat must proceed through the rites of passage, through loneliness, anxiety, and frustration to an understanding of himself and others. At first he flees from all the horror of his life and escapes his mean environment through drugs. He is afraid to join others and be dependent upon them. When he leaves his isolation and loneliness, he finds that he has responsibilities and in carrying out those responsibilities he must make sacrifices. The world of *Psion* is a grim world, an environment in which one would expect the characters to grow up alienated and hostile. Dr. Siebeling, director of the institute's psi group, is a man who hates himself because he could not protect his wife from death. Jule is ashamed for having been born a psion and thus disgraced her family. Cat learns to develop a relationship both with Siebeling and Jule and to support them both as his "family." All three learn to trust one another, to care, to love, to maintain their communications in a world where the norm is hatred, corruption, and insensitivity. Cat's exciting adventures are continued in the novella, "Psiren."

The Snow Queen. The Hegemony rules the preindustrial world of Tiamat in a period long after the collapse of the Old Empire. Only the rulers of the Hegemony have achieved star travel and Tiamat is accessible through a star gate only 150 years out of 250. During these 150 years, Tiamat is dominated by the Winters, who sell to the Hegemony an elixir of long life taken from the blood of slaughtered sea beasts, the gentle telepathic mers. In return for this elixir, they are given the use of minor technology which the Hegemony controls. During the remaining 100 years, the rustic Summers rule, worshipping the Lady of the Sea, holding the mers inviolate, and consulting the sibyls.

The novel opens as Winters' reign nears its end and the Stargate is closing. The Snow Queen Arienrhod, ruthless, powerful, and beautiful, plots to ensure her continued control when the offworlders and their technology leave. The Snow Queen is determined to change the shape of society by outlasting the periodic cycle and retaining the Hegemony technology so that society does not revert to a primitive state. By injections of the Mer elixir, Arienrhod has sustained her youth and beauty. She intends to outlast the Summer cycle by cloning herself. Her clone, Moon Dawntreader, while also powerful and beautiful, is compassionate and loving as well. Moon, raised as a Summer, becomes a sibyl, but loses her childhood sweetheart, Sparks, when he is unable to pass the Sybil test. Divorced from the Summers by her resemblance to Arienrhod and holding sibyl powers that are feared by the Winters as causing death and madness, Moon uses her psi powers to travel to Kharemough, center of the Hegemony, where she discovers that the function of sibyls is to retain and transmit the

Old Empire knowledge which is maintained in a computer data bank below the Winters Castle. During her absence, Sparks is corrupted by the Snow Queen, who takes him as her lover. Arienrhod, thinking her original scheme has failed, prepares to unleash an epidemic that will annihilate all the Summers, but she is thwarted by the police inspector Jerusha. Moon returns to the planet in time to participate in the necessary transitional sacrifice of the Winter queen to the Sea and the rise of the Summers' reign.

This is one of Vinge's most successful novels combining fantasy, myth, and romance. It is a story of love lost, betrayed, and regained; the battle of evil against good; a story of love between two alienated individuals. The creation of the planet Tiamat with its complex sociology, culture, and political organization is a major achievement, as are the believable characterizations of both major and minor figures. There are close parallels in *The Snow Queen* to Hans Christian Anderson's fairy tale of the same name. Sparks, at first the innocent lover, is turned into an evil being by the cold and insensitive Winters Queen and is later restored by Moon. Moon, like Gerda in the fairy tale, travels through snow and ice to save her love and restore his self respect. The story is also strongly influenced by Robert Graves' *The White Goddess*, the triple faced goddess of the moon with powers to create and destroy. The ancient Babylonian mother goddess was also called Tiamat. By making Moon the clone of Arienrhod, Vinge allows the new phase of the moon to supplant the old and bring forth renewal. Vinge also uses the archetypal myth of the death and revival of vegetation to symbolize the psychological development of her characters. The Winters' period is similar to the death or alienation period, while Summers' represents the regenerative and healing period. Moon also represents fertility, while Arienrhod is sterile from drinking Mers water. In the fertile, regenerative period, Moon has the possibility of integrating the Winters and the Summers to bring a revival of the higher culture of the Old Empire. As in most fairy tales, through the power of love, good triumphs over evil and change may come to benefit the entire society.

Biographical/Bibliographical Readings

Len Hatfield, "Joan Vinge," in *Twentieth-Century Science-Fiction Writers*, ed. Curtis C. Smith (St. James, 1986), p.755-56. "Joan Dennison Vinge," in *Something about the Author* (Gale, 1984) v.36, p.194-96. Charles Platt, "Joan D. Vinge," in *Dream Makers* (Berkley, 1983), v.2, p.211-17. [Judith R. Bernstein]

VONNEGUT, KURT, JR.

Life and Works

Kurt Vonnegut, Jr., was born in Indianapolis, Indiana, on November 11, 1922. After attending public schools there, he studied chemistry at Cornell University. He was a battalion scout during World War II and was captured by the Germans during the Battle of the Bulge. While being held prisoner of war, he witnessed the destruction of the city of Dresden, a disturbing experience he felt able to draw on only much later, in his best-known novel, *Slaughterhouse-Five* (1969), the title of which refers to the abatoir under which he was kept (locked safely in a meat locker) while the firestorm raged above him, killing more people than the bomb dropped on Hiroshima. After the war Vonnegut married a childhood friend, Jane Marie Cox, who was to bear him three children. He was accepted as a graduate student in anthropology at the University of Chicago (1945-47) and also worked as a police reporter for the Chicago City News Bureau in 1946. His longest job was in public relations at the Research Laboratory of the General Electric Company in Schenectady, New York. It was in his last year there (1950) that he started selling short stories to *Collier's.* With the money from these stories, he was able to leave his job and begin work on *Player Piano* (1952), a novel which he claims mocked General Electric.

At this point he moved to Cape Cod and became a free-lance writer. Some time later, around 1966, following the republication of his novels *The Sirens of Titan* (1959), *Cat's Cradle* (1963), *Player Piano*, and *Mother Night* (1961), an absurdist treatment of Nazism, Vonnegut entered a new phase in his career, gaining literary acceptability as a self-conscious fabulator and becoming something of a counter-culture hero figure. In addition to his novels, the best of his science fiction short stories are "Harrison Bergeron," "The Barnhouse Effect" (his first published story), "The Euphio Question," and "Epicac." All of these were collected, along with an excellent later tale about an overpopulated future where sex has been made unpleasurable as the title story, in *Welcome to the Monkey House* (1968). Since then he has held various university teaching posts, beginning with the Writers Workshop at the University of Iowa, has been the recipient of academic grants, and has obtained a Ph.D. in literature.

Themes and Style

There is an oft-quoted passage in his novel *God Bless You, Mr. Rosewater* (1965) in which Vonnegut has Eliot Rosewater pay tribute to science fiction writers, and in particular to Kilgore Trout, a character who has a significant role in another of Vonnegut's novels, *Breakfast of Champions* (1973). Rosewater declares that only science fiction writers are willing to talk about the *really* terrific changes going on; they are the only ones courageous enough to *really* notice what machines do to us. But in the real world it works the other way around: tackling such themes will inevitably give one's work some of the attributes of the science fiction genre, and being sold as science fiction can restrict the reviews and readership of an author's books. Not surprisingly, in an article entitled "Science Fiction" first published in *The New York Times Book Review* in 1965, Vonnegut declared that he would like out of the artificial category, the file drawer labeled "science fiction." All the same, the ingenious claims he makes that *Player Piano* was simply a novel about life in the present day and therefore necessarily a novel about people and machines hardly takes stock of the carefully established near-future dystopian context, which is what gives credibility to the plot and to the single-minded obsessions of his characters. In the same place Vonnegut writes affectionately enough of the science fiction community, although he considers it to be one of many meaningless social aggregations.

Probably, in fact, the only completely generic science fiction of Vonnegut's is to be found in early short stories such as "Unready to Wear," a witty tale about humans learning to live without their bodies, or "Tomorrow and Tomorrow. . . ." (originally called "The Big Trip up Yonder), a satirical portrait of life in 2158, when "gerasone" secures unlimited life. Both of these first appeared in *Galaxy* in the early 1950s. Vonnegut's continuing interest in the genre is shown by his recent *Galapagos* (1985). This is a wistful fable about the devolution of a handful of people marooned on the Galapagos Islands, and their transformation, in the course of a million years, into a seal-like, furry, rather dim-witted new species. The narrator is Leon Trotsky Trout, who has been decapitated and exists as a ghost on the islands. In the course of Vonnegut's writing career, science fiction seems to have supplied a repertoire of literary conventions and motifs (such as space and time travel) which Vonnegut rather deliberately parodies even as he makes use of them--especially in his sophisticated space fantasy, *The Sirens of Titan*. Its mock-mythic opening plainly debunks the generic sense of wonder proper to the emerging space age and offers instead empty heroics, low comedy, and pointless death. This is in keeping with a consistent theme of Vonnegut's; that human beings will always be their own worst enemies. New technologies, the new frontiers of space, will only open further arenas in which human folly will parade itself once more. It is a reconsideration of the notion of a flaw in human nature in the framework of a systems view of the human predicament. The interaction of human short-sightedness with a highly complex world inevitably produces undesirable effects among its many surprises: people are guilty not of being evil but of being outwitted by the range of possibilities they are subject to. The most succinct illustration of this theme is to be found in *Cat's Cradle*.

As a consequence of this conviction about the complexity of our world, Vonnegut produces a generalized satire, with no specific ultimate targets. Everything that insulates a person from awareness of the situation Vonnegut presupposes; this potentially absurd premise of the absolutely unfathomable mysteries of life is potentially dangerous. The notion of "necessary lies" is very much in keeping with Nietzche's philosophy and with current postmodern thought. As its implications pervade all of Vonnegut's subsequent work, his emergence as a literary figure may have a good deal to do with the contemporary appeal of this underlying preoccupation. In his science fiction works, Vonnegut has concentrated on the way such "fomas," or harmless falsities, can become rigidified into systems of belief which artificially reduce complexity so as to insulate a group of people from harsh realities. He appears to have somewhat ambiguous feelings toward pseudoreligions. Bokonism, in *Cat's Cradle*, is a case in point. Its rituals are at least partly effective in bringing people closer together, and seem intended to be rather endearing, even if futile or pathetic at the same time. Vonnegut ascribes a similar function to the wildly inventive science fiction of his character, Kilgore Trout.

Like the authors of the so-called New Wave science fiction, Kurt Vonnegut, Jr., seems to be interested in reviewing problems of human life which are usually resolved in moral terms in other, more neutral and less rigid, ways. Much of what he does as a writer, from his pithy, throwaway style and jokes to his consciously implausible plots, seems intended to protect him from the risk of letting a sense of high moral seriousness do his thinking for him. His best work, notably *Slaughterhouse-Five*, shows him pulling ever more inventive tricks out of the bag so as to be able to open up his readers' responses to ever more repressed facts of life, without the author laying down any clearly interpretable guidelines for them.

Plot Summaries of Major Works

Cat's Cradle. The narrator-protagonist of this short novel links together its two parallel and ultimately convergent lines of development when he is chosen to beome leader of the republic of San Lorenzo, a mock-utopian island in the Caribbean where two-thirds of the story takes place. For, in this unlikely setting--a grotesque parody of the dictatorship of Duvalier in Haiti--he encounters, and is converted to, "Bokononism," an incoherent pseudoreligion which parades the falsity of its doctrines and the impossiblility of making sense of a brutal and absurd world. He also, however, unearths the last of the family secrets of Dr. Felix Hoenikker, one of the fathers of the atomic bomb, and his strange children. This ultimate disclosure is that of the catastrophic power of "ice-nine", the science-fictional element in the novel, a form of water which melts only at very high temperatures.

This is a deceptively small work, divided--apparently arbitrarily--into 127 short chapters with whimsical titles such as "Bell, Book, and Chicken in a Hatbox." The other immediately noticeable feature is the string of seemingly nonsensical terms, such as "karass" and "granfalloon," invented by Bokonon. But even these prove to be pertinent. Appearances, indeed, are deceptive, as this is a cleverly plotted novel in which everything finally slots into place. It has many literary allusions--the opening parodies that of *Moby Dick*, to choose the most obvious example--and makes skilled use of the conventions of the detective story, science fiction, and the picaresque tradition. Finally, though, the absurdism loses its playfulness and in the apocalyptic ending the bitter implications of the story are given great force. The aimless, almost accidental, unleashing of ice-nine gives the novel a powerful culmination: in a flash it corrupts a world of inexhaustible possibilities, too rich to be either good or bad and too complex to be dominated, reducing it to a pitiful travesty of itself. In all this it repeats and condenses the essence of the human predicament as Vonnegut portrays it throughout the novel.

Player Piano. The story at first is centered on the manager and engineers of the Ilium Works, New York, a vast automated industrial center typical of many others throughout this near-future America. The nation is now run by the National Industrial, Commercial, Communications, Foodstuffs, and Resources Board and a restricted executive class of Ph.D.s with high I.Q.s, while the mass of the population has been made redundant by automation--originally as part of the war effort. In Ilium they live in Homestead, over the river from the centers of production and power, and are conscripted into either the Army or the Reconstruction and Reclamation Corps (the "Reeks and Wrecks") if they are unable to survive economically alongside the machines. The narrative follows the actions of the manager of the Ilium Works, Dr. Paus Proteus, as he attempts to build new links with the Homesteaders. Instead he becomes the figurehead of a machine-wrecking revolt led by the mysterious Ghost Shirt Society. This would-be revolution inevitably ends in failure, but for its instigator, a Protestant minister named Lasher, it was never intended to be anything but a symbolic gesture, like that of the Indians of the 1890s who were massacred by the U.S. Calvary while wearing the Ghost Shirts, which represented their desire to resist being taken over by an alien force, but which were ineffectual against their opponents' bullets.

In writing this lengthy first novel Vonnegut drew on his experiences as a public relations official at General Electric in Schenectady, New York. This probably helps to explain the convincing images of machinery at work and the authenticity of the office talk. The ultimate vacuity of the mentality of his technocrats, and the clumsy insensitivity of their emotional life, is especially well conveyed. Indeed, the backbone of this biting satire is really located in the subplots, where the later Vonnegut's sense of the absurd and the ridiculous is already apparent. The encounter of the visiting Shad of Bratpuhr with the massive computer EPICAC and with a typical American citizen provide moments of delightful satire, as do the scenes in the Meadows, a country retreat where the corporation men (and their wives) indulge in an orgy of morale-building games and fun, fake Indians, and all.

The negative utopia of the inhumanly systematized society in which a kind of "lawlessness" prevails (given the absolute right of machines over humans) is perhaps best seen as a nightmare extrapolation of the dangers inherent in uncontrolled mechanization. However, the main plot, with its sardonic ending (the saboteurs cannot resist trying to restore the machines they themselves had damaged shortly before) does not directly address the underlying--tremendously involved--socioeconomic issues. It concentrates on Paul Proteus's sense of the cost, in terms of an individual's self-realization, of accepting the premises of a technocratic society. To him, and to everyone else in the novel, pianos can only be conceived of as player pianos. Using machines means becoming dependent on them, with the machines calling the tunes.

The Sirens of Titan. The story opens in Newport, Rhode Island, some time between the Second World War and the Third Great Depression, with a crowd awaiting the materialization of Winston Niles Rumfoord, a millionaire with style and a private spacecraft, and his pet hound Kazan, who now exist as wave phenomena--apparently pulsing in a distorted spiral with its origin in the Sun and its terminal in Betelgeuse. Rumfoord had run into a space/time warp (a "chrono-synclastic infundibulum") and is now dispersed through space and time, able to see everything that has happened and will happen. He and his dog are, however, permanently materialized on Titan, one of Saturn's moons. He has masterminded the colonization of Mars and will have his "Martian" army launch a farcical invasion attack against Earth in which almost all of them will be killed. The idea is to shock humankind into a mood of mature cynicism receptive to the launching of his new religion, "The Church of God the Utterly Indifferent." The man he chooses to be its first martyr is Malachi Constant. This immensely wealthy but unfulfilled businessman will be abducted, have his memory erased and will be taken to Mars where he will be known as "Unk" to his fellow soldiers. His relationships, with Rumfoord's wife Beatrice and with his commander Boaz, and his various adventures on Mars, Mercury, Earth and Titan, form the main thread of the plot. However, in the end the real guiding force behind it all turns out to be the alien beings on the planet Tralfamadore in the Lesser Magellanic Cloud. They are prepared to mold the destinies of millions of distant Earthlings, shaping whole chunks of Earth history, provided this will save time in obtaining a spare part for one of their spaceships. Their endearing messenger, Salo, has been grounded some 200,000 years on Titan: without the needed part it cannot continue on its supposedly important mission of carrying the message of "Greetings" across the universe.

The Sirens of Titan is a witty novel profuse in outlandish ideas and inventive details. Its theme is the endless human urge to put in doubt any apparent solution to the problem of the meaning of life. Vonnegut's implied viewpoint is that of a cat playing around with a mouse; he is aloof from the situations he has his characters cast into, but seems to enjoy the game. This works well with spurious solutions such as hedonism (Malichi in Hollywood) or the soft utopia chosen by Boza among the "cute little" harmoniums of Mercury, but Vonnegut's tone does not allow him to convey the anguish people can feel when their value systems break down in the face of unacceptably harsh realities. But it could be said that Vonnegut's ability to ridicule with such flair even the most serious and profound aspects of the human situation is actually his greatest gift--as when Malachi faces the seventy-three knobs, switches, and buttons of Salo's spaceship. The controls were anything but a hunch-player's delight in a universe composed of one trillionth part matter to one decillion parts black velvet futility.

Slaughterhouse-Five, or The Children's Crusade. The narrator of this story introduces it as a failure. Instead of the level-headed exposure he wanted to produce on the subject of the tragic destruction of the lovely German city of Dresden in the Second World War (when 135,000 people, mostly civilians, were killed by British and U.S. bombers), he gives us the story of Billy Pilgrim. This is told in a chatty style, interspersed with quotations from other, more orthodox works on warfare and on Dresden's history, with cartoon drawings and with the recurrent use of the phrase "So it goes" whenever the subject of death--even that of champagne bubbles!--comes up. This lack of seriousness or moderation makes the pathos ambivalent.

The central character, who as a young prisoner-of-war was housed in the cellar of a slaughterhouse in Dresden during the fire-bombing, has become "unstuck in time," and the narrative follows his leaps backward and forward. Billy's innocence is as clearcut as his misfortune. There are three main sequences which can be pieced together from the disjointed episodes: that of the war years, that of his professional life as a successful optometrist and his marriage in Ilium, New York, and that of his time on the planet Tralfamadore. The last sequence is the science fiction aspect of the novel. Billy claims that he was (or will be) kidnapped at the age of forty-four by a flying saucer and taken to Tralfamadore to be exhibited naked in a zoo, where a mate is later brought to him. She is Montana Wildhack, a movie star. Together the two of them come to live a parody of the normal life of a young Earthling couple, watched all the while by hundreds of Tralfamadorians.

The science fiction devices of time travel and an alien viewpoint allow Vonnegut to make his case--that war is too senseless to even begin to reason against--while demonstrating, in the very structure of the book, the emotional disturbance it provokes and which, for those with direct experience of its horrors, is what counts most against it. However, he manages this with a great deal of wit and some hilarious scenarios while carefully balancing righteous indignation against resignation and quietism.

Biographical/Bibliographical Readings

Charles L. Elkins, "Kurt Vonnegut," in *Science Fiction Writers*, ed. E. F. Bleiler (Scribner's, 1982), p.551-62. Robert Group, "Kurt Vonnegut, Jr.," in *Twentieth-Century American Science-Fiction Writers* (Gale, 1981), v.2, p.184-89. Jerome Klinkowitz and John Somer, *The Vonnegut Statement* (Delacorte, 1973). Asa B. Pieratt, Jr., and Jerome Klinkowitz, *Kurt Vonnegut, Jr.: A Descriptive Bibliography and Annotated Secondary Checklist* (Shoestring Press, 1974). Thomas L. Wymer, "The Swiftian Satire of Kurt Vonnegut, Jr.," in *Voices for the Future*, ed. Thomas D. Clareson (Bowling Green University Popular Press, 1976), v.1, p.238-62. **[Jonathan K. Benison]**

WELLS, H. G.

Life and Works

Herbert George Wells was born on September 21, 1866, in Bromley, Kent, not too far outside of London. He was the fourth and last child of Joseph Wells, a struggling shopkeeper, and Sarah Wells. Wells' childhood was not particularly unhappy despite the family's hardships. His father encouraged his reading and, although his schooling was not high quality, he managed through a love of reading to become quite well educated. He was apprenticed to a firm of drapers but was so unhappy that he left it and became an assistant master at Midhurst Grammar School. While there he won a scholarship to the Normal School of Science in South Kensington where he studied under T. H. Huxley. In 1890, he graduated from the University of London with a degree in zoology. In London, he was actively involved with a number of groups which were to shape his thinking and influence his later writing. Many of these were socialist groups, such as the Fabian society with which he was associated for a number of years. He also met a number of influential people, including George Bernard Shaw and William Morris. His predilection toward religious scepticism and socialism were already formed by this point in his life. Wells' first marriage ended in divorce after only one year and in 1894 he married a former student, Amy Catherine Robbins. Despite his devotion to her, he had several serious liaisons, the most famous of which was with Rebecca West, which lasted for eleven years.

A year after his second marriage, Wells published his first novel, *The Time Machine* (1895). This was to be the first of his science fiction novels. The year 1896 brought *The Island of Dr. Moreau*, followed by *The Invisible Man* in 1897. *The War of the Worlds* was published in 1898 and in 1899 Wells published both *When the Sleeper Wakes* and *Tales of Time and Space*. After *When the Sleeper Wakes*, Wells wrote several additional novels in the scientific mode; however, he moved further and further from the imaginative brilliance of his earlier works and focused on perfecting his utopian ideas within the novel form. *The First Men in the Moon* was published in 1901. After this point, Wells turned more and more to his sociological novels and nonfiction. In all, Wells published approximately 120 books in his lifetime. Wells died on August 13, 1946, having seen in two world wars many of the horrors he had prophesied in his novels.

Themes and Style

The fantastic elements that Wells introduced in his science fiction novels were only partly responsible for their immense popularity. He was a critically acclaimed writer whose plots served as a vehicle for his more sophisticated ideas and philosophy. They were imbued with the socialistic pessimism of the Fabians and other freethinkers of the time. In *The Time Machine*, Wells comments extensively on the separation of the classes. That Wells was a brillian writer is undeniable. His novels *Tono Bungay* and *Ann Veronica*, both published in 1909, and his nonfiction, such as *The Outline of History* (1920), surely have given him a place among worthy twentieth-century writers, and his literary merits have been highly recognized. Yet it is the early writings, the fantastic science fictional novels of the 1890s, that cause the acclaim for which Wells is known today.

Plot Summaries of Major Works

The Invisible Man. Griffin, a physicist, discovers the secret of making objects invisible, first experimenting with inanimate objects, then with a cat, and finally doing the ultimate experiment upon himself. The results of his experiment are successful only in the scientific sense, for he discovers that true invisibility can be a hindrance. Griffin, though invisible, can feel the dogs nipping at his feet and the icy snow on his naked body. He decides that he must find a way of reversing the condition. Retreating to a small English village, Griffin makes initial attempts to remedy the situation but too soon is discovered by the villagers. He flees and in time comes upon the home of a former college acquaintance, now a country doctor. Assuming that Dr. Kemp will aid him, Griffin determines that his future holds power and that he will begin a reign of terror. However, Kemp realizes the danger to society that Griffin threatens and ultimately aids in his capture and death at the hands of the villagers.

Wells has created a strong sense of tension in this novel. Griffin is a driven man and it is the terror created within himself that eventually creates the sense of terror that overwhelms the countryside. Wells has developed a character who is outside the social order of the time. He is a man without morality in a totally moral setting. He cannot relate to his fellows because of his invisibility, and ultimately the mob turns on him. His beating is the ultimate act taken against an antisocial outcast. Wells clearly defines the social order in this world. The educated class (represented by the doctor), the villagers and the innkeeper, and the naked Marvel (the drunken vagabond whom Griffin uses) all play their parts in determining the fate of Griffin within the social order. Although Wells' science fiction focuses on the fantastic, he does not belie in any way his later reputation as a social critic. The terrorist, the man who attempted to put himself above society, is tracked down and killed by the rational man, Kemp, and the members of ordinary society.

The Island of Dr. Moreau. When Prendick is saved from a shipwreck and taken to the island of Dr. Moreau by Montgomery, Moreau's assistant, he does not realize immediately that this is the same Moreau who scandalized London with his bizarre and inhumane experiments on animals. Prendick realizes this as he sees all of the grotesque lifeforms on the island. Assuming that these are human beings on whom Moreau has experimented, he attempts to escape. When this fails, he threatens suicide in order to avoid the terrible fate which he suspects is awaiting him. Moreau, however, is not quite so evil as Prendick assumes, being interested only in turning animals into humans. Although his experiments are enough to make any animal lover despise him, he does not destroy human life. Indeed, he is frustrated in his attempts to make permanent any of his changes; the animal/people seem to revert to their elemental form after a time. Moreau attributes this to the fact that he has been unable to find the basic part of the brain which makes a living thing human. Prendick accustoms himself to life on the island, but soon things begin to go wrong for Moreau. A number of the things created from feral beasts revert to their natural form and Moreau and Montgomery are killed by their creations. Prendick manages to cope with the situation and finally attempts an escape. He is picked up by a passing ship and returned to society. The strain on him has been severe and he determines that he must live an isolated life in order to survive.

A number of standard Wellsian themes are woven throughout the novel. Wells has made use of his studies with Huxley and the evolutionary process. After Prendick returns from the island, he is unable to see that humans are very different from the beasts. He envisions the animal tendencies within a human and could not persuade himself that the people he met were not also human/beast, somewhat of a reversal of Dr. Moreau's experiment. Likewise, Wells points out that religion is no salvation. The beast people had developed a religion of sorts, following the laws laid down by Moreau. Wells' treatment of the ceremonies and repetitious litany performed by the beast people is bitter indeed as he describes the sly and devious deviations from Moreau's law and the total breakdown as the animals revert to their original forms.

The Island of Dr. Moreau does not present a positive picture of civilization. Wells is trying to convince his readers that within humanity there is a dark side, that there exists the potential for totalitarianism, for cruelty, for barbarism, and that the totems of humanity, e.g. religion, will not save civilization from reverting to its primal state.

The Time Machine. The Time Traveller recounts to a group of skeptical dinner guests his journey forward in time. He has invented a machine in which he travels into the future. He arrives in the year 802,701 to find himself in a bucolic setting inhabited by an innocent, simple people called Eloi. The first bit of trouble occurs when the Time Traveler discovers that his time machine has disappeared. He assumes that the Eloi have simply moved it for safekeeping, although he wonders at their ability to do so. An omnious sense begans to pervade the Traveller as he observes that night brings a change in the Eloi from joyous and playful to fearful. Soon he discovers that the Eloi are not alone, but are merely the above-ground inhabitants. The Morlocks, the underground dwellers, appear during the night and feed on the Eloi, and it is the Morlocks who have hidden the time machine. Finally, the Time Traveller manages to retrieve it and travels still farther into the future, watching the decay of Earth. He stops his travels as the Earth is dying and returns to his drawing room where he tells his strange tale. His friend, the narrator, visits him just in time to see the Time Traveller disappear in his time machine, this time never to return.

In *The Time Machine*, Wells bitterly satirizes the class structure of English Victorian society. The effete upper class are represented by the decadent Eloi, who spend their days playing in the halycon countryside. The Morlocks are the working class, toiling in the underground world of the machines. However, it is the Morlocks who now control society, having succeeded in reducing the Eloi to the level of domesticated animals to be used for food. Through the Time Traveller, Wells gradually moves from the idea of a utopian society to one that is a dark prediction of things to come, from perfect harmony to langour and decay. Ultimately, Wells' vision of the universe is despairing, cold and lost as his Time Traveller visits the shores of a dead sea with the only life form a round black blob hopping about.

The War of the Worlds. Into the peaceful evening of the Surrey countryside comes a cylinder. At first it is thought to be a falling star. Excitement is generated and a holiday atmosphere prevails. Soon, however, excitement becomes panic and then mass terror as the Martians and their terrible war machines emerge from the cylinder and begin the devastation of the countryside. A total of seven cylinders fall on Earth on seven successive nights and, as cylinders fall and the smoke and red moss pervade the countryside, the horror becomes worse. The Martians, who take the fresh blood of other living creatures and inject it into their own veins, are monsters who prey on the humans they capture. As they make their way to London, it seems as though nothing can stop their progress toward the complete destruction of Earth. Yet, ultimately, the Martians fall victim to simple bacteria and die.

Wells' depiction of the plight of humanity is vivid, horrifying, and even more effective because of his ability to portray the prosaic aspects of English life with all of its trivialities and banalities. The sharp contrast of the self-satisfied, contented lifestyle with the horror and devastation that occurs with the arrival of the Martians is skillfully handled. Wells accomplishes the description of the invasion through a single narrator, although he later alters the focus of the book from the narrator to his brother, based in London. Not only does this allow for a broader scope, it permits Wells to depict strong contrasts in characterization. The narrator encounters a curate who accompanies him in his travels and who is killed by the narrator and finally eaten by the Martians. In the curate, Wells describes a despicable human being, cowardly and hyprocritical. Nicely contrasted is the narrator's brother, who is depicted as a good, helpful man who comes to the aid of a young woman and her female companion. The other character of note is the artilleryman who first appears as a deserting soldier and later as a comic revolutionary who has a visionary plan for the lower classes to survive. Wells has not ignored the social statement in these characterizations. The hyprocritical curate, the clownish revolutionary, the intellectual narrator, the kindly brother, are all aspects of the society Wells lived in and he shows it clearly with all of its foibles. Even without Orson Wells' famous radio broadcast of 1939, *The War of The Worlds* would probably be H. G. Wells' most popular and most read novel.

When the Sleeper Wakes. Graham, an insomniac driven to the brink of suicide for lack of sleep, is more than astounded to discover that he has indeed fallen asleep and has awakened two hundred years in the future. During this period, he was cared for by friends and became something of a curiosity. As the years passed, his estate acquired more and more wealth and the Sleeper, as he was to be known, acquired the aura of a messianic figure. When he awakens, he discovers that he is the "master of the world" and the godhead of the working classes. "When the Sleeper Wakes" has become the rallying cry of the workers who have become the downtrodden people in a totalitarian society. After waking, Graham is too awestruck by the marvels of the new and unfamiliar world to alter the political chaos that has surrounded his reemergence into the world. Indeed, the marvels of moving walkways, video cylinders and television, broadcasting, and airplanes--all yet in experimental forms in his time--are sources of amazement for Graham. It is not until one of the leaders of the revolt, Helen Wotton, a young woman in awe of the Sleeper, begins to educate Graham about the plight of the workers that he begins to assume the role of leadership that has been cast upon him. He realizes that Ostrog, the Boss, has used and betrayed him. In a final air duel, Graham kills Ostrog but is also killed himself, leaving the future of the revolution unresolved.

When compared to his other scientific romances, *When the Sleeper Wakes* seems a ponderous and lifeless work. Wells himself rewrote the work in 1910 with the title *The Sleeper Wakes*. He admitted to being dissatisfied with it and so shortened it considerably but without altering the concepts to any great extent. It is, within the early group of novels, his most philosophical work. Wells' main focus is the social structure of the future society, one in which society has been divided into two major elements--the rulers and the ruled. It is, perhaps, the continuation of the Eloi and the Morlocks of *The Time Machine*. Wells questions the advantages of progress if the circumstances lead to class separation.

Not one of Wells' more popular novels, one can still see the influence on later writers. Huxley's *Brave New World* and Orwell's *1984* are reminiscent of the totalitarian society Wells depicts. The Labour Company workers in their blue uniforms, living without privacy and totally controlled by the council, reflect Wells' personal view of a future nightmare. It is a grim view, not enlightened by all the technological advances Wells so creatively imagined.

Biographical/Bibliographical Readings

Brian W. Aldiss, "H. G. Wells," in *Science Fiction Writers*, ed. E. F. Bleiler (Scribner's, 1982), p.25-30. J. R. Hammond, *An H. G. Wells Companion* (Macmillan, 1979). Norman and Jeanne Mackenzie, *The Time Traveller: The Life of H. G. Wells* (Weidenfeld and Nicolson, 1973). Frank McConnell, *The Science Fiction of H. G. Wells* (Oxford University Press, 1981). **[Jeanne M. Sohn]**

WILHELM, KATE

Life and Works

Born Katie Gertrude Meredith on June 8, 1928, in Toledo, Ohio, she married Joseph B. Wilhelm in 1947. Working as a model, a telephone operator and in several other positions, Wilhelm turned to writing full time in 1956. Divorced in 1962, the same year her first book, *More Bitter Than Death*, appeared, she remarried the following year, this time to fellow science fiction writer and editor Damon Knight. Her first collection of short stories, *The Mile-Long Spaceship*, appeared in 1963. Selected to codirect the Milford Science Fiction Writers Conferences, Wilhelm rapidly built her reputation as an exceptionally fine writer. With the publication of *The Killer Thing* in 1967, and the 1968 Nebula award for her short story, "The Planners," Wilhelm began to be regarded as more than just another promising science fiction writer. While coauthoring *The Clone* (1968) and *The Year of the Cloud* (1970) with patent attorney Ted Thomas, Wilhelm continued to sharpen her craft through the Clarion workshops. In 1971, she lectured at Tulane University on science fiction, then began a succession of novels, most notable being *Abyss* (1971), *City of Cain* (1973), and *The Clewiston Test* (1976). Remarkably, at the same time she worked on several nonscience fiction titles including *Margaret and I* (1971) and *Fault Lines* (1976). In 1977, *Where Late the Sweet Birds Sang* won the Nebula and Jupiter awards. In 1980, she received an American book award nomination for *Juniper Time*. Her latest book is *Huysman's Pets* (1985). Presently living in Eugene, Oregon, she is the mother of three sons, two from her first marriage and one from her second.

Themes and Style

Kate Wilhelm has an incredible ability to develop characters while obscuring their thought processes. Concealing the subconscious and yet retaining a view of the world from within, Wilhelm allows the dialogue to reveal the thoughts of her characters. In fact, with this technique Wilhelm is often able to grasp the reader's attention and create an aura of suspense. The swirl of activity and dialogue that surrounds her characters obscures their motives and creates a highly believable, moody atmosphere. This ability is particularly well displayed in her latest novel, *Huysman's Pets*, in which the principle character is either acting deliberately or accidentally revealing insanity. Her books are often set against an apocalyptic tapestry, be it the famines of *Juniper Time*, the earthquake in *Fault Lines*, the ecological disasters of *Where Late the Sweet Birds Sang*, or the experimental serum of *The Clewiston Test*. In each novel, she does not attempt to judge the sweep of the disaster, but instead devotes her energies to the personal effect, the individual's tragedy and will to survive against an unfeeling, unresponsive system. Her characters reveal Wilhelm's innate belief in the integrity of the person when confronted with insurmountable odds and in the ability of the human race's infinite capacity to heal itself. Wilhelm's scientific interests are in the area of genetic research, with several of her works--*Where Late the Sweet Birds Sang* and *Huysman's Pets*--dependent upon the actions of geneticists. Yet, she does not involve the reader in the nuts and bolts of science and technology. Her writing has been termed feminist, as she often creates situations in which the female character must struggle against the bonds which suffocate individuality and creativity, as in *The Clewiston Test* and *Juniper Time*. Her male characters are equally sympathetic, even when chained by the strictures of society as in *Where Late the Sweet Birds Sang*. Her concern is for the human, the persons, both psychologically and philosophically. The Sisyphean tasks awaiting her main characters drain the reader with their intensity and complexity, from the savage desert planet battles of *The Killer Thing* to the incredibly complex *Juniper Time* with its elegy for the American Indian, the ravaged planet Earth, and the foundering space program. Wilhelm has progressed with each novel, revealing a poetic talent for allegorical cautionary tales, increasingly complex imagery, and a frightening personal vision of the Earth's future.

Plot Summaries of Major Works

Huysman's Pets. Set in present-day Eastern United States, little Lisa Robbins is enigmatically caught in a telepathic link; she and her mother are being pursued by a faceless enemy. Other children are similarly pursued and terror-stricken. Drew Lancaster, a second-rate writer with a first-rate talent for eccentricity, is a man obsessed with his failing marriage. He is willing to undertake almost any task to regain his wife, except that of writing a biography of her wealthy, powerful father. The federal agent Leon Louder, looking for a counterfeiter and bookdealer named Sorbies, enters the scene, certain that Drew knows his whereabouts. Against this increasingly complex weave, a young couple, T. M. and Michelle, are being inexplicably hounded by the I.R.S. for a minor tax irregularity. What do all of these have in common? Their relationship to the mysterious dead geneticist, Huysman. They are all being drawn closer to Huysman's experimental genetic hospital. The pets of Huysman are his children, a hundred genetic constructs with remarkable talents.

The beginning of this novel reads much like Van Vogt's *Slan*, with the telepathic children pursued by mysterious anonymous figures. Also like *Slan*, the state has been made the villain, though seemingly in this case, an unknowing and perhaps uncaring depersonalized federal research and development office, that pours out funds for many years without seeming to look too closely at the nastiness of the project. The character of Drew Lancaster is very believable. Wilhelm allows the reader to see the world and Lancaster's actions from within his perspective, and yet never reveals his motivations. Other characters are drawn into the complex web, and other lives spun out in strange and wondrous shapes, but never is the entirety of any character revealed. Wilhelm does not address directly the moral issue of creating Huysman's children, but instead deals with the personal struggle that each character must face against the corrupt power and manipulation of politicians, government agents, and glory-seeking scientists. A cautionary tale in which the reader is left to worry where our single-sighted, blinders-on scientists are leading us, *Huysman's Pets* is a thoughtfully and finely crafted novel with no wasted words or characters.

Juniper Time. The time is the near future. The United States has been brought to the edge of cataclysm by decreasing resources and economic instability. The space program has been wrecked by a series of tragic accidents and greedy manipulative politicians. The daughter of one of the dead space heroes, Jean Brighton, is a survivor of the terrible camps, called Newtowns, that have been established to try and deal with the huge mass of unemployed, starving citizens. Jean is raped and brutalized in the camp, and retreats to the high plains desert of her childhood in Eastern Oregon, where she is restored to health by an elderly American Indian friend of her family. After becoming steeped in the Native American philosophy of being one with the land, Jean is forced back into contact with the world outside. She is the leading linguist of her time, and the space agency needs her to translate a cryptic alien message found in space. As she is drawn into the government circles as a translator, and realizes that her father's dream of space exploration may not have been in vain, Jean begins to suspect that she is the victim of an elaborate hoax that threatens to destroy her integrity and sanity in one bitter moment of irony.

Juniper Time is a complex ecological thriller, with as many victims as heroes. The catastrophic atmosphere created is believable, as such devastations are seldom simple cause and effect. The fascinating scenario of a world in which drought has created famines that unbalance the United States' economy and tip the economics of the disastrous space program is stunningly prophetic in light of the public response to the Challenger tragedy and the

African famine. The characterization of Jean is well crafted, creating a portrait of the scandal that rocks society today with its capacity to create and educate genius, but its unwillingness to support such genius unless some practical use can be made of his or her talents. Jean's rape is not just a betrayal by fellow sufferers, but reflects a far deeper and more cosmic rape of the individual, a brutalization of the ego by an uncaring bureaucracy. With the introduction of the mystical and philosophical structures that have permitted some desert Indian cultures to survive, Wilhelm seems to be saying: strip away the trappings and return to contact with our native soil. Only in these roots will we find the keys to our survival, either as individuals or as the human race. This is an outstanding novel which offers haunting and evocative images of a world on the edge of disaster.

Where Late the Sweet Birds Sang. The Sumner family has gigantic land holdings along the Shenandoah valley, in a world approaching ecological ruin. Recognizing the signs of a rapid decline of the human race, through a sudden inexplicable drop in the birth rate, the family begins preparations to survive the coming storm. Using cloning experiments at their own private hospital, David Sumner and his uncles develop an answer to the increasing sterility. Creating clones of the Sumner family members, the experiment proves successful, but not in time to save the human race or most other warm-blooded species. No bird, no deer, and only a few genetically cloned livestock breeds survive. With each generation the Sumner family finds a reduction in fertility, eventually being forced to resort to sexual reproduction in the fourth generation. The offspring produced exhibit an individuality and creativity that the clan finds disturbing. The last child created by sexual union is driven from the valley, only to return when his talents are discovered necessary to the survival of the species.

With haunting images of a desolate, depopulated, contaminated world, this story is superior to the many other survivalist novels that have recently appeared. Wilhelm's fascination with genetic engineering and the double-edged sword created by its realization find fruitful ground within the story. The complex multileveled generations of cloned individuals with six Meriams, watching over their six identical sisters, each consumed with narcissism, leaves strange images in the reader's mind of the ties that bind a family together to the edge of their own destruction. The will of the individual within even this small group is shown by Wilhelm to be in danger of destruction by the tyranny of the majority. The beauty of Wilhelm's language, the poetic and lyrical quality of her writing, are pervasive, softening the harsh indictment of our environmental policies. The novel of the ultimate ecological catastrophe was well received, being awarded both the Hugo and Jupiter awards in 1977.

Biographical/Bibliographical Readings

John Clute, "Kate Wilhelm," in *The Science Fiction Encyclopedia*, ed. Peter Nicholls (Doubleday, 1979) p.655. Anne Hudson Jones, "Kate Wilhelm," in *Twentieth-Century American Science-Fiction Writers* (Gale, 1981), v.2, p.194-200. Richard Low, "Science Fiction Women: Victims, Rebels, Heroes," in *Patterns of the Fantastic: Academic Programming at Chicon IV* (Starmont House, 1983), p.11-20. Jim Villani, "The Women Science Fiction Writers and the Non-Heroic Male Protagonists," in *Patterns of the Fantastic: Academic Programming at Chicon IV* (Starmont House, 1983), p.21-30. [Colleen Power]

WILLIAMSON, JACK

Life and Works

Jack Stuart Williamson was born on April 29, 1908, in Bisbee, Arizona. His family lived in Mexico and Texas before moving to eastern New Mexico in 1915. Life on their small farm was difficult; the work was hard and money was scarce. Williamson sought escape from this isolated world through reading and through his imagination. In 1926, he discovered the world of science fiction in *Amazing Stories*, and soon began writing short stories. His first published story, "The Metal Man," appeared in 1928 in *Amazing Stories*.

Williamson attended West Texas State College, but left school to concentrate on writing. In the 1920s and 1930s, he wrote numerous stories and became part of the science fiction community of authors and fans. For the first time, he felt as though he was a part of a group other than his own family. In 1934, WIlliamson began publishing one of his most memorable creations with the serialization in *Astounding Science Fiction* of *The Legion of Space*, published as a novel in 1947. This novel and its sequels, *The Cometeers* (1950) and *One against the Legion* (1950) are space operas distinguished by their characterization and their shift away from the total reliance on technology that dominated most of the genre at that time.

In the 1940s, John W. Campbell encouraged Williamson to improve his writing style, suggesting that he must do so in order to grow within the field. Williamson wrote his antimatter series, *Seetee Ship* (in *Astounding Science Fiction* in 1942 and 1943 and as a novel in 1951) and *Seetee Shock* (in *Astounding Science Fiction* in 1949 and as a novel in 1950), for Campbell, publishing them under the name of Will Stewart. In 1949, his best known novel, *The Humanoids*, was published. This book about robots whose mission to protect humanity leads to the denial of all initiative and freedom was partially influenced by Williamson's difficulties readjusting to civilian life after his service as a weather forecaster for the U.S. Army Air Force during World War II.

In 1947, he married Blanch Slaten Harp, whom he had known as a child, and they settled in Portales, New Mexico. Williamson worked for the local newspaper for a time, but soon returned to writing science fiction. In the early 1950s, he wrote a science fiction comic strip, *Beyond Mars*, for the *New York Sunday News*, which took most of his creative energy. His only novels during this time were collaborations in which his original stories were reworked by James Gunn and Frederik Pohl. With Gunn, he wrote *Star Bridge*, published in 1955. Pohl collaborated with Williamson on the Undersea series which consists of *Undersea Quest* (1954), *Undersea Flight* (1955), and *Undersea City* (1958).

In the mid-1950s, Williamson returned to college, receiving his B.A. in the spring of 1957 and his M.A. in the fall of 1957 from Eastern New Mexico University. In 1960, he began teaching English there. In 1964, he received his Ph.D. from the University of Colorado. His thesis was published as *H. G. Wells: Critic of Progress*. Teaching became his primary career; his main science fiction writings during his teaching period were collaborations with Pohl. In the early 1960s, they published the Starchild trilogy, consisting of *Reefs of Space* (1964), *Star Child* (1965), and *Rogue Star* (1969). In 1975, the first of their novels about the world known as Cuckoo, *Farthest Star*, was published. He promoted the use of science fiction in the classroom and edited *Science Fiction Comes to College* (1971) and *Teaching Science Fiction: Education for Tomorrow* (1975).

Williamson retired from teaching in 1977 and began concentrating on writing science fiction again. In 1979, he explored genetic engineering in *Brother to Demons, Brother to Gods*. A sequel to *The Humanoids--The Humanoid Touch*--was published in 1982. *Manseed* (1982) used efforts to seed the universe with humanity as a means of considering individual freedom and the role of technology. He again collaborated with Pohl on *Wall around a Star* (1983), the sequel to *Farthest Star*. The same year saw the publication of a new story about the Legion, *The Queen of the Legion*. *Lifeburst* (1984) is an exploration of politics, family relations, and alien psychology. Also in 1984, he published his autobiography, *Wonder's Child: My Life in Science Fiction*. *Firechild* (1986) expands some of the concepts of the potential use and abuse of genetic engineering and evolution that he had begun to address in 1972 in *The Moon Children*.

Jack Williamson has been honored with many awards. In 1968, he received the First Fandom Science Fiction Hall of Fame Award for his career in science fiction. He received the Pilgrim Award from the Science Fiction Research Association in 1973 for his encouragement of the academic study of science fiction and for his work on H. G. Wells. In 1976, he received the Nebula Grand Master Award for lifetime achievement in science fiction. Eastern New Mexico University awarded him an honorary doctorate of humane letters in 1981, and in 1982, it named the Jack Williamson Science Fiction Library in his honor. He currently still resides in Portales, New Mexico.

Jack Williamson has been writing science fiction for sixty years, publishing over thirty books and numerous short stories. He is one of the few writers who successfully adapted to the changes in science fiction throughout his development. When he began writing, the term "science fiction" had not been invented and there was only one pulp magazine. Now there are many magazines and thousands of books published each year, and science fiction is taught at many universities. Williamson grew with the field, using topics such as antimatter, genetic engineering, and artificial intelligence to explore humanity's evolution, the role of technology, and the theme of individual freedom. As with any prolific writer, not all of his works are equally good, but Williamson's best works are both entertaining and thought-provoking. His ability to appeal to readers for over sixty years has made him one of science fiction's most well-known and respected authors.

Themes and Style

There are several themes that pervade Williamson's work. Throughout his career, he has written about the positive and negative impacts of technology on humanity. In presenting technology as the salvation of humanity's independence in "The Equalizer" and as the destruction of freedom in *The Humanoids*, Williamson maintains that technology has no innate value of good or evil; it is merely a tool.

Williamson also frequently addresses the theme of the tension between individual freedom and the restrictions of society. The need for independence may conflict with the expressed needs of the community. This is shown most dramatically in *The Humanoids*, where the society is preserved at the expense of all individual freedom. Williamson believes that there is an obligation to strive for as much individual freedom as possible while maintaining a responsibility to one's society. It is a continual question of balancing these needs.

Many of Williamson's works concern the evolution of humanity--morally, intellectually, and physically. In *The Queen of the Legion*, some people have a newly evolved ability to navigate through space without depending upon technology. Several works, including *Firechild*, *Manseed*, and *Brother to Demons, Brother to Gods*, deal with genetic engineering as a means of speeding up evolution or of creating new races. One possible explanation of the protectiveness of the humanoids is that their guardianship will force humanity to evolve intellectually and psychologically. Williamson sees science as one of the forces that will cause humanity to continue to evolve.

Williamson's protagonists are usually ordinary individuals placed in circumstances where they must use all of their abilities to survive and overcome their problems. They are not superhuman, but they find that they must perform heroic deeds. Some of his works reflect the archetypical pattern in which the outsider gathers a small group of friends to help overcome the enemy, as shown in the Legion of Space series.

Throughout his work, Williamson attacks all varieties of extreme beliefs. He has presented the dangers of exaggerated militarism, pacifism, religion, and capitalism. He portrays evil as destructive and silly. This theme, while present in all his works, has become much stronger in his later novels such as *Firechild*, which attacks extreme religious and political conservatism.

Plot Summaries of Major Works

The Humanoids series. Jack Williamson's most successful stories are about the humanoids, the shining, sleek, perfect black robots created to serve, obey, and guard humans from harm. Their protection brings an end to war, crime, poverty, menial work, illness, and unhappiness. The humanoids prevent anything harmful to human beings, but this prohibition includes smoking, sports, cooking, scientific research, and even reading works about unhappy people. They anticipate every need and provide everything except freedom, thereby destroying creativity and innovation.

The Humanoids. First appearing in "With Folded Hands. . . ." in 1947 in *Astounding Science Fiction*, the protectiveness of the humanoids left humanity with nothing to do but sit with folded hands. The idea was expanded into a novel, *The Humanoids*, serialized in 1948 as ". . . And Searching Mind." Clay Forester, who discovered the science of rhodomagnetics, is in charge of a secret military project created to defend his world from neighboring planets. In his attempts to find a unified theory that would explain all reality, Forester neglects his wife, Mary, and their marriage begins to fail. Forester is approached by an unusual group of people, nearly all of whom have psychic abilities. They warn him that the humanoids will come to take over the world. Forester's knowledge of rhodomagnetics, the science that created the humanoids on another world, might allow humanity to defeat the humanoids. The arrival of the humanoids does prevent the approaching planetary war, but at the cost of a passive, drugged population. Mary is among those accepting the humanoids, Forester gratefully accepts the humanoids as benefactors who enable humanity to pursue intellectual development, and he prepares to take the benefits of the humanoids to other human worlds. Humanity's only means of resisting the smothering protectiveness of the humanoids seems to be in the development of psychic abilities. This shift from technology to thought may indeed have been a goal of the humanoids, an attempt to balance the uncontrolled explosion of technology by forcing the growth of mental abilities. The conclusion to *The Humanoids* is ambiguous; it has been interpreted in different ways by various critics. One interpretation sees the humanoids as tools whose helpful protection enables humanity to restore the balance between technology and the intellect by advancing the life of the mind. Another interpretation proposes that the ending, in which the resistance to the humanoids changes to acceptance of their benevolent protection, shows the total defeat of humanity. Williamson has said that the ending, while deliberately somewhat ambiguous, was intended to be seen as coming from the view of brainwashed, reengineered individuals.

The Humanoid Touch. In the sequel, published in 1980, humanity finds a way of overcoming the humanoids without destroying them. Refugees fleeing the humanoids have developed very different civilizations on two neighboring planets. Kai has a harsh climate and very little metal; its people rely on technology to survive and envy the ore that is mined on neighboring Malili. On Malili, the people have developed psychic abilities because technology is not possible due to a native virus that destroys machinery. The inhabitants of Malili share a racial memory, are telepathic among their race, and find aggression an alien concept. The humanoids, led to the area by the bombs used on Kai to sterilize a mining site on Malili, take over Kai, but decide that the natives of Malili do not require their services because they are not threats to the humanoids or to each other.

The works about the humanoids have been Williamson's most successful--they have been translated, reprinted, and analyzed frequently in the thirty years since their first publication. The series makes use of several of Williamson's favorite themes. He explores the relationship between humanity and machines, considering the dependence upon technology, the imbalance between developments in technology and morality, and the potential abuse of technology. Williamson also presents the theory that science will influence the ongoing evolution of humanity, whether by encouraging the development of psychic ability or exposing humanity to alien influences.

An underlying theme of the series involves the tension between individual freedom and the constraints of society. The protection of the humanoids is accepted by nearly everyone, and it does save humanity from war and destruction, but only by destroying individual freedom of choice. Williamson's presentation of the questions concerning an individual's obligation to society and the role of technology are effectively combined with his creation of the seemingly benevolent, yet sinister, humanoids in one of his most thought-provoking works.

The Legion of Space series. The longevity of the Legion of Space series is surpassed only somewhat by that of its creator. *The Legion of Space* and its sequels, *The Cometeers* and *One against the Stars*, first appeared in *Astounding Stories* in the 1930s. Nearly fifty years later, in 1983, *The Queen of the Legion* was published. The series tells of the adventures of the Star family, descendants of former emperors whose tyrannical rule was overthrown by the democratic Green Hall. Democracy and humanity are protected by AKKA, a mysterious weapon of incredible power. AKKA can be used only by a young woman known as the Keeper of the Peace who can manipulate and destroy matter and energy through her mental use of the weapon. The Legion of Space is the military peace-keeping and exploration force which also has the responsibility of guarding the keeper.

The Legion of Space. Aladoree, the keeper, is abducted by traitors who have allied with the alien Medusae in an effort to restore an empire to be ruled by the Ulnar family. John Ulnar remains loyal to the keeper and, with the help of Kalam, Samdu, and Habibula, rescues her. In recognition of his service, he is given the name John Star.

The Cometeers. Bob Star, son of John and Aldoree, works with Kalam, Samdu, and Habibula to save humanity from an invasion of aliens who inhabit an immense artificial comet.

One against the Legion. The third novel tells of Chan Derron's struggle to defeat a master criminal. The legion believes that Derron is guilty of murder and theft. With Habibula's support, Derron, Habibula's grandson, clears his name, destroys the criminal, and rescues the leaders of humanity.

The Queen of the Legion. The final novel is about Jil Gyrel, a descendant of the Ulnar family, and her struggle to save humanity from an invasion of alien parasites that control minds. Aided by the immortal Habibula and by a descendant of John Star, she defeats the aliens and becomes the new keeper.

The series is space opera at its best with fast-moving adventures, loyal heroes, and evil villains. It rises above most of this genre because of its skillful writing and character construction. Williamson's style is clean and precise and his plotting is careful. His characterization is relatively complex for the early period of science fiction. Williamson has said that the series was influenced by Dumas' *The Three Musketeers*. Williamson's three legionaires are the intelligent and thoughtful Jay Kalam; the strong Hal Samdu; and the talkative, complaining Giles Habibula. Habibula, also derived from Falstaff, is the the only character to appear in all of the stories.

The aliens are convincingly described, whether they are the evil Medusae in *The Cometeers* or the helpful allies such as Miss Williams in *The Queen of the Legion*. The protagonists are not superhuman; they are determined individuals who must do everything within their power to overcome evil. Habibula is often frightened, always hungry or thirsty, and continually complaining, but he will continue to resist the enemies.

The series reflects a shift away from the traditional space opera reliance upon technology. AKKA was mainly a weapon of the mind; its tiny mechanical triggering device was used to focus the thoughts of the Keeper of the Peace. This use of mental or mystical powers in space opera was unusual at that time. Most stories of the period indicated that any advances in technology would be beneficial; Williamson proposes that the value of technology lies in how it is used. The Legion of Space stories have entertained readers for fifty years. Like their author, they continue to appeal to each new generation.

Biographical/Bibliographical Readings

"Jack Williamson," in *The Sound of Wonder: Interviews from the Science Fiction Radio Show* (Oryx Press, 1985), v.1, p.126-58. Sam Moskowitz, "Jack Williamson," in *Seekers of Tomorrow* (World, 1966), p.84-100. Robert E. Myers, *Jack Williamson: A Primary and Secondary Bibliography* (G. K. Hall, 1980). Alfred D. Stewart, "Jack Williamson: The Comedy of Cosmic Evolution," in *Voices for the Future*, ed. Thomas D. Clareson (Bowling Green University Popular Press, 1976), v.1, p.14-44. Jack Williamson, *Wonder's Child: My Life in Science Fiction* (Bluejay, 1984). **[Linda K. Lewis]**

WOLFE, GENE

Life and Works

Gene Rodman Wolfe was born in Brooklyn, New York, on May 7, 1931, but spent his formative years in Texas. He attended Texas A & M at College Station in 1949 and 1952, but left without a degree to spend the years 1952-54 in the army. He received a B.S. in engineering from the University of Houston in 1956. From then until 1972, he was employed by Procter and Gamble as a project engineer. His first published story, "Mountains Like Mice," appeared in *Worlds of If* in 1966, but more important was "Trip, Trap," his first story in Damon Knight's New Wave anthology *Orbit 2* (1967). He continued to publish annually in *Orbit* and elsewhere (his first novel, *Operation ARES*, appeared in 1970), though when he finally left Procter and Gamble in 1972, it was to take the post of senior editor for the professional journal *Plant Engineering* in Barrington, Illinois.

Wolfe hit his artistic stride with the 1972 publication of *The Fifth Head of Cerberus*. The volume consists of three interconnected novellas; the first--the title story--had already appeared in the 1972 *Orbit*. Also produced in the 1970s were two nonscience fiction novels--*The Devil in a Forest* (1976) and *Peace* (1975). Wolfe also published poetry in *Orbit* and elsewhere, and in 1978 received the Rhysling award for verse.

In 1973, Wolfe's story "The Death of Dr. Island," also from *Orbit*, won the Nebula award. It appeared again as part of another triptych in the 1980 collection *The Island of Dr. Death and Other Stories and Other Stories*. In 1980 appeared the first volume of Wolfe's masterwork thus far, *The Shadow of the Torturer*, the four-volume science fantasy entitled The Book of the New Sun. This meticulously composed tetralogy won Wolfe many awards: the 1982 Nebula, Locus, World Fantasy, and British Science Fiction Association awards, the 1983 British Fantasy award, and the 1984 John W. Campbell Award. During the appearance of The Book of the New Sun series, Wolfe published other books as well: a short story collection entitled *Gene Wolfe's Book of Days* (1981), and two nonfiction collections--*The Castle of the Otter* (1982) and *The Wolfe Archipelago* (1983). Wolfe has just commenced another series of novels with *Soldier of the Mist* (1986), a fantasy about an amnesiac mercenary in ancient Greece who discovers he can communicate with the world of the supernatural.

Themes and Style

Considering Wolfe's career as an engineer, one would expect his science fiction to fit the hard-core technological paradigms of the John W. Campbell tradition, heavy on hardware, scientific rationalizations, and fast-moving plots, minimal in style and character development. In fact, just the reverse is true, as his long association with Knight's anthology suggests. Few writers within the genre can match Wolfe in stylistic sophistication or literary subtlety, and rarely does science or technology exercise a central function in his work. Wolfe belongs to that group of writers--like Le Guin or Ellison--one could call fabulists, who use the conventions of science fiction to modernize fantasy in pursuit of largely thematic concerns. Indeed, the list of authors Wolfe cites as influences--including writers as different as Proust, Chesterton, Maugham, Wells, Tolkien, and Borges--demonstrates the breadth of his literary background and purpose.

Wolfe's early stories played upon subtleties and ambiguities, usually challenging the reader to read between the lines in order to piece together details of plot and character. "Trip, Trap," for instance, appears as a series of letters giving two perspectives of the same events, one human, one alien. What results when they face a common foe is a darkly humorous story. "Seven American Nights" is the diary of a sophisticated Iranian tourist visiting a decadent, crumbling United States where, among other ironies, the meaning of "The White House" has been forgotten.

Wolfe's first novel, *Operation ARES*, failed to meet the standards of his short fiction, however. On one level, it reads like a Heinlein juvenile: a group of Martian colonists reinvade home planet Earth to persuade a weak, Soviet-controlled America to take up space exploration once again. The plot moves are modeled on chess (like Brunner's *Squares of the City*), but the action is uncharacteristically rushed for Wolfe.

In *The Fifth Head of Cerberus*, all three stories take place on the twin worlds of Sainte Anne and Sainte Croix, settled inexplicably by French colonists and possessing a stereotypical Gallic blend of moral laissez faire and institutional fallibility. But the stories themselves are anything but stereotypical. "The Fifth Head of Cerberus" concerns a boy who is the heir to a powerful and corrupt family, and--it turns out--to a self-replicating heredity. It is a model Wolfe tale, having as its main character an innocent subsumed by his morally decadent reality. The second novella, "'A Story,'" by John V. Marsch," is purportedly an anthropologist's rendition of a legend of Sainte Anne's mysterious autochthones, while "V.R.T."--a Kafkaesque exploration of punishment, bureaucracy, and the relativity of truth, ingeniously suggests that John V. Marsch, who appears in all three stories, may not be what he seems.

The Island of Dr. Death and Other Stories and Other Stories, like the novellas in *The Fifth Head of Cerberus*, has three related stories, though soley by theme in this case. The title story, "The Island of Dr. Death and Other Stories," focuses on a boy trapped in a morally decadent situation: his drug-addicted mother is having an affair with a younger man. The lover gives the boy a book derived from Wells's *The Island of Dr. Moreau*. Unable to understand the real world around him, the boy escapes into the more manageable horrors of the fictive world, actually meeting the characters of the pulp adventure in his own surroundings.

In the award-winning story "The Death of Dr. Island," the main character is again a boy, trapped in the interior of an artificial satellite designed to treat mental illness. While the robot system observes and comments--as artificial waves, trees, and monkeys--the youth learns that he is part of the therapy of the most important patient of the three in the satellite, a homicidal genius. This therapy is, by moral standards, cruel and inhuman, sacrificing human life for human sanity. Once more Wolfe toys with the excruciating ambiguities of moral choice. "The Doctor of Death Island" has a character imprisoned under a life sentence in a world where natural death has been eliminated. Besides the

"Island" stories, this volume contains other pieces of Wolfe's short fiction.

The Book of the New Sun volumes are set presumably on a far-future Earth under a dying sun, where technology has moved forward and then decayed; it traces the travels of one Severian through a landscape that blends the medieval with the futuristic and even the extraterrestrial. Raised amid the guild of torturers, Severian shows mercy to a prisoner against the rules of the guild and is exiled to a post in distant mountain town. In the process of getting there, which carries Severian through the first book (*The Shadow of the Torturer*) and the second (*The Claw of the Conciliator*), the hero--surprisingly passive and innocent despite his grotesque calling--has a number of adventures, many verging on the surreal.

Through these and the subsequent volumes--*The Sword of the Lictor* and *The Citadel of the Autarch*--we follow the protagonist through events which are violent, hideous, and erotic; we meet strange characters--among them an android, a giant, creatures from other stars, and a woman resurrected from the dead; and we learn much of this bizarre world where our own time is forgotten in the distant past. And as in all of Wolfe's work, we find ourselves challenged to make sense of the subtle complexities of plots within plots, tales within tales.

Plot Summaries of Major Works

The Book of the New Sun series. This award-winning science fantasy tetraology was published as four volumes: *The Shadow of the Torturer*, *The Claw of the Conciliator*, *The Sword of the Lictor*, and *The Citadel of the Autarch*, from 1980 to 1982. The series traces the rapid ascent of Severian, a young man raised as a torturer in the Order of the Seekers for Truth and Penitence, from his apprenticeship, through his elevation to journeyman, and subsequent exile for crimes against the rules of the guild, to his eventual advancement after many adventures to the highest place in his culture, that of autarch.

The Urth of the story appears to be a far future Earth, orbiting a dying, ruddy sun. Human civilization is ancient and decadent, medieval in its institutions, barbaric in its amoral social code, Byzantine in organization. Urth is littered with the crumbling remnants of massive, half-inhabited cities, with forests and deserts haunted by alien life brought from an earlier age of space travel, and with the myths and legends left over from forgotten eras.

The Shadow of the Torturer. The first novel opens with a mysterious episode in a graveyard, then goes on to Severian's life as an apprentice with the guild of torturers. When, as journeyman, he shows mercy to Thecla, a high-born woman prisoner who has befriended him, by giving her a knife with which she can end her own torment, Severian barely escapes a similar fate himself. His master sends him off instead with the gift of a powerful sword to become an executioner in the distant town of Thrax. Along his journey, he passes through the massive city of Nessus, where among other adventures, he inadvertently brings a woman back from the dead and makes a mortal enemy of another by killing her brother, and where he falls in with a troop of traveling players run by an android and a giant.

The Claw of the Conciliator. Severian continues toward his post at Thrax, for the most part in the company of Jonas, half-man and half-machine, who eventually returns to the stars from which he traveled. He is also pursued by a variety of deadly alien creatures apparently being set intentionally upon him. He meets the rebel leader Vodalus and devours a portion of his beloved Thecla, thereby incorporating her memories. And he learns that an artifact that has come into his possession may be the Claw of the Conciliator, a talisman of great power.

The Sword of the Lictor. Severian comes to Thrax, still pursued by danger, though he practices his craft there for only a short while before again committing mercy and fleeing. This volume ends with Severian leading a rebellion against the brutal tyranny of Baldanders, the ever-growing giant of the earlier troupe of players.

The Citadel of the Autarch. Severian joins the war going on in the north, where he meets the autarch--whom he has met as other persons before--and takes on his role by devouring him and his memories, as he had Thecla's. When we last see him, Severian is preparing, under the guidance of an alien race, to renew the dying sun and bring life back to his Urth.

True to Arthur Clarke's dictum that a technology advanced enough would resemble magic, Wolfe's Urth provides a fertile setting for a sword-and-sorcery adventure, though with the author's characteristic literate subtleties and ambiguities. A simple summary such as this can only suggest the many-leveled complexity of Wolfe's masterpiece, and leaves out much that is central to the plot and Wolfe's thematic concerns. Of the latter, it is worth noting that here again Wolfe confuses innocence and guilt, especially in his main character, who is at once enforcer of a brutal justice and practicer of forbidden mercy, a torturer and a savior, executioner and life-giver, naive and all-knowing. In reference to this work, Wolfe himself observed that even Christ, as a carpenter, must have built instruments of pain. To approach this dense and difficult tetralogy properly, one must abandon the conventional distinctions between moral absolutes.

The Fifth Head of Cerberus. This 1972 volume contains three novellas connected by setting, theme, and a single character. The setting is the twin worlds of Sainte Croix and Sainte Anne, inhabited by the descendents of French colonists; as such, they possess both the charm and decadence associated with the Gallic temperament: moral laxness linked with a lapsed Roman Catholicism, a corrupt and inefficient if rigid bureaucracy.

The title story is the first-person account of a boy--known simply as Number Five for most of the story--who receives a brutal education at the hands of his cold and powerful father. It turns out that he is being trained to pursue a family calling--continuing research into biological engineering, financed by a highly successful brothel--and that the boy is the fifth generation clone of one individual. Outraged by his inheritance, he murders his father, but after a long stay in prison assumes the family burden anyway.

A minor character in the first story, anthropologist John V. Marsch, provides the subject matter for the next two stories. "'A Story,' by John V. Marsch" purports to be a reconstruction of a legend of the elusive aborigines of Sainte Anne. The aborigines themselves seem to have disappeared; some believe that they never existed, others that they were shapeshifters who have blended with the human population. Marsch's story is a fantastic narrative in Amerindian style about spiritual questing, blood sacrifice, sibling murder, and shifting identities.

In "V.R.T.," Marsch is an inmate in a Sainte Croix prison, held under wretched and even torturous conditions on the grounds that he is a spy from Sainte Anne. As a bureaucrat pores through journals, tapes and papers in a half-hearted attempt to decide Marsch's case, there is a hint that the prisoner, if not a spy, may not be the anthropologist either, but an aborigine who has taken his form.

Thematically, all the stories deal in one way or another with one of Wolfe's favorite subjects, the contrast of moral absolutes and ambiguity, and especially the nature of innocence and guilt. Each of the tales, though different in detail, uses the pattern of blood-brothers--whether clones, siblings or spiritual companions--trading identities in death and thus trading relative guilt and innocence as well. These moral polar opposites become indistinguishable in each case. The ingenuity and ambiguity of these carefully composed and interwoven novellas make them models against which Wolfe's other fiction may be compared. As a whole, *The Fifth Head of Cerberus* suggests the intricacy and subtlety of which Wolfe is capable, and expresses best the moral conundrum at the heart of his work.

Biographical/Bibliographical Readings

Thomas D. Clareson, "Gene Wolfe," in *Twentieth-Century American Science-Fiction Writers* (Gale, 1981), v.2, p.207-10. Idem, "Variations and Design: The Fiction of Gene Wolfe," in *Voices for the Future*, ed. Thomas D. Clareson and Thomas L. Wymer (Bowling Green University Press, 1984), v.3, p.1-29. Gene Wolfe, *The Castle of the Otter* (Bibliography) (Starmont House, 1982). **[Stephen W. Potts]**

WYNDHAM, JOHN

Life and Works

Better known by his Christian names, which he adopted as his signature after World War II, John Wyndham Parkes Lucas Beynon Harris was born on July 10, 1903, in the village of Knowle, War- wickshire, England. His parents separated when John was eight years old, after which he and his brother (Vivian B. Harris, also to become a writer) no longer had a settled home. The two boys and their mother formed a very close family group, however, and John enjoyed a happy childhood and adolescence. He went to a series of boarding schools, spending three years at the the last, Bedales, in Hampshire, an advanced coeducational school which did much to form his character. In the following years, he tried his hand at farming, prepared to study law at Oxford University, changed his mind, and worked in commercial art and advertising. He started writing short stories in 1925, but without much success, and was supported financially by his family.

Wyndham's career as a science fiction writer can be traced back to 1929, when he came across a copy of *Amazing Stories*. In 1930, he won $100 from Hugo Gernsback's *Air Wonder Stories* for his proposed slogan, "Future Flying Fiction" (which was never adopted as a title). The first story he sold, "Worlds to Barter," ap- peared in *Wonder Stories* in 1931. It was a cleverly contrived time travel story, the first of many similar tales he published (under the name of John Beynon Harris) in *Wonder Stories* and *Tales of Wonder* during the 1930s. A collection of the stories was published with the title *Wanderers of Time* (1973). His first novel was *The Secret People* (1935, using the name John Beynon, reissued in 1964 as by J. B. Harris, and in 1972 as by John Wyndham). This was followed by *Planet Plane* (1936), better known as *Stowaway to Mars* (1953), an interesting though flawed story about the conquest of Mars, set in the year 1981, with England still a victorious world power.

During the war, Wyndham was in the civil service, although he joined the Royal Signal Corps in time to take part in the Nor- mandy invasion. When he returned to writing, he struggled at first to leave behind the world of space opera, but finally hit upon the idea of reworking the English disaster novel tradition as exemplified in H. G. Wells's "The Sea Raiders" and *The War of the Worlds*. The first of these novels was *Revolt of the Triffids* (1951), which was immediately popular and has been reprinted many times since. Its British title was *The Day of the Triffids*. It established Wyndham's name and induced a taste for this new kind of intelligent, calmly related, realistic catastrophe story. His later novels in the same vein are *Out of the Deep* (British title: *The Kraken Wakes*) (1953), *Rebirth* (British title: *The Chrysalids*) (1955) , and *Village of the Damned* (British title: *The Midwich Cuckoos*) (1957). Wyndham married very late and lived the last part of his life in seclusion in the English countryside he was so fond of, dying on March 11, 1969.

Themes and Style

Perhaps the hallmark of John Wyndham's writing is his smooth, measured style, with its deliberate use of sufficient detail to create, almost at once, a credible framework of everyday sights and familiar human behavior within which the unfamiliar will emerge--usually in a compulsively readable plot. He is a "literary" writer whose allusive and erudite use of cultural knowledge and generic conventions to give substance and variation to the work were already apparent in *Stowaway to Mars*. That novel includes tongue-in-cheek reworkings of the pistol duel (from westerns) and carefully plotted intrigues (Wyndham had written a detective novel himself in 1935). It makes reference to previous descriptions to Mars (H. G. Wells' example is never far from the author's mind). There are speculative debates about the role of machines in society and the social position of women--a theme dealt with at greater length in "Consider Her Ways." The knowledgeable exchange of ideas is another constant of Wyndham's fiction.

Wyndham went on writing short stories even after the war, and here especially there is evidence of his commitment to the possibilities the science fiction genre allowed him and of his success in making it more flexible. He presents his stories in the foreword to *The Seeds of Time* (1956) as experiments in adapting the science fiction motif to various styles of short story. In this aim he was backed up by a whole generation of writers who came to science fiction after the war.

In Wyndham's stories, as in those of Wells, the focus is generally on the consequences of a single abnormal factor. The treatment of the human response to the resulting crisis is particularly sensitive, and full of plausible details, in his catastrophe novels. The disaster or threat is used to show up the weaknesses and to generate the missing strengths of the society in question. In a sense, the underlying theme always derives from the question of the possible future evolution of the human race. In *Village of the Damned*, for example, the alien prodigies are described as a group of brains that can join forces. As with the spiders in *Web*, posthumously published in 1979, the interest in seeing Wyndham's characters measure themselves against this united front is that the strengths of the alien force make sense precisely as versions of potential human qualities which, in the twentieth century, are constantly invoked, but which remain no more than a series of unrealized hopes and unachieved ambitions.

Plot Summaries of Major Works

Out of the Deeps (British title: The Kraken Wakes). Series of fireballs are seen descending in mid-ocean and disappearing without trace in the deepest parts of the sea. The deep-sea probes and bathyscopes sent down to investigate are lost, their cables fused. Naval vessels are destroyed by unknown means, apparently involving vast electrical forces. A theory is proposed that some alien life form, adapted to the the conditions of enormous pressure and total darkness that exist in the ocean depths, has begun to establish itself on Earth and has commenced large-scale engineering works in these inaccessible zones. The "xenobaths," as they come to be called, extend their attacks to the surface, gaining control of the sea routes and making incursions on land by means of "sea-tanks" presumably masterminded from the deep. After a brief period of illusory calm, they turn to a more drastic strategy apparently designed to adapt the planet as a whole to their requirements. However, this move threatens the very existence of the human race, which finally acts decisively to rid itself of the menace. Mike and Phyllis Watson are a husband and wife team of radio script writers who decide to write a personal account of the invasion of the aliens. They present the events through newspaper clippings, interviews, eyewitness reports, recollections, and through conversations with Dr. Bocker about his theories, the only scientific voice which rises to the exceptionality of the occasion.

The striking opening of the novel, with its description of icebergs disintegrating in the English Channel, gives the reader a vivid foretaste of the immense power of the waking "Kraken"--a term taken from a poem of Tennyson's. Wyndham's choice of a husband and wife team of radio writers as his central characters is an astute one, as it means he can plausibly have them draw on a wide range of sources. The solitary figure of Dr. Bocker as a visionary in a world dominated by Cold War divisiveness is almost too isolated to be really credible. In the end Wyndham suddenly turns from the English viewpoint which governs the novel and has the Japanese produce a technological panacea to clear the deeps. But this hardly matters, since the main interest of the story lies less in the transformation of the outside world than in the process of adaptation to these unforeseen disruptions within the relationship of a typically English middle-class couple.

Rebirth (British title: The Chrysalids). It is perhaps one, or possibly two thousand years after a global catastrophe--presumably a nuclear war--destroyed the civilization of the "Old People." The simple farming community of Waknuk, in Labrador, is typical of many in the area. Genetic mutations are common and the objects of fear and loathing. The slightest deviation is rejected; crops are burnt, mutants are either killed or rendered sterile and left to survive as best they can in the "Fringes," the harsh country that borders the vast zones where nothing now lives. These purges are governed by a code so strict that a person with six toes, for example, infringes the "purity standard," which is justified and sustained by a virulent Puritanical religious creed. All mutant forms are held to be the work of the devil because they corrupt the perfect models established by God. In this oppressive atmosphere of surveillance and bigotry, a group of eight telepathic children struggle to grow up undiscovered and, when the time comes, to escape. The youngest of the children has astonishing and disconcerting mental powers of an as yet unknown kind. With her aid, the children are able to contact another society in New Zealand which has preserved a higher standard of technology and which represents the solution to their problems, since mutations into a "superior variant" are welcomed there.

There was a glut of stories in the 1950s about mutants in a postnuclear world, so Wyndham's theme here is not a new one by any means. His treatment of it nevertheless stands out for several reasons. It is the work of a skilled storyteller: the contrasts between characters, the strands of the plot, and the matching opening and closing images of the more advanced society are carefully conceived. The author's smooth prose style is effective in conveying the anguished feelings of the characters, but he also manages to escape sequence excitement despite its predictable ending. As usual, Wyndham fills out the plot with much sensitive and thoughtful speculation, this time on the subjects of conceptual rigidity--whether based on science or religion--and the justifiability of violence and discrimination. This novel, along with *Village of the Damned*, gives the reader a very real sense of the difference, or even alienness, of children in the midst of the world of adults. The fact that the narrator is one of the children softens this effect and in some ways reaches beyond it.

Revolt of the Triffids (British title: The Day of the Triffids). Bill Mason wakes up in the hospital with his eyes still bandaged following a minor operation. He is puzzled by the eery silence broken only by shuffling noises and occassional sobs and cries. Unsettled, he pulls away his bandages and encounters a world in which almost everyone has suddenly become blind, presumably as a consequence of staring at some mysterious bright green flashes in the sky. Soon afterwards, he finds an attractive young woman, Josella Playton, who has also retained her sight, but after a few shared experiences, they are separated and forced to take part in an ultimately futile attempt to help save the blind population of

the increasingly overrun and disease-ridden city. Only a chosen
few can survive, it seems, especially when the "triffids" spread everywhere. These are monster plants, as tall as a person, which
have been bred all over the world for their precious oils. They
may have originated on other planets but are more likely to be the
outcome of biological meddlings. Triffids are carnivorous, are
able to lurch about on their three-pronged root, can detect noises,
and have fatal stings that they whip out at their prey. The threat
they pose becomes more obvious in the English countryside, with
its few isolated communities of survivors, as Bill searches for
Josella.

John Wyndham succeeds in telling an engrossing and imaginative story in a very polished way. It is probably the careful, ar-
ticulate, descriptive style and the life-likeliness of his charac-
ters--he is a master of natural sounding dialogue--that makes it all
seem strangely plausible. But if this approach also means that the
cataclysm is treated unsensationally, almost incidentally, this is in
accordance with the fact that it is merely the backdrop for the
real concerns of the novel. What is at stake is the conflict between the conventional way of life and the pull of peculiar circumstances. There is an ethical dilemma: can one simply turn
one's back on less-well-endowed groups of people? There is also a
suggestion that the universal blindness may have been caused by a
misfiring of some experimental radiation weapon in orbit around
the Earth. As human beings go out of existence, the triffids represent mistreated nature coming into its own; unlike humankind,
they apparently possess a grasp of social organization which is
their passport for the future.

Village of the Damned (British title: The Midwich Cuckoos).
The sleepy little village of Midwich is visited by an alien spacecraft and isolated from the rest of the world. Anyone who tries
to enter the affected zone during what the villagers later refer to
as the "Dayout" falls to the ground and loses consciousness. The
curious phenomenon ends and everything apparently returns to
normal. However, it soon becomes apparent that all the women of
child-bearing age in the village are pregnant, and in due course
they give birth to sixty-one babies, perfect in every way, but all
of them with striking golden eyes. They also prove to have inexplicable mental powers and communicate with each other as if
they were parts of a single collective being. As time goes by, the
sinister and threatening aspects of the growing "cuckoos" (birds
which lay their eggs in the nests of other, weaker species) become
apparent to all and a way must be found to rid the planet of this
insidious menace.

The unruffled narrative style combines an evocative portrait
of English village life with a carefully paced mystery story. The
main characters are well filled out, especially that of Gordon
Zellaby, a much-traveled and well-read landowner who acts as a

mouthpiece of Wyndham's philosophical bent and introduces much of the ideological content of the novel. The conversations touch with subtlety and humor on many issues, from the role of women in society to the workings of the press, and from the theory of evolution and scientific dogmatism to the difficult moral and legal issues raised by the potential struggle for survival against this cunning takeover bid. This novel gives thought-provoking depth to a readable and credible tale of how a close-knit community might come together to confront the incredible. Wyndham makes sure that Zellaby at one point puts Richard, the narrator, into the picture over the increased complexity of this invasion as compared with H. G. Wells' Martians (which nevertheless belong in the same tradition). It is pointed out by some critics how different (and, it is implied, more plausible) is the reaction recounted in this novel compared with those typical of American science fiction. A film was made of this novel in 1960.

Biographical/Bibliographical Readings

E. F. Bleiler, "Luncheon with John Wyndham," *Extrapolation* 25:4 (Winter, 1984), p.314-17. Walter Gillings, "Modern Masters of Science Fiction: John Wyndham," *Science Fiction Monthly* v.1 (1974). Sam Moskowitz, "John Wyndham," in *Seekers of Tomorrow* (Hyperion, 1966), p.118-32. John Scarborough, "John Wyndham," in *Science Fiction Writers*, ed. E. F. Bleiler (Scribner's, 1982), p.219-24. [Jonathan K. Benison]

ZAMIATIN, YVGENIJ

Life and Works

Evgenij Ivanovich Zamiatin was born in 1884 in the central Russian town of Lebedyan where his father taught at the local gymnasium and his mother was a pianist. Upon graduating from the Voronezh Gymnasium in 1902, he enrolled at the St. Petersburg Polytechnic Institute for Naval Architecture. As a Bolshevik revolutionary he was arrested both in 1905 and 1911. However, he was able to finish his studies at the Polytechnic in 1908 and was given a lectureship in marine architecture, where he continued to teach until his departure from Russia in 1931. This same year his first short story was published. It was not, however, until his second exile from St. Petersburg in 1911 that he wrote "Tales of a District," about provincial backwardness, which made his name known in Russian literary circles. In 1916, he was sent to England to supervise the construction of Russian icebreakers. Here he wrote two satirical pieces on the provincial behavior of the English, "The Islanders", and "The Fisher of Men." On his return to Russia in 1917, he became very active in literary circles and was one of the founders of the Petrograd section of the All-Russian Union of Writers. He edited several literary periodicals, served on editorial and theatrical boards, began writing plays and gathered around him authors like Gorkii who were later identified as the most talented of Soviet writers.

Disenchanted with the excesses of the Bolshevik regime, he proceeded to write articles, stories and fables criticizing the regime and decrying its belief that the revolution was completed. One of his most important polemical essays was "Scythians?" published in 1918, in which he expounds his view that the true revolutionary devotes himself or herself to constantly working for change and improvement, rejecting the Bolshevik thesis that they had accomplished the final revolution. While it was expected that he would become a leader of the new Soviet literature, he also became a "fellow-traveler," a term invented by Trotsky to describe writers who did not follow the party line but were in general sympathetic to the revolution. Zamiatin was very active in the publishing house World Literature. World Literature was established to translate and publish non-Russian literary works with an introduction and extensive annotation to each volume. From 1917 to 1921 he wrote extensively, turning out a novel, plays, tales, short stories, and articles. It was during this time that he edited three volumes of H. G. Wells' works as well as the twelve-volume collected works of Wells not published until 1924-26. Two public lectures on Wells that he delivered early in 1921 were also later published as essays. In 1922, he also published a biography of Robert von Mayer, a pioneer in modern thermodynamics, in which he discusses entropy and the role of the heretic in modern society.

His most famous work, *We*, was completed in 1921 and was undoubtedly stimulated by the ideas of the scientific socialist utopia he found in Wells work. It was the forerunner of the two later famous antiutopian novels, Huxley's *Brave New World* and Orwell's *1984*. Never published in the Soviet Union, *We* was translated into English in 1924 and only published in the original Russian in New York in 1952. However, it probably circulated in manuscript form in the Soviet Union during the 1920s. In the 1920s he was arrested several times, had difficulty in finding publishers, and was considered antagonistic to the Soviet regime. He continued, nonetheless, to produce numerous biographies, critical essays, and book reviews, of which the most important for an understanding of his philosophical ideas was "On Literature, Revolution, Entropy and Other Things," which elaborated on the ideas expressed in "Scythians?". In 1928, during the formation of the first five-year plan, there was a major change in policy in the U.S.S.R. towards literature. All literature was to be subordinated to the party line. It was at this time that excerpts from *We* appeared in a journal in Prague and then in the Soviet Union. Zamiatin was accused of having written a parody of communism. He became the object of a campaign of villification, was dismissed from his editorial posts. Magazine and publishing houses were closed to him and his plays were banned. He resigned from the Russian Writer's Union and asked Stalin for permission to leave the Soviet Union. With Maxim Gorky's intercession, he was allowed to leave Russia. He settled in Paris where he lived until his death in 1937.

Themes and Style

Zamiatin believed that the essence of life was change. Revolution was a cosmic universal law. On the other side of revolution are the forces of entropy, which represent stagnation and death. He felt that dogmatism in science, religion, social life, or art was the entropy of thought. Dogmatism is the attempt on the part of reason to establish absolutes and final patterns onto life. Zamiatin saw both the state and religion as edifices which imposed final answers for humanity. To Zamiatin there was no fixed truth; the truths of today would be the errors of tomorrow. Humans, according to Zamiatin, need to be free, to be continually asking the questions "Why?" and "What next?" Entropy must be combated with energy if the social system is to remain viable. However, he was aware that most people want fixed answers and live by the law of entropy. Only a few strong people, the heretics, exist to bring salvation and life into the world. *We* exemplifies Zamiatin's style of satire and irony in a work imbued with symbol, metaphor, simile, allusion, and other powerful images. Zamiatin was not concerned with technological achievement; in fact he was suspect of Wells' technologically perfected utopia. He was concerned with depicting the position of the individual in a state which has carried the ideas of scientific reason to their ultimate and horrific culmination.

Plot Summaries of Major Works

We.   *We* takes place 1000 years in the future. The human being has been reduced to a simple number, a cog in the machinery of the One State. The narrator is a mathematician, D-503, who is building the *Integral*, a glass spaceship whose mission will be to subjugate to reason beings on other planets. In the walled city all activity is regulated by the Tables, which are modeled on the greatest of all monuments of ancient literature, the Official Railroad Guide. Every morning with six-wheeled precision, at the same hour, at the same minute, millions wake up at once. At the very same hour, millions like one begin work, and millions like one, finish it. The Numbers live in houses with glass walls since there is no longer a need for privacy. Any desire to be different is treated as a disorder or a crime. Sex is regulated under the Sex Laws which allow any Number to obtain a license to use any other Number as a sexual product, thus doing away with the disorders of love. In spite of the attempts of the State to impose complete happiness, there are those who stray from the regulations and must be liquidated by the Well-Doer, head of State.

Into this ironic portrayal of an idyllic regulated life comes I-330, for whom D-503 develops an uncontrollable passion. I-330 is part of a revolutionary group who live outside the walled city where primitive nature still exists and who are preparing to sabotage the flight of the *Integral*. In a series of diary entries, D-503 sets down his emotions from his first meetings with I-330 until the revolutionaries are seized and executed. D-503, a most rational man, is torn between his abhorrence for the irrational, exemplified by his early reaction to the introduction of the square root of minus one, and his primitive and irrational passions for I-330. At the same time that he yearns for the mathematical order and security of the State, he is prey to the primitive urges of passionate love. I-330 tries to convince D-503 that, just as there is no last number because numbers are infinite, there is no final revolution. As revolution breaks out, D-503 flees to a public toilet and there finds an old man, logarithmic table in hand, who claims to have solved the problem of infinity. The old man and D-503 go together to have their creativity surgically excised by the State. As the novel ends, D-503 sits by with no emotion as I-330 is executed.

We is one of the three classic dystopian novels of the twentieth century, along with *1984* and *Brave New World*, and has been called the pivotal work of the antiutopian tradition after Wells. The plot of *We* clearly is a vehicle for a profusion of symbols and images. "I" is the mathematical name given to the square root of minus one. 503 is a prime number, thus implying that D-503 is unique and not totally part of the one Numbers. I-330's features remind him of an X--the unknown, and she leads him to the Ancient House which symbolizes the past of paganism and untamed lawless passions. There is a clear allusion to the Biblical Book of Revelations. The walled city is similar to the New Jerusalem in its geometric design, with its wall to protect it from the natural world. The plaza of the one state is surrounded by 66 concentric circles, 666 being the number of the Beast. The idea that the United State is the New Jerusalem is confirmed by the Well-Doer who reminds D-503 that in paradise they know no desires anymore, no pity, no love, there they are blessed. Eternal peace is also eternal nonfreedom. To Zamiatin both the State and religion impose dogmatic order on society that is inimical to growth and creativity. Zamiatin incorporated both the ideas of Hegel of process and change and those of Dostoevsky of the irrational, primitive person as the guarantor of humanity's freedom and individuality in this paradigmatic, antiutopian novel. His belief that revolution is continuous is clear in his sympathetic portrayal of the revolutionary Mephi's (an obvious allusion to Mephistopheles). I-330 exemplifies the irrational primitive nature which is necessary for individuality and creation. D-503 is the average individual torn by the desires to feel and create but who is finally unable to live with the pain of being free.

Biographical/Bibliographical Readings

Alex M. Shane, *The Life and Works of Evgenij Zamjatin* (University of California Press, 1968). [Judith R. Bernstein]

ZELAZNY, ROGER

Life and Works

Roger Joseph Zelazny was born in Cleveland, Ohio, on May 13, 1937. He spent his childhood in the rural town of Euclid, Ohio, where he began to show his talent for writing in school. Although he initially majored in psychology at Western Reserve University in Cleveland, he changed his major to English in his junior year. He graduated with a B.A. in English and went on to receive a master's degree in English at Columbia University. After receiving his M.A., he returned to Cleveland, where he began to work for the Social Security Administration. During this time, he began writing short stories, sending them to science fiction magazines with the idea of eventually turning to full-time writing. His first published story was "Passion Play," published in *Amazing* in 1962. Within a matter of months, he published stories in several magazines, including *Amazing*, *Fantastic*, and *The Magazine of Fantasy and Science Fiction*.

He made his mark after publishing "A Rose for Ecclesiastes" in 1963. This was shortly followed by a number of popular stories that made him a highly marketable success: "The Doors of His Face, the Lamps of His Mouth" (1965), "He Who Shapes" 1965, and ". . . And Call Me Conrad" (1966). He expanded the latter two works into the novels *The Dream Master* (1966) and *This Immortal* (1965), respectively. When he began producing more novels than short stories, he attained enough monetary stability to quit his civil service job in 1969 and write full-time. Early in his career, he received several Hugo and Nebula awards, and his works were translated widely all over the world. Early Nebula awards were received in 1965 for *The Dream Master* and "The Doors of His Face . . . ." Among his Hugo award winners were ". . . And Call Me Conrad" and its expanded novel, *This Immortal*, in 1966. His novel, *Isle of the Dead* (1969), received the first French Prix Apollo.

In the 1970s, Zelazny produced the Chronicles of Amber series, made up of five novels: *Nine Princes in Amber* (1970), *The Guns of Avalon* (1972), *Sign of the Unicorn* (1975), *The Head of Oberon* (1976), and *The Courts of Chaos* (1978). He is working on a new trilogy of Amber novels in the 1980s. Two of the novels have been completed, *Trumps of Doom* (1985) and *Blood of Amber* (1986).

Themes and Style

When he entered the science fiction community in the 1960s, Zelazny became readily associated with the New Wave, that is, writers who deal more with human problems and mores within some fantastic situation, rather than the earlier, more gadget-oriented science fiction authors. With his background in English literature, Zelazny used his knowledge to imbue his fiction with arcane references and literary quotations from the classics. He brought to science fiction a fresh literary style that was one of the factors that allowed the genre to emerge from its "pulpishness" to enjoy a social relevance akin to mainstream fiction. His love for the science fiction he read as a boy is evident in his early homages to Burroughs and others when he depicts a habitable Mars of red sands in "A Rose for Ecclesiastes" and a watery Venus in "The Doors of His Face, the Lamps of His Mouth." His stories and novels have made use of a wide spectrum of themes such as alien contact, immortality, robot and machinelike intelligences, time travel, and Earth after the holocaust, but he often molds these themes around strong characters undergoing emotional turmoil. His use of such standard themes is shaped by a strong and abiding interest in explaining how things work, describing the processes involved. Even in his works of fantasy, he has a need to explain processes, including the workings of magical spells, in a rational way. This expression of rationalism is prevalent in virtually all of his works.

Zelazny's stories and novels reveal his keen interest in the relationships of people and the maturation of a specific type of hero. The hero is usually tall, powerfully built, and highly cultured. However, this individual is also emotionally flawed because of a failed relationship with someone in the past. Both Gallinger in "A Rose for Ecclesiastes" and Carlton Davits in "The Doors of His Face, the Lamps of His Mouth" fit this description. Both protagonists are shown to mature through current relationships that parallel their earlier counterparts.

In the novels *Lord of Light* (1967) and *This Immortal*, Zelazny complicates the theme of a heroic figure maturing through relationships by adding complex political and religious problems that the hero must resolve. Sam, in *Lord of Light*, has gone through drastic physical changes that echo maturational growth by means of a reincarnation machine, placing his psyche within a newly grown body. The changes that Sam undergoes are not merely physical; his experiences with other characters, especially as alliances change among them, help Sam to grow emotionally. In *This Immortal*, Conrad Nomikos is an immortal human on a postholocaust Earth who has had a long and rich history as a rebel against the ruling order. Through his encounter with an alien being as he leads a tour of friends and acquaintances through the "hot spots" of the radiated planet, Conrad matures in his understanding of the xenophobic relationship between the people of Earth and the aliens. For Sam and Conrad, maturation comes in part from self-realization of their places in the world which they occupy. By placing these characters in worlds of political and religious upheaval, Zelazby is exercising his rational approach in showing how people may become gods, or showing the telling differences in attitudes between human and alien.

The Chronicles of Amber series depict the growth and changes of fortune of Corwin, a Prince of Amber, the archetypal world of which all others are mere shadows. Corwin resembles the other heroic figures of Zelazny: he is tall, powerful, and possessed of a poetic, cultured quality. He is a pragmatic and shrewd character who can be ruthless when ncessary. The novels in the chronicles recount Corwin's changing fortunes and various meetings with the other members of his bickering family. The reader watches the maturation of Corwin, as he changes from unwitting outsider to challenger to the throne. His story becomes a vast panorama of political intrigue and lust for power. However, it is more than that: the story posits a mystical philosophy about the creation of the universe. The Earth, as we know it, is only on one level of reality; Amber is the true reality, with physical laws that are quite different from ours. Earth is merely one of many Shadows that reflect--imperfectly--the real world. Zelazny puts forth this philosophy with humor but never with tongue-in-cheek. He reminds us that we people of Earth are not necessarily the masters of our universe.

Plot Summaries of Major Works

The Chronicles of Amber series. Written during the decade of the 1970s, The Chronicles of Amber have been so closely identified with Roger Zelazny that the author incorporated himself under the company name of The Amber Corporation. The series consists of five novels: *Nine Princes in Amber*, *The Guns of Avalon*, *Sign of the Unicorn*, *The Hand of Oberon*, and *The Courts of Chaos*. Together, they form a large-scale mosaic of political intrigues among the minions of a royal family that spans several parallel worlds. They trace the adventures of Prince Corwin, his father,

Oberon, and his brothers and sisters as they seek power over one another in a magical world called Amber. Amber is the primal city, the original world created out of Chaos. All other worlds, including our own Earth, are imperfect copies, or Shadows, of Amber.

Nine Princes in Amber. In the first novel, Corwin awakes in a hospital on our Earth, suffering from amnesia after an automobile accident. Finding an ally in his brother Random, Corwin regains his memory by walking through a mystical, mazelike tracing called the Pattern. The land of Amber and all the parallel worlds of the universe owe their existence to the Pattern, traced on a dungeon floor in Amber. Corwin learns that he is possessed of exceptional powers: he has supernormal strength, remarkable regenerative control over his body's healing capacity, and, like the others in his family, he can travel into parallel worlds under his own volition.

Corwin finds himself embroiled in war with his siblings. His greatest adversary is his brother Eric, who has usurped the throne in the absence of their father Oberon. In his attempt to destroy Eric and take command of Amber, Corwin is captured by his brother. Eric puts out Corwin's eyes and tosses him into a dungeon to spend the rest of his years. He regains his eyesight because of his amazing recuperative powers and escapes from the dungeon. At the novel's end, he swears vengeance on Eric as he leaves Amber.

The Guns of Avalon. In the second novel, Corwin makes new acquaintances as he begins to gather an army of Shadow-beings to do battle against Eric. Zelazny introduces several elements that make this novel more than mere fantasy-adventure. One of these is Corwin's use of firearms to help him wage war in a land of broadswords. With the use of firearms, Corwin gains control of Amber and takes over the reign from the deceased Eric.

Sign of the Unicorn. The third novel picks up the story with Corwin's uneasy rule in Amber. His brothers and sisters continue to create mischief, making Corwin suspicious of all of them. Acting very much like the classical detective in a mystery novel, Corwin interviews suspect and follows up "leads" to find out who is behind the murder of Caine, another of Corwin's brothers, and the attempted murders of his brother Brand and himself. While seeking the solution to these mysteries, Corwin finds himself enshrouded by a larger mystery involving the nature of Amber itself.

The Hand of Oberon. As the fourth novel opens, Corwin discovers a Pattern that no one knew was in existence previously. Apparently, this Pattern was the true original that had created the Amber universe, and not the Pattern in Amber that he was familiar with. In this novel, another brother, Brand, emerges as the archvillain. Brand's intention is to destroy the Amber universe and forge a new Pattern that would invoke a whole new universe out of his own evil psyche.

The Courts of Chaos. The final novel of the series brings Corwin together with his allied brothers and sisters against an evil army of beings from the world of Chaos. Reflected by Corwin's battle with the army of Chaos is the universal mythos of the forces of good battling the forces of evil. The forces of good are victorious, but not without suffering losses and disappointments. For one thing, Corwin learns that he is not the chosen one to rule in his father's place; his brother Random is selected to be the new ruler of Amber. But Zelazny concludes the Chronicles of Amber with the wondrous possibility that Corwin has opened a doorway into a completely new universe by tracing another Pattern on the ground in a distant Shadow world. At the end of *The Courts of Chaos*, Corwin is eager to explore this possibility.

Although the Chronicles of Amber series is a complex story of politics and power, it is also a human drama in which the reader watches as Corwin grows and matures. Like the reader on first reading *Nine Princes in Amber*, Corwin is an innocent. He senses danger all around him, but he does not know why. He picks up mere bits and pieces of a life he cannot remember, trying to puzzle them out just as the reader must. When Corwin comes to full realization of his identity, he recognizes, as does the reader, that he is not an innocent; he has been ruthless, even criminal, in the past, and he is a member in good standing of a rather nasty family. The reader grows with these discoveries, having been joined with Corwin in innocence, only to learn that the protagonist is not entirely deserving of sympathy. With Corwin's pragmatic approach to life, however, the reader enjoys the smirking cynicism that aids Corwin in his accomplishments. In a magical world that does not allow for the use of firearms, Corwin finds a way to use firearms to defeat an army of evil beings that attack Amber. With unchivalrous dispatch, Corwin mortally wounds a fencing master who sought Corwin for a relatively petty cause at a time when Corwin was concerned with setting right the universe. Thus, we see Corwin as a human with large faults, but these faults grow out of a very real paranoia, because the dangers he faces are real. Small matters cannot stand in the way of the winning of a universe, and that is what Corwin ultimately seeks. Corwin's meeting crisis with cruelty is a necessary means to reach a nearly incomprehensible end. The reader cares about Corwin precisely because of these faults; they make him a fully rounded character acting without remorse against terrible odds. Zelazny's rational approach to even the most fantastic predicaments, along with his humor and literary allusions, brings to the common human experience a whole range of real yet utterly magical possibilites.

Damnation Alley. Taking place on a postholocaust Earth, *Damnation Alley* is an adventure novel about an unlikable protagonist on a mission of mercy. Hell Tanner is a last remnant of the notorious Hell's Angels motorcycle gang who is coerced into joining a small group of drivers carrying badly needed medicine from California to Boston. Only the most courageous and daring drivers could make the journey because the final atomic war has created ferocious atmospheric conditions and terrifying mutant beasts. These phenomena are especially bad in the central states, giving the name "Damnation Alley" to that savage corridor of the country.

Although Denton, the Secretary of Traffic for the Nation of California, recognizes the need for Tanner's survival abilities on the mission, he despises Tanner for his criminal past. He offers Tanner full pardon if he will join a band of drivers who are taking Haffikine antiserum to the plague-ridden people of Boston.

Tanner drives one of three armored vans. They meet danger almost immediately: one van is crushed by a giant gila monster, and the second van is lost in a furious sandstorm. In the remaining van, Tanner is paired with a tall, idealistic, part-Indian named Greg. When their journey becomes especially difficult, Tanner and Greg change ideological positions, so that Greg wants to give up their mission while Tanner wants to continue. Tanner is forced to knock Greg out and leave him with a farming family in Pennsylvania. Continuing alone, Tanner finds the greatest danger coming from roving motorcycle gangs. Taking on a female passenger called Corny, Tanner is soon forced to give up the protection of the van to ride the remaining way by motorcycle. Attacked by a lone sniper, Corny is killed, but Tanner survives to ride into Boston with the Haffikine. True to his image, Tanner writes graffiti on the base of a statue erected to him in Boston Common by the grateful populace and then leaves Boston.

Zelazny originally wrote this story as a novella that was little more than an action-adventure tale on a nuclear bomb-ravaged Earth. When he expanded it to novel length, the sections he added did little to further the action-adventure premise. Two appended episodes are meant to take us into the mind of Hell Tanner: one is a mystical, overextended philosophy about life and creation, and the other is an image that relates to a Japanese form of drama. Other appended episodes reveal scenes of tragedy and stagnation among several people affected by the plague in Boston. None of these additions really further the story, and the two secions taking the reader into Tanner's mind are too oblique for this kind of adventure. Even Zelazny has professed that he prefers the shorter version.

The Dream Master. Dr. Charles Render is a neuroparticipant therapist, known as a Shaper. Using a futuristic device, he is able to join his patient in a dream state and manipulate what the subject dreams. By doing this, Render is able to bring out the subconscious cause of the patient's problems. Render's downfall comes from putting his faith into a young blind woman, whose motivation has already led to one person's tragic state of insanity. Inevitably, Render's life come to a tragic end because of his own actions and emotional "blindness."

Zelazny sets the tone for a classical tragedy by introducing us to Render while at work. He is engaged in a therapy session with a man in high political office who fears failure at the hands of others. In order to bring this knowledge to his patient's consciousness, Render leads him into a dream that is taken directly from one of Shakespeare's tragedies: the assassination scene in *Julius Caesar*. This initial episode of the novel is only a prelude, and is one of several hints that Render will embark on a tragic course. At an exclusive club of which he is a member, Render meets Eileen Shallot, a young psychiatrist who has achieved her professional status though blind from birth. Amazingly, Eileen seeks to become a neuroparticipant therapist like Render, and wants him to take her through several dream sessions so that she may learn to "see" in her dream state. Although his colleagues warn him of the danger in entering a dream state with Eileen, and although Render himself realizes that their minds could become intertwined and irrevocably locked in a form of madness, he agrees to the sessions. He develops an obsessive interest in her, losing sight of his professionalism as he becomes further involved. As Eileen's psyche manipulates more of their dream sequences, Render becomes more susceptible to entrapment within the dream state. The tragic elements develop from their final dream session.

One of Zelazny's most structured experiments, *The Dream Master* describes the professional life and personal relationships of a unique type of psychiatrist of the near future. The novel was expanded from his Nebula Award-winning novella "He Who Shapes." It is a highly experimental work in which Zelazny channeled his story to fit the dramatic form of classical Greek drama, using Aristotle's definition of tragedy as his guide. According to Aristotle's precepts, tragedy depicts a great man who comes to a dramatic fall through his own inner flaw. Zelazny establishes that Render is such a "great man" by the admiration he receives from his employees and the high respect paid to him by his colleagues. Render's tragic flaw, however, is a sense of false pride and deliberate unwillingness to recognize personal danger. In that respect, Render is similar to Shakespeare's King Lear.

Zelazny draws upon medieval and classical tales as metaphors for Render's tragedy. Besides the mode of Shakespearean tragedy alluded to in the opening sequence, Eileen compares Render to the Greek artificer Daedalus who allowed himself to be trapped by King Minos because of pride in his work. Throughout the sessions describing the involvement of Render with Eileen, knighthood and chivalry are fixed with their relationship. Render is the innocent knight Tristam, entrapped and doomed because of the deceit of Isolde of the White Hands. Zelazny wants to draw the reader's attention to the classical proportions of their fate.

Although *The Dream Master* is rich in classical allusions, it forces the reader to see Dr. Charles Render as a man with a narrow perception. This is quite different from many another Zelazny protagonist, who shares his or her innermost thoughts with the reader and evolves into a more mature individual as a result of some traumatic experience. In this case, Render does not share his inner thoughts or doubts, and he certainly does not mature in the experience. Thus, the novel is unwaveringly fatalistic. It is probably Zelazny's most deliberate and humorless work.

Lord of Light. Sam is a member of a space expedition that had landed on a primitive planet ages ago. He, and the other members of the expedition, had developed futuristic technological devices that gave them highly advanced powers. To the indigenous people on the planet, the Earth colonists became gods. These gods took on the names and roles of the ancient gods of the East Indian pantheon. Sam finds the ruling gods in "Heaven" to be oppressive, and he schemes to take over their reign. Sam's psyche is regenerated into a newly constructed body by means of a kharma machine that the gods use routinely to maintain eternal existence in many guises. Because Sam had been disintegrated and dispelled into the atmosphere surrounding the planet, his reincarnation has caused him to be named Mahatsamatman, or "Great-Souled Sam." In episodic flashbacks, the reader is taken back to Sam's earlier days when he first began to rebel against the repressive rule of the Trimurti, the three ruling gods. He goes through numerous incarnations, including those of Siddhartha and the Buddha called Tathagatha. He changes both physically and experientially with each incarnation.

There are two mighty battles between Sam's forces and the armies of the Trimurti. They are called the Battle of Keenset and the Battle of Khaipur. Sam is defeated at the Battle of Keenset and his body is transpersed into the atmosphere and then reincarnated. With his new alliance with Yama, Sam plans to fight the ruling gods in the Battle of Khaipur in the final chapter. He succeeds in upsetting the Trimurti, but instead of remaining to initiate a new rule, he wanders away and becomes the stuff of legend.

Heading each chapter of this novel is a passage from the Indian holy books, most particularly the Upanishads of the Hindu religion. Zelazny uses these as a means of giving a folklorelike flavor to the novel. These passages also contrast with the colloquial style of the dialogue and the informal narrative. The awkward construction of the novel--a "frame" of present events surrounding the unfolding of Sam's past--is likely to confuse the reader at first. Many seemingly disconnected actions occur in the first chapter. But once the reader gets through the first chapter, he or she will be rewarded with the view of a marvelous tapestry of human frailties, sly political maneuverings and wry good humor. The particular charm of this novel is the way in which Zelazny humanizes these so-called gods, showing them to be far from omnipotent, much less omniscient. The character of Sam, after all, is known to be a charlatan, and another character admits that Sam's greatest strength is his insincerity. They are memorable characters because we recognize their flaws, and, at times, we can laugh at them. *Lord of Light* shows Zelazny at his most playful, combining serious philosophical and religious arguments with a gentle poking at human nature and all its foibles.

This Immortal. On a nuclear-blasted Earth of the future, the remaining people, and the flora and fauna of this most exotic planet, have become points of interest for tourists from another world. Conrad Nomikos is commissioner of the Earthoffice Department of Arts, Monuments, and Archives, and in that capacity he is hired to conduct a tour of Earth's radiated "Hot Places." He is also a human who has lived for more than two hundred years. His services have been hired by an extraterrestrial from the planet Vega, a wealthy member of Vegan society named Cort Myshtigo. Conrad finds reason to despise Cort in the alien's supercilious attitude toward human civilization. The Vegans are fascinated by a civilized race of creatures that has virtually committed suicide by atomic war. With utter disregard for human sensitivity, Cort insults the poetry of another long-lived friend of Conrad's, and proceeds to lambaste the whole human history of Christianity.

Covering up his former identity, Conrad leads a group of friends, acquaintances, and the obnoxious Vegan on a tour of the burnt-out cities in Greece. This expedition enables them to meet several bizarre creatures, and the climax occurs when the tour encounters a mad doctor and an enormous Albino mongoloid idiot that feeds on blood. Real tension builds from Conrad's personal relationships with several members of his party. In one instance, an old acquaintance, Hasan, has joined the tour in an apparent attempt to assassinate Cort Myshtigo, and part of Conrad's job is to protect the extraterrestrial.

Conrad is one of Zelazny's most fully realized characterizations, having many facets, some which the reader senses are "going on in the wings," as it were. The reader learns much of early background that is unique, and Conrad's love for the girl, Cassandra, shown briefly, is genuinely touching. The characterization of Conrad draws the reader's interest; he is an example of rugged individualism in the Hemingway vein, but he is also cultured, introspective, and physically flawed. Zelazny depicts Conrad as having some deformities--a short right leg, his face partly discolored from a fungus, and one blue and one brown eye. In the face of such physical deformities, one female character notes that he is so ugly that he is attractive.

Written in the first person, the novel allows the reader to understand and sympathize with the protagonist. Along with Conrad, the reader is surprised to learn the truth about Cort Myshtigo, his mission on Earth, and the hidden motivations of the Vegans. Conrad discovers that he has a pivotal role in altering the state that the Earth is in, from a shattered world dependent upon the good will of Vega to an independent and autonomous world once again. His willingness to keep Cort alive during his visit to Earth is crucial to this goal. When Conrad realizes this, he finds a new maturity. *This Immortal* shows a man who matures, not only by facing real dangers in his society, but also by maintaining his integrity in the face of internal conflicts. The novel finds its power in the evolution of a flawed man who gradually becomes whole. The novel becomes a joyous celebration in identifying humanity's place in the creation.

Biographical/Bibliographical Readings

Theodore Krulik, *Roger Zelazny* (Ungar, 1986). Daniel J. H. Levack, *Amber Dreams: A Roger Zelazny Bibliography* (Underwood/Miller, 1983). "Roger Zelazny," in *Speaking of Science Fiction: The Paul Walker Interviews* (Luna, 1978), p.78-84. Joseph L. Sanders, *Roger Zelazny: A Primary and Secondary Bibliography* (G. K. Hall, 1981). Carl B. Yoke, *Roger Zelazny: Starmont Reader's Guide 2* (Starmont House, 1979). **[Thedore Krulik]**

Appendixes

A. SCIENCE FICTION MAGAZINES AND CRITICAL JOURNALS

Basic Magazines with New and Original Stories, Novelettes, and Serialized Works

Amazing Stories (1926). Bimonthly. TSR, Inc., Box 110, Lake Geneva, WI 53147. ISSN: 0279-1706.

Analog Science Fiction/Science Fact (1930). 13 issues a year. Davis Publications, Inc., 380 Lexington Ave., New York, NY 10017. ISSN: 0161-2328.

Galaxy (1950). Monthly. UPD Publishing Corp., 720 White Plains Rd., Scarsdale, NY 10583. ISSN: 0016-4003.

Galileo (1976). Bimonthly. Avenue Victor Hugo Publishing Company, 339 Newberry St., Boston, MA 02115. ISSN: 0162-3805.

Isaac Asimov's Science Fiction Magazine (1976). 13 issues a year. Davis Publications, Inc., 380 Lexington Ave., New York, NY 10017. ISSN: 0162-2188.

The Magazine of Fantasy and Science Fiction (1949). Monthly. Mercury Press, Inc., Box 56, Cornwall, CT 06753. ISSN: 0024-984X.

Omni (1978). Monthly. Omni Publications, 1965 Broadway, New York, NY 10023. ISSN: 0149-8711.

Critical Journals

Extrapolation (1959). Quarterly. Thomas D. Clareson, ed., Kent State University Press, Kent, OH 44242. ISSN: 0014-5483.

Foundation (1972). 3 issues a year. Science Fiction Foundation, North East London Polytechnic, Longbridge Rd., Dagenham, Essex RM8 2A5, England. ISSN: 0306-4964.

Locus (1968). Monthly. Locus Publications, P.O. Box 13305, Oakland, CA 94661. ISSN: 0047-4959.

Science Fiction Chronicle (1979). Monthly. Algol Press, Box 4175, New York, NY 10163. ISSN: 0195-5365.

Science Fiction Studies (1973). 3 issues a year. SFS Pubs., McGill University, Arts Bldg., 853 Sherbrooke St. W., Montreal, Quebec H3A2T6 Canada. ISSN: 0091-7729.
SFWA Bulletin (1965). Bimonthly. Science Fiction Writers of America, Montrose Publishing Co., Box H, Wharton, NJ 07885. ISSN: 0036-1364.
Thrust (1972). Semiannually. Thrust Pubs., 8217 Langport Terrace, Gaithersburg, MD 20877. ISSN: 0198-0686.
Vector (1958). Bimonthly. British Science Fiction Association, 114 Guildhall St., Folkestone, Kent, C7201ES, England. ISSN: 0505-0448.

B. NEBULA AND HUGO AWARD WINNERS

Listed below are the winners of the Nebula and Hugo awards for various forms of science fiction. There are numerous other awards, some presented sporadically and some on a more regular basis, but the Nebula and Hugo awards are undoubtedly the most important. They have been the subject of controversy; the granting of any literary prize is filled with the potential for politicization, whether the voters are hard-core fans (the Hugo awards), or professional writers (the Nebula awards). The winners of both are presented here as interesting and perhaps useful information.

Nebula Awards

Given by the Science Fiction Writers Association, the Nebula awards began in 1966, given for writing published in 1965. The awards in various categories always recognize work from the previous year. The award winners are selected by a vote of the membership of the Science Fiction Writers Association.

Nebula Award Novels

1965   *Dune*, by Frank Herbert
1966   *Flowers for Algernon*, by Daniel Keyes and
         Babel-17, by Samuel R. Delany
1967   *The Einstein Intersection*, by Samuel R. Delany
1968   *Rite of Passage*, by Alexei Panshin
1969   *The Left Hand of Darkness*, by Ursula K. Le Guin
1970   *Ringworld*, by Larry Niven
1971   *A Time of Changes*, by Robert Silverberg
1972   *The Gods Themselves*, by Isaac Asimov
1973   *Rendezvous with Rama*, by Arthur C. Clarke
1974   *The Dispossessed*, by Ursula K. Le Guin
1975   *The Forever War*, by Joe Haldeman

1976   *Man Plus*, by Frederick Pohl
1977   *Gateway*, by Frederick Pohl
1978   *Dreamsnake*, by Vonda N. McIntyre
1979   *The Fountains of Paradise*, by Arthur C. Clarke
1980   *Timescape*, by Gregory Benford
1981   *The Claw of the Conciliator*, by Gene Wolfe
1982   *No Enemy but Time*, by Michael Bishop
1983   *Startide Rising*, by David Brin
1984   *Neuromancer*, by William Gibson
1985   *Ender's Game*, by Orson Scott Card
1986   *Speaker for the Dead*, by Orson Scott Card
1987   *The Falling Woman*, by Pat Murphy

Nebula Award Novellas

1965   "The Saliva Tree," by Brian W. Aldiss and
         "He Who Shapes," by Roger Zelazny
1966   "The Last Castle," by Jack Vance
1967   "Behold the Man," by Michael Moorcock
1968   "Dragonrider," by Anne McCaffrey
1969   "A Boy and His Dog," by Harlan Ellison
1970   "Ill Met in Lankhmar," by Fritz Leiber
1971   "The Missing Man," by Katherine MacLean
1972   "A Meeting with Medusa," by Arthur C. Clarke
1973   "The Death of Dr. Island," by Gene Wolfe
1974   "Born with the Dead," by Robert Silverberg
1975   "Home Is the Hangman," by Roger Zelazny
1976   "Houston, Houston, Do You Read?" by James Tiptree, Jr.
1977   "Stardance," by Spider and Jeanne Robinson
1978   "The Persistence of Vision," by John Varley
1979   "Enemy Mine," by Barry Longyear
1980   "The Unicorn Tapestry," by Suzy McKee Charnas
1981   "The Saturn Game," by Poul Anderson
1982   "Another Orphan," by John Kessel
1983   "Hardfought," by Greg Bear
1984   "Press Enter," by John Varley
1985   "Sailing to Byzantium," by Robert Silverberg
1986   "R&R," by Lucius Shepard
1987   "The Blind Geometer," by Kim Stanley Robinson

Nebula Award Novelettes

1965   "The Doors of His Face, the Lamps of His Mouth," by
         Roger Zelazny
1966   "Call Him Lord," by Gordon R. Dickson
1967   "Gonna Roll the Bones," by Fritz Leiber
1968   "Mother to the World," by Richard Wilson

1969   "Time Considered As a Helix of Semi-Precious Stones,"
        by Samuel R. Delany
1970   "Slow Sculpture," by Theodore Sturgeon
1971   "The Queen of Air and Darkness," by Poul Anderson
1972   "Goat Song," by Poul Anderson
1973   "Of Mist, and Grass, and Sand," by Vonda N. McIntyre
1974   "If the Stars Are Gods," by Gregory Benford and Gordon
        Eklund
1975   "San Diego Lightfoot Sue," by Tom Reamy
1976   "The Bicentennial Man," by Isaac Asimov
1977   "The Screwfly Solution," by Racoona Sheldon (James
        Tiptree, Jr.)
1978   "A Glow of Candles, a Unicorn's Eye," by Charles L.
        Grant
1979   "Sandkings," by George R. R. Martin
1980   "The Ugly Chickens," by Howard Waldrop
1981   "The Quickening," by Michael Bishop
1982   "Fire Watch," by Connie Willis
1983   "Blood Music," by Greg Bear
1984   "Bloodchild," by Octavia E. Butler
1985   "Portraits of His Children," by George R. R. Martin
1986   "The Girl Who Fell into the Sky," by Kate Wilhelm
1987   "Rachel in Love," by Pat Murphy

Nebula Award Short Stories

1965   "'Repent, Harlequin!' Said the Ticktockman," by Harlan
        Ellison
1966   "The Secret Place," by Richard McKenna
1967   "Aye and Gomorrah . . . " by Samuel R. Delany
1968   "The Planners," by Kate Wilhelm
1969   "Passengers," by Robert Silverberg
1970   No award
1971   "Good News from the Vatican," by Robert Silverberg
1972   "When It Changed," by Joanna Russ
1973   "Love Is the Plan, the Plan Is Death," by James Tiptree, Jr.
1974   "The Day before the Revolution," by Ursula K. Le Guin
1975   "Catch That Zeppelin!" by Fritz Leiber
1976   "A Crowd of Shadows," by Charles L. Grant
1977   "Jeffty Is Five," by Harlan Ellison
1978   "Stone," by Edward Bryant
1979   "giANTS," by Edward Bryant
1980   "Grotto of the Dancing Bear," by Clifford D. Simak
1981   "The Bone Flute," by Lisa Tuttle, declined by the author
1982   "A Letter from the Clearys," by Connie Willis
1983   "The Peacemaker," by Gardner Dozois
1984   "Morning Child," by Gardner Dozois

1985   "Out of All Them Bright Stars," by Nancy Kress
1986   "Tangents," by Greg Bear
1987   "Forever Yours, Anna," by Kate Wilhelm

Nebula Grand Master Awards

1975   Robert A. Heinlein
1976   Jack Williamson
1977   Clifford D. Simak
1979   L. Sprague de Camp
1984   Andre Norton
1986   Arthur C. Clarke
1987   Isaac Asimov
1988   Alfred Bester

Hugo Awards

The Science Fiction Achievement Awards are almost universally known as "Hugo's," the popular title coming from Hugo Gernsback, the legendary editor of early science fiction magazines. They are awarded at the World Science Fiction Conventions, with different rules pertaining at different times since the first awards in 1953. Unlike the Nebula awards, these awards are listed for the year in which they were presented, although the work so honored most often has a copyright date from a previous year.

Hugo Award Novels

1953   *The Demolished Man*, by Alfred Bester
1955   *They'd Rather Be Right*, by Mark Clifton and Frank
          Riley
1956   *Double Star*, by Robert A. Heinlein
1958   *The Big Time*, by Fritz Leiber
1959   *A Case of Conscience*, by James Blish
1960   *Starship Troopers*, by Robert A. Heinlein
1961   *A Canticle for Leibowitz*, by Walter M. Miller, Jr.
1962   *Stranger in a Strange Land*, by Robert A. Heinlein
1963   *The Man in the High Castle*, by Philip K. Dick
1964   *Way Station*, by Clifford D. Simak
1965   *The Wanderer*, by Fritz Leiber
1966   *Dune*, by Frank Herbert and
          This Immortal, by Roger Zelazny
1967   *The Moon Is a Harsh Mistress*, by Robert A. Heinlein
1968   *Lord of Light*, by Roger Zelazny
1969   *Stand on Zanzibar*, by John Brunner
1970   *The Left Hand of Darkness*, by Ursula K. Le Guin

1971   *Ringworld*, by Larry Niven
1972   *To Your Scattered Bodies Go*, by Philip José Farmer
1973   *The Gods Themselves*, by Isaac Asimov
1974   *Rendezvous with Rama*, by Arthur C. Clarke
1975   *The Dispossessed*, by Ursula K. Le Guin
1976   *The Forever War*, by Joe Haldeman
1977   *Where Late the Sweet Birds Sang*, by Kate Wilhelm
1978   *Gateway*, by Frederik Pohl
1979   *Dreamsnake*, by Vonda N. McIntyre
1980   *The Fountains of Paradise*, by Arthur C. Clarke
1981   *The Snow Queen*, by Joan Vinge
1982   *Downbelow Station*, by C. J. Cherryh
1983   *Foundation's Edge*, by Isaac Asimov
1984   *Startide Rising*, by David Brin
1985   *Neuromancer*, by William Gibson
1986   *Ender's Game*, by Orson Scott Card
1987   *Speaker for the Dead*, by Orson Scott Card

Hugo Award Novellas

1968   "Riders of the Purple Wage," by Philip José Farmer
      and "Weyr Search," by Anne McCaffrey
1969   "Nightwings," by Robert Silverberg
1970   "Ship of Shadows," by Fritz Leiber
1971   "Ill Met in Lankhmar," by Fritz Leiber
1972   "The Queen of Air and Darkness," by Poul Anderson
1973   "The Word for World Is Forest," by Ursula K. Le Guin
1974   "The Girl Who Was Plugged In," by James Tiptree, Jr.
1975   "A Song for Lya," by George R. R. Martin
1976   "Home Is the Hangman," by Roger Zelazny
1977   "Houston, Houston, Do You Read?" by James Tiptree, Jr.
      and "By Any Other Name . . . ," by Spider Robinson
1978   "Stardance," by Spider and Jeanne Robinson
1979   "The Persistence of Vision," by John Varley
1980   "Enemy Mine," by Barry Longyear
1981   "Lost Dorsai," by Gordon R. Dickson
1982   "The Saturn Game," by Poul Anderson
1983   "Souls," by Joanna Russ
1984   "Cascade Point," by Timothy Zahn
1985   "Press Enter," by John Varley
1986   "24 Views of Mount Fuji, by Hokusai," by Roger Zelazny

Hugo Award Novelettes

1955   "The Darfsteller," by Walter M. Miller, Jr.
1956   "Exploration Team," by Murray Leinster
1959   "The Big Front Yard," by Clifford D. Simak

1967   "The Last Castle," by Jack Vance
1968   "Gonna Roll the Bones," by Fritz Leiber
1969   "The Sharing of Flesh," by Poul Anderson
1973   "The Goat Song," by Poul Anderson
1974   "The Deathbird," by Harlan Ellison
1975   "Adrift Just off the Islets of Langerhans: Latitude 38
          54"N, Longitude 77° 13"W," by Harlan Ellison
1976   "The Borderland of Sol," by Larry Niven
1977   "The Bicentennial Man," by Isaac Asimov
1978   "Eyes of Amber," by Joan D. Vinge
1979   "Hunter's Moon," by Poul Anderson
1980   "Sandkings," by George R. R. Martin
1981   "The Cloak and the Staff," by Gordon R. Dickson
1982   "Unicorn Variation," by Roger Zelazny
1983   "Fire Watch," by Connie Willis
1984   "Blood Music," by Greg Bear
1985   "Bloodchild," by Octavia Butler
1986   "Paladin of the Lost Hour," by Harlan Ellison

Hugo Award Short Stories

1955   "Alamagoosa," by Eric Frank Russell
1956   "The Star," by Arthur C. Clarke
1958   "Or All the Seas with Oysters," by Avram Davidson
1959   "The Big Front Yard," by Clifford D. Simak
1965   "Soldier, Ask Not," by Gordon R. Dickson
1967   "Neutron Star," by Larry Niven
1968   "I Have No Mouth and I Must Scream," by Harlan Ellison
1969   "The Beast That Shouted Love at the Heart of the World,"
          by Harlan Ellison
1970   "Time Considered as a Helix of Semi-Precious Stones," by
          Samuel R. Delany
1971   "Slow Sculpture," by Theodore Sturgeon
1972   "Inconstant Moon," by Larry Niven
1973   "Eurema's Dam," by R. A. Lafferty and
          "The Meeting," by Frederick Pohl and C. M. Kornbluth
1974   "The Ones Who Walk Away from Omelas," by Ursula K.
          Le Guin
1975   "The Hole Man," by Larry Niven
1976   "Catch That Zeppelin," by Fritz Leiber
1977   "Tricentennial," by Joe Haldeman
1978   "Jeffty Is Five," by Harlan Ellison
1979   "Cassandra," by C. J. Cherryh
1980   "The Way of the Cross and Dragon," by George R. R.
          Martin
1981   "Grotto of the Dancing Bear," by Clifford D. Simak
1982   "The Pusher," by John Varley

1983   "Melancholy Elephants," by Spider Robinson
1984   "Speech Sounds," by Octavia Butler
1985   "Crystal Spheres," by David Brin
1986   "Fermi and Frost," by Frederik Pohl

Hugo Award Short Fiction

1960   "Flowers for Algernon," by Daniel Keyes
1961   "The Longest Voyage," by Poul Anderson
1962   The Hothouse series, by Brian W. Aldiss
1963   "The Dragon Masters," by Jack Vance
1964   "No Truce with Kings," by Poul Anderson
1966   "'Repent, Harlequin!' Said the Ticktockman," by Harlan
        Ellison

Sources

Anatomy of Wonder. Ed. Neil Barron. 2nd ed. New York, Bowker, 1981.

---. 3rd ed. New York, Bowker, 1987.

A Reader's Guide to Science Fiction. Ed. Baird Searles et al. New York, Facts on File, 1979.

Science Fiction and Fantasy Reference Index, 1878-1985. Ed. H. W. Hall. Detroit, Gale, 1987.

The Science Fiction Encyclopedia. Ed. Peter Nicholls. Garden City, N.Y., Doubleday, 1979.

The Science Fiction Reference Book. Mercer Island, Wash., Starmont House, 1981.

The Science Fiction Sourcebook. Ed. David Wingrove. Harlow, Essex, Longman, 1984.

Science Fiction Writers. Ed. E. F. Bleiler. New York, Scribner's, 1982.

Twentieth-Century American Science-Fiction Writers. Ed. David Cowart and Thomas L. Wymer. Detroit, Gale, 1981.

Twentieth-Century Science-Fiction Writers. Ed. Curtis C. Smith. New York, St. James, 1986.

Ulrich's International Periodicals Directory. 26th ed. New York, Bowker, 1987.

Title Index

In this index are included all titles for books and short stories for which plot summaries appear. Works in series are listed under the series and under their unique titles.

Marilyn Fletcher is the head of the Serials Department at the University of New Mexico's General Library. She is also an associate professor of library science at the University and author of *Science Fiction Story Index* (ALA, 1981).